The Bloomsbury Introduction to Children's and Young Adult Literature

The Bloomsbury Introduction to Children's and Young Adult Literature

Karen Coats

Bloomsbury Academic
An imprint of Bloomsbury Publishing Plc

BLOOMSBURY
LONDON · OXFORD · NEW YORK · NEW DELHI · SYDNEY

Bloomsbury Academic

An imprint of Bloomsbury Publishing Plc

50 Bedford Square
London
WC1B 3DP
UK

1385 Broadway
New York
NY 10018
USA

www.bloomsbury.com

BLOOMSBURY and the Diana logo are trademarks of Bloomsbury Publishing Plc

First published 2018

British Library Cataloguing-in-Publication Data
A catalogue record for this book is available from the British Library.

ISBN: HB: 978-1-4725-7554-8
PB: 978-1-4725-7553-1
ePDF: 978-1-4725-7556-2
eBook: 978-1-4725-7555-5

Library of Congress Cataloging-in-Publication Data
Names: Coats, Karen, 1963- author.
Title: The Bloomsbury introduction to children's and young adult literature /
Karen Coats.
Description: London; New York: Bloomsbury Academic, 2017. | Includes
bibliographical references and index.
Identifiers: LCCN 2017010082 | ISBN 9781472575548 (hardback) | ISBN
9781472575531 (pb)
Subjects: LCSH: Children's literature–History and criticism. | Young adult
literature–History and criticism. | BISAC: LITERARY CRITICISM /
Children's Literature.
Classification: LCC PN1009.A1 C55 2017 | DDC 809/.89282–dc23 LC record available at https://lccn.loc.
gov/2017010082

Cover design: Eleanor Rose
Cover illustration by Nicholas Stevenson

Typeset by Deanta Global Publishing Services, Chennai, India
Printed and bound in India

To find out more about our authors and books visit www.bloomsbury.com. Here you will find extracts, author interviews, details of forthcoming events and the option to sign up for our newsletters.

This book is dedicated to the memory of Shelby Wolf and J. D. Stahl.
I couldn't have wished for better mentors, and children's literature had no
better friends. If books had fairy godparents who watched over them, surely
this one had you two. You are sorely missed.

Contents

Acknowledgments

Ever since I started on my academic journey, I've been blessed with great teachers of children's and young adult literature, starting at Virginia Tech with Pat Kelly and Bob Small, and later the inimitable J. D. Stahl. And as everyone who works in this field knows, there are no more generous colleagues, mentors, and friends than the ones I've found through the Children's Literature Association, the International Research Society for Children's Literature, and in my teaching at Illinois State University and Hollins University. So while I have dedicated this book to the memory of J. D. and my dear friend and mentor Shelby Wolf, I also dedicate it to all of my colleagues, since it couldn't have been written without you. Your work in the field is changing the landscape of academia and uplifting the lives of children all over the world, and it is my humble hope that this will prove to be one more tool to bring to that service.

I have a few groups that deserve special thanks: first, the folks at the Center for Children's Books at University of Illinois Urbana-Champaign, where I spend my Wednesday mornings talking about children's and young adult literature with some of the smartest, most dedicated, most hilarious people I know. Second, the wonderful authors and illustrators I have had the pleasure to spend time with at Hollins, who welcomed me, a boring academic, into their critique group, and gave me invaluable feedback on and contributions to this manuscript. My Tuesday night Bible study ladies are prayer warriors; through health issues and deadlines, they have helped me keep my eyes on our infinitely generous Father, who provides all the words in His time. And finally, I want to give special thanks to my students. For more than thirty years, you all have inspired me, taught me, and made my work an utter joy.

The authors and illustrators who contributed to this book deserve emeralds and pearls—they donated both their time and their wise words, so please buy their books!

I also thank David Avital for his patience and support, and the team at Bloomsbury Academic.

And finally, of course, always, I thank my family: Will, Emily, Blair, and my parents—you are unfailingly patient, wise, kind, and tolerant; thanks for letting me borrow your stories, and steal time that rightfully belonged to you.

Introduction

In 1953, literary critic M. H. Abrams proposed two evocative metaphors for understanding literature: the mirror and the lamp. I'd like to start our study of children's and young adult (YA) literature by asking you to dwell on those metaphors for a bit.

When we think of mirrors, we think of them as reflecting what is in front of them in a straightforward way; that is, we believe that what we see in a mirror is an accurate imitation of the real world. Picturebooks with naturalistic art or photographs, realistic novels and chapter books, or even fantasy novels that feature recognizable psychological or emotional responses in their characters seem to present reliable pictures of how the world actually works, and how people actually think and feel. But what if we think more carefully about the qualities of the mirror itself, rather than what it reflects? I daresay that all of us have had the experience of looking into a mirror that distorts reality in some way—a fun house mirror, for instance, that elongates and shortens parts of the body, or a dressing room mirror that makes us look thinner than we expected, or a fractured mirror that breaks apart or doubles parts of our face. Mirrors also have edges or frames that limit, focus, and contain the field of what they reflect. They only show surface features, and they don't generate their own light, though they can amplify a light source by reflecting it. And what about our behavior in front of mirror? When we look in a mirror, we can't help but interact with what we find there: we almost always judge what we see against what we expected to see (and are often surprised!); we may zoom in on certain features to check them out more closely or back off to get a better sense of the whole; we may even check to see to if a discrepancy we notice is due to a property of the mirror, a feature of what's in front of it, or a mismatch that happens somewhere between the image and the viewer.

If we consider literature as a mirror according to those features, we come up with some new ideas about seemingly realistic or even nonfiction literature. First, it doesn't fully reflect or represent reality in a transparent and unproblematic way. Instead, it selects particular moments, highlights them, and puts a frame around them. While this enables us to focus on certain aspects of a situation, it also may limit or ignore important contexts. The author's perspective might act like a distorted mirror, exaggerating some aspects and giving others short shrift, idealizing or stereotyping characters or exposing their cracks and flaws. Sometimes, more often in YA literature than in books for younger children, a book that strives to mirror a difficult reality doesn't light the way forward out of a bad situation; that is, it reflects the murk of the situation exactly as a mirror would, without imposing a light source not visible from within the situation itself, or even suggesting that the room (society) around the individual situation is so dimly lit that the subject is confined by the darkness surrounding it. Other times, a solution to a difficult problem comes from a source that is highly unlikely given the reality that the story proposes to imitate—a happy ending appears out of nowhere to satisfy the expectations or desires of a reader.

Our mirror metaphor allows us to think about what we do when we read as well. As we do with actual mirrors, we come to a text with expectations, and we tend to judge what we see against those expectations as much as by what we find on the page in front of us. Our methods of interpretation may involve close readings of particular elements or more context-driven analysis based on an assessment of the whole. Even if we are not engaged in critical analysis of a text or an image, we never just passively absorb what we read or view; we act on it in some way, filling in gaps, posing questions, evaluating textual answers against what we know of the world it reflects. Literary mirrors have an important function in that they frame experiences and situations and offer them back to us for analysis and contemplation; they reflect in their ways so that we can reflect in ours.

Mirrors can be evocative literary metaphors in and of themselves. Think of Narcissus who couldn't turn away from the beauty of his own reflection and as a result lost the will to live. Harry Potter faced a similar temptation of not wanting to leave the Mirror of Erised (Rowling 1997). Lewis Carroll's Alice fell *through* the looking glass over her mantel into a world of danger and wonder where everything was inverted from the real world (1871). Teen vampires, like Chris in M. T. Anderson's *Thirsty* (1997), desperately fight against the loss of themselves in adolescence, figured through their inability to see their reflection in a mirror. The wicked queen in "Snow White" had a talking mirror that commented on who was the fairest in the land, prompting contemporary poet Christine Heppermann to proclaim that, for teen girls faced with the beauty myths of contemporary culture, "now all mirrors chatter" in a continual, self-loathing critique of their bodies (2014: 5). Children's and YA books are full of mirrors, and they almost always signify something—a temptation, a danger, a misrecognition, or a portal to a place where the characters will learn something about themselves.

In addition to mirrors, Abrams also drew on the metaphor of the lamp as a way to think about what literature does. The lamp can be considered here as an illumination of the writer's soul, or of the characters'; through literature, we can see ideas, thoughts, and emotions that might remain silent or concealed in everyday experience. In real life, I can really only see what's in front of me—for instance, my messy desk, my computer screen, the contents of my office, my hands on the keyboard. But all of these present things have histories and futures that I can only access through memory and projection. The lamp of literature facilitates both of these processes, casting a spotlight on pasts that I have not experienced and lighting possible paths into multiple kinds of futures. Here again, lamps operate as metaphors within texts as well as metaphors for what literature can do. Aladdin's lamp opens a world of possibility and danger, the chief danger, perhaps, being the loss of his own authenticity, while Weetzie Bat's lamp lights her way to the realization of her heart's desire (Block 1989). Literary critic Rudine Sims Bishop (1990: x), focusing attention on multicultural books, conceived of literature as a window and a door as well as a mirror, highlighting the fact that while children need to see themselves reflected in literature, they also need to view lives and lifestyles that are unlike theirs in order to understand "the multicultural nature of the world they live in, and their places as a member of just one group, as well as their connections to all other humans."

Obviously, these metaphors can open out in ways other than those we have considered here. Think for a moment about the role mirrors play in your life. How do you use them? What do you do in front of them? How are lamps and other light sources (spotlights, twinkly ropes of outdoor lights, the flashlight app on your phone) important in your life? How do windows position viewers, and how do doors work, as in, what is required of you when you approach a door? What metaphoric connections to literary experience and self-understanding can you make from your reflections?

Throughout this study, I will ask you to stop and make reflections such as these. I do this because I want to encourage you toward greater self-understanding as well as an understanding of the content in this book, and this can only happen if you take the time to stop and reflect on what you are reading and make it meaningful for yourself. Reflecting on children's and YA literature and your interactions with it is an especially effective way to do this, because we have all, in some way, been affected by the literature we read as children and teens. In fact, children's literature in particular bears all the weight of making a first impression, not only in terms of the way it reflects or illuminates or allows children to see the world, but also in terms of its own structures and forms; children's literature apprentices children into ways of seeing and reading that set their expectations about how representation can and should work. This is not to imply that young readers, listeners, and viewers are passive consumers of the texts adults share with them, but it does suggest that the literature we read as children has an enormous impact on the adults we become. Throughout this book, we will explore how and why this literature is so important to our development as individuals and as a family of human beings, negotiating our way through cultural differences, spiritual and moral values, physical challenges, consumerist longings, and the never-ending quest for a self that we like and respect.

The literary texts produced for young readers are incredibly varied and have a long history. In addition, the methods and theories that scholars and educators use to study them are richly diverse. As a result, I can't stress enough that this is only an *introduction* to the wealth of materials that can support and deepen your study of children's and YA texts and their contexts. What you will find in this book are some of the tools and frameworks you can use to increase your understanding of not only the literature itself but also the various ways to study and write about it. I have tried to include attention to as many of the concerns circulating among critics of children's and YA literature as possible without producing an overwhelming brick of a book, but the field is growing so large that my task is happily impossible. Hence, my ultimate goal is to induce in you a deep dissatisfaction with your level of knowledge about youth literature as well as an enthusiasm to learn more; in other words, I want to whet your appetite without satisfying it, to give you a taste that inspires you to seek out and partake of a much fuller banquet.

I have also asked some authors and illustrators to offer their perspectives on the topics addressed in the chapters. I figured that was only fair since the creators of literature for young people often have very different ideas about their craft than the critics do. At the beginning of each chapter, I have suggested some texts that you might want to read or view alongside the information so that you can test my ideas against your own impressions and insights, but these aren't meant to limit your choices; hopefully, the frameworks offered in the chapters will be relevant to any text you enjoy, and inspire you to think more deeply about, and thus enjoy more fully, your favorite children's and YA books. Certain terms that are especially relevant to the study of children's and YA literature are in bold, and explained further in the glossary. I have also included suggestions for further reading and research; questions for discussion, writing or thinking about; activities that you might develop for yourself or incorporate into your own pedagogy; and case studies that provide models of how some of the ideas presented in the chapters might work in application to specific texts. Finally, though, I hope that you will read this in the company of others, including a teacher who will challenge, offer additional context, and even occasionally disagree with what I have to say; after all, it's only through listening to, analyzing, and arguing through multiple perspectives that we find our own.

A word from your author:

Since I will be using "I" a lot in this textbook, and since I mean the book to be, in many respects, a conversation, I thought it might be wise to introduce myself. I grew up in a small town in northern Maryland on land that was part of my family's farm. I read a lot, so much so that my uncle called me a "house mouse," which I think was hardly fair, since I spent a good deal of time on the farm, in the woods, and exploring the creek near my house. In the early 1980s, I attended Virginia Tech for an undergraduate degree in English with an Education option, and taught junior high and high school in Virginia and North Carolina for four years, including a brief stint as a teacher's aide for first and second graders, before returning to Virginia Tech for my Master's degree in English. I had my first baby, Emily, who has Down syndrome, and we moved back to live in the farmhouse in Maryland while I got my PhD at The George Washington University in an interdisciplinary field called Human Sciences. While pursuing that degree, I had another daughter, Blair, and I taught adults preparing for their high school equivalency exams as well as college students. Since then, I have taught children's and YA literature at Illinois State University at the graduate and undergraduate level. I also teach at Hollins University and review books for *The Bulletin of the Center for Children's Books*. So, to sum up, the "I" in this book is a middle-class, white, married woman in her mid-1950s, with over thirty years of teaching experience at various levels. You can call her Karen.

Literature references

Anderson, M. T. (1997), *Thirsty*, Somerville, MA: Candlewick.

Block, F. L. (1989), *Weetzie Bat*, New York: HarperCollins.

Carroll, L. (1987), *Through the Looking Glass, and What Alice Found There*, London: Macmillan.

Heppermann, C. (2014), *Poisoned Apples: Poems for You, My Pretty*, New York: HarperCollins.

Rowling, J. K. (1997), *Harry Potter and the Philosopher's Stone*, London: Bloomsbury.

1

Ideologies of Childhood and the History of Children's Literature

Suggested texts to read alongside this chapter

The Brownies' Book (full text of select issues available here: http://childlit. unl.edu/topics/edi.brownies.html).

Comenius, John Amos, *Orbis Sensualium Pictus* (full text available online).

Fine, Anne, *Madame Doubtfire*; *The Tulip Touch*; *Flour Babies*.

New England Primer (full text available online).

Rousseau, Jean-Jacques, *Emile, or On Education* (full text available online).

Stevenson, Robert Louis, *A Child's Garden of Verses* (full text available online).

Yang, Gene Luen, *American Born Chinese*.

How histories of childhood and children's and young adult literature are constructed

In Lenore Look's *Alvin Ho: Allergic to Dead Bodies, Funerals, and Other Fatal Circumstances* (2011), anxiety-ridden second-grader Alvin is worried about his first test on the colonial history of his hometown of Concord, Massachusetts. His older brother, Calvin, comes up with the ingenious plan of drawing symbolic pictures to help his brother remember significant historical events. He starts by drawing a dinosaur, and then Pangaea, then the Egyptian pyramids, the Trojan War, the Great Wall of China, the Vikings, Benjamin Franklin, Henry David Thoreau, and finally,

Fenway Park. Of course, none of these selective tidbits will be of any help to Alvin on his test, but Calvin has hit on some of the key problems of writing a history: when to start your history, and what to include. Your own teachers over the years have likely warned you often enough not to begin any essay with some variant of "since the dawn of time," and yet even the distinguished scholar Seth Lerer (2008: 1) begins his magisterial history of children's reading with the sentence: "Ever since there were children, there has been children's literature." While this is very likely true, it requires a feat of informed imagination to reflect on the forms that literature took before print, as well as to extrapolate from the bits and scraps that have been preserved over time in order to make some generalizations about what young readers might have read and enjoyed prior to our present age; well-loved books, like well-loved toys, may not have survived the ravages of time and rough handling as well as those items that were not subjected to everyday use. Yet this kind of imaginative reconstruction is precisely what we must do to fully account for the stories, educative texts, and poetic forms shared with young people throughout the course of human history.

Conceiving a history of children's and YA literature requires a writer to consider three overarching questions: First, what will count as literature? Second, what do we mean when we say children and YAs? And third, how does literature fit into broader cultural, **ideological**, and historical contexts? The answers the historian frames for these questions guide the selection of what to include in the history of a literary **genre**. The overly broad sweep proposed by Calvin in his march through planetary history toward the contemporary state of a small town in North America is certainly meant to be comic, but it reminds us that history is always colored by conscious and unconscious perspectives and biases, as well as by the degree of specificity the project needs or can afford. In this introduction to children's and YA literature, for instance, I am dedicating a single chapter to the history of a **genre** (some would argue two **genres**, separating out children's from YA literature) that has received far fuller treatment in multiple book-length studies from diverse perspectives and with various levels of specificity. My goal in this chapter is to bring together historical and **ideological** contexts from antiquity to the present in order to explore how and why Western children's and YA literature has developed into the forms it takes today.

Why history matters to the study of children's literature

But, some of you may be saying, I am not really all that interested in the history of youth literature; I plan to teach contemporary youth literature to contemporary children, tweens, and teens. Or: I want to write for young people, so my goal is to understand what's happening in the literature today and where it's headed. Fair enough—the historical study of children's and YA literature as an end in itself may be more relevant to those seeking to become professors and literary critics. However, no reader, adult or child, approaches a children's or YA text without a distinct attitude toward its intended audience, without, in other words, an **ideology** of childhood or what it means to be a teenager. Such an **ideology** is a set of conscious and unconscious ideas, beliefs, and values that influence how we read and understand the literature as well as how we think about ourselves and how we respond to actual children. Since our ideas seem natural to us, they don't feel like beliefs or values at all, but rather common sense or, simply, truth.

Studying the history of youth literature, however, reveals that ideas about childhood have a particular point of emergence and that they have changed over time. Our present attitudes rest on the tip of a very large iceberg. Considering the rest of the iceberg—the foundations on which those attitudes rest—shows us that what people have believed about children and childhood in the past is different, in some cases markedly so, from what we believe now about children and childhood. Let's take a pause and consider what **ideology** means and what its implications are for the study of youth literature.

Icebergs and Ideologies

If you are sitting in a room with a window, look at it and consider what you see. When I ask my students to do this, they usually tell me what is visible outside—the leaves of a tree, the next building over, people tossing a ball or studying under the trees on the campus lawn. In other words, they are looking *through* the window, and why not? This is one of the things windows are for, after all, so why else would I be asking? But then I point out that nobody mentioned the window itself—the shape of it that limits the range of what they can see (i.e., only part of the tree, building, and lawn rather than the whole thing), and the fact that there are smudges, fingerprints, and a mesh screen that they ignored, not recognizing the distorting effects these have on what they see. Once they scold (and forgive) me for my trick question, I also point out that, even with this limitations, they wouldn't be able to see anything at all if the window weren't there.

In a similar way, **ideology** acts as a framing device that enables and also limits or distorts what we can see. **Ideology** refers to the consciously and unconsciously held beliefs and values that structure and inform our attitudes and actions. We can usually give accounts or defenses for our actions and attitudes—what we see in front of us. The challenge is to be able to look at

(Continued)

the **ideologies** that inform or underlie them—in other words, to redirect our attention to the window through which we see, rather than what we see on the other side.

Consciously held **ideologies** are usually not that hard to locate and explain, and we can discuss them as goals or values even when we don't always act in ways that are consistent with them. They are those positions that we have thought through and adopted because we see in them some benefit toward creating a society that we want to live in; political **ideologies** and belief systems, including atheism, for instance, are usually consciously adopted positions. But even though we consciously espouse certain beliefs or values, we also hold unconscious **ideological** positions that we have absorbed to the point where they seem like common sense; these are values that we take for granted, so much so that we are surprised when we find that other people perceive things differently. These positions are often related to the ways in which we think about ourselves with relation to other people, so they include our racial and ethnic attitudes and prejudices, our attitudes toward gender and family structures, and our expectations toward what constitutes a good society and a happy life. Since these unconscious **ideologies** are, by definition of the word unconscious, absorbed from birth without thought or reflection through encounters with the world around us—our families, our cultural products such as books and other media, and our schooling— it becomes important for those who study child culture to examine how **ideologies** appear and are reinforced in youth literature. In other words, we need to look *at* the window rather than merely through it, to drill down to what motivates our thoughts, opinions, and, most importantly, our emotional, kneejerk reactions to the things we see and hear, and ask ourselves where these responses came from.

As you read through this chapter, be on the lookout for the ways that cultural attitudes toward childhood have shifted. A quick summary of the evolution of **ideologies** of childhood that have informed much of the literature produced for them looks like this:

- Children, though they require different levels of physical care than adults, only need practical training in tasks that fit their role in their social group, and don't need special stories that would prepare them for life outside of their own communities.
- Children are immature adults that need to be shuffled along to adulthood as soon as possible.
- Children are special gifts from God but are infected with original sin and thus need to be cherished but also corrected and instructed according to the dictates of their faith. A secular version of this is that children are born with aggressive tendencies in the service of their

own self-interest. In either case, they can and should be allowed to read stories that show natural and imposed consequences to aggressive and antisocial actions in order to develop their moral sense as well as self-control.

- Children are blank slates that can be positively or negatively influenced by their surroundings and education. Their education should be both robust and moral, emphasizing humans' superiority over the natural world along with their obligation to protect and develop their understanding of it.
- Children are born naturally and innocently good, with an innate sense of justice and compassion, and should be protected from negative influences, including stories with sloppy or ambiguous morals, that emerge from adult society.
- Young people are our only hope to save the world and make it a better place.
- Children are diverse in intelligence, temperament, experience, and interest, but are all capable of learning given the right approach, and all need positive representation in literature and other media in order to understand their embeddedness in human communities and to realize their full potential as individuals. Moreover, there is a time between childhood and adulthood that is distinctly different from either, and thus deserves its own attention as a stage of life.

Despite the fact that I have indicated various **ideologies** of childhood as discrete positions, it is also important to understand that once certain ideas about what it means to be human come into the world, they don't simply go away. Instead, newer ideas dialogue with older ones, refining, challenging, sometimes reinforcing and sometimes transforming those ideas beyond recognition. Thinking historically allows us to recognize and trace connections and disruptions, and to consider what conditions enable us to hold our present attitudes. Looking backward in time, we can ponder the question of whether it is the children and teenagers who have changed, as Anne Fine does in the Author Talkback to this chapter, or whether it is our interpretation of and attitudes toward their concerns that have changed. Related questions then emerge regarding how such a change happens; that is, does the literature change in response to the needs of its audience, or does the audience change in response to the literature?

Seth Lerer (2008: 1) frames an answer to some of those questions this way: "The history of children's literature is inseparable from the history of childhood, for the child was made through texts and tales he or she studied, heard, and told back."

The first part of that sentence seems inarguable: in order to have a literature specially dedicated to young people, a culture has to have a sense of who and what that audience is and what they need to know as they grow into adulthood. The contemporary idea that we should also consider what will make them happy is a more recent notion, as is the rather curious claim expressed in the second half of the sentence, that children are somehow *made* through stories. This is an idea we will consider in more depth in future chapters. However, if you read around in the history of childhood or children's literature, at some point you will come across the statement that the concept of childhood as a separate stage of life didn't exist in traditional Western societies before the Middle Ages. This strange idea grows out of the work of French historian Philippe Ariès, who states provocatively in his 1960 book, *Centuries of Childhood: A Social History of Family Life*, "In medieval society, the idea of childhood did not exist" (128). Such a statement was bound to meet with challenge, and it has, repeatedly, in the works of scholars interested in childhood and family life during the classical and medieval periods. Hugh Cunningham (2014: 30), for instance, points to a translation problem in the sentence, arguing that what has been translated as "idea" was something more like "sentiment" in the original French. Understood this way, Cunningham argues that our tenderly nostalgic sense that childhood *should be* a time set apart and deserving of protection from adult troubles, even if it isn't actually like that for many of the world's children, is in fact an invention of the 1600s, which we have been refining ever since. Eva M. Simms (2008) elaborates the provocative idea that the issue wasn't that we didn't have a sense of what childhood was so much as we lacked a sense of what constituted adulthood. During much of human history prior to the eleventh century, she explains, adults and children participated in communal rituals on an even basis; they played the same games, sang the same songs, told the same stories. The advent of the Crusades and the practice of embarking on spiritual pilgrimages marked the first time that many people ever left the villages of their birth. Simms argues that it was only when YAs began to loosen their ties to their families and communal traditions to follow such private destinies that a new psychological awareness of individual personality and maturity developed. Consider this in light of the very common trope of the road trip in YA fiction: taking off in an unreliable vehicle with a few friends and a load of snacks constitutes a modern-day pilgrimage on the road to maturity. "Children become children," Simms argues, "when adults become more 'adult'" (199). In any case, while childhood has been understood differently over the years in terms of age, sentiment, accountability, and psychology, world historian Peter N. Stearns (2006) notes that there is now a general agreement among historians that all societies in all times have had some way of designating a fundamental difference between childhood and adulthood.

No matter how dubious his conclusions are, credit is due to Ariès for inaugurating the scholarly study of children in society. His work prompted scholars from disciplines other than psychology and biology to view childhood as a social construct that draws from and influences the entire range of **discourses** that define a culture. What do children mean to a culture politically, economically, and spiritually? How should they be educated? What should their lives look like, and what responsibilities should they bear with respect to the welfare of the family? How complex are their emotions, memories, and inner lives? When do they become adults, and what markers distinguish childhood from adulthood? Are the teenage years special in some way, and if so, what are the expectations for those years? Are the concerns of childhood so fundamentally different from those of adulthood that we perceive children themselves as wholly "other"? Do children themselves have any influence, agency, or voice in how they are perceived, or are they wholly subject to what adults imagine them to be? These are the sorts of questions posed by researchers in the rapidly growing field of Childhood or Children's Studies, and the answers you come up with for yourself as you read this book as well as other critical and primary texts and engage in class discussions will help you form a more cohesive picture of why you respond to children's and YA literature in the way that you do.

To formulate scholarly, critically informed answers to such questions, we will begin by considering how they have been answered in the context of historical developments. What follows will contain a lot of generalizations, both about the sweep of history and the function of stories and storytelling. To some extent, this is inevitable given the vast amount of time under consideration; as I've said, we need to perform acts of imaginative reconstruction when it comes to the whys and wherefores of youth literature and culture, and that is especially true when we lack written records. But we also have to consider the role of literacy in fomenting more rapid and granular social change. For the hundreds of years when alphabetic literacy was limited or nonexistent, ideas and traditions were shared property, and any innovations required the approval and uptake of the whole group; anyone who's ever served on a committee has an inkling of how long that process can take! But when more individuals began to have access to more and more varied ideas through print, the pace of cultural change exploded. So if I make it seem like things stayed pretty much the same for the first forty thousand or so years of human history, you might think about the difference in speed of flow between a glacier and a viral internet video. However, my hope is that you will add your own insights, talk back to some of mine, and be inspired to seek out more in-depth studies of the youth literature written in the time periods that interest you. As your study of children's and YA literature deepens and develops, you will be able to ask more pointed questions and challenge some of my assumptions based on your own research; what I am attempting to model here is the profound interconnectedness between a culture's material, economic, and **ideological** circumstances and the kinds of stories it produces for its young people.

The development of children's and young adult literature from the preprint era to the early twentieth century

Before print: From cave paintings to agrarian folklore

Despite shifting attitudes toward the nature and importance of childhood, children have always needed special attention, care, and training in order to prepare for adult roles in their communities. Much of that training comes through stories, poems, and songs, and of course, in the era before alphabetic literacy, all of the instruction and stories that enabled the survival of individuals and communities would have been conveyed orally or through drama, dance, and visual art. At the risk of reaching all the way back to prehistory like Calvin Ho, our story of the development of children's literature, then, starts with hunter-gatherer societies. While we don't know much about their oral literary practices, cave paintings and other artifacts discovered on nearly every continent, some dating from forty thousand years ago, suggest a tradition of representational storytelling. But wait, you may say, these are pictures and sculptures, not literature! And that indeed links us back to our question of what constitutes literature in the first place. As children's literature professor Barbara Kiefer (2011) speculates, these paintings and other artifacts likely served a similar function in their time that picturebooks do in ours; that is, they combined the visual and the verbal in the service of storytelling for preliterate people. What is perhaps more interesting for our purposes here is that paleobiologist R. Dale Guthrie (2005) has convincingly argued that some of these paintings depicting scary hunting scenes and sculptures of generously proportioned females were likely created by adolescent males, making them a kind of proto-YA literature, expressing the fears and longings of teenage boys in a pictorial way as they considered their transition from childhood to adult responsibilities in their family groups. Hunter-gatherer groups still exist in many places in the world, and based on evidence gleaned from such contemporary groups, Stearns (2006) argues that birth rates were likely low because children were a drain on limited resources, and couldn't contribute very much to their own welfare. Children would not have been involved in hunting until they were around fourteen years old, and work for the entire group would have comprised only a few hours a day, leaving lots of time for play in the community. There wasn't much division between adults and children during their leisure activities, and the dangers and triumphs related through story were relevant to everyone in the community, so it's probably safe to speculate that little thought was given to creating separate kinds of stories for children; instead, children would have learned and perhaps even contributed to the stories of their group alongside their adults, implying that children's and adolescent literature started long before print culture developed and alphabetic literacy became widespread.

Stearns (2006) notes that the development of agriculture around 9000 BCE marked the first significant change in human economies. While cities began to develop around 3500 BCE, agrarian life was the most common lifestyle for most of the world's children until the 1800s. Even now, the legacy of the agrarian lifestyle lives on in the school calendar; what are now the summer months of vacation were originally freed up to enable children to work in the fields. This is important to highlight because it gives us a context for understanding what children's daily lives were like as well as why there is such an emphasis on pastoral or rural settings in children's literature; in the landscape of ideas, we have tended to associate the condition of being young with the early days, or "childhood," of culture itself. Moreover, many people idealize a rural lifestyle as simpler, purer, and more natural, all adjectives that we associate with the contemporary ideas we hold of childhood, if not its reality, then or now. For in reality, rural life was an existence of hard work in which children were expected to participate as fully as they were able. Unlike hunter-gatherer societies, which had little work that children could actually do until they were older, agricultural societies feature tasks, such as caring for domestic animals and working in a garden, that children as young as four or five could manage. As people began to realize the potential for children to contribute useful work on farms and in-home manufacturing, birth rates went up, and parents had to figure out ways to keep older children emotionally tethered to home as well as economically dependent so that they would continue to contribute their labor to the family.

> Children, though they required different levels of physical care than adults, only needed practical training in tasks that fit their role in their social group, and didn't need special stories that would prepare them for life outside of their own communities.

The growth of agriculture marks, then, the true birth of adolescence as an extended period between childhood and adulthood. During this time, the teen's ability to perform meaningful work was expected and valued, but also enforced through the establishment of property rights and inheritance protocols that were meant to ensure that young adults remained obedient and dependent as long as their parents were alive.

Stearns (2006) goes on to argue that the agricultural context also involved greater task differentiation between males and females. In hunter-gatherer societies, the work of females was just as important as the work of males to the daily life and survival of the family. When it came to farming, however, men took on the economically more productive outside work and gained power through laws of property ownership, resulting in the growth of patriarchal attitudes in family life. Children, particularly girls, were viewed as property that the father could dispose of as he liked, and neither boys nor girls had much power to resist the fates their parents mapped out for them. Over time, an economy grew up based on land ownership, the threat of conquest, and the subsequent need for protection, resulting in the development of a rigid class hierarchy; peasant farmers would provide labor and sometimes sons and daughters to a landowner in return for military protection from invaders. Rites of passage, which in traditional societies marked the change in social status that came from being a hunter and a warrior for boys, and marriageable for girls, slowly transformed into markers of spiritual importance, but did little to change a young adult's material or economic circumstances. The stories that grew out of this environment were thus aimed at legitimating gender roles and distinctions as well as, possibly, meeting psychological needs of escape from the clutches of grasping adults through fantasy scenarios. Instead of a rigid division between stories for adults and stories for children, the chief distinction was between stories for the lower classes and stories for the wealthy, each aimed as representing the world in such a way that class distinctions were confirmed and naturalized. Consider the fact that many fairy and folktales that we give to very young children today center on adolescent concerns like leaving home, defeating giants and ogres, seeking one's fortune, and finding a mate or being forced into marriage with a beast or a stranger. This seems strange when you think about contemporary childhood experience in democratic societies, but it makes sense that these were, in fact, literature for young people in light of their historical provenance. These stories were thus likely shared with children of differing ages to reconcile them to the lives and restrictions that they had little choice but to just accept.

The growth of education from the first century BCE to the 1500s

With the advent of the classical civilizations of the Mediterranean came formal education for a small minority of elite children who could afford to enter the tuition-based schools, often taught by educated slaves. Literature was still transmitted through the temporal arts, such as oral poetry, drama, music and dance, and through visual storytelling in murals, tomb and vase paintings, frescoes, bas-relief sculptures, carvings, and mosaics. The key purpose of education was moral and practical. Moral instruction came through classical literature featuring the exploits and failures of great men and women, as well as mythology and the animal fables of Aesop; students would have learned such classical texts as Horace's *Odes* (c. 23 BCE), Ovid's *Metamorphoses*

> Children are immature adults who need to be shuffled along to adulthood as soon as possible.

(8 CE), and Virgil's *Aeneid* (29-19 BCE) as well as the earlier Homeric epics, the *Illiad* and the *Odyssey*, which are still taught in today's secondary schools. Young scholars would also learn literacy and numeracy in the service of rhetoric, political history, geography, law, rigorous critical thinking, and proper conduct. While not much attention was given in extant documents to young children, older children, especially teenage boys, were the subject of both anxiety and instruction, so much so that Socrates was officially tried and put to death for the crime of "corrupting the youth" by teaching young men to question the belief systems and authority of their parents. There was general agreement among the Greeks and Romans that young people, while aesthetically pleasing, needed strict adult guidance and should be pushed to adopt adult perspectives as soon as possible. Such an attitude militates against the development of a literature specifically aimed at children, either for instruction or entertainment; to learn to think and behave like an adult, after all, you must read what adults read. While education was mostly limited to the wealthy, poorly spelled, bawdy graffiti found on the walls of Pompeii indicates that there was some degree of literacy in the broader population as well. However, because of the cultural disparagement and legal disenfranchisement of youth and the often harsh treatment of children as part of their education, very few adult writers looked back on their childhoods with fondness.

> Children are special gifts from God but are infected with original sin and thus need to be cherished but also corrected and instructed according to the dictates of their faith.

The religions of the book that grew in the midst of Mediterranean culture were profoundly important to the spread of literacy as well as instilling a new, more positive attitude toward children in general, making Judaism, Islam, and Christianity essential to the development of Western children's literature. Stearns (2006: 35) notes that these religions "all highlighted the pride and responsibility of parenthood, and particularly fatherhood (though Christianity, uniquely, also had the strong image of the loving mother of Jesus)." Children were perceived as a gift from God rather than a financial boon or burden; they possessed a unique soul from birth, and the responsibility to instruct them in the beliefs and traditions of their religion became an imperative act of stewardship for which parents were accountable to God. During the early centuries after the life of Christ, the Church Fathers taught the classical curriculum alongside Christian texts so as to emphasize the superiority of the Christian religion. Once again, though, concerns that children may be corrupted precipitated legal action, this time involving official censorship when Julian, the Roman Emperor who feared that Christianity was gaining too much power, banned Christians from teaching the classical curriculum at all. Christian teachers thus increasingly turned to allegorical stories and plays that built on biblical texts. One such drama was *The Play of Daniel*, which was written and performed by students of the Beauvais Cathedral school in 1234. In addition, children and adults would have learned the stories of the Bible and the saints through the iconography of Catholic and Orthodox churches, which often related the narratives in sequential panels rich with symbolism, much like contemporary wordless picturebooks or comics, one of which we will discuss in the case study for this chapter.

While such artwork joined memorization and oral recitation as the primary means of transmission of approved texts for most people, the rich and complicated nature of the scriptures both required and inspired the acquisition of alphabetic literacy. More importantly, though, the Pauline injunction to "work out your own salvation with fear and trembling" (The Bible, Phil. 2:21) necessitated the ability to read and understand the scriptures for oneself, thus prompting the growth of literacy and translation, despite lethal consequences for translating the scriptures from Latin to the ordinary languages of the people. For instance, the Roman Catholic Church burned John Hus, an advocate of individuals having access to the scriptures in the language they actually used, at the stake in 1415 using manuscripts of John Wycliffe's English translations of the scriptures as kindling. Still, we know that parents were committed to teaching their children to read and memorize scripture, as *Foxe's Book of Martyrs* (1563) records that seven people were executed in 1517 for teaching their children to recite the Lord's Prayer in English rather than Latin. And during the various Inquisitions that began in the twelfth century and lasted through the early nineteenth, Jews, Muslims, and Christians whose beliefs were deemed heretical in the affected countries continued to teach their children to read and memorize their sacred texts in secret. But whether officially sanctioned or dangerously private, the upshot for children and their literature was that nearly all schooling after the dissolution of the Roman Empire in the fifth century, whether at home or through the church, was undertaken under religious auspices; the idea of secular education didn't reappear until universities at Bologna and Padua were established in the late twelfth century, and much later in England and the United States.

This early background helps us understand the contexts that conditioned the development of children's literature. People needed to have a compelling reason to learn to read, and a culture of schooling needed to be in place. Additionally, attitudes toward children and young adults had to reach a point where they were seen as being in need of teaching, worth teaching, and teachable. Further, the instruction of children had to be cast as a political or religious duty so that children would be given the time away from other work to pursue learning. High-born children bore the special responsibility of establishing and/or maintaining friendly relationships with others of their rank in order to maintain the strict delineations of class in the feudal economies of medieval Europe. Books of courtesy, manners, and conduct thus supplemented religious texts for young royals and nobles, often directly linking courtly manners with religious piety, as does *The Babees Book* (c. 1500 CE), the introduction of which gives a nice presentation of the common practice of fostering—sending noble children to live with other noble families in order to forge alliances—in medieval culture. But conduct and manners were also taught through *Aesop's Fables* and the **romances** found in works like the *Gesta Romanorum* (Acts of the Romans) and the Welsh tales that would later form the *Mabinogion* and the Arthurian **romances**. While these tales had an ostensibly moral purpose, their draw for children was probably based on their exciting plots, which featured a lot of magic, fighting, and tests of honor. A later conduct guide, "Youth's Behaviour, or, Decency in Conversation amongst Men, composed in French by Grave Persons, for the use and benefit of their Youth, now newly turned into English, by Francis Hawkins, nephew to Sir Thomas Hawkins. The tenth impression. London, 1672," included the following recommendations for girls' reading:

> To entertain young Gentlewomen in their hours of Recreation, we shall further commend unto them, Gods Revenge against Murther; and, the Arcadia of Sir Philip Sydney; Artemidorus his Interpretation of Dreams. And for the business of their Devotion, there is an excellent book entitled Taylor's Holy Living and Dying; The Duty of Man, in which the Duty to God and man are both comprehended (in Hewins 1888: 2) .

Such a list indicates that young women of noble birth were expected to be literate and to read both secular and sacred texts.

The development of print texts for children from the 1400s till 1600s

Hand-copied books of courtesy were only circulated among the upper classes, however. The next development necessary for the evolution of a recognizable youth literature was a new technology: mechanized printing. In the time periods we have canvassed thus far, books were not the primary education materials, even in schools. Books were rare, expensive and precious, and for good reason: a single hand-copied edition of the Bible could take up to three years to produce, and children's hands are often sticky. Prior to the development of print technologies and the invention of paper, literacy was taught through the use of wax tablets, and even when printed books became more readily available after the invention of the Gutenberg press in the 1400s, they weren't generally allowed in the hands of children. Instead, schoolchildren would use **hornbooks**, which typically contained an alphabet, the Lord's Prayer, common vowel and consonant combinations, and Roman numerals. These were printed on sheets of vellum or paper that were then pasted onto wooden paddles and covered with a thin layer of transparent horn or mica, which protected the printed material. In fact, it wasn't until 1658 that a book of words and pictures was written and published especially for children to be used in schools, *Orbis Sensualium Pictus* (*The Visible World in Pictures*), by Czech educator John Amos Comenius (1592–1670).

Comenius was incredibly important to the development of children's literature not simply because this particular text established the tradition of using illustrated books for children for educational purposes, but also because of his general philosophy of education, which included a commitment to universal instruction, the teaching of reading through ordinary or vernacular language, and the idea of starting with pictures of objects familiar to children in order to introduce new words and concepts. He wanted children to enjoy their studies; in short, he introduced the idea that children needed materials specifically designed for their experiences and abilities so that learning would be intrinsically motivating. This makes him a relatively unsung hero in the history of children's literature, even though the US National Council of Teachers of English (NCTE) does give an award in his name for the best nonfiction books for children each year. But Comenius's democratic attitudes toward education, inspired by his own poor upbringing and his Protestant beliefs that every person was responsible for his or her relationship to God and thus needed to be able to read scripture and to understand the marvels of creation, marked something of sea change in how education for young children was conceived. Comenius established the progressive organization of schooling from kindergarten through university that we use today, wrote textbooks for various age groups, and championed a model of education that would enable all students to gain a comprehensive knowledge of their world and its history. His early textbooks were thus among the first printed works especially designed for young audiences.

Comenius shared with the Puritans and other Reformation thinkers like John Calvin (1509–64) the belief that children were made in the image of God, but tainted by original sin from birth and in need of salvation. The most important task of education, then, was to make children aware of the consequences of following their natural inclinations toward sin and to encourage them to seek salvation through grace and then pursue good works. Consider this stanza from a poem written by a seven-year-old (!) Isaac Watts (1674–1748):

> I am a vile polluted lump of earth,
> So I've continued ever since my birth,
> Although Jehovah grace does daily give me,
> As sure this monster Satan will deceive me,
> Come therefore, Lord from Satan's claws relieve me. (Bond 2013: 14)

Clearly, even at seven years of age, Watts had internalized the prevailing view of childhood for religious thinkers in the seventeenth century, but this little poem also suggests that he was adept at the most prevalent method of instruction in early children's literature: the rhyming poem. Watts would continue writing such verse throughout his life, convinced that the pleasing nature of rhyme is the best vehicle for learning as well as for elevating the mind toward contemplation of the divine. Many of his poems were included in the various versions of *The New England Primer*, which first appeared between 1687 and 1690 and was used by children in New England for over a century. Contemporary English-speaking children who attend church or celebrate Christmas, however, are still familiar with Watts' work through his hymns, which notably include "Joy to the World" and "O God, Our Help in Ages Past." Watts' work shared the same **ideological** bases as that of John Bunyan's *Pilgrim's Progress* (1678) and James Janeway's *A Token for Children: Being an Exact Account of the Conversion, Holy and Exemplary Lives, and Joyful Deaths, of Several Young Children* (1671). Each of these broadly contemporaneous works has a similar goal—to direct children away from sin toward salvation—but they enact that goal through distinctly different tones. Bunyan's allegorical tale has the thrilling clarity of a heroic quest, while Janeway's sentimental tales of children finding faith and inspiring others before dying young seem particularly maudlin to modern tastes until we consider the popularity of books like John Green's *The Fault in Our Stars* (2012), which also focuses on the heroism of dying adolescents. Watts' poems encode religious doctrine and moral instruction into forms so persistently memorable that, 150 years after they were published, they became fodder for Lewis Carroll's parodies in his Alice books, but still find their way into contemporary religious education. Hence, works such as these represent more than quaint artifacts that reflect outmoded ways of thinking and stories we no longer tell; rather, they establish a way of thinking about children that persists in contemporary culture. Indeed, whether or not you believe in the particular **ideological** substrate that informs these works, it is important to note that their project as well as their various methods are foundational to children's and YA literature today. Contemporary literature for young people shares with these early texts the idea that memorable poetry, fantasy quest narratives, and melodramatic realism are useful vehicles for conveying the **ideology** of a culture to its readership. Whether we seek to save our children from a biblical hell or from the hells of climate change and social bigotry, we have never meant to simply entertain our children through their literature; we have always wanted to make them better.

John Locke's new way of thinking about children

While the emphasis on moral and religious instruction dominated children's literature in the 1600s, the development of print enabled secular texts to be more widely circulated as well. Children had access to horror stories as well as traditional tales and ballads through the stories told by exasperated nursemaids anxious to scare their charges into compliant behavior, as well as through the circulation of **chapbooks** and **broadsides**. **Chapbooks** were short, poorly made pamphlets sold by peddlers in Britain, usually for a penny, starting in the sixteenth century. They contained poems, abridged versions of popular works, and woodcut illustrations. Broadsides were large sheets of paper printed on one side that sometimes contained

> Children are blank slates that can be positively or negatively influenced by their surroundings and education. Their education should be both robust and moral, emphasizing humans' superiority over the natural world along with their obligation to protect and develop their understanding of it.

news, but more often ballads, poems, and woodcut illustrations. The tabloids of their day, the cheap publications aimed to titillate their readers with stories about brave knights, dangerous fairy folk, and monsters such as "Rawhead" and "Bloody Bones." English philosopher John Locke (1632–1704) objected to the sharing of such stories with children, not just because they were secular or irreligious but because they went against the project of the European Enlightenment, which sought to encourage reason and individualism over and against tradition and superstition. Unlike the Puritans, Locke rejected the idea of original sin, and believed instead that children's minds were what he called *tabulae rasae*—blank slates. Locke believed that, like the soft wax tablets on which former children had been taught to read and write, the minds of children were susceptible to impressions given to them through stories; therefore, it was imperative that those stories did not perpetuate the superstitions that would make children fearful. Instead, children should be introduced to the natural world without fictionalizing, fantasy, or superstition, and made to understand that their distinctly human minds made them naturally superior to lesser beings. Locke followed Comenius in advocating for simple books that would charm children as well as educate them. They should learn about and care for their environment, but not be subject to it, and they should be taught that any problems they encounter could be solved through knowledge and reason. They must always seek to make progress in understanding the natural world and facilitating better social structures and institutions that promote the education and well-being of more and more people.

Locke's basic idea, that children are born blank slates, has come to dominate contemporary thinking about children. Today we call this a **social constructivist** position, meaning that children are largely products of their environment. I say largely because in the next chapter we will encounter some theories that call the limits of constructivism into question, but for the most part, scholars in the humanities and social sciences take as an article of faith that children's perceptions, values, beliefs, tastes, dispositions, and expectations about the world are embedded in the environments in which they are reared. What is different about these contemporary positions versus a strict adherence to Lockean principles is the positive value we now give to imaginative literature. Locke's emphasis on a completely naturalistic and rational education for children disallowed any metaphorical explorations of fear and inordinate desire, which he believed would not exist in children's minds if they weren't implanted by stories. By contrast, our current understanding of children leads us to consider that they may be attracted to stories of the sort Locke would not approve because such stories meet some innate psychological need. Such needs might grow out of an existential fear of abandonment, say, or of being consumed; they come from our embodied experiences, rather than scary stories. Engaging with such stories, then, may lead to exorcizing fears as much as implanting or reinforcing them.

There is also a subtle but important difference in outcome between Locke's notion of the tabula rasa and the traditional Christian idea of original sin. Interestingly, Christian belief in original sin has more in common with Sigmund Freud's positions about innate aggressions, desires, and jealousies than Locke's; while all three positions contend that childhood experience is crucial to the development of the kinds of adults each considers healthy and well-adapted, both the Freudian and Christian positions agree that children have some inborn problems to confront and overcome. Locke, on the other hand, held the optimistic belief that proper educational methods would prevent irrational fears and superstitious beliefs from existing in the first place.

> Children are born with aggressive tendencies in the service of their own self-interest; they can and should be allowed to read stories that show natural and imposed consequences to aggressive and antisocial actions in order to develop their moral sense as well as self-control.

> Children are born naturally and innocently good, with an innate sense of justice and compassion, and should be protected from negative influences, including stories with sloppy or ambiguous morals, that emerge from adult society.

One hundred years after Locke penned his ideas about the nature of children, Jean-Jacques Rousseau radicalized the notion of human nature even further by suggesting that children were born with a carefree, innocent goodness that is ultimately corrupted by adult society: "Everything is good as it leaves the hands of the Author of things; but everything degenerates in the hands of man" (Rousseau 1762, 1979: 37). Rousseau believed that children's minds are in between those of animals, who act in their own self-interest and can't be considered good or bad, and the decadence of a depraved adulthood which once again chooses self-interest but does so out of pride and envy, in the full knowledge of right and wrong, and is thus culpable. "Love childhood," he says, "promote its games, its pleasures, its amiable instincts. Who among you has not sometimes regretted that age when a laugh is always on the lips and the soul is always at peace?" (79). In *Emile, or On Education* (1762), Rousseau laid out his ideal education plan for a fictional child, arguing against childhood reading as burdensome and proposing instead that children should be reared in the company of a tutor who would answer questions and encourage the child's natural curiosity. Rousseau's equations of childhood with nature, innocence, and peaceful pleasure formed the basis of the Romantic view of childhood, which was more effusively articulated in Wordsworth's "Ode: Intimations of Immortality from Recollections of Early Childhood" (1807): "But trailing clouds of glory do we come/ From God, who is our home:/ Heaven lies about us in our infancy!" A clear contrast from Watts's "I am a vile polluted lump of earth," Wordsworth's vision of childhood adds to the historical spectrum of **ideologies** of childhood that we continue to respond to today as we consider what we believe about childhood and how it should be lived and valued. In general, we accept that children are unique individuals from birth, and thus have the ability and the responsibility to pursue a future largely of their own choosing. Beyond that, however, questions remain: Are children born sinful and in need of salvation? Are they blank slates and in need of protection? Are they innately good and in need of preservation? Is there some synthesis or middle ground between these viewpoints? Most authors (and critics) are not going to come right out and explicitly state where they stand on these issues, but as we will see in the case study that follows this chapter, variations on these and other basic beliefs inform how writers write and how readers read.

The effects of industrialization on the children's literature of the eighteenth and nineteenth centuries

Eliza Dresang (1999) argues that the belief in childhood innocence and goodness began to take precedence in the later nineteenth and early twentieth centuries. Generally speaking, a belief in natural human goodness is an *interested* perspective, by which I mean that, while Romantic in origin, it serves the aims of the European Enlightenment as well as the popular uptake of the Darwinian theory of evolution, which took hold in the mid-1800s. Political, economic, and social change was afoot, and Europeans were making what looked like healthy human progress through evolution and revolution. A belief in human nature as naturally good subtends the faith that it is possible to make the world a better, more just place if only we can preserve and augment that goodness through proper education methods. Interestingly, the material history of childhood up to that point stands in contrast to Rousseau's representation of it; as we noted above, agrarian childhoods were harsh, and the Romans considered childhood a stage to be hurried through as quickly as possible. So what changed, culturally speaking, so that a nostalgic attitude toward an idyllic, carefree childhood marked by essential goodness gained traction?

Matthew O. Grenby (2009) points out that, beginning in the early 1700s, a new way of thinking emerged that encouraged the sentimental attachment between middle- and upper-class mothers and their children; such a shift in parenting practices away from harsh discipline toward more tender treatment would certainly make recollections of childhood sweeter for the economically privileged, literate child. But I would also suggest that the effects of increasing industrialization, sometimes called the Industrial Revolution, had a lot to do with changing attitudes toward childhood. Beginning around 1760, new manufacturing methods spurred the growth of factories and afforded families the opportunity to improve their incomes, at least in theory, if they moved to cities. However, industrialization brought with it a sense of alienation; operations once performed at home by family groups were now outsourced to impersonal factories, and workers in those factories were unable to afford the goods they produced. Birth rates went up, though child mortality was still quite high. But most significantly, child labor became a valuable commodity. Since all factory-based manufacturing processes were new, there was no such thing as skilled labor, and children could be paid less and fit into small spaces around machines and in mines to perform dangerous tasks. Living and working conditions were horrific for children. Additionally, pollution was a major concern in cities; cities were grimy and smelly, and the soot-laden air was hard to breath. These conditions were noted by William Blake (1757–1827) and reflected in his poetry, particularly in *Songs of Innocence* (1789), where he gave voice to a nostalgia for a rural childhood that had to be better than the present conditions for both adults and children living in an industrialized city. Such nostalgia is an important impetus to take up writing for children in the first place, whether it be in fond, fuzzy remembrance of a childhood untainted by the effects of industrialization, or in a desire to *invent* such a childhood as an alternative to present horrors.

In addition to encouraging a more sentimental view toward one's own childhood, the growth of industrial practices generally made children's publishing something you could make money doing, with Thomas Boreman's Gigantick Histories series beginning in 1740, and Mary Cooper's collection of English nursery rhymes, *Tommy Thumb's Pretty Song Book,* as well as John Newbery's *A Little Pretty Pocket-Book,* appearing in 1744. Newbery went on to publish more than twenty books for children to read for pleasure, as well as *The Lilliputian Magazine* (1751–52), the title indicating widespread familiarity among young readers with Jonathan Swift's *Gulliver's Travels* (1726). Publishers found that oral folk and fairy tales sold well in print, increasing the availability of fiction of a nonreligious variety. In fact, the success of pleasurable books for children, including English-language versions of Charles Perrault's *Tales of Mother Goose* in 1697 and *The Arabian Nights Entertainment* in 1706, led to a backlash of moral and didactic work. Leading the charge was Sarah Trimmer (1741–1810) who became the first children's book reviewer with her aptly named publication *The Guardian of Education* (1802–06). Like Locke, as well as like many contemporary critics, she was opposed to fairy tales for the ideas they perpetuated, so it could also be argued that she inaugurated the cultural criticism of children's literature as well. Trimmer was joined in her efforts to improve the moral and educational quality of children's literature by Anna Laetitia Barbauld (1743–1825), Hannah More (1745–1833), Maria Edgeworth (1768–1849), and Mary Martha Sherwood (1775–1851).

Both Barbauld and Edgeworth championed the use of children's ordinary language in their domestic stories, establishing a wholly new way of writing for children. Sherwood's three-volume *History of the Fairchild Family* (1818, 1842, 1847), however, hearkened back to earlier styles with its graphic descriptions of naughty children meeting grisly ends and suffering the tortures of hell as a result. While women authors began to take center stage in writing for children during this period, Thomas Day's school story, *Sandford and Merton* (1783), also enjoyed a robust readership. Hence while the popular books of the day still aimed at moral teaching, they were less overtly religious and more concerned with presenting white children of various social classes in everyday situations.

Framed in this way, then, industrialization seems as though it was as good for the growth of children's literature as it was bad for the lives of poor children. But of course things are not so simple. The attention paid to the voices and virtues of ordinary children in literature made the spectacle of child labor that much harder to bear. Sunday schools were established in the 1780s to educate factory children, often alongside their parents, on their one day of the week off. But the **ideology** of the Romantic child set against the actual lives of urban children inspired public outrage and activism that resulted in the first child labor laws being enacted in England. The Cotton Regulation Act of 1819 set the minimum working age at nine, with paid inspectors coming on the scene through the Regulation of Child Labor Law of 1833. Later, the Ten Hours Bill of 1847 set a limit of a ten-hour workday for women and children. Twenty-eight of the then forty-five United States had laws regulating child labor by 1899. These laws may seem ridiculous by today's standards, but recall that life had always been difficult for working-class children and continues to be so for most of the world's children even today. In that light, these reforms represented a slow but steady movement toward a better standard of living in industrialized countries with accountable governance structures. The period from 1760 to 1870 saw significant growth in the middle class and sustained growth in per capita income in such countries, and the addition of steam technology to printing processes meant greater availability of books for all classes of people.

Despite the efforts of Trimmer and her like-minded contemporaries to remove fantasy from children's books, folk and fairy tales continued to find their way into children's hands. Indeed, in the eighteenth century, collecting and transforming traditional oral tales into lasting literary versions came into fashion as a way of preserving the treasures of an oral tradition that was being gobbled up by print culture. Jeanne Marie de Beaumont (1711–80) in France, Elizabeth Newbery (c. 1745–1821) in England, Alexander Pushkin (1799–1837) in Russia, and Jacob (1785–1863) and Wilhelm (1785–1863) Grimm (1786–1859) in Germany collected, revised, and published collections of folk and fairy tales indigenous to their countries. Inspired by the Grimms, later collectors such as Joseph Jacobs (1854–1916) and Andrew Lang (1844–1912) in England and Peter Christen Asbjørnsen (1812–85) and

Jörgen Moe (1813–82) in Norway searched the countrysides of their native lands for folktales. Hans Christian Andersen (1805–75) pulled motifs from the folktales of Denmark to create his own original literary fairy tales, which set Christian themes in fantasy settings. As noted earlier, given their concern with marriage and seeking one's fortune, it is probably more precise to consider many of these folk and fairy tales as YA rather than children's literature, but writers over the years have drawn from this rich source material to produce new work for a range of ages, from the cheerfully metafictive picturebook rendition of *The Three Pigs* (2001) by David Wiesner for young readers to the LGBTQ-friendly short story collection *Kissing the Witch: Old Tales in New Skins* (1999) by Emma Donoghue.

The golden age of children's books: The nineteenth to early twentieth centuries

Beginning in the mid-1800s, a rising middle class, a flourishing publishing industry, greater levels of literacy, an inflamed social conscience, a more pronounced distinction between the sacred and secular, and increased nostalgia for an idealized childhood all combined to create a robust children's book trade that has come to be referred to as the golden age of children's books. A wider variety of books appeared, some supporting and others challenging the overt didacticism of their predecessors. For older readers, humor, parody, and nonsense appeared on the scene, with Catherine Sinclair's *Holiday House* (1839) poking gentle fun at family life in the tradition of Jane Austen, Heinrich Hoffmann's outrageous *Struwwelpeter* (1844, English translation 1848) launching a direct attack on the genre of the cautionary tale, and Edward Lear's *A Book of Nonsense* (1846) making language play its own reward. While the **didactic** literature of Barbauld, Trimmer, and More was overtly invested in religious instruction to justify and preserve the social and economic status quo, religion and sentiment were also combined in the service of social critique in Harriet Beecher Stowe's antislavery novel, *Uncle Tom's Cabin*, published in 1852.

This period saw the development of the first texts beyond the folk tradition that specifically focused on teenagers as well. A strong emphasis on manliness and self-reliance threaded through the European, Australian, and North American ideal of character, aided and abetted by Rousseau's recommendation of Daniel Defoe's *Robinson Crusoe* (1719) as acceptable reading for Emile as a teenager in 1762, preached by Johann David Wyss to his four sons in his novel, *The Swiss Family Robinson* (1812), and trumpeted by Ralph Waldo Emerson in his 1841 essay "Self-Reliance." Despite her loss of the American colonies, England was still invested in maintaining an international empire, and the infant United States had troubles of its own with the Barbary pirates; such conditions necessitated inspiring young men and women with a patriotic love of country and a taste for adventure and the glories of battle. Captain Frederick Marryat thrilled young readers on both sides of the Atlantic with his semiautobiographical accounts of swashbuckling battles during the Napoleonic Wars beginning with *Frank Mildmay* (1829) and continuing through the more well-known *Masterman Ready* (1841). Though occasionally bogged down with intrusive moral lessons, his books established the exciting sea story as adolescent reading, inspiring other authors, such as Robert Ballantyne and Captain Mayne Reid to develop their own stories of war, manly adventure, and escape from home. G. A. Henty became famous for his historical novels featuring resourceful young boys, and sometimes young girls, behaving admirably in difficult times. Other boys' adventure stories followed, including Robert Louis Stevenson's *Treasure Island* (1883) and *Kidnapped*, first published as a serial novel in the magazine *Our Young Folks* in 1886. Adolescent literature was growing in America as well, with Mark Twain's *The Adventures of Huckleberry Finn* (1884 UK & Canada; 1885 US) and Louisa May Alcott's *Little Women* (1868–9), both taking their teenage characters' moral development, as well as their country's moral health and need for reform, as their subject (Trites 2007). An early Australian text, *Seven Little Australians* (1894), by Ethel Turner, mirrors *Little Women* in some ways, highlighting teen rebellion as thirteen-year-old Judy chafes at the expectations imposed on her as she grows into a young woman.

New printing technologies prompted some of the most prominent illustrators of the day to turn their attention to illustrating children's books. George Cruikshank, Walter Crane, John Tenniel, Randolph Caldecott, Kate Greenaway, and Arthur Rackham all became well known, and reasonably well paid, for their children's book illustrations. Children's poetry and nursery rhyme collections appeared in illustrated editions, and proper picturebooks, such as Helen Bannerman's controversial but highly successful *The Story of Little Black Sambo* (1899) and Beatrix Potter's *The Tale of Peter Rabbit* (self-published in 1901 but picked up and released by Frederick Warne in 1902) became standard fare for younger children. New kinds of fantasy emerged as children fell down the rabbit hole with Alice in 1865, traveled with Dorothy to Oz in 1900, and flew away to Neverland with Peter Pan in 1904. They sought treasure with the Bastables in 1899, and mucked about in boats with Ratty and Mole in 1908. While these works were trumpeted by critics as having finally shed the **didacticism** of their predecessors, many of them nevertheless took their stand quite firmly against adult society and customs, which is a lesson and critique in itself. Gentler messages were found in the realistic texts of the period, which focused primarily on girls healing their communities through their cheerfully tenacious optimism; examples include Kate Douglas Wiggin's *Rebecca of Sunnybrook Farm* (1903); Frances Hodgson Burnett's *A Little Princess* (1905) and *The Secret Garden* (1911); Lucy Maud Montgomery's *Anne of Green Gables* (1908), and Eleanor H. Porter's *Pollyanna* (1913). But while this spate of girls' titles set against boys' adventure tales makes it seems as though the line between gendered reading was firmly drawn, Edward Salmon (1888: 29) noted after surveying a large group of British students that girls of the period "don't care for Sunday-school twaddle; they like a good stirring story, with a plot and some incident and adventures—not a collection of texts and sermons and hymns strung together." Fortunately, they were finding plenty of stories to their liking. Children's magazines flourished during this time as well, the most famous, perhaps, being *St. Nicholas* which began under the editorial guidance of Mary Mapes Dodge in 1873 and remained in publication until 1940. Master storytellers Rudyard Kipling, E. Nesbit, and Kenneth Grahame all contributed to this truly golden period of enduring and beloved children's literature.

The **ideological** projects, if not the character depictions, carried through youth literature in the nineteenth century were becoming more diverse. Imperialist and anti-imperialist sentiments found their way into young people's books, with religious sentiments pressed into service on both sides. Nonwhite characters were occasionally represented in the texts, but almost always in positions of inferiority, as was the case with characters who were Jewish or Irish. Many adventure stories, for instance, followed in the tradition of *Robinson Crusoe*, with their attitude of benevolent paternalism toward the peaceful indigenous characters the young explorers met on their journeys. Works of this ilk, such as Catharine Parr Traill's *Canadian Crusoes: A Tale of the Rice Lake Plains* (1852), show indigenous characters working cooperatively with the white protagonists, but ultimately emphasize the superiority of Western civilization and Christianity, an attitude also reinforced by stories in religious tracts aimed at encouraging zeal and donations for missionary work. Michelle J. Smith (2011: 178) notes, however, that other Robinsonades, as these books are called, such as Mrs. Herbert Strang's *The Girl Crusoes* (1912), "to some degree revise[] the idea of the British castaway civilizing a non-white Other" by portraying nonwhite characters as genuine friends. But even texts that appear to take their white characters to task for mistreating their nonwhite peers often do so from a perspective of entitled superiority, as Michelle H. Martin (2004) notes in her even-handed and thoughtful comparison of Hoffman's "The Inky Boys" (in *Struwwelpeter*, 1845) and Helen Bannerman's *Little Black Sambo* (1899). Whereas the white boys in Hoffman's tale are scolded and then punished for taunting a silent, unnamed black boy, their punishment is to be turned black themselves, making the story "explicitly antiracist yet implicitly racist" (Martin 2004: 9). Bannerman's text, on the other hand, while chastised over the years for its far-reaching role in the establishment of damaging racial stereotypes, presents an appealing, resourceful child character who is loved by his parents and celebrated for his cleverness.

More ambiguous is the position taken in a text like Robert Louis Stevenson's *A Child's Garden of Verses* (1885). The poem "Foreign Children," for instance, certainly seems to promote British superiority by asking a list of ethnically identified children, "O! don't you wish that you were me?" The second stanza, however, catalogs a series of appealing things these children have seen and done that are unavailable to the British child, who is "safe and live[s] at home." Given the wistful longing for a larger world that the child speaker intones throughout the entire collection, the declaration of "safe . . . at home" begs to be read ironically, or at least as an attempt to convince oneself of the superior benefits of being confined and excluded from a world of wonders. Tracing **ideologies** of the period through these texts, then, requires care and subtlety as they reflect both explicit and implicit attitudes circulating at the time regarding race, class, ethnicity, and gender. Given the class-driven economics of publishing, print youth literature remained, however, a primarily white, middle-class enterprise.

The emergence of adolescence as a life stage distinct from childhood and early adulthood: Divergent views

At various points throughout this chapter, I have noted the presence of conditions and themes that fall under the category of what we would today call adolescence or young adulthood rather than childhood. From cave paintings to folktales to novels by Twain, Alcott, Henty, and others, there is an implicit acknowledgment throughout literary history that the changes that come between childhood and adulthood—learning a trade, separating emotionally from parents, dreaming about a partner of one's own—require some sort of special attention, even if that attention is framed in negative terms, as in Shakespeare's *A Winter's Tale*: "I would that there were no age between ten and three-and-twenty, or that youth would sleep out the rest; for there is nothing in the between but getting wenches with child, wronging the ancientry, stealing, fighting" (act 3, scene 3). The term "adolescence" comes from the Latin *adolescere,* which means to mature or become established, as a plant does. It didn't come into the popular vocabulary in reference to people, however, until the publication of American psychologist G. Stanley Hall's two-volume study called *Adolescence: Its Psychology and its relations to Physiology, Anthropology, Sociology, Sex, Crime, and Religion* in 1904.

Like Ariès, Hall deserves some pride of place for opening an interdisciplinary conversation about adolescence. But also like Ariès's, Hall's work has engendered strong critique. For instance, Hall coined the phrase *Sturm und Drang,* "storm and stress," to refer to the mood disruptions, conflict with parents, and risky behavior associated with the teenage years. While Shakespeare would likely agree with Hall, subsequent researchers have taken issue with his thesis that adolescence is a necessarily turbulent period on both individual and cultural levels, as have authors of literature for children and young adults. There is, of course, some biological basis for moodiness and risk-taking during the teen years, but authors have long believed in the power of literature to actively socialize and redirect rather than merely reflect and enforce what comes naturally. Consider, for instance, that there would be no need for a commandment to honor one's father and mother if it were natural to do so. Hence, early nonfiction books stressed obedience and proper conduct as a way to stave off conflict, while folk and fairy tales offered a means for imaginative release and wish fulfillment as well as subtler indoctrination of cultural norms and expectations regarding gender in particular (boys seek their fortune, slay dragons, and rescue damsels; girls wait, usually unconscious, for a reviving kiss), but also providing general blueprints for what makes for happy ever after (e.g., heterosexual marriage, a kingdom to rule over, and great wealth).

But stories can also make their readers itch for social and economic change, as did the tales that glorified outlaws and robbers like Robin Hood in an age of economic exploitation and rigid class hierarchies. This sort of storytelling exacerbates conflict rather than bedding it back down and can become a catalyst for changes in the conditions under which one matures or becomes established in life. As economies and social hierarchies change, the need for certain types of personalities and values change as well, and this may be one way to understand Lerer's idea, cited at the beginning of this chapter, that the child is *made* through stories. Teenagers are especially vulnerable to personal exploration through external models, for reasons we will discuss in the next chapter. Empire building, exploration, an entrepreneurial spirit, and scientific advances call for people willing to take risks; the adventure novels of the late 1800s and early 1900s, from Marryat and Stevenson to the Stratemeyer Syndicate, purveyors of the Bobbsey Twins (1904–79), Nancy Drew (1930–2003), and the Hardy Boys (1927–2005) among countless other teen series, responded by painting a picture of adolescence as a time of excitement and adventure. Teenagers, both boys and girls, are overwhelmingly competent in these tales, whether they are fighting pirates or solving crimes. They don't spend their time moping or fighting with their parents, and their risky behavior is championed as necessary and nearly always rewarded with success.

In the early days of the twentieth century, then, the relative optimism and faith in human progress that had characterized Western civilization since the European Enlightenment allowed for the development of a literature that allowed children to engage in unfettered imaginative play and encouraged adolescents to proceed confidently into the future. Oh, sure, there were social injustices to be addressed, but if one just had pluck, determination, and a group of hardy chums, one could entertain great expectations. On the pages of children's and adolescent literature, the empire was flourishing. New worlds were waiting to be discovered. Battles were glorious. Dragons were conquerable. Villains were easily thwarted. It truly did seem to be something of a golden age. And then came the world wars.

Children's and young adult literature from the early twentieth century to the present

The golden age of children's texts is generally considered to have ended around 1915. As we discussed when we unpacked the various metaphors for literature in the introduction, the aesthetic artifacts of a culture are not straightforwardly mimetic; they exaggerate some things and hide others. They imagine more and sometimes differently than the histories or realities out of which they are born. They operate according to a logic of desire rather than fact. In particular, the literature a culture produces for and about its young reflects more than its current state of scientific and theoretical knowledge; instead, it functions as a barometer of its fears, beliefs, and aspirations for itself.

Conquest, human and environmental abuse and oppression, and war always require stories to inspire and justify participation. The stories we tell both before and after conflict, especially for young people, often establish clear boundaries between aggressor and defender that are much less clear in real life. But no matter how romanticized the stories, the actual, lived horrors and atrocities of conquest and war shake humanity's faith in itself, especially when we begin to listen to the stories of the victimized, and realize that any war that is supposed to end all wars simply doesn't. Even when our side is victorious, we look back on the mess and ask: How did we let this happen? What might we have done differently? Shouldn't we, with all our scientific knowledge and achievements, be better people than this? It is in this context of a shaken faith in the soundness of humankind's ability to make beneficial social progress that children's and YA literature developed in the twentieth century.

Eva M. Simms's (2008: 199) assessment of the dynamics of age in the Middle Ages, that "children become children when adults become more 'adult'," played out in the early decades of twentieth century as adults looked back with a kind of existential exhaustion on the hopefulness of their youthful ideals. Imagining life as a glorious battle that could be faced heroically and won through the force of our own pluck gave way, according to literary theorist Alan Friedman (1966: 9), to a postmodern understanding of life as a continual buffeting of "assaults and offers" that require often compromised responses. As a result, the more exhausted adults became after decades of war and economic crisis in the twentieth century, the more they needed childhood to be a protected, contained space of hope and renewal. The youth literature of the war years reflects this need. Children's publishing had become an established marketing sector with vocal advocates, particularly in libraries; the American Library Association was founded in 1876, specialized training for children's librarians began in 1898, and a prestigious awards system began developing in 1922. Indeed, the gulf between children's and adult literature became more and more distinct as the century progressed, in part so that adults could hold on to the narrative that, despite our failures to resolve problems without recourse to violence, there might still be hope if we can just make our children's lives havens of peace, social justice, and heroic amity between diverse peoples and nations.

Children's literature in the decades during and after the world wars offered such havens through the fantasies of A. A. Milne, J. R. R. Tolkien, and C. S. Lewis, the historical fiction and alternate histories of Rachel Field, Laura Ingalls Wilder, Geoffrey Trease, Arthur Ransome, and Joan Aiken, and the family stories of Noel Streatfeild, Elizabeth Enright, and Eleanor Estes. Kathy Merlock Jackson (1986: 1) argues that "prior to World War II, the image of children in American films was one of unqualified innocence"; children were "happy, basically good, and endowed with a sense of childlike tenderness and wonder." Walt Disney put children's stories on the big and small screens, helping to make movies and television avenues of escapism; MGM's *The Wizard of Oz* (1939) became an emblem of the American spirit. Children's picturebooks became increasingly diverse in artistic style and subject matter, and children's inner worlds were given their due through more complex stories and character depictions. Travel opened up for both actual and armchair tourists, with authors such as Astrid Lindgren and Langston Hughes developing texts designed to promote intercultural understanding rather than colonialist appropriation.

On the other hand, though, as the century progressed, more actual knowledge about the world de-romanticized the lure of the unknown to some extent, and led to a desire for new frontiers. This desire teamed up with Einstein's theories about time and relativity, anxieties over technology fueled by the development of atomic weapons, and the Space Race between the United States and the Soviet Union that

> Young people are our only hope to save the world and make it a better place.

began in the 1950s to inspire science fiction for young adults. As the millennium turned, contemporary YA dystopian novels continue to explore anxieties over new technologies, invasive and authoritarian political structures, and environmental devastation through plots that position teenagers as society's only hope. And in fact, our social and personal technologies have engendered children's and YA fantasies that foreground an emergent **ideological** framework, **posthumanism**, that challenges—in dialogue of course—all of the **ideologies** of childhood we have addressed in this chapter, and will be discussed at length in the chapter on fantasy. In general, the youth literature of the twentieth and into the twenty-first century has expanded its reach into all aspects of the human and posthuman story, but it has carved out a special role for young people in that story, as those who can succeed and prosper when adults fail.

Diversity in youth literature: An ongoing quest

In the early twentieth century and continuing to the present, however, there has also been a growing recognition by librarians, writers, teachers, scholars, and social activists that all children are not equally served by the children's and YA literature on offer. In fact, children of various ethnic and racial heritages and/or non-normative genders, and those who have physical disabilities or neurological differences, if they are represented at all, are more likely to be confronted with either belittling or romanticized stereotypes than fully realized character representations. As noted above, some adventure and frontier novels of the 1800s included nonwhite characters, but these characters were most often used in the service of promoting the imperialistic project or encouraging a patronizing benevolence in the white, able-bodied main characters without disturbing their sense of entitlement. Even though the first books explicitly for and about nonwhite children were published as early as the 1890s and there was a smattering of texts throughout the first few decades of the twentieth century, the imagery in these early efforts tended to reinforce rather than challenge racist and ableist stereotypes.

To counteract the persistently negative imagery that black children were faced with in their daily lives as well as their literature, W. E. B. Dubois (1919: 286) started a children's magazine for black children in 1920 called *The Brownies' Book* that listed the following purposes:

a To make colored children realize that being "colored" is a normal, beautiful thing.
b To make them familiar with the history of the Negro race.
c To make them know that other colored children have grown into beautiful, useful, and famous persons.
d To teach them delicately a code of honor and action in their relations with white children.
e To turn their little hurts and resentments into emulation, ambition, and love of their own homes and companions.
f To point out the best amusements and joys and worthwhile things of life.
g To inspire them to prepare for definite occupations and duties with a broad spirit of sacrifice.

Prominent black authors such as Nella Larsen, Langston Hughes, and Effie Lee Newsome published work in *The Brownies' Book*, while well-known black artists such as Albert A. Smith, Laura Wheeler, and Hilda Rue Wilkinson contributed cover art; unfortunately, this significant publication saw only two years in print. The American Library Association's Newbery Award in 1928 went to an Asian American writer, Dhan Gopal Mukerji, for *Gay-Neck: The Story of a Pigeon,* and Pura Belpré, the first Puerto Rican librarian in the New York Library System, published the first US Latinx book for children in 1932. Despite these and other standouts, and despite continued efforts of librarians and critics to champion books that featured non-stereotypical depictions of indigenous and non-European characters written by authors who hailed from these groups, though, children's literature of the early twentieth century retained its publishing origins as a mostly white, middle-class enterprise, as Nancy Larrick noted in her landmark 1965 article, "The All-White World of Children's Books." And indeed, the landscape hasn't gotten much more colorful: statistics compiled by the Cooperative Children's Book Center in

> Children are diverse in intelligence, temperament, experience, and interest, but are all capable of learning given the right approach, and all need positive representation in literature and other media in order to understand their embeddedness in human communities and to realize their full potential as individuals. Moreover, there is a time between childhood and adulthood that is distinctly different from either, and thus deserves its own attention as a stage of life.

2014 show that only 14 percent of the books written for young readers were about nonwhite protagonists, and with the exception of Latinx literature, 57 percent of those books were written by authors who were not from the culture from which they drew their characters (Ehrlich 2015). Most recently, a push for diverse literature for young readers has taken social media by storm, and publishers are taking note of the #weneeddiversebooks movement, but debates that began in the 1960s with the publication of Ezra Jack Keats' *The Snowy Day* (1962) still rage. White author Keats created a young everyboy Peter as his main character enjoying a walk in a city neighborhood transformed by snow, but was critiqued by Larrick and others for not overtly acknowledging or celebrating the fact that Peter was black. The question of how central one's ethnicity is to one's character, the ways it can and should matter, is unresolved in current debates, and likely unresolvable.

While many make the argument that children's literature as a profit-driven enterprise is responsible for the continuing dearth of diverse characters, the situation is much more complicated. One of the key factors is **ideology**. Robin Bernstein (2011), for instance, has argued that the Romantic **ideology** of childhood innocence and goodness has implicitly and explicitly excluded nonwhite children. This attitude would certainly have served the aims of European empire building and the exploitation of children as workers who were not entitled to protected childhoods like their middle-class white counterparts. Thus the representation of indigenous people in particular has long been in the hands of their invaders and colonizers who often used such characters as **tropes** that supported their **ideological** messages. Only in the mid to late twentieth century have authors emerged who write from within their own cultures, exploring their own cultural aesthetics and explicitly and implicitly critiquing the premises on which white cultures operate.

One of these salient **ideological** differences that multicultural literature surfaces and critiques is the relative value of the group versus the individual: that is, which seems to matter more in the book's explicit or implicit messaging? Oppressed and underrepresented people groups tend to have a strong sense of their corporate identity; members cluster together for safety as well as community strength and positive recognition that they don't get from people outside their group, value their racial history and language as an ongoing legacy, and perceive harm to one person as an affront to all. As a result, you will find more emphasis on history, intergenerational memory and respect for elders and traditions, and narratives of strong community responsibility in books from minority cultures. Members of the dominant culture, on the other hand, are more likely to individuate. Part of this stems from a desire to avoid responsibility and guilt; by dismissing group affiliation, a person can disavow personal involvement in the perpetuation of systemic injustice—the "I've never oppressed anybody" defense. But another part comes from a philosophical tradition that has developed since the advent of the warrior/hero culture inspired by historians and bards such as Homer and the Beowulf poet who glorified individuals in their epics. Wars are fought by nations and groups, but songs are sung about named individual heroes. Christianity contributed the notion of taking personal responsibility for inborn sin, and being willing to leave family and ethnic affiliations for multiethnic communities of faith. Obviously, not everyone believes in these particular **ideologies**, but remember the iceberg? Such individualistic notions of both the possibility of fame and recognition and personal responsibility for one's own behavior inform **discourses** of one-person-one-vote majority-rules governance, capitalism, private property, family structures, child development, and personal aspirations to stand apart from the group. This stress on individual achievement often causes conflict for characters negotiating between cultures, such as Junior in *The Absolutely True Diary of a Part-time Indian* (Alexie 2007); as his friend Gordy puts it, "'Well, life is a constant struggle between being an individual and being a member of a community'" (132). As we shall see in multiple discussions of diversity throughout this book, including the case study at the end of this chapter, the different levels of importance given to individual achievement, recognition and blame versus group affiliation, representation and solidarity often strike at the **ideological** heart of the debates that surface regarding multicultural literature for young people.

The literature directed specifically at teenage readers that emerged in the 1970s has a slightly better track record in terms of diversity, featuring more nonwhite writers as well as texts that frankly explore the problems of class, ethnicity, sexual orientation, and gender. Rather than construct adolescence as an apolitical world inhabited by energetic and resourceful heroes, these newer texts responded to the social problems of their day and admitted that justice doesn't always prevail, and not everyone survives. Today's YA literature continues in this mode, featuring books that focus on **intersectionality**—that is, how race, ethnicity, class, embodiment, gender, and sexual orientation combine to create complex social identities that result in multiple forms of discrimination and oppression. As a largely character-driven genre with an emphasis on negotiating identity, contemporary YA texts respond quickly to changing demographics and shifting cultural concerns. However, contemporary children's and YA literature is still disproportionately white by the numbers, and even more so by genre count, as we will see when we address specific genre in later chapters. Diversity is on everyone's minds in the early decades of the twenty-first century, but it has a long way to go to claim equity on the shelves in the children's and teen section.

Conclusion

In this chapter, we have explored the **ideological**, economic, and social conditions that enabled the development of a special literature devoted to children and adolescents. We have developed a framework for understanding that children's and YA literature emerges in dynamic response to those conditions. We might sum it up this way: what we believe about children and ourselves determines what we write and buy for them. Further, these acts of sharing the world with young people are indicators of what we hope for them, and what we think they need to survive. It is also important to remember that while ideas may have histories, they also have futures; once an idea comes into the world, it weaves its way into the fabric of our ways of thinking, often without our realizing it. In subsequent chapters, we will nuance our understanding of the **ideologies** that thread through children's and YA texts even further as we focus more specifically on the various forms and genres available to young people today.

Extending your study

Reading:

Lerer, Seth. *Children's Literature: A Reader's History, from Aesop to Harry Potter* (Chicago, IL: University of Chicago Press, 2008).
   A comprehensive, readable history of children's literature with an emphasis on the role it has played in developing the cultural imagination.
Marcus, Leonard S. *Minders of Make Believe* (New York, NY: Houghton Mifflin, 2008).

Overview of the development of three hundred years of American children's literature through the context of ideological battles around what counts as good reading for children.

Stevenson, Deborah. "History of Children's and Young Adult Literature." In Shelby A. Wolf, Karen Coats, Patricia Enciso, and Christine A. Jenkins, Eds. *Handbook of Research on Children's and Young Adult Literature* (New York, NY: Routledge, 2011).

Informative overview of the problems inherent in constructing a genre history before embarking on a history of children's and YA publishing from the classical era through the nineteenth century.

Townsend, John Rowe. *Written for Children: An Outline of English-Language Children's Literature* (Lanham, MD: Scarecrow Press, 1996).

Comprehensive overview of youth literature produced in England, the United States, Australia, and Canada, including many texts often overlooked, from medieval times to 1996, with a 2003 postscript.

Writing:

1 What do you believe about the nature of children and childhood? What factors inform this belief? Was there a moment when your beliefs about childhood changed? If so, describe the incident that sparked the change. If not, describe an incident that confirms your present beliefs.

2 C. S. Lewis wrote The Chronicles of Narnia (1950–6) in the aftermath of the Second World War; Madeleine L'Engle wrote *A Wrinkle in Time* (1963) during the Cold War era; James Lincoln Collier and Christopher Collier wrote *My Brother Sam is Dead* (1974) during the Vietnam era. Choose one of these books and explore how it is an imaginative response to the war of its time.

3 Compare and contrast girl characters from two different eras. For instance, you might compare Harriet from *Harriet the Spy* (Fitzhugh, 1964) with *Pollyanna* (Porter, 1913). What are the cultural expectations for each girl? What role does she play in her community? What characterizes her interactions with others? Ultimately, what does your analysis suggest about the **ideologies** related to girls in each time period?

4 After reading the case study (below), choose a picturebook and develop two different readings based on different **ideological** frameworks. For instance, you might look at *Mufaro's Beautiful Daughters: An African Tale* (Steptoe 1987) from a multicultural framework and a Christian framework, similar to the work done in the case study, or you might consider *The Wolves in the Walls* (Gaiman 2003) from the perspective of someone who believes that horror is beneficial for children or someone who takes a more Lockean view. Another

suggestion would be to look at *Where the Wild Things Are* (Sendak 1963) and construct an argument from two opposite perspectives on appropriate methods of punishment. (Should the mother have isolated Max and threatened to withhold food—yes or no?)

5 Choose a character from a middle grade or YA novel and decide which **ideology** of childhood best informs his or her depiction. Is she, for instance, clearly a product of her environment and upbringing, as in a Lockean model? Or does he conform more readily to a Romantic view that he is basically good, and immune from the influences of poor treatment and abuse? Or, by contrast, is she basically selfish and in need of punishment or reform? Write an essay in which you describe the character's behavior and traits in light of the **ideological** position that seems most applicable. Remember, of course, that such attitudes toward children are rarely pure, so you may find yourself arguing for a blend.

Discussing:

1 How might future historians construct an **ideology** of childhood or adolescence in the early days of the twenty-first century based on contemporary literature? What do we seem to believe about the nature of children or teens and what they should like and know?

2 Based on your discussion of the previous question, what are some reasonable limits and values of understanding historical attitudes through the reading of literary and artistic artifacts?

3 Read "Cinderella: or the Glass Slipper" by Charles Perrault, available here: http://www.pitt.edu/~dash/perrault06.html. Consider some contemporary versions and riffs on the Cinderella story. What changes are evident in the new versions versus Perrault's version? What do these changes suggest about what contemporary storytellers think children need and like?

4 Throughout history, the distinction between childhood and adulthood has been more or less clear. In traditional and medieval societies, for instance, adults and children shared games, stories, and other activities, whereas in the nineteenth century, sharp lines were drawn between what was appropriate for children and what was appropriate for adults. How would you rate the sharpness of the distinction between the two in contemporary culture? What indicators lead to your answer?

5 After reading Anne Fine's talkback for this chapter, discuss whether or not you think children today are different from how they were ten or fifteen years ago. Discuss this question with your parents to get their perspectives on their own childhood versus yours. Share and compare your findings with those of your classmates.

Responding:

1 Create a replica of a hornbook. Research and select a poem of scripture that would have been used on an authentic hornbook, or produce a parodic version of your own based on actual examples.

2 Visit a church or cathedral with stained glass windows or other iconography. Imagine you are a preliterate child in that church. What stories are told through these visual elements, and how effective is the storytelling?

3 Google directions for making paper and give it a try. With your finished paper, make a book (or you can skip this step and make a book out of premade paper). Consider what you would include in a primer for very young children. Share your project with others, discussing how you made your decisions about what was important to include. What does this exercise tell you about your own **ideologies** of what children like and need to know?

4 Read Robert Louis Stevenson's *A Child's Garden of Verses*, available through Project Gutenberg (http://www.gutenberg.org/files/25609/25609-h/25609-h.htm). Code the poems in terms of the type of literature or the themes you think they represent, such as didactic or morally directive, history, fantasy, psychological, realism, and nature. Now, code the types of poems found in a contemporary anthology. Present your data in a graphic organizer or infographic of some kind so that the comparisons are easily visible. What do your findings tell you about the kinds of literature that were considered appropriate and necessary for children at the end of the nineteenth century? What has changed? What has stayed the same?

Online exploration:

1 The guide to the children's literature collections at Indiana University at Bloomington. See especially the exhibition catalogs that are linked to the page in the resources box:
http://www.indiana.edu/~liblilly/collections/overview/lit_child.shtml

2 The late Kay E. Vandergrift created an extensive collection of resources related to children's literature. Here is her page on the social history of children's literature.
http://comminfo.rutgers.edu/professional-development/childlit/HistoryofChildLit/

3 A list of web and print resources about the history of children's literature from the School Collection, University of Illinois at Urbana-Champaign:
http://www.library.illinois.edu/sshel/s-coll/index.htm

4   Guide to resources on historic children's literature at the British Museum: http://www.bl.uk/reshelp/findhelpsubject/literature/chillit/childhist/childhistorical.html

5   The website of the We Need Diverse Books organization: http://weneeddiversebooks.org/where-to-find-diverse-books/

6   The Reading While White blog, written by white librarians who seek to confront racism by allying with indigenous people and people of color. http://readingwhilewhite.blogspot.com/

Case Study: How Ideologies Influence Interpretations

The theme of Gene Luen Yang's *American Born Chinese* blooms differently when considered from different **ideological** perspectives. In this graphic novel, the Monkey King aspires to join the other deities of Heaven for a dinner party, only to be rebuffed at the door by a guard who says: "Look. You may be a **king**—you may even be a **deity**—but you are still a **monkey**" (15). After his rejection, Monkey King is even more determined to assert his worth, so he masters the arts of kung fu and wreaks vengeance on all of the other Chinese deities who will not accord him the proper respect. They appeal to Tze-Yo-Tzuh ("He Who Is"), who explains to Monkey King that he must accept who he is, since he (Tze-Yo-Tzuh) created him in that form. The Monkey King defies and attacks Tze-Yo-Tzuh, and ends up buried under a mountain of rock until he releases his attachment to kung fu and his desire to be a god and accepts his true form. He then becomes an emissary of Tze-Yo-Tzuh.

In a parallel story developed in the novel, young Jin Wang longs to be a transformer, and after his family moves to a mostly white neighborhood, he tries his best to distance himself from his Chinese identity. He rejects and hurts another Chinese classmate, Wei-Chin, who tries to befriend him. He has successes and failures throughout elementary and junior high school, but he eventually transforms himself into Danny, an athletic blond teen who is tormented by yearly visits from his embarrassing cousin Chin-Kee, who embodies all of the hyperbolic Western stereotypes of Chinese culture. After a fistfight, Chin-Kee reveals himself to be the Monkey King. He tells the parts of his story that overlap with Danny's (now returned to his original form of Jin), leaving him with this insight: "You know, Jin. I would have saved myself from **five hundred years' imprisonment** beneath a mountain of rock had I only realized how **good** it is to be a **monkey**" (223).

(Continued)

This text is often included in the curriculum in American high schools because it surfaces issues of stereotyping and the difficulties people face in negotiating multicultural environments. In the end, it explicitly conveys the theme that, in order to be happy, one must accept who one is and not attempt to conform to the dominant culture. In Jin's case, the dominant culture is visually depicted as middle class and white. In the story of the Monkey King, the dominant culture is shown as the traditional deities and spirits of Chinese mythology. From an **ideological** viewpoint that embraces human diversity as its core value, this seems to be a solid, affirming moral that has relevance across a variety of circumstances. In fact, most teaching guides for this text feature some variation of the questions: "Have you or someone you know transformed him or herself in a similar way to the transformations of the characters?" "How do the characters' feelings about themselves influence how they think they are perceived or how they are treated? Do their attitudes toward themselves make them feel better or worse?" (https://multcolib. org/american-born-chinese). This line of questioning implies that identity construction is largely a matter of personal choice, and that all that really matters when it comes to being happy is whether or not we like ourselves. It also implies that our negative feelings about ourselves are the main factor in the way others treat us.

However, the plot of the story shows that Jin is bullied at school, and cannot date the girls he likes simply because he is Chinese. As Mike Cadden (2014) argues, the parallel narrative of the Monkey King indicates that for Jin to accept who he is means, ultimately, that he has to accept being inferior in his society. This creates a problem for a sunny interpretation of this text from a multicultural perspective, because it implies that the perks of the dominant culture are inherently better and more desirable, and that some people are going to have to accept that they will always lack access to the things they want. Cadden concludes that while "neither race-erasing delusion nor laughable stereotypes are acceptable options," the question Jin poses of "so what am I supposed to do now?" (Yang 223) remains unanswered in any satisfying way.

Starting from an alternative **ideological** standpoint yields a different perspective on this text. Yang states in interviews that he is a Christian who embraces the theology of Roman Catholicism, and he includes iconography in this text from Christian traditions as well as from Chinese culture. For instance, the emissaries of Tze-Yo-Tzuh are a lion, an ox, a human, and an eagle. In Christian art dating from the eighth century, these four creatures represent the four evangelists, Mark, Luke, Matthew, and John, respectively. When the Monkey King completes his test of virtue, he meets the infant Christ, whom readers will recognize because his mother and father are depicted in iconic fashion. Therefore, it is not presumptuous or out of place to consider this text from the standpoint of Christian **ideology**. From such a perspective, certain ideas become intelligible that are not available from a secular multicultural perspective, because Christianity differs markedly from the world system of dividing people up according to markers such as nationality, ability, or race. Instead, the creator, Tze-Yo-Tzuh, calls all of his creations good, and, throughout both testaments of scripture, repeatedly stresses the virtue of humility and service over prideful assertions of one's own worth. Hence, the Monkey King's problem is not that he is inferior, but that he seeks to assert his own superiority. The consequence is that he is buried under the world system that he seeks to dominate, and yet continues to perceive Tze-Yo-Tzuh's offer of freedom as a more insidious form of enslavement.

The monk Wong Lai-Tsao voices Yang's explicit character lesson here; all of his efforts to achieve legendary status through feats of discipline fail, but he excels in acts of service. When questioned about his commitment to the ungrateful vagrants, he replies, "I am no more worthy of love than you, yet Tze-Yo-Tzuh loves me deeply and faithfully, providing for my daily needs. How can I not respond in kind?" (137). Even as he is being impaled by demons, the monk continues to challenge the Monkey King: "To find your true identity . . . within the will of Tze-Yo-Tzuh . . . that is the highest of all freedoms" (149), a lesson the Monkey King conveys to Jin before he leaves him. Under this reading, the text challenges all of the ways identity is asserted and valued in contemporary culture. Attempts to ground one's identity in a cultural, racial, or national heritage, or even one's talents, abilities, appearance or self-esteem, are ultimately doomed to dissatisfaction and failure because the humans who have established these criteria of value are, in Wei-Chin's words, "petty, soulless creatures" (219). Jin re-establishes his relationship with Wei-Chin, who turns out to be the Monkey King's son, by repenting, the ultimate act of Christian humility.

Author talkback: Anne Fine

In this essay, award-winning author and former Waterstone Children's Laureate Anne Fine talks back to many of the issues considered throughout this chapter, including how her books respond (or don't respond) to changing social conditions and **ideologies** of childhood. She also addresses the question of whether children have changed or our attitudes toward them have. For more information about Anne Fine, visit http://www.annefine.com/.

Start as you mean to go on, they say, and I started writing with no thought for publishers or the market. I knew nothing about either. Stuck in the house with nothing to read during a blizzard, I simply started to write the sort of sunny, easy-going comedy I'd have enjoyed as a ten year old reader. The snow cleared, but I kept on writing.

The next four books followed the same pattern. We lived abroad. I'd never met my publishers. I just wrote what I wanted, and the lovely agent who had pounced on me at a party when my first unpublished manuscript was the runner-up in a competition placed them, one after another, with the same editor. Only later did I realise how very introspective those first books were, and how I was working my way through insecurities and emotional concerns that stemmed from my own childhood.

We came back to Britain, and finally I met the people who published my work just at the time when I was psychologically ready to take less interest in myself and more in the world around me.

This was the 1980s—a splendid time to want to write about what the journalist Neal Ascherson referred to as "that murky, impenetrable little community" of the family. Marital breakdown numbers appeared to be skyrocketing. Step-parenting—never a cakewalk—fuelled complications in so many people's lives. But just as parents were no longer judged so harshly for divorcing or remarrying, so children—especially teenagers—were no longer viewed, like Cinderella or Hansel and Gretel, as totally vulnerable innocents. I wrote about what has always interested me most in life—the refractions of emotions in families—and the books concerned, *Madame Doubtfire*, *Goggle-Eyes*, *Step by Wicked Step*, *Flour Babies*, proved that a ready market had arisen for stories about honest feelings in "broken" or "reconstituted" families. Though I wrote about all sorts of families, these were the books that won the big prizes and sold most strongly. It was my impression that, in a few areas, there was a level of disapproval about this supposedly new subject matter. Indeed, one edition of the Companion to English Literature contains a scathing remark to the effect that most of the writing for children produced since the sixties might play some part in the history of sociology but has little or nothing to add to literature. Thus, with a brief nod to one or two undismissable classics, forty years of children's writing was passed over in less than a paragraph.

I carried on writing whatever I wanted, switching to novels for adults whenever the topic that fascinated me was of little or no interest to younger readers. I never signed a contract till a book was finished, so never felt the need to hurry or skimp, or try to kid myself my daughters didn't need as much of my time as they often did. I do remember getting occasional suggestions from editors about what to write, and for which age group, and queries about when things I was working on might be finished. But maybe because I'd been so isolated from publishers at the start, I never felt pressured. I doubt if many writers who've come into the profession recently could say the same.

Over the years, like every other children's author I know, I've had the sense that the bean-counters and sales people have taken over. Where once the editor's decision about whether or not to publish a book appeared to be final, it certainly isn't now. I know of more than one occasion when an experienced editor has been both startled and humiliated by a decision that's bounced back from these other departments. And this is deemed very bad news for writers who don't much care to tread old ground. Books in series are far more popular with publishers than one-off publications since the advertising put into any one title of a series effectively works for them all.

Not long into my career, I remember a publisher telling me that she and her colleagues wouldn't dream of putting guns on the covers of books for children, and they avoided graphic descriptions of violence, or cruel scenes. In the feminist eighties it was also unacceptable to pitch books as "for boys" or "for girls." Since cash became king, and "whatever sells most" has become the watchword, violence and cruelty have crept steadily into much children's fiction, even for younger readers. The sense that what a child reads has a parental or educational imprimatur has taken a real knock, and many parents would be truly shocked if they realised exactly what their children are reading.

Have all these changes left me with the elegiac sense that my day as a writer is almost done? No, not at all. I'm certainly not confident I would have succeeded in this more recent world. It took me several books and several years to grow into the style that continues to serve me well. I'm not sure today's new writers are given the chance to develop through lacklustre sales while an editor keeps faith. Many current career trajectories have an astonishingly instant peak and an almost equally precipitous collapse.

But I was lucky, and I'm still here after nearly forty years. I used to claim that, though childhood changed a good deal over the years, children themselves didn't, so someone of my age could still write for someone of theirs. I'm not so sure of that now. I recognise that young people aren't so much addicted to their phones and computers as to the social contact with their friends that these devices provide. But as I look around I rarely see anyone over the age of eleven just being alone, not trying to make contact with anyone, so I do have to ask myself if one of the staples of childhood—self-reflection—isn't being seriously eroded, if not lost.

Then I cheer up. Writers have always had to work their way around difficulties. I don't have to deal with a government censor. I don't work in a freezing garret. I'm not a refugee who suddenly has to learn to work in a whole new language. My grandchildren fall about laughing, lose their tempers, and get worried in exactly the same way my own daughters did, and no doubt I did too. I might be mistaken, but I'd like to think that children aren't all that different now from how they were when I began to write for them. So if I have to remember that certain sorts of plots won't wash ("Why didn't he use his *mobile*?" "How come she didn't know that already? Wasn't she even on *Facebook*?"), I can find others. Even more cheeringly, the books still sell, so I must have plenty of readers. That's all I wanted when I started, and it's basically all I want now.

I'd also like to believe that, if a writer came along tomorrow who was just like I was back then, there would be an editor out there somewhere who would take her on,—and keep her even if her career, like mine, began so slowly no one even noticed.

I really, really hope that that's still true.

Literature references

Alcott, L. M. (1868, 1869), *Little Women*, Boston: Roberts Brothers.

Alexie, S. (2007), *The Absolutely True Diary of a Part-Time Indian*, New York: Little Brown.

Arabian Nights Entertainment. (1706), London: Grub Street.

Bannerman, H. (1899), *The Story of Little Black Sambo*, Philadelphia: J. B. Lippincott.

The Holy Bible: English Standard Version (2001), Wheaton, IL: Crossway.

Blake, W. (1789), *Songs of Innocence*, London: Catherine Blake.

Boreman, T. (1740–43), *Gigantick Histories* Series, London: T. Boreman.

Bunyan, J. (1678), *Pilgrim's Progress*, London: Nathaniel Ponder.

Burnett, F. H. (1905), *A Little Princess*, London: Warne.

Burnett, F. H. (1911), *The Secret Garden*, London: Heinemann.

The Babees' Book: Medieval Manners for the Young (2000), (E. Rickert and L. J. Naylor, trans.), Cambridge, Ontario: In parenthesis Press, www.yorku.ca/inpar/babees_rickert.pdf [Accessed August 18, 2014].

Comenius, J. A. (1659), *Orbis Sensualium Pictus*, (C. Hoole, Trans.), London: J. Kirton. [Original work published 1658].

Day, T. (1783), *The History of Sandford and Merton*, London: Stockdale.

Defoe, D. (1719), *Robinson Crusoe*, London: W. Taylor.

Donoghue, E. (1999), *Kissing the Witch: Old Tales in New Skins*, New York: HarperTeen.

Emerson, R. W. (1883), "Self-Reliance," in Emerson, R. W., *Essays* (pp.45–88). Boston: Houghton Mifflin. [Original work published 1841].

Foxe, J. (1563), *Actes and Monuments of these Latter Perilous Times Touching Matters of the Church*, London: John Day.

Gaiman, N. (2003), *The Wolves in the Walls*, Illus. D. McKean, New York: HarperCollins.

Green, J. (2012), *The Fault in Our Stars*, New York: Dutton.

Hoffmann, H. (n.d.), *Struwwelpeter: Merry Stories and Funny Pictures*, New York: Frederick Warne & Co. [Original work published 1844]. www.gutenberg.org/files/12116/12116-h/12116-h.htm [Accessed August 18, 2014].

Janeway, J. (1671), *A Token for Children: Being an Exact Account of the Conversion, Holy and Exemplary Lives, and Joyful Deaths of Several Young Children*, London: D. Newman.

Lear, E. (1846), *A Book of Nonsense*, London: Thomas McLean.

Lilliputian Magazine (1751–52), London: John Newbery.

Little Pretty Pocket-Book (1744), London: John Newbery.

Look, L. (2011), *Alvin Ho: Allergic to Dead Bodies, Funerals, and Other Fatal Circumstances*, New York: Random House.

Marryat, F. (1829), *Frank Mildmay, or The Naval Officer*, London: Richard Edward King.

Marryat, F. (1841), *Masterman Ready, or The Wreck of the "Pacific,"* London: Blackie & Son, Ltd.

Montgomery, L. M. (1908), *Anne of Green Gables*, Boston: L. C. Page & Co.

Perrault, C. (1697), *Tales of Mother Goose (Histoires, ou contes du temps passé, avec les moralitéz*, Paris: Barbin.

Porter, E. H. (1913), *Pollyanna*, Boston: L. C. Page.

Potter, B. (1902), *The Tale of Peter Rabbit*, London: Frederick Warne & Co.

Rousseau, J. J. (1979), *Emile, or On Education*, (A. Bloom, trans.), New York: Basic. [original work published 1762].

Sendak, M. (1963), *Where the Wild Things Are*, New York: Harper & Row.

Sherwood, M. M. (1818, 1842, 1847), *The History of the Fairchild Family:, or, The Child's Manual*, London: J. Hatchard and Son.

Sinclair, C. (1839), *Holiday House*, London: Ward, Lock & Tylor.

Steptoe, J. (1987), *Mufaro's Beautiful Daughters*, New York: Lothrop, Lee & Shepard.

Stevenson, R. L. (1883), *Treasure Island*, London: Cassell and Company.

Stevenson, R. L. (1885), *A Child's Garden of Verses*, London: Longman, Green.

Stevenson, R. L. (1886), *Kidnapped*, London: Cassell and Company.

Stowe, H. B. (1852), *Uncle Tom's Cabin; or, Life Among the Lowly*, Boston: Hammatt Billings.

Strang, H. (pseud.) (1915), *The Girl Crusoes: A Story of the South Seas*, London: Humphrey Milford.

Swift, J. (1726), *Gulliver's Travels*, London: Benjamin Motte.

Traill, C. P. (1852), *Canadian Crusoes: A Tale of the Rice Lake Plains*, London: Arthur Hall, Virtue & Co.

Turner, E. (1894), *Seven Little Australians*, London: Ward, Lock and Bowden.

Twain, M. (pseud.) (1884), *The Adventures of Huckleberry Finn*, London: Chatto & Windus.

Tommy Thumb's Pretty Song Book (1744), London: Cooper.

Wiesner, D. (2001), *The Three Pigs*, New York: Clarion.

Wiggin, K. D. (1903), *Rebecca of Sunnybrook Farm*, New York: Houghton Mifflin.

Wordsworth, W. (1807), "Ode: Intimations of Immortality from Recollections of Early Childhood," in *Poems in Two Volumes*, London: Longman, Hurst, Rees, and Orme.

Wyss, J. D. (2007), *The Swiss Family Robinson*, (J. Seelye, ed.), New York: Penguin Classics. [Original work published 1812].

Yang, G. L. (2006), *American Born Chinese*, New York: First Second Books.

2

Contemporary Insights into Child and Adolescent Development

Suggested texts to read alongside this chapter

Dulemba, Elizabeth, *A Bird on Water Street.*
Henkes, Kevin, *Little White Rabbit; Chester's Way; Owen.*
Stone, Tanya Lee, *Almost Astronauts: 13 Women Who Dared to Dream.*
Wilson, Jacqueline, *The Illustrated Mum; The Story of Tracy Beaker; Dustbin Baby.*

Ways of thinking about children and young adults

It is certainly possible to read and study children's and YA literature without thinking about its target audience. Considering the texts as **aesthetic** artifacts in themselves, for instance, need not include any overt reference to who might be reading them and what those readers might take away from the experience; the literary or cultural critic might focus entirely, for instance, on how certain **motifs** and symbols provide depth in a YA novel, how patterns of sound in a poem contribute to its meaning, or how the word–picture interaction functions in a picturebook. Such a strict adherence to textual features has been important over the years for scholars in English departments, since their project has been (and in many cases continues to be) to gain a foothold for youth literature in a discipline that seeks to study works that offer the richest expressions of the human experience. In order to be taken seriously by their peers, literary scholars in particular need to overcome the persistent prejudice of their colleagues that children aren't capable of deep thought or critical reading, and that books written for the young are simplistic and disengaged from serious issues. Thus, if these critics consider a reader at all, they consider him or her only as an abstract entity called the **implied reader**, that is, the reader the author seems to have had in mind who would have the skills and dispositions to understand and appreciate the text.

But a desire for professional viability is not the only reason many scholars have avoided consideration of actual children and teens in the study of literature marketed to them. A further objection to considering children's and YA literature in light of its readership is an **ideological** one. Some critics worry that when we take children and teens as objects of study, we distance ourselves from them and construct them as "other." Marah Gubar (2013: 450) has helpfully named this way of looking at children as the "difference model," explaining that such a model separates adults and children so firmly that children are seen as "a separate species, categorically different from adults." One problem with such a model is that it may render young people incomprehensible. Some critics believe that we can't know who children really are without projecting adult-informed assumptions onto them, which is a misuse of power and privilege. Alternately, by constructing children as the absolute "other" of adults, we turn them into empty screens on which to project a sense of our own lost purity on the one hand, and our outlawed desires and unresolved fears on the other. In our exhaustion with the acquired knowledge of living, adults often come to desire an Eden of human experience—unselfconscious, sexually naïve, open to a responsive universe of goodness, acceptance, and provision—what we discussed in Chapter 1 as the Romantic view of childhood. Our life experiences have rendered us cynical on those points, and indeed the entire genre of YA realistic fiction seems bent on disabusing readers of their possibility, but we still seem to need a place to preserve and refresh that desire, so we place it on the shoulders of children, who seem less inhibited in their expressions of the pleasures of embodiment. Many young children, for instance, luxuriate in the rage and tantrums adults must suppress, weep openly at cheesy sentiment, and are unashamed to ask for comfort when they are afraid. But at the same time as we grant them some license to express those fears and desires, we strive to make them more like us; that is, to bring those passionate displays under rational control. Many critics have referred to this process as "colonizing" children— we exploit their resources of imagination, energy, and existential refreshment in exchange for protecting and "civilizing" them according to adult standards. As Maria Nikolajeva (2010: *passim*) explains in her coinage of the term **aetonormativity**, adult thinking is the norm, and children are the deviants who must be brought in line. Our thinking about childhood can thus lead to us considering children as imperfect adults. Gubar (2013: 450) refers to this as the "deficit model" of childhood, where children are primarily defined by what they lack, which is primarily "the abilities, skills, and powers that adults have."

These objections can be laid to rest, I think, with a richer understanding of developmental frameworks within what Gubar calls a "kinship model" (450), which allows us to think about adults and children in terms of "relatedness, connection and similarity without implying homogeneity, uniformity and equality" (453). The word "development" seems to be the sticking point here—we tend to think of child development as linear and synonymous with progress, and thus consider adult thinking and accomplishments superior to those of children because they are farther along that timeline. But if we think of development in its secondary definition as a significant change in circumstances, then we are able to understand both the gains and losses involved in growing older. It is undeniable that children and adolescents accumulate experiences over time, and that the processing of these experiences changes the way they think. Some developments are in the main positive, some are negative, and some are merely interesting. Moreover, as we shall see shortly, there are significant differences in the way adults and children process experience; some of the factors involved include brain architecture, cultural inputs and expectations, and temperaments. In this light, while we can maintain the idea that children and adolescents as a group and as individuals may process experience differently from adults (again as a group and as individuals), they are not fundamentally "other" or incomprehensible. Rather, as Kieran Egan (1990: 2) points out: "Childhood is not something we leave behind. The achievements and experiences of childhood are *constituents* of our later selves." As such, any romanticizing or colonizing we do in our thinking about children and teens needs to be reconceptualized as part of a fluid and dynamic construction of the nature of what it means to be human; understanding childhood is key to understanding personhood.

Other points of contention with regard to a focus on actual young readers, as Nodelman and Reimer (2002) point out, include the unreliability of the data and the dangers of overgeneralization of the findings, particularly when it comes to applying the various assumptions of child development research to our stance on the appropriateness of their literature. Nodelman and Reimer and others mount strong critiques of theories that carry the scent of **biological determinism**—that is, that human beings are the way they are because of innate biological traits and capacities— but are in reality based on the assumptions of white male Europeans who see their ways of thinking as the pinnacle of human development. In the latter decades of the twentieth century, however, the pendulum of thinking on child development, at least in the social sciences and humanities, swung away from biology toward the idea of **social construction**, particularly with regard to gender. **Social constructivists** argue, for instance, that girls and boys behave the way they do not because of any differences in hormones, brain function, or embodiment, but because the images we offer them in books and media image teach them how to behave, and teach others how to behave toward them. Change those images, and we can remap the social order. The same will hold true for other cultural markers such as race and class.

As we shall see, this is certainly a valid argument and goal, but contemporary thinking in developmental psychology holds that children are in fact products of nature as well as nurture. Certainly, when the values and practices of nurture change, so will the kinds of skills and personalities they produce, at least to a certain extent. The old adage that "children learn what they live" is true in a cultural as well as familial setting. It may well have been that in an era that valued "logico-mathematical" thinking and abstract moral reasoning above other kinds of learning, the behaviors children exhibited in these areas could readily be interpreted as progressive strands of development by controversial researchers such as Jean Piaget and Lawrence Kohlberg. Moreover, the inputs children received through their books and media may have reinforced that kind of thinking over the social intelligence we are more apt to emphasize today. That doesn't mean, however, that the careful observations of these researchers and the conclusions they drew from them are utterly wrong for our time and can therefore be dismissed out of hand. In fact, Nodelman and Reimer concede that some assumptions about children and childhood may in fact be valid despite flawed research models or outdated paradigms precisely because such assumptions influence the way we rear children. If we believe that children cannot access certain types of stories and concepts, we don't offer opportunities for them to prove us wrong, and so they don't. If we believe, as did psychologist G. Stanley Hall, that the teenage years will be full of turbulence and dangerous behaviors, we might respond preemptively with overbearing restrictions that lead to self-fulfilling prophecies of rebellion and challenge.

But I would also argue, from my admittedly time-bound stance of the early twenty-first century, that nurture and the reinscription of cultural values doesn't tell the whole story here. Nature persists. Children's and teen's brains grow in both size and complexity, and as we learn more about the ways in which brain architecture and chemistry affect skills and behavior, it can make sense in some cases and strains of literary criticism to bring that knowledge to bear on the way we study children's and YA literature. Furthermore, an understanding of developmental stages and concerns can in fact help adults decide what sorts of literary experiences are likely to have uptake with children at various times in their lives—not to limit their exposure to texts according to a rigid stage model but to recognize **developmental age** differences and respond with the kinds of texts that might help children mature through periods where specific concerns predominate.

Relating theories of child development to literary understanding

Literature has a powerful effect on human understanding. As noted in the introduction, it acts as a mirror, reflecting experience back to us in a framed and manageable way that enables us to think through concepts and relationships by pinning them to events and characters, and as a door and a lamp, enabling us to see beyond surface appearances and behaviors into other minds and motivations, and beyond actual worlds into possible ones to explore and extend our sense of ethics and what could be. If this is true for adults, it is even truer for children and teens, whose apprehensions of the world are less overdetermined by habit and long experience. In terms of brain growth and development, children's and teen's brains are more busily engaged in synaptogenesis and synaptic reorganization and pruning—the processes of making the connections and associations that will shape their interests and capacities—than adult brains. Environmental factors, including the expansion of imagination and emotional awareness obtained through reading, are influential during these critical periods of the brain's self-organization. Understanding even a little bit about these processes can help adults make informed cases for advocacy of minority genres, such as poetry and fantasy, in environments that belittle those genres as nonserious, or consider them unnecessary or inappropriate for students of varying abilities, or even object to them as culturally irrelevant.

Learning about child and teen development can also help us understand our own preferences better, especially if we remember that developmental stages are not tied to particular ages nor are they gates or levels that, once worked through, are no longer relevant. Close observation of children indicates that developmental stages do seem to follow a certain order of initial appearance based on multiple factors, such as growing physical abilities and expanding experiences. But the concerns of each stage don't disappear once a certain outcome has been achieved. Rather, each stage offers what Michael J. Parsons (1987: 11) calls "a cluster of ideas" that we can then work with to consider a problem or analyze a situation or a work of art. When we combine what we know about the developing brain and psyche with what we know about literary and critical theory, we have a strong basis from which to analyze texts aimed at young people.

There are multiple stage models one could work from in analyzing literature, including the **psychoanalytic** models of Sigmund Freud and Carl Jung, but one that offers particularly interesting and relevant clusters of ideas for youth literature study is Erik Erikson's theory of psychosocial development (1950). Erikson's stages are organized around a set of basic conflicts that we must work through as we grow. The way we resolve each of these conflicts establishes a pattern of response that may recur throughout our lives as we encounter new situations. Erikson further suggests that each of these growth crises gives rise to certain imaginative themes or **motifs** that show up in cultural myths and stories as well as individual dreams. David Gooderham (1995) and Michael Howarth (2014) have extended Erikson's theory of imaginative themes to consider the appeal of various elements of children's fantasy and horror literature, respectively, arguing, among other things, that children in the midst of working through one of these conflicts will respond more readily to the imaginative themes that characterize that particular stage. Their applications can be productively extended beyond fantasy and horror to all types of texts, including the kinds of jokes we find funny. Understanding these imaginative themes can help us clarify our own emotional states by helping us understand why, even as adults, we find ourselves "in the mood" for a particular type of story.

Another method of thinking about how development matters in children's and YA literature comes through the emergent field of **cognitive poetics**. Variously called cognitive narratology or simply cognitive studies, this framework seeks to situate literary response and understanding within what we know about how the brain works. Ellen Dissanayake (2009) and Ellen Winner (1982), for instance, explore the role that early childhood experience plays in priming children to be producers and consumers of the arts; Brian Boyd (2009) looks at the origins, structures, and functions of stories from the perspective of evolutionary biology; Hugh Crago (2014) explores the conflicts and coordination of old and new brain functions, detailing the right-brain capacities we have for experiencing stories alongside characters even while we exercise our left-brain roles as spectators who analyze and reflect on the action. For increasing our understanding of youth literature in particular, it is important to seek out and perform studies that honor emotions as a key element in cognitive studies. Research strongly suggests that the parts of our brain that control emotional response are far more developed in the early years than our capacities for detached, rational contemplation, so considering what Michael Burke (2011) terms "emotional cognition" is central to thinking about young people's responses to literary experiences.

Structuralist versus universalist thinking

I'd like to proceed with caution, then, into the territory of child and adolescent development, offering a story of that development that should be understood as structural rather than universal. The difference between thinking in terms of universals and thinking in terms of structures can be understood by considering the difference between saying that all humans naturally prefer sweets and saying that all humans develop taste preferences over time and through experience. The former is universalizing and demonstrably untrue, while the latter allows for variations within a common structure. The former makes a claim for biology as a common determiner and unsurmountable destiny by implying that all beings with a particular sort of embodiment will share certain specific traits, in this case, a preference for sweet tastes. The latter, on the other hand, doesn't exclude biology, but claims it alongside cultural intervention and variation as well as individual difference, so that children growing up in a culture where spicy or savory foods predominate may develop a preference for those tastes, but individual results will vary. In addition, a structural approach suggests that these things—biology, culture, and individual variation—are interrelated within a larger system that enables us to see what we have in common as well as how we differ. **Structuralism**, then, seeks out those elements that can be said to remain invariant despite change or differences in individual expressions or manifestations. So, in our example, we can say that every person develops taste preferences based on factors such as experience and biology that we can analyze and explore, but we can't say for sure what those taste preferences will be.

Diversity within structural similarities

What, then, are some of the elements that remain invariant across cultures and through time in terms of human development? I would argue that there are three underlying structural features that must be taken into account in understanding what it means to be human, and thus what children and teens need to negotiate as they move through their early years: we are embodied; we use language and other systems of representation; and we live in communities. Let's consider each of these in more detail before moving on to an integrated story of children's and teen development as it relates to their reception of literary experiences.

We have specifically human bodies

First and foremost, we are embodied. This seems almost too obvious to point out, but much theory in literary and cultural studies focuses on the cultural construction of identity and the self, discounting any sort of similarities that might be a consequence of the fact that we live in bodies. The issue of nature versus culture is a vexed one in theoretical debates. It came to the fore during second-wave **feminism**, for instance, when feminist theorists objected to the idea that people had essential differences based on their biological sex or race that forced or fitted them for particular positions in society. This kind of **essentialist** thinking had justified the "natural" superiority of free, white males over women, slaves, and nonwhite populations since the days of Plato and Aristotle, but had received an ideological booster shot through Darwinism and, later, through the naturalist philosophy of David Hume. Cultural or social constructivists argue that people do not possess essential qualities, but are completely the products of their environments. From such a perspective, forms of embodiment—race, gender, ability—are given relative measures of significance through cultural systems that celebrate some forms and denigrate others, as we saw in the case study for *American Born Chinese* (Yang 2006), resulting in discriminatory social and political practices that diminish one's ability to pursue individual forms of happiness and success.

In *Almost Astronauts: 13 Women Who Dared to Dream* (2009), a middle-grade nonfiction book about the women who attempted to join the US space program in 1960, author Tanya Lee Stone explores this dilemma of how physical differences between the genders mattered in American culture of the early 1960s. The results of the physical and psychological tests established to determine a candidate's fitness for space exploration proved that women's bodies and minds would likely bear up better under extreme conditions than men's bodies, but these findings were ignored by NASA and the US government because they didn't fit the larger cultural narrative of women being the weaker sex. Children internalize the prejudices of their societies almost as soon as they notice differences between themselves and others, which is why diverse images in children's literature matter so much. One of the ways in which a critical awareness of embodiment matters to the study of youth literature, then, is through its visual and verbal representation. YA texts are more likely than children's books to explicitly problematize issues of embodiment, considering weight, ability, and the visibility of racial difference in light of dominant cultural narratives. But reading all texts with a view to how they treat embodiment, including how bodies move around in their physical environments, can be enlightening in terms of understanding how these cultural narratives are formed and reinforced.

But embodiment also matters when it comes to the capacities of readers. Children's brains are quite amazing in their information-processing capacities, but they are not fully developed at birth. As neuroscientists learn more about the distinct areas of specialization within the brain as well as neural plasticity, their discoveries alternate between affirming long-held beliefs based on close observations of children's and teens' behaviors, and challenging what we think we know. For instance, we now believe that the prefrontal cortex of the brain houses the CEO of the brain, making it important for what is called executive function, which includes working memory, inhibitory control, and mental flexibility. The prefrontal cortex is underdeveloped at birth, it experiences a rapid overproduction of cells just before puberty, and it isn't fully developed and hooked up with the rest of the brain until a person reaches the early twenties. Its fully functional presence enables the ability to strategize, focus, reason, reflect, assess risk, inhibit impulses, and predict outcomes, but its relative underdevelopment from birth through the teen years has fascinating implications for the study of children's and YA literature. For instance, here's a nibble: Alison Gopnik (2009) cites studies that demonstrate that children as young as three years old can entertain counterfactuals—that is, they can imagine things that haven't happened. This ability enables them to understand conditionals, the "what-if-things-were-different" side of situations, as well as to pretend. Because their prefrontal cortexes are immature, they are actually better able to fully enter into their pretend play and fantasies than adults because they are not inhibited by the functions of that part of the brain—the part that says, "yes, but that's not logically possible," or "that would never happen." As their prefrontal cortexes grow, tweens and teens are more attentive to logic, which explains why they might require more internally consistent textual worlds in their fantasy texts, or they might reject fantasy altogether, preferring realist texts or nonfiction that affirms their sense of the possible.

We use language and other systems of representation

Humans are undeniably **multimodal** communicators, but our dominant mode of communication is language, both oral and written. Even images, which are supposed to "be worth a thousand words," change significantly when we choose a few of those thousand words to describe them. Many theories of how language relates to the world have been proposed from various disciplinary standpoints, but most agree that language has a significant material effect on perception, a concept we will explore further in the chapters on poetry, picturebooks, and stories. The key finding is that when we use words, we aren't merely describing an event, experience, or object; instead, we are to some degree creating or changing events, experiences, and objects through the words we use to talk about them. When I was in graduate school first learning about some of these theories, I had a dream of two boxers in a ring. As they delivered their blows, they shouted at each other, saying things like "Thought pre-exists language—language just expresses what you're already thinking!" POW! "No way! You can't have thoughts without language, so language is what is creating your thoughts!" SMACK! "But things EXIST, whether we have words for them or not!" THWACK! "Ha! Certain things only exist BECAUSE we have words for them!" UGH! I woke up before there was a clear winner, but I think that's because there can't be one. But these are the essential kernels of the debate: Can we have mental concepts independent of language, or are all of the mental concepts we have dependent upon and determined by the language we use to talk about them? Clearly, I had a **multimodal** impression of the conceptual debate—it became an actual fistfight between two people, but I wouldn't have understood what they were fighting about without their dialogue.

Consider this fascinating, interrelated facet of child development: Sometime during the first year of life, babies develop what Piaget (1963) called "object permanence," that is, the ability to understand that something continues to exist even when they can't see it. What this must mean is that they have developed a durable **mental model**—an internal representation of external reality—of the object in question. Researchers disagree about exactly when object permanence manifests, with some saying as early as three months in opposition to Piaget's original determination of between eight and twelve months (Baillargeon and DeVos 1991), but this ability generally corresponds with the development of separation anxiety, and the ability to understand a few oft-repeated words, such as the baby's own name, the names of his or her caregivers, and of a few privileged objects, even if he or she cannot yet say the words. Before object permanence develops, separation anxiety doesn't really exist, since any warm body capable of performing the caregiving functions will serve. But when the baby knows that the caregiver still exists even when he or she is no longer present, this induces a desire to call the caregiver back. Interestingly, the presence of a **mental model** and a word that corresponds with that model creates both the problem of separation anxiety and points to its solution; even as adults, when we find ourselves missing someone or something that is absent, we can draw upon a **mental model** and comfort ourselves by talking about it, either out loud or internally. But even before our first year of life is over, we have established a structure where the representation of a thing stands in for the thing itself.

Although language is our preferred mode of communication, representations created and expressed through language are dependent on **multimodal** experiences. **Mental models**, for instance, are not primarily linguistic, even though it's hard to think about them without translating them into words. The New London Group (1996), a team of academics who wanted to reimagine a literacy pedagogy more responsive to new millennial modes of information transfer, coined the term **multiliteracies** to describe the ways meaning can be communicated. They draw attention to verbal, auditory, visual, gestural, spatial, and tactile ways of creating and conveying meaning in a digital age where text is almost always accompanied by other forms of representation. Children's and YA literature has always been responsive to these **multimodal** communication techniques. The oral stories and songs, picturebooks, and media images that we encounter in the first years of life augment our **mental models** and supplement our representations, particularly for things we might not regularly encounter in real life, like giraffes or people who don't look or act like our own family members. The **mental models** also involve what cognitive psychologists call **schemas** and **scripts**, which are patterns of thought and event sequences for common activities, like eating or going to the store. Baby brains avidly collect these patterns. I like to think of this process as filling up our image banks, since these are the **mental models** that we continue to draw from for the rest of our lives to create expectations, test reality, and imagine possibility. Certainly the models change over time, but those changes happen through accumulation and nuance rather than outright replacement, which may be one of the reasons why consciousness-raising and sensitivity-training efforts to overcome stereotypical ways of thinking aren't all that effective later in life. Greater efforts toward filling our image banks with diverse representations in the first place are much more effective than trying to reform our attitudes later, so that's a strong argument for diverse children's literature.

That said, however, we need to consider that language and other modes of representation come online for children through a process of differentiation that is largely driven as much by brain development as by cultural inputs. As our left hemispheric functions develop, we sort things into categories and give the things in our environment both individual and categorical labels. One of the things that gets sorted into categories this way is gender stereotypes. Research (Martin and Ruble 2004; Trautner et al. 2005) shows that children learn gender-related characteristics in ordered phases. During their toddler and preschool years, children accumulate data related to how their culture associates particular words and images differentially with regard to boys and girls. When they enter school, their category knowledge of gender-related characteristics takes on a rigidity that is hard to dislodge no matter what new data are presented to them; girls dress and behave in a certain way, and boys in another way, and anything that challenges those expectations is regarded as a violation or mistake. The good news, however, is that around age seven, the categories start to open up again, and children can begin to accommodate and assimilate more flexible notions of gender characteristics, preferences, and identities.

We live in communities

In 2002, I did an independent study with a teacher from Zimbabwe who wanted to become familiar with Golden Age Anglophone literature. She was struck by the number of orphans in the books she read: Tom Sawyer, Anne Shirley, Mary Lennox, Dorothy Gale. She asked me if losing one's parents was a widespread lived reality for English and American children of the time, and I assured her it was mostly a literary device to get parents out of the way so the child characters could take center stage. She was excited to take these stories home with her, though, because being orphaned was in fact a common occurrence for her students. As a result of the AIDS epidemic, almost none of her teenage students had living parents, and her elementary students were absent on a regular basis due to the need to attend funerals of their parents and other relatives. Oftentimes, her orphaned students were treated poorly by the relatives who took them in. In these books, she found orphans who were able to create communities of affection among their relatives and peers, and she thought they would give her students hope for their own futures.

Human beings must have communities; it is part of our embodiment as mammals that we require the presence of other mammals to thrive, and part of our embodiment as humans that we need other humans in order to learn a human language. Different kinds of communities support language development in different ways. In her cross-cultural study of language acquisition, linguistic anthropologist Elinor Ochs (1988) reported that American and British caregivers tend to treat their infants as conversational partners, asking questions and pausing for babies to answer even before they can make understandable utterances. Samoan caregivers, on the other hand, do not converse with their babies, although they sing to them. As the babies start to use words, American and British caregivers validate their imperfect utterances by imitating them, often making the baby's mispronunciations part of the family lexicon. Not so Samoan caregivers: they correct their children's mispronunciations, insisting that toddlers speak correctly, and making them repeat themselves until they do. As a result, Samoan children as young as three years old can repeat a complicated message to an elder with no mistakes, a feat nearly impossible for the normally developing Western child.

These findings have some interesting implications. First, the rate and degree of development of a child's abilities in any given area is often dependent on community expectations, standards, and norms. Second, those norms are embedded in the ideologies of a culture. In Western culture, we have tended to value the individual over the community, so we encourage our children to express themselves in idiosyncratic ways. Treating infants as conversational partners by asking them questions and imagining their answers cultivates the sense that their individual thoughts and desires matter, which is crucial for the sustainability of Western economies. Fairly soon, children will be able to express their desires loudly and forcefully enough to command attention, exercising what marketers call "pester power" to induce weary parents to buy them what they want. When they enter school, adults will ask them to tell stories "in their own words," preparing them for a world where even words and ideas are commodities with property rights. What is repressed in such a system is that there are no such things as "our own words," so our individuality is constrained by publically available words and symbols. Samoan culture depends more overtly on communitarian values, and their language socialization practices reflect that. Children are not encouraged to have "their own words," but are instead taught the norms of expression in their communities so that they can fully participate in a social structure that depends on cohesion.

This example shows one way in which communities both enable and regulate human development and behavior. In contemporary Western culture, our emphasis on the individual carries within it an implicit demand to cultivate a unique identity that we then express as a performance of self. With the entire world available to us via a keystroke or two, we seem to instinctively seek ways to make our world smaller and more manageable by selecting niche communities with which to identify ourselves. Think of the online quizzes you take, the groups to which you belong, the social media sites you frequent, each of which contributing to or reflecting an aspect of your identity that you value and enact. Young children become obsessed with cartoon characters, and adults oblige by buying costumes, toys, and housewares to surround them with their fictional heroes. Teens identify themselves and find like-minded peers through shared fandoms focusing on sports teams, music, video games, and YA books and characters. Contemporary getting-to-know-you conversations might include questions like "Are you a Joss Whedon fan?" or "Are you team zombie or team unicorn?" Our everyday language is peppered with movie quotations or references, and the people who recognize them are our people. The degree to which we use story worlds and fictional characters to craft our identities is astounding, and of course can have great relevance to the study of children's and YA literature if we consider the means through which this happens. Let us turn our attention, then, the ways bodies, representations, and communities work together to form the story of us.

Prebirth to preschool

Our responses to literary language are primed in the womb. By about eighteen weeks of gestation, neurotypical babies have developed the apparatus needed for hearing, including the bones of the inner ear and the nerve endings that send the signals to the brain. The sounds they hear and feel throughout their entire bodies include the mother's heartbeat and the susurrations of shifting fluids. By twenty-four weeks they have become habituated to internal noises, and can hear environmental sounds, such as their parents' and siblings' voices. Psychologists (DeCaspar and Fifer 1980; Kolata 1984) tested the effects of prenatal reading by having mothers read Dr. Seuss's *The Cat in the Hat* (1957) to their unborn children twice a day for six and a half weeks prior to birth. Within hours after birth, they then tested their sucking rates as they heard *The Cat in the Hat* and then another poem with a different rhythm. Their sucking rate increased with the familiar poem, but not the unfamiliar one, leading researchers to believe that they recognized the book they heard before they were born. Certainly, there could be other variables involved. For instance, both the mother's familiarity with the text and the nature of the poetry itself might have led her to read the Seuss text faster than the unfamiliar one. The baby might then be adjusting her sucking tempo to the rhythm of the text itself, demonstrating attunement rather than recognition. In either case, though, it's clear that babies are born with a sensitivity to and perhaps even a preference for patterned, poetic language over everyday speech.

Those findings are borne out by research conducted by David S. Miall and Ellen Dissanayake (2003). They analyzed the poetic features of **infant-directed speech** and found that a baby's first encounters with speech are steeped in poetic devices, which they argue lay the foundation for future responses to literature and other arts. More importantly, Dissanayake (2009) stresses that this way of talking isn't something that we teach babies to like, but rather something that they train us to produce through their responses. Infants are more likely to respond to utterances that are "simplified, repeated, exaggerated, and elaborated" (23). Adults adjust their responses until the interactions take the form of what researchers call "communicative musicality" (Malloch and Trevarthen 2009). In other words, when you were born, your caregivers sang to you, and you sang back. It might not have sounded like

Mozart or Beyoncé, but it had rhythm, tune, emotion, and even harmony, as your grown-ups adjusted their voices to get you to respond in pleasing ways. This communicative musicality is the foundation for all acts of communication that we participate in throughout our lives.

Despite its role in laying the foundation for **aesthetic** intelligence and response, the most critical aspect of communicative musicality for the infant lies in the communicative part. Human infants are born with only three basic survival skills: sucking, swallowing, and breathing, and even breathing can be irregular. As a result, they cannot survive without the delivery of food in a form they can access, but more importantly, both accidental and intentional studies with human infants and other mammals indicate that mammalian infants will fail to thrive without close physical contact with another, caregiving mammal. Pediatrician Harvey Karp (2003) thus calls the first three months after birth the "fourth trimester," and emphasizes that this period should replicate womblike experiences as closely as possible. To the five Ss he recommends—swaddling, side or stomach position for sleeping, shushing, swinging, and sucking—I would add singing, since the muted sounds of voices were also part of the womb environment. In addition, singing and talking, especially in the rhythmic vocalizations that characterize poetic language, have a measurable influence on the coordination and regulation of breathing and heart rate (Cysarz et al. 2004). As those physical rhythms synchronize within and between infant and caregiver, the pair experiences emotional bonding as well, laying the foundation for participating in joint attention activities such as book sharing, as well as establishing the cognitive precursors for understanding intentionality and representation. For instance, if a caregiver always sings the same song at bath time, it isn't long before an infant comes to associate the sound with the activity and its emotional response, realizing that this song *intends* or points to bath time; in time, the song can evoke the emotion in the absence of the activity itself, as its representation.

In these early months, sighted infants are rapidly developing visual acuity. Their initial focal length is 7–30 inches, and they are better able to see things that are at the perimeter of their vision rather than straight ahead. By three months of age, they can see the full spectrum of colors, but their preferences seem to be for high-contrast, fully saturated colors, simple, schematic shapes, and slow-moving objects, especially faces, with their high contrast of eyes, brows, hairlines, and mouths that are almost always in motion (Eliot 1999). By six months of age, babies can even anticipate the path of a moving object, looking slightly ahead of where it actually is toward where it's going. At birth, input for each eye is channeled separately and competes for space within the brain, but over the first four months, if that competition is not impeded by strabismus or some other problem, the ability to see binocularly, or in three dimensions, develops. This explains why even very young children can recognize two-dimensional representations of three-dimensional objects; binocular vision enhances but doesn't replace the ability to recognize schematic or cartoon-like depictions in picturebooks and media. This also explains an early preference for simple, brightly colored, high-contrast images on the page and screen.

Since babies obviously can't fill out questionnaires or free associate, what's happening psychologically, morally, and intellectually is a matter of conjecture based on close observation. Erikson posits that the first two years of life are spent learning whether the world is a trustworthy place. In matters of feeding, sleeping, eliminating, and attention, babies are seeking patterns of response from their caregivers as well as from their own bodies. In some respects, then, the rituals of story-, song-, and poetry-sharing with infants are what matter most at this stage, with the meaning of what we share being largely indifferent. The primary importance, though, lies in setting aside time to read to babies, and developing vocal patterns that signal the specialness of literary language. Such reading rituals help create both an actual and metaphorical "holding environment," which psychologist D. W. Winnicott (1965) stresses is crucial for infants so that they can feel as though their bodies and the world are safe places in which to live. In fact, books offer a special and enduring kind of holding environment, evident in the phrase "curling up with a good book," which implies multiple kinds of safe, pleasurable enclosure.

From the rootstock of bias to the flowering of identity

But while the activity of reading at this point seems more important than the content of what is being read, we have to remember that we start filling up babies' image banks at birth. There is some evidence that even before their first birthdays, babies are developing preferences for puppets they understand to like what they like, such as graham crackers versus oat rings, and those that seem helpful to others rather than obstructive (Bloom 2013). Through these experiments, researchers have found that the seeds of bias develop much earlier than we thought, and for reasons other than markers of status in culture, such as race, class, or gender. The infants studied identified patterns of behavior—in this case, taste preferences—as either like them or unlike them, and they not only wished to see those who were like them given help, but they also wanted to see those who were not like them punished or obstructed from their goals. Ouch! So we can extrapolate from these findings to possible literary interventions: It is clear from these infant experiments that even before they are one year of age, children are already gaining a sense of self by identifying and disidentifying with others. Hence, it is crucial to introduce images of people who have diverse physical appearances to very young infants, but we also need to pay attention to the situations and contexts in which they are introduced. We should, in our talk around these images, highlight the way the characters like the things that the baby likes, giving the baby multiple possible sites of connection beyond outer appearance, and also be intentional about showing diverse images of people who are doing things that are obviously prosocial and helpful.

In terms of intellectual development, Eliot notes that infants quickly become bored with unmoving visual stimuli and follow the demands of their rapidly growing brains to seek out novelty, so it's important to share a variety of books that they can mouth and manipulate as well as access visually. The one image that babies can't seem to get enough of, however, is the mirror image of themselves. French psychoanalyst Jacques Lacan (2006) argues that children first recognize themselves in a mirror between the ages of six and eighteen months, and that this is a pivotal moment in the establishment of a sense of self. From that moment forward, we understand ourselves through an image that we identify with, rather than simply through the body we inhabit, so in some sense, this is when our identifications become more visually oriented rather than, as noted above, through other senses such as taste. In fact, Lacan asserts, we prefer the image over our body, because it represents a visual coherence, control, and completeness that we might not experience through our bodies. The baby's experience of his or her body is one of dependence and impotence; the baby can see and want things that he or she can't reach for himself or herself. What the baby sees in the mirror, by contrast, is a being that moves of its own accord, and appears more capable than the baby feels. This image thus gives the baby a sense of autonomy, which is, of course, an illusion, but it is a generative one in that it propels him or her to reach for autonomy as a desire and possibility. A baby's first sense of being an individual self, then, comes through identification with an external visual image.

Of course, such a theory is speculation on Lacan's part because infants can't express their relation to the mirror image, but its validity is borne out by the way we continue to use our mirror images in later life. We use mirrors to check what we look like or how we appear, regardless of how we feel. We also use mirrors to compare and correct our appearance so that it aligns with what we desire it to be, to see what we look like when we make certain facial expressions, and to organize our movements. These common activities remind us that we often give more weight to our visual image than we do to our internal feelings. The relevance for this attachment and preference for visual images can't be overemphasized for the study of children's and YA literature, because once we begin recognizing ourselves in and through an external image, we begin to rely more on representations and images than individual sensual experience to organize our worlds and our sense of self.

These images are not restricted to mirrors or images of ourselves, but extend to all manner of representations, including those in books and other media. In that initial recognition of ourselves in a mirror, we establish a structure whereby we idealize the image; the baby desires autonomy, and the mirror image of the baby seems to have it, so the image becomes an ideal for the baby. Structurally speaking, the image gains more authority than the thing it represents. Visual images in picturebooks are then viewed through this structure of idealization of images; in looking at them, babies collect images of what mommies and daddies look like, what pirates, cowboys, and princesses look like, what homes and bedrooms and castles look like, and ultimately, what happily ever after looks like. Moreover, their busy little brains associate these images with both words and affects, so that a signifier like "princess" slides over iconic images in their books and films, as well as their sense of self, since they may be called princess by their caregivers and/or associate the word "princess" with all females. For example, before my daughter could read, an older friend asked her the name of her primary school principal. She replied, "Oh we don't have a principal; we have a princessipal," because her principal was female, and her ear told her that princess was the right term for a female.

A potential problem that emerges out of this structure then becomes evident: if all the princesses they see in their books and films are white with blond hair, for instance, that association may become locked for them, creating a problem for both self-image and inclusion if there is a disconnect between the image they have of themselves, the images they see in media, and the signifiers that connect to them. Recent research shows that infants are attentive to the visual aspects of racial difference as early as six months of age (Kelly et al. 2007), and that their attitudes toward racially defined social differences are formed between the ages of four and seven (Katz 2003; Paley 1979; Vittrup 2007). The problem for intervention is that there is no way to predict the associations that individual children will make, but the findings do argue for intentionally diversifying the image bank, with plenty of positive affect attaching to accompanying verbal signifiers, as early as possible.

Humor, temperament, and **Theory of Mind**

Because **mental models** and patterns are busily forming during this early stage, a nascent sense of humor also emerges from about six months of age based on the perception of incongruity—a disruption or violation of an expected model or pattern. Incongruous stimuli can provide the novelty for children's brains to grow either through accommodation or assimilation, but their initial appearance requires an affective interpretation: Is this incongruous thing dangerous or harmless? When a caregiver or sibling behaves in a way that violates the baby's expectation, the baby may respond with either alarm or laughter, depending on her assessment of the threat level. Gentle silliness during reading, such as affecting a funny voice or sound effect for a character, facilitates the development of a sense of humor, but babies younger than two usually are not yet ready to disturb the connection between a person or object and its name. This is because while a one-year-old typically has a receptive vocabulary of around seventy words, mostly nouns and social expressions, they tend to assume three things about words: (1) words refer to whole objects, rather than their parts, (2) words refer to classes of items, and (3) objects have only one name.

Hence books that present and name objects in classes, such as dogs, cats, and farm animals, are useful for vocabulary and category development. Simple stories told or read well, with a rise and fall in vocalization that corresponds with the plot movement, will help instantiate a sense of story structure. Books can also play a role in facilitating fine motor skills; between twelve and eighteen months, babies develop controlled release, meaning that they can willfully open their hands and let go of something they have grasped, so page turning becomes possible as does manipulation of simple mechanisms such as sturdy pull tabs and lift-the-flap reveals.

By the age of two, young children are developing a range of physical skills that make them eager to develop a sense of independence, a stage that Erikson called "autonomy vs. shame and doubt." Their expressive vocabulary is expanding rapidly, though there is around a five-month delay between understanding a word and being able to say it. However, once they hit the magic number of being able to say approximately fifty words, they start to acquire as many as eight new words a day, and the pattern of understanding-first-and-saying-later reverses. They may, for instance, use a word correctly in a sentence or situation and then ask what it means. In terms of book and story sharing, then, it is perfectly fine and even desirable to read and tell stories with words they aren't likely to know; at this point, they are absorbing **aesthetic** forms through the feeling states they produce, and when they hear a new word in context, they can adopt it into their lexicon even if they aren't quite sure of its precise meaning. Their quests for autonomy in moving around the environment, feeding themselves, and learning proper toileting behavior are likely to introduce conflict into their social environments, so plot-driven stories that mirror everyday situations and demonstrate love and successful conflict resolution will help bridge the gap between image and embodiment, providing reassurance that the world is still a trustworthy place even when caregivers respond in new, often more negative ways.

As conflict and social interactions increase for the preschool child, his or her temperament will likely become more pronounced. Nurses in neonatal wards testify that temperament is evident at birth; some newborns are quiet and wide-eyed, while others are fussy and hard to pacify. As they grow older, temperaments affect how children approach tasks and other people, as well as how their environment affects them. Problems occur when there is a mismatch between parental or teacher expectations and children's behavioral styles. Fortunately, many books for young children highlight that mismatch, offering reassurance for caregivers and children that "normal" has a wide definitional range. Maurice Sendak's groundbreaking *Where the Wild Things Are* (1963), for instance, opened the door to exploring a child's often chaotic inner world. Max displays what researchers call a "spirited" temperament, and while he was preceded by Kay Thompson's psychologically simpler but every bit as rambunctious *Eloise* (1955), his descendants are much more numerous, including characters found in books like Ian Falconer's *Olivia* (2000), David Shannon's *No, David* (1998), Spike Lee's *Please, Baby, Please* (2002), Michael Buckley's *Kel Gilligan's*

Daredevil Stunt Show (2012), and Yuyi Morales' *Rudas: Niño's Horrendous Hermanitas* (2016). On the other end of the behavioral spectrum are the "easy-going" or "timid" child characters, such as Lucille Clifton's Everett Anderson, Charlie from the Charlie and Lola series, Gerald from Mo Willem's Elephant and Piggie books, and many of Kevin Henkes's mice characters. All of these depictions show how characters' temperaments lead to problems and solutions that ultimately validate individuality and autonomy even when the character is overtly scolded.

Regardless of temperament, most children cycle through bursts of independence and demands for freedom tempered by a need for reassurance from the time they are eight or nine months old until late in their teen years. At each stage of development, children and teens experience some measure of frustration at their relative lack of power. Erikson's third stage of development, which begins around age three, centers on the conflict of initiative versus guilt. At this point, children who have had caregivers who encourage conversation and narrative memory will begin to show signs of storytelling, shaping the concerns of their days into patterned speech that sound like songs or poems, or incorporating those concerns in their pretend play. They are beginning to feel the effects of power turned against them as they struggle to do what they want against the demands of adult rules and schedules, and they respond by exerting their own power over their toys in pretend play. Books that feature personified animals or toys that come alive and have adventures, like Mini Grey's *Traction Man* series (2005, 2008, 2012) and David Wiesner's *Mr. Wuffles!* (2013), facilitate imaginative play through modeling, while domestic tales like Russell Hoban's Frances books and Lauren Child's Charlie and Lola show children that their problems are not unique or unsolvable. But while such domestic settings may mirror their realities, they are, for the four-year-old itching for adventure, quite possibly a bit tame, so picturebooks modeled on folk and fairytale narratives, such as Julius Lester and Jerry Pinkney's *Sam and the Tigers: A Retelling of Little Black Sambo* (1996), Janet Stevens's *Tops and Bottoms* (1995), and Julia Donaldson's *The Gruffalo* (2005), which show less powerful characters overcoming threats and obstacles, meet psychological needs for empowerment and growth when bodies still need to stay close to home.

Somewhere between ages three and five, children develop an early version of **Theory of Mind (ToM)**. **ToM** is the ability to imagine that other people have intentions, beliefs, desires, and knowledge that may be different from your own. It's called a theory because it's not visible from the outside, so it requires some cognitive abilities to develop before it comes online. One of those abilities is the flexibility to understand that words and objects are not organically linked. A child must understand that a word can mean more than one thing, and that objects can go by different names. This is important for **ToM** because it means that children can understand that the way they talk about the world isn't necessarily the way the world is. This is a very sophisticated mental achievement, one that we lose to some degree when we stop asking "why?" all the time and just accept the world as given to us through our ideological blinders. But one of the tests to determine **ToM** is the false belief test, where a toy is hidden beneath a cup in front of two children. One child leaves the room, and the examiner moves the toy. The child who stays is then asked where the absent child will say the toy is. A three-year-old child will simply point to where the toy actually is, reflecting an inability to divorce the truth from what someone else might think is the truth. By contrast, most five-year-olds will point to where it was originally, before the first child left the room. They are able to consider that someone might believe something about the world that they know is not true. That understanding opens a space between minds that enables children to understand irony, and to consider further that other people might not share their ways of thinking. Understanding a picturebook like *Rosie's Walk* (Hutchins 1968) or *Lily Takes a Walk* (Kitamura 1987) requires at least a nascent ability to separate out what someone might be thinking in contrast to what is actually happening in the world, and in fact, working through a book like this with an adult reader can facilitate the development of **ToM**.

Another skill a child needs in order to understand **ToM** is how to read gesture and other visual and auditory clues to emotion. Emotions are internal, but they are expressed **multimodal**ly, through gesture, posture, tone of voice, etc. Sometimes these cues are accompanied by a direct verbal expression of the emotion, but sometimes they require inferences. The ability to make inferences from gesture and other nonverbal signs is key to a robust **ToM**. Stories help children develop **ToM** because they are able to associate words that describe feeling states with episodes that trigger them and gestures that typically accompany them. To a large degree, picturebooks and novels teach children how to perform or display emotion in ways that are recognizable in their culture. While some degree of **ToM** must be present for a child to understand motivations and cause and effect sequences in a character-driven story, character-driven stories continue to enhance **ToM** throughout one's reading life. **ToM** is also important for understanding verbal humor. Children begin to use joke forms, such as knock-knock jokes, when they are four to five years old, but they usually aren't funny. But once children understand that words can have more than one meaning, and have a sufficiently developed **ToM** to understand that someone else can be led to misunderstand which meaning is operative in a particular situation, then they can tell jokes and riddles that are actually clever plays on language.

Much recent research relates **ToM** to empathy and ethical action, often blurring the lines between them. The hope is that if children and teens can understand a character's inner thoughts and emotions, they will respond with greater compassion. But this is where it is important to pry apart the relevant brain functions, cultural inputs, and individual differences involved in reading and responding to literature. The ability to *feel with* another person or a character, which is what empathy involves, is a right-brain function. As such, it rests on **multimodal** inputs, that is, words are not always the most important conveyor of meaning when it comes to empathy. Consider, for instance, the way the audience comes to feel with the immigrant in Shaun Tan's (2007) wordless book, *The Arrival*. Even when words are used, with or without visual images, empathy depends not just on what words mean, but how they sound, the visual and visceral images and memories they elicit, identifications we make with others through them, and the contexts surrounding them. These features are available to very young children, and, as Crago (2014) notes, continue to be available to us throughout our lives through well-made stories.

ToM, on the other hand, is a left-hemisphere function; it depends on the ability to analyze whatever data are available and reflect on what it might mean. This is why **ToM** is not evident in children younger than four years old; their brains have not developed sufficiently to reflect on experience from a detached perspective that considers the difference between what is happening and what they or others think or feel about what is happening. Further, **ToM** is not dependent on emotion, though it might draw on emotional mirroring to produce its interpretations. You can understand what someone thinks or believes without feeling with or identifying with them. This is why **ToM** doesn't always arc to empathy, or further stretch toward more compassionate behavior (Keen 2007). While reading can lead to a more well-developed **ToM** through enhanced understanding of people's motivations, and also generate empathy if the author's words create the necessary atmosphere for feeling with a character, the motivation for acting compassionately or morally depends on wholly different kinds of inputs. For young children, according to Kohlberg (1984), those inputs include memories of getting in trouble or being rewarded for certain behaviors; for older children, they come from internalizing social rules and weighing the costs and benefits of their actions in light of likely peer and adult response. Still older children and adults might choose to act according to abstract moral codes, even if they understand and empathize with others, or they may choose to use their ToM to manipulate others (a skill as useful for benevolent teachers as for Machiavellian types). All of these variables mean that the optimistic belief that reading leads to more compassionate or moral behavior is generally unsupported.

The development of a sense of humor is critical at this preschool stage because it is a defense against the increasing encroachment of adult rules and authority. Most of the social rules a child learns prior to starting school are related to the proper use of one's body and socially approved expressions of emotion. These are subtly and not so subtly nuanced by race, class, and gender. Because books are the source of ideal images for children to model and emulate, they have enormous influence on how children and YAs come to perceive what is expected of them. They model both conscious and unconscious developmental processes, in realistic or metaphorical ways, and they allow readers to test limits and explore fears in safe ways. What if I left my favorite toy at the Laundromat and couldn't make anyone understand? What if I woke up and my mom was gone? What if I decided to eat everything in the entire world except green beans? While many books for preschoolers tackle such problems as these from a realistic standpoint and offer comforting resolutions, others take the fear to a point of absurdity so that children experience a sense of superiority over the problem.

The school years

Once children start school, adherence to social rules becomes even more urgent, and they focus on a conflict Erikson calls "industry vs. inferiority." They are usually less interested in their own inner worlds and more interested in learning how to use the world around them. They focus on their peers and how they measure up. The books they are interested in, then, have themes of friendship and developing competencies (such as mysteries and easy science fiction), but reading itself is a competency they must develop, so for a time they gravitate to books that reinforce, but don't necessarily stretch, their skills, such as formulaic series books. Their humor is generally focused on transgressive or taboo subjects—authority figures in diapers, for instance, or machines that produce noxious sounds and smells—that place those in power in absurd situations. Mikhail Bakhtin (1968) calls this sort of transgressive humor "carnivalesque" and suggests that, since medieval times, it has had a basically conservative function; during the "Feast of Fools," those without power could blow off steam by ridiculing their oppressors without getting in trouble. Once the pressure of living under rigid social hierarchies was thus vented, things could go back to normal until the next opportunity for controlled anarchy. Maria Nikolajeva (2010) argues that carnival is the structuring principle for nearly all children's books, since they turn adult-dominated culture topsy-turvy and allow children to be in charge for a limited time until order is restored in the end. In their school worlds, then, children learn to follow rules, while in their books they are permitted to challenge and thwart those rules with impunity.

The rules they are interested in challenging are not merely social, however. Middle childhood is a time of testing and chafing against existential limits. Henry Wadsworth Longfellow's "Let us, then, be up and doing" might well be considered the anthem of middle childhood, as their concerns are more focused on developing their embodied agency than on reflecting on their character or identity. Their ability to understand how the world actually works expands, but their ability to entertain counterfactuals without the inhibitory function of a fully developed prefrontal cortex means that they aren't quite willing to accept the limitations of realities like, say, physics or bank accounts. In other words, they know they aren't getting their letters to Hogwarts, but they don't know how unrealistic it is to think that they will become rock stars or professional athletes (although of course, a few of them will). As a result, they are highly invested in imagining fabulous if unlikely futures for themselves as heroes in their chosen fields of endeavor. Kieran Egan (1997) heralds this time period as one dominated by what he calls "romantic understanding." Romantic understanding, in Egan's view, builds on the insights of earlier "mythic understanding," whereby young children learn about the world by means of binary oppositions such as good-evil, love-hate, free-oppressed, and organize their experiences into simple story structures that turn these binaries into concrete images and metaphors. Romantic understanding then continues this story building in a more reality-based vein; school-aged children want to think about ideas, concepts, and technologies as the outcome or product of human activity, so that they can imagine how they might participate in knowledge making. Nonfiction, then, is most engaging when it tells a human story. Mysteries and survival stories are also popular because they often combine heroic action with the competent use of the environment in extreme conditions.

Books for this middle-childhood age continue to offer reassurances, though, that the world is a safe place that makes sense, and they often feature, as Nodelman (2008) points out, a home-away-home pattern that rewards autonomy and initiative without leaving the hero alone and stranded. Here you can begin to see why various stages of development can't be considered over and done with at any particular age. The patterns established in early childhood continue to evolve and resurface throughout our lives. Every new circumstance requires a renegotiation of trust and testing of the limits of our autonomy and initiative. The quests of a fairy tale hero fire the imagination of the preschool armchair traveler every bit as much as heroic fantasy quests for the tween and road trip novels and travel romances do for the teen reader for the same reasons; our psychological needs to venture out into the world, gather allies, and face and overcome dangers aren't often met by our physical ability to do so. Our focus shifts as we encounter different circumstances and develop new cognitive abilities, but patterns recur because we need them to, because we never fully and finally "finish" any part of our developmental process.

Adolescence

The advent of puberty brings with it a host of bodily changes over which we have little control, which sends us right back to mirror stage thinking: that is, preferring our body image to our actual bodies. This may sound odd, considering that many of us are somewhat embarrassed by our teen body image, but by preferring our body image over the real body, I mean caring for and obsessing over our image rather than necessarily having a positive feeling toward it. The reasons for this preference are similar to the reasons we had as infants: the body image gives us at least an illusion of control and stability that the lived body does not. We can't control the release of hormones, but we can manipulate, to some extent, how we appear to others. We continue to build our sense of self based on external images and models, and our ToM continues to evolve. Brain scans show that teens are still making sense of the world through their emotions, so the drippy pages of melodrama and the heart-stopping action of horror, which are often considered inferior genres by adult readers, rightfully claim space on teen shelves as much now as they did in the 1700s. However, a growth spurt in gray matter in the area of the prefrontal cortex occurs around age eleven, and the remainder of the teen years into the early twenties is spent linking up the new abilities to reason, understand, assess risk, and inhibit impulses with more archaic functions such as motor skills and emotion. If we have successfully navigated our way through Erikson's conflicts, we have a basic trust in the world, our primary relationships, and our own abilities, we aren't afraid to assert ourselves and take risks, and we feel reasonably confident of our ability to learn new things. If not, we may seek out ways to continually engage those themes that have tripped us up, either through acting out or through imaginative repetitions. But Erikson argues that the key project of the teen years is the development of a stable identity in the face of role confusion.

At the time of Erikson's writing in the mid-twentieth century, the public face and expectations of gender roles and adult behavior were more clearly defined and reinforced throughout the range of social institutions and media. The revolutions of the late 1960s surfaced questions about the adequacy of those expectations, with teens themselves rebelling against what they saw as a stifling climate of conformity. As a result, it is perhaps unrealistic today to talk about role confusion, because the model governing contemporary identity incorporates the ability to move fluidly among the various roles we adopt and enact throughout our lives—what we have hinted at in the previous chapter as a move toward "**posthumanism**." It's not that we think of ourselves as cyborgs necessarily, but that we reject the idea of the unified, autonomous self that traditional philosophical "**humanism**" posited as the end goal of a mature adult person. The searching question of the 1960s, "Who am I?," is now something more along the lines of "How do I present myself in this situation?" Representations in media and books become even more important in such an environment not because they reinscribe cultural ideologies or provide models to imitate, but because they offer sites to question and contest the efficacy of certain identity memes. The mean girl who gets her comeuppance, the jock who has to recover from a crippling injury, the nerd who suddenly finds herself popular, the nonwhite character who has to negotiate his place in an all-white school, the girl or boy who falls in love with someone outside his or her ethnicity or class—these stock characters in middle-grade and YA fiction interrogate the terms of identity construction. Surely, the lesson learned is most often one that could be crudely termed "be yourself," but the story that teaches that lesson has many moving parts for readers to ponder along the way.

Egan's (1997) categories are instructive here: The binary oppositions of mythic understanding haunt the adolescent, but he or she now have enough experience in the world to know that good does not always triumph, nor is it always easy to completely separate from evil. The stories teens tend to be interested in are usually more focused on how things break rather than how they work. Internal struggles such as mental illness, ethical dilemmas, gender fluidity, addictions, the aftermath of abuse and victimization; total social collapse figured through dystopias, zombie apocalypses, climate crises and race relations; and more private relational problems with siblings, divorces, break-ups, parents who don't care, unplanned pregnancies, and deaths: these are the topics that have dominated YA literature from its inception and continue to be reworked through countless iterations. But these serious topics are counterbalanced by rich expressions of humor, often trenchantly directed at adult or peer pretentions, heroic fantasy quests, lighthearted friendship novels, and cotton-candy romances. The prevalence of the latter leads me to suggest that, at least in terms of the representations in the literature, the developmental crisis Erikson reserves for the years immediately following the teens, "intimacy vs. isolation," is very much on the minds of today's teens as well.

Moreover, we see shades of Egan's (1997) further developmental categories, "philosophic understanding" and "ironic understanding" in play throughout YA literature. In their early teen years, Egan argues, young people develop a more theoretical approach to the world that in some ways hearkens back to the binary categories of their early childhood; that is, they begin to think in terms of large structures and problems, but now words like society, culture, environment, racism, and politics make sense to them on both a personal and impersonal level. They take sides on issues, often stridently so, because they still tend to lead with their emotions. In contemporary dystopias, for instance, it is almost always clear where the evil lies, and the characters have to claim their agency as they take up arms against it. The characters in both realistic and fantasy YA novels experience moments where they see through the phoniness of systems of oppression (or think they do), and finally, finally understand why they have always felt so out of place; they *get it*, emerging out of confusion about what matters into a firm sense of identity. As they move toward ironic understanding in their adult lives, however, they develop the capacity to reflect back on their own complicated relationships to social structures, shedding some of their idealistic passion and acknowledging their complicity in maintaining oppressive structures.

While Egan argues that stories matter throughout the lifespan, and is a strong advocate for storytelling as both a goal and the means of education, he doesn't fully acknowledge the role that literature and the media play in facilitating the transitions between these levels of understanding. The stories a culture tells about itself and the ideologies that inform those stories shift, as we have seen in the previous chapter. Global interaction, political turmoil, local fights for social justice and freedom, and the wars of the past two centuries have exposed children and teens to actual experiences and vicarious stories that promote an awareness of how larger social structures can impact daily life. Moreover, today's authors are less likely to adopt a protectionist attitude in the literature they write for young people. Instead, through their stories, they ask readers to imagine and empathize with young people enmeshed in and victimized by the systemic problems of the twentieth and twenty-first centuries: concentration camps, drug and human trafficking, institutional racism, gang culture, environmental abuse, and the list goes on. Hence, I would argue that contemporary children and teens are a lot savvier and more ironic about their place in the world a lot sooner than Egan posits precisely because of the range, depth, quality, and availability of the texts produced for them.

Conclusion

In this chapter, we have looked at the physical, psychological, and social structures within which children develop. By bringing together what we know about the developing brain with literary theory, we can make a strong case for the importance of visual and storied representations of everyday life and fantasy worlds in youth literature. The developmental needs of children and teens are addressed in and through their literature, helping them feel at home in the world, and giving them a safe space to explore dangerous ideas and situations. Their books also help them develop a more nuanced understanding of other people and the social structures that envelop us all, so that they can reflect on their responsibility in the face of them.

Extending your study

Reading:

Burke, Michael. *Literary Reading, Cognition and Emotion: An Exploration of the Oceanic Mind* (New York: Routledge, 2012).
Though not focused on children's literature, Burke's exploration of emotional cognition is readily applicable to children's and YA texts, particularly his discussion of the roles literary-induced imagery and particular themes play in evoking emotion.
Crago, Hugh. *Entranced by Story: Brain, Tale and Teller, from Infancy to Old Age* (New York: Routledge, 2014).
Employing clearly explained theories of the stratified brain and the bicameral mind, Crago goes on to explore why and how certain stories are important to us at particular periods of our life.

Egan, Kieran. *The Educated Mind: How Cognitive Tools Shape Our Understanding* (Chicago: University of Chicago Press, 1997).

An argument and practical suggestions for reimagining education in light of what we know and can observe about how children and teens think at various stages. Part One describes his stage theory, with chapters devoted to each stage; Part Two draws implications for education reform.

Gooderham, David, "Children's Fantasy Literature: Toward an Anatomy," *Children's Literature in Education* 26, no. 3 (1995): 171–83.

Uses Erikson's stage theory to explore the types of fantasy written for various ages.

Kümmerling-Meibauer, Bettina (ed.), *Emergent Literacy: Children's Books from 0 to 3* (Amsterdam: John Benjamins, 2011).

Essays by scholars of various disciplines addressing the cognitive, **aesthetic**, linguistic, and psychological dimensions of books for very young children.

Writing:

1   After reviewing Erikson's stages of psychosocial development, identify and discuss the ways in which a picturebook or middle-grade novel of your choice addresses the needs of children in a particular stage. Use the case study below as a model.

2   Alternately, research Egan's model in order to expand the work of the case study, considering *A Bird on Water Street* (2014) (or a text of your choice) in light of how it portrays a young teen's growing awareness of how his life is impacted by larger economic and environmental forces.

3   Write an essay in which you explore the developmental interests addressed by an early chapter book.

4   Find three books that address a difficult subject such as divorce or death: a picturebook for young children, a middle-grade novel, and a YA novel. Compare and contrast the ways in which the problem is presented, addressed, and handled.

5   Working with a book of your choice, analyze the way the book encodes community or cultural norms regarding embodiment.

Discussing:

1   What are the principal dangers in analyzing and choosing literature based on developmental stage models?

2   How might knowing about stage models enable you to help a child in distress choose an appropriate book?

3   Come up with a list of nursery rhymes or fairy tales that are familiar to people in your discussion group. What cultural and personal themes do they

address? Are these themes appropriate for preschool children on a practical level? A metaphorical level? What do you think some of the purposes of folk literature such as these are?

4 Do you have a "comfort read," a book for younger readers that you return to such as Jacqueline Wilson discusses in the talkback to this chapter? Why do you think it provides comfort for you? What does this suggest about how reading and stages of development interact?

5 Like Jacqueline Wilson in the talkback, consider how you feel about the practice of putting age guidance on the covers of books. Consider also that on Scholastic's website, they have two categories: interest level and reading level. For Stephenie Meyer's *Twilight*, the reading level is listed as fourth grade, but the interest level is listed as ninth-twelfth grade. Given Wilson's experience, do you think that reading level or title is an adequate indicator of interest level? What other signposts do publishers have at their disposal to indicate the intended audience for a book? Which are helpful and which may not be?

Responding:

1 Research and watch an episode of a television show aimed at young children. Reflect on how well you think the show meets the needs of its target audience.

2 Watch the PBS documentary *Merchants of Cool*: http://www.pbs.org/wgbh/pages/frontline/shows/cool/ What surprises or dismays you about what you have learned? What ideologies of teen identity and identity formation processes does it surface?

3 Go to a library or bookstore and "lurk" in the children's or teen section. (Take a notebook so you won't look like a creeper.) Observe how the books are organized and marketed in terms of age distinctions. Observe, if possible, how children and teens choose books. Talk with a librarian or bookseller about their feelings toward helping patrons choose age-appropriate books.

Online exploration:

1 A wealth of resources, including short videos, explanations, and external links, exploring temperament:
https://www.b-di.com/

2 Dr. Dipesh Navsaria is a pediatrician who also holds a master's degree in library and information science, specializing in youth services. Dr. Navsaria is a strong advocate of early literacy as a way to improve the lives of children as well as their lifelong health. The links are to a page that lists various literacy initiatives that he is involved in, and to a document he has

composed that shows how books for children are related to their developmental needs.

http://www.navsaria.com/home/professional.html http://www.navsaria.com/home/document-library/dormouse.pdf

3 This link is for a report on the findings of a study focused on the impact of early reading on brain development.

http://pediatrics.aappublications.org/content/early/2015/08/05/peds.2015-0359

4 This video shows the puppet show referenced in the chapter about how babies relate to stories and develop bias:

https://www.youtube.com/watch?v=FRvVFW85IcU

5 Kieran Egan's webpage has links to his articles and further information about his developmental model:

https://www.sfu.ca/~egan/

Case Study: Industry and Inferiority in a Middle-Grade Novel

Elizabeth O. Dulemba's *A Bird on Water Street* (2014) offers a clear picture of a young boy working through the conflicts of industry versus inferiority. Our introduction to Jack comes through his contemplation of the effects of acid rain on his mining community. His teacher insists that the students learn about the various types of trees, even though no trees grow anywhere near the copper mine that dominates his town. As the book progresses, Jack learns more about the ecosystem of his town, coming to understand how trees, water, bugs, frogs, and birds are interrelated. But he's not just interested in ecological systems; he wants to know what role people have played in creating the barren landscape, and he vows, with true middle-childhood bravado, "I'm gonna bring nature back" (56). He reads all he can on the subjects that interest him, and he seeks out the resources he needs to grow a garden and nurture a tree.

In addition to Jack's intense interest in his environment and his commitment to making a difference, he demonstrates the fluidity of stages past and stages yet to come. When the miners strike to protest a series of layoffs, Jack is conflicted. He values the stability of his community, and he wants to help everyone, including himself, feel safe during the times of uncertainty. But he also wants to assert his autonomy. His father sees him as a seventh-generation miner, but Jack does not want to join his father underground. His desire is to establish his own identity while maintaining the relationships that have always made him feel safe. So while he is reaching back toward safety, he is also looking forward toward seeking a viable identity and future intimacy.

Author talkback: Jacqueline Wilson

In this talkback, prolific and popular author Jacqueline Wilson discusses the dilemmas she faces as she considers the needs of the audiences for which she writes. For more information about the author and her books, visit her website at http://www.jacquelinewilson.co.uk/.

A few years ago there was a big dispute in the world of British children's literature. The major publishers decided it would be a good idea to have age guidance on the covers of all their children's books. As many children's books were now ordered online or bought from supermarkets it was felt that purchasers needed help choosing age appropriate stories.

The publishers were surprised when the majority of their children's authors were emphatically opposed to this idea. Many argued that they didn't write for specific age groups and made the valid point that reluctant teenage readers who might otherwise enjoy a particular title would hate to be seen reading a book clearly labeled for the under tens.

I had to make a decision on this myself. I found it difficult. I could understand both points of view, which wasn't much of a help. I didn't really like the idea of age or gender guidance on any kind of book. I'd certainly be highly irritated if I were only encouraged to read books labeled for women of sixty-plus. I know that people of all ages read my books. Young children of seven read all my Victorian books about Hetty Feather with great enjoyment, though I would probably think them more suitable for the ten plus age group. Older readers in their mid teens who now choose adult novels often fixate on one of my books for seven- to eleven-year-olds as comfort reads when they're stressed or depressed.

However, there are some books by me still in print that are categorically teenage reads, like *Kiss* (a girl having to come to terms with the fact that the boy she loves is gay) and *Love Lessons* (a girl falls for her art teacher and they start an inappropriate relationship). These are definitely not suitable for young children. I'd hoped that their titles might indicate this but during signing sessions I'd seen various proud parents buying them for six-year-olds. When I gently suggested they might read the books first themselves and then maybe pop them away in a cupboard for a few years they assured me that their children were brilliantly competent readers. I realized that many people confuse reading progress with an ability to understand and absorb a complex subject.

I therefore compromised and so for a while any of my books considered mildly controversial were clearly labeled *For older readers*. It's a vague term but manages to give some indication of content.

But although I still like to think most of my books can be read by anyone from six to sixty or beyond, I admit I do generally have an age range in mind when I write my books. I don't decide on a subject and then make detailed notes about my characters.

The process is much more nebulous. It's more like the imaginary games I played as a child. I make up my main character first, and then I "play" with her inside my head. I discover all sorts of things about her. I know what she loves most, what frightens her, what she's really worried about. As I see her more clearly I learn her family background, her looks, and most importantly her age, though I don't always make this clear in case it puts off a potential reader. But *I* know and that helps me get the tone right. I nearly always write in the first person and so I imagine my girl talking to a special friend around the same age, using the sort of language that seems right. I also try to deal with the theme of the book in an appropriate and understandable way.

I often choose demanding subjects for a children's book. Having just glanced at twenty or so of my titles at random, I can see that many deal with big emotional subjects like inadequate or missing parents, illness and death.

I try to deal with these issues in different age appropriate ways. I think of the child reader I'm aiming at. If they're under ten I try to be as comforting as possible and would never go into distressing details. If they're twelve or above I might try to be more truthful, and although I always aim for an upbeat ending I wouldn't necessarily have my characters living happily ever after.

My most popular title for perhaps seven- to eleven-year-olds is *The Story of Tracy Beaker* (with over a million sales and a long-running award winning television series). It's about a feisty little girl in a children's home desperate to be fostered. She's writing her own story—and although she is an unreliable narrator, fantasizing constantly about her absent mother, the young reader is fully aware of her anger and despair. I don't go into any sordid or upsetting details about the backgrounds of Tracy and her friends in the children's home. I try to make sure there are many tension-easing humorous passages in the text so it isn't a grim read. I engineer a reasonably happy ending for her, though not quite the ending Tracy herself longs for.

I deal with another unwanted child in a book for teenagers called *Dustbin Baby*. The plot concerns fourteen-year-old April as she's trying to reconstruct her past and find the unknown mother who abandoned her as a young baby. I allow more distressing detail in this book, and expect my readers to understand April's lack of a true sense of self and her sadness when she pieces together half-forgotten events in her life. I try to keep April a realistic teenager though, angry that her staid foster mother won't let her dress in a flamboyant fashion or own a mobile phone. The ending is bittersweet, and possibly will make my reader a little tearful, but in a good positive way.

Mothers or mother figures loom large in my books. *The Illustrated Mum* is aimed at the mid-range ten- to twelve-year-old, a story of two sisters and their bi-polar mother who is loving but completely unreliable, a disturbed woman covered in decorative tattoos. The story is told by the younger sister, Dolphin, who adores her mother in spite of everything, while her older sister, Star, resents her bitterly. This is mostly a sad book and my publishers did initially have doubts about including one particular scene where the mother has a break down and has to be hospitalized—but ever since it was published nearly twenty years ago I haven't had a single complaint. I think children can deal with distressing subject matter, so long as there's reassurance and no truly graphic detail.

I write about the death of a loved one in several of my books. The nineteenth century world of children's literature dealt with death straightforwardly. Who hasn't shed a tear over the death of Beth in *Little Women*? But for more than a century we shied away from death in our children's books, though that's far from the case now, with the huge success of John Green's *The Fault in our Stars* and many other authors and titles.

I try to write about death in a truthful but age-appropriate way. I realized that for most children the demise of a beloved pet is the first time they have to deal with death. I wrote my short chapter book *The Cat Mummy* about a child called Verity growing up in a family who never discuss death because it's too painful, so Verity deals with the death of her poor old cat Mabel by trying to turn her into a mummy— she's been learning about the Ancient Egyptians at school. (I promise there aren't any gruesome details). When the remains of Mabel are eventually discovered, Verity's understanding teacher tells her about *The Egyptian Book of the Dead* and Verity is comforted by writing her own book about Mabel. Tender-hearted cat-loving adults finish the book in tears but I haven't discovered a single small child who has cried.

Young teenagers often write to say they cried over *Vicky Angel* or *My Sister Jodie*, but thankfully they've stressed that they've enjoyed a good cry and found it cathartic. In the first title, Jade has to cope after her best friend Vicky has died running across the road. I've had quite a few letters saying this book has helped young people cope with the death of their own friends. Vicky comes back to haunt Jade as a very ebullient ghost—or does she? I deliberately left the text ambiguous so that my readers could make up their own minds.

There's no doubt that there's a tragic unexpected death at the end of *My Sister Jodie* but this has proved one of my most cherished novels and many readers have invented their own sequels. I think this exchange of ideas by email and letter is one of the most rewarding aspects of being a children's author. I try to reply to as many as I can. I'm delighted to be connecting with so many young people. It's a way of keeping in touch with taste and development in a rapidly changing world.

Literature references

Buckley, M. (2012), *Kel Gilligan's Daredevil Stunt Show*, New York: Harry N. Abrams.
Child, L. (2000-present), *Charlie and Lola* series, New York: Grosset & Dunlap.

Clifton, L. (1970–92), Everett Anderson series, New York: Henry Holt.

Donaldson, J. (2005), *The Gruffalo*, New York: Dial.

Dulemba, E. O. (2014), *A Bird on Water Street*, San Francisco: Little Pickle Press.

Falconer, I. (2000), *Olivia*, New York: Atheneum.

Grey, M. (2005), *Traction Man is Here!*, New York: Knopf.

Grey, M. (2008), *Traction Man Meets Turbo Dog*, New York: Knopf.

Grey, M. (2012), *Traction Man and the Beach Odyssey*, New York: Knopf.

Hoban, R. (1948–70). *Frances the Badger* series, New York: Harper.

Hutchins, P. (1968), *Rosie's Walk*, New York: Simon & Schuster.

Kitamura, S. (1987), *Lily Takes a Walk*, New York: Dutton.

Lee, S. (2002), *Please, Baby, Please*, New York: Simon and Schuster.

Lester, J. (1996), *Sam and the Tigers: A Retelling of Little Black Sambo*, New York: Puffin.

Morales, Y. (2016), *Rudas: Niño's Horrendous Hermanitas*, New York: Roaring Brook.

Sendak, M. (1963), *Where the Wild Things Are*, New York: Harper and Row.

Seuss, Dr. (pseud.). (1957), *The Cat in the Hat*, New York: Random House.

Shannon, D. (1998), *No, David!*, New York: Blue Sky Press.

Stevens, J. (1995), *Tops and Bottoms*, New York: Harcourt Brace.

Stone, T. L. (2009), *Almost Astronauts: 13 Women Who Dared to Dream*, Somerville, MA: Candlewick.

Tan, S. (2007), *The Arrival*, New York: Arthur A. Levine.

Thompson, E. (1955), *Eloise*, New York: Simon and Schuster.

Wiesner, D. (2013), *Mr. Wuffles!*, New York: Clarion.

Willems, M. (2007–present) *Elephant and Piggie* series, New York: Hyperion.

3

Thinking Theoretically about Children's and Young Adult Literature

Suggested texts to read alongside this chapter

Carroll, Lewis, *Through the Looking Glass, and What Alice Found There.*
Hunt, Peter, *Backtrack.*
Nodelman, Perry, *The Same Place but Different.*
Silverstein, Shel, *The Giving Tree.*

Every piece of good critical analysis begins with wonder. As you read a book or view a film, it brings you joy, or it horrifies you, or makes you angry, or leaves you cold. If you are an analytical thinker, you start to wonder why it affected you that way, or how the text produced those effects, or whether others share your experience. Each of these avenues of wonder—the personal or interpersonal, the **textual**, and the **contextual**—leads you down a separate rabbit hole into the warren of contemporary literary and critical theory.

The purpose of this chapter is to help you consider how your wonder might be developed into coherent arguments and analyses of children's and YA texts. The field of literary and cultural criticism of children's and YA literature has made enormous gains in scope and gravitas over the past fifty years, such that virtually every **theoretical paradigm** that has been applied to literature for adults has found a voice in the critical discussion surrounding youth literature. In the late 1990s, I developed a way of introducing **theory** to my students by showing how interpretations of Shel Silverstein's *The Giving Tree* (1964) changed when considered through different "isms"—such as **feminism**, **Marxism**, **ecocriticism**, **formalism**–and other critical lenses–such as religious study, child development, and psychology. I posted the idea on the online discussion group child_lit, and people took the ball and ran with it, adding their own favorite **theories** to my initial list, demonstrating the growing range of perspectives that have been fruitfully applied to children's texts. Clearly, we can't discuss every possible critical lens in a single chapter; instead, we will focus our attention on certain principles, research strategies, and methods of critical engagement with texts and their contexts, offering some general frameworks for thinking theoretically about children's and YA literature. Some people find the idea of literary **theory** exciting, others find it intimidating, and still others actively resist it, believing that any type of analysis is overanalysis that threatens to drive the wonder out of the experience. But my position is that we are always already theorists; that is, we each have an implicit or explicit system of ideas or suppositions that we use to explain the things we encounter, and that is the very definition of a **theory**: A **theory** is an overarching system of ideas or a model that serves to explain a group of things; it's usually external to the thing it explains, and it helps us understand how or why the thing exists, works the way it does, or appears in the form it takes. When it comes to literature, someone, somewhere, at some point in time has systematized each of these habitual ways of making sense of our experiences into a **theoretical paradigm**.

Natural-born theorists

Consider the following scene: A teenage girl, Carly, is approached by Evan, a boy for whom she has long harbored an unrequited crush; he asks her a rather mundane question about the homework in a class they share, and then follows up by asking if she will be at Friday's game. When she says, "yeah," he replies "cool," and walks away. She immediately grabs her group of friends and heads for the bathroom to analyze the conversation. Each of her friends has a different question. Siobhan asks her to repeat *exactly* what Evan has said. Daphne wonders about his underlying intentions: Does his asking about homework mean he thinks she's smart, and is that a good thing or a bad thing? Does asking her about the game really mean that he wants to see her more, and perhaps date her? Rebecca sees balance in his questions: Since he is exposing a vulnerability in his academic prowess, he is anxious for her to see that he is good at sports. Beatrix starts analyzing Evan rather than his words, bringing up rumors she has heard to warn Carly of his reputation and interpreting his questions as an attempt to make her one of his conquests. Tamara asks about body language and intonation: Did he lean in when he talked to her? Did he raise his eyebrows or wink when he said "cool"? Did his question about the game sound like a private invitation? Sylvia asks Carly what she thinks he meant, and how it made her feel. Finally, Mitzi rolls her eyes and says, "Maybe he just missed the homework and wondered whether you were going to the game. Sometimes people just mean what they say. Or maybe he didn't mean anything—he just said something to end an awkward conversation."

Each girl's question reflects a way of thinking about "text" that has been developed into one or more recognized ways of doing literary criticism:

*Siobhan, the **bibliographic** critic*: By asking Carly to repeat the conversation exactly, Siobhan is doing something called "establishing the text." Texts often go through multiple revisions and versions, sometimes even after they are published. A famous example is *Peter Pan*, which started life as a short section in an adult novel and became a stage play before becoming two different versions of a novel, all by J. M. Barrie. It has also seen multiple adaptations, revisions, and continuations by other authors over the years. **Bibliographic critics** establish **authoritative editions** of texts by combing through archives to find out what they can about the process of their creation. Sometimes, they find deleted scenes, misleading translations, and/or letters to and from editors, enabling them to produce an essay or book chapter that explains the process of production, or perhaps even a variant of a "director's cut" or **annotated edition** of a book. They may or may not speculate as to why particular changes were made, but their work with original manuscripts allows others to do interpretive work on the most reliable versions of the texts. Even if **bibliographic** work doesn't interest you, it is always important to use a recognized, unabridged edition and reread a text very closely, often multiple times, before embarking on any interpretation.

*Daphne, the **psychoanalytic deconstructionist***: Daphne's question about intentions can take a critic in many directions. She wants to read more into what Evan said, to suss out what his motivations were for asking his questions, but also how his words might be covering over, rather than straightforwardly expressing, his real meaning. She is convinced that his simple questions mean something more or maybe even something different from what they are ostensibly about. She assumes that language is not a transparent conveyor of what's really going on in any situation. Instead, she thinks that every utterance sits atop a layer of unexpressed motives and desires, and that **signifiers** always refer to other unspoken, repressed **signifiers**. As a result, we always say both more and less than what we mean. Analyzing language for what it doesn't say as well as what it does is one of the starting points for **deconstruction** and **psychoanalytic criticism**, but it is important to understand that the source of any repressed meanings is not the personal psychology of the author or character. Instead, the source resides in the system of language and representation itself. Representation in the form of image and language is what we rely on to establish our sense of self, connect with others, and express ourselves. But as I have noted in Chapter 2, we do this by identifying with publicly available symbols and words rather than "our own words." Inquiring about author's intentions in a deeply personal way, then, is out of favor in literary criticism, because authors, just like everyone else, are dependent for their means of expression on the available resources, both **ideological** and material, of their time and culture, and because they always say more and less than what they mean.

Rebecca, the **textual** *or* **formalist** *critic*: Noticing form within a text and extrapolating how the form contributes to the meaning requires, first and foremost, a detective's eye in close reading. **Textual** and **formalist** critics pay attention to the way sentences work on their own and in combination, as does Rebecca when she recognizes balance in Evan's questions. We will focus closely on this type of **textual criticism** in the chapters on poetry, picturebooks, story, and film, considering how to do close readings of story structure, images, figurative language, poetic form, and other linguistic conventions. It is particularly important to note, however, that Rebecca also brings the "so what?" to her observations about **form**. She could have simply stopped by noticing that Evan's first question was about academics and his second about sports. Instead, she found the symmetry of his questions and attributed meaning to her observations within the context of the situation.

Beatrix, the **contextual** *critic*: Beatrix's contribution to the conversation goes beyond the text to the external social contexts of the situation. Rather than doing a close reading of what was said, she references what she knows and believes about Evan before going into the bathroom, and judges his actions within that wider context. Critics likewise bring outside contexts into their readings of texts. These contexts take many forms; indeed, we could say that all critical positions are external to the original text, and operate as lenses through which we view situations. So, for instance, bringing your knowledge of child development to bear on your interpretation of a text is a contextualized, interdisciplinary way of reading, but so is drawing on your knowledge of how figurative language works when analyzing a poem. Other contexts are more overtly driven by **ideology**. Some of you, for instance, may be troubled by my entire example because it plays on sexist and heteronormative stereotypes; your response may reflect a preference for **feminism**, **gender studies**, or **queer theory** as an interpretive context. Beatrix herself is demonstrating a way of doing criticism that moves from her interpretive presuppositions to the text at hand, rather than from text to interpretation, which I would suggest is something to be careful about. Nothing in Evan's utterance actually supports Beatrix's interpretation, which makes it harder to defend. That does not mean it is indefensible; it just means that you will need to find additional **textual** and **contextual** examples to craft a persuasive argument. It also means that not everyone will agree with your reading, because not everyone shares or will be convinced by your **ideological** positions or frameworks, which is, in the end, the fate of all interpretations.

Tamara, the **rhetorical** *critic*: Although rhetoric is concerned with language, and, in the case of visual rhetoric, image, it is not merely about what words and images mean or even the representations they construct. Instead, rhetoric is concerned with the ways in which the delivery of a message produces effects on its audiences, so elements of affect (feelings or emotions), gesture, and presentation matter as much as the words themselves, especially when the message is being communicated to readers at different stages of development, as we have seen in Chapter 2. **Rhetorical theory** is gaining traction in the study of children's and YA literature as critics begin to think more about the role of the body in meaning-making as well as the **multimodal** nature of children's and YA texts.

*Sylvia, the **reader response** critic*: In tandem with considering how a text communicates is the consideration of how it is received by its audience. The ways a text affects us, like the preferred avenues of wonder we pursue, are embedded in our dispositions, memories, and experiences. **Reader response criticism** is a favorite method among teachers because it starts conversations and helps students see that there is more than one way to read a text. From that insight teachers and critics can launch into discussions that point to certain **textual** and **rhetorical** devices that engender particular responses, or into discussions that surface **ideological** positions and expose them to interrogation. Indeed, analyzing our own responses can teach us as much about ourselves as it does about the texts we read.

Mitzi, the eye-roller: Freud was supposed to have said that "sometimes, a cigar is just a cigar." But our impulse to make meaning from texts is so strong that a position like Mitzi's is one most of us view with some suspicion. Mitzi either resists or doesn't believe the idea that language is anything more than a transparent way to convey information, or that people always say more and less that what they mean. She also resists or doesn't understand the fact that social and **rhetorical contexts** matter in analysis. As a result, the other girls might do some eye rolling of their own at Mitzi's naïve assessment of the situation. While some analyses of texts certainly seem to go against common sense, we know from everyday experience that what we notice and think of as common sense isn't necessarily the same as what others pick up and understand. And since there are different ways of interpreting any text, that means that all texts are interpretable. Of all the girls called into the bathroom, Mitzi's call for a literal interpretation is certainly the least interesting, and ultimately the least satisfying, because we all know that's not how texts work. The next time there is a conversation to analyze, Mitzi will probably not be invited back.

That said, in the critical analysis of children's and YA literature, though, there are Mitzis out there. Frederick Crews (1963, 2001), for instance, has written two books where he uses *Winnie-the-Pooh* (1926) to poke fun at literary and cultural **theory** itself, seeking to expose the fondness of its practitioners for particular kinds of terminology, often called jargon, as so much silliness that needlessly complicates our approach to interpretation. His use of Milne's book to make his points, however, is a double slam at applying literary criticism to children's and YA literature, taking aim not only at the **theory**, but also at its use with texts he considers completely straightforward and transparent.

Identifying your own path of wonder

Over the next few days, pay close attention to the way you and your friends tell stories and assess situations. Look for patterns that reveal your preferred avenue of wonder. In 1953, M. H. Abrams argued that all literary theories could be broadly classified under four basic categories: mimetic theories, which are interested in the way texts represent the world; expressive theories, which concern the way works reveal the inner world of the author; pragmatic theories, which focus on the ways texts affect their audiences; and objective theories, which look at the texts themselves as self-contained objects for **aesthetic** contemplation. This systematic way of viewing literary criticism is appealing for its tidiness, but it was already being challenged by a series of influential lectures delivered in 1955 by J. L. Austin, later collected in a little book called *How to Do Things with Words* (1962). Austin argued that language didn't merely give expression to preexisting thoughts and constructs, but was an action in and of itself; that is, language actively creates what it seems to merely describe. This idea thus calls into question any sort of mimetic theory that would argue about how accurate or true a **textual** representation is in reference to some external reality.

Austin's conception of language as "performative" rather than representational joined the theory of language developed by Ferdinand de Saussure in lectures given from 1906 to 1911 and published as *Course in General Linguistics* (1959). Saussure also claimed that language didn't just label independently existing concepts, objects and structures, but played an active role in constructing these things. Student movements in the 1960s expanded these insights to include the linguistic and cultural construction of identity and worldviews, arguing that if language and other representational systems had created these things in the first place, then language could recreate them in ways that challenged existing political hegemonies and elevated the status of formerly marginalized people groups; change the way we talk and use images, and we'll change the way we think. Such close attention to the power of language and visual image to construct reality continues to open new avenues of wonder around the consideration of history, identity, and representation.

These avenues are especially important for children's literature critics because of the power imbalance between an adult author or illustrator shaping reality the way he or she sees it and a reader with less real-world experience against which to test that text-driven reality. Psychoanalyst Jacques Lacan (1988: 49) argues that the "child . . . is prodigiously open to everything concerning the way of the world that the adult brings to him." The work of a responsible children's literature critic or teacher is to analyze texts within the multiple **contexts** of their production and reception, realizing that texts are in fact a form of action; they help shape identities and worldviews and evoke emotions that attach to their constructions, forming lasting memories through which we process present experience. In this way, they produce effects on readers.

The remainder of this chapter will provide a brief introduction to ways of thinking theoretically about literature, highlighting special adjustments I think are useful in writing about children's and YA texts.

Thinking with "isms" about children's and young adult literature

There are multiple guides that explain **theoretical paradigms** and how to apply them to texts. Discrete schools of thought are given separate names and chapters, often with sets of questions that help focus your thinking and guide your analysis. This approach is helpful in identifying what's at stake and what might be missing in a particular way of reading and interpreting a text, but it can also have a one-note, cookie-cutter feel; that is, you have a feminist-shaped or psychoanalysis-shaped cookie cutter and you use it no matter what the text itself seems to be doing (now, my husband did make me a pancake once that looked exactly like Karl Marx when I was studying **Marxism**, but that was just an irrelevant accident . . . I think). At any rate, that's what Frederick Crews does in his books, and what I did in my opening example. By now, though, you have probably sensed a little bit of the problem with dividing up the world in this way—while you or some of your colleagues and friends may have a preferred or dominant mode of theorizing the texts you encounter, others may work from a hybrid model, or use different approaches with different texts. In other words, you might have said that sometimes you think like Beatrix, keying to issues outside the text, and sometimes you think more like Tamara, thinking about how a particular **form** worked to communicate a particular message. And sometimes you want to bring Beatrix's or Tamara's way of thinking together with Sylvia's concerns about how a reader will respond to a text. So the lines between the different kinds of **theoretical paradigms** blur, and that's perfectly okay.

Of special consideration to children's and YA literature, however, is the fact that Crews took existing **theoretical paradigms** developed for peer texts—that is, books by adults meant to be read by other adults—and mapped them onto a children's text without altering them to account for the text itself or the **implied audience** of the text. Interestingly, people have found his books very useful in understanding the theories he lampoons. So there is an argument for using children's books to understand complex theoretical positions; in fact, when I teach literary theory courses, I suggest that my students read a chapter of *Through the Looking Glass and What Alice Found There* (Carroll 1871) every night before they go to bed, so that the theoretical ideas they are learning can percolate alongside a rich text that plays with language and representation. You can certainly learn about various kinds of

theory through applying them to children's texts. The question is, can you learn more about children's and YA literature through the use of **theory**?

Unlike Crews, I believe that smartly conceived, theoretically informed readings of children's and YA texts are crucial for understanding not only how a text works but also how a society thinks. After all, every theorist was once a child learning his or her book, and those early experiences matter enormously in giving concrete expression to both individual and cultural anxieties and desires. If we think back to the structural terms of embodiment, representation, and community introduced in Chapter 2, thinking theoretically involves having research-based, critically informed theories about these elements, as well as how they work together. This trio of embodiment, representation, and community is like the inner workings of a kaleidoscope: three mirrors that form an inward-facing triangle and bend, reflect and refract images of the bits and pieces of history, people, objects, and texts into an endlessly morphing, interconnected web of theoretical perspectives. The web has gotten far too complicated to discuss in the space I have, but there are certain concerns peculiar to children's literature that bear scrutiny because the tendency to map theories developed for peer texts directly onto youth literature collapses a space that might more productively and ethically be left open. What follows are thus two things: some, but by no means all, of the **theoretical paradigms** that are useful in thinking theoretically about children's and YA literature, and some special considerations when thinking theoretically about various aspects of children's and YA literature.

History, with attention to diversity

As we have cautioned in Chapter 1, the history of a **genre** is rife with gaps and biases regarding what counts as literature, as well as what is considered pertinent **context**. Clearly, if you are interested in a particular aspect or the entire sweep of the history of youth literature, you will have no lack of resources to help you with an overview or to zero in on a particular **genre** or period. However, it is important to read those resources with a healthy degree of skepticism, and to be sure to read the actual children's books of the period alongside the history in case your interpretive framework differs from that of the historiographer you are reading. Did you catch that? I said historiographer, as in, someone who *writes history*. What that means is that you are not really studying past events so much as you are studying "the changing interpretations of those events in the works of individual historians" (Furay and Salevouris 1988: 223). The case study at the end of this chapter demonstrates how you can engage in respectful conversation and at the same time challenge and extend a critic's biases and presuppositions. Such scrutiny is particularly important when researching the history of multicultural literatures. Not only have conscious and unconscious biases excluded discussion of the literatures of cultural and linguistic minorities from standard histories of children's and YA literature, but also, as Katharine Capshaw (2014a) persuasively argues in her book, *Civil Rights Childhood: Picturing Liberation in African American Photobooks,* what discussion there is of those literatures is often limited to majority-approved critical positions such as celebratory multiculturalism, individual heroism, or the power of childhood friendship to heal systemic racism. Capshaw demonstrates how such tamed interpretations deracinate and de-radicalize the impact of texts by people of color focused on ethnic experiences.

Capshaw (2014b: 3) calls for "a more materialist, interventionist critical practice, one that links the ideas we study to the lived experience of young people." As an -ism, this methodology is closely aligned with **New Historicism**. **New Historicism** seeks to place a literary text in its historical contexts, which include the **ideologies** of the time in which it was written, but also the material conditions under which the book was written and disseminated. **New Historicists** emphasize that a work of literature does not express some sort of universal truth about human nature (a claim commonly made about classic children's texts), but instead is one of many artifacts of a particular time and place that together produce the **ideologies** of a culture that affect the way individuals think, work, form relationships, and otherwise live their daily lives. While it may be called **New Historicism**, the practice carries over into the study of contemporary literature within the present moment as well. Whether you intend to include a historical argument in your own teaching or writing, or if you wish to consider the full contexts of a contemporary text, it is crucial that you acquaint yourself with the material practices and cultural **ideologies** in circulation at the time of a work's construction.

Paul Du Gay (1997) points to five principal processes that must be accounted for in order to situate a text within its historical context: representation, identity, production, consumption, and regulation. When investigating texts, we need to cast a critical eye over all of these processes, looking especially for absences and gaps, and being wary of ascribing a monolithic view of people or cultures that turns them into "zoological specimens" without the "potential for liberation or for change" (Prashad 2001: 11, in Capshaw 2014b: 11). Youth literature has long been dominated by white, middle-class publishers, authors and critics, and it is critical to interrogate what that mode of production and consumption means for representation and identity, especially of diverse populations. Moreover, we need to have a broad understanding of regulation, considering not only the regulation of diverse voices but also the self-limiting **ideological** biases within our own critical practice.

For instance, literary critics and youth services librarians, more so than teachers and parents, tend toward a preference for texts that wear their **didacticism** lightly. As a result, a text that is overly earnest is likely to be condemned as purposive or preachy. But that prejudice comes from the earliest days of children's publishing, when John Newbery sought to make money by delighting (white) child readers rather than educating them, or instructing them in social or religious mores. The preference for entertainment over instruction is even more pronounced these days when it is out of fashion to be caught trying to impose a singular system of morality in a pluralistic society (although this is certainly an arguable point when we consider that there is what we might call a new **didacticism** toward the values of pluralism. Discuss.). On the other hand, however, earnestness can in fact be an aesthetic element of certain literary traditions. I am thinking here in particular of African American children's literature, which, *in general*, having emerged under specific conditions of a need for racial pride and an unfortunate and often conflicting need to learn social "rules" that might save one's life, contains elements of admonishment as part of its distinctive style. In fact, Laretta Henderson (2005: 303) argues that African American children's literature should be critiqued "in accordance with the criteria set forth by some theoretical framework based in African American literary scholarship and community." Other critics of diverse literary traditions might advocate for similar attention to the particularities of their **aesthetics** as an antidote to imposing historically white values onto multicultural literature. Unconscious bias, masquerading as objectivity, can emerge when we assume that all literary traditions have the same values, goals, styles, and structures. Hence, it is important, when approaching a work of children's or YA literature, to understand that there is no objective or universal basis for assessing quality or appeal, but that our criticism can be better informed by understanding a text according to the terms of its own tradition.

Another of the live debates circulating among children's literature critics, reviewers, publishers, and general readers is whether or not people can write about cultures of which they are not members, or review such books with the required sensitivity (see, for instance, the comments section in Sutton 2015). This is analogous to what Henderson prescribes about critiquing the literature, namely, that critical discussion of multicultural literature should be undertaken only in light of the literary tradition of the people groups it represents. But the danger here lies in the opposite direction, and that is that viewpoints regarding the representation of people of a certain culture or identity can evolve into a new theoretical orthodoxy that is just as limiting or damaging to individual writers and readers as what it seeks to replace. In other words, in seeking to impose socially or community defined limits on who can represent characters and how they can be represented, we may risk silencing the very voices that we need most to hear because they offer diversity within diversity—that is, they may have stories to tell that run counter to our theoretical certainties about what living as a minority in a dominant culture actually feels like.

Textuality

The term **textuality** refers to ways in which language and, in our case, images are used in print and other forms of media. The assumption that undergirds studies of **textuality** and **narratology**, which we will discuss in the chapter on stories, is that language is not simply a transparent method for recording reality or conveying thoughts and intentions. As I have noted above, several lines of inquiry emerged in the 1960s regarding how language works and how it is related to the world. These inquiries changed the landscape of literary criticism. Instead of thinking of language as referring to the external world or some preexisting emotion in a speaker or writer, Jacques Derrida picked up Saussure's claim that a word only has meaning because of its difference from other words. In other words, language is a closed system that does not refer to anything outside itself, so the work of the literary critic is to show how words and other signs depend on other words and signs, both in contemporary usage and in a historical progression of meaning. By exposing these interrelations, this critical work of **deconstruction** can highlight the irreducibility of meaning, but also the power relations that circulate within language. Take, for instance, the conversation Alice has with Humpty Dumpty in *Through the Looking Glass* (Carroll 1871). After an exhausting linguistic battle where Humpty Dumpty inverts and subverts all traditional ways that words are related to their objects, he finally says, "When *I* use a word . . . it means just what I choose it to mean—neither more nor less."

"The question is," said Alice, "whether you *can* make words mean so many different things."

"The question is," said Humpty Dumpty, "which is to be master—that's all." (213)

Humpty Dumpty begins by asserting what Derrida would call a misguided "metaphysics of presence" in his claim that a word means only what he says it means; that is, its meaning depends on his presence and his use of that word in the present circumstance. This is, as Alice notes, impossible, because words have complex and contradictory histories, and they are related to other words; every word is in some way haunted by all of the words the author might have used but didn't, and all of the opposite words and concepts the author represses by putting forth this word. The will to power, then, can be read in Humpty Dumpty's insistence that he is somehow immune to this property of language. He imagines that he is language's master, rather than recognizing that he, as a personified, speaking egg, is actually *nothing more than a creation of language itself.* Language made him, and it will ultimately destroy him. (Voila, Humpty Dumpty, an omelet of **deconstruction**! I crack myself up! I'll stop now, but isn't this method of analysis kind of fun?)

Another line of inquiry took the form of a debate about ordinary versus literary language. The case began to be made that since ordinary language was so infused with devices formerly associated with poetic language, such as **metaphor**, **irony**, and distinctive **rhythms**, the distinction between poetic language and ordinary language was no longer necessary (Fish 1973; Pratt 1977). Newly emerging theories of how literary language affects the brain differently than other kinds of language are challenging the terms of that debate, but thus far most of the studies about how readers process literary language have been conducted with adult readers (Miall 2006; Burke 2012). The findings that relate to how literary language works to invite a reader into the world of a text, generate emotional effects, and manage closure, however, map onto children's and YA text with surprising ease (Coats 2016), suggesting two things: first, that most children's texts are not all that different, from a rhetorical standpoint, from adult texts, and thus bear up well under similar analyses of language use and story structure, and second, that children's and YA texts function well as apprentice texts for understanding the linguistic and visual rhetorics of a culture as well as its adult literature. Therefore, studies that compare how language is used in peer texts and children's texts, as well as theoretical and **empirical** studies that consider linguistic and **textual forms** in terms of **rhetorical theory**, **deconstruction**, **reader response**, **speech act theory**, and **multimodal discourse analysis,** all offer promising avenues of wonder to pursue.

In addition, multiple studies have been undertaken with children as they read and respond to picturebooks (e.g., Arizpe and Styles 2003; Arizpe, Colomer and Martínez-Roldán 2014; Sipe 2008), suggesting that children are capable of quite sophisticated apprehension of the tensions that exist between different modes of representation. However, as we will discover in the picturebook chapter, approaches to picturebooks that emerge out of art criticism do sometimes suffer from an **aetonormative** bias, whereas approaches that have a communicative basis offer a wider range of possible responses, given the particular modes of attention that children give to images.

Authors, readers, diversity and more **ideology**

The gap between adult authors and their child readers has long bothered the theoretical **discourse** surrounding children's and YA literature. Jacqueline Rose (1984) famously averred that since the child in children's literature was a cultural fetish, an innocent, asexual construct that didn't exist outside the pages of a book, children's literature itself was in fact an impossibility; its target audience are adults who need to imagine childhood as a space outside the messiness of human relations, so that its very existence is a contradiction in terms. Since she put forth this argument, many critics have disagreed with her in many ways, challenging her constructions of childhood and children's literature with ones of their own (see, for instance, Lesnik-Oberstein 1994; Nodelman 2008; Rudd 2013). Nodelman (2008) argues that every children's text is haunted by adult authorial control over what kinds of knowledge the text allows the child to access. Nikolajeva (2010) proposes the concept of **aetonormativity** as the theoretical modality uniquely suited to the study of children's and YA literature; no matter what happens throughout the course of the text, the norm of adult perceptions and behaviors is ultimately somehow reinforced such that childlike forms of being and thinking are rendered deviant, temporary, and insufficient. What these thinkers emphasize is the power imbalance between adults and children, an unfairly weighted seesaw that destabilizes both real and literary children. Marah Gubar (2009) and David Rudd (2013), on the other hand, argue for childhood agency; yes, they argue, children are constructed through language and are hence affected by, and even to a large extent created by, the texts they read, but so are we all, and adults and children co-construct the stories that shape our subjectivities.

None of these positions proceed primarily from interactions with real children as readers and viewers—they are the theoretical postulates of literary critics who build on, among other ideas, Louis Althusser's influential theory of Ideological State Apparatuses. Althusser (1971) argued that there are two methods by which societies exert power over individuals: through Repressive State Apparatuses, like the police and the military, and through Ideological State Apparatuses, such as the family, the church, the media, literature, and the other arts. The latter are more insidious and effective in controlling a populace, because they work through a subtle indoctrination of values that people internalize and come to see as reasonable and/or natural rather than openly repressive, rendering people willing to police and limit themselves rather than having to be physically controlled. Literature and media are seen as particularly strong conveyors of **ideological** messages, prompting literary critics to fret over the effects literature has on children.

But media studies professor Joseph Tobin (2000: 3) argues that we need to get beyond what he calls the "effect paradigm," that is, the idea that "movies and television [and I would add books here as well] are . . . dangerous forces that have the power to reach out and grab children," infecting them with pernicious and damaging ideas. Like Gubar and Rudd, he suggests that children have the ability and wherewithal to talk back to media messages; unlike most literary theorists, however, he set out to find out if his theories were in fact true by actually talking to children. He does, however, draw extensively from literary **theory** to interpret the "texts" of his data— that is, he treats the children's responses to movie clips as he would a literary text, deconstructing their utterances to interpret what conditions might have inspired them. In particular, he uses **performance theory**, recognizing that his child informants were in fact drawing from and critiquing language that they have heard from adults and other media sources in their responses to his questions. He also zeroed in on responses that surprised or puzzled him in order to create a rich interpretation of the children's understandings of violence, gender, race, colonialism, and middle-class values in the filmic images.

The mix of ethnically diverse children he worked with recognized and actively resisted messages about racism and colonialism, but were less resistant to the signs of patriarchal family and work structures. Given what he knew about the children's home and school lives, then, his findings led him to conclude that "instances of resistance to dominant ideological messages in the popular media are most usefully understood as reflections not of an individual's strength of character or level of cognitive development but of the individual's participation in a discourse community that includes compelling resistant voices" (146). This conclusion verifies not only Gubar's and Rudd's positions but also those of V. N. Voloshinov (1927/1976), who argues for the kind of **psychoanalytic criticism** that I have suggested in the recap of Daphne's concerns at the beginning of this chapter—that is, "a psychoanalysis not of individual psyches and intentions, but instead of the anxieties, concerns, and tensions of the large society as verbalized in the utterances of individuals" (Tobin, 2000: 13). When we consider a text or a child's response to it, we would do well to listen or read for those moments that grant us insight into the way texts and readers are picking up, reflecting, refracting, and resisting overt and covert **ideological** messages. We also need to be alert to texts that persuasively present counternarratives that actively resist dominant **ideologies** so that children and teens know, even if they question or even reject the counternarratives in those texts, that they have wiggle room to perform resistant readings in whatever direction they choose. After all, as people with situated power who care about developing and empowering children's independent critical skills, we have to be wary of asking them to replicate our values in their performative responses.

In any case, consideration of the relationship of children and adults as characters, implied narrators and audiences, and actual authors and readers in a complex **ecosystem** argues against the simplistic mapping of theories that explore other kinds of power imbalances, such as **feminist** or **Marxist** critiques that focus on the imbalances between two adults of different genders or economic circumstances without considering the special circumstances of children. **Feminist** critics of children's and YA literature such as Roberta Seelinger Trites (1997), Lissa Paul (1999), Christine Wilkie-Stibbs (2002), and Lisa Rowe Fraustino (2015) have crafted and inspired thoughtful and important arguments regarding the implications of children's continual exposure to literature that implicitly and explicitly champions patriarchal, bourgeois values, but such **ideological** criticism of children's and YA texts tends to operate from an **aetonormative** stance. Critics often weigh matters of fairness, status, and representation in terms that situate children and adult women as coequal in terms of systems of oppression, without considering that children of any gender actually need more protections and have less agency and subsequent responsibility than adults of any gender.

In addition, critics make their arguments using prefrontal cortex executive functions such as reflection, naming, and the rational inhibition of emotions. They are able to interpret representations with an emphasis on larger systems of political and social oppression and threat. Recent research in neuroscience strongly suggests that young brains process information differently, making them potentially more susceptible to interpellation by well-managed, **multimodal rhetorical** messaging and less able to take a detached, evaluative view. However, given the relative localness of their worldview, their perceptions of threat, fairness, and status may rest on foundations wholly different from adult accounts of political and systemic forms of hegemony and oppression; for instance, the individual friendship solution to the problem of racism and white privilege may be exactly what children can understand and actually do something about, even if it doesn't come close, from an adult perspective, to solving a large social problem. Hence, young people's perceptions of their own power and the ability to shift the terms of status and threat must be understood in local terms in order to engage them in meaningful conversations about the literature they read. This is not to say that young readers don't somehow "get it," that is, that they don't understand how a representation might be offensive or stereotypical or only a small step in solving a big problem. It does indicate, however, that adult sensitivities may differ from child and teen sensitivities. While we can say whatever we want in our scholarship, it would be worthwhile to listen to our children and teens as they sort through their responses to a text rather than impose a reading they aren't developmentally prepared to receive.

Posts

Although I have been reading and teaching literary theory for over twenty years, I still find myself somewhat stymied when it comes to giving quick, accessible definitions of words like **poststructuralism, postmodernism, postcolonialism**, and now, **postfeminism, postmemory,** and **posthumanism** (and yes, you will note by the font shift that they are all in the glossary, so I have obviously found a way to define them, but so much is left unsaid.). Part of the problem lies in the prefix post-, which seems like it should mean to come after something, and that the thing it comes after is somehow over. That gets complicated with some of these terms, especially when we think about children and YA; as I have noted in my cautions about stage theories, the clusters of ideas that emerge in each stage are never fully and finally in the past. But the biggest problem is with the ideas that inform **poststructuralism** itself: **poststructuralism** is based on the theories of language and **textuality** we have already discussed. If it's an inherent feature of the theory itself that meaning can never be secured because the nature of language is such that it always refers to and depends on something else, then the term **poststructuralism**, at least, can never be fully and finally defined. But in order to make this an idea that is useful to you in your readings of texts, let's settle on this: most of the theoretical work in this book is based on **structuralist** principles. **Structuralists** look for patterns and similarities across a range of individual examples. So when I talk about developmental concerns, story grammars, plot patterns, and visual forms, I am describing structural and systemic frameworks that provide some conditions under which children's and YA literature becomes intelligible. Familiarity with these principles will enable you to understand and interpret any number of texts according to those patterns.

What you will find, however, is that what makes a text really interesting is the way it adapts, challenges, and even explodes the structures of meaning that you have been expecting. And when a text violates an expectation, you become consciously aware of two important things: first that you were in fact expecting something to happen that didn't, so you have to ask where that expectation came from, and second that texts can, to some degree, make their own rules. The key insight of **poststructuralism**, then, is that structures and systems of intelligibility are not natural, universal, or inevitable, but instead are **socially constructed** and must be learned anew by every new member of a society. In its historical emergence in academic **discourse**, **structuralism** came before **poststructuralism**, but as an idea, the post- of **poststructuralism** seems kind of backward—maybe it's just my way of thinking, but if the key insight of **poststructuralism** is that structures must be learned, doesn't it follow that the structures learned come after that insight? Certainly, the literature produced for and shared with children and teens functions as an apprenticeship into the forms, values, beliefs, and practices of a particular time and place, but as Tobin argues, children and teens often find ways to talk back to and resist the **ideologies** of these texts. Put a two-year-old in front of a camera, for instance, and observe what he or she does; the child knows what is expected, but responses might range from making a comic face, adopting a supermodel, superhero, or otherwise exaggerated pose, hiding, or pasting on a demure smile. The very fact that they parrot and parody such **scripts** demonstrates not only their knowledge of conventions but also their knowledge that they *are* conventions, and as such they are available for imaginative recasting.

Imaginative recasting of conventional **scripts**, then, is at the heart of **postmodernism**. For a beautifully clear summary of the confusing terminology that harries discussions of **postmodernism**, I refer you to the introduction of Cherie Allan's text on **postmodern** picturebooks, *Playing with Picturebooks: Postmodernism and the Postmodernesque* (2012). As with **poststructuralism**, the post- in **postmodernism** has more to do with the historical emergence of the **theory** than with the concept itself. **Postmodern** literature disrupts conventions of realist fiction in specific ways, many of which are found in texts that predate the historical period— that is, after the Second World War—usually associated with the term. Whereas **modernism** was or is concerned with constructing texts that focus on linear, progressive, totalizing narratives that treat disruption and fragmentation as a besetting problem, an ache, if you will, as is pictorially represented by Edvard Munch's *The Scream* (1893), **postmodern** texts celebrate fragmentation, recursive structures, open endings, historical reimaginings, multiple perspectives, and **metafictive** techniques that highlight their own constructedness. Since the 1990s, the **postmodern** picturebook form has flourished and been the object of much study; fewer but still significant YA texts, such as those by Robert Cormier, Peter Hunt, and Francesca Lia Block, have engaged in the **postmodern** "incredulity toward [western] metanarratives" (Lyotard 1984: xxiv) of progress, capitalism, democracy, etc. More recently, **postmodern** experiments in YA literature have expanded in scope and complexity, with authors like Libba Bray, Andrew Smith, Sean Beaudoin, and Shaun Tan creating works that stylistically disrupt narrative, ethical, and ontological norms, borrow from, blend and parody traditional genres, and raise provocative questions of how texts are put together.

Postcolonialism has also made its mark in children's and YA literary criticism, as critics focus their attention on how Anglophone literature for the young has historically supported notions of empire and how even today it normalizes first-world experiences. Obviously, the United States, Canada, and Australia were all once colonies under British rule, but the exigency of **postcolonial** criticism for these successful, majority-white colonizers is not on establishing or understanding what might be considered quintessentially American, Canadian, or Australian in the aftermath of their independence from England, but on the recovery of literatures and cultural understandings of the indigenous and enslaved peoples they have displaced, and the ongoing ways in which actual colonization has been replaced by the global dissemination of Western ideologies through media flows. In fact, for many critics, the post- in **postcolonial** is little more than wishful thinking, since children and teens all over the world are more likely to gobble up Western texts through the internet than vice versa.

Postfeminism, **postmemory**, and **posthumanism** are emerging areas of inquiry for youth literature critics. In each case, the "posts" are used in contradictory ways by various critics, so it's important, if you are taking up one of these perspectives, to read widely and decide which definition you intend to work with. **Postfeminism**, for instance, conveys the sense that the political need for feminist critique has exhausted itself, and we are now in a space where girls are able to have all the choices and freedom their foremothers fought for. (Cough, cough—ahem, sorry, got something caught in my throat there—I think it was my inability to stomach comforting illusions. Moving on.) On the other hand, **postfeminism** has been used as a term that calls into question the idea of a homogeneous, one-size-fits-all conception of the female subject and her concerns. It leans toward and opens up a discourse of **intersectionality**, where a character like Judy Hopps in Disney's *Zootopia* must face discrimination and limited expectations not only because of her gender but also because of her size and species, and yet she can't morally or politically align with Assistant Mayor Bellwether simply because they are both female and fall into the category of prey. Similar questions are opened up in E. Lockhart's *The Disreputable History of Frankie Landau-Banks* (2008) and Renée Watson's *This Side of Home* (2015); there's a paper or two in there just waiting to be written.

Postmemory has its own set of controversies. The term was coined by Marianne Hirsch (1997) to designate how memories are formed and transmitted outside of personal experience. Much writing for children about the Holocaust, American slavery, cultural displacements, and various wars around the globe is produced by descendants of those traumatic experiences rather than by the victims themselves, indicating a need to understand and theorize how children carry forward and invest in the memory of events that have never happened to them. Critics of the concept of **postmemory** argue that there is a danger of losing the specificity of lived experience in such intergenerational writing, but there is also a special ethical concern when it comes to asking children to bear witness to traumas that are theirs only through family or cultural history and not by their immediate social context. **Postmemory** studies therefore have a strong familial connection to **trauma theory**, which attends to the experience and the artistic representation of both personal and cultural traumas. The prevalence of trauma narratives in children's literature has caught the attention of critics who explore the complicated ethical questions surrounding how one defines a trauma, why readers are drawn to trauma narratives, and how the representation of trauma in children's and YA texts might engender healing (Elliot 2015).

I will save a discussion of **posthumanism** for Chapter 11, but I want to give brief mention to other areas of inquiry that are finding purchase in children's and YA literature. Given the long connection between children's literature and the pastoral tradition, it seems fitting that attention should be given to **ecocriticism**, which is the study of the relationship between literature and the environment (see, for instance, Dobrin and Kidd 2004). Similarly, engagement with the emerging **discourse** of **animal studies** seems like a particularly natural fit for a literature that regularly personifies animals in the service of conveying **ideologies** (see Fraustino 2014; Ratelle 2014). As I have noted earlier, there is no way to canvas all of the positions and theories that scholars are using to enrich our understanding of children's and YA literature. I will thus refer you to the journals that I list in Chapter 12 and suggest that you find your kindred spirits among the wealth of literary critics represented there. However, there are a few more avenues that I would like to suggest as fruitful possibilities for exploration.

Other ways of thinking theoretically about children's and young adult literature

Reading texts in terms of a particular –ism or named paradigm is only one way of thinking theoretically about children's and YA literature. The theories we have discussed so far have only recently been applied to youth literature (and I should note that my idea of recent means the past thirty years or so—your idea of recent may be very different). Now that youth literature has a more robust presence in colleges and universities and is attracting new scholars, theoretical interest in the field is on the move. However, we have a lot of interesting work to do when it comes to situating youth literature within the discipline of English studies.

For instance, the curriculum in literature departments as well as much literary scholarship is organized around more or less aesthetically cohesive periods and genres, such as Renaissance drama, British Romanticism, Victorian literature, modernist poetry, and postmodern literature, but these courses and studies typically do not include texts written for young people. To be sure, children's literature critics do identify distinct artistic movements within the development of children's literature, such as the golden age we have discussed in Chapter 1. But only recently have critics begun to position children's and YA books alongside texts for adults to consider the ways they adopt and/or challenge and revise the characteristics that define literary movements such as Romanticism, modernism, and postmodernism. Deborah Cogan Thacker and Jean Webb take that as their project in *Introducing Children's Literature: From Romanticism to Postmodernism* (2002), alternating between overviews of the literary movements themselves and essays that perform close readings of individual texts to demonstrate how they participate in those movements. In 2007, Karin E. Westman guest-edited a special issue of *Children's Literature Association Quarterly* on children's literature and **modernism**, arguing that "the exclusion of children's literature [from discussions of literature as such as well as literary history] and its emphasis on genre" (283) have resulted in a paucity of critical discussion that seeks to interrogate the features of children's and YA texts as they correspond to the concerns of **modernist** literature in general. Also in this vein of tracing the concerns of a literary period on children's texts, the contributors to James Holt McGavran, Jr.'s *Romanticism and Children's Literature in Nineteenth-Century England* (1991) highlight how Romantic preoccupations with creativity and sensory cognition led to new emphases in children's books. Studies of this sort are multiplying, but more work needs to be done to show how children's and YA texts dialogue with the aesthetic preoccupations of their time, so it is worth considering such a focus for a potential research project.

In addition to placing children's and YA literature within literary history proper, remembering that literature for young people does not appear and grow in its own artistic and cultural bubble can help us understand the dynamic, reciprocal influence of adult and youth culture. Literary and cultural critics, to say nothing of parents and grandparents, often worry that children will be exposed to adult concerns too early through their literature, with the result that they will "grow up too fast" or "lose their innocence," as the clichés go. What is less widely acknowledged is that children's and YA cultural artifacts exercise a significant influence on adult culture as well. Reflecting critically on your own reading and viewing past should alert you to the fact that your **aesthetic** tastes as well as your expectations for what makes a good story are deeply embedded in the books and films you experienced as a child, even if your response to those texts is now a negative one. Authors and illustrators are not immune to this influence, but as generators of new texts, they have to operate in dynamic response to their own pasts and their present audiences, balancing familiarity with innovation as society changes. But the material they work with—language, story structure, visual styles, conscious and unconscious beliefs, etc.—and their attitudes toward that material are largely influenced by their experiences with children's texts. Juliet Dusinberre (1987) suggests, for instance, that the children's fantasies of the Victorian and Edwardian period seeded the ideas for the modernist experiments of writers like Virginia Woolf and D. H. Lawrence. More recently, Kimberley Reynolds (2007) has proposed that children's literature, as a space where authors and illustrators can experiment with new forms, is actually the driver of aesthetic change in contemporary culture. Analyzing children's and YA texts in light of their artistic challenges to the status quo requires an integrative cultural studies approach that reaches beyond traditional literary research.

Another way to approach researched writing about children's and YA literature, then, is to pursue interdisciplinary connections. Katharine Capshaw (2014b) suggests that the study of youth literature has greater potential than has yet been realized to intersect with other area studies. On the one hand, she argues, the specialized insights and critical paradigms of ethnic, gender, Holocaust, and working-class studies, to name just a few of the interdisciplinary programs within the contemporary academy, can help move children's and YA literary theory out of isolating frameworks that seek to seal childhood experience itself into an ahistorical, apolitical never-never land. Exposure to critical positions not focused on children's and YA literature can thus serve as a corrective to an overly limited perspective. But on the other hand, if Kimberley Reynolds's (2007) thesis that children's literature is a driving factor behind political and artistic change is valid, then the inclusion of youth literature in those areas has the potential to deepen our understanding of how society works.

However, two cautions: First, interdisciplinary study requires a commitment to understanding the research protocols of a particular area from the inside out. Such understanding might begin by taking a class in the area, or searching for online syllabi to get a sense of topics and essential readings. Browsing the journals dedicated to the area will also be helpful in giving you a sense of what scholars are researching and what theoretical texts they come back to again and again. Second, as I have noted above, **theories** developed for peer texts (i.e., written by adults for an adult audience) should not simply be mapped onto texts written for young people. While the kinship we have discussed in Chapter 2 exists between adults and children, there is also a space between that must be negotiated in an ethical and liberatory way. I think that the work of a children's literature scholar must balance a desire for seasoned adult perspectives on topics such as social inequities and histories of oppression with the need for the imaginative development of counterfactuals that have not been overwhelmed by social and historical realities. Not everyone in the field shares my perspective on this, so it's worth discussing.

Conclusion

In this chapter, we began by looking at some of the ways that we prefer to interpret texts. Out of those preferences can come informed critical readings. However, I suggested that we should always be attentive to the special features of children's and YA literature, especially the gap in perspective between adult authors and critics and child and teen readers, as we seek to perform theoretical readings of texts.

Extending your study

Reading:

Grenby, M. O. and Immel, Andrea. *The Cambridge Companion to Children's Literature* (Cambridge: Cambridge University Press, 2009).
   A collection of essays demonstrating a range of critical perspectives on various aspects of children's literature.
Hunt, Peter. *Understanding Children's Literature* (London and New York: Routledge, 1999).
   Though the essays are dated, they provide an overview of the types of theoretical perspectives that structured the field in the last decades of the twentieth century.
McGillis, Roderick. *The Nimble Reader: Literary Theory and Children's Literature* (New York: Twayne Publishers, 1996).
   McGillis offers an argument as well as an accessible model for reading theoretically.
Nikolajeva, Maria. *Power, Voice and Subjectivity in Literature for Young Readers* (London and New York: Routledge, 2010).
   Nikolajeva defines and explores the concept of aetonormativity. The introduction is particularly useful as it gives an overview of the ways in which theory has been used to analyze children's texts.
Op de Beeck, Nathalie. *Suspended Animation; Children's Picturebooks and the Fairy Tale of Modernity* (Minneapolis: University of Minnesota Press, 2010).
   Op de Beeck demonstrates the possibility of situating a particular form of children's literature within a broader aesthetic and cultural context.

Writing:

1 Read an article from a journal devoted to children's literature. Perform a rhetorical analysis of the article. What is the thesis of the article? Write a one sentence summary of each paragraph and then reflect on how it has been structured. How does it incorporate outside research? Could you detect a specific theoretical framework for the article?

2 Go back to an essay you have written on a children's or YA text and consider how it might be expanded through research. Alternately, consider how you might make a new or more sophisticated argument by thinking theoretically about your topic. Revise the essay.

3 Experiment with a theoretical paradigm. Consult a handbook of literary theory or perhaps one of the essays in one of Frederick Crews's books. Apply your theoretical perspective to a text you know well. Close your essay by reflecting on what you have learned about the theory or the text through your experiment.

4 Go to Thomas E. Wartenberg's website, http://www.teachingchildrenphilosophy. org/wiki/Main_Page. Click through to some of the book modules. Choose one, research the philosophical perspective using both the children's book and online resources. Write an essay explaining how the book illuminates the philosophical concept.

Discussing:

1 Discuss the opening scenario of the chapter with your classmates. Which perspective do you find most intriguing or frustrating? Where do you fit in that scenario? Is there a perspective missing?

2 Choose a book module from Wartenberg's site (above) and conduct a philosophical discussion with your classmates.

3 What has been your experience with doing literary analysis? What is your general attitude toward thinking theoretically about children's and YA texts? What do you see as its advantages or disadvantages?

Responding:

1 Take a paragraph or two from a theoretical article on a children's or YA text and feed it through an online word cloud generator. What terms are most prominent? What does this tell you, if anything, about the theoretical perspective of the article?

2 On a large sheet of paper, write down all the titles of your favorite books in a random arrangement. Using different colored markers for setting, main

character type, theme, and plot type (romance, dystopia, action or adventure, etc.), draw lines between the titles with similar features. So, for instance, if you use blue for setting, connect all of the books with similar settings with blue lines. What do you learn about your intertextual preferences?

Online exploration:

1 This site offers tips for writing about literature, including a brief introduction with questions to ask of a text from various theoretical perspectives. https://owl.english.purdue.edu/owl/section/4/17/

2 The Johns Hopkins Guide to Literary Theory and Criticism offers articles to help you expand your knowledge of theory. http://litguide.press.jhu.edu/index.html

3 Here is a list of theoretical readings specifically chosen for a course on children's literature and literary theory: http://www.circl.co.uk/reading/theory.htm

Case Study: How to Incorporate Research that Challenges a Common Ideological Bias

Most contemporary historians will begin their studies by being forthright about their parameters. They define what they mean by children's literature, and justify their focus. This is a good practice, but as critical readers and researchers, we need to be aware of unconscious biases and gaps. Histories build on one another, so that the summaries, errors, and oversights of prior sources get repeated and magnified over time, not unlike the children's game of "gossip" or "telephone," where the message related at the end of the process can be quite distorted from where it began. This is particularly true when we read and teach about texts without actually reading the original material, or when we only read excerpts. As Marilynne Robinson (1998: 99) astutely points out with regard to the *New England Primer*, for instance, a work that is often cited and vilified for its overtly Puritan messaging, we assume we know everything we need to know about it, so we accept that it can be "faithfully summarized in cliché and canard." The provocative snippet, "In Adam's Fall, we sinned all," is often the only bit cited in historical studies, and it is used to indicate, in something like a code, the presumed abuse the caricatured "Christian right" continues to visit upon their young due to their rigid intolerance and conservatism. Further reading into the actual text, however, reveals

(Continued)

that most of the principles that are now considered politically progressive, such as caring for the poor, rejecting greed, stewarding the earth, being kind to immigrants, and championing the rights of all people, are seeded throughout the Puritan poetry through which American children were taught to read for over a hundred years.

Similarly, Robinson calls us to revisit what we think we know about the McGuffey Readers (1836–1960), a series of graded primers that purportedly indoctrinated young readers into the material interests of the rising white middle class in America. A common complaint, she argues, is that the Readers were blithely inattentive to the social reforms of their time, including abolition and the rise of the labor movement. To the contrary, she points out that, given the known radical politics of the early contributors, it is more likely that the lack of explicit engagement with social issues such as slavery was an effective tactic to encourage the popularity of the Readers in areas where resistance to social change was strongest: "For [McGuffey and his circle], education was the method as well as the substance of reform, yet education in the Middle West, as well as in the South, would have to take account of intense hostility toward the antislavery movement" (Robinson 1998: 116). The project of the McGuffey Readers was to promote widespread literacy and modest prosperity earned through individual effort and character, but these goals, even today, run counter to economic systems based on the aristocratic and feudalistic ideologies that inspire slavery and other abusive labor practices. Therefore, Robinson implies, a directly critical approach would have resulted in limited uptake of the Readers in the places where they were most needed, specifically the American South with its feudal economy, and the Middle West, where the economic system had yet to be established when the Readers were first published. "The McGuffey Readers acknowledge neither slavery nor the factory system outright, but they teach an ethic so consistently opposed to both of them that they are arguably the subject of the books" (118). Whether or not you accept Robinson's perspective, her call to read original texts in their entirety as well as to investigate the social and ideological conditions of their production and distribution can help you uncover interpretive bias, correct errors, and even propose new insights regarding historical claims about children's and YA literature.

Author talkbacks:

For this chapter, two prominent children's literature critics, Perry Nodelman and Peter Hunt, share their very different experiences in turning from their primary identities as critics toward writing the fiction they critique.

Perry Nodelman is Professor Emeritus of English at the University of Winnipeg. Since 1975, he has studied, taught, and written extensively about children's and YA literature, publishing over one hundred articles. He has also written three groundbreaking books (and counting) that continue to shape the field: *Words About Pictures: The Narrative Art of Children's Picture Books*; *The Pleasures of Children's Literature*; and *The Hidden Adult: Defining Children's Literature*. His nonfiction is known worldwide. As an author of fiction, he has written four novels, and co-authored, with Carol Matas, two fantasy series for YAs.

The Critic as Novelist, and the Novelist as Critic

Perry Nodelman

I began to write children's fiction after I was a full professor of English and a published critic of children's literature—and almost by accident. In the late 1980s, after an exhausting few years in which I taught full time, I wrote an academic book (*Words About Pictures: The Narrative Art of Children's Picture Books,* The University of Georgia Press, 1988) as well as a number of articles, acted as Editor of the *Children's Literature Association Quarterly* and then as President of the Association, and tried to find a few hours each day to spend with my wife and children. I was feeling exhausted. It was time for a sabbatical—but the last thing I wanted to do was begin a new research project. Then I remembered the few pages of a children's novel I had begun on a whim and then just as quickly abandoned many years earlier. Why not apply for a sabbatical to write that novel? My colleagues in the English department might be just blind enough to my lack of fictional writing skills to agree to it. I could try it, and of course it wouldn't work out, because I really wasn't a fiction writer, right? And then I could spend the rest of my year off any way I wanted. Sleeping a lot, maybe. The department committees could hardly blame me for turning out to be unable to write fiction. So I applied for the sabbatical, and much to my surprise I was granted it, and then even more to my surprise, I found the task of novel-writing tremendously pleasurable. Not only did I finish the book, I even actually found a publisher for it.

Did my ability to write a publishable children's novel emerge from my knowledge of children's literature as a scholar and critic? I know that in a way it did. My first novel, *The Same Place But Different*, involved figures described in Katharine Briggs's *Encyclopaedia of Fairies* that I learned about through my scholarly work. Reading about scary bogies and boggarts, I'd found myself wondering how somebody nowadays would react if creatures like these appeared in a neighbourhood like mine—and the somebody, a smart-ass boy with a lack of respect for authority, might well have emerged from my reading of YA novels. Most of all, I have to acknowledge that knowledge of my work as a critic, and an endearing hope that my reputation might lead to sales, was what led editors at both Groundwood in Canada and Simon and Schuster in the United States to first look at my manuscript.

Beyond that, though, I'd rather not think all that much about how my scholarship affects my fiction. Much as I love a lot of children's literature, my critical stance towards it tends to be pretty suspicious, a matter often of teasing out not necessarily healthy ideological implications that writers themselves might not be all that conscious of. Logic suggests that it would be difficult if not impossible for the critical me to become aware of what the novelist me assumes unconsciously. Even if I could do it, I don't want to. I would rather not discover too much about what kind of gullible fool I am or what ugly untruths I have blindly been taking for granted or how much I have been perverting the minds of my young readers. I was surprised about how relatively painless I found most of what Richard Flynn had to say about the intersection of my fiction and my criticism in his article "Ambivalent, Double, Divided: Reading and Rereading Perry Nodelman" (*Jeunesse: Young People, Texts, Cultures* 3.1 [2011]: 137–51); but I suspect there is more to be said about these matters than Flynn says that I might enjoy knowing less.

On the other hand, I have a clear sense of how my fiction writing has affected my criticism. In his article, Flynn says, "I am convinced that becoming a novelist has made Nodelman's sharp critical eye that much sharper" (149). I like to think that that's true. What I have learned as a writer has certainly had a profound effect on my work as a scholar.

For me, the most obvious effect emerges from my new experience as a writer of how publishing for young readers works, and especially, my growing awareness of how little what gets published has to do with what writers might ideally want to write or what readers might be most stimulated by reading—how little it represents the ideas about creativity or individual expression or delighting young readers that govern much of our discourse about producing fiction. I learned how very much writing is a team sport, the team including not only agents and editors, but also, book designers and marketing people and especially, those in charge of a publishers' bottom line. I learned more than I had expected to find out about a wide range of factors that constrain and shape what publishers are willing to offer: ideas about what genres (and what sections of bookstores) books might fit into; beliefs about reading levels based on misunderstood theories of childhood development; convictions about what kinds of words and what aspects of experience children of various ages should and, more importantly, should not have access to; views about what boys or girls like to read or ought to read; the topics and periods of history that school curriculums tend to focus on and need historical fiction about; authors' previous sales records. I had always rather vaguely understood that the market for children's books more immediately involves adult purchasers like parents, teachers, librarians, and booksellers than it does children. Through interactions with astute literary agents and publishers, I came to develop an acute understanding of how what most children's book buyers not in the book business—parents and teachers and librarians— thoughtlessly take for granted about who children generally are or what children of certain genders or ages generally like or should learn about have far more influence on the publishing of books than does any concern with what might actually appeal to child readers.

Perhaps most important, I came to understand how much publishing is a business, how much market forces and market values predominate, not just in the selection and distribution of books and decisions about matters such as what authors to support with advertising campaigns and which ones to drop, but also in terms of what values the books themselves can be seen to support or recommend. Mostly controlled by profit-hungry multinational corporations, mainstream publishers of children's books are clearly not in the business of encouraging children to develop the sort of anti-corporate values that might one day have a negative impact on the bottom line.

Or in other words: my experience as a novelist has made me an even more suspicious critic than I once was. I have learned to look for evidence in the texts I study of how publishing and market forces might have helped to shape them, and to be especially wary of claims texts or their admirers make for the texts being rebellious or anti-establishment. I have also learned to be suspicious of critical engagements with texts for young readers by other scholars that don't consider such possibilities—that seem innocently accepting of the innocence of writing for children.

My fiction career has gradually slowed down in recent years, mostly because my publishers lost faith in my ability to engender a profit for them. While agents and editors were enthusiastic about my novels, they never did sell all that well. Maybe they were never that good. Maybe, as I prefer to believe, they were just a tad too unconventional to suit the preconceptions of most adult purchasers. And as what seems most likely to be profitable has become even more constrained in tough economic times and a sadly diminishing marketplace, I have found myself unwilling to follow what are, in essence, unwritten rules.

For instance, I recently accepted an invitation to produce a draft of a book to be considered for publication in a series directed specifically at young male readers. But as I wrote about the boy at the centre of my story, he insisted on becoming more thoughtful, more sensitive about the subtle confusions of moral issues, more unlikely to act without thinking, more like me than like the typically boyish boys that most adult purchasers believe young males want to read about. I finally realized I had made him too human, as I understand human beings, to fit into the series and conventional assumptions about what appeals to boys.

Nevertheless, my knowledge of the forces that have made it ever more difficult for me to be a successful children's fiction writer has made me, I believe, a much wiser and much more useful critic of children's literature.

Peter Hunt

In the 1980s, Peter Hunt published four novels for children: *The Maps of Time* (1983), *A Step off the Path* (1985) (translated into Danish as *På Afveje* [1986]), *Backtrack* (1986; paperback 1992) which Neil Philip in the London *Times* called "the first postmodernist children's book," and *Going Up* (1989, paperback 1991,1993) and two books for younger children *Fay Cow and the Missing Milk*, and *Sue and the Honey Machine* (1989, paperback 1992). In the same period he produced 37 academic papers and reviews and one scholarly edition of a children's classic.

Since 1990, he has published 25 academic books and critical editions, over 160 papers and book chapters, 120 reviews, and 130 encyclopedia items in 18 volumes. And no fiction.

Peter Hunt reflects on this.

I may be doing critical theorists and literary critics of children's literature an injustice, but I suspect that many of them know that they have a novel inside them, and not just any old novel, but the novel that redefines the nature of the novel and the reading process. It is not simply jealousy despite the fact that even today at children's book conferences the authors of children's fiction address huge audiences in the main auditorium, while theorists address small audiences in the basement. Even for theorists, the novel (if not the novel and the child) is ultimately *the thing*—but what happens if you are a novelist and a theorist? Are the two habits of mind fruitfully compatible?

Yes, if you're Umberto Eco or Aidan Chambers; if you're Peter Hunt, applying theory to fiction apparently means that nobody wants to publish it. Of course, the explanation for this might *not* be that publishers are all craven Barabbases, afraid to experiment or to allow children anything but the conventional: it just might be that Peter Hunt has been writing lousy novels.

My own interest in theory back in the 1980s was principally about how texts work—style, structure—and how they might be interpreted/misinterpreted/reconstructed by a non-peer audience. I was also deeply concerned with the book as book, rather than, as now, text in any form. My novel-writing didn't stem directly from theory—I've been a fiction writer from the egg—but I found that I was more interested in how the story was told—how stories exist—rather than the story itself (my favourite undergraduate reading was—honestly—*Tristram Shandy*)—and I assumed that my audience would be as fascinated as I was, and as willing to play with the idea of text and how it could be manipulated by writer and reader.

In both respects I was at considerable variance with publishing wisdom—such weird books were not what children wanted—or rather, not what they were allowed to want. But I was lucky—I was published by one of the most influential editors of the period, Julia MacRae, one of the last of a breed, an editor who could give her protégés several chances to make good (her imprint finally became part of Random House).

My first novel, *The Maps of Time*—which Julia admitted that she didn't fully understand—has four Chapter 9s—parallel versions of "reality," which today might be more suited to computer presentation. *A Step off the Path* had a third person external narrator telling a story, and a character *in* the story telling (more or less) the same story. One of the reviewers objected (clearly not having come across Carolyn Keene or Enid Blyton) to the number of child characters (seven), so my third novel, *Backtrack* had only two characters who appeared in the "present" narrative—a technical achievement of which I am still proud—although, of course, nobody noticed. *Backtrack*, like Aidan Chambers's near-contemporary and much (more) celebrated *Breaktime* (1978) used forms of multimedia—maps, handwritten letters and diaries, newspaper clippings, extracts from other books—almost all of them spurious.

The only other place where you could find such mildly radical stuff at the time was in the picturebook—then, as now, commonly cited as the hot- (or warm-) bed of innovation (although when in 1990, I got to read and review all the picturebooks published in the UK that year—around 300—I found no more than eight that pushed at the envelope of convention, and I very much suspect that I might get the same result today.)

Those were heady days—I even published a pamphlet on my dual role [*Woodfield Lecture XIII,* Woodfield and Stanley, Huddersfield (1990) pp. 17 *reprinted as* "Critic into Author, The Woodfield Lecture," *International Review of Children's Literature and Librarianship*, 5 (1) (1990): 39–56.] and I had entries as both author and critic in the third edition of St. James Press *20*th *Century Children's Authors* [ed. Tracy Chevalier, Chicago and London, 1989]. Prophetically, Keith Barker wrote in my entry: "His writings have not often achieved easy popularity with either critics or children. There are some who maintain that for this reason he would be wise not to pursue any experimentation." (284)

Ah, hubris: and he was right. The more I knew about possible structures of novels, and the more I came to respect and suspect the abilities of developing-readers, the more I wanted to test the limits of both. Not with just a pony book in which all the characters hated ponies (hardly fiction), or a suite of eight books of different genres and for different age-groups, all covering the same events (still a great idea)—but with a book with 21 first chapters, in which the characters argue about how to tell the stories, or a novel that includes 142 pastiches of children's books. In this last case, I almost (almost) ended up sympathising with the publishers—where would they find an audience who has read enough books to see the jokes?

It might be said (and undoubtedly it *is* said by many publishers) that there is no reason why books should be experimental, or disruptive of conventions—or postmodern—after all, relatively few readers *really* read Eco or Joyce, or Carroll or William Mayne—even if reading theoretical critics and their favourite objects of examination might make us suppose differently. But there is every reason why *children's books* should be experimental: adult readers read the conventional at least partly because as children they were trained to respond to the conventional. As has often been observed of education—especially with regard to poetry—acquiring literacy (and *literary* literacy is not exempt) is a process of repression.

Adult—and especially postmodernist—theorists have repeatedly demonstrated the spectacular ways in which *all* texts *could* be read. However, tragically (from a liberal-humanist point of view), the universal utilitarian movement in education, and the almost total mind-control exercised by the commodification of childhood and the instruments of commodification (in which publishers are implicated) mean that the idea that some children—or *any* kind of child—*could* read those texts in those spectacular ways is diminished.

After all, the fundamental distinctive feature of children's texts is *control*: consequently, the theory of children's literature, especially any theory overtly (and more usually covertly) bound up with a faith in the written word bound into books, must extend to the true begetters of texts—the accountants behind the multinational venture capitalists who ultimately control mainstream publishing. (Check out the literary-sociological work of Dan Hade, and Jack Zipes, among others.)

Sad to say, despite all the undoubted creativity flying around, children's books were, in the 1980s, and are, in the 21st century, a missed opportunity. In the 1980s, challenges to the conventions of the book may have been welcomed by individual editors, but were not regarded as commercially viable. Even now most literature (and not especially children's) validates itself by reference to ideas of established patterns of story, or of community ("folk") narrative, of closure, of semiotic sets and intra-textual conventions that are ages old. And this in the face of everyday ways of telling stories (multimedia, games, astonishing filmic techniques, social-media thought patterns) that are radical beyond the imaginations of a generation ago. Somewhere there is a video-text for children that does not have its ancestors in eighteenth century convention, or its justification in linear grunts around campfires (with the "folk"). Even more challengingly, somewhere, yet unborn, is a children's-literary-theory that matches the speed-cutting of a music video, engages with the ever-changing volatility of all types of text, and does not seek to freeze in order to observe.

In short, what a few of us were trying to do in the 1980s within the confines of printed text *should* be being done now in the infinitely variable texts of the multimedia, electronic age. What we were groping for in theory then should be taking on the *now*. Then, a small group of writers and illustrators (to be invidiously selective)—Ellen Raskin in the USA, Gary Crew in Australia, Diana Wynne Jones in the UK (and some "sci fi" writers)—were trying to *break* the book. There were, and are, plenty trying to *perfect* the book—and many have been brilliant at it but we mustn't confuse the two. The breakers did what they could, and I'm pleased to have been around at the time.

I grow old and I have no ideas what the storying of the digital, interactive, screen-age, or the theory/criticism that might address it could possibly look like; similarly it may well be—in fact it *must* be—I am stupendously ignorant of the talent that is out there, playing with the new media. What I am sure of is that the role of the theorist is to see possibilities in text and in texts—and that the role of the publisher is to see the practicalities. Whether those two poles of children's texts can ever be resolved productively . . . I live in hope.

Literature references

Carroll, L. (1871), *Alice Through the Looking Glass, and What She Found There*, London: Macmillan.

Lockhart, E. (2009), *The Disreputable History of Frankie Landau-Banks*, New York: Disney-Hyperion.

Silverstein, S. (1964), *The Giving Tree*, New York: Random House.

Watson, R. (2015), *This Side of Home*, New York: Bloomsbury USA.

Zootopia/Zootropolis (2016), Directed by Byron Howard and Rich Moore, Burbank, CA: Walt Disney Studios.

4

Poetry and Poetic Language

Suggested texts to read alongside this chapter

Poetry for young children:

Janeczko, Paul, *Firefly July: A Year of Very Short Poems*.

Lawson, JonArno, *A Voweller's Bestiary*.

Rosen, Michael, *A Great Big Cuddle*.

Thomas, Joyce Carol, *Brown Honey in Broomwheat Tea*.

Worth, Valerie, *Peacock and Other Poems*.

Poetry for older readers:

Adoff, Arnold, *Slow Dance Heartbreak Blues*.

Duffy, Chris, ed., *Above the Dreamless Dead: World War I in Poetry and Comics*.

Heppermann, Christine, *Poisoned Apples: Poems for You, My Pretty*.

Zephaniah, Benjamin, *Talking Turkeys*.

Verse narratives:

Frost, Helen, *Diamond Willow*.

Koertge, Ron, *Shakespeare Bats Cleanup, Coaltown Jesus*.

Nelson, Marilyn, *How I Discovered Poetry*.

The aim of the previous chapters has been to set the stage for a more in-depth study of children's and YA texts. As we consider the historical progression of the material and ideological contexts in which the texts are produced (Chapter 1) and the relative changes in the way young brains process information over time (Chapter 2), we can pursue multiple critical directions through which to understand the ways that culture and individual development intersect in the production, consumption, and reception of children's and YA texts, both by their intended audience and by us as adult critics (Chapter 3).

In the next three chapters, then, we will focus on the essential building blocks of children's and YA literature: words, pictures, and stories. Our focus in these chapters will be on the forms, rather than genres or subjects, that children's and YA literature takes. Both nonfiction and fiction are presented to young readers in the forms of poetry, picturebooks, and illustrated texts, and story, so it's important to take some time to figure out how these forms work.

What poetic language is, what it does, and why it matters

I want to start this chapter with a theoretical discussion of why and how poetic language matters to children and young adults (and ultimately, everyone at every age). Poetic language is a way of using language that appeals to the senses as well as the intellect, and it appears in both prose and poetry. However, most people distinguish poetry from prose by virtue of the qualities of the language; the word prose derives from a Latin word meaning direct or straightforward, so that's somewhat helpful, whereas the origins of the word poetry refer more generally to an author or a maker. Poetry has appeared in so many forms that it is difficult to propose any sort of definition at all; in fact, I would argue that poetry is something that we sort into categories or types rather than define outright. According to poet and poetry theorist Lewis Turco (2012), there are three major types of poetry: **lyric**, which are personal expressions characterized by their musicality; **narrative**, which are story poems; and **dramatic**, which are written in dialogue between one or more speakers. Some people, he says, want to insist that **lyric poetry** is the only "pure poetry" (3). Indeed, most of the forms that you will have no doubt encountered throughout your school years, such as the sonnet, the ode, the elegy, the haiku, the cinquain, the sestina, the blues, and the verses on greeting cards, fall into the category of **lyric poetry**.

But limiting poetry to the **lyric form** puts a straitjacket on what we can consider when we talk about poetry. Instead, Turco argues that poetry is a **genre** whose focus is on "the *art of language*" (2012: 4); I disagree that it's a **genre**, for reasons I explain in Chapter 9 and three quarters, but the focus on language as an art seems right. **Verse** is a way of writing poetry that is characterized by a specific **meter**, or count of stressed and unstressed syllables in a line. If you are counting syllables, you are writing **verse**; if you are not, you are writing prose. Either way, according to Turco, you might be writing poetry if your main intention is to attend to the quality of your language at four distinct levels: typography, sound, **tropes** (such as metaphors and other figures of speech), and theme (5); we will pay attention to all of these in our discussion of poetic language and children's poetry, but we will also consider why the art of language matters to children and young adults.

As we have noted in Chapter 2, children's first encounters with language, no matter what their cultural origin, are poetic in nature—that is, both **infant-directed** speech and young children's first utterances are characterized by many of the features in the accomplished poet's toolkit, such as rhythm, repetition, balance, **consonance, assonance, alliteration, onomatopoeia, condensation, metonymy, synecdoche**, and **personification**. This is because early oral language generated by children as well as traditional and new poems for very young children form a bridge between a child's sensory, embodied experience and the socially understood linguistic expressions of his or her culture (see Coats 2013). To perform this task, the sounds and pulses of the language have to replicate in some fashion the movements of the body, which are characterized by balance and symmetry (as in, for instance, the bilateral movement of the feet and arms while walking), and the periodicity of tension and release (as in such functions as breathing, eliminating, and working up to an explosive wail). This early language is literally nonsense; that is, it has no semantic content. What it means is what it does.

To understand how this works even in adulthood, think of a single line from a nursery rhyme, such as "hickory, dickory, dock." Stand up and walk across the room while reciting the line, stopping your recitation sharply at the word dock. What happened? Did your walking rhythm "hiccup"? Or did you feel a need to extend the rhyme in order to keep walking? Chances are that your footfall conformed to the **meter** of the line—that is, your foot hit the ground in time with each accented syllable, so that when it came to the final accented syllable, you had to either stop walking or keep chanting. Stopping abruptly is difficult because walking is a type of organic cycle; if a foot is raised, it must be put down, and when one foot is down the other goes up unless you have made a conscious effort or plan to stop. Try the experiment with other nursery rhymes and notice how your walking rhythm synchronizes with the verse, and how difficult it is to separate the two or perform them out of phase with each other. You might also notice how your head moves while you recite the poem. This simple demonstration of how the brain synchronizes movement in and through patterned speech gives you some idea of how and why early poetic language helps children organize embodied experience, and how the body's rhythms and processes are replicated in poetic language.

As they become more adept language users, children repeat and innovate on the sounds they hear to set their worlds in order, converting emotions that distress or delight them into repetitive and patterned vocalizations. Psycholinguist Ruth Hirsch Weir (1962) noticed that her infant son babbled when he was alone in his crib before naptime and before going to sleep for the night. She recorded his speech, and began noticing phonetic patterns and meaningful associations with his daily experience in what first seemed like merely musical-sounding gibberish. Hugh Crago (2014) elaborates on Weir's and other similar findings, suggesting that "Here, at the earliest beginnings of language, we can observe the start of the impulse to take a painful or perplexing subject and 'work it' into something ordered and meaningful" (17). Compare this language use of very young children to Robert Frost's claim that poetry enacts "a momentary stay against confusion" (2002/1939: 440), or William Wordsworth's assertion that "all good poetry is the spontaneous overflow of power feelings" (1802). Even if their utterances don't have the sophistication we have come to expect from published poetry, they are apparently using poetic forms for the same purposes as these recognized master poets.

In addition to the musical ordering of nonsense phonemes into a comforting pattern, children are using their store of words to make their experiences meaningful and solve problems. Crago cites the example of two-and-a-half-year-old Emily, who works out her distress over a broken TV in her pre-bedtime monologue (2014: 18). She uses repetition, balance, and comparisons between things that are broken and things that get fixed. She associates the TV with a car, a tank, and a boy, showing, perhaps, an emerging ability to create **metaphors**. While Russian poet and linguist Kornei Chukovsky (1965: 13) points to children's difficulties in understanding idioms and figurative language, Ellen Winner (1988) finds that by the time they are three or four, children are capable of both understanding and generating simple **metaphors** that suggest similarity between objects based on the same sense modality, such as sight, sound, movement, or touch, as long as they have sufficient knowledge of the two things being compared. For instance, Valerie Worth's implicit comparison of an umbrella to a bat—"Slack wings/ Folded, it/ Hangs by a/ Claw in/ The closet" (2002: 5)—draws on the modality of sight, and would be understood by most three-year-olds who have experience with both umbrellas and upside-down-hanging bats. Moreover, the comparison would bring them pleasure because of its novelty in connecting two ordinary things to form a richer idea in their developing imaginations.

Are children natural poets?

Noting all of these innovative tendencies in children's use of words, some linguists and literary critics argue that children are not just using poetic language, but that they are actual poets. Chukovsky, for instance, argues that "in the beginning of our childhood, we are all 'versifiers,'" and that poetry composition is the next logical step: "Making up verses begins when the aimless pronouncing of rhymed and other sounds stops and meaning is introduced" (1965: 64). As a first language, however, the poetic qualities of child language seem to be ephemeral, either voluntarily put aside or drummed out of us by adult expectations. In implicit laments, Margaret Meek says that "children are natural poets, singing before they can speak, metaphor-making before they prose their way to school," and Neil Philip agrees: "From the moment they can talk till the moment we finally convince them that what they have to say isn't important, children are producing poetry all the time" (qtd. in Chambers 2009: 43, 86). Meek and Philip nevertheless set forth this idea of children's natural poetic facility as a challenge to those who would write poetry for children: Adult-written children's poetry must be at least as good—that is, as energetically fresh, as sonically pleasing, and as conceptually daring—as what children produce by themselves.

Many people disagree with this way of thinking about child language and poetry, however. They argue that true poetry is a carefully cultivated way of using language to express deep emotions and complex concepts, and as such is inaccessible to children as either producers or consumers. Influential children's poets from Anna Laetitia Barbauld in the eighteenth century to Myra Cohn Livingston in the twentieth have argued that children's aesthetic sensitivities and intellects are not yet well enough formed or informed to appreciate good poetry. To allow them access to inferior drivel, or to give the impression that their compositions merit the name of poetry, then, does a great disservice to their developing sense of the beauty and grandeur that ought to inhere in poetry. After first complimenting Isaac Watts's accessible and beloved *Divine Songs Attempted in Easy Language for the Use of Children* (1715), Barbauld goes on to complain,

> But it might well be doubted, whether poetry *ought* to be lowered to the capacities of children, or whether they should not rather be kept from reading verse, till they are able to relish good verse; for the very essence of poetry is an elevation in thought and style above the common standard; and if it wants this character, it wants all that renders it valuable. (1781: v)

In speaking of children themselves as capable of producing poetry, Livingston writes:

> No one questions that the writing of children . . . may be an expression of child art, but the idea that it is *literature*, in the sense that it is a broadening, enriching body of work that has survived because it humanizes mankind and because it extends self and social consciousness for others, is debatable. (1984: 182)

For these critics, poetry worth the name is molded and judged by culturally nuanced **aesthetic** values that, though they seem to be ever-evolving, maintain a certain commitment to difficulty; that is, a good poem is something that challenges and stretches its readers, either emotionally or intellectually. At best, children can memorize, understand, and mimic singsong-type rhyming **verse**, but this is not what these people consider poetry.

Adherents of both sides of this argument make their point based on their own terms and definitions of what poetry is and what it's for, so it's worthwhile to clarify for yourself what you believe children's poetry and poetic language is or does, even if

I resist defining it for you. If you believe that poetry is a higher form of expression that elevates and ennobles human emotion and encases it in multivalent, sometimes difficult, **metaphors** that we can understand only through extended and informed contemplation, then poetry composed by children, and a good deal of that composed by adults for children, does not merit the name. But everyone produces and responds to poetic language, and this merits an exploration.

In Chapter 2, we have introduced the idea that children's first introduction to language is through a form of "communicative musicality" (Trevarthen and Malloch 2009, *passim*). Trevarthen and Malloch developed this concept to account for the ways in which we construct our sense of self and our sense of community through what they call synrhythmia—the "mutual psychosocial regulation of intentions and experience between mother and infant" (Mazokopaki and Kugiumutzakis 2009: 203). In their view, poetic language always already "extends self and social consciousness for others," a trait Livingston would limit to *literature* in snooty italics. For these researchers, by contrast, this extension of the self toward the other occurs through our earliest forms of poetic language; in fact, that's its job. Moreover, this early use of poetic vocalizations is important not only for individuals but also for the development of culture as a whole. Drawing on the work of multiple researchers as well as their own work, Katerina Mazokopaki and Giannis Kugiumutzakis conclude that "imitation, rhythms, rhythmic imitations, melorhythmic structures and lyrical music . . . are, all together, basic talents for growth of music, language, 'mind reading', empathy, sympathy and intersubjectivity in a child, as they certainly were in the early evolutionary stages of the process of hominization" (2009: 203). According to this view, then, the poetic language and poetry we share with children, and the poetry and poetic language they produce in response, are what binds us to others both psychologically and socially; without such shared musical language, we risk losing a sense of empathy and social cohesion right from the start.

Finding the chocolate in poetic language

If these theories are correct, and children use poetic language to shape their experiences and share their worlds, the question remains as to how this works: how does language in general, and poetic language in particular, help us express, communicate, and gain some control over the experiences of the feeling body, and how might that process change over time from childhood through young adult experience? After all, feelings and words are never a direct match. To better understand how this works, I propose that you perform the following experiment:

Procure several high-quality dark chocolate bars, a few friends, and some paper, pens, and glasses of room temperature water for everyone.

Divide the chocolate among your friends, making sure they each have two pieces of chocolate. Have everyone drink some water to clear the palate. Now, guide everyone through an exploration of the chocolate with all five senses, jotting down notes about the experience as you all do so. Look closely at the piece of chocolate, and notice its colors and sheen; rub your fingers across its surface and notice its texture; bring the chocolate to your nose, closing your eyes and cupping your other hand to enclose the chocolate with your nose, and inhale deeply; hold the chocolate close to your ear and break it. Finally, taste the chocolate by placing it on your tongue for a few seconds and then pushing it up to the roof of your mouth, allowing it to melt slowly. As you do this, take a deep breath through your nose. Make a note of all of the different flavors you taste as the chocolate melts. Compare your notes with each other.

Now, read the following words to your friends: "Dark chocolate has top notes of cherry, red berries, and balsamic vinegar, followed by middle notes of salt, leather, and tobacco, and finishes with hints of smoke and charred oak." Have them smell and taste the second piece of chocolate, and record their findings.

Follow up with a reflective discussion about the experience.

Whenever I perform this activity with my university students, they notice several things as we discuss our findings. First, they are nearly always disappointed with their sense vocabulary. They find that the adjectives they come up with are common and trite; words like "smooth" and "rich" don't come anywhere near what they tried to communicate about their experience and even, upon reflection, seem odd as descriptions of taste, since smooth is a texture and rich more commonly refers to the possession of wealth. They are impressed with the swirls of color that they see when they really look closely at their chocolate samples, especially as they tilt them at various angles from the light source, when they look at them "slant," as Emily Dickinson might say. Inevitably, they use an **onomatopoeic** word to describe the sound of their breaking chocolate, such as "snap" or "crack" or even a nonsense syllable like "phhht." Finally, they are a bit awed by the fact that their second taste of the chocolate samples is slightly different than the first; as one student said, "Wow, that hint of tobacco is weird—it's definitely there, but I wouldn't have known what it was before you said that."

So, what are we to make of this experiment? Our experience with the chocolate tasting teaches us several things about the mismatch between sensory experience and ordinary language. We have to approximate what we feel and sense in words that other people can understand if we want to communicate our needs and experiences effectively. The frustrations and embarrassment my students feel with the poverty of their ready store of descriptive vocabulary vividly shows us how ordinary language flattens out **multimodal** sensory experience: we *love* chocolate, we *love* our pets, we *love* a song, we *love* our partners, but each of these experiences is qualitatively different (I hope!). This is why we often turn to poetry, or self-consciously poetic language, to express particularly strong or special emotions, and, in turn, why poetic language has the power to elicit emotion when we hear it. Ordinary language, by virtue of its everyday familiarity, blurs distinctions, whereas poetic form and figurative language defamiliarize their subject matter so that we pay more and different kinds of attention to it.

Indeed, perhaps the most interesting aspect of our chocolate tasting experience is the effect that the descriptions had on the second tasting. These descriptions weren't poetic, but by focusing the tasters' attention on specific perceptions and mental images of what things taste like, these words actually changed how they experienced the taste of the chocolate. According to their reports, my students couldn't taste or didn't notice certain flavors until they had the right word for them; those words enhanced or directed their perception of what common sense tells us should be unchangeable—after all, shouldn't our experience of a sensory phenomenon such as taste be a result of nerve endings, physical properties and wavelengths, chemistry, and the facticity of our bodies? As it turns out, even something as seemingly natural as sense perception is culturally mediated, and much of that mediation comes through language. We have a common sense belief that sensory experience precedes conceptual understanding; "seeing is believing," we say. But this experiment proves that what we perceive with our senses is at least in part determined by the language we have available to talk about the experience.

This ultimately means that *words alone have the power to change our sensory and perceptual experience*. This is profound, and profoundly important to grasping the importance of poetic language in the lives of children as well as adults. This power is one of the pragmatic aspects of poetic language; that is, it is one of the functions such language performs. Linguists often think about pragmatics in terms of specific kinds of speech acts, such as making requests or demands, asking questions, making promises, and showing respect. In this view, poetic language is often seen as merely ornamental, unnecessary in the traffic of daily lives and transactions. But close observation of children reveals that they use language, specifically forms of language with poetic or musical qualities, to calm themselves, impose order on chaotic emotions, express deep feelings, amplify joy, or indulge in sadness. Nor does this stop with childhood; think of the last time you chose a musical playlist to alter your own emotional state. Our lives are random and complex; the communicative musicality of poetic language moves a potentially overwhelming holistic state into a more manageable, orderly action while preserving some of the qualities of full sensory immersion.

Jerome Bruner (1983) points out that many of the preverbal behaviors of children are goal directed, and that "much of early infant action takes place in constrained, familiar situations and shows a surprisingly high degree of order and systematicity" (28). How boring! Further, Derek Bickerton (1981) argues that even before they acquire language, babies develop a set of basic theories about time, space and causality such as specific/nonspecific, punctual/recurrent, causative/noncausative, and states/processes. (When you think about it, that's kind of miraculous, given how hard it is relearn these things as adolescents in science classes.) Hence, toddlers and preschool children enter language-seeking pattern, order, and regularity to "specify, amplify, and expand distinctions that the child already has about the world" (Bruner 1983: 30). However, the human brain soon tires of familiarity and even tends toward stagnation, so that we can only taste in the chocolate what we expect to taste. In order to learn new things, grow, and be refreshed, the brain craves novelty and surprises. Ordinary language can give expression to the familiar, but poetic language restages the familiar in novel ways, affirming order through formal patterning but surprising through pattern-breaking syntax and domain-crossing imagery.

Here's a quick example of how poets play with the familiar, setting up patterns to create expectations and then surprising us through their disruption: I saw the Disney movie *Frozen* (2013) in a theater crowded with small children. In his tragically misguided hymn to the glories of summer, the snowman, Olaf, sings the lines "Winter is nice to stay in and cuddle, but put me in summer and I'll be a," at which point the music pauses. When that happened, a jubilant young voice in the theater piped up "puddle!" This young viewer obviously took great pleasure in completing the sonic pattern; indeed, it seems he couldn't resist it, just like it's hard to resist completing an organic cycle (remember the object lesson of walking while saying "hickory dickory … "). Furthermore, his choice affirmed what he knew about what happens to snowmen in the real world. The songwriters obviously depended on viewers making just that inference, and broke both the semantic and the sonic pattern to create an effect of humor and sympathy with the naïve character when Olaf finishes his song not with the word our ears expected, but with the words "happy snowman!"

Meek's and Philip's laments that children lose their poetic views of the world as they enter school might thus be thought of as the fate of all wonder. At first, we are delighted or troubled by a new stimulus, whether it's an object, person, feeling, or idea; we play with it literally or in our imaginations, turn it over, and seek to discover its qualities and limits. Very young children do this by using language that is repetitive, imagistic, and patterned. Older children, adolescents, and adults also reach for poetic language to describe something new; we wax eloquent at the start of a new romance, or when we first encounter a striking view. But soon enough what had once been new becomes familiar and ordinary, at least in part because we have put it into words, encased it in a shell of sorts that renders it less stimulating. This is, generally speaking, a good thing for children, who are encountering genuinely new stimuli more regularly than adults, and who have to learn the limits of expressing their strong emotions in public.

Perhaps, then, children become less poetic as they grow older because fewer things they encounter are new to them, and because the prosody of poetic language has done its first work of providing a containment system for strong emotion. If this is the case, then the purpose of poetry in children's lives shifts as life settles into a banal routine of sameness and already named and claimed experiences. Instead of providing a method for ensuring stability and structure, poetic language becomes a site of resistance to everyday life and language as it is. Much of the impetus behind nonsense poetry comes from just this impulse to reject the imposed meanings of grown-up language while preserving the sonic silliness and relation to the body that nonsense delivers. Other kinds of children's poems often take as their subjects small, everyday things, things that children already know something about and that may have thus lost their wonder, and then introduce a new way of thinking about them—a way that refocuses our attention, or opens up a perspective we haven't considered. In this way, they bring new life to something we have come to take for granted, burnishing qualities that have faded, reawakening wonder. Just as our introduction of new taste words made the chocolate taste chocolatier, Russian critic Victor Shklovsky argues, "To make a stone feel stony, man has been given the tool of art" (1990: 6).

Devices to make stones stony

Many of the literary devices and much of the figurative language that poets use to draw attention to their subjects evoke our senses directly. They do this through their sound, and/or through calling to mind specific sense memories. We know, logically, that there is no necessary correspondence between how a word sounds and what it means, but we still employ onomatopoeic language to exemplify or even emphasize the meaning of our utterances. Actual onomatopoeia, for instance, occurs when we use a word like "snap" or "crack" to approximate a sonically similar environmental sound, but even a word like "smooth," with its susurrating consonants and elongated vowel sounds, arouses the feeling of the meaning to which it refers, and thus connects sound with touch. Actual onomatopoeia, then, is not the only sonic screwdriver in the poet's toolkit: alliteration, assonance, consonance, rhyme, and repetition all depend on the use of sound (and sometimes vision, if you are reading a poem and notice what's called an **eye rhyme**—two words similar in spelling but pronounced differently) to produce a multisensory experience that enhances the literal meaning of the words.

The tempo or pace of poetic utterances also has the power to call to mind embodied experience through simulating movement and duration. We use the words "long" and "short" to describe vowel sounds because, quite simply, it takes a fractionally longer time to articulate a long vowel sound than it does a short one. Hence the contrast between using "snap" to describe the sound of the quick breaking of chocolate feels right to us, while stretching out the word "smooth" mirrors the longer process of chocolate melting on our tongues. In poems, words and collections of words work together to form the meter of a poem, which, if done well, slows down and speeds up according to the subject matter. Ordinary language occasionally does the same thing, speeding up when we're excited and slowing down when we are tired or wish to calm ourselves or our listeners; so does well-wrought prose, moving us quickly through action scenes, manipulating reading speed through suspenseful scenes to build tension, and then slowing down to indicate resolution. But poems do it with more intentionality, using specific forms of meter.

Meter is the rhythm established by the poem. It is defined by two things: the number of syllables in a line, and the pattern of stressed and unstressed syllables. Individual rhythmic units are called feet, and the number of feet in a line determines what the **meter** is called. Most (but not all) children's poems have a clearly recognizable **meter**. Literary critics have come up with a series of terms to define **meter**. For example, a pattern of an unstressed syllable followed by a stressed syllable (da DUM) is called an iambic foot, or simply an iamb. A common **meter** for children's poetry is iambic tetrameter, meaning that there are four iambic feet in a line, as in this first line from Robert Louis Stevenson's "Farewell to the Farm": "The coach is at the door at last." Another common **meter** in children's poems is anapestic tetrameter. An anapestic foot has two unstressed syllables followed by a stressed one (dada DUM). Anapestic tetrameter has four of these feet per line. Sometimes the first syllable is left out in the line, but it's still mostly anapestic tetrameter. Many a student's pleasure in poetry has been extinguished by teachers forcing them to memorize the various names for different kinds of feet, and I have no intention of doing that here. The important thing to remember is that **meter** in poetry is manipulated to enhance the sensual experience of the poem and thus can be crucial to fully understanding its meaning and the effect it has on you as a reader or listener. For instance, consider the opening lines from Dr. Seuss's *The Cat in the Hat* (1957):

> The sun did not shine. (da DUM da da DUM)
> It was too wet to play. (da da DUM da da DUM)
> So we sat in the house (da da DUM da da DUM)
> All that cold, cold wet day. (da da DUM DUM DUM DUM)

The emotion established by these opening lines is boredom, so the poetry has to drone on in a regular, monotonous way, with a dead fall and full stop on the final syllable of each line. But this is escalating boredom, a piling on of dreariness if you will, so the final line breaks the pattern with a series of words that each have their own emphasis, like a drumbeat to doom. To ensure that we read it in the spirit it was intended, Seuss inserts a repeated word in the middle with a comma that requires us to pause and fully enunciate the word whose position in the preceding lines is buried in an unstressed syllable.

In addition to sonorous devices and meter, poetic language does its work of making stones stonier and chocolate chocolatier through other kinds of figurative language, some of which fall in between meaning and sound. An isocolon, for instance, is a series of parallel words, phrases, or clauses that are put together for balance or emphasis. If there are two items, such as "Don't worry, be happy," it's a bicolon; three constitutes a tricolon, as in the Wizard's pronouncement in the 1939 MGM film *The Wizard of Oz*: "You are talking to a man who has laughed in the face of death, sneered at doom, and chuckled at catastrophe." While the power of the bicolon may rest in the ways in which it mirrors the symmetry and balance of the body and/or the play of opposites, the tricolon assuredly takes its rhetorical force from the storytelling trope of the **Rule of Three**, which we will explore in more depth in Chapter 8. In either case, however, an isocolon responds to our embodied expectations of an organic cycle (breathing in and out, for instance, or proceeding through originating stimulus, rising tension, release) to create a felt sense of completion; hence these devices are often used at the end of a poem.

Metaphors children learn by

Other figures of speech are used to great effect in children's poetry and poetic language, and lists with examples abound on the internet. But perhaps the most important one to understand and explore in depth is metaphor. A **metaphor** is a comparison of one thing to another based on similar attributes, and whether we are aware of it or not, we use them all the time, especially when we are trying to reach across the gap from sensual experience to linguistic expression. For instance, when we are trying to describe how chocolate tastes, we tend to favor **synesthetic** and **conceptual metaphors** rather than literal depictions; what does it mean, after all, to say that something tastes "smooth" or "rich"? There are multiple kinds of **metaphors** and a vast body of research concerning them, but all agree that they consist of two parts: a subject that is being described, and an object from which the attributes for description are taken. For instance, when I wouldn't let my daughter, who has Down syndrome and was five at the time, have a second brownie, she responded with "mommie . . . pig." (I was thrilled—it was her first metaphor!). In this example, mommie is the subject to be described. Metaphor theorists have various names for this part: tenor, ground, or target. A pig, then, possesses the qualities that Emily wanted to ascribe to me in that moment; theorists call this the vehicle, figure, or source, respectively. Sometimes the vehicle is not explicitly named, only implied by the invocation of its qualities; this is called an implied metaphor. For instance, when poet Ernest Slyman (2010) says that lightning bugs (the title of his poem) "take snapshots," he is implying that the on and off flashes of the lightning bugs resemble a camera flash.

Synesthetic metaphors are ones that cross sensual domains to link tenor and vehicle. For instance, we might use a haptic term, which refers to the sensation of touch, to describe something we perceive visually: orange is a "warm" color. Or we might use an aural term to indicate a visual phenomenon: He wore a "loud" tie. We say we are "moved" by a work of art even though no part of our bodies actually changes position, or that an expression or action that we only observe from afar is "touching." **Conceptual metaphors** also depend on crossing domains, but they compare ideas more so than sensory perceptions, although these ideas are often grounded in embodied experiences. To say a food is rich, then, is more of a **conceptual metaphor** than a **synesthetic** one, since the word "rich" implies an idea of wealth, fullness, or abundance that maps onto the way rich food makes you feel full or overloads your sense of taste. Such ways of talking seem completely ordinary to us, and it's only when we look at them closely that their semantic strangeness comes into view.

Ellen Winner (1988) distinguishes between several different kinds of sensory metaphoric connections, arguing that some are more available to children than others. Multiple studies show that preschool children can most easily apprehend simple comparisons based on a single sensory trait, such as "clouds are pillows" (64), because they look alike. Interestingly, children as young as four years old could just as easily perceive cross-modality metaphors, as long as the comparisons are grounded in certain kinds of perception, such as the relationship between brightness and loudness. For instance, by age four, children can connect brightness in color with high pitches and loud sounds, and dimness with lower pitches and quiet sounds. However, it isn't until around age eleven that connections can reliably be made between high pitches and small size, and low pitches and large size. While Winner points to innate neurological substrates to account for an earlier ability to make certain connections and not others, arguing that we are born with some understanding of cross-modal similarities, it might also be the case that infants have learned that the bright world outside the dim womb is much louder than the muted, darker environment they have left behind, and daytime sounds, accompanied by bright sunlight, are usually louder than the sounds of the night. Whether this ability is inborn or learned, however, it is important to note that sense-based **metaphors**, even **synesthetic** ones, are accessible to children's understanding long before they learn to read, and that this ability can be enhanced by exposure to clever, deliberate **metaphors** in children's poems. Moreover, children's poems often use first-person **personification** that encourages children to engage in metaphoric thinking by making comparisons between themselves and inanimate objects or animals, as in Karla Kuskin's (1972) "I liked growing" where the speaker is a strawberry.

Winner also discusses nonsensory metaphors, distinguishing between relational and psychological-physical **metaphors** (1988: 66–67). Relational **metaphors** compare dissimilar objects that perform similar functions. The child narrator in Joyce Carol Thomas's *Brown Honey in Broomwheat Tea* (1993) says "My mother says I am / Brown honey in broomwheat tea," indicating, at the level of function, that she sweetens her family's lives in the same way that honey sweetens tea. The vehicle of a **metaphor**, however, always brings other meanings into the mix as well. For instance, in this case, the description of the honey as brown functions to associate the daughter's brown skin with sweetness, beauty, and light, since honey has a translucent, lit-from-within quality. Broomwheat tea has already been introduced in the book as something that is *"good for what ails you, especially when poured by loving hands,"* and the illustrations amplify the association of the sweetness and joy of family life with light-infused brown honey hues throughout, unifying visual and textual inputs.

The second kind of nonsensory **metaphor** that Winner describes is the psychological-physical **metaphor** (1988: 67). These **metaphors** compare sensory attributes with psychological qualities, as when we say someone has a sour disposition. Not surprisingly, these are the most difficult for children to comprehend. Winner speculates that this is likely because of the relatively late acquisition of nuanced knowledge of the psychological domain. That is, children's understanding of states of mind appears gradually and through talk and exposure to literature, which allows children to peek into the minds of others. As we have noted in Chapter 2, the capacity for the development of **Theory of Mind** comes online sometime between four and five years of age, but a complex understanding of the psychological domain is something we continue to develop over a lifetime. Thus talking through poems like Shel Silverstein's "Sour Face Anne" (1981: 91) can help a child make the cross-domain connections between the physical and the psychological in steps: First, a child might be able to put together the face one makes when one tastes something sour with someone who is disappointed or unhappy, then the poem itself points out how that maps onto a person's inner sensation of never being satisfied with what he or she gets.

This transition from external sensory experience to internal states of mind and emotion is key to understanding how children's relationship to poetry and poetic language changes as they grow older. While poetry for young children is most often about things and situations in their everyday experience, or conventional outliers like exotic animals or imaginary creatures, poetry for older children and teens takes an inward turn. Generally speaking, we could say that poetry for very young children helps the child cross the bridge from body to language, depending primarily on sound to do so, while poetry for older readers moves them from outward experience to inner experience, combining sound with meaning. From containing emotion and helping young children create a more navigable, predictable world, poetry for older children moves to stimulating new perspectives and refreshing our attention. This is not to say that older children and teens don't also use poetry to express those "thoughts that do often lie too deep for tears," but they also use poetry as a form of protest against a world gone stale and restrictive.

Poetry as protest

Once children learn to feel at home in the world of words, their active brains impel them to test the limits of the words-to-world correspondence. This fits with the developmental stages where children are beginning to feel confident enough to assert themselves against authority by taking initiative and testing the limits of their autonomy. The poems children create and favor at this stage tend to be ones of exaggerated valor, a sort of celebration of the wonder of themselves (Chukovsky 1965: 68–69), and poems that stage a protest against propriety and limits. Throwing a tantrum is certainly one such form of protest, but for children who have learned the effectiveness of words, humor is a more affectively pleasant and socially sanctioned way of saying no to the tyrannies of authoritative structures—structures that would insist on making sense with your words, a single definition of a word, a single use for an object, a single notion of the right way to do or say things. Verbal humor is in general terms a form of poetic language, in that it is not literal, but it is also a dominant **aesthetic** choice in children's poetry for this very reason: humor in children's and YA poetry is a refusal of the tyranny of ordinary language itself and the authoritative structures of politeness and convention it suborns. This is why playground taunts often rhyme; to say a mean thing in ordinary language is just, well, mean, but to craft it into a rhyme: "Happy birthday to you. / You live in a zoo. / You look like a monkey, / and you smell like one too!" takes a hackneyed convention of well-wishing and turns it upside down in a way that shows that the manipulation of the convention is intentional. It says "I refuse conventions of form and politeness not because I don't know them, but because I won't be bound by them!" When children first encounter Dixon Lanier Merritt's 1910 rhyme of pelican with "belican" and "helican," they are delighted not only with the clever nonsense coinages that make sense to the ear even if they are not proper words (in the limerick, the sense of "belican" is "belly can" and the sense of "helican" is "hell he can"), but also with the anarchic use of a swear word, something they might get punished for saying if it weren't so clever.

Humor, like other cognitive and emotional attainments, develops in stages. Babies as young as six months old respond with a laugh when a trusted caregiver behaves in an exaggerated, incongruous way. Verbal humor comes on board once a child has developed a sense of self that is immutable to verbal naming. When a child is first learning the terms for things, his or her goal is to get things right, to pin things down into a stable, predictable world. However, once children learn that people and objects stay the same even if you change their names, the incongruity of calling mom dad or making up nonsense words strikes them as very funny. Incongruity is key to all types of humor. Our brains are pattern-building machines, so we experience pleasure when we can create or recognize a pattern. When an anomaly or violation of a pattern appears, we have to assess whether or not it is threatening or harmful; if it's not, or if we can resolve it into a new pattern, we find it at least interesting, and often "funny" in some sense of that word.

Interest and humor in poetry can thus depend on nonsense, understatement, exaggeration, or hyperbole, all of which function outside the expectations of ordinary life. But humor is also profoundly social; children make jokes and memorize funny poems not only to entertain themselves but also to elicit responses from others. Humor can thus also depend on the assertion of superiority or the shock of scandal. Once a child understands that words can have more than one meaning, and has sufficient **Theory of Mind** to know that people can be fooled into misunderstanding which meaning is met, then the world of riddles, innuendo, and double entendre opens up. Alternately, as noted above, children use humor to channel their aggression in socially approved, or at least clever, ways, allowing them to get their own back against authority figures, bullies, and the social rules that oppress them.

While humorous poems for children expose the absurdity of conventions, they often do so in carnivalesque ways that, though they imagine hilarious mayhem, ultimately reinforce the status quo. For instance, Shel Silverstein's "Sarah Cynthia Sylvia Stout Would Not Take the Garbage Out" (1974: 70–71) contains a gleefully disgusting recitation of the consequences of Miss Stout's refusal to do her chore. Readers are led through this anarchy to its absurd and comically grim consequences. Message: take the garbage out. Indeed, even the act of reciting absurd, taboo-violating poetry can enable a pressure-release-valve for children learning to contain the excesses of their bodily energies.

Clever resistance to the authority of language rules appears in **concrete poetry** as well. While **concrete poetry** is most commonly thought of in its visual form as "shape" poetry, children are more likely to be familiar with phonetic (sound) and kinetic (movement) poems, as preschool media are filled with them. Media producers combine text, image, music, and movement to create decidedly poetic, multimodal presentations of the letter "C," for instance, and while professional phonetic and kinetic poets are much more intent on using poetry as a disruptive art form, their practices bear a strong family resemblance to children's educational media. As children enter school, however, these slickly produced **multimodal** presentations are less prevalent, and children are instead inundated with rules for the right way to do things, including the proper and conventional form for writing sentences. In gaining this competence, they lose a degree of sovereignty over their fully embodied forms of expression, a loss that is not often recognized as such but which is significant nonetheless. As they grow older, the rules that bind them have more to do with social expectations, the violation of which can lead to isolation. **Concrete poetry** challenges conventional rules by using spatial arrangement and typeface variations in playful ways. On the one hand, it showcases the connection of language to the things it represents by shaping the words into pictorial representations related to the subject of the poem. On the other hand, however, this very practice surfaces the disconnection between the world and the conventions of language and propriety we use to interact within it; we take the busy, buzzy, tactile world of experience and write it down in a controlled linear fashion that completely divorces it from its objective and individual presence.

Visual **concrete poems** are often hard to read aloud, because their meaning is dependent on their reader's ability to take them all in at once and make the intuitive leap from the visual presentation to its metaphorical referents. For instance, in Arnold Adoff's (1995) adolescent collection, *Slow Dance Heart Break Blues*, he includes a **concrete poem** built around a single sentence: "There is hair on my upper lip." On the left side of the page, he titles the poem "He:", indicating that a boy is speaking or thinking this line, which is lineated with one word per line. On the right, he repeats the line and its lineation, but in reverse, as if in a mirror, and headed by the word "She:". Readers confronted with this poem first need to adjust their expectations of written language to understand that both lines are the same, even though the mirror image is at first hard to read. The lineation matters because it slows the line down, highlighting a sense of wonder and maybe even disbelief as the adolescent confronts this physical change. But the inferences of the poem become immediately clear in the mirror image; whereas the boy can be public, straightforward, and even proud of his facial hair, the girl with the same growth wishes to hide it. Moreover, the fact that her words are backward subtly suggests self-consciousness—the girl is having these thoughts while staring into a mirror. Conventions of reading right to left also play a significant role here, as they become a metaphor for moving forward or making progress; facial hair is usually heralded as a positive move toward maturity for a boy, while it is a source of shame and turning away from the changes of puberty for a girl, signifying a longing to go back in time rather than forward.

Emotions and diverse identities in YA poetry

While YA poetry is more likely to drift toward melancholy and anger than nonsense and hyperbolic silliness, it can still be read as a literature of protest against the banality of everyday life and emotions and the social rules and taboos that confront the developing teen. Depending on how you look at it, adolescent poetry is less about containing embodied emotions than it is about expressing or invoking them, though these actions may seem like two sides of the same coin, given that either way, embodied experience is transferred to words. As both their linguistic abilities and frontal lobe functions have grown in complexity, psychological-physical **metaphors** are more available to adolescent readers, but brain-imaging technologies reveal that teens are still leading with their emotions, so poetic language remains an important channel for directing overwhelming emotion into socially sanctioned expression. In fact, given the social prohibitions on public displays of emotion for teens in social life, reading and writing poetry becomes for many a safe, private activity through which they can make sense of their inner lives.

The latter decades of the twentieth century saw the growth of both multicultural poetry and poetry for YAs, often in tandem as the recognition and formation of gendered and ethnic identities became the primary task of adolescence in wealthy Western cultures that have tended to marginalize their nonwhite, nonheteronormative citizens. In contemporary multicultural poetry for children, the emphasis is often on celebrating one's heritage and ethnicity, even when there is an edge of warning, as in the title poem of Joyce Carol Thomas's *Brown Honey in Broomwheat Tea* (1993), where the narrator's parents celebrate her beauty and the sweetness of their family life while warning her that some in the outside world have prepared a "bitter brew" for children of color. YA poetry, on the other hand, is far more likely to take explicit aim at oppressive structures. Christine Heppermann's *Poisoned Apples: Poems for You, My Pretty* (2014), for instance, flips fairy tales on their heads to offer darkly funny, trenchant, and incisive critiques of the beauty myth that suborns eating disorders, rape culture, and self-harm in contemporary teens; her collection is complemented by haunting art photography that echoes the themes of the collection. Naomi Shihab Nye has published several collections of translated poems from all over the world in order to highlight how teens face the similar issues of entering adulthood under significantly different cultural stresses and values.

In addition to poetry collections for YAs, many contemporary prose novels have poetry and therapeutic claims for poetry embedded within them. Emily Dickinson and Sylvia Plath are favorites for such treatment, and rightly so, as many of their poems express a deep-seated rage at being overlooked and silenced by rules of social etiquette and gender expectations, things teens experience and to which they need to give expression. In novels such as Jenny Hubbard's *And We Stay* (2014), Jacqueline Woodson's *Feathers* (2007), and Meg Wolitzer's *Belzhar* (2014), characters use poetry to understand their own emotions in more complex ways. A more formal concept is taken up by Kate Hattemer's *The Vigilante Poets of Selwyn Academy* (2014); the main characters, having learned about Ezra Pound's "The Cantos", undertake the task of "revisionary mythopoesis" by adopting the long poem themselves as their form of protest against the takeover of their school by a reality television show.

Verse novels

While much contemporary poetry for young people takes the form of lyric poems (poems that focus on personal response to emotional experiences), narrative and dramatic poetry (poetry that tells a story and/or employs multiple voices) continues to have a strong presence. Combining individual **lyric poems** into a coherent story has resulted in another trend that has taken hold in recent years: the novel-in-verse. The tradition of the long **narrative poem** has been with us at least since the days of Homer, and children's poems such as "Casey at the Bat" (Thayer 1888) participate in this epic tradition through mocking it; instead of treating a heroic subject in elegant language that conveys the values of a culture, this mock epic elevates a trivial subject in the language of a sportscaster, which perhaps also ironically conveys the values of our iconoclastic culture. Ballads, whether anonymously composed or written by poets such as Samuel Taylor Coleridge, Rudyard Kipling, Christina Rossetti, Alfred Noyes, and Langston Hughes, have been taken up by children because of their richly emotional stories and catchy rhyming stanzas. The Schoolroom Poets (also known as the Fireside Poets) of nineteenth-century America—Henry Wadsworth Longfellow, John Greenleaf Whittier, William Cullen Bryant, Oliver Wendell Holmes, Sr., and James Russell Lowell—spun long story poems that mythologized American history. While the novel-in-verse is indebted to this rich history, it is quite different.

The novel-in-verse is composed of separate poems that work together to tell a story. Joy Alexander suggests that free verse is the "house style" of the verse novel, but Turco takes issue with the term "free verse." As you will recall, **verse** in his definition pays attention to the number of syllables in each line, and establishes a metrical pattern based on that; hence, "free" verse is simply a contradiction in terms. He argues instead that the term for such an unmetered yet still stylized mode should be prose poetry. Postmodern poets such as Rachel Blau duPlessis (1997) stress that the defining feature of poetry is its attention to the line, and still others complain that many novels in verse a contain not a speck of anything that might be considered poetry (Grimes, in Vardel & Oxley 283). I'll split the difference and call it lineated prose. While some so-called verse novels are written entirely in lineated prose, in many the poetry varies in form; indeed, in the best verse novels, the poet uses form to enhance the reader's understanding of the themes in the book. Helen Frost, for instance, uses existing forms or creates her own to mirror the dominant ideas of her books. In *Keesha's House* (2003), for instance, she uses form to highlight the contrast between adults and teens; the teens speak in the fluid, interconnected sestinas, while the adults present their perspectives in isolated, rigid sonnets. In *Diamond Willow* (2008), she creates shaped poems that look like the irregular patterns that appear in a diamond willow branch stripped of its bark and sanded to reveal the dark heart at the center of a diamond shape. Frost effects a visual representation of this by highlighting a few words in bold at the center of each poem; these highlighted words reveal a secret fear or emotion that haunts the main character, Willow, in the midst of her activities. As the narrative develops, the **metaphor** deepens; Willow is stripped of her own outer shell as secrets that relate to that inner diamond are revealed.

The novel-in-verse is thought by many teachers to be a boon for reluctant readers because of the abundance of white space on the pages and the relative paucity of extraneous detail that prose adds to the texture of a narrative. While this is certainly valid in some ways, it also does something of a disservice to both readers and the texts themselves. A good verse novel is not just an abridged version of a more complex narrative, but is instead an artistic creation where attention must be paid to **form** as well as content. The lower word count may in fact be a boon to insecure readers, but, as Ron Koertge notes in his talkback to this chapter, it is important to spend time thinking about what the poetry is doing rather than merely focusing on the story; poetry must be more than "prose hacked into pieces like kindling." In fact, the distinctive features of the poetry—the sounds, beats and textures of the words and the images they conjure—may be the real draw for readers whose preferred modalities are aural, kinesthetic, and visual rather than keyed to written prose.

In addition, though, it is interesting to consider the verse novel as a form steeped in the **ideology** and material expression of contemporary adolescence; the everyday lives of contemporary teens are composed of emotionally laden, disconnected fragments of experience distilled into moments—social media status updates, intellectually isolated school subjects, Instagram and Snapchat exchanges, work, sports, drama, sex, spirituality, relationships—that they must somehow bring together into a coherent sense of a self fully alive in the present yet tending toward an imminent and imposing future. The pressure to be constantly busy, constantly social, constantly plugged in leaves little time for the reflection required to craft one's life as a sustained, coherent prose narrative. The verse novel offers a different way to tell one's story, and to recognize it as a story with underlying themes and concerns that connect across its various fragments.

Conclusion

Poetry for young people has a rich and varied history. It has been part and parcel of every ideological and material shift we have noted in Chapter 1 with regard to children's and YA literature as a whole, beginning in oral chants around a communal fire, developing as a form of storytelling, lament, and worship, participating in both sacred and secular pedagogy, and forming an impressive percentage of the whole of children's print culture up to the present day. Linguistic anthropologists believe that humans could sing before they could talk, and Daniel J. Levitin (2008) argues that six fundamental types of songs—songs of friendship, joy, comfort, religion, knowledge, and love—have actually directed the evolution of the brain and human society. After years of well-documented neglect, scholarly attention to children's and YA poetry has seen tremendous growth in the early decades of the twenty-first century, with books and articles focusing on historical and **aesthetic** movements and trends. If we take into account picturebooks, anthologies, single-authored collections, novels and nonfiction in verse, and nonprint resources, children's and YA poetry today is a robust segment of a robust publishing sector.

What I have attempted in this chapter is to lay out a framework for thinking about poetic language in general as well as children's and YA poetry. From the moment we are born, we begin teaching our mouths to form sounds, joyfully playing with these new toys that are our bodies and our voices, coordinating our sounds with and directing our calls to the "other." Swiftly, words become ways of expressing specific needs and desires, as well as laying claim to those things in the world that are ours—our parents, our siblings, our toys, our comfort objects. As our words help us turn *the* world into *our* world, we also learn to say "no!," offering up an enthusiastic, if not always efficacious, protest to authoritative and restrictive rules. And all the while, we are playing—playing with sounds, playing with words, and finally, playing with meaning. For once we have learned the right word for something, the conventional word, we have to test its limits—if I change the word, will I have changed the thing it refers to? What can my words do in the world? Can they call someone to me, or push someone away? Can I make someone smile or laugh with just my words, or make someone angry? Can words create a me that he, or she, or they, will notice and admire, even love? Can words create a world, or destroy one?

Neil Philip avers that "there is in the best children's poetry a sense of the world being seen as for the first time, and of language being plucked from the air to describe it," and while he concedes that as much could be said of adult poetry, he goes on to say that "immediate sense perceptions have an overriding importance in children's poetry, quite beyond the workings of memory and reflection, or the filters of spiritual, philosophical, or political ideas" (1996: xxv). Inherent here is the sense of a trajectory, from the immediacy of just the right language to evoke a sensory image of the external world to the reworking of those images in and through the interior world. And indeed, this is precisely what poetic language is for—the working of sensory perception into mental concepts, and the reworking of mental concepts through the fresh invocation of embodied perceptions. In other words, children's poetry, or poetry for children, tethers us to the world through sensual concrete language, helping us to contain the enormity of the world and our feelings toward it into images we can taste, touch, see, and smell, while poetry for older children and young adults draws on those images to encode and enrich our interior lives.

Extending your study

Reading:

Chambers, Nancy (ed.), *Poetry for Children: The Signal Awards 1979-2001* (Stroud: Thimble Press, 2009).
   Collection of essays in response to the poetry awards given by the now defunct children's literature journal, *Signal*.
Sorby, Angela. *Schoolroom Poets: Childhood, Performance and the Place of American Poetry* (Lebanon, NH: University of New Hampshire Press, 2005), 1865–1917.
   Maps the dissemination and importance of the popular story poems of the "schoolroom" or "fireside" poets of the nineteenth and early twentieth century in America.
Styles, Morag. *From the Garden to the Street: Three Hundred Years of Poetry for Children* (London: Cassell, 1998).
   Provides a comprehensive and accessible history of British and American children's poetry and poets from John Bunyan through the late twentieth century.
Styles, Morag, Joy, Louise, and Whitley, David (eds.), *Poetry and Childhood.* Stoke-on-Trent (United Kingdom: Trentham Books, 2010).
   A set of academic essays that approach children's poetry from a range of critical perspectives.
Thomas, Joseph T., Jr. *Poetry's Playground: The Culture of Contemporary American Children's Poetry* (Detroit: Wayne State University Press, 2007).
   Situates children's poetry within the concerns of adult poetic discourse and movements, emphasizing its antic and subversive character.

Writing:

1   Research the life and work of a particular poet and write an essay about dominant themes in his or her work and what those themes say about his or her ideology of childhood.
2   Read this introduction to the special issue of the *Children's Literature Association Quarterly* devoted to children's poetry: Tarr, A. and Flynn, R. (2002), "'The trouble isn't making poems, the trouble's finding somebody that will listen to them': Negotiating a Place for Poetry in Children's Literature Studies," *Children's Literature Association Quarterly* 27.1: 2–3. Drawing on your own experiences with poetry taught in schools, write an opinion piece that details why you think the criticism neglects this art form.
3   For the next week or so, keep a journal where you record incidents of what you consider poetic uses of language as defined and elaborated in this chapter.

These can be quotations from books or other media, snippets of conversation, or your own thoughts. Look back over your notes and consider the following: What situations tend to prompt the use of poetic language? How does the language reflect or actively affect your emotional response to the experience? Transform your reflections into a statement of your own about the role of poetic language in everyday life.

4   In his talkback to this chapter, Ron Koertge gives equal weight to good storytelling and good poetry. Read one of his verse novels and write a paper that explores how the poetry supports the storytelling.

Discussing:

1   What was your favorite poem as a child? In what context did you hear it?
2   Can you recite a poem from memory? If so, what sort of poem is it and why do you think you still remember it?
3   In what ways can poetry enrich children's lives?
4   How is the practice of writing, reading, and sharing poetry related to empathy? Think about poems as banal as those on greeting cards and expressed as sports cheers and revolutionary chants as well as poems that express profound insights. What do people's responses (including your own) to these things tell you about poetry's effect on helping people share the emotions of others? What are the implications for society of not having a robust poetry curriculum for children?
5   Working in small groups with an anthology of children's poems, locate and categorize the metaphors you find. Use Winner's categories of the sensory, relational, and psychological-physical. Which types are more prominent in the poems in your anthology?

Responding:

1   Perform a children's poem using your entire body, perhaps with props and costuming.
2   Put a children's poem to original music and perform it.
3   Listen to a poem from the Children's Poetry Archive or Poetry Foundation website (see below for links). As you listen, draw or paint whatever images come to mind. Then, write your own poem based on what you have drawn.
4   Find the meter in a children's poem by using one of the following techniques: (1) Recite the poem while walking. Notice how your footfalls correspond to stressed syllables. (2) Put your elbow on the table or desk in front of you, and put your chin in your elbow. Read the poem aloud and notice how your mouth drops in accordance with the stressed syllables.

Online exploration:

1 Searchable archive of children's poets reading their poems:
   http://childrenspoetryarchive.org/?_ga=1.210829014.2111141854.1432217922

2 Online network with resources for poets up to age twenty-five, with short
   articles about aspects of poetry, writing tips and challenges, and
   announcements and information about contests, publishing venues:
   http://www.youngpoetsnetwork.org.uk/about-young-poets-network/

3 Children's section of the Poetry Foundation website, featuring book picks,
   articles, videos, and features on children poets:
   http://www.poetryfoundation.org/children/

4 Active ad-free blog maintained by professor, author, and editor Sylvia Vardell
   on all things related to children's poetry:
   http://poetryforchildren.blogspot.com/

5 A website chock full of videos and information about children's poets:
   http://www.nowaterriver.com/resources/

Case Studies: Poetic Language in Poetry and Prose

Because poetic language is not only found in poetry, I have included two brief
case studies here. In the first, a poem by Robert Louis Stevenson is analyzed
for its use of figurative language and poetic devices. Then, based on that
analysis, I show how knowledge of these devices can be used to create an
(clearly inferior!) imitation of the poem.

"Farewell to the Farm" (*alliteration*)		
The coach is at the door at last;	A	*Rhyme Pattern*
The eager children, mounting fast	A	*Four-line Stanzas (Quatrains)*
And kissing hands, in chorus sing:	B	*Iambic tetrameter: da DUM da DUM da DUM da DUM*
Good-bye, good-bye, to everything!*	B	
To house and garden, field and lawn,	C	
The meadow-gates we swang upon,	C	*(inverted sentence order)*
To pump and stable, tree and swing,	B	
Good-bye, good-bye, to everything!*	B	
And fare you well for evermore,	D	
O ladder at the hayloft door,	D	*(apostrophe)*
O hayloft where the cobwebs cling,	B	*(apostrophe)*
Good-bye, good-bye to everything!*	B	
Crack goes the whip, and off we go;	E	*(onomatopoeia)*
The trees and houses smaller grow;	E	

| Last, round the woody turn we swing: | B | |
| Good-bye, good-bye, to everything! * | B | *repetition of last line of each stanza |

By Robert Louis Stevenson, from *A Child's Garden of Verses*

Imitation of "Farewell to the Farm" By Karen Coats (with help from her children)	"Leaving the Magic Kingdom" We end the day with one more line
--*Iambic tetrameter (mostly)*	Aboard the monorail we climb, (*inverted sentence order*)
--*four-line stanzas*	And looking back, we <u>s</u>adly <u>s</u>ing: (*alliteration*)
--*repetition of last line (mostly)*	Good-bye, good-bye to everything!
--*similar rhyme scheme (mostly)*	
	<u>O spinning teacups</u>*, <u>fl</u>ying <u>f</u>ast,
(*consonance*)--	<u>O Mickey, Stitch, and the res</u>t <u>of the cast</u>,*
	<u>O princesses who love to s</u>ing,*
	*(*apostrophes*)
	Good-bye, good-bye to everything!
	And as we <u>s</u>adly <u>s</u>ay farewell, (*alliteration*)
	We leave with many tales to tell.
	Of Dumbo, Aladdin and the Lion King:
	Good-bye, good-bye to everything!
	Boom and crack the fireworks sound, (*onomatopoeia*)
	As our day is winding down.
	Onto the monorail we climb:
	Good-bye, good-bye, until next time!

For the second case study, I have included some prose passages from Frances Hardinge's *Fly By Night* (2005) that make elegant use of poetic devices to create strong images. The passages are quoted as they appear in the book, and then glossed for poetic devices:

There were traces of past riot as well as present revelry. A couple of boys in battered, broad-brimmed hats dawdled by houses that were freckled by musket fire, and used clever little knives to pick out the shot when no one was looking. In the old marketplace a burned-out sedan chair tilted on a pile of blackened timbers, and Mosca's heart lurched as she saw what seemed to be a charred human figure inside. As she passed, however, she saw that beneath an enormous, singed wig shaped like a wasp's nest, the white face

(Continued)

was chill and unmarred, except for the chin, which the flames had tiger-shaped in bars of soot and sallow. It was a marble statue of the Duke that had been clumsily dressed and given to the pyre. (Hardinge 2005: 472)

There were traces of <u>past riot</u> as well as <u>present revelry</u> [*notice alliteration and balance between the phrases—past riot is over and therefore shorter, while present revelry, which is still going on, is longer, stretching out*]. A couple of <u>b</u>oys in <u>b</u>attered, <u>b</u>road-<u>b</u>rimmed [*alliteration*] hats <u>dawdled</u> by houses that were <u>freckled</u> [*personification to evoke emotion, but also perfect visual description, double lines under vivid verbs*] by musket fire, and used <u>clever little knives</u> [*makes a clicky noise which is what that action would sound like—continues with pick*] to pick out the shot when no one was looking. In the old marketplace a burned-out sedan chair <u>tilted</u> on a pile of blackened timbers, and Mosca's heart <u>lurched</u> as she saw what seemed to be a charred human figure inside. As she passed, however, she saw that beneath an enormous, <u>singed wig shaped like a wasp's nest</u> [*notice all of the s's, w's, g's and p's—assonance, but also a more defined pattern: sgwg, then spwp, and vowels: ii, then aa, and singed wig/shaped wasp*], the white face was chill and unmarred, except for the chin, <u>which the flames had tiger-shaped in bars of soot and sallow</u> [*brilliant image—evokes Blake's poem "Tyger, tiger, burning bright/ In the forests of the night," but look also at the alliteration there—white face/which flames, chill/chin, soot/sallow, plus sallow meaning a sickly yellow color, but also sounds like tallow, which is nasty, stinky material for making candles*]. It was a marble statue of the Duke that had been clumsily dressed and given to the pyre. (Hardinge 2005: 472)

Familiar pains were throbbing behind his eyes, and he paused to let them pass. Little pale points came and went before his sight, as if a giant cat were kneading the tapestry of the world and letting its claw tips show through the cloth. He sighed, swept away the crumbs and dipped his quill to continue with his writing, then looked up at the baby one last time, as if she had said something to interrupt him. (Hardinge 2005: 9)

Familiar <u>p</u>ains were <u>throbbing</u> behind his eyes, and he <u>p</u>aused to let them <u>p</u>ass. Little <u>p</u>ale <u>p</u>oints came and went before his sight, as if a giant cat were <u>kneading</u> the tapestry of the world and letting its claw tips show through the cloth [*notice the vivid picture that image draws in your mind. The explicit comparison of pain with the cat's claws overlies an implicit comparison of his head to the whole world, which is where the whole world is, really, to a writer. The repetition of the sharp "p" sounds enhance the prickly feeling.*]. He sighed, swept away the crumbs and dipped his quill to continue with his writing [*This construction of three phrases that are parallel in structure but with each one getting longer is called a tricolon crescens—it is a form of an isocolon where parallelism is formed by the use of two or more words, phrases or clauses. The parallelism creates emphasis and balance. The crescens, though, means that each phrase gets a little longer, and here it shows how the action itself is extended.*], then looked up at the baby one last time, as if she had said something to interrupt him. (Hardinge 2005: 9)

The courtyard was paved with great, six-sided tiles, glazed in creams and shades of caramel. Across it extravagant figures lolled in sedans, or strolled idly like sun-struck drones over a giant honeycomb. Along the darkened colonnade, footmen paced briskly in cloth-soled shoes, and serving girls tripped with baskets of dry lavender, beating them with pestles to fill the air with its scent. (Hardinge 2005: 279)

Another strongly evocative visual image—all of the colors and shapes and nonspecific activity is exactly like looking at a honeycomb in a beehive. But also, the image works particularly well because it symbolizes all of this activity in the service of an unseen queen bee.

Also, the verbs! Three different verbs for walked—strolled, paced, and tripped—each indicating the character and station and attitude of the walker, even the verb that indicates the people too important and indolent to walk— lolled.

Senses appealed to: glazed in cream and caramel, honeycomb—taste words as well as vision words; sight, obviously; the feeling on your skin evoked by sun-struck; and the smell of lavender.

Author talkback:

Ron Koertge is a poet and a novelist, and sometimes he combines the two to write novels in verse. This talkback is a reflection on the relationship between good poetry and good storytelling, what compels him to combine the two, and what's at stake when he does.

A Good Story Compellingly Told

By Ron Koertge

Twenty or so years ago, I was happily writing novels for young adults when I hit a patch of black ice and skidded off the road. I was publishing with Orchard Books when—I'm going to wring everything I can out of this winter metaphor—there was a sudden freeze in the Orchard, my editor left, and I was out in the cold.

I've been a published poet since about 1965, so I knew I'd always write. Maybe the YA novels were an anomaly. So I happily returned to poetry.

I still liked novels, though, and one of the things a librarian friend turned me onto was the novel-in-verse. What was this interesting hybrid, anyway? One reviewer simply called the genre a narrative in verse. Another identified it as a story in short lines. But short lines do not a poem make. There had to be more to it than that.

Emily Dickinson said she knew something was poetry when a book made her whole body so cold no fire could ever warm her. But a novel-in-verse is not poetry at its purest. So would a novel-in-verse just make her reach for a sweater?

I was teaching at the city college in Pasadena, California, when there was a gun scare on campus in the late 1990s. I started brooding about the new phenomenon of school shootings. Pretty soon I was working on what would become my first Novel-In-Verse, *The Brimstone Journals*. But it started as blocks of prose.

Brimstone has fifteen speakers, each writing in his or her private journal. Early on in this project, the question to myself was this: How can I make these secrets from troubled kids into something compelling?

Here's a journal entry about halfway into the narrative arc. It's written by a young woman, Sheila, tangentially involved with the through-line of possible carnage, but more concerned with her attraction to another girl:

> I went to talk to Monica about living together outside the city. There are commune things for just girls. Women and girls. We've got gym together, so I stopped her after and showed her this article about the communes. Wow. Big misunderstanding. Called me names and everything. What a mistake. Took it totally the wrong way.

As prose, that would advance any narrative: What will Sheila do now? But it doesn't belong in a novel-in-verse. It may be part of a story but falls woefully short of any definition of poetry. So I made some adjustments.

Sheila

Oh, man. I showed Monica that commune thing
and *she just freaked.*

Told me no way. Told me to just forget it.
Told me to quit bothering her!

She said, "I'm not like you. I'm no dyke!"

I'm no dyke, either. I'm just in love
with Monica.

That was more like it. First of all, it decorated the page like a poem. Then there's the brevity, the cool line break in the second-to-last line and the repeated "Told me," which for the scholars among you is a rhetorical device called anaphora.

If "Sheila" didn't always meet Rita Dove's definition of poetry as "language at its most distilled and most powerful," it was nevertheless more distilled and more powerful than the prose version.

After *Brimstone*, I worked on poems and scribbled drafts of traditional YAs. For someone like me who likes both fiction and poetry, there was an interesting and vital symbiosis. One fueled and informed the other. If one of the elements of poetry is brevity or compactness, my fiction for young readers got shorter and tighter all the time. And I'm not the only one. Everybody I know who writes both fiction and poetry celebrates the fact that Poetry and Prose live on the same block and play together.

Here, for example, is one of the opening paragraphs from a high-octane YA of mine, *Margaux with an X*:

> The drive is okay: AC on HIGH (it's torrid in Los Angeles with the usual muslin-clad sky), radio up, some gratifying also amiable also envious also admiring also lubricious glances. But she has to park at the top of a new structure, following a ramp so circuitous it's like an inner ear. Is she going to emerge under the invisible stars on Level 5, blue level, or get lost inside some enormous Osseous Labyrinth? Who would ever find her if she did?

It's close to Poetry because it does something Prose rarely does, and that is it draws attention not to just the story but the language of the story: the muslin-clad sky, the simile with the inner ear, the fun with all the s's.

When I wasn't working in prose that flirted with poetry, the lure of the pure novel-in-verse continued to call to me. And if I ever wanted inspiration or an example of how to build a verse-novel, I turned to Karen Hesse's terrific *Out of the Dust,* which is as raw-boned and spare as her subject—the Dust Bowl in the 1930s.

Over the years, my list of verse novels for young readers has expanded exponentially. If I name ten novels-in-verse now, I have to leave out a hundred. So that's good, isn't it? More books to read. More kids to like poetry. Well, yes and no.

As the popularity of verse novels grows, I can't help but notice the emphasis on *novel* and in some cases the neglect of *poetry*. Poets are careful about lineation. Basically, that's a concern with the line: where it breaks in a poem. How it slows readers down or goads them. Sometimes, however, lineation is reduced to prose hacked into pieces like kindling. Damp kindling that would never start a fire. What follows I made up for my students, but it's a fair approximation of what I'm talking about:

> We look through Mom's old things.
> We're both crying a lot. What to
> keep. What to give away. It's dusty
> where we are. We can hardly look at
> each other even though we're sisters.

Why does that qualify as verse? Mostly because lying there on the page it looks like a poem. Well, an unconscious man looks like a man. The stanza is carelessly assembled (lines two and four ending on prepositions) and there's that numbing repetition of the plural pronoun. It is in a word—flat. And whatever poetry is—and it is a lot of things—it's not supposed to be lifeless.

Octavia E. Butler, the great sci-fi writer, kept a hand- printed card that said this: No entertainment on earth can match a good story compellingly told.

Can poetry help a story to be compelling? Sometimes. Can someone who isn't a poet write a Verse Novel? Maybe. Just for fun, should writers of all kinds experiment with the novel-in-verse? Of course they should. And publishers can disseminate anything they want. Still, Christopher Fry said, "Poetry is the language in which man experiences his own amazement."

When it comes to the novel-in-verse, then, the more amazement the better.

Literature references

Adoff, A. (1995), *Slow Dance Heart Break Blues*, New York: Lothrop, Lee & Shepard Books.
Barbauld, A. L. (1781), *Hymns in Prose for Children*, London: J. Johnson
Dr. Seuss (1957), *The Cat in the Hat*, New York: Random House.
Frost, H. (2003), *Keesha's House*, New York: Farrar, Straus & Giroux.
Frost, H. (2008), *Diamond Willow*, New York: Farrar, Straus & Giroux.
Frost, R. (2002), "The Figure a Poem Makes," in *Robert Frost Reader: Poetry and Prose*, ed. Edward Connery Lathem and Lawrence Thompson, pp. 439–42, New York: Holt. [Original essay published 1939].
Frozen (2013), Dir. by Chris Buck and Jennifer Lee, Burbank, CA: Walt Disney Studios.
Hardinge, F. (2005), *Fly by Night*, London: Macmillan.
Hattemer, K. (2014), *The Vigilante Poets of Selwyn Academy*, New York: Knopf.
Heppermann, C. (2014), *Poisoned Apples: Poems for You, My Pretty*, New York: Greenwillow.
Hubbard, J. (2014), *And We Stay*, New York: Delacorte.
Koertge, R. (2003). *Shakespeare Bats Cleanup*, Somerville, MA: Candlewick.
Kuskin, K. (1972), *Any Me I Want to Be*, New York: Joanna Cotler Books.
Philip, N. (1996), *The New Oxford Book of Children's Verse*, Oxford: Oxford UP.
Silverstein, S. (1974), *Where the Sidewalk Ends*, New York: HarperCollins.
Silverstein, S. (1981), *A Light in the Attic*, New York: Harper & Row.
Slyman, E. (2010), *Poems that Make You Laugh*, Smashwords, Digital File.
Stevenson, R. L. (1945), *A Child's Garden of Verses*, New York: Puffin. [Original work published in 1885].
Thayer, E. (1888), "Casey at the Bat: A Ballad of the Republic Sung in the Year 1888," *The Daily Examiner* (June 3, 1888).
Thomas, J. C. (1993), *Brown Honey in Broomwheat Tea*, New York: HarperCollins.
Watts, I. (1715), *Divine Songs Attempted in Easy Language for the Use of Children*, http://www.gutenberg.org/cache/epub/13439/pg13439.html.

Wolitzer, M. (2014), *Belzhar*, New York: Dutton.

Woodson, J. (2007), *Feathers*, New York: G. P. Putnam's Sons.

Wordsworth, W. (1802), *Lyrical Ballads with Pastoral and Other Poems*, Longman: T. N. Longman and O. Rees.

Worth, V. (2002), *Peacock and Other Poems*, New York: Farrar, Straus & Giroux.

Worth, V. (2007), *Animal Poems*, New York: Farrar, Straus & Giroux.

5

Reading (with) Pictures

Suggested texts to read alongside this chapter

Crew, Gary, *The Watertower*, Illustrated by Steven Woolman.
Gregory, Nan, *How Smudge Came*, Illustrated by Ron Lightburn.
Hinds, Gareth, *Macbeth.*
Rocco, John, *Blackout.*
Yang, Gene Luen, *Boxers and Saints.*
Three or four picturebooks of your choice.

Alice was beginning to get very tired of sitting by her sister on the bank and of having nothing to do: once or twice she had peeped into the book her sister was reading, but it had no pictures or conversations in it, "and what is the use of a book," thought Alice, "without pictures or conversations?" (Carroll 2013/1897: 11).

What use, indeed, we may wonder, is a book *for children* without pictures? For many people, the presence of illustrations is necessary for a book even to be considered a book for children. Furthermore, parents, teachers, and unfortunately a great many children regard a book without pictures as a mark of growth with regard to literacy, since more experienced readers are thought not to *need* pictures as they read. Under that assumption lies the premise that people who are learning to read *do* need pictures, and underlying *that* assumption is that pictures are somehow more transparent or available to meaning than words. These two assumptions have been solidly trounced by children's literature critic Perry Nodelman in his authoritative work on picturebooks (see Nodelman 1988; Nodelman and Reimer 2002). But consider this: in this paragraph, I have used italic font to emphasize certain words, because I wanted them to sound a certain way in your ear as you read them. I didn't use pictures to make my point, but I did manipulate a visual code in order to produce my desired effect, since fonts represent a kind of pictured sound (think, for instance, of how capital letters are taken to represent shouting in internet and text discourse). But in order to know how to interpret that shift in font, you needed to know what the convention for italic font means in this context—it's not something that comes naturally. Visual representations are replete with such codes and conventions. Children's literature offers an important apprenticeship in how those codes, conventions, and contexts function and matter in culture. In this chapter, then, our assumption will not be that children *need pictures* in order to learn to read words, but that we as literary critics *need words* in order to learn to read pictures.

Why you won't find pictures in this book

Despite Alice's complaint, though, this chapter, unlike many analyses of picturebooks, will not include reproductions of individual pages or images from picturebooks or graphic novels to illustrate the principles of analysis we will discuss. Instead, I encourage you to gather a stack of picturebooks and a few graphic novels to keep by your side as you read; I have made some suggestions at the beginning of this chapter, but they are by no means meant to restrict your choices. My reasons for this decision are many. First, any analysis of the way images work should have broad applicability. In my research on picturebooks, I have found that critics come back to the same illustrators again and again—Anthony Browne, John Burningham, Maurice Sendak, Anthony Browne, Chris Van Allsburg, Trina Schart Hyman, David Wiesner, and more Anthony Browne—and to be sure, these artists are exemplary in their use of visual design for the purposes of storytelling. Indeed, they are among the best makers of the best picturebooks. But children don't always and only read the best books, and we all have a book or two in our past that we were very fond of even though its banality embarrasses us as adult critics. If we want to understand how these books became favorites—that is, why they were so influential and affective for our younger selves and continue to attract young readers—we need to develop strategies for analysis that travel; that is, they should be applicable at some level to any book children may happen to pick up. The degree to which certain compositional strategies are in evidence, however, will also give us a framework for telling the good from the bad, the artistic from the pedestrian.

    Another of my reasons for not including images is that I am reluctant to call out specific illustrators and their books as either good or bad. That is not to say I don't have my own opinions or critical judgments with regard to aesthetic quality. However, I am sensitive to the problems of the academic canon formation of children's books that Deborah Stevenson (1997: 111, 112) elaborates, especially her distinction between a "canon of sentiment" and a "canon of significance." Certainly, as she notes, "scholars are likelier to discuss books about which they have something to say" (112), and I will be doing a lot of that in this chapter. But a robust set of critical tools drawn from **formalist** criticism as well as cultural studies and other methodologies should enable us to have something to say about any book we pick up, as well as a good deal to say about film and new media products, rather than limiting our study to a few well-known masters of the **form** and giving less attention to newcomers to the field and/or to artists whose work, while appealing to children, seems less technically challenging or innovative to literary critics. Indeed, we need critical tools to account for that appeal in order to understand how books and other forms of visual storytelling that make some adult critics wince or say "meh" nonetheless nestle firmly into the hearts and minds of child readers, helping to shape their **aesthetic** sensibilities and form their **ideologies**. Perhaps more importantly, though, the majority of books academic critics focus on are by white artists doing things we expect them to do with figures, colors, shapes, and formatting, and even challenging their readers and breaking rules in ways that we expect those rules to be challenged and broken. Not only does this perpetuate a limited canon of what counts as quality, but it also tends to relegate books by nonwhite authors into the categories of socially important or useful for curricular purposes. Such categorization nearly always, and sometimes unfairly, sounds the death knell for such books to be analyzed for their aesthetic techniques and value. (There are some controversial bits in this paragraph. Discuss.)

The most important reason for my decision not to include reproductions of individual pages or images, however, has to do with the nature of the picturebook itself. Barbara Bader (1976: 1) offers this compelling definition of a picturebook:

> A picturebook is text, illustrations, total design; an item of manufacture and a commercial product; a social, cultural, historical document; and foremost an experience for a child. As an art form it hinges on the interdependence of pictures and words, on the simultaneous display of two facing pages, and on the drama of the turning page.

Given this emphasis on "total design" and the work as an *experience* for the reader, I think it does something of disservice to isolate and reproduce a single page or image, even for heuristic purposes. Size, color, the weight, sheen, and texture of the paper, the position of the page within the book, the images before and after, even the smell of the ink: all of these things matter in the total experience of book. They constitute what David Lewis (2001: 46–60 *passim*) calls the "ecology" of the picturebook experience; his metaphor of the picturebook as an **ecosystem** disinclines me toward presenting an image outside of the full context of the book as an object to be held, manipulated, smelled, read, and experienced in its totality. After all, an **ecosystem** is a network of interconnecting and interacting parts, so no one element can be understood on its own, and if an element is removed or changes, every other element is affected, and the entire experience is distorted. Therefore, I would encourage you to read picturebooks alongside your reading of this chapter, stopping now and again to think about how the ideas presented here are reflected not only in the texts themselves, but also in your whole experience of reading the books.

Images, ideology, and diversity

As we have noted in Chapter 1, pictorial representations of events, such as those found in cave paintings and iconic sacred art, have long functioned as a form of storytelling in preliterate cultures as well as in cultures where print literacy was not widespread. Cave paintings were likely a representation of wished-for success in the hunt as well as a record of actual successes, and a walk through a cathedral immerses the viewer in the sequential storytelling of tales that define its faith tradition. Belligerent cultures decorated the walls of their royal palaces with panels that depicted the building of their empires and the torture and defeat of their enemies (see, for instance, the Assyrian panels in the British Museum). These artifacts remind us that illustrations tell powerful stories that are meant to appeal to the viewer's emotions and convey cultural values. This is no less true today that it ever was, and therefore it is important to understand how illustrations in children's and YA texts participate in the emotional and ideological structuring of contemporary enculturated subjects.

Illustration has been a prominent feature in texts written for children since the 1600s, when educational philosophy and print technologies developed to the point that people like Comenius could produce early textbooks. These books used illustration not only to facilitate literacy but also to introduce readers to the wonders of the world that were outside their everyday experience. Unfortunately for their readers, however, children's books through the eighteenth century were illustrated using the cheaper, less-refined method of wood cuts, which could be set along with the letter blocks and could run through the press at a single pass, rather than the more delicate and precise multistep process of engraving, which was how illustrations in adult books were more often created and printed. However, in the early nineteenth century, educational philosophy and printing technologies came together to create the demand and possibility for higher quality illustrations, and market forces entered the picture: the Locke-inspired demand for rational, scientific inquiry in children's education and the intentions of empire-building nations to expand their territories required more precise depictions of the natural world in their illustrated books to instill in their readers a desire for travel and exploration, blending curiosity with entitlement. Illustrated books that featured Australian, Canadian, African, and South Asian settings, for instance, began to appear in the 1840s and 1850s. At first mostly by visitors rather than settlers, these illustrated texts were variable in the authenticity of their depictions of indigenous flora, fauna, and peoples, but they were intended to serve two overarching goals: first to exoticize the locales now open to colonization in order to engender a pioneer spirit and taste for adventure, and later to emphasize Australia and Canada in particular as desirable domestic spaces for would-be settlers; these latter books were often written and illustrated by women who were rearing children in these locales. While engraving and color-printing technologies had developed to the point where precision and attractive decoration became feasible, there were as yet few skilled engravers in the colonies, so most of the books in Canada and Australia were imports. However, a rising middle class throughout the British Empire and the United States in the early 1800s, with aspirations for their children, inspired the production of and created a market for books with the inclusion of a few, high-quality, often hand-colored pages of illustrations, called plates. Publishers and entrepreneurs such as William Darton, John Harris, Henry Cole, and Joseph Cundall commissioned artists to provide illustrations for their children's books, so that by the second decade of the 1800s children's book illustration became a viable occupation for working artists.

While the original impetus for improved quality in children's illustrated books may have been to enhance the pedagogy of the text, promote scientific inquiry and, more implicitly, spark a desire for travel and exploration in the service of empire, shifts in attitudes toward the purpose of children's literature, namely from moral and scientific instruction to entertainment, also freed artists to present a world that only existed in the imagination—a world of mythical creatures that existed somewhere between heaven and hell, between symbolic allegory and outright fantasy. Wolves that dressed like grannies, rabbits in waistcoats, dancing dishes, and fairy creatures that inhabited the woods became some of the dominant images of the Golden Age, as illustrators like Randolph Caldecott (1846–86), Walter Crane (1845–1915), Kate Greenaway (1846–1901), Beatrix Potter (1866–1943), Arthur Rackham (1867–1939), and John Tenniel (1820–1914) in the United Kingdom, and Windsor McCay (1867–1934), Maxfield Parrish (1870–1966), Howard Pyle (1853–1991), and Jessie Wilcox Smith (1863–1935) in the United States turned their attention to children's book illustration. The success of these books with their intended audience (who wouldn't like such interesting and beautiful objects?) solidified the necessity for illustrations in a profitable children's book.

I would argue, in addition, that these illustrators participated in a far more significant **ideological** shift that has had far-reaching consequences with regard to how we think about knowledge itself. Scientific discoveries in the field of optics in the early 1600s combined with the perfection of perspective in Renaissance art to place a new emphasis on the visual as a form of knowledge; telescopes, for instance, showed observers what objects in the sky really looked like stripped of mythology, and paintings using perspective depicted scenes that looked realistic instead of stylized to demonstrate abstract principles. This turn toward the visual as the source and guarantee of what is real and knowable about the world marked a profound shift in our understanding of reality. The Platonic worldview argued for a distrust of any information gained through the senses; true reality existed in the unseen world of Ideal Forms, and what we experienced in our daily lives were only appearances and imitations of these Forms. But thinkers in the seventeenth century, such as Galileo, Kepler, Newton, and Descartes, argued that reality lies in the perceivable world, and that our ideas appear to us as images based on sense perceptions. While Descartes (1639) is justly famous for his mistrust of the senses and a total dependence on thinking as the basis for self-understanding ("I think, therefore I am"), he worked through his ideas to the point where he ultimately realized that his ability to see the world was in fact his guarantee that he existed:

> For if I judge that the wax exists from the fact that I see it, it certainly follows still more evidently that I exist myself, from the mere fact that I see it. For it might be that what I see is not really wax; it might be as well that I do not even have eyes for seeing something: but it cannot happen that when I see, or when I think I see (which I no longer distinguish from seeing), I who am thinking am not something.

So we connect the dots: Descartes argued that our capacity to see things in the world guarantees that we exist and also provides us with knowledge about that world; the things we perceive visually become internal images that we work on (process, sort, theorize, etc.) with our reason and emotion. We then project these thoughts back out onto the world as ideals.

As this visual turn has taken hold, we have invested more and more heavily in the importance of vision and visual images to convey knowledge about the world, but also to connect us with that world through our own processing of visual images into internal **mental models**. The images in the *Orbis Pictus* or a nineteenth-century book about Australia gave children information about a world they'd never seen, and they transformed that information into ideas and knowledge about the world, whether those ideas were true or not. Pierre Bourdieu (1991: 166, 170) represents the logical extension of Descartes's system by arguing that today, the media has the power to "construct reality"; that is, "a power of constituting the given through utterances, of making people see and believe, of confirming and transforming the vision of the world and thus the world itself." Thus this historical turn in the realm of ideas—that seeing is not just believing, but *knowing* the world through our vision of it—has particular relevance to the contemporary practice of sharing picturebooks with children; through picturebooks, we offer children knowledge about the world, regardless of whether that knowledge is accurate or complete. The question then becomes: what sort of knowledge, especially social knowledge, are they taking in, processing, and then projecting back onto the world as truth?

It has become a critical commonplace that "children need to see themselves in books." As a commonplace, though, that claim is rarely interrogated or explained. American author and educator Nancy Larrick, for instance, in her landmark 1965 article "The All-White World of Children's Books," says this: "Across the country, 6,340,000 nonwhite children are learning to read and to understand the American way of life in books which either omit them entirely or scarcely mention them. There is no need to elaborate upon the damage—much of it irreparable—to the Negro child's personality" (63). I would argue that this *is* a need to elaborate, and that the visual turn of the seventeenth century plays a large role in understanding the critical importance of representation of nonwhite, non-able-bodied children in their visual media. If visual images are our main source of knowledge about the world, then a lack of representation in those visual images can have a profound impact on children's ability to feel connected to the world in which they are expected to perform. Media critic George Gerbner (1972: 43) claims that "representation in the fictional world signifies social existence, [therefore] absence means symbolic annihilation." While Descartes argued that the act of seeing and thinking about what he had seen guaranteed his existence in the world, being represented and being seen in today's mediated culture is what confers symbolic and thus social existence (think, for instance, of the internet meme, "pics or it didn't happen"). This is why the representation, and particularly the visual representation, of diverse characters is so crucial in contemporary picturebooks, illustrated texts, and graphic narratives.

Market demand, new print and digital technologies, and this post-Enlightenment way of thinking about the importance of the visual image have come together in contemporary culture to produce a range of illustrated forms that stretch across the spectrum of children's and YA literature and into adult literature as well. Traditional picturebooks that contain words and text working together to tell a single story are just one form to consider. There are wordless picturebooks, alphabet books, movable and pop-up books, wimmelbooks (loosely translated from the German as "teeming picturebooks," these feature crowded scenes that ask readers to find things or construct stories from the activities depicted), **early concept books**, poetry picturebooks, informational picturebooks, illustrated novels, and various other types of graphic narratives. Some of these forms, such as the wordless picturebook, *The Arrival* (Tan 2006), are both challenging and accessible to readers of various ages. While Tan's book tells the story of a man leaving his family to immigrate to a new city where he doesn't know the language or the customs, a preschooler, immigrant or not, might relate to the abstract and concrete depictions of the man's fears and alienation through his or her own experience of entering school for the first time. An older reader, on the other hand, might focus more specifically on the immigrant experience as an outsider or insider to that experience, thinking through the emotional effects of the loss of home and the practical needs to find shelter, food, employment, companionship, and a sense of belonging in a place where nothing is familiar.

While Tan's book is conceptually accessible for a range of readers at different levels of development, Bettina Kümmerling-Meibauer and Jörg Meibauer (2011) point to other picturebooks, such as the experimental Pop Art books of the 1970s, that, though explicitly marketed to children, may miss their mark as engaging and transgressing boundaries simply because they don't offer enough cognitive or affective tags for children to latch on to in the first place. Therefore, instead of being defamiliarizing or estranging in an artistic way, such books are just experienced as strange, and fall into the category of curiosities, or picturebooks for teens or young adults. Books that address their audiences on more than one conceptual, artistic, and/ or narrative level, however, are often called crossover picturebooks (see Beckett 2012). Such books present a theoretical challenge to those who don't accept the kinship model of childhood discussed in Chapter 2, but also a more practical challenge for teachers and librarians who want to be attentive to the **developmental ages** and abilities of young people while offering them opportunities to reach for new ideas. But the point is, as Barbara Kiefer (2011) notes, that picturebooks have become an attractive format for the artist at play, and as such they are not something to be put away at a particular age or stage of development in favor of print texts.

In addition to crossover picturebooks, comics, graphic novels, and other densely illustrated texts have become something of a cause célèbre in the world of contemporary children's and YA publishing and scholarship. Comics have a long history as controversial reading fare for young people; in 1954, the United States Senate Subcommittee on Juvenile Delinquency, taking seriously the claims of psychiatrist Frederic Wertham (1954) that the reading of comics led to juvenile delinquency, poor body image for girls, and interest in homosexuality for boys, held hearings on the appropriateness and possible corrupting influence of the popular horror and crime comics of the day. The result was the development of the Comics Code Authority by the industry itself to self-police content and thus forestall government regulation. Librarians and teachers also rejected comics, believing that in addition to questionable content, they encouraged the use of slang and bad grammar (the horror!). Over the years, however, comics remained popular with young (and old) readers, and have achieved a legitimacy that testifies to the important role of images in storytelling. Scott McCloud (1994: 9) offers this definition of comics:

> **comics** (kom'iks) **n.** plural in form, used with a singular verb. **1.** Juxtaposed pictorial and other images in deliberate sequence, intended to convey information and/or to produce an aesthetic response in the viewer.

McCloud elaborates on his definition by arguing that today's comics participate in the full range of storytelling **genres** and artistic styles, using whatever materials a creator chooses. Contemporary graphic novels (which use the comics form but are published as stand-alone books) span the range of **genres** that we will discuss in subsequent chapters, including realistic and speculative fiction, traditional folk stories and epic narratives, and various kinds of creative nonfiction. As a result, their nomenclature is still in flux, with some critics preferring the term "graphic narrative" instead of "graphic novel". It should also be noted that graphic narratives are crossing not only **genres** but age groups as well. From simple stories with limited vocabulary that support new readers, to energetic historical and contemporary narratives for middle graders, to fiction and nonfiction that address the social problems of teens and emerging adults, graphic narratives have overcome their bad reputation among educators and are now seen as a **form** that combines engagement with an opportunity to promote **multimodal** literacies and develop literary competencies.

Indeed, today's graphic narratives transcend boundaries between the enduring popular art form of serial comic books that proved so attractive to young people in the early twentieth century and the classics that the literary elite admire and wish to pass on to young people as a cultural heritage. Graphic novelist Gareth Hinds, for instance, has taken as his subjects works such as *Beowulf* (2007), *The Merchant of Venice* (2008), *King Lear* (2009), *The Odyssey* (2010), and *Macbeth* (2015). His works are self-conscious apprentice texts for young readers, with notes on his process of adaptation as well as guidelines for how to read the images. These guidelines sometimes make strong arguments in favor of the **form** itself; for instance, he notes how some of the scenes in *Macbeth* are actually more effective in comics that they are on stage; an imaginary dagger or hovering ghost, for instance, can come off as cheesy in a stage production, while an illustrator can use color, shading, perspective shifts, and blurred panel outlines to indicate an unreal presence in contrast with the flesh-and-blood characters. The use of the **form** proves similarly effective in Chris Duffy's edited collection, *Above the Dreamless Dead: World War I in Poetry and Comics* (2014). This collection puts the poetry and songs of the "trench poets" in the hands of various comics artists. The gaps between and movement represented within the panels highlight the significance of the lineation of the poetry, while the pictures and fonts heighten the atmospherics and draw out the **irony** and trauma implicit in the verbal imagery. These visual qualities enhance readers' understanding and appreciation of the poetry.

How to study picturebooks and other illustrated narratives

Given this incredibly broad range of image-based or image-assisted literature, literary and cultural critics, **multimodal** theorists, and education practitioners and theorists are rapidly expanding the methodologies for their critical study as well. Gillian Rose (2012: 19) suggests that there are three areas to consider in the interpretation of visual images: "the site of *production*, which is where an image is made; the site of the *image* itself, which is its visual content; and the site where the image encounters its spectators or users, or what this book will call its *audiencing*." She further specifies that there are three aspects worth considering within each of these sites: the technological, which refers not only to how an image is made but also to how it is disseminated and displayed; the compositional, which includes its content and materials and its relation to other texts; and the social, which is a broad category that can include any and all of the interpersonal meanings that flow between authorial intent and audience reception.

The theoretical perspectives of our critical theorists in the bathroom conversation in Chapter 3 remain relevant within Rose's conceptualization of visual methodologies.

However, the elements and the modalities within and between the methodologies render the distinctions we have made between them kaleidoscopic, which is appropriate considering the multifaceted nature of sequential art and visual storytelling. Throughout these next sections, I will make a mention of various critics who approach the picturebook and other sorts of illustrated texts from various perspectives; these references serve as both recommended research sites and mentor texts for developing your own investigations. While I summarize some of the methods these researchers have developed and provide some examples of how a particular element might work, I don't go into detail or advocate for any single approach. Instead, I point you to the main things you should pay close attention to as you read a picturebook or do research from a particular perspective, and then offer an example of how you might do a close reading of one aspect of a picturebook's design in the case study that follows the chapter.

Focus on production

To build our understanding of how your natural inclinations might support research interests in the study of visual texts, let's start with Siobhan, our **bibliographic critic**. With her interest in establishing the text, she is likely to be interested in getting to the source of its production—looking at working sketches; reading and perhaps conducting interviews with artists; thinking about how technologies and techniques, from pencil to paint to collage to Photoshop, enable, constrain, and transform an artist's vision of his or her subject; and more generally, considering the fate of the picturebook across changing technologies of production. Critics like Leonard Marcus (2012) and Phil Nel (2003, 2012) research and/or interview makers of picturebooks to gain insight into how their lives and cultural milieus intersect with their production. Nathalie op de Beeck (2010), on the other hand, focuses her attention more generally on how picturebooks of the early twentieth century expose ambiguities between nostalgia and a desire for progress. Margaret Mackey takes a wholly different tack in some of her research, investigating how children's picturebooks get disseminated and transformed across spin-offs and merchandising (2011b), what her own **multimodal** interactions with the texts of childhood can tell us about the development of literacy, and how print narratives are transformed as they are disseminated through other kinds of image-based media (2007, 2011a).

In addition to studies by literary critics, many illustrators of children's books have websites that offer insight and even tutorials into the methods they use to create their books. Classic texts such as Joseph Schwarz's *Ways of the Illustrator* (1982) and Uri Shulevitz's *Writing with Pictures* (1985) still inspire picturebook artists, as do newer texts like Martin Salisbury's *Illustrating Children's Books* (2004) and Karenanne Knight's *The Picture Book Maker: The Art of the Children's Picture Book Writer and Illustrator* (2014). Surveying these texts can form a foundation for critical analysis on the basis of the technological and compositional aspects of production.

Some related issues with regard to the social production of texts would be of interest to our **rhetorical critic**, Tamara. Recall that Tamara was interested in Evan's body language and style of delivery, particularly whether his message seemed to be a private one, even though it was delivered in a generic form of address. Such interest, broadly understood, might lead in multiple directions in terms of the production of texts. For instance, it might lead to an investigation of the forms in which texts were originally transmitted to their audiences. Mathew O. Grenby (2009) argues that children's literature criticism is fixated on the origin stories of texts; that is, there is something peculiarly self-validating about a book when we find out that it has been written for a specific child. This fascination with the person-to-person transmission of texts might thus prompt an inquiry into how the social identity of the artist affected the venue he or she has chosen. Beatrix Potter, for instance, was born into a wealthy family that nurtured her natural artistic talent as a child through private instruction in drawing and painting with watercolor. The summers she spent in the countryside shaped her interest in the natural sciences and conservation, and her close observation of the natural world and the small pets she kept led to the finely detailed illustrations that fill her books. She wrote the first version of many of her tales of Peter Rabbit and his fellow creatures in picture letters to the young children of her former governess. When she published her imaginative tales, they appeared in small texts for small hands, which was the currently fashionable publishing trend. All of these features of an artist's life and culture feed into a complex understanding of the production and transmission of his or her stories, opening up multiple avenues of exploration, including archival research into original materials.

What is also interesting from the production angle of approach is to realize that contemporary authors often have little control over who illustrates their story or the final book design. An author submits a manuscript to an editor, but the editor is usually the one who chooses an illustrator. The book's design, including such things as font style, placement of words with respect to images, cover design, end papers, etc., is handled by yet another person employed by the publisher. The distinctiveness of these processes is invisible in the final product, and not much critical work has been undertaken by children's literature critics with regard to this aspect of book-making, though it is an area gaining traction in literary studies, especially with regard to the collaborative work of producing a graphic narrative. However, picturebook artists are using their websites and interviews to discuss at least some of their own thought processes and artistic techniques and processes on the way to publication, as does John Rocco in the talkback to this chapter.

Focus on image

Another direction that Tamara's interest in multimodal rhetoric could take in the study of picturebooks might be to focus on the embodied rhetoric depicted through the images themselves. Images speak to us emotionally, intellectually, and socially, but their messages are not transparent; they are mediated through our embodied memories and experiences as well as our experiences with other texts in our culture. And these texts are also mediated through artistic styles, trends, and media that build on one another and go in and out of fashion. Because contemporary culture is so image-saturated, educators at all levels feel a strong imperative to teach themselves and their students how to analyze and interpret images so as to understand their persuasive force, especially when they are combined with other forms of expression, including words and music.

One of the ways that picturebooks and other illustrated texts facilitate greater understanding of **multimodal discourse** is through the use of gesture and facial expression. Mo Willems, for instance, has created a wildly expressive yet simply rendered character in his pigeon books, beginning with *Don't Let the Pigeon Drive the Bus* (2003). As the eponymous pigeon attempts to persuade the audience to let him drive a bus against the express wishes of the bus driver, he cycles through the various types of rhetorical appeals and fallacies. As he shifts from logos ("I'll tell you what: I'll just steer.") to ethos ("My cousin Herb drives a bus almost every day!"), to pathos ("I never get to do anything!"), his body posture and facial expressions change, highlighting for readers the fact that rhetorical effectiveness is a full body affair for both the persuader and the one whom the rhetoric is supposed to persuade. By asking child readers to attend carefully to the embodied depiction of emotion, adult interlocutors can help them develop their **Theory of Mind**; young viewers can make inferences about what characters are feeling and thinking based on their gestures, body postures, and facial expressions, and test those inferences against the information provided through the words. Such discussion can also help them develop a critical understanding of how visual rhetoric works in conjunction with text as a mechanism of persuasion that coaxes them to feel a certain way about a character or situation.

This sort of attention given to how pictures and text work together necessarily draws together a wide variety of interdisciplinary research methods in order to serve the interests of **textual** or **formalist critics** like Rebecca; they are keen to analyze **form**, but also to understand how **form** contributes to meaning. Analysis of how the images contribute to the atmosphere and storytelling in picturebooks began in a rather subjective way with the thoughtful review work of Betsy Hearne and Zena Sutherland in the late 1970s and early 1980s, but at that point it lacked a technical vocabulary to support sustained critical work. As a result, most reviews and studies of picturebooks gave the pictures short shrift, focusing on the story told through the words, and, distilling that even further, adopting an educational focus that concentrated on the "lesson" of the story. William Moebius (1986), Perry Nodelman (1988), Molly Bang (1991), and Jane Doonan (1992) were among the first to introduce critical **aesthetic** and communicative frameworks for the serious study of picturebooks. These pioneers in the criticism of picturebooks as works of literature rather than pedagogical tools recognized that methodologies rooted primarily in art theory and developed for the appreciation of still, isolated images could not account for the narrative structure of art that is intended to move a reader through a story. Hence they began to borrow from **semiotics**, the study of the signs and symbols of human communication. Nodelman also drew from psychology and literary theory to develop a comprehensive and usable model from which to study picturebooks as a total "experience" for the reader. With the tools and methodologies developed by these theorists, children's picturebook criticism bloomed alongside the growth of the form itself, inspiring similar eclectic work that enables sophisticated close readings of not only how pictures work but how they interact with text to produce what Larry Sipe (1998) has called the "synergy" and David Lewis (2001) calls the "ecology" of the picturebook. Other critics (Agosto 1999; Nikolajeva and Scott 2001) have coined other terms and developed taxonomies to name different types of word–picture interaction and explore the complexities of how it operates. Do the pictures replicate, extend, or contradict the words, for instance? Because that relationship may vary over the course of a text, however, I find Lewis's metaphor of a constantly shifting **ecosystem** most useful in analyzing a complete book.

This concern to approach picturebooks from an integrative perspective has sparked a more recent model called **multimodal discourse analysis (MDA)**. **MDA** innovates on the work of Gunther Kress and Theo van Leeuwen (2006), who developed a "grammar of visual design." Introduced to the study of picturebooks through Lewis (2001), the model has been considerably expanded by linguistics researchers Claire Painter, J. R. Martin, and Len Unsworth (2013), and Arsenio Jesus Moy Guijarro (2014), and turned into useful pedagogy by Frank Serafini (2014). This methodology proposes that all texts carry three types of meaning, called metafunctions. Ideational meaning concerns how a text represents a real or imagined world. Interpersonal meaning refers to the relationships and roles between the characters and also between the book's creator and the reader. Textual meaning focuses on how a text is organized—the layout and composition of the pages with regard to how the images and figures within them are arranged, if and how borders are used, and how the text is positioned with regard to the images. All of the decisions that authors and illustrators make emerge out of what the form makes available to them, and the three metafunctions work in tandem to create the overall experience of the picturebook. While Painter et al. establish a comprehensive system for analyzing picturebooks in their capacity as apprentice texts that enable children to develop bimodal literacies, they focus exclusively on the texts themselves; Guijarro, on the other hand, includes attention to the likely capacities of young readers as they develop their abilities to understand how texts work. Serafini expands the applicability of **MDA** across picturebooks, graphic narratives, film, and digital media, offering a comprehensive overview followed by unit plans that teachers can adapt for their purposes in teaching **multimodal** literacy.

So what do textual critics focus on when they perform analyses of picturebooks and other sequential art narratives? Well, everything really. As we have noted, the elements of book design, which include font style, end papers, cover art, orientation (landscape or portrait), size and shape, special features such as die-cuts, flaps, fold-out pages, and the inclusion and placement of paratextual features such as dedications, author and illustrator notes and bios, and copyright data require interpretation for their total effect on meaning.

Consider *The Watertower*, by Gary Crew (1999), a picturebook in the horror genre where a town is overshadowed by the menacing presence of a water tower of unknown origin. Two boys, Bubba and Spike, decide to escape the heat by swimming in the tower, but when Spike leaves Bubba alone for a while, Bubba emerges from his swim irrevocably changed. The story is creepy and disorienting, with no answers as to what power the water tower has or the exact nature of the threat, but it is clear that the townsfolk, and ultimately Bubba, are in the thrall of the sinister tower because its shape is reflected in the pupils of their eyes. The book's design enhances the sense of mystery and disorientation by forcing readers to gradually rotate the book 270 degrees as they read, following a circular pattern that is imprinted on the outside of the tower itself. The suggestion is that the reader, too, is sucked into the same hypnotic control the water tower exerts over the rest of the town. One page turn evokes a literal jump when, after settling into page after page of dark pictures on a black background, the next **opening** suddenly reveals Bubba's clearly frightened, bright peachy-orange face in a **full-bleed**, double-page spread. A dominant **motif** in the book is the presence of concentric circles that radiate out from the water tower into the air around it but also that form ripples on the dark green surface of the water within; that this pattern is replicated through the movement required by the book and in the image on the back cover heightens the effect of feeling totally enclosed within the mysterious pull of the water tower. Creepy!

In addition to considering the features of the book's overall design, critics look at the elements that make up the individual images. Color, shape, linework, and artistic media and style all create different impressions on readers, and while these impressions are subjective, they tend to follow certain embodied and cultural patterns of meaning. Color, for instance, carries both cultural and individual meanings. Studies have shown that our ability to distinguish color depends to a great degree on the words we have for it (Adelson 2005), a finding that relates to what we have learned in the previous chapter through our chocolate experiment. In the English-speaking world, we distinguish color by **hue**, **saturation**, and **tone**. **Hue** refers to the color itself, that is, its position on the spectrum that identifies it as blue, red, green, etc., or even blue-green, or reddish-orange. We divide the spectrum into warm and cool **hues**; warm **hues** are reds, oranges, and yellows, and cool **hues** are greens, blues, and purples. Brown is also a warm **hue**, since it results from a combination of more warm **hues** than cool ones. **Saturation** refers to purity of a **hue**—we say that a color is fully saturated when it is at its most intense. By contrast, **tone** refers to **hues** that have been mixed with white, black, or gray to change, say, pure red into burgundy or pure blue into sky blue. These aspects of color translate into both idiosyncratic and more generalizable preferences. For instance, older children and adults tend to prefer cool **hues** to warm ones, whereas children up to age eight or nine tend to prefer fully saturated, high-contrast colors regardless of whether they are warm or cool (Winner 1982: 114), a distinction that we should bear in mind when we make evaluative judgments about artistic choices in picturebooks. For instance, what adults find "garish" might be very appealing to younger eyes (which is not to say it isn't still garish, but we might use a term that is less judgy).

Colors also work in relationship with each other to create different effects; high contrast between fully saturated colors ramps up the energy of an illustration, while **tones** with low contrast create a more sedate or emotionally consistent atmosphere. The **openings** of *Goodnight Moon* (Brown 1947) alternate between bright, warm **hues** and gray **tones**, causing viewers' pupils to dilate and constrict and their eyes to blink as they turn each page. This creates a visual pattern that ideally combines with the soothing rhythm and content of the words to literally cause children to feel sleepy. Bang (1991) points out how contrasting colors can generate emotions, connect characters, and create dynamic tension. While particular **hues** carry specific meanings in various cultures, our experience of **tone** is also closely related to our embodied experience. Darkly colored backgrounds, for instance, tend to be scarier for humans because we see better in the daytime, but a bland, featureless expanse, even if it's rendered in a pale **tone**, can also be frightening because it offers no orienting horizon or perspective. It's worth taking a minute here to pause and look at a picturebook and assess it in terms of how you respond emotionally to the colors; even better, share that experience with someone else and see how your impressions compare and contrast.

Color can also help readers keep track of a character through transformation or disguise, as in Gerald McDermott's *Raven: A Trickster Tale from the Pacific Northwest* (1993). In this trickster tale, Raven transforms from a bird to a pine needle to a child. Such shifts could be very confusing for an inexperienced reader, but all readers need some consistency in order to recognize characters as they appear and reappear in a story. McDermott maintains such consistency in his character by replicating the colors and patterns of Raven's bird form in the clothes he wears when he is transformed into a boy. Strategic use of color also solves a tricky moral dilemma in this tale: Raven's goal in changing into a boy is to steal the sun from the house of the Sky Chief and give it to the Tlingit people who live in perpetual dark and cold. While young readers may object to stealing as unequivocally wrong no matter how good the intentions, the box in which the sun is hidden bears the same colors and marks as Raven, so that his taking possession of it seems less like stealing and more like reclaiming something that is rightfully his in the first place.

In **MDA**, color works across the three metafunctions in different ways. For instance, in terms of ideational meaning, color often corresponds in expected ways to the things it represents in the real world: green grass, white snow, various skin tones. When it doesn't, it indicates that the world represented is not necessarily this one, giving readers an important clue as to how to approach the story. In terms of textual meaning, Painter et al. suggest that "colour may be used contrastively to highlight or foreground some element within a composition to make it especially salient for the viewer, or repetitions of a colour may be used cohesively as a kind of visual rhyme to link different parts of a narrative" (2013: 35). This use of color can be readily seen in Gene Luen Yang's paired graphic novels *Boxers & Saints* (2013). Yang uses color selectively throughout these books to highlight the two main characters' different belief systems. In *Boxers,* Bao falls in love with the gods of the operas presented at the local fairs in his village. These gods are portrayed in costumes and masks that all feature vivid colors, including fully saturated reds, that do not appear in the settings and clothing of his normal life and thus contrast sharply with the pale tones of the other images. When he fights as a member of the Society of the Righteous and Harmonious Fists, he believes that he and his fellow warriors are possessed by their gods, and the pictures show them taking their form as they fight. Their outlines when they are gods are no different from the outlines of the other characters, indicating that their god forms are as real as their human ones. By contrast, Vibiana, a Chinese convert to Christianity in *Saints*, has visions of Joan of Arc. The artwork in *Saints* is entirely rendered in various sepia tones with black linework on the characters, except for the scenes depicting Joan and, later, Christ, which are yellow and gold with darker gold outlines. Joan also has an aura—a fuzzy halo of gold—surrounding her on the cover, indicating that she does not share the same reality as Vibiana. This differential use of color highlights the different relationship the two characters have with their gods; Bao's experience of his gods is material and immediate, while Vibiana's reflects her vacillation between faith and doubt. Readers tend to be sympathetic to both characters, but most have an easier time understanding and connecting with Vibiana's experience insofar as it shows, through color and linework, a more typically Western attitude toward religion as something we experience outside ordinary sensory experience. Color's most immediate role, then, is to create an affective, interpersonal link with the reader. Color affects our emotions, and thus contributes to the ambience of a picturebook in very specific and powerful ways.

Bang's (1991) other principles refer to shape, position, and relative size of pictorial elements, and these accord with assessments by Moebius (1986) and Nodelman (1988). Generally speaking, rounded shapes make us feel more secure, while pointed or elongated shapes signify threats. Larger shapes convey a greater sense of power than smaller ones. Horizontal shapes and planes induce a sense of calm and stability, while vertical ones suggest energy and power. Put those vertical shapes on a diagonal or tilt a horizontal shape and you get the impression of movement and instability, which induces in the reader a need to mentally complete the implied action. **MDA** brings the notion of **vectors** to bear here, both on how the shapes and figures are positioned and how they relate to one another through visible or invisible lines of connection. For instance, one character looking at another creates an imaginary line or vector connecting the two. Figures might also be physically inclined toward or away from each other, indicating a relationship that may or may not be reinforced by the words, and thus require the reader to construct meaning based on the way the images and words work together.

Kress and van Leeuwen (2006) suggest that figures and situations that appear on the left side of a page represent what is given or ordinary about a situation, while what appears on the right is potential or new, and Nodelman (1988) stresses that this positioning has a cultural significance as well: in alphabetic systems that read from left to right, characters facing or moving in that direction are perceived to be making progress, while characters facing or moving from right to left are experiencing obstacles or impediments. Kress and van Leeuwen also suggest that elements that appear on the lower half of an image are experienced as real, whereas the ones on the top half are conceived as ideal. All of these interpretations of shape, position, and vectors draw on **conceptual metaphors**—metaphors that have their basis in embodied experience—and thus their interpretation is largely situated as interpersonal. They are certainly a good place to start with image analysis, but it bears reminding that picturebooks develop their own codes and processes as they go along, so that your interpretive results may vary.

The style of character depiction is another salient feature of interpersonal meaning. Painter et al. (2013) argue that the style of character drawing affects how we feel about characters and the degree to which we engage with their stories. A minimalist style, for instance, is one that uses simple circles or ovals for heads, dots or blank circles for eyes, and only schematic accuracy in proportion—you might think of it as variations on a stick figure. Generic depictions add a few more details, such as shading to indicate musculature and dimension. Naturalistic depictions offer the most detail; the characters give the impression of being real, individual people. Each of these ways of drawing characters tends to correspond to a particular type of text and evoke a different level of emotional engagement. Books that are primarily "message-y" and focus on social commentary or critique, such as Shel Silverstein's *The Giving Tree* (1964), tend to use a minimalist style; readers maintain a level of emotional distance in order to appreciate or glean the main point of the story. This style is often used in humorous texts which, as we have noted in Chapter 4, usually encode some form of protest against social rules or abuses. The generic style is more often deployed in the service of injunction, "implicitly expecting child readers to see themselves in the protagonist role and to 'be/do like this'" (Painter et al. 2013: 33). The naturalistic style, which features characters and settings most like real life, asks for the highest level of emotional investment so that readers can be led through the events sympathetically and come to an understanding of right and wrong through the specific story situation rather than as a message applicable to life in general.

Linework and borders also draw much attention in picturebook criticism. Thinner lines, including outlines of objects and figures as well as detail work, suggest more agility and movement, while thicker lines indicate stasis or confinement (Moebius 1986: 150), although this is not always the case with artists like Chris Raschka or Yuyi Morales, whose thick linework enhances the sense of movement (so this is why we need to treat each book as its own ecosystem). Jagged lines indicate strong emotions, usually negative ones like anger or fear, while fluid, wavy lines suggest powerful organic flows that herald change. Lines also enclose pictures in borders. Borders and framing act as powerful **signifiers** in picturebooks and are always worth paying attention to. Framed pictures, for instance, give a sense of an enclosed, fictional world; the reader is positioned on the outside of the frame as a little god surveying a total but limited world. Unframed pictures, especially **full-bleed** ones that extend to the edges of the page, suggest an insider's perspective; the reader is positioned inside a world without visible borders, much like the real world. When a picture extends beyond a previously established frame, it usually indicates that a **metaphor** of some sort is being enacted; a situation is getting out of hand, a character has escaped a confining situation, or you as a reader are being invited into the world to take up a perspective as an insider. Max's imaginative wildness, for instance, overflows the boundaries of his mother's authority in *Where the Wild Things Are* (Sendak 1963).

When a character does breaks out of a framed picture, as happens in David Wiesner's *The Three Pigs* (2001), the reader is forced to confront and acknowledge the fictionality of the framed world; it loses its totalized aspect and becomes unstable. This sort of frame-breaking is one of the hallmarks of postmodern picturebooks, a name given to picturebooks that go beyond being merely playful to actually challenging the traditional frontiers and conventions of storytelling. Think of frames here as metaphorical rather than physically depicted as lines on a page: a traditional story is "framed" in that it asks you to enter its world and stay a while. Even if it's a world where animals talk and wear clothes, the story generally unfolds in linear time, and stays within the boundaries, rules, and logic established by the world they create, no matter how zany those rules may be in comparison to the real world. A **postmodern** picturebook, on the other hand, breaks boundaries and exposes the artifice of its creation. This self-conscious reminder that the book is a story is called **metafiction**, and it is accomplished in various ways. Characters may talk back to their illustrators, for instance, or move in and out of other stories within their story, blurring the lines between narrative space and time. Characters may also acknowledge the reader, as do Gerald and Piggie in Mo Willems's *We are in a Book!* (2010). Piggie goes on to point out features of book design such as page numbers and speech bubbles. The Little Red Hen in Jon Scieszka and Lane Smith's *The Stinky Cheese Man and other Fairly Stupid Tales* (1992) similarly calls explicit attention to the book design, complaining that the

ISBN bar code on the cover is ugly, which speaks to a wider critique of the commercialization of children's culture. The stories within this book are all parodies, another **postmodern** form popular in picturebooks. Parodies call attention to the conventions of traditional storytelling and culturally accepted morals and values by making fun of them, and they are somewhat controversial in literature for children, because they require familiarity with the original works in order to understand the jokes. They are wildly popular with older children and teens, however, as they resituate the locus of authority in storytelling.

In terms of **form**, however, it is important to understand that **postmodern** picturebooks aim at disrupting the kinds of knowledge that the visual world of traditional picturebooks and other media present to children. Sylvia Pantaleo and Lawrence R. Sipe (2008) have edited a collection of essays devoted to the various techniques and concerns that characterize **postmodern** picturebooks, and Cherie Allan (2012) provides a comprehensive study of the ways in which such books challenge modes of representation and authorized versions of history, promoting diversity as a positive value. By introducing the notion that the boundaries between worlds and stories within those worlds can be breached, by playing with the conventions of traditional storytelling, and by surfacing the mechanisms whereby visual knowledge reinforces frames that exclude nonnormative subjects, **postmodern** picturebooks use provocative images to expose the expectations and affect the worldview of audiences.

Focus on audience

Picturebooks have a long history of use as pedagogical tools to teach morals and convey information. More recently, their influence on audience identity and the acquisition of **aesthetic** literacies and **ideological** frameworks has become a focus of critical work. Researchers are interested in sharing picturebooks with children to assess their actual, as opposed to theoretical and speculative, effects on developing readers. They are particularly interested in how children account for books where the text and the pictures tell contradictory or asymmetrical stories. They thus begin by performing close textual analyses of the books themselves, and then pose questions aimed at discerning how readers of various ages make sense of challenging picturebooks. Most, like the essays in Janet Evans's edited collection, *Talking Beyond the Page* (2009), and Evelyn Arizpe and Morag Styles's *Children Reading Pictures: Interpreting Visual Texts* (2002), focus on young readers of primary school and above, but there is one notable collection that focuses on books for the very young: Bettina Kümmerling-Meibauer's *Emergent Literacy: Children's Books from 0 to 3* (2011).

Another way of approaching image-based literature through a concern for audience is to read texts like our **contextual critic**, Beatrix. You'll remember that

Beatrix was suspicious of Evan because of what she knew about him prior to his interaction with Carly, and sought to read his words in light of what she knew about how he had acted in other contexts. Like Beatrix, **contextual critics** of children's picturebooks see these books as conveyors of **ideologies** that go far beyond the present situation of one single story. They are therefore concerned with how the world is represented to children, particularly when the representations are distorted mirrors that don't reflect actual conditions, or when representations rely on damaging stereotypes. In the early 1970s, for instance, some social scientists seeking the roots of society's racist and sexist attitudes turned their attention to children's books to see what messages about the world those books were sending to young readers. A landmark 1972 study (Weitzman et al.) found a huge disparity of representation between images of boys and girls in picturebooks; in a five-year period of Caldecott award-winning books, boys were pictured ten times more than girls. Other researchers focused on the content rather than the numbers, and found that boys were more likely to be portrayed as active and successful in problem-solving, while girls were more often portrayed as needing help or being dependent on others. More recently, in 2011, McCabe et al. examined 5,618 (!) children's books published throughout the twentieth century and found that boys appeared twice as frequently as girls in titles, and 1.6 times more than girls as central characters. But, you might argue, that was then, this is now; surely it isn't still the case in the twenty-first century! To which I would challenge you to go to the nearest bookseller and do your own counts. Pay particular attention to animal characters, where the predominance of male characters is even greater than it is for humans. And while Thomas Crisp and Brittany Hiller (2011) have noted an uptick in ungendered characters in Caldecott winners, empirical research shows that most adult readers gender such textually ungendered characters male when they read these books to children (Arthur and White 1996).

The Beatrixes of the critical world have found the numbers related to race and ethnicity even more dismal. The Cooperative Children's Book Center at University of Wisconsin-Madison generates annual statistics on the numbers of books published each year by and about people of color; until very recently, their findings report that fewer than 14 percent of the books published in the United States in any given year are by or about nonwhite **protagonists**. Even factoring in that approximately half of all of the picturebooks published in a year feature nonhuman **protagonists**, CCBC director K. T. Horning (2013) found that "children of colour make up 7.8 percent of the total number of picturebook protagonists." What is interesting about these findings is that the raw numbers have gone down since the late 1990s, despite more recent calls through social media such as the #weneeddiversebooks movement. The findings of the McCabe study may point to one reason why: in their sweep through the twentieth century, they discovered that there was more gender equity in the books during periods of social activism, that is, prior to the 1930s during the first wave of feminism, and during the heyday of the second wave from 1970 to 2000. Such findings are consonant with the CCBC statistics on periods of social activism and multicultural literature, indicating that when the culture pays explicit attention to these sorts of inequities, things improve a little, but in the end, children's picturebooks, as well as graphic novels for older readers, are dominated by representations of white, cisgendered males.

Conclusion

There is no question that we live in an image-saturated culture. We accept images, even unreal ones, as sites of knowledge about the world and our place in it. This makes the critical analysis of the texts that apprentice readers into the codes of visual culture an incredibly serious cultural imperative, but it's also an endlessly fascinating joy. I encourage you to follow your theoretical inclinations in the direction of research that interests you most, diving into the sources that I have included throughout this chapter, and scouring their bibliographies for even more resources. Most of all, however, I would encourage you to continue to read picturebooks and graphic novels with an eye to your own pleasure, but also with the understanding that these books are providing children with knowledge about themselves and the world. Looking at pictures gives preliterate as well as newly reading children a **multimodal** site of meaning-making while a more competent reader is sharing the words, and the children actively make connections and associations not only between the words they are hearing and the pictures in front of them, but between those words and images and their own experiences and memories. They find the joy of affirmation in seeing aspects of their lives represented in addition to learning how their inner worlds can be expanded through imagining things that they have never experienced, or seeing objects depicted that don't exist in their everyday environment. And while they don't necessarily *need* illustrations to envision a scene described in words, coupling pictures with words in picturebooks offers a model for doing so, which will serve them well when they encounter text without pictures that they have to make sense of.

Picturebooks and graphic novels offer an implicit apprenticeship into the codes active in visual communication in other media that critical reading seeks to make explicit; they foster visual literacy as well by teaching children how to read the potential action, emotional content, and power dynamics conveyed in and through pictures. This is certainly an essential skill for navigating today's highly visual world, especially as children become both critical consumers of images as well as **prosumers**—that is, people who produce and promote, rather than just consume, visual media through social networks. The problem is that picturebooks start performing this work at a time before children have sophisticated filters or critical awareness of how they are being influenced by the images. Very young children are actively researching category distinctions like gender and racial difference in order to develop a sense of who they are and how the world works, so the images available to them in picturebooks have the potential to be enormously influential in structuring their attitudes through visual representations of how boys and girls of different ethnicities are valued in their culture, and how they can and should interact. By understanding the practices and codes of visual communication from the perspectives of production, image, and audience research, we can guide our visual apprentices toward a greater awareness of how to read (with) pictures.

Extending your study

Reading:

Allan, Cherie. *Playing with Picturebooks: Postmodernism and the Postmodernesque* (Basingstoke: Palgrave Macmillan, 2012).

Clear, readable survey of postmodern aesthetic practices in picturebooks.

Arizpe, Evelyn, and Styles, Morag. *Children Reading Pictures: Interpreting Visual Texts* (London: Routledge, 2003).

Describes a two-year study with children of various ages responding to picturebooks. Offers a nice overview of picturebook theory and Michael J. Parson's theory of aesthetic development.

Lewis, David. *Reading Contemporary Picturebooks: Picturing Text* (New York and London: Routledge, 2001).

Includes discussion of the formal features of modern and postmodern picturebooks as well as exploring how young readers interact with and understand picturebooks.

McCloud, Scott. *Understanding Comics: The Invisible Art* (New York: HarperCollins, 1993).

Indispensable guide to reading and understanding how comics work.

Nodelman, Perry. *Words about Pictures: The Narrative Art of Children's Picture Books* (Athens, GA: University of Georgia Press, 1988).

Essential, comprehensive text for analyzing the formal features of picturebooks from a literary studies perspective.

Painter, Clare, Martin, J. R., and Unsworth, Len. *Reading Visual Narratives: Image Analysis of Children's Picture Books* (Sheffield: Equinox Publishing, LTD., 2013).

Demonstrates a useful new paradigm for understanding picturebooks through multimodal discourse analysis, a branch of systemic-functional theory.

Serafini, Frank. *Reading the Visual: An Introduction to Teaching Multimodal Literacy* (New York: Teachers College Press, 2014).

Reviews and synthesizes recent research in multimodal literacies, and offers unit plans for teaching picturebooks, illustrated novels, graphic novels and comics, advertisements, film, and digital media. Excellent resource for prospective teachers.

Writing:

1 Locate two picturebook versions of a fairytale; one written in the past ten years, one written before then. Analyze the art in each version according to the principles detailed in this chapter regarding color, character depiction, vectors, and shapes. How does the art contribute to the storytelling? Compare the two versions. How do you account for the differences?

2 Read Chapter 3 of Scott McCloud's *Understanding Comics.* Using a graphic novel of your choice, identify the types of closure that appear on 3–5 consecutive pages. Write an essay that discusses how readers will need to fill in the gaps between the panels and how that might affect the pace and understanding of the story.

3 Find two picturebooks that deal with a similar problem, such as bullying, or the death of a pet, or going to school for the first time. Analyze how shape and vectors contribute to the understanding of the story.

4 Look carefully at a picturebook of your choice. What conceptual metaphors of power, comfort, and movement can you find and describe? Pay close attention to the linework and any borders of the pictures. How do you interpret the use of line as a metaphor?

5 Do a careful reading of a picturebook of your choice. Are there any metaphors or use of figurative language? How do the words correspond to the pictures? Is there any sense of irony (words meaning more or the opposite of what they seem to be saying)? In what ways does each author use sentence structure with page turns to keep the story moving? When does the story slow down and how does the use of language (or the absence of language) affect the pace of the story? Because comparisons help you see better, choose another book and consider these same questions in regard to the use of language.

Discussing:

1 How does color affect your response to a picture or a work of art? Do you think this is a culturally conditioned response, and if so, in what ways have culture and language influenced the way you perceive color?

2 When you read a children's picturebook with animal characters behaving like humans, do you tend to think of them as animals or people? Does it make a

difference as to how you understand their actions? If not, why do you think the illustrator chose to use animals instead of people?

3   Ellen Dissanayake (2009) argues that infants and very young children prefer language that demonstrates simplification, exaggeration, repetition, and elaboration. How are the qualities of simplification, exaggeration, repetition, and elaboration used in picturebook art?

4   Characterize the diversity of the books you chose to look at while reading this chapter in terms of gender, embodiment, race, ethnicity. How do they correspond with your own subject position and values? Did you make a conscious decision to include diverse books? Why or why not?

Responding:

1   Get some tracing paper and trace just the shapes and vectors of a picture from a sequence of pictures within a picturebook. Analyze the composition of the figures and vectors and consider how they contribute to the meaning of the story.

2   Using the techniques described on Eric Carle's website, make your own art paper and use it to create an animal of your choice.

3   Using the principles of line, shape, color, and style discussed in the chapter, draw or use other materials to create a visual representation of a character or setting from a nonvisual text. Explain your choices.

Online exploration:

1   Informative site maintained by Denise I. Matulka, featuring slide shows and key definitions and examples of artistic media, elements of picturebooks, and a historical timeline, among other resources. Associated with a fee-based service, but this site is free:
    http://pingb.picturingbooks.com/

2   The professional website of author and picturebook artist, Elizabeth Dulemba. Includes advice for writing and illustrating as well as interviews and guest blog posts with many contemporary illustrators:
    http://dulemba.com/index.html

3   Picturebooks Artists Association Website. Includes sample pictures and links to member sites:
    http://www.picturebookartists.org/

4   The Picturebook Manifesto:
    http://www.thepicturebook.co/

5   Children's Picturebook Database at Miami University. Contains abstracts of
    5,700 picturebooks, search by keywords or browse by categories.
    http://dlp.lib.miamioh.edu/picturebook/
6   A step-by-step guide to one way of doing a picturebook analysis:
    http://comminfo.rutgers.edu/professional-development/childlit/Syllabus/
    pictureanalysis.html

Case Study: The Use of Visual Perspective to Situate Readers

For this case study, I am going to focus on how perspective is deployed
to implicate the reader in an ethical stance in Nan Gregory's *How Smudge
Came* (1995). The story concerns a young woman named Cindy who finds
a stray puppy and struggles to keep it even though the rules of her house
prevent her from having a pet. The cover art is a full-bleed illustration showing
a hand patting the head of a puppy. The vector produced by the hand and the
puppy's head moves the reader's eye up and to the right at a diagonal, but the
fact that we see only the hand reaching down creates the impression that the
reader is the one doing the patting; after all, if I were patting a dog's head, I
would be looking down from above and I might see my hand and the puppy
in the same positions as they are depicted on the cover. This manipulation of
perspective invites readers to identify with Cindy.

The title page and the first opening show Cindy walking through a
rainstorm. Her features are indistinct, and in the second opening she is turned
away from the viewer on the **verso** (the page on the left), while the **recto** (the
page on the right) repeats the cover image. Hence, while we are now looking
at her from the perspective of an observer, our identification has not been
broken and is actually reinforced through the replication of the cover image. It
has also been reinforced by the words. The first line establishes a refrain that
is repeated throughout the book, "If there's one thing that Cindy knows . . . ."
While the narration is in third person, this phrasing and the clipped sentence
structure suggest an inner dialogue; we are given immediate access to
Cindy's self-talk, which strengthens our identification because we are inside
her head.

It is not until the fourth opening that we see Cindy's face as she is being
handed a large piece of layer cake. My personal experience tells me she
has Down syndrome, though it may not be obvious to all readers. Note that
this information was withheld until readers had established a position of
identification with Cindy. Now, though, the hands that hold the cake come
from the lower left side of the page, which shifts the reader's identificatory

(Continued)

position in the book. The hands that are presenting the cake are coming from the same position someone would be in if she were holding the book; in other words, as readers, we are now in the position of the cake holder. The vector of Cindy's gaze is toward that person, and Cindy is holding what the words tell us is a napkin full of stew under the table, away from the implied gaze of the figure holding the cake, but still visible to the reader. Cindy refuses the cake politely, but her refusal still establishes that she is not cooperating with this person. The **recto** of this opening, however, positions the reader at an impossible height looking down on Cindy as she sits on the floor feeding her dog. This combination of images places us in a position of authority over Cindy, authority that she is defying.

The fifth, sixth, and seventh openings show Cindy going about her day and night, and while she is faced out, her eyes are never directed at the reader. It is clear from the context of the words, however, that she lives in a home where she is not allowed to have a dog, and where the authority figure is not related to her. We are on a level with Cindy once again, indicating a sense of being in her space as an equal. At the eighth opening, though, we are returned to the impossibly high perspective, this time looking down on Cindy being scolded by the owner of the arm that offered her cake, Mrs. Watson. We only see the tops of everyone's heads, but we recognize Mrs. Watson by the sleeve of her outstretched hand. At the ninth opening, our perspective has shifted once again: now we are on a level with Cindy. Her face is full-size, perhaps even slightly larger than an adult face, cut in half by the edge of the page, and she is faced out to us. The vector of her gaze is toward the **verso**, where a man is taking her puppy away from her, but the angle is oblique so that she can't really see the puppy. What stands out, though, is the tear falling from her eye.

At this point, we have become implicated into two perspectives for character identification—the perspective of Cindy, and the perspective of Mrs. Watson—and one of outside observer. This stance as an observer positions us to make an ethical decision about whether or not Cindy should be allowed to keep the puppy. When we are first asked to identify with Mrs. Watson, our acceptance of that identification is manipulated in two ways: Up until this moment, we have only seen Cindy in terms of her body postures and hands, so even though the illustrations are naturalistic, we can still identify with her as a person with a body that is similar to ours. But when neurotypical readers get their first indicator that Cindy has Down syndrome through a close-up of her face, they may be distanced from her even if they had identified with her before. We therefore need someone else to identify with, so we accept the position of the person offering cake, which is a nice thing to do. By the tenth opening, however, we have become more sympathetic to Cindy, who has clearly shown that she is capable of taking care of her dog even if she is not allowed to do so by Mrs. Watson. The **verso** of the tenth opening, then, solidifies our stance against Mrs. Watson. Once again we are put in her position with her hand emerging from the bottom left of the page, but this time it is imperiously pointing Cindy up the stairs, accompanied by the all caps text, "'GO TO YOUR ROOM, CINDY.'" Since Cindy has just been crying and had her puppy taken away, this seems unreasonably harsh. For most of the remainder of the book, we are once again set at an equal height with Cindy, even once seeing her face reflected in a window while we don't see her—meaning that we are in the position she would be, making her reflection ours. But our ethical position is clear: we have seen the problem from both sides, and we are not on the side of Mrs. Watson.

There are many aspects to consider in the way this book communicates with the reader; I have limited my discussion to the above perspective in order to show how a close reading of a single aspect might work to guide a reader's empathy over the course of a complete narrative.

Author talkback:

In this talkback, award-winning illustrator John Rocco shares his insights on the choices an illustrator makes to produce images that work in the service of storytelling.

Some Things I've learned About Picturebook Making
By John Rocco

Before embarking on a career in the children's book field, I worked as an art director in the entertainment business. Movies, television, theme parks and games were my media, and my job was to make breathtaking cinematic imagery that would be projected or displayed on a screen of some sort. It took me a few years and several failed attempts to realize that this approach does not translate well into picturebook making.

I thought if you had a good story and thirty-two amazing pictures you would have a fantastic picturebook. I was wrong. That is not to say that you don't need a good story, and at least a few amazing pictures, but as I'd learn, it takes much, much more than that.

One of the things I needed to understand was that a picturebook is a physical object that a person holds in their hands. How big is it? Is it a tall vertical book? Horizontal? Does it have glossy paper or matte? Do the pictures fill the entire page or do they rest within the page? These are some of the many questions I now ask myself as I begin the creation of a book. Publishers will definitely have some say in the answers to these questions, as many affect the price of producing the book, but the more of them I can be aware of the better. For example, if I am telling a story that takes place in an interesting landscape and that landscape is important to the story I might choose to create a book that has a horizontal format. When I was creating the imagery for my book, *Fu Finds The Way*, I used tea stained paper to give the pictures a certain aged quality. The publisher and I tested the final prints on both matte and glossy paper. Because my pictures had very subtle tonal variations the quality of the image looked better on the glossy stock paper, but in the end I chose to go with the matte paper. I did this for two reasons, the first being that the story took place a long time ago, so I wanted the paper to feel old. The second reason was that on the glossy paper, the tea stained pictures looked like photographs of paintings, whereas on the matte paper it looked like the book was actually aged and stained itself.

Another incredibly valuable lesson I learned came to me after studying the works of Uri Shulevitz and Maurice Sendak. I realized a picturebook is more like a play than a movie. The page serves as the stage and your characters come and go from that stage acting out their story. Nowhere is this more apparent than in Sendak's wonderful little book, *Hector Protector and As I Went Over the Water*. Even the cover looks like a theatre set piece. In *Hector*, you see the characters acting out their scene in their home, as Hector gets ready to visit the Queen. He sets off toward the castle and we follow him as he goes from left to right on the page, just as we read a book. Arriving at a new set (the castle) he continues this left to right movement, and eventually he is sent home. How does he get home? Does he turn around and walk back, right to left, which would mean going against the page turn? No! He continues to walk left to right and somehow he manages to get home. Do we question this? Did he walk around the world to get back to his house? Of course not, but as a reader we do not question the logic of such a thing because of how we turn the pages. The character must move from left to right otherwise he wouldn't be able to arrive on the next page.

When I am thinking of a new picturebook, it usually plays out like a little movie in my head. So when I was coming up with ideas for my book, *Blackout*, I first had some pretty cinematic images in mind. I really wanted to draw these beautiful dark cityscapes using a horizontal format that would show off the vastness of the city. But as I developed the story I realized that this story wasn't about the city as much as it was about the people inhabiting it. I decided to create a stage for my characters to act out their parts. Take a look at two versions of a scene where the lights go out and in the cityscape you only see one window illuminated by the family's flashlight. In the early version you see a very dramatic angle looking down a street of buildings where the perspective lines draw you towards the window. The sketch is done on a long horizontal layout showing lots of details of the city.

Now if you look at the later sketch you will see that I have flattened everything out, gotten rid of the perspective, and created a more theatre-like set for my characters to act out their story.

I've also gone ahead and changed the physical layout of the book so that it is more vertical, as this would allow me the opportunity to stack panels of the story on top of one another like a comic book.

I am definitely thinking differently now that I am a creator of picturebooks, as there are a myriad of decisions to be made and every one of them will impact how the story is presented. I always try to remember that every choice I make must support the story.

Literature references

Brown, M. W. (1947), *Goodnight Moon*, Illus. C. Hurd, New York: Harper.

Carroll, L. (2013/1897) *Alice in Wonderland*, New York: W. W. Norton and Co.

Crew, G. (1998), *The Watertower*, Illus. S. Woolman, Brooklyn, NY: Crocodile Books.

Duffy, C., ed. (2014) *Above the Dreamless Dead: World War I in Poetry and Comics*, New York: First Second.

Gregory, N. (1995), *How Smudge Came*, Red Deer: Red Deer College Press.

Hinds, G. (2007), *Beowulf*, Somerville, MA: Candlewick.

Hinds, G. (2008), *The Merchant of Venice*, Somerville, MA: Candlewick.

Hinds, G. (2009), *King Lear*, Somerville, MA: Candlewick.

Hinds, G. (2010), *The Odyssey*, Somerville, MA: Candlewick.

Hinds, G. (2015), *Macbeth*, Somerville, MA: Candlewick.

McDermott, G. (1993) *Raven: A Trickster Tale from the Pacific Northwest*, New York: Harcourt Brace Jovanovich.

Scieszka, J. and Smith, L. (1992), *The Stinky Cheese May and other Fairly Stupid Tales*, New York: Viking.

Sendak, M. (1963), *Where the Wild Things Are*, New York: Harper & Row.

Silverstein, S. (1964), *The Giving Tree*, New York: Harper & Row.

Tan, S. (2006), *The Arrival*, New York: Scholastic.

Yang, G. L. (2013), *Boxers & Saints*, New York: First Second.

Willems, M. (2003), *Don't Let the Pigeon Drive the Bus*, New York: Hyperion.

Willems, M. (2010), *We Are in a Book!*, New York: Hyperion.

Wiesner, D. (2001), *The Three Pigs*, New York: Clarion.

6

Thinking about Story

Roland Barthes had this to say about stories, a term he uses interchangeably with narratives:

> The narratives of the world are numberless. Narrative is first and foremost a prodigious variety of genres, themselves distributed amongst different substances—as though any material were fit to receive man's stories. Able to be carried by articulated language, spoken or written, fixed or moving images, gestures, and the ordered mixture of all these substances, narrative is present in myth, legend, fable, tale, novella, epic, history, tragedy, drama, comedy, mime, painting . . . stained glass windows, cinema, comics, news item, conversation. Moreover, under this almost infinite diversity of forms, narrative is present in every age, in every place, in every society; it begins with the very history of mankind and there nowhere is nor has been a people without narrative. All classes, all human groups, have their narratives. . . . Caring nothing for the division between good and bad literature, narrative is international, transhistorical, transcultural: it is simply there, like life itself. (Barthes 1977: 79)

Usually, when someone makes such a sweeping statement, we are apt to regard it with skepticism; the world is a big place, full of many different cultures and types of people who have vastly different lifestyles, practices, and values. However, in this case, Barthes isn't wrong: humans are what Jonathan Gottschall (2012) has called the "storytelling animal." In this chapter we will consider why we tell stories as well as examine the elements of storytelling.

Most children, if they're lucky, will have heard a wide range of stories before they start to read. And indeed this early exposure to orally shared stories, with and without accompanying picturebooks, will assist their ability to enjoy reading for themselves, as they will have developed a repertoire of voices and images to bring onto their mental stage as they translate words on a page to moving pictures in their heads. But they will also learn how stories are shaped in their culture—what beginnings and endings sound like, for instance, and how events relate to each other. If storytelling is, as Barthes and Gottschall suggest, a universal practice of endless variety that in fact makes us human, then it's important to think analytically about story forms and elements in children's and YA literature.

Why we tell and sometimes censor stories

My daughter Blair returned home from her first day of kindergarten with a strangely triumphant apology on her lips. She explained to me in great detail how she had been unable to stop talking while the teacher was talking, and thus received a warning in the form of a green card. Angered, she told the teacher that she would not keep quiet, at which point she was issued a yellow card and told to stand by the door. When the teacher looked away, Blair reported, she lifted her dress and showed the rest of the children her underwear, and this resulted in a red card, and she had to stand in the hallway until snack time. Needless to say, I was mortified, and apologized profusely to her teacher the next day when I dropped her off. The teacher looked perplexed, and when I told her what Blair had told me, she smiled and said, "Well, yes, that would have been just terrible, except it never happened!"

So, what was really going on here? Was my daughter developing into a pathological liar and exhibitionist? Could she not separate reality from fantasy? Should we be putting a psychoanalyst on speed dial? Her teacher and I talked it over, and she told me that what had actually happened the day before was that she had explained her color-coded discipline system to the children—a green card for a warning, a yellow card for a second offense, and a red card that resulted in a punishment, usually a time-out. Blair, in order to make sense of the logical but abstract system, had imagined concrete behaviors that would warrant such a progression from green card to red card into a story with herself as the protagonist. Her story wasn't a lie so much as a way to assimilate new information about her expanding world and give her a sense of agency within that world. She had been confronted with new knowledge, but its presentation was limited to knowing *that* something exists and knowing *how* it worked. Her imaginative story closed the gap of knowing *what it would feel like* to experience the system at work. An emergent strand in cognitive literary criticism points us to emotional cognition as one of the key roles storytelling plays in children's lives; stories are an essential epistemological tool—a way of knowing—that engages their reasoning in tandem with their feelings (Burke 2010; Damasio 1999; Oatley 2011, 2012; Vermeule 2011).

Blair's story also hints at some more general facts about stories that can be mildly troubling for parents and educators, if not children's literature scholars, such as: the worst decisions make for the best stories; trouble, violence, and death are *interesting*; and things that are good for us are not as appealing as things that aren't. Gottschall (2012: 52) quotes Charles Baxter's pithy observation that "Hell is story-friendly." Parents and educators know that children often model themselves and their behavior after storybook heroes, and so they tend to follow Plato in desiring that children be offered models that wed desirable behaviors and moral virtue with intellectual development—in other words, stories with culturally acceptable morals or lessons. Of course, what is culturally acceptable or desirable changes over time and across cultures. But there are certain lessons that we seem to want all children and teens to learn in order to function in social groups, such as kindness, cooperation, overcoming selfishness, and taking responsibility for one's actions. Many parents, then, are concerned by the proliferation of tales for younger children where the characters behave badly without consequence or even with approbation, or where the general flavor of the story is one of protest against legitimate or illegitimate authority figures. YA literature is especially notorious for its focus on social and moral problems and its morally ambiguous endings.

Evolutionary theorists think that this darker mode of storytelling is probably an adaptive behavior keyed to survival and the development of new ways to solve problems. That is, we tell stories about when things go wrong in order to warn our community members about dangers that they need to be aware of and problems that need to be solved collectively. And we are more interested in the abnormal or new thing than we are in familiar things, because we need to assess whether an unfamiliar thing is dangerous or helpful. Such storytelling helps establish standards of justice and community identity as the group works through processes of interpretation, but also eventually expands the community through the assimilation of new ideas. Many (though by most counts not nearly enough) notable children's books are overtly activist in this way through the depiction of family and community structures, identities, and moral situations that challenge white, class-based, heteronormative values, while others tacitly reinforce those values. The challengers have almost always met with some form of attempted censorship. Over the years, for instance, conservative censorious readers have objected to the use of talking animals on religious or educational grounds, citing either an affront to their conception of God or a concern that such depiction might confuse children. Explicit sexual content and vulgar language are almost always deemed unsuitable for young readers, such that bawdy passages from Jonathan Swift's *Gulliver's Travels* (1726) were removed in children's versions of the story, and YA novels like Robert Cormier's *The Chocolate War* (1974) and Sherman Alexie's *The Absolutely True Diary of a Part-Time Indian* (2007) are taken to task for their discussion of masturbation. An app called Clean Reader has been developed that will replace "offensive" words in uploaded e-books with alternatives its creators deem inoffensive, such as substituting "chest" for "breast." Books that feature nonheterosexual relationships also appear regularly on lists of banned and challenged books, as do books that present adults, religious institutions, and governments in an unfavorable light.

Since the 1970s, however, some progressive parents and educators have joined their conservative counterparts as advocates of official and unofficial censorship, citing sexist, racist, and homophobic content as unsuitable for young readers. Progressive parents, for instance, will often leave out or alter passages that strike them as overly restrictive in their portrayal of gender roles. In response to the public outcry against racist content in books commonly used in schools, Mark Twain scholar Alan Gribben (2011) has published an edition of Twain's novels about Tom Sawyer and Huckleberry Finn where the offensive word "nigger" has been replaced throughout by the word "slave." These censors firmly believe in the power of children's and YA literature to shape community values, and they don't trust young readers to read skeptically or recognize **irony** or social critique in the stories they encounter.

In addition to the survival of the group and perpetuation or confrontation with its values, however, we also use stories to fight for our individual survival within a group, telling our side of the story to generate understanding and empathy, or even inventing a fiction to defend ourselves against community censure. Storytelling in the service of self-justification may take comic or serious, ironic or straightforward, morally questionable or utterly righteous guises. Consider, for instance, Laurie in Shirley Jackson's widely anthologized story, "Charles" (1949). Laurie, a boy just starting kindergarten, tells his parents stories about a classmate Charles who does naughty things. His parents tut-tut about how difficult this Charles must make things for the teacher and can't wait to meet his parents at a school function. To their surprise, the teacher informs them that there is no Charles, and readers, who have been following the clues all along as to Charles's true identity, are affirmed in their suspicions that Laurie is the real perpetrator of all of the disruption. In Jon Scieszka's *The True Story of the Three Little Pigs* (1989), the wolf explains how his intentions regarding the three pigs have been completely misunderstood in the official version of the story. In a more serious vein, an ant must argue for his right to survive in Phillip M. Hoose's *Hey, Little Ant* (1998), a picturebook that inspires philosophical reflection on power and responsibility, animal rights, and peer pressure among other things. Walter Dean Myers puts the storytelling media of the screenplay and the personal journal in the hands of his character Steve in *Monster* (1999) to highlight the manifold differences between the true and false stories our communities tell about young men of color and the true and false stories they tell about themselves. Laurie Halse Anderson's *Speak*

(1999) shows the extreme social ostracism that results when Melinda, a girl who has been raped by a popular upperclassman the summer before she enters high school, literally cannot tell her side of the story. Giving the perpetrator's perspective, Kier, the main character in Chris Lynch's YA novel, *Inexcusable* (2005), seeks to justify his sexual assault on his friend Gigi by insisting on all the ways he is a good guy; good guys don't rape their friends, he reasons, so what he has done to Gigi could not have been rape. Sutter Keely, the alcoholic teen in Tim Tharp's *The Spectacular Now* (2008), desperately seeks to earn his friends' (and the reader's) love by locating all of his questionable decisions in a framework of natural beauty and self-denying ethics, forcing readers to draw on real-world understandings of the distorted effects of reasoning under the influence of too much whiskey.

Whether these self-revealing or self-justifying tales engender sympathy or deploy **dramatic irony** to make social statements, they point us toward other aspects of storytelling. Most importantly, they teach us that no one has a god's-eye view of the world; instead, all stories emerge from a particular perspective. And while we have a tendency to believe in the veracity of a first person, I-was-there account, narrators can be **unreliable**, so that not all personal stories are true. And in fact, as Mike Cadden (2000) points out, since children's and YA books are almost always written by adults, first-person narration in the voice of a young person is inherently ironic if not completely untrustworthy. **Dramatic irony** is achieved when the writer and audience know something more or different than the character, so what Cadden works out here is that, since the author has an adult perspective on the emotions and situations that confront a young character, any account of events that purport to be present tense and in first person is in fact a retrospective narrative from a distanced viewpoint that already knows the significance of things that are presented as happening in real time. But even third-person, seemingly disinterested narrators write from a particular perspective; they have a reason for telling a particular story in a particular way. Good storytellers can manipulate their hearers into believing what they want them to believe. They create characters to carry their **ideological** perspectives, and then use a character's appearance, actions, situations, and language to make readers like or dislike them. Imagine, for instance, how readers might have responded if Harry Potter had been to the manor born and Draco Malfoy had been shoved into a cupboard under the stairs; their actions, speech, and motivations would have been cast in an entirely different light.

In and through stories, we can imagine ourselves as someone else, and that someone else may be better or worse than we really are. In fact, we even go so far as to construct our sense of self based on specific characters and character types that we identify with and dis-identify with. Once again, I turn to my daughter's storytelling proclivities to illustrate a few salient points on the ongoing development of a sense of self through narrative imitation: In first grade, she got in trouble for kissing a boy on the playground. He was not pleased. When I asked her what happened, she said,

"Oh, mommy, when a hero rescues you from a flow of hot lava, you just have to kiss him. It's what princesses do!" I sighed; while her familiarity with traditional story conventions was clearly well-established, this was an epic fail for Feminist Parenting 101. But, as noted in Chapter 2, the rigidity of attitudes toward gender ebbs and flows along a developmental line, and sure enough, a couple years later, eight-year-old Blair stunned a class of college students she was sitting in on by asking, "Um, why does the princess always have to marry the prince just because he rescues her? Whatever happened to 'thank you'?" Through stories, then, children test identities and pick up clues about how to manipulate truth and respond to situations, and this all feeds into their developing sense of self (Tobin 2000). By looking into the minds of characters, they recognize aspects of themselves that they want to cultivate or expunge, and by seeing how actions are met with consequences, they can determine what might be worth pursuing and what is better left on the page or screen.

Terry Pratchett treats this tendency to fashion our lives after story with wonderfully layered irony in *The Amazing Maurice and His Educated Rodents* (2001). In this novel, a group of newly sentient and literate rats long for the society depicted in a children's book called "Mr. Bunnsy Has an Adventure," where animals and humans live in harmony. Similarly, a human that they meet called Malicia Grim structures her expectations around fairy tale tropes. Over the course of the novel, Pratchett alternately pokes fun at and reinforces the idea that real life works like a story: for instance, Malicia's expectation that a thug's lair will have a hidden door to a secret room is presented as laughable until one actually appears, and the rats' religious faith in their book is undone when Malicia reveals that it is a silly fiction but then reaffirmed when the rats actually do negotiate with humans for a space of their own. Such multivalent **metafictive** reflection on the relationship between stories and real life, and between stories and other stories, has its roots in Golden Age books such as *Alice in Wonderland* (Carroll 1865), *Anne of Green Gables* (Montgomery 1908), and the works of E. Nesbit (1858–1924), and continues into the present through books such as Cornelia Funke's Inkworld trilogy (2003–08) and Lemony Snicket's Series of Unfortunate Events (1999–2006).

Another reason young people tell stories is related to the reason they use poetic language: stories, like poetry, can both contain and structure the world, making it manageable while simultaneously making everyday events more intense and exciting. Running around on a playground can be a pretty dull activity for your mind if not your body; being chased by a dinosaur and rescued by a brave knight is thrilling by contrast, whether you are the dinosaur, the knight, or the victim. A perfectly safe camping trip takes on a deliciously frightening dimension when eerie stories imply threatening presences looming outside the campfire circle. Alternately, stories can transform horrific events into safe, or at least safer, closed narratives. Mildly scary episodes often become humorous when they are transformed into stories. Unpleasant experiences can be shared and redeemed through story, as Sharon Flake beautifully articulates in her talkback to this chapter. And the representation of truly traumatic events through stories can enable victims to bear witness to their own pain—to, in effect, double themselves as both character and teller, witness and victim—in ways that can be therapeutic if not completely healing.

So while it may be instructive to tell imaginative tales about ordinary events going exactly as planned, or good people making good decisions with good outcomes, those stories really aren't that engaging. They don't draw on the same resources of quick-witted, innovative thinking or fear responses that excite the mind and body through the temporary release of cortisol that increases focus and provides a shot of energy. As Plato lamented and Aristotle found emotionally useful, we enjoy things in stories that we would hate to happen in real life. Knowing my daughter, her kindergarten teacher's displeasure in real life would have sent her into tears, but in story, she was a defiant heroine, a little Katniss shaking her fist at an authoritative Capitol. Even at five years of age, she learned that "in literature only trouble is interesting" (Burroway 2003: 82).

Studying story

Now that we have some idea of how young people might use the stories they read and tell, we will turn our attention to three critical questions: What exactly *is* a story, what do we need to know to analyze stories critically, and why do we need to know it? Taking the last question first, a vocabulary for thinking about story is useful no matter what type of critical method or theoretical framework most appeals to you as a scholar. **Ideology**-driven **contextual** methodologies like **feminism** or **Marxism**, as well as **rhetorical**, **formalist**, **structuralist**, **deconstructionist,** and **reader response** approaches, all benefit from close reading of a story's component parts in relation to each other and to the outside world; your theoretical analysis must be underwritten and supported by **textual** evidence. Likewise, if you want to be a writer or a teacher, you need to know how stories work so that you can go about your own writing or assist students with their understanding.

But a reason beyond academic or creative work for understanding stories analytically is implicit in what we have just discussed: We come to know the world through the stories we encounter as children, and we come to understand ourselves and other people through stories as well, so being able to break stories down into their component parts helps us understand why we think like we do, and what the advantages and limitations of those ways of thinking might be. Stories don't just passively represent the world as it is; they actively construct it through multiple modes of expression. **Narrative theory** or **narratology**, which attends to how people make sense of and use stories as well as how stories represent and structure experience, is therefore something of a baggy monster, traversing multiple disciplines and picking up new questions and critical concerns as people begin to recognize how much of our **aesthetic**, scientific, and practical pursuits are embedded in storied frameworks. Hence experts in the study of narrative can be found in the fields of anthropology, architecture, all of the visual and temporal arts, artificial intelligence, interior and environmental design, history, law, natural and human sciences, philosophy, psychology, and religion. Recent developments in neuroscience give pride of place to narrative knowledge as we come to understand more fully just how the brain uses stories to make sense of the world. Cognitive literary critics such as Michael Burke, Hugh Crago, Patrick Colm Hogan, David S. Miall, Peter Stockwell, Mark Turner, and Lisa Zunshine bring these findings to bear on story processing, and while they haven't worked with children, their research offers a fascinating validation of common sense findings and empirical observation of how children come to understand the world through story. Researchers who have worked with children to understand story processing include Lawrence Sipe, Evelyn Arizpe, and Morag Styles. Many other researchers in the fields of developmental psychology and literacy studies have undertaken **empirical research** with children; these studies reached their heyday in the late twentieth century and have since waned, so this is an area of research that would benefit from refreshment given new possibilities in neural imaging.

What is a story?

Given the multifaceted and consequential roles that stories play in shaping our understanding, then, it's a good idea to define what we are talking about when we use the word "story." Let's start by thinking about what it is not: a story is not merely the recitation of one event following another, nor is it a mere description of a character or setting or the revelation of certain facts. As John Rocco has pointed out in his talkback to the previous chapter, a set of thirty-two beautiful paintings does not make a story. These are all elements of story, but a story emerges in the defined and complex relationships between these elements, and every element relates in some way to the larger framework of the story. In the most cohesive stories, the elements of character, setting, plot, and conflict, and the language and imagery used to describe these things coalesce around a unifying subject or theme, and follow a recognizable shape or rhythm that proceeds temporally from a spark of interest or conflict through causally connected events, mounting tension, and a culminating experience to a resolution that restores the peace and releases the reader back into the world outside the story.

Obviously, there can be many variations built on that scaffold, and some **postmodern** picturebooks and YA novels seek to actively disrupt the structure altogether. **Postmodern** experimentation in children's and YA storytelling may take the form of simultaneous narratives, as in David Macaulay's *Black and White* (1990), where one episode of each of four interrelated stories appears on each opening, and it's up to the reader to pull the details into a coherent story by the end. Alternately, the presence of multiple perspectives is a hallmark of **postmodern** storytelling for children. The strategies involved in interactive texts such as the *Choose Your Own Adventure* series and various console games, where the narrative may move back and forth depending on reader or player choices, produce another kind of plot structure that we might call recursive. Some of these structures reject closure or a unified meaning altogether, preferring instead to present plot as a series of open-ended challenges.

Another experiment that is sometimes seen in YA literature involves providing a level of minute, hyperreal detail that obscures the sense of a narrative arc and focuses attention on the banality and ongoingness of everyday life. These experiments tend to be exceptions that prove the rule that most stories for young audiences have both structure and unity. In fact, this may be one reason why children's and YA literature is experiencing a publishing renaissance; while adult literary fiction is managing some brilliant assaults on our **aesthetic** expectations, resulting in more art and experiment than linear, closed plots, readers often long for a coherent story, masterfully told. Longer stories and novels may repeat the pattern of mounting tension and release over and over again through an episodic structure or the development of subplots, but this general story shape is what we mean when talk about a story rather than some other kind of abstract or experimental narrative form.

Perry Nodelman (1992) suggests that children's literature as a whole functions as a repertoire—a stock of familiar plot lines that are repeated in various ways. In suggesting this, he is thinking like a **structuralist**. **Structuralist** critics of narrative seek to locate the patterns that underlie seemingly disparate stories. **Structuralists** may also seek to identify what is referred to as a "grammar" of story; Tzvetan Todorov (1977), for instance, constructed a notion of story grammar based on the model of the sentence. In his model, the subject and verb of a sentence become the equivalents to the protagonist and action of story, with adjectives and adverbs describing the state or quality of the protagonist as something happens to him or her or as he or she performs an action. Introducing a character through a name or a physical description implies a kind of originary stasis or condition. A predicate can then indicate a change or movement that introduces disequilibrium, one of the conditions for a story structure. In longer narratives, just as in compound or complex sentences, multiple changes or movements may be introduced that relate to and complicate the central problem before resolution and return to a refreshed stasis is achieved (see also Prince 1987).

Scripts and intertextuality

Children can actually be thought of as natural **structuralists** insofar as they actively seek and unconsciously absorb patterns to structure their daily routines and activities. These patterns develop into what Roger C. Schank (1990) has called "**scripts**," which are mental representations of the basic actions needed to complete a more complex action that is common to daily experience. Many **early concept books** for very young children are simple rehearsals of these **scripts**, describing the steps involved in going to bed or taking a bath. Books such as these mirror back to children the activities of their days, transforming a **script** into an ideal expression of a daily ritual. While they are certainly narratives in that they narrate a sequence of events, they aren't necessarily good stories, because a good story develops out of a scenario that violates a **script** in some way. So, for instance, one oft-repeated way of telling the story of going to bed features a child deploying innovative delaying tactics that disrupt the normative bedtime **script** that might include taking a bath, changing into night clothes, brushing teeth, getting into bed, reading a book, and finally, turning off the light and going to sleep. However zany the disruptions, though, they depend on an underlying recognition of a bedtime **script**.

Scripts can be drawn from life experience or other stories, so all stories are either implicitly or explicitly **intertextual**. **Intertextuality** refers to the practice of evoking or alluding to one text within another. If we think of our lives as a kind of text, then the **scripts** we use to make sense of a literary text are a kind of implicit **intertextuality**. But often, authors use **intertextuality** explicitly by referring to other literary texts within their own. For instance, when Mary, in Frances Hodgson Burnett's *The Secret Garden* (1911), remarks that Colin's eyes look as big as the wolf's from Little Red Riding Hood, she is drawing on a familiar story to make sense of a phenomenon— Colin's eyes open particularly wide when he first sees his mother's walled garden. At the level of understanding what is happening with the character, we might say that Mary is making sense of both the story and Colin's reaction by relating them to each other; upon seeing Colin's widened eyes, she draws on a remembered context where big eyes occurred, and since it happened in an exciting part of the original story, the emotional response of heightened tension carries over into her present circumstance. This is, in fact, one of the ways we use stories in real life. But for the interpreting reader (and perhaps for Mary, though it's never explicitly noted in the text), this reference to Little Red Riding Hood also evokes a sense of threat. Little Red Riding Hood notices that the wolf's eyes are exceptionally large just before he eats her. And indeed, allowing Colin into the garden that Mary has so lovingly tended signals the beginning of the end for Mary's importance in the story; once Colin enters the garden, the story shifts from Mary's awakening sense of self to Colin's physical recovery and his assumption of his place as lord of the manor, such that Mary doesn't even appear in the final chapter of the book. The big-eyed boy metaphorically consumes Mary just as the big-eyed wolf literally consumed Little Red Riding Hood.

As these examples illustrate, the use of **scripts** and more overt **intertextual** references enables authors to employ a kind of shorthand in their storytelling by evoking a scene, context, or theme rather than actually describing it. Cognitive theorists interested in the way people process stories have noted that at the beginning of stories, readers draw heavily on their own **scripts** to make sense of the story world they are entering. Compelling stories for children, then, begin with some sort of emotional or situational point of connection that anchors readers in their own experiences and memories. From there, stories beckon readers to follow the story's path into the new or unknown. Texts that inspire this kind of balancing between **scripts** that readers are likely to know and violations of those **scripts** are the most engaging for readers, as they can fill in gaps with their own knowledge and experience, but also expand that knowledge by imagining and assimilating new experiences. In discussing these examples from a **structuralist** perspective, though, we are already getting into some of the elements that make stories work, so it's time to turn our attention more directly to the elements of stories.

Elements of stories

Plots and conflicts

As we have indicated above, good stories have recognizable structures—beginnings, middles, and ends with events that occur not only in a sequence but build from each other through a relationship of cause and effect; this is what is known as the plot. Types of plots fall into different categories. For instance, the plot structure that we have already alluded to, featuring an originary stasis or exposition, an inciting event, mounting tension, a climactic moment, falling action, and resolution is known as a **climactic plot**. Most European-based folktales and picturebook narratives follow this plot, so they apprentice children into an expectation of this structure. This plot may feature a single character or group of characters working from the start toward a common goal, or it may result from what's known as a **cumulative plot** structure, where new characters are added to the story in parallel ways until a breaking point occurs, as in Jan Brett's *The Mitten* (1989), Julia Donaldson's *Room on the Broom* (2001) and *A Squash and a Squeeze* (2003), and *There Was an Old Lady Who Swallowed a Fly* (1997), by Simms Taback.

A longer story or chapter book for new readers, then, may make use of this climactic structure by creating chapters with individual episodes that each contain a mini version of this plot. Taken together, this is called an **episodic plot** structure, and it's something we often see in series books. Sometimes each episode stands alone like a self-contained short story, as in Louis Sachar's Wayside School series. Lenore Look's Alvin Ho series is another example of this type of episodic plot structure. Each of the books in the series is organized around a particular set of things Alvin is afraid of, and each chapter in each book features a plotted episode that relates in some way to that fear. In some novels with episodic plot structures, each episode contributes to the mounting tension that will ultimately result in a larger climax and lead to a resolution where a character or situation has changed due to all of the events that have gone before. This is more likely to happen in series where the character is actually aging throughout the series, as in L. M. Montgomery's Anne books, or working toward some overarching goal, as in J. K. Rowling's Harry Potter series.

Episodes in **climactic plots** for children and YAs tend to follow the guidelines set out by Aristotle some twenty-three hundred years ago. He identified five persistent elements of plot that are key to a satisfying story: Stories often begin with some sort of *reversal* of fortune, usually from good or middling fortune to bad, and the remainder of the story charts the journey back to good fortune. Along the way, protagonists make *discoveries* about themselves related to their past, their flaws, their gifts, or their motivations, or other significant people in their worlds. They also encounter *complications* that stand between them and their goals. These complications are often the subject of episodes with their own mini-climaxes as they overcome them. Finally, though, they are faced with a *catastrophe*—something bigger than a mere complication occurs and forces a confrontation of some sort. How this catastrophe is handled determines the outcome of the plot. The *resolution*, then, proceeds logically from the events and discoveries of the plot. It is not a miracle or an unlikely outcome.

These elements form themselves in various ways around specific content. Perry Nodelman (1992) has suggested that the range of children's stories may be best understood as variations on a few generic plots that function as a repertoire. And while there is some resistance to reducing the marvelous variety of children's and YA books to a limited number of plotlines, I find it useful to have some system of categorization in order to map the territory. I will offer a few here for your consideration. For instance, you might think in terms of the nine plots that Christopher Booker (2004), a British journalist, claims are archetypal. With some adjustments, the plots that he identifies for mostly adult texts are prominent in children's and YA texts as well. These plots include:

- Overcoming the Monster: The hero learns of a great evil and sets out to destroy it. This plot also applies to a character overcoming an "inner demon."
- Rags to Riches: Surrounded by dark forces who wish him or her ill, the protagonist eventually overcomes the evil and obtains riches, a home, and a mate.

- The Quest: The hero learns of a great boon and sets out to find it.
- Voyage and Return: The protagonist journeys to a far-off land where he or she triumphs and returns home with a more mature outlook.
- Comedy: A friendly, familial, or romantic relationship (or relationships) is (are) initially strained through misunderstanding and/or other obstacles, but the obstacles are overcome and the relationship is healed.
- Tragedy: The protagonist desires something he or she can't or shouldn't have. His or her quest is unsuccessful, or the inner conflict it produces is unresolved.
- Rebirth: The protagonist makes a fatal mistake of some kind, and is restored to life and happiness by the intervention of another character's loving act or by his or her own repentance. Alternately, the character's own sacrifice may result in the reward of rebirth.
- Mystery: The outsider to a crime or other horrendous act must find the truth and ensure that justice is meted out.
- Rebellion against "the One": The protagonist resists or rebels against an illegitimate power, ultimately causing its downfall. This differs from Overcoming the Monster in that the power is often institutional or ideological rather than another character or an "inner demon."

As you were reading through those brief sketches, I am sure you were thinking of stories you know that fit those plots. You probably also realized that some stories, or certain episodes within larger books, fit into more than one category. Another system for thinking about plot that seems to me particularly useful for youth literature was developed by Norman Friedman (1955). He sets out three basic categories, which he then nuances according to the types of characters involved.

- Plots of Fortune are:
  ◦ Sentimental when a weak character wins
  ◦ Tragic when a strong character loses
  ◦ Punitive when a bad character gets his or her just deserts
  ◦ Admirable when an ordinary person wins

- Plots of Character can be about:
  ◦ Maturation when a character moves through a life transition
  ◦ Reform when a fallen person is restored
  ◦ Testing when a noble person undergoes trials
  ◦ Degeneration when an attractive character falls from grace

- Plots of Thought center on:
  ◦ Education when the protagonist learns something
  ◦ Revelation when some point of ignorance is abolished
  ◦ Disillusionment when there is a loss of ideals with consequent effects
  ◦ Affective tension when thought and feeling are at odds with each other

In either of these categorical frameworks, you might also have noticed that certain story types are more prevalent in books for different age groups. It is hard, for instance, to name a tragedy, "rebellion against the One" story, or a plot of thought that centers on disillusionment for very young children, while there are many that come to mind for YA novels. This is because the conflicts in children's and YA literature tend to be keyed toward common developmental concerns, focusing on problems that readers can see an end to or at least be able to cope with if they can't be resolved, but also because we are **ideologically** resistant to offering despair as an endpoint in a story for young readers. In traditional literary study, the core conflicts are categorized in terms of abstract struggles of a fictional character:

- character vs. character
- character vs. society
- character vs. nature
- character vs. self
- character vs. supernatural
- character vs. technology or machines

Children's and YA books set these abstract conflicts into stories that reflect both common experiences and fantastic adventures, and their resolutions often embed a culture's **ideological** wish list for its future. As I have noted above, however, there are books that eschew plot altogether for one reason or another, confronting readers and viewers with abstractions that require interpretation, and perhaps, in their intentional rejection of traditional story form, reminding young readers that plots and conflicts are imposed upon events and are therefore open to revision, to the possibility of telling a new story.

Setting

While the plot outlines defined above are generic enough to be continually reinvented in any setting, conflicts take on the specific colorations of the times and places in which stories are set. Not only material conditions and circumstances but social mores and ideas about what constitutes a good life change over time and in different places, so the setting of a story to a large extent determines the kind of dilemmas a character will find him- or herself in. **Narrative theorists** pay attention to how story worlds are built, and how space and time are portrayed and managed as both material aspects of the story world and as thematic elements. Different kinds of places create different storied associations, based on readers' personal or intertextual experiences, so, for instance, a hut in the woods will conjure different expectations than a busy urban street. And even though the plot structure or central conflicts might be very similar, a story set in the distant past will create a different feeling than one set in the future. Sometimes time and space are considered together as what Bakhtin (1981: 84) called a **chronotope**, the "intrinsic connectedness of temporal and spatial relationships . . . expressed in literature," but also, there are studies that treat them separately, focusing specifically on space, place, and the environment in children's and YA literature, and how time is portrayed, managed, and understood in various kinds of youth literature.

Characters

Of course, plots must be enacted by characters. Characters in books for young children are often iconic—that is, they appear more as types than visually or psychologically real human beings. Scott McCloud (1993) argues that the fewer the details in a face, the more people a character could look like, and this invites identification. **Multimodal discourse analysis**, however, proposes an opposite theory, suggesting that visually iconic characters with few realistic details impose a critical distance from which readers can evaluate, rather than identify with, a character. By contrast, more naturalistically drawn characters invite greater degrees of identification and empathy. I propose a middle ground between these two views based on the functions of characters within stories and the developmental needs and abilities of their readers. We have noted in previous chapters that children's **Theory of Mind (ToM)**—their ability to ascribe motives, beliefs, and intentions, including ones that differ from their own, to other people—is a work in progress starting from around age four or five. But children respond to characters according to type long before that. For instance, researchers at Yale's Baby Lab have designed simple puppet shows to test whether babies prefer characters who perform helpful actions over those who are harmful or obstructive. An astonishing 80 percent of the 3- to 5-month-old babies tested prefer the puppets who perform helpful actions. These findings suggest that babies don't respond to character based on appearance, but rather function; they prefer helpers over nonhelpers.

This function-based assessment of character likely continues until children begin developing a more robust and complex **ToM**, so as long as characters in picturebooks and multimodal storytelling feature high-contrast, fully saturated colors, simplified features, exaggerated gestures, and identifiable relationships, children are likely to make simple judgments based on the roles they play in their stories. For this purpose, **flat characters** and character types, as long as they don't tip over into offensive stereotypes, may be more likely to appeal to very young viewers. Psychological complexity, which is characteristic of what are known as **round characters**, is not only not necessary but it can also be confusing.

As children grow into their own sense of a complex interior self, however, they seek characters that they can identify with rather than just evaluate. Character types still remain important as heroes, helpers, mentors, and foils, and plot-driven narratives such as mysteries, action or adventure stories, comedies, and formula romances draw on stock characters rather than developing highly mimetic, fully realized characters. But protagonists in stories aimed at middle childhood and adolescence have, at least since Maria Edgeworth's creation of Rosamond in 1796, spoken and behaved more or less like real children and teens. Such protagonists tend to be both **round** (i.e., demonstrating multiple traits and facets) and **dynamic** (i.e., they appear to undergo an arc of development that leads from a state of innocence or immaturity to a state of greater knowledge or maturity). I use the verb appear here to highlight the fact that they don't in fact grow—literary characters are made of ink and ideas, after all, but we do treat them as though they were real, a trick of the mind that has been explored by **cognitive literary theorists** such as Lisa Zunshine, Blakey Vermeule, as well as by Maria Nikolajeva and Roberta Seelinger Trites. Even so, however, the idea of a character arc that mimics the enlargement of perspective and the acquisition of a more complex capacity for emotion is so pervasive as to almost seem a requirement of serious realistic fiction for teens.

A comprehensive theory of character in children's literature that extends far beyond this brief discussion has been developed by Nikolajeva in *The Rhetoric of Character in Children's Literature* (2002), where she suggests, among other things, that contemporary characterization in children's books focuses on the imitation of real people with whom children can identify and empathize rather than role models for them to aspire to. She also explores the various effects produced through the use of collective characters, which tends to support the illusion that the experiences they have are real (even and especially in fantasy) because they are shared; individual protagonists who, because of their limited and often naive perspective, cast doubt on the veracity of the events depicted; and intersubjective protagonists who, by multiplying perspectives, may go some way to mitigate problems of gender or age bias. Since the publication of that book, Nikolajeva has continued her research into character by exploring how consciousness and emotions are represented in children's picturebooks.

Narrators

A critical question to ask when analyzing a story is who is telling it. Narrators can be part of the story world, appearing as characters, or they can exist outside of it, but even if they exist outside the story, they are not synonymous with the flesh-and-blood author. **Narrative theorist** Seymour Chatman distinguishes between the various participants in a story conceived as an act of communication. There is, first of all, a *real author*, the actual person who wrote the text. When young readers connect with a text, they often desire to connect with the real author, and teachers encourage such interaction by having their students write letters or invite the authors to give talks and readings at their schools. Contemporary children's and YA authors have achieved something of a celebrity status on the interwebs; successful marketing of their work often involves a substantial web presence that allows readers to feel as though they have a personal connection to the author of their favorite book.

In scholarly discourse and analysis, however, the real author is not to be confused with the **implied author**, which is the sense of the author you get from reading the text. Consider, for instance, an author like Louis Sachar. The Louis Sachar who wrote *Holes* (1999), a middle-grade novel that focuses on the themes of justice, friendship, the burdens of history, and racial reconciliation is not experienced as the same Louis Sachar who wrote the Wayside School series, a trilogy of chapter books characterized by their zany humor, quirky characters, and stand-alone chapters. The **implied author** of *Holes* uses mild **irony**, interconnected digressions, and a climactic narrative structure to convey a serious philosophical and social message. The **implied author** of the Wayside School books, on the other hand, uses an **episodic plot** structure, fantasy setting, gross-out humor, and clever wordplay to make readers laugh. When analyzing a text for how its language, structure, and characterization contribute to its themes, we are discussing the *implied* **author's** decisions, motives, and qualities, not the *real* author's. It's customary, therefore, when writing about a book, to use the present tense verbs to talk about what an **implied author** does in a text, as I have done above, but past tense when discussing real events that took place in the real author's life: for example, Sachar won the Newbery Award for *Holes* in 1999.

One of the reasons for prising apart the real author from the **implied author** is to avoid what literary critics have called the "intentional fallacy" (Wimsatt and Beardsley 1946). This refers to the notion that the real author does not have the last word in determining what a text means. Instead, the **implied author** is constructed by the reader through his or her interpretation of the text. In his influential essay, "The Death of the Author" (1977/1967), Barthes asserts that the author is "born simultaneously with the text," arguing that the meaning of a work, rather than being located within an author's head, or even within the work itself, is instead created anew with each reader's interpretation. Michel Foucault's assessment of the role of the author is slightly different. In his 1969 essay, "What is an Author?," he argues that authors are constructs that we use to limit interpretations. When we say "Sachar of the Wayside School Stories," for instance, what we are doing is constructing the **implied author** as what Foucault called an "author-function" that allows us to create certain expectations; "oh yeah," we say, "we know him—he's wacky," and we don't expect any serious content in the books themselves as a result. Interestingly, some authors choose pseudonyms perhaps in part to work with these expectations or establish different ones for different types of books. For instance, an author named E. Lockhart writes YA fiction that focuses on complex relationships and psychologies of teen girls. However, the same person uses the name Emily Jenkins when she writes picturebooks for younger readers.

The next level of participant in Chatman's model is the narrator. As we have noted above, narrators can be characters, or they can exist outside of the story world. Likewise, they can address their narration directly to a narratee who is another character, or to someone who is not present in the story, or to a general audience. Narrators who are characters in the story may be main characters or secondary characters, and they refer to themselves as "I" throughout the story. However, this does not necessarily mean that the use of the word "I" indicates first-person narration; Lewis Carroll's narrator in the Alice books occasionally says I, and directly addresses the reader as narratee, but neither the narrator nor the narratee is a character in the story. First-person narrative voice, by contrast, means that the person doing the talking is a character in the story. Epistolary stories—stories told through letters—are examples of narrators who are characters addressing their narration to another character, whether that character ever actually appears in the story or not. Paul, in Edward Bloor's *Tangerine* (2001), writes his first-person narrative as a journal that he will hand over to the police to implicate his brother for his crimes. S. E. Hinton's *The Outsiders* (1967) is written in first person as a school assignment so that Ponyboy can make up for the year of school he has lost. Narrative situations like this are common in middle-grade and YA fiction, and in fact, it might not be going too far to say that first-person narrative voice is the house style of contemporary YA fiction. A variation of this is the plural first-person narrative, where chapters alternate between characters to provide differing perspectives on the same events and relationships.

Third-person narration is more often found in stories for younger readers, though it is often used to good effect across the spectrum of children's and YA literature; all of the Harry Potter novels, for instance, are written in third person. Third person comes in multiple varieties. For instance, a third-person narrator may limit him or herself to just relating the actions of the characters, revealing no **ideological** position or personality, or offering any evaluative commentary. Alternately, the narrator may intrude on the story, posing questions for the reader. The third-person narrator in *Holes* (Sachar 1999: 115), for instance, directly addresses the reader after telling the tragic story of the teacher-turned-outlaw, Katherine Barlow, and Sam, the onion man, saying, "You make the decision: Whom did God punish?" This style of direct address is sometimes referred to as an "intrusive narrator" or "breaking the fourth wall," a term borrowed from theater. A traditional stage set has three walls with the front open to the audience, an arrangement aimed at giving the illusion that the story space is self-contained; the "fourth wall" that separates the cast from the audience is imaginary. Sometimes, however, the actors address the audience directly. Because this highlights the fact that what is happening on stage is in fact a story performed by actors, this is a **metafictive** technique similar to the ones we have discussed in Chapter 5. An intrusive narrator imposes a distance from which readers or viewers can evaluate what's happening; such a narrator serves as a reminder that this is a story that is being crafted and told for specific purposes, rather than maintaining the illusion that what is happening is real.

Another variation of third-person narration is to take a god's-eye, or omniscient, view that sees and knows everything that is happening or being thought of in a story. Now, it would be extremely tedious to read the thoughts and actions of everyone all the time in a story, so even a third-person omniscient narrator selects what he or she reveals. But third-person omniscient narration can manipulate **dramatic irony**. For instance, in the picturebook *Officer Buckle and Gloria* (Rathman 1995), the story is told from a third-person omniscient perspective, and the pictures offer us a visual analogue of that point of view. We see the actions and know the thoughts of Officer Buckle and the children. Additionally, while we see the antics of the dog, Gloria, who stands behind Officer Buckle while he delivers his boring safety speeches, Office Buckle is not privy to her actions until he sees her on TV. The omniscient point of view in that scene is cleverly handled with a mirror behind Office Buckle's back, so that we not only see Gloria and him watching TV, but we also see what he is seeing. The third-person omniscient point of view thus allows the children and the audience to know more than the character, which is the definition of **dramatic irony**. This book also illustrates the difference between a narrator and an **implied author**. In third-person omniscient point of view, the line between an **implied author** and the narrator is often hard to distinguish. However, in this book, the narrator recounts the events and dialogue in a straight-faced, humorless tone, while the **implied author** is clearly taking an ironic stance on the seriousness of police officers and the need for children to be entertained while they are learning important information.

Third-person narration can also be limited or restricted to a single character's perspective. Different theorists have different names for this limited perspective; the character through whom the action is seen is alternately called a filter, a reflector, or a **focalizer**. Sometimes the entire story is focalized through a single perspective, but I find that rare in children's and YA texts; if an author wants to provide a singular perspective, he or she will use a first-person point of view. However, there are many exemplary texts that shift **focalizers** in third person for various effects. Robert Cormier, for instance, focalizes through different boys at different times in *The Chocolate War* (1974) to show the far reach of and varied responses to the oppression exercised by Archie and the Vigils. Sachar mostly focalizes through Stanley throughout *Holes* (1998), creating sympathy for his plight, but breaks that focalization to provide important story information that Stanley couldn't know. J. K. Rowling plays with focalization throughout the various books in the Harry Potter series. While we usually stay within Harry's knowledge and perspective, there are moments when we need to know more than he does. For instance, at the beginning of the first book, Harry is a baby, so he doesn't really have a perspective yet through which to focalize. However, we can't view the scene through the eyes of unsympathetic characters, so Rowling provides an observer, Professor McGonagall, to filter our perspective on the drop-off of baby Harry with his relatives. In the beginning of *Harry Potter and the Goblet of Fire* (2000), we are faced with a similar problem. Voldemort is discussing information that we need to know, but there is no one outside his circle to focalize through, so she uses the caretaker, a muggle like us, to overhear what's going on.

What is behind this technique of focalizing through a specific character is the manipulation of our emotions, identification, and **ideological** stance. A first-person narrative voice invites us to take on the perspective of the speaking character; we are used to using the pronoun "I" to refer to ourselves, so it doesn't take a huge leap of imagination to get behind the eyes, so to speak, of a character who uses that pronoun. However, we still maintain a sense of evaluative distance precisely because we know that his or her "I" is not ours. As a result, we can more readily detect an **unreliable narrator** by testing his or her perspective against what we would think or feel in a similar situation. A third-person **focalizer**, however, works differently. Third-person narration is more likely to feel inherently trustworthy, since it doesn't, at first blush, seem to have a perspective at all. So when a third-person narrator is focalizing through a character, and asking us to see the world through his or her eyes, we are more vulnerable to **ideological** manipulation, since we are given that person's perspective, but we are given it through a narrative voice that seems to take an external, objective stance on events rather than an internal, subjective one.

You will no doubt have noticed that I have left out second-person point of view. It is rarely used in fiction, and even more rarely in children's and YA fiction, rendering it a notable experiment. To understand how it works, we first have to distinguish second-person narration from direct address. When a narrator makes a direct appeal to the reader, as discussed above, this is not second-person point of view. Instead, second-person narration occurs when a **protagonist** is addressed as you, as is the case in Charles Benoit's *You* (2010), Tim Wynne Jones's *Blink & Caution* (2011), Beth Kephart's *Going Over* (2014), and Heather Davis's *Wherever You Go* (2011). Because the occurrence of second-person narration is so rare, no theoretical consensus on its effects has emerged, and each instance must be judged on its own terms. For instance, Benoit's use of the point of view is meant to be confrontational and accusatory, emphasizing the main character's sense of alienation and his unwillingness to be accountable for his own decisions. Kephart, Wynne Jones, and Davis, on the other hand, infuse their second-person narration with a sense of longing, creating sympathy for the characters who use it by highlighting the unbridgeable distance they feel from the "you" they are describing. Interestingly, these three books have multiple narrators, and only one in each book uses second-person narration, so readers get to know the characters addressed as "you" on their own terms, whereas Benoit only provides the angry perspective of his narrator.

The final two participants in Chatman's model are the **implied reader** and the real reader. The **implied reader** is constructed by the assumptions made by the text: What would a reader have to know, what scripts or intertextual information would he or she need to bring from prior experience into this text to fully understand it? Many YA novels, for instance, include a lot of pop culture references that make cross-cultural reading or even reading outside one's social class challenging. But while we argued in the previous chapter that seeing oneself in literature is important, it is equally important to see the "other" as well, so it's best not to interpret the implied reader too narrowly. Good authors supply the information young readers need to engage with their stories not by dumbing a story down or explaining every detail, but by providing enough context so that readers can figure out things that might initially confuse them. The work of a real reader, though, might well involve some research, which is rarely a bad thing.

Conclusion

Every day, stuff happens. We eat, we sleep, we play, we work, we worship, we love, we hate, we complain, we cry, we laugh. And through it all, we use stories to make sense of the world we find and to shape it so that it becomes our world. In the past three chapters, we have focused on the building blocks of children's and YA literature: words, images, and stories. The remainder of this book will turn now to the various kinds of stories that dominate children's and YA literature.

Extending your study

Reading:

Theories of Storytelling in Human History:

Boyd, Brian. *On the Evolution of Stories: Evolution, Cognition, and Fiction* (Cambridge, MA: Harvard University Press, 2010).
    Explores the evolutionary origins of art and storytelling and provides an application of his approach through Homer's *Odyssey* and Dr. Seuss's *Horton Hears a Who*.
Gottschall, Jonathan. *The Storytelling Animal: How Stories Make Us Human* (Boston: Houghton Mifflin, 2012).
    Combines research from neuroscience, psychology, and evolutionary biology into a readable, unified theory of storytelling.

Cognitive Approaches to Story:

Burke, Michael. *Literary Reading, Cognition, and Emotion: An Exploration of the Oceanic Mind* (New York and London: Routledge, 2012).
Densely researched and highly informative account of the factors that make literary reading appealing and affective.

Hogan, Patrick Colm. *The Mind and Its Stories: Narrative Universals and Human Emotion* (Cambridge, UK: Cambridge University Press, 2009).
Cross-cultural exploration of story patterns that evoke particular kinds of emotions.

Narrative Theory and Children's Literature:

Cadden, Mike (ed.), *Telling Children's Stories: Narrative Theory and Children's Literature* (Omaha, NE: University of Nebraska Press, 2011).
Essay collection from leading scholars in children's literature, divided into four sections: "Genre Templates and Transformations," "Approaches to the Picture Book," "Narrators and Implied Readers," and "Narrative Time."

Nikolajeva, Maria. *The Rhetoric of Character in Children's Literature* (Lanham, MD: Scarecrow, 2002).
Comprehensive discussion of the types of characters that are most often found in children's literature and how they are depicted.

Writing:

1 This is a partner assignment. Together, choose a character from a children's or YA book. Working independently, analyze the ways he or she is revealed through illustration (if applicable), physical description, dialogue, and actions. Exchange papers and compare your analyses. At what points did you differ? Write a reflection on how **scripts** and prior knowledge contributed to your construction of the character.

2 Choose an episode from a novel written in third person. Rewrite the episode in first person. Reflect on the process, considering how your feelings toward the character differed as you imagined the story from his or her perspective.

3 Write an essay in which you discuss how setting and conflict are intertwined in a particular story. What elements of the landscape or time period create the conditions for the conflict to unfold? What **ideological** concerns of the culture or time period influence what counts as a good outcome or resolution? What **ideological** concerns of the culture or time period at the time of the writing (if different from the setting of the story) influence the depiction of the conflict and its resolution?

4   Choose a story from Sharon Flake's *Who am I Without Him?: Short Stories about Girls and the Boys in their Lives* that made you think about a situation in your own life differently. Freewrite about what aspects of the story spoke to you and how it changed your perspective. Did you identify emotionally with the characters? Or did you view and evaluate their behaviors as more of an outside observer? If you had read this story before or when you were going through a similar situation, how might you have handled yourself differently? What wisdom do you have now about relationships that you didn't have before reading the story? For a more formal paper, then, work out your own theory of how and why stories can be useful in helping young people understand others and navigate relationships better.

Discussing:

1   Share a time where you felt a strong need to tell your side of a story. What were the circumstances? Did sharing your story change things for you?

2   Tell about a story that helped or changed you in some way, or about a time when you shared a story in order to help someone else. What do you think might have happened if you hadn't heard or shared the story?

3   Tell about a story you once believed to be true but don't any longer. What changed? Why is the new truth more compelling than the old story? How does storytelling help or hurt your ability to learn something?

4   After reading the case study below, read the rest of *Sam and the Tigers* and continue to identify what scripts are at work in the book. Discuss why you think this was an important project for Lester and Pinkney to undertake, and how they met the objectives they had set forth in their author's and illustrator's notes.

Responding:

1   Locate passages from a novel that describe the setting of a particular episode (for instance, the arena in Suzanne Collins's *Catching Fire*). Using whatever materials you wish, create a three-dimensional model of the space. Explain the choices you have made to create your model.

2   Create a story box of a book: using a box of some kind, place items in the box that relate to the story. Why did you choose each object? How do these physical objects represent important moments in the story?

3   Read or tell a story to a group of children or peers. Ask them to draw the most important part of the story. Compare the drawings and reflect on how personal experience determines our assessment of what matters in a story.

Online exploration:

1 Kurt Vonnegut on the Shapes of Stories: https://www.youtube.com/watch?v=oP3c1h8v2ZQ
2 Glen C. Strathy's Summary of Christopher Booker's nine basic plots: http://www.how-to-write-a-book-now.com/basic-plots.html
3 An article on the neuroscience behind storytelling: http://lifehacker.com/5965703/the-science-of-storytelling-why-telling-a-story-is-the-most-powerful-way-to-activate-our-brains
4 Further details on how settings are important in stories: http://www.writersdigest.com/tip-of-the-day/discover-the-basic-elements-of-setting-in-a-story

Case Study: How Scripts and Intertextuality Enhance Meaning in a Picturebook

For this case study, we will look at the way **scripts** and **intertextuality** work in the opening page of Julius Lester's *Sam and the Tigers* (1996). The first line of the text reads, "Once upon a time there was a place called Sam-sam-sa-mara, where the animals and the people lived and worked together like they didn't know they weren't supposed to." Most obviously, the use of the opener, "Once upon a time," draws on the conventions of the folktale, signaling to both novice and experienced readers that this story is meant to be read as a story in that tradition.

But from here the intertext becomes more complicated, and may be less available to the novice reader. Experienced readers, however, may know from the outset or from reading the **peritextual** notes of the illustrator, Jerry Pinkney, and the author that this is a revision of the controversial book, *Little Black Sambo*, written by Helen Bannerman in 1899. Lester notes that the setting of Bannerman's text is neither Africa nor India, but a mythical place. But over the years, readers have taken issue with Bannerman's casual blur of actual geography, so Lester takes care to create a place that is clearly mythical. Lester also notes that Sambo was a centuries-old derogatory nickname for people of nonwhite descent. Thus, the play on the word "Sambo" in the name of the town both calls attention to and critiques the earlier version by transforming it into a melodious nonsense word, somewhat in the manner of protest described in Chapter 4.

The controversy surrounding Bannerman's *Little Black Sambo* has to do not only with the use of the nickname Sambo, which stripped the main character of his individuality as well as implying his inferiority in an age when quasi-scientific claims were being made about racial hierarchies, but also with its pictures, which caricatured African hair and facial features. The pictures that appear on the **recto** of this **opening** in *Sam and the Tigers* immediately challenge those problematic features of the original text by showing three naturalistic watercolor and colored pencil portraits of a black boy, his mother, and his father that, while resembling each other in the way that genetically related families do, are nevertheless each distinct, smiling, and attractive, with no exaggerated features.

Lester's opening line and Pinkney's **full-bleed verso** illustration of the town also evoke **scripts** that will be understood differently by novice and more experienced readers. When he says, "The animals and the people lived and worked together like they didn't know they weren't supposed to," he challenges a **script** that even very young children will have figured out: animals like the elephants, giraffes, alligators, storks, and foxes depicted in the busy town scene do not live, dress, walk, and work like humans. This category distinction between humans and animals is established in the first years of life. But the clever wording of the phrase also evokes the racial tensions of the Jim Crow era. Animal characters are often used as metaphors to indicate racial or ethnic difference, so to claim that animals and people were able to coexist "like they didn't know they weren't supposed to" is a sly, knowing reference to the legacy of a time when black and white people in certain parts of America **did** know that, either by law or custom, they "weren't supposed to" live and work together. Similarly, Lester alludes to the erasure of black individuality through imposed collective nicknames and the consequently resistant practice of black naming in this introductory spread, in fact turning this on its head by explaining that even though all of the people in Sam-sam-sa-mara were named Sam, "nobody ever got confused about which Sam was which, and that's why nobody was named Joleen or Natisha or Willie."

Because this entire story is an adaptation based on a prior text, we can say that the entire story is **intertextual**. However, the invocation of multiple **scripts** in this beginning render the tale original and multifaceted, creating different and satisfying readings for both novice and experienced readers.

Author talkback:

Sharon G. Flake is author of nine novels and short story collections for middle grade and young adult readers, including *The Skin I'm In* (1998), *Money Hungry* (2001), *Begging for Change* (2003), *Who am I without Him?* (2004), and *Unstoppable Octobia May* (2014). Here, she talks about one more crucial reason we tell stories: to overcome our fears and reach out to others. Sharing her story has empowered other young readers to "cope with their own stuff," letting them know that they are not alone. Flake lives in Pittsburgh, Pennsylvania. You may learn more about her at sharongflake.com, sharonflake (Facebook), or @sharonflake (Twitter)

The Girl Who Hid Among the Pots
Or
How Fear and Insecurity Shaped My Life as an Author
By Sharon G. Flake

At Lehigh Elementary, where I attended school, my teacher Mrs. Brown would occasionally say, "Sharon Flake, do I need to put horse blinders on you?" For years I thought I must have been cheating or copying off other people's papers. But that is so not like me. So when I rethought my school days a few years back, in light of the person I am now and have always been, I came to the conclusion that I wasn't cheating at all. Most likely I was double checking, doubting myself. Unsure as I have often been, afraid of making a mistake, of being wrong. Yet in spite of my fears, I have always had this other side of my personality—a counter weight of sorts—a brave, risk-taking, people person who does not mind leaping without a net. Over time, I have come to understand that it is both the scared, insecure side of Ms. Sharon G. Flake, as well as the side of me that will climb any mountain, that has shaped my voice and career as an author.

Sometimes I think I was born afraid. My family often recounts the time I ran and hid among the kitchen pots. And what was I running from? A vicious dog? Bullies? A tease of a brother? No. I was avoiding my grandfather who was visiting and handing out money to his grandchildren. Everyone else understood the value of a penny it seems, except me. I took off running, dashing under the kitchen cabinet sink. He was a tall, boisterous, animated fellow so perhaps that's what frightened me. "What a foolish child," my grandfather said. And I suppose he was right because who would turn down money, especially then when two pennies could buy you cookies the size of saucers? I was not feeling so brave that day I imagine, much like the times I decided I needed to gauge the accuracy of my work against my peers' at Lehigh School. Yet it is those very feelings of inadequacy and fear that Maleeka Madison wrestles with in my internationally acclaimed novel, *The Skin I'm In*.

I guess you can say Maleeka created me as much as I created her. For two years, I wrote the book in the wee hours of the night, simultaneously working a full-time job and raising a daughter actively involved in sports. My daughter is dark skinned. I always wanted her to know she was as pretty and loved as anyone else on the planet. So while the book was not about her, she was my motivation for writing it. For a very long time, I did not see any connection to the novel and myself. Now I've come to recognize a few. I have a strong voice like Maleeka and struggled with being insecure too; there is a quirky side to me like the teacher Tai, and similar to Miss Saunders I am strong-willed and spent years in the public relations field.

For nine years I was head of public relations at the business school at The University of Pittsburgh. And wouldn't you know it: after working so hard to overcome my insecurities and fears, the girl who hid among the pots strolled into that position right along with me. It shouldn't have come as a surprise I suppose; after all I had struggled with panic attacks in my thirties. But you see, I have this way of saying yes to opportunity and the business school gig was a great one. Managing budgets, putting out a magazine multiple times a year, overseeing the redesign of the school's logo and public image (all things I had no previous experience with), meant I was very visible. I received raises and glowing reviews, and yet there were days I closed my office door and cried, overwhelmed with thoughts that I wasn't doing a good enough job, frightened at the idea that people could truly see me after all my years of hiding in plain sight.

So often we have no use for emotions like fear and insecurity. We want to rid ourselves of them instantly, to be strong and confident when all the while we may be crumbling inside. But what we can learn from the most self-assured characters (i.e., Anne of Green Gables and Unstoppable Octobia May), or those lacking confidence (i.e., Maleeka and Celie in *The Color Purple*) is that everyone can teach us something. And that even when we are feeling less than exceptional, we have it within us to help guide someone else on their journey.

Years after *The Skin I'm In* was published, I realized that my self-doubt and insecurity had found a home in my most recognizable protagonist—Maleeka. And that the two of us—the creator and the creation—had miraculously joined forces and used our insecurity for good. Young people across the globe still write to me about the book. One girl recently said she did not know she was a bully until she read *The Skin I'm In*. Many high school students write whole college entry essays about the novel and how it helped give them a more positive sense of themselves. A student who read the novel in elementary school and loved it turned to it once more in graduate school. One of the few people of color in her program, she began to doubt herself and her abilities. So she pulled out the book and read it. And realized again that she could do anything. I am hearing from many college students like her these days, who are still guided by the book.

I had no expectations when I wrote *The Skin I'm In*. I wanted the book published, but had not thought about next steps. That's what you do when you are insecure. You jump without thinking because if you don't you fear standing in one place forever. So with the book published, I leaped. When schools and libraries invited me to speak, I shouted yes; never mind that I had avoided public speaking most of my life, even at the business school. I think young people and I made a sort of unspoken pact, though. During visits I would tell them my deepest innermost fears, and they would listen, open up or even email me about theirs. I would sometimes shake like a leaf because of stage fright, and they would listen to the why behind my nerves and accept me for who I was. I hugged them. I asked what they were good at and I did not take "I don't know" for an answer. I wrote long, winding sentences in their books, encouraging them to fly. In return they dared to be vulnerable. Boys who some teachers said never read stood boldly in front of hundreds of their peers and shared their thoughts of the book—surprising teachers and themselves. One even proposed to me.

I wish I could say that the girl who hid among the pots is standing fully in the light at last, but it wouldn't be the entire truth. On occasion her eyes still shift where they shouldn't, checking to see if she has gotten it right. Wishing she were better at writing, at being a friend or even a daughter. But what I know now that I did not know as a child, is that all of me has value—even the pieces that seem broken or bent. And because I was given the gifts of fear and insecurity, I have also been able to help millions of fans and readers cope with their own stuff—often moving past it or growing through it. Not bad for a scared-y cat, huh? Not bad for a character in a book either, who will never know what I know, that because she—Maleeka Madison— was created, people around the globe see themselves in a more positive light.

Literature references

Alexie, S. (2007), *The Absolutely True Diary of a Part-Time Indian*, New York: Little Brown.

Anderson, L. H. (1999), *Speak*, New York: Farrar, Straus and Giroux.

Bannerman, H. (1995/1899), *The Story of Little Black Sambo*, Bedford, MA: Applewood Books.

Benoit, C. (2010), *You*, New York: Harper Teen.

Bloor, E. (2001), *Tangerine*, New York: Harcourt.

Brett, J. (1989), *The Mitten*, New York: Putnam.

Burnett, F. H. (1996/1911), *The Secret Garden*, New York: Grosset & Dunlap.

Cormier, R. (1974), *The Chocolate War*, New York: Pantheon.

Davis, H. (2011), *Wherever You Go*, New York: Houghton Mifflin Harcourt.

Donaldson, J. (2001), *Room on the Broom*, New York: Dial.

Donaldson, J. (2003), *A Squash and a Squeeze*, New York: Macmillan.

Flake, S. G. (1998), *The Skin I'm In*, New York: Hyperion.

Flake, S. G. (2004), *Who Am I Without Him? Short Stories about Girls and the Boys in their Lives*, New York: Hyperion.

Gribben, A. (2011), *Mark Twain's Adventures of Tom Sawyer and Huckleberry Finn: The NewSouth Edition*, Montgomery, AL: NewSouth Books.

Hinton, S. E. (1967), *The Outsiders*, New York: Viking.

Hoose, P. M. (1998) *Hey, Little Ant*, Illus. Hannah Hoose, Berkeley, CA: Tricycle Press.

Jackson, S. (1949), *The Lottery and Other Stories*, New York: Farrar, Straus and Giroux.

Jones, T. W. (2011), *Blink & Caution*, Somerville, MA: Candlewick.

Kephart, B. (2014), *Going Over*, Chronicle.

Lester, J. (1996), *Sam and the Tigers*, New York: Dial.

Lynch, C. (2005), *Inexcusable*, New York: Simon & Schuster.

Macaulay, D. (1990), *Black and White*, New York: Houghton Mifflin.

Myers, W. D. (1999), *Monster*, New York: HarperCollins.

Pratchett, T. (2001), *The Amazing Maurice and his Educated Rodents*, New York: Doubleday.

Rathman, P. (1995), *Officer Buckle and Gloria*, New York: G. P. Putnam's Sons.

Rowling, J. K. (2000), *Harry Potter and the Goblet of Fire*, New York: Scholastic.

Sachar, L. (1998), *Holes*, New York: Random House.

Sachar, L. (1998), *Sideways Stories from Wayside School*, New York: HarperCollins.

Scieszka, J. (1989), *The True Story of the Three Little Pigs*, Illus. Lane Smith, New York: Puffin.

Swift, J. (1726), *Gulliver's Travels*. London: Benjamin Motte.

Taback, S. (1997), *There Was an Old Lady Who Swallowed a Fly*, New York: Viking.

Tharp, T. (2008), *The Spectacular Now*, New York: Random House.

7

Drama, Film, New Media, Oh My!: Children's and Young Adult Literature on Stage and Screens

Walt Disney's *Zootopia/ Zootropolis* (2016) begins with children performing what appears to be a school play. It's a stylized condensation of the history of predator-prey relations, climaxing in a pretend attack that features Judy Hopps, a bunny, being viciously killed by a tiger classmate, with red ribbons and ketchup standing in for spurting blood. The two main characters are then encased in cardboard boxes highlighting their need to be kept apart, but when the boxes are lifted, both tiger and bunny are wearing white robes, resurrected as evolved, aspirational creatures that no longer live in an antagonistic relationship. The modern predator dreams of hunting tax deductions rather than prey, as he plans to be an actuarial, and Judy, our hero, wants to be the first bunny police officer. All the while, an offstage critter punctuates the scenes with comically conventional sound effects.

The children's play not only serves as an introduction to the character and goals of Judy Hopps, but it also offers in miniature the source of the conflicts she will encounter and the emotional arc of her story: for the remainder of the film, despite the outwardly peaceful coexistence of predators and prey in their present society, she will face danger followed ultimately by triumph. Buoyed by her performance (and her cop costume), she continues to perform in the role of a police officer after the play is over, facing in real life what she has enacted on stage, and again emerging triumphant, even though she has been hurt by her bullying fox classmate. She reprises her dramatic performance one more time later in the film, suggesting that the acting skills she has learned in childhood continue to serve her in good stead as an adult, but at that point her ruse serves also as a sly **intertextual** allusion to the technique Hamlet used to snare Claudius into admitting his guilt: "the play's the thing/ Wherein I'll catch the conscience of the King" (Shakespeare 2.2); in Judy's case, her performance does indeed provide her with all the evidence she needs to convict a criminally ambitious politician. Hence her use of playacting resonates in many ways: as a method for presenting social history and development, as a performative promise of a life to come, and as an art form that reflects humanity (animality?) back to itself in such a way that our best and worst sides are laid bare for contemplation and correction.

Playing the stories

This technique of a play-within-a-story is nothing new in children's literature—the March sisters in *Little Women* (Alcott 1868) entertain themselves by staging morally uplifting living-room dramas, Anne Shirley gets her friends involved in acting out Romantic poems (Montgomery 1908), and the very first scene of the stage drama of *Peter Pan* features the children "doing an act" (Barrie 1995: 89). It serves different thematic functions in each instance, but for our purposes here it functions as a reminder that children have never been content just to listen to or read stories; they must play at them. Full-bodied drama, complemented with as much staging, costumes, and movement as is practically available to them, is as much a part of their everyday lives as eating and sleeping. Alternately, they may play the role of director, moving their toys around as actors in improvised and evolving scenes; if other children are involved, the creative process becomes an exercise in collaboration, cooperation, and self-regulation as groups of children work out their own roles and rules. Wise parents and teachers encourage this sort of playacting, knowing that it provides opportunities for the alchemical transformation of inner stresses and problem-solving into artistic forms, similar to the ways children use self-generated poetic language as discussed in Chapter 4. In a seemingly paradoxical way, speaking in someone else's voice, taking on the role of a character, builds *self*-confidence; identities in process can find and expand the edges of themselves through experimenting at being someone or something else. One would think, therefore, that we would see a lot more print literature in the form of scripts that children and teens could enact, but that isn't the case; original plays written for young audiences are nowhere near as common as picturebooks, poetry, and prose novels. But then again, perhaps it isn't all that strange that there is so little published dramatic literature for children and teens in the forms of plays and scripts; after all, in terms of staging their own plays or producing their own skits or YouTube videos, all kids really need are some stock plots, a few interesting characters, and their imaginations, and they are off to their own **intertextual** never-never lands.

In fact, though, people who work with children and teens have always been aware of the tendency of and even need for children to act out stories. Children have performed in religious theatre productions and pageants under the auspices of the Roman Catholic Church at least since the early Middle Ages; before they had theories and research studies on how children learn best, teachers had an intuition that enacting a story was the best way to get its message into the heads of both the actors and spectators. Educationists in the sixteenth century also recognized the advantages of dramatic performance in developing elegant posture and diction. However, as Peter Hollindale (1996) notes, a prejudice against children acting in theatrical performances instead of being engaged in more rational pursuits had already been creeping into public discourse by the early 1600s, and children's theatre experienced something of a hiatus for the next two centuries. There remained exceptions in terms of drama in the service of education, Hollindale notes, as documented by Jonathan Levy in his anthology, *The Gymnasium of the Imagination: A Collection of Children's Plays in English 1780-1860* (1992), which contains plays by Maria Edgeworth among others notably committed to rational pedagogy. Beginning with the Victorian era, however, theatre for young audiences got a new lease on life: the **pantomime** became a popular form of family entertainment; a stage musical of *The Wonderful Wizard of Oz* (Baum 1900) was produced in 1902; Alice Minnie Herts opened the Children's Educational Theatre in the United States in 1903; and the first performances of *Peter Pan* were mounted in London in 1904 and in New York in 1905. Hence, the stage was set for Mark Twain to opine that "[it] is my conviction that children's theatre is one of the very, very great inventions of the twentieth century" (qtd. in Ward 1939/1950: 33–34).

How to study multimodal children's and young adult literature

Of course, children's theatre wasn't the only very, very great **multimodal** storytelling medium that was invented as the nineteenth century rolled over into the twentieth, and each one has had a significant impact on the way children's and YA literature has developed. Each emergent medium—radio, film, television, and digital media—has been involved with the transmission of children's texts since its inception; recall, for instance, that Alexander Graham Bell's first voice transmission over telephone in 1876 and Thomas Edison's first phonograph recording in 1877 were both recitations of the children's poem, "Mary had a little lamb," by Sarah Josepha Hale. Silent film versions of *Alice in Wonderland* and *The Wonderful Wizard of Oz* premiered in 1903 and 1910, respectively. YA literature was not left out either; Booth Tarkington's novel *Seventeen: A Tale of Youth and Summer Time and the Baxter Family Especially William*, for instance, published in installments in 1914 and collected as a novel in 1916, was made into a silent film in 1916, a play in 1918, a musical comedy in 1926, a radio broadcast in 1938, a talking film in 1940, and a new musical in 1951. Other texts were similarly dispersed across various media, as they are today, and, as Michael Rosen (1996) points out, the paths flow in many directions: book to script; script to novel; radio play to novel; book to film; film to novelizations, other stories, and sequels for various age groups. Nowadays, we can add in TV, video and live-action role-playing games, interactive tablets, e-books, audiobooks, apps, toys, household items, clothing, fan fiction sites, museum exhibits, and theme parks as sites where children can access and interact with both long familiar and new stories at different levels of immersion.

In this chapter, then, I have two simple goals. First, I want to offer some ideas of how to approach interactive and multimodal children's texts critically. Second, I want to provide some useful ideas to think with regarding how texts in different media weave through each other to change the forms of youth literature as well as how we think about its stories and its audiences. That should get you started on a research tangent that interests you. But it's important to note that each of these types of **multimodal** story sharing has developed its own presence in academic study, so, as with history and the other theoretical models I have introduced, you will have a wealth of resources to draw from in whatever direction you choose to extend your study.

To begin, then, here's an overview of some of the useful search terms in each area. Both the professional performance and scholarly study of children's theatre are called in some places Theatre for Young Audiences (TYA) and in others Theatre for Young People (TYP), while some programs that focus on theatre's role in education label it Theatre in Education (TIE). (I should also note that, when searching, you should try spelling theatre with either an -re or an -er at the end, as these are used interchangeably.) Scholars who work in this field often cross the creative/critical divide, as does Nicole B. Adkins, who wrote the talkback for this chapter. ASSITEJ, the International Association of Theatre for Children and Young People, is a global organization dedicated to promoting diverse, inclusive, high-quality theatre for young people, including innovative professional theatre for babies and people with disabilities, so their website provides a wealth of information, including an online journal with research that emerges out of their conferences.

Children's and teen film and TV are taken up in media studies, and academics who study interactive video games are creating a field called game studies, which blends insights from **narrative theory**, **adaptation theory**, and **fidelity criticism**, conflicting paradigms of audience effects research, education research, and **performance theory** among other methodologies as scholars seek to understand how people interact with games and how that interaction differs from other forms of storytelling and response. Within each focus, scholars seek to chart histories and developments of their areas of inquiry, how the texts themselves function as artistic artifacts and social practices, and how children and teens respond to plays, TV, films, and games. Hence, they follow many of the same protocols we looked at when we considered visual images in Chapter 5—what Rose (2012) called sites of production, image, and audiencing from the perspectives of technology, composition, and the interpersonal or social meanings that are engendered by a different multimodal forms.

Much of the early research on film, TV, and video games was heavily invested in surfacing the negative effects these types of multimedia productions are thought to have on children, ranging from mild dismay to full-blown moral panic. Scholars seem to have a persistent bias either toward the past, when youth literature and culture was obviously more intellectually challenging and more wholesome, as were children and teens themselves (we're talking about our own childhood selves after all!), or to print, because the "original" book is always considered more artful and worthwhile than its film or game adaptation. But at some point, such arguments have to exhaust themselves as technologies change faster than the human brain, more ethnographic studies are carried out, and we realize that these **multimodal** means of sharing stories and other types of art and information seem to be having good, bad, and neutral effects on viewers and users (see Gee 2003; "Video" 2007; Tumbokon 2014).

In fact, given the theoretical nature as well as the problematic research design and single-cause fallacy that tend to limit the validity of many of these arguments, Joseph Tobin (2000) argues that we need to move beyond an audience effects paradigm altogether. That is, most of these studies either don't actually talk to children at all, or they isolate small segments from films and have young viewers respond to them out of context, or they ask stupid questions: "Does watching a violent film make you want to behave violently?" Well, honestly, what is a child supposed to say to that? Young people participate in and respond to media as one aspect of their entire lives, so we can't assume a direct line from media causes to behavioral effects. Still, even as I write this, there are commercials airing on American television that feature worried-looking moms (all moms, incidentally, hmmmm . . .) expressing concern that their toddlers are addicted to devices, refusing to let go of mommy's phone, or to leave their console games to go outside, or to use the tablet purchased to facilitate reading practice for anything other than games. While I can't say that such fears aren't justified, surely the decision of whether they are or not has to be made, if at all, at the end of an analytic process. That is, a thoughtful literary critic should approach the analysis of **multimodal** texts with an eye toward understanding how they work and what social, affective, and intellectual ends they serve. In addition, it is increasingly imperative as critics and teachers of children's and YA literature that we develop practices and vocabularies adequate to analyzing and assessing the affordances of the various forms that youth literature takes.

Levels of children's drama

The spontaneous, improvisational pretend play of young children is a precursor to what Moses Goldberg (1974) named "creative dramatics," one of three categories in his taxonomy of children's drama. "Creative dramatics," or what Vivian Gussin Paley and Resa Matlock (2002) call "story acting," is more structured than pretend play, in that it involves asking children to enter into a self-aware if informal performance of a story. Paley, for instance, creates a performance space by outlining a section of the floor and having the children sit around the perimeter unless they are involved in the acting. Following such performances, Shelby A. Wolf (2003) notes, even young children can engage in guided critical activity as they assess the degree to which the actors brought the story and the characters to life convincingly. This activity of **transmediation**—from creative story to enactive drama to evaluative discussion—facilitates any number of cognitive and affective learning outcomes, but it also instantiates a practice of critical, self-reflective awareness that we are separate from our stories even as we participate in them. This in itself is a strong argument against naïve effects research. As Tobin (2000) and Becky Parry (2013) have discovered in their work with children, young people try on identities from stories not to adopt them or passively succumb to their values but to test and critique them.

Goldberg's next category is "recreational drama," a term that is somewhat misleading, in that it suggests an activity done for enjoyment outside the confines of work. If we consider that the most common forms of this sort of drama, as Goldberg explains it, are "school pageants, camp skits, or recreation department programs in which children act for other children" (5), the connotation of Goldberg's term is that such projects are not in fact part of the work of childhood, and that they are voluntary rather than assigned or otherwise coerced. But these two levels of children's drama point up a larger issue to consider with respect to the role of theatrical performances in young people's lives, and that is the persistent need to justify them as something more than or outside the realm of artistic pleasure or even the conveyance of story. Even more than reading, viewing or acting in a performance on stage has consistently been cast in light of educational and social aims, and if it can't make its case there, its value to education administrators, politicians, and nonprofit funding sources is on shaky ground indeed. This is largely why Goldberg's third category, "children's theatre," which is the professional publication and performance of plays specifically designed for young audiences, remains an outlier in the realm of children's literature and culture, at least in the Anglosphere.

Of course, money matters in theatre for young audiences. As we have noted, market forces have always played a huge role in the production, quality, and dissemination of children's literature. Nowhere is this truer than in the consideration of children's drama. A professional stage play can be expensive to put on, and expensive to attend. Production rights must be purchased, halls must be rented, actors, directors, and crew must be paid, and all of that is before the expense of renting or making costumes and props and designing and building sets. An amateur production bears many of these costs as well. Since live productions can usually only bring in money locally, through actual audience attendance rather than the residuals earned through video production and sales, a show has to attract a wide audience with enough disposable income to risk buying a ticket for a young viewer who might, in the middle of the performance, decide he or she is bored and become squirmy and disruptive. Even then, ticket sales sometimes only account for 25 percent of operating costs. You can see where I'm going with this—professional children's theatre is a chancy if not impossible business when it's built on a for-profit model.

For this reason, as well as for the persistent distaste many adults feel about targeting children as consumers, much children's theatre in the United States, Great Britain, Canada, and Australia has been constructed on a not-for-profit, donor-supported, and/or public-funding model, spearheaded by committed visionaries who believe that children deserve the best not only in **aesthetic** productions but also need to be cultivated as audiences and performers who will carry their love of live theatre into adulthood. But early advocates of children's theatre also stressed its socializing and educative functions, particularly in immigrant neighborhoods, with a strong emphasis on teaching what these advocates viewed as appropriate at the time. Social activist Jane Addams, for instance, argued that the stage should be "a reconstruction and reorganization of accepted moral truths" (qtd. in Bissel Brown 1999: 188). Playwright Constance D'Arcy Mackay (1918: 14) wanted to steer children away from the commercial entertainments of vaudeville and Buffalo-Bill type shows, claiming that "through love of beauty, which is the love of art, can commercialism be overcome!" While this latter sentiment seems to make a strong argument for high-brow aesthetic quality in children's theatre, in the first half of the twentieth century aesthetics was seen more as a means rather than an end, particularly in a field where the consumer is not the same as the buyer. That is, the theatre that was produced for children, at least until the 1960s, was not necessarily aimed at pleasing young viewers, but rather at being deemed acceptable and educationally significant by teachers and community workers who sought to make children assimilate middle-class values, ideals of cooperative social organization, and individual aspirational goals. Hmmm—kind of like the play at the beginning of *Zootopia*.

Is this necessarily a bad thing? Of course not, but it does limit the potential for experimentation, decisively separating children's drama from adult drama at the level of purposes and goals, and rendering TYA a somewhat conservative enterprise, even today. Contemporary theatre companies are pushing the envelope, especially with conceptual theatre for babies, but they still need to find that sweet spot where donors and the schools that would invite them in are pleasantly surprised and challenged rather than shocked, confused, or offended by their productions. As Adkins notes in her talkback, one of the most important aspects of theatre is that it is an intensely collaborative and interactive art form, and as such, it is perhaps beholden more than other arts to the values of local communities. For instance, Adkins discusses the difficulties of performing David Saar's (1997) YA play, *The Yellow Boat*, in some schools because they feared the intensity of the audience responses. On the other hand, we see audience response played for mild laughs when Judy Hopps' parents show their dismay at their daughter's performance, and then try to talk her out of her plans afterward, and when the bully, Gideon Grey, loudly jeers at Judy during the performance.

From these three anecdotes, we can see three different concerns with regard to audience in TYA studies. First, there are the concerns of appropriateness. As we have noted at various points throughout this book, appropriateness is a moving target, keyed to **ideology**. In TYA studies, the way scholars and critics judge appropriateness is most tied to what they understand and expect live theatre experiences to accomplish. Whereas in the early days of children's theatre, the experience was supposed to be socially and morally uplifting, nowadays the public face of children's theatre most often advertises itself as joyful spectacle, fun for the entire family! Assumption: public displays of happiness and wonder, with colorful sets and elaborate costumes, are what sell, but artistic forms that may lead to cognitive challenge and the public expression of genuine sadness? Not so much. Aristotle claimed that the purpose of spectacle was to augment the catharsis of powerful emotions, particularly fear and pity, engendered by the other elements of a drama; one would be hard-pressed to make such a claim for dancing candy canes. Maybe the public pedagogy of Disney's *Inside Out* (2015) will make more people rethink that assumption, but given that the holiday spectacular and humorous fairy tale adaptation are what many people expect from TYA, complex, issue-based shows, no matter how moving or socially important, will likely remain a tough sell to schools as well as the general public.

However, the reactions of Judy's parents indicate that adults recognize the power of theatre, and they do expect children to be influenced by what they see. In general, parents today seem more worried about their children being sad, troubled, or bored than they are about their children coming to expect that every day will be a zany, brightly colored extravaganza. But the version of that concern that Judy's parents express is that she really will think that her life can be like the utopian dream she has enacted on stage. The remainder of the film challenges and complicates that message, but offers a consolation prize when Judy's parents admit that because of her play, they have changed, and are now working with Gideon Grey, something that would have never happened if they hadn't seen her vision. The social message of the play had real effects on their community.

Gideon's rowdy response during the play is an aspect of audience study that is much more interesting in TYA than it is in the study of adult theatre, because contemporary adult theatergoers behave themselves—that is, they sit quietly, they don't interact with the players, they titter responsively to humor, and clap when the curtain falls. Children, on the other hand, must be wrangled into such behaviors by accompanying adults, who are not always successful in curbing the enthusiasms of their charges. This enforced quiescence often works against the goals of the actors themselves, who want their young audiences to interact with their performances, to blend their energies with what is happening on stage to create moments of syncretic attunement. Tinkerbell dies if the audience members don't clap their hands, and while adult critics have cast a jaded eye over this scene as a crude manipulation that forces children to perform belief for world-weary adults, the invitation to *participate* in the story world is a laudable recognition of a deep-seated need. As Adkins suggests, relevant research on audience responses is best done during a performance rather than after, so to do research of this kind, get a seat in the back and take a notebook when you take in a TYA show, and record your observations of audience response in real time. (What? You don't take notes when you are watching a play or film? I hereby grant you a literary critic's nerd license to do just that.)

How to read a children's or young adult play

The problem with doing critical work on a piece of dramatic literature is that it is meant to be performed, not read in silence. And the problem with doing critical work on a live performance is that your experience of it cannot be replicated for study and analysis later. So, a lot depends on what your goals are—Are you doing a review of a live performance, or are you analyzing a play as a work of dramatic literature? Either way, you want to start by reading and/or viewing more than one play written or performed for a young audience. Qualities stand out in comparison with other objects of the same type, so it's wise to get a general sense of what TYA is like, so that the entire experience isn't so estranging that you end up comparing it to something it isn't, such as theatre for adults, or films, or novels. Now, I realize that comparative analyses such as these are perfectly legitimate approaches, but what I am proposing here is an analytic framework that builds on the specific affordances and expectations of the play as an exemplar of a particular form. After you have that down, you can move on to comparative approaches from a position of deeper understanding.

Once you have some immersive experience with the conventions of TYA, you are ready to begin thinking analytically about a single work. First, read the play. I know that some scripts are not readily available, so this might not be possible. But if you have access to the written text, do make use of it. Even if you are going to see the show performed, it would be good if you could read the script before you go. As you do so, you should take some notes, and either subvocalize (which means creating specific voices silently in your head for each character) or read aloud. I prefer the latter, which makes me very popular at coffee shops or on public transportation—that nerd license comes in handy. The notes you take are on moments that you find important, surprises, lines that reveal something about a character, relationships between characters and when they enter and exit scenes, how acts begin and end, what staging, lighting, and props are called for, and how these theatrical elements might be symbolic or recurrent motifs.

David Ball (1983) recommends reading a play backward after you have read it forward—in fact, his techniques for reading a play are so good that my feelings would not be hurt if you stopped reading this right now and read his book instead, and I can just meet you back at the next subheading. The genius of Ball's idea is that by reading backward, you are forced to pay attention to what caused each effect, and this makes certain details that seemed insignificant or mere background information about character stand out as important plot elements. In particular, it is often difficult to isolate what exactly a character wants, and what leads him or her to take certain actions that seem like delays or detours. I have used this technique with verse novels to great effect as well, which often behave like play scripts. So, once you have read the play from beginning to end, start at the end and see how each scene is dependent on what has come before.

As you read, try to imagine how the play might be staged. If you are going to a live performance, find out a little bit of context about the playhouse and the company. What kinds of shows do they do? Do they include children in their productions? Is there a mission statement that guides their performance decisions? Even if you are not seeing the play on stage, find out what you can about the playwright and his or her sociohistorical contexts and goals. I have given you a very scant bit of TYA history here, but it's important to remember that playwrights are products of their cultures, and that plays are part of an activity system of dramatic performance that includes the kinds of stages that are available, the director's vision, history, and reputation, the actors' approaches to interpretation, the general and specific beliefs about young audiences, what age range the play is aiming to reach, whether the play is intended for professional or amateur production, and the historical and current **intertexts** of literature, film, visual media, and theatre. Many stage sets for professional productions of children's plays, for instance, are designed by picturebook artists, indicating a cross-fertilization not only at the level of story but also at the level of visual interpretation. The fact that contemporary children and young adults can be expected to have a good deal of experience with film and TV even if they are unfamiliar with the conventions of live theatre can affect pacing, character development, sound, and the use of special effects in both subtle and more direct ways; ask yourself how. Also, remember that we live in an age of presentism and parody, which affects how directors reimagine the scripts of the "classics" for young audiences.

At this point, your method of analysis will diverge, depending on whether you are viewing a production or analyzing a written text. In the case of a live performance, you will want to attend to elements of set design, such as backdrops, costumes, props, lighting, sound, and makeup; directing decisions, especially if they represent departures in style or significant cuts from the script you read; acting, including casting, movement, and line delivery; and any special effects. You also want to watch the audience and record their reactions as the play proceeds. Your goal here is twofold: first to closely observe all of these elements, and second to analyze how they contribute to or detract from the play's overall unity and effectiveness. Taking notes along the way is therefore essential.

If you are working from a written text instead, you can deploy any of the theoretical models outlined in Chapter 3. Since you have done a close reading of the play, for instance, you can assess its rhetorical qualities—that is, how it uses language to convey its message to a young audience—or you can set in the context of an **ideological** –ism. You can consider it in the light of the history of TYA, or in its broader sociohistorical context, or in comparison with the writer's other work. If the play is an adaptation of a novel, you could analyze it in relation to its source text, but I would caution you to avoid the assumption that a comparison must indicate which one is "better."

Film, TV, and video games

With apologies to Joseph Tobin (2000), I want to focus our attention in this section on media effects, but not in sense of the effects that film, TV, and video games have on young viewers and gamers. Rather, I want to consider how these different kinds of texts have changed, animated, and influenced each other in terms of **form**. But since I promised to provide some ideas to think with and resources for you to explore on your own, I will begin by doing that.

Ideas to think with about multimedia texts

As I have noted above, the thrust of most of the studies of these media has been on their negative effects on children (see Goldsen 1977; Postman 1983; Winn 2002). The American Academy of Pediatrics (2016) discourages exposure of children to any screen media before the age of two, and suggests that older children and teens limit their usage to one to two hours per day of high-quality programming. As Rosen (1996: 532–33, 532) points out, the critiques of visual media are "moral, aesthetic, educational, cognitive, developmental, political" as TV and other visual media "'leave nothing to the imagination', prevent children from thinking, turn them into passive couch potatoes, render them subject to consumerism, turn them into atomized, separate non-collective, non-communitarian individuals." And this was before the onset of widespread internet use and console gaming!

But here's the interesting contradiction in the effects research: If one of our worries is that children will become atomized, non-communitarian, passive consumers of what they see, it's likely because TV and film act as lamps illuminating what we don't like about ourselves and prefer to hide. As Kathy Merlock Jackson (1986) points out, "Films, because they are the product of several creators' efforts and ideas and because they are designed to appeal to a mass audience, are perhaps more reflective of a collective unconscious than other more individualistic art forms" (3). In other words, young people who are avid consumers of mass media will likely be *more* in tune with the values of their community than children who spend their time reading alone in their rooms, which is what detractors of mass media consumption would prefer they do. But of course, **ideologically** speaking, we've been here before: In *The Hunchback of Notre Dame* (1995/1883), Victor Hugo embarks on a philosophical digression about how the cathedral used to be the center of communal and religious life; all arts and industry were devoted to the construction of this structure, which represented "the great book of humanity, the chief expression of man in his various stages of development, whether as force or as intellect" (242). "The general characteristics of all theocratic architecture," he summarizes, "are immutability, a horror of progress, a retention of traditional lines, a consecration of primitive types, a constant tendency of all human and natural forms towards the incomprehensible caprices of symbolism" (249). But then, Hugo's character Frollo laments, came the printing press, "that gigantic machine which untiringly sucks up all the intellectual sap of society, [and] unceasingly vomits forth fresh material for its work" (258). With the ease and relative speed of being able to publish a book that relies on an individual intellect rather than a community effort and critique at the site of its production, a splintering and proliferation of artistic energies isolated people as writers and readers, with the result that "the book will kill the building" (238). Of course, nowadays the book is as revered by traditionalists as the cathedral, but do you hear in this a similar complaint made by contemporary critics of new media forms—that just as the isolating book killed the communal building, mass media will kill the book? Any kind of new media undoubtedly changes what we think and how we feel about human capabilities to some degree. The problem is that we can't figure out what we value more, so we are continually recycling old fears and complaints about individuality versus community, distinctiveness versus inclusion. Film, TV, and new media represent sites around which new forms of community and identity appear, both in terms of production and reception, drawing us out of the isolation of silent reading and individual interpretation into the responsiveness and responsibility of common understanding on the one hand, and niche identities, in-group/out-group separatism, and team loyalties on the other.

To give a few anecdotal examples, my family and I went to a midnight launch party at our local bookstore for the final volume of the Harry Potter series (at least we thought at the time it was the final volume!). It was really crowded. As we were threading our way through fans in costume and excited readers of all ages, I started up the chant from the Potter Puppet Pals YouTube video, "The Mysterious Ticking Noise." Immediately, complete strangers joined in until a whole section of the bookstore was participating in this obscure bit of online fanfic that had obviously gone viral—in the midst of a loyal community organized about a literary experience, a spontaneous eruption of performative empathy emerged through a shared knowledge of related mass media that parodied what we loved.

Another example comes from various screenings of *Bend It Like Beckham* (2002) in my YA literature classes. I first saw this movie on an international flight, and knew I had to get a copy. It has everything I like to talk about in my YA literature classes, namely identity issues related to culture, ethnicity, gender, class, body image, sexual orientation, and intergenerational conflict. In addition to these themes, the formal features of the film—its creative use of cuts, music, point of view, setting, etc.—enable me to explore film as a storytelling medium. What I didn't expect was the community-building that would happen with the audience. The first time I showed the film, it hadn't yet been released in the United States (don't ask how I got a copy), so it was new to all of my students. When Joe and Jess kiss at the end, and Joe does that cute thing of biting his lip, an audible swoon-y sigh went around the room, and I was surprised that it came from everyone, from the twenty-something young women who made up the bulk of the class, to a seventy-year-old woman who was taking the class and the forty-something professor teaching it, to the three young men in the class who may or may not have been gay. We all agreed that there was something about that moment that breached our expressive thresholds and engendered a sense of longing that we all recognized at some level. Most recently when I showed this film, however, the female students in my class complained *en masse* about that scene. They said that they were tired of films about girls who triumphed in their lives but still experienced conflict in their female friendships over a guy, and whose ultimate triumph had to be tied to a successful romance. What a difference ten years can make on the **collective unconscious**!

Most young people are avid movie and pop culture consumers—it's one of the chief ways they form community with their peers, and establish their identity as separate from the older and younger generations of their families. As a result, they have lots of experience with the story conventions of contemporary teen books and films, which almost inevitably feature a romance plot or subplot that presents the making of a couple as a necessary accomplishment for a girl protagonist, no matter how much she accomplishes in other areas of her life. When I first started showing *Bend It Like Beckham* in 2002, Buffy the Vampire Slayer was one of the few teen icons who put her career ahead of her heart, and we didn't have characters like Bella Swann, Katniss Everdeen, Tris Prior, Sookie Stackhouse, and Lorelai and Rory Gilmore as characters who set expectations for female heroines to combine relationships with other goals. In the intervening years, we do have these **intertextual** referents, combined with varieties of **postfeminist** rhetoric, a distinct shift in attitudes toward compulsory heterosexuality, and an increase in female heads of household whose successes and failures are watched closely by their daughters. In light of these cultural shifts, it's unsurprising (though I admit I was surprised, given my own social and textual contexts from having grown up in a different era) that my female students' responses to Jess and Joe's relationship were so adamantly negative.

Intertextuality

I'm making an argument here that asks you to think more expansively about the concept of **intertextuality** in children's and YA literature. **Intertextuality** doesn't just refer to the practice of making specific allusions to other texts, though that is part of its definition. However, it also refers to specific and nonspecific connections between texts and contexts that readers and viewers recognize on both conscious and unconscious levels. In other words, the sites of a text's production, form, and audience response are webbed and mutually informing, so that we can never say that we are reading or viewing a straightforward, linearly conceived adaptation of an "original" source text, and nor can we analyze it purely on those grounds. A child viewer, for instance, will likely encounter a filmed version of a text long before or even instead of its print version, so which, for her, is the original? In addition to thinking diachronically—as in, from one text to the next in a chronological or historically progressive way—we need to consider texts synchronically—that is, how they relate to the systems and practices of their own time and genres as well as ours, since no matter when they were made, our responses are always made in the context of viewing them now. All stories make use of other stories, and all books, films, and TV shows draw on the techniques and conventions of other books, films, and TV shows in subtle and overt ways, at the level of form and content.

For instance, contemporary novels often include or are sometimes written entirely in online genres, such as text messages and emails. Alternately, voice-over narration and chapter titles such as in the film *Babe* (1995) indicate a film's stylistic indebtedness to books. The titular character in *Scarlett Epstein Hates It Here* (Breslaw 2016) is a "BNF" (an acronym for Big Name Fan, a term used in online fandom communities to indicate that her **fanfic** and live tweets have earned her a significant following) of a TV show that is a clear analogue to *Buffy the Vampire Slayer* (1997–2003). When it goes off the air, she consoles herself by writing fan fiction, which is included as part of the book and relates to what it happening with her character in real life. Patrick Ness's *The Rest of Us Just Live Here* (2015) is also indebted to Buffy, as he imagines what it would be like for the characters who live in a town like Sunnydale but aren't the Chosen Ones. All of that's overt. But the use in much new fiction for children and teens of short, episodic chapters, quick cuts within chapters to change the perspective on the action, stock characters to round out scenes, and wacky action-packed sequences at the conclusion of a book, among other techniques, seems to reflect the subtle cross-fertilization between TV or film and books. In addition, the serialized narrative, which gained popularity in the magazines and newspapers of the 1800s, merged seamlessly into radio and television dramas of the twentieth century, and has migrated to online publications of fan fiction, web comics, and online novels in installments through sites and apps like FanFiction.net and Serial Box.

Young people's receptions to these texts come from their varied experiences with stories and films as well as other forms of discourse, such as news and opinion shows and blogs, reality TV, fashion, and trends, the kinds of philosophical conversations they have with their friends and families about their values and frustrations, etc. As Kimberley Reynolds (2007: 164) points out, "Young readers today acquire media literacies alongside conventional literacy, meaning that they come to texts of all kinds as transliterate readers." These transliterate relationships between texts and contexts are not linear, but enmeshed and dynamic, so that readings of texts change over time, both individually and, as we have seen with the example described above, collectively.

Changing **aesthetics**

Another way in which mass media and children's and YA literature are in dynamic, **intertextual** conversation is at the level of **aesthetics**. Sianne Ngai (2012) suggests that the dominant **aesthetic** categories of contemporary culture are the cute, the zany, and interesting. She doesn't make her arguments by looking at youth in media or media for youth, which is odd, because I would argue that youth culture *owns* at least the first two of these, and is deeply engaged in the third as well. Instead, she focuses on modes of production and consumption of adult fare by adults under postindustrial capitalism. While I think she is right in highlighting these three **aesthetic** categories, and her arguments are rich and complex, it's interesting to tease out what she misses by focusing more on her **Marxist** paradigm than considering the influence of youth culture on our visual and cultural **aesthetic** tastes and expectations.

So, a quick summary of her premises: Cuteness is tied to a logic of consumption that links tenderness with aggression in "an eroticization of powerlessness, evoking tenderness for 'small things' but also, sometimes, a desire to belittle or diminish them further" (3). The zany speaks to our anxiety regarding the wavering between playfulness and desperation, especially in our affective labor, that is, the work of relationship building and inducing or changing emotional responses in people. The **aesthetic** category of interesting is linked to the circulation of discourse and commodities, responding to our desire for novelty but dependent upon the coproduction of boredom.

To fill in some important gaps in her argument, then, we need to start by remembering that youth literature and culture has been intertwined with each new medium at the point of its emergence. This makes intuitive and practical sense—intuitive perhaps because the felt experience that these inventors were giving birth to something new might have unconsciously led them to call upon childhood's poems and stories but also practical because the linguistic forms of childhood could lend a comforting familiarity to technologies that were considered alien and frightening to many people of the time. Of course there were other reasons as well. Jackson (1986) places the Lumière Brothers' *Watering the Gardener* (1895) as the first children's film; it features a boy stepping on a garden hose and then stepping off in order to douse the gardener who was investigating the cause of the clog. In other words, it is both cute, insofar as the child bests the adult, and zany, in that it turns on the physical comedy of the practical joke. This sets a pattern for the use of children in films, as well as for films themselves—zany comic antics would become a staple of the industry with the child, Jackson argues, acting as instigator. But children and infants were also deployed for their visual beauty and as icons of innocence and cuteness. Jackson argues that the "innocent child in jeopardy" (35) was a dominant **trope** in pre-First World War films, suggesting exactly what Ngai highlights in her articulation of the blend of tenderness and aggression in the aesthetics of the cute—evoking compassion for small things while also belittling them in fact and **ideology**, as victims of those who seek to do them actual harm and as vulnerable persons in need of rescue.

A similar combination of tenderness combined with belittlement plays out in comic strips that feature mischievous and naïve children. *Buster Brown*, for instance, was a strip created in 1902; the main character is an inveterate practical joker who cross-dresses, pranks his neighbors, and damages property. Though he gets punished in nearly every strip, he never changes or repents of his hijinks. His character was leveraged across theatre, film, radio, television, and various advertising platforms, and children participated in his story through creating playground rhymes and wearing versions of his clothes and shoes that were explicitly marketed through his image; I daresay many of the women reading this book have worn "Mary Jane" type shoes, which were named for Buster's companion. Later films came to feature what Jackson calls the "fix-it kid," whose cuteness is derived from his or her earnest desire to take care of a dysfunctional parent, and whose version of zaniness often involves harrowing action sequences and chase scenes where the child is in almost over his or her head, as in *The Goonies* (1985) and *Catch that Kid* (2004), among countless others.

The **aesthetics** of the zany plays equally at the sites of production, text, and reception. Filmmakers and creators of children's media quest frantically for the next new sensation, and their products often feature frantic kids behaving frantically. There is a persistent sense that there is something not only odd but also creepy and *wrong* with the child who sits quietly, as do the children in *The Cat in the Hat* (Seuss 1957) until the antic

Cat and their zany alter egos, Thing One and Thing Two, show up. Few contemporary children's films avoid a manic chase scene. Such zany energy is the dominant trend in children's theatre productions as well, and the children audience is expected to perform their happiness in demonstrative ways for the actors on stage as well as for the adult who paid for their tickets.

That leaves interest to be considered. Interest emerges when a reader is engaged, and engagement for young readers is fueled most readily by interaction. As Reynolds (2007: 156–59) points out, interactive texts for children are as old as children's commercial publishing itself, and have evolved from pop-up books, paper toy theaters, books that incorporate simple mechanisms for revealing and changing the pictures, and toy books to electronic and online games that respond to a shake of the device, the touch of a finger, or the click of mouse or joystick. Interactivity within these texts and games is variable. "Sandbox" games, for instance, allow users to create characters and change both the virtual world in which they move around and the story itself, while progression-style and emergent games have more complex storylines that a player moves through, more akin to the print "choose your own adventure" type books they resemble, where the story moves forward according to the outcomes of certain decision points. Most games, especially ones that allow for multiple players working together, combine these elements in the service of generating and maintaining interest, because working your way through a book or game where all the answers are already given generates boredom after all its secrets are revealed.

Interest is also generated in a text through a sense of ownership of the story—that is, to have an interest in something implies that you have some sort of stake in its outcome. This is where fandom studies come into play, as scholars seek to discover how such communities of interest and ownership are created and maintained. **Fan fiction** keeps the interest of a story alive and circulating by enabling readers to contribute their own revisions and extensions, and it's worth studying because of the way in which it demonstrates how young readers-turned-writers understand characters and make inferences. Obviously, the perceived intimacy afforded by the internet is a huge contributor to interest as well; some readers become particularly invested in stories or poems if they can establish a connection with their creators, so authors are strongly encouraged by their agents and publishers to maintain an active online presence. But also, the cross-marketing of peripheral merchandise—toys, bedding, wallpaper, games, costumes, everyday clothing, kitchenware, jewelry, soundtracks, and school supplies (What have I missed that is in your home *right now*?)—related to children's and YA films and TV series allows both new and nostalgic consumers to take ownership of a story in an embodied way that feels connected to one's individual identity and/or communal affiliation. It is more realistic than cynical, then, to suggest that interest is in fact driven by the desire to make money through the continual flow of discourse and commodities, and that more money is spent on commodities related to youth media than on any other cultural forms.

Adaptation

The above was just a brief introduction to the ways in which studying youth literature and the way it travels across media contributes to the **aesthetic** categories of the cute, the zany, and the interesting; I hope as I was citing examples that you came up with a zillion more. I have suggested that many, but by no means all, of the multimedia texts of children's culture are adaptations of stories that first appeared in other forms. In fact, a good many published essays focus on how **transmedia** products relate to their print sources, and such comparisons are regular essay assignments in children's and YA literature classes. But I have suggested more forcefully (I hope) that the forms a text takes depend as much on social expectations, **ideological** concerns, and **genre** conventions as they do on any source text. This broad-based understanding of **intertextuality** and its generalized effects on cultural products causes problems for **adaptation theory**, which, according to Tom Leitch (2003), needs a complete overhaul from its basis in **fidelity criticism** in order to be viable, as it depends on certain fallacies that are patently false, such as that novels are always better and can create more complex characters than films, or that fidelity to the original is the sine qua non of a good adaptation. But as we will discuss further in the chapter on folk tales, adaptations are writing *into* a living culture as much as they are drawn *out of* a source text. Furthermore, while each form has different affordances due to technology and delivery system, none of these forms has a lock on complexity, though some deliberately choose to simplify or make a text more complex in its adaptation. A ballad, for instance, offers "plots with all the motivations left out," says Delia Sherman, who builds in those motivations in her novels based on ballad plots (qtd. in Windling 2015). In film, a character could monologue about his or her motivations, but unspoken motivations of a character can also be made clear through gesture, facial expression, tone of voice, relationships and dialogues with other characters, lighting, locations, **non-diegetic** musical scores, and costuming, all of these working in conversation with filmic and other visual conventions to aid viewers in making inferences about what is left unsaid. While this might seem overly subtle and out of interpretive reach for young viewers, Parry (2013) makes the point that extensive film viewing actually teaches children how to read films, and I would add that all of their experiences with literature, from picturebooks to poetry to novels, feed into that process; what scholars and teachers do is to isolate the elements and provide useful vocabulary to help them structure their analyses.

How to read a children's or young adult film

Parry (2013) notes that most of the criticism on children's film takes square aim at vilifying anything that comes out of the Disney Studios, with the unfortunate result that a lot of potentially productive air gets sucked out of the critical space. Single-authored, book-length explorations inside and outside the Disney canon, aside from Parry's, which focuses on her work with children, include Thomas J. Harris' (1989) *Children's Live-Action Musical Films: A Critical Survey and Filmography* and Ian Wojcik-Andrews' (2000) more comprehensive *Children's Films: History, Ideology, Pedagogy, Theory*. Kathy Merlock Jackson's (1986) *Images of the Child in American Film: A Sociocultural Analysis* focuses, as the title suggests, on the uses of children in film rather than on children's films, but her history and context is instructive, and a good method for finding out more about what has been written about children and film is to go to any of these texts and peruse their bibliographies, and actually go to where they are shelved in a brick-and-mortar library (gasp! to suggest such a thing in this of all chapters!) and see what's around them. Several essay collections address various aspects of the children's literature on stage, screen, and gaming platforms (Rollin 1993; Collins and Ridgman 2006; Neighbors and Rankin 2011; Papazian and Sommers 2013; Stephens 2013; Brown and Babington 2015), and various articles that focus on single films appear with regularity in media studies and children's literature journals. Margaret Mackey (2007, 2011) has investigated how readers and gamers understand narrative across various forms. Nearly all of these works consider films for their content or their audiences rather than their form, which is what I propose to do in what follows. I will be using some film terminology, but not a lot. As with drama, I want to empower you to read a film carefully in a way that is accessible to everyone, not merely a professional film critic. Note: these detailed explanations of the elements of film interpretation join with the notes on how to read a play to replace a separate case study for this chapter.

Previewing the film (and other multimodal productions)

In what follows, I refer exclusively to film, but these techniques are also applicable to TV shows and series and even some highly narrative multimodal games. It would be cumbersome to keep listing all the separate forms, so I have chosen what seems to be the most inclusive term, and trust you to fill in any gaps. Because I want you to think of the film as separate from any book it might be based on, I will not be suggesting that you read the book first. Some films aren't even based on books, but even if the one you are watching is, I think it's more useful to consider them as distinct art forms, so comparison at this point should be put on hold. However, you might want to come back to any original source material after you have engaged in your analysis, because it can help you see what a director is doing if you are contrasting it with choices he or she might have made. But if you go into a film with a clear expectation or desire that it will be faithful to what you remember from your reading, you will likely miss what it *is* doing in favor of what it isn't. So bracket off those expectations, and try to consider the movie in light of other movies, rather than as an adaptation of a book.

However, it is a good idea to give some consideration to the hype surrounding the film. How do the promotional materials work as visual images? What scenes are included in the trailer? What mood does the sound in the trailer establish? What is the genre of the film and how do you know? Who is the target audience and how do you know? What type of merchandise is being sold to go along with the film? I received a catalog from a high-end toy store, for instance, that featured a full page of action figures, crafts, and games to go with the new version of *The Little Prince* (2015), which had not yet been released in the United States even though it won awards around the world and was already in theaters elsewhere. Marketing for this film in my small US town was thus aimed at wealthy, educated parents who would know about international films or at least shop at high-end toy stores (or people who had put themselves on mailing lists for purely professional purposes, ahem) and who would be expected to take their children to this film when it was released. Those children, then, would be at an age where they would want to play the story with their action figures, make complicated models, and have friends or siblings who would play the board game with them, indicating, perhaps, that their parents would not be the sort who allowed them to play video games all day; there were no electronic toys on offer in this catalog related to the film.

Entering the story

After you have surveyed the preliminary material surrounding the film, the first thing you want to ask when screening a movie for analytical purposes is how you as a spectator are invited into the world of the film. Disney uses birds. Not always, but very often, a Disney animated film begins with a flock of birds flying in a trajectory that starts from the upper right side of the screen and swoops down toward the left. As the birds fly in, the "camera" seems to pan from an impossible height down to a human-height level in the immediate setting of the film. Then those particular birds disappear, taking no further role in the film. I often asked myself, "what's up with those darn birds?" until I realized that they were the spectator's path from the living room or the theatre into the story world. As a spectator, I am outside the story in a larger world, so taking my eyes down and to the left draws me into a framed narrative space. The movement down and to the left is also significant because it goes against the conventional direction that signifies progress. As Nodelman (1988) points out, since we read from left to right, we experience that movement as going forward, and, in the language of conceptual metaphor (Lakoff and Johnson 1980), going up signifies moving on or making progress. By going down and to the left, I am being invited to sit down, stay a while, and regress to a state of quiet, passive readiness to be enveloped in a story.

Another method that films sometimes use is called "suture," which is the way a film positions you, stitches you in, as it were, as a viewer. One of the things a camera almost never does is pan more than two-hundred-seventy degrees, and it mostly stays within a one-hundred-eighty-degree radius. Why? Because the human head can't turn that far around. In order to give the impression that you are part of the film, you can only see what it in front of you, or to either side. Often, a film sutures you in at the beginning through a progression called a shot-reverse shot—you see a scene (that's the shot), and then the camera turns around and shows you who in the film was observing that same scene (that's the reverse shot). This way, according to theorists of suture, you take on the ideological position of that character, seeing the rest of the film through his or her metaphorical eyes because you saw that first scene as if you were seeing it through his or her literal eyes. A good example of this comes at the beginning of *The Sound of Music* (1965). The camera starts at an impossible height above the Alps, and pans down toward people height, but then it starts a spin, traversing the one-hundred-eighty-degree mark, and the two-hundred-seventy-degree mark (wait, what?), until it's gone a complete three-hundred-sixty degrees. This is an impossible view for a human until the reverse shot happens, and you realize that the reason the *camera* can give you a complete circle view is because the *character who is seeing the view* is spinning in a circle. With that shot-reverse shot, you are stitched into Maria's perspective, and you remain her ally for the rest of the film.

A final example comes from the movie *Babe* (1985). This film begins with a title sequence that, like the opening scene in *Zootopia/Zootropolis* (2016), presents the arc of the plot in miniature. Starting with music that features a mild fanfare as the ornate script of book title appears, the music shifts as the impression is given of a book opening. The music then is soft and tinkly as the camera pans across a sequence of wall art that first pictures benign, three-dimensional pig portraits. When one of the portraits opens up to reveal the possible meat products that can be derived from a hog, the music begins to change. It gets louder and a bit more antic. The next art piece is a pig in a chef's hat, followed by an animated piece that features a pig jumping through a hoop and then a group of pigs dancing in a chorus line. Meanwhile the music slips briefly into a minor key with some dissonance before producing a more assertive fanfare as the camera tracks finally toward and then zooms into a framed photograph of sleeping pigs. The initial soft music motif returns as the photograph takes on realistic colors and then becomes unframed live action. Thus we have been taken through the entire emotional arc of the narrative, from initial stasis, to threat and conflict, to triumph through performance, all before we are led into the framed space and present time of the narrative.

Mise-en-scène

Mise-en-scène is a French term roughly translated as "put into the scene." In film studies, it refers to all the people, places, and props that are evident in a film. Let's break it down:

- Set design: The setting of a film is always chosen and designed with care to create a sense of place, mood, atmosphere, and to provide inferences about characters. In many children's films, such as *Willy Wonka and the Chocolate Factory* (1971) or *Babe* (1995), the filmmakers are careful not to specify any particular country or city, so little things like license plates and signs are removed or rendered nonspecific. This creates an impression of universality for the story, turning the setting into something like a timeless republic of childhood. As Charlie goes about his paper route and walks home from school, he goes down lonely, desolate, darkened alleys, and passes the enigmatic chocolate factory, settings that highlight his current despair and his longing to transcend it. In other films, the particular cities matter very much as signifiers, allowing filmmakers draw on associative stereotypes; for example, in *Inside Out* (2015), Riley moves from Minnesota, where her favorite hobby was ice hockey, to San Francisco, where they eat broccoli on pizza. Note the change from an unnamed town in a Midwestern state to a well-known city in California; both locales are rich with stereotypes, but like Charlie, Riley travels down empty streets in muted colors, even though it's daytime, on her way to the bus station as she plans to run away. The Bhamras of *Bend It Like Beckham* (2002) live close to Heathrow, which is something of a class marker while also providing an opportunity to foreshadow Jess's future of leaving London, as scene changes repeatedly show airplanes flying over their house. Indoor environments are even more carefully designed to reflect characters. Jess has a poster over her bed of David Beckham that she talks to so that we can get an idea of her frustrations and hopes. Her posters also provide the impetus for a discussion with her father that deepens our sense of the conflict, and she has to remove them when guests arrive for her sister's wedding. When thinking about set design, then, you'll want to pay close attention to small details—everything from the smallest tchotchke in a room to type of landscape in which a scene takes place has been specifically chosen to produce an effect.

- Lighting: Lighting serves to create atmosphere. Dark environments can create intimacy or a sense of foreboding, while brightly lit landscapes are favored in comedies and lighthearted moments in a drama. Cinematographers manipulate where the light comes from in a scene so as to create or alleviate shadows or focus attention on foregrounds, backgrounds, characters, and their interactions. When Babe is taken from the piggery, strong contrasts between dark and light bars of light suggest a sinister mood very different from the voice-over narration, which suggests that pigs are in no danger when they leave. The effect signifies **irony** for the knowing viewer, but can allow a more naïve viewer to protect him or herself from knowing too much. Follow the light throughout this film, and you will come to understand the various ways light and dark relate to the emotions of the characters.

- Space: Like lighting, spatial distances are manipulated to highlight themes and focus attention. Whereas a print text like *Holes* (Sachar 1998) might suggest long distances and empty space by slowing down the narration with detailed descriptions, a camera can use a long shot or a slow pan to highlight the vastness of a landscape, or the distance between a character and his or her goals. On the other hand, space can be compressed to suggest imminent danger or confinement. Jess and Jules each have alternate environments when they play soccer—the park, the pitch, and their backyards. While it may seem like no more than realism to show them playing in each area, the larger point made is that they are confined and limited in the parks and their backyards, but that worlds of possibility and freedom open up for them on the fields. When the action moves from inside to outside, when distances seem to open up or contract from scene to scene, you can be sure that the director is making a point that goes beyond the placing of characters in realistic settings.

- Costume, makeup, hair styles: With these elements, filmmakers create a sense of character that reveals much without verbal descriptions. An obvious manipulation happens in the film of *Nanny McPhee* (2005), where each child is clothed according to his or her personality, and Nanny McPhee herself has large facial moles and crooked teeth that disappear and straighten, respectively, as the children learn to behave themselves. Animation can be both more and less subtle. What my students discover when they look closely at what colors are worn by heroes and villains in animated films is that heroes tend to wear primary colors, such as red, blue, and yellow, while villains are more likely to wear secondary colors, such as purple, orange, or green. Weird. They also tend to have darker skin tones and hair—not only weird, but objectionable. The exception, of course, are characters like Draco Malfoy, whose blond hair and Aryan features are packaged with his family's attitudes toward Mudbloods to make reference to . . . well, we know what they are references to.

- Composition: As the word suggests, composition puts set design, lighting, space, and character into a shot that pulls everything together to create a unified effect for that scene, as well as to move your eyes around the scene while focusing attention on the important bits.

- Film stock or media type: Film stock refers to whether the analog film is shot in black and white or color, and whether the texture is grainy or sharp. Now that cinematography is mostly digital, the replication of these techniques, and of course the development of many new textures and techniques, is done on computer. While exploring these techniques from the site of production can take you down many fascinating rabbit holes (or not, depending on your interests), what you want to focus and reflect on are the effects of the different styles of animation. Maybe it's just me, but I find that attempts to use motion capture to create digitally altered but still human-looking characters, as with the characters in *The Polar Express* (2004), have a distancing effect that reminds us that we are watching unreal humans even within a fantasy medium, whereas

I accept Dobby, a CGI house elf produced with similar technology, as completely real and worthy of real tears when he . . . spoiler alert! . . . dies. On the other hand, computer-animated human characters such as those in *Toy Story* (1996) and *Despicable Me* (2010) have more in common with hand-drawn cartoons in the way they appear and move, so they don't have that uncanny, almost-but-not-quite human character that distracts from full immersion in the story. These are my subjective opinions, of course, but part of your analysis of any film should try to account for how style affects your subjective responses.

Editing

Editing and camera positions work in ways similar to the page turns of picturebooks. Stories move from scene to scene with gaps that the viewer fills in; otherwise, a film would be interminable and interminably boring. So watching where the camera is, what it focuses on, and how it moves between scenes reveals a lot of thematic information. For instance, in the first Harry Potter film, the camera spends an inordinate amount of time on two things: panning the castle, and focusing on Harry looking with wonder at the new delights of Hogwarts and gazing out of its windows. This focus establishes the castle as something like a character, but mostly like a home for the abused orphan. The scenes where he looks out the window suggest that he is still lonely and longing— he has found a place, but he hasn't yet found his family—but at least now he is on the inside looking out rather than vice versa. Additionally, as we are being shown the castle, we are supposed to react with a wonder similar to Harry's, with whose perspective we have been sutured by the shot/reverse shot editing technique.

Cuts between scenes create associations in various ways. For instance, in *Bend It Like Beckham*, there are several training montages set to lively music. These have become an obligatory feature of sports films since the Rocky franchise, but the fact that the athletes are girls makes a point important to the film. There are also lots of quick cuts that showcase women's bodies as active and strong instead of the usual fare of women as passive objects to be looked at. My absolute favorite use of rhythmic cuts in any film anywhere comes when Jess is playing soccer while Pinky is dancing at her reception. The back and forth between one possible future and another very different one is perfectly balanced, concluding with both women being literally lifted up—Pinky by her husband and Jess by her teammates—in metaphoric moments of equally exultant joy.

Sound

There are basically two kinds of sound in a film: **diegetic** and **non-diegetic**. **Diegetic** sounds are sounds that come from the environment of the film itself, such as birds chirping, conversations, sirens, and the scraping of chairs. **Non-diegetic** sounds are sounds that are not part of the story, but are added to augment the mood of a scene.

For instance, when Fly's pups are being sold in *Babe*, she sits quietly watching, while wistful violin music plays to suggest that she is mourning their loss. In *Bend It Like Beckham*, the juxtaposition of British pop music and traditional Indian music enhances the thematic messages of a clash between cultural values, as well as maintaining a high energy level during some scenes, and toning it down in others. Sounds are thus used to create reality effects and mood-enhancing effects, and their volume and quality shift according to what's needed in a scene. In a film like *Babe*, where you have talking animals that interact with humans in an otherwise realistic setting, sound is used to draw a distinction between what's real for the story and what's real outside the story. When Babe is having a conversation with the elderly sheep Maa, for instance, we hear their voices, but we also see Mrs. Hoggett listening, and what she hears is a pig noise and a sheep's bleat. Similarly, when Rex and Fly have their fight, we hear their angry words, but Farmer Hoggett only hears growls. Another method of using sound is for a character to have his or her own musical motif. This anchors the character in a viewer's mind through both the style of the motif and its repetition. The questions of how sound is used in a film include what type of diegetic and non-diegetic sounds are used, how volume is manipulated within scenes, what effects the absence of sound is used to create, and how sound is used conventionally as well as innovatively.

Ideology and modifying "The Bechdel Test"

Once you have done your close reading of the film or TV show you are watching (because the same techniques apply to a TV show), you can step back and assess how the elements relate to the general **ideological** messages of the film. Most children's and YA films speak to fairly simple binary oppositions, such as real/imaginary, childhood/maturity, home/away, freedom/oppression, and poverty/wealth. In addition, they tend to center around finding, creating, or repairing homes, families, and communities. Even teen horror films often focus, at least thematically, on these issues. These themes tend to be explicit, and are supported in various ways by the techniques of the filmmaking, so you can build arguments around how, for example, diegetic and non-diegetic sounds produce different impressions and levels of reality, or how editing creates metaphoric connections that are important to the messaging of the film.

But there are also implicit themes that hitch rides along with these techniques. For instance, a film that seems to imply that having a strong family is better than being super-rich, and yet obsessively lingers over the visible signifiers of wealth, is certainly sending a mixed message; it's a television cop show commonplace, for instance, that the criminals have better cars and boats than the beleaguered police officers we are supposed to admire. Race and gender are other sites of contention. Debbie Olsen (2011) points out that the absence of black children in science fiction is particularly problematic, for instance, since these films are set in the future: Are we projecting a white-only future for humankind, or entire galaxies? Frank Serafini (2014: 158) suggests that students might consider applying the criteria Alison Bechdel laid out in 1985 in her comic strip *Dykes to Watch Out For.* Bechdel's test consists of three criteria:

1   The movie has to have at least two women in it,
2   who talk to each other,
3   about something besides a man.

Serafini also adds that the women should have names. While this test seems apt as it is for YA films, I think it needs some further modifications in order to make the test more relevant to children's films. For instance, I would suggest that the female characters included in the count should be children—after all, it feels somewhat like cheating if the adult females' names are "mom." However, if the females in the movie are the moms, then their conversations should be about something more than childrearing. When I had my students do this test on films of their choice, they found over and over again that the women in the films talked to other women, as well as their male partners, about their worries and concerns for their children, but rarely discussed anything else.

Conclusion

In this chapter, I have attempted to do three things: first, to introduce and provide some guidance on how to approach a much neglected form of children's and YA literature: drama and theatre for young audiences. I have also provided some guidelines for how to read films and other multimedia texts critically by looking at some of the formal features that they share. Finally, though, I have suggested some ideas that we might consider in future study about the aesthetics that youth media draw on and perpetuate in the larger culture. Walt Disney is reported to have said, "We just make the pictures, and let the professors tell us what they mean" (in Bell, Haas, and Sells 1995: 1); the filmmakers and playwrights are doing their part, so we must attend to ours.

Extending your study

Reading:

Mackey, Margaret. *Narrative Pleasures in Young Adult Novels, Films, and Video Games* (London: Palgrave Macmillan, 2011).
    Theorizes a study undertaken with 18–21-year-old interpreters of narratives in various forms.

Neighbors, R. C. and Rankin, Sandy. *The Galaxy is Rated G: Essays on Children's Science Fiction Film and Television* (Jefferson, NC: MacFarland, 2011)

Theoretically informed essays on science fiction texts ranging from the 1950s to the present.

Papazian, Gretchen and Sommers, Joseph Michael. *Game On, Hollywood!: Essays on the Intersection of Video Games and Cinema* (Jefferson, NC: McFarland, 2013).

Fourteen essays that focus primarily on narrative as it passes through adaptations.

Reynolds, Kimberley. *Radical Children's Literature: Future Visions and Aesthetic Transformations in Juvenile Fiction* (London: Palgrave Macmillan, 2007).

Chapter 8 and the conclusion of this book focus on the ways in which children's literature and interactive texts intermingle.

Tobin, Joseph Jay, *Good Guys Don't Wear Hats: Children's Talk about the Media* (New York: Teacher's College Press, 2000).

Brings insights from poststructural theory to bear on the interpretation of young children's responses to film clips in light of violence, gender, race, colonialism, and family.

Wojcik-Andrews, Ian. *Children's Films: History, Ideology, Pedagogy, Theory* (New York: Garland, 2000).

Comprehensive overview and close readings of children's films from various angles delineated in the title.

Writing:

1 Although I have stressed the problems with book-to-adaptation comparisons, it's an inevitable starting place, so write an essay in which you compare a book to its **transmediation** in another form. Begin your prewriting by analyzing the works separately according to the elements discussed in this chapter and the preceding one, and then focus your analysis on one aspect, such as character, theme, setting, or plot.

2 Closely observe and analyze one element of a film, such as music or style, in its relation to the overall theme or emotional content of the film.

3 Mount an **ideological** critique of the portrayal of children, teens, and/or teens in a film or a set of films. In what ways are young people presented as cute, zany, or interesting, for instance, and to what ends and with what effects?

4 Go to http://www.gkidsfilms.com/ and peruse their films. Choose one to view and analyze and write an essay that considers how it differs from a film produced by a larger studio. Consider issues of style, pace, and content.

Discussing:

1 Continue the discussion of the categories of cute, zany, and interesting based on your own experience with children's and YA media. What examples of these categories do you find? Do you agree with Ngai that these are the dominant **aesthetic** categories of today's media? Are there any categories that you might add?

2 What story forms do you find the most satisfying? What constitutes the appeal for you? If you are a gamer, discuss how the stories you find or create in games compare to stories in other forms.

3 What plays have you been to or participated in? Have they been specifically designed for young audiences? If they were adaptations from works for adults, what modifications were made? Were they necessary, in your opinion?

Responding:

1 Working in groups, script a game adaptation or storyboard a movie from a book. What key scenes will you include? What might you leave out? How would you maintain a coherent narrative arc?

2 Take a picturebook or a scene from a novel and rewrite it as a script. What staging would you need? What costumes and sets would help you delineate character? Bonus: produce your play.

3 Explore several book-related apps and write reviews of them that are similar in style to the reviews on commonsensemedia.org.

Online exploration:

Resources for studying film:

1 A list of basic vocabulary words related to the art of film:
http://www.wabashcenter.wabash.edu/syllabi/w/weisenfeld/rel160/filmterm.html

2 A helpful reference guide to film studies terminology written by college students for college students
https://collegefilmandmediastudies.com/about/

Resources for investigating children's drama and TYA

1 The website of the International Association of Theatre for Children and Young People includes an online research journal.
http://www.assitej-international.org/en/

2 TYA Theatre Companies:
   Australia: Australian Theatre for Young People: http://www.atyp.com.au/
   Canada:
   Carousel Theatre for Young People: http://www.carouseltheatre.ca/
   Vancouver Symphony: http://www.vancouversymphony.ca/series/15KIDS/
   The Bumbershoot Theatre, Kelowna, BC: http://www.bumbershoottheatre.com/
   Four Seasons Musical Theatre, Victoria, BC: http://www.fsmtheatre.ca/
   Western Canada Theatre, Kamloops, BC (adult and children's productions):
   http://wctlive.ca/default.htm

Author talkback:

Nicole B. Adkins has taught classes and workshops to students of various ages at theatres, K-12 schools, and universities. Her plays have been performed at Hollins University, Mill Mountain Theatre, Studio Roanoke, Children's Theatre of Charlotte, Creative Drama Children's Theatre in Winston-Salem, NC, SkyPilot Theatre in Los Angeles, the American International School in Guanghzou China, and other theatres, festivals, schools, and museums nationally and abroad. *Playwriting and Young Audiences: Collected Wisdom and Practical Advice from the Field,* a book co-written with Dr. Matt Omasta of Utah State University, is slated to be published by Intellect Press in 2016. Nicole has four plays published by YouthPLAYS (www.youthplays. com), where she is also Artistic Associate. Awards include the 2011 National Waldo M. and Grace C. Bonderman Award and recognition in the 2012 Beverly Hills Theatre Guild Marilyn Hall competition. Hollins University Children's Literature MFA graduate and Core Faculty in the Writing For Youth Concentration in Hollins Playwriting MFA program, Nicole is also a member of Dramatists Guild and TYA/ USA. www.nicolebadkins.com

Playwriting, Collaboration, and the Collective Moment
Nicole B. Adkins

Theatre is inherently a collaborative art. It begins with the script, pours through the hands, hearts, and minds of a wide variety of specialized artists, and culminates with the audience. The end goal and marker of a script's initial success is for it to be performed. The play and the audience are not complete without one another.

One of the most beautiful and frightening things about theatre is the unique and unpredictable nature of the audience. It can be composed of people of varying age, sensibility, culture, politics, and aesthetic taste. These individuals form a temporary community, experiencing and responding to a play in a distinctive way.

An audience of young people or families is no less unique. Even an audience of say, fourth graders who may have a class, teacher, school, and/or certain developmental markers in common, is still composed of distinct individuals who can and will respond differently from another audience of fourth graders. They may respond differently on a Tuesday than they would on a Friday, or differently in a darkened theatre than they would in a cafetorium.

Audiences do not, furthermore, respond in isolation. Audience members' oral and physical reactions are immediately accessible to all artists present as well as to each other. Individuals often measure personal response against a collective response. This may serve to amplify warranted response—laughter when others laugh, silence when a hush falls. The audience feeds the energies of the players on stage with their rejoinder, completing the collaboration between all parties involved.

As a professional actor in a Theatre for Young Audiences (TYA) touring company for two years, I had the extraordinary pleasure and terror of performing four plays a year in rotation in every space imaginable. We played to school audiences and family audiences in communities across the social spectrum. In age, they ranged from two-year-olds to eighth graders to teachers and grandparents, and in experience, from connoisseurs of the theatre to those who were experiencing their very first play. The most satisfying performances occurred when we were able to create a completely mutual experience with the living sum of a diverse audience.

When a moment like this occurs in a show, everyone knows it. Something primal in the play, the production, the performance, or all three together, communicates itself to each member of the audience. When a two-year-old and her grandfather are able to surpass barriers of understanding such as language or life experience by processing the same moment in the *same way*, it can be a profoundly validating experience for all. The amazing thing is that it can have so little to do with the physical or temporal environment—it can happen in a gym with a squeaky floor as easily as in a professional black box theatre. It can happen in every performance at the same place in the script, or occur only once as a seemingly magical anomaly.

To give an example: in our production of *The Velveteen Rabbit* (adapted by Scott Davidson), regardless of the space in which we were performing, there was always a hush followed by quiet murmurs when the rabbit silently noticed that his legs were no longer stuffed but *real*. It was a brief moment between lines of dialogue, a space for discovery by the director, designers, and actors for which allowance had been made within the script. The production team achieved this moment simply: the director staged our surreptitious removal of the "bag" that had served as part of the costume to make the rabbit's lower half look more like a stuffed animal, the sound designer provided a bit of enchantment music, and we actors responded to this "miraculous" physical change. The magic transpired in the union of all these elements. The dramatic question of this play (what will happen to the rabbit?) began to be answered, and the response was satisfying to the audience.

In such moments of transformative understanding, players and audience alike become participants in an original experience. This is so even when individual interpretation of that moment differs. The Holy Grail for a playwright is when an *entire performance* captures the audience this way and allows everyone present to leave changed. A step above this is when the experience recurs in separate performances, or even in productions by different companies.

One of the shows we toured was David Saar's original memoir play, *The Yellow Boat*. It chronicles the real-life journey of the playwright, his wife, and their son, Benjamin, a spirited and artistically gifted boy who was born with congenital hemophilia. He contracted HIV through a blood transfusion and subsequently died of complications from AIDS at the age of eight. Though it charts heartrending terrain, the play is remarkably filled with joy and humor. It was our favorite show to perform, though unfortunately we performed it far less than any other show. Learning the topic, many schools shied away. They felt unequipped to handle the questions the play would raise. Especially courageous schools brought in counselors to lead a post-show discussion forum. Those schools reported their surprise at the level of empathy, maturity, and understanding on the part of their students, and their pleasure at the shift it led to in their school culture. We felt it. Our audiences were perhaps more engaged and present than in any other show we toured, either year. The most notable example of a bridge the production helped to create occurred at the home theatre, at a public performance. After the show a mother brought her six-year-old boy to meet us back stage. Through her tears, she thanked us. She explained that she had been trying to explain to her son for years what had happened to his older brother, how and why he had died, and that through watching the show together they were finally able to truly connect and to begin a new process of mutual healing.

So how do playwrights (or playmakers) create plays that are effective in this manner? Yes, the production quality makes an enormous difference, but how can a playwright best prepare her/his script for a wide range of interpretation? That which gives a good script potential for *transcendence* can be difficult to pinpoint and even more rare to achieve; but, there are ways to open oneself and one's writing to the possibility. Beyond ongoing study of the art of playwriting, and a fearless resolve to write what most challenges and compels a writer personally, I believe it is crucial to make theatre in a role other than that of playwright. In fact, it is helpful if the writer seeks experiences participating in multiple artistic roles.

The manner in which a playwright writes affects every possible collaborator. It is much easier for a writer to understand how to write dialogue when she or he has had experience as an actor. The lyrical, alliterative line prized by the playwright could turn out to be the trickiest tongue twister imaginable when spoken aloud. Complicated technical requirements written into a script (frequent set changes, intricate lighting . . . a working helicopter) may limit the creativity of a set designer or render the play un-producible by most companies. A playwright is more likely to avoid this pitfall if she or he has had experience backstage. A writer who has directed knows how a playwright's overuse of stage directions may hinder the director and ultimately rob a play of golden, shared moments.

It is also vital for a playwright to have regular experience as an audience member, both as a reader of scripts and as a live theatre attendee. A play that translates beautifully to the stage may not read half as well, and vice-versa. It is only possible to fully understand how this works if one reads many scripts. Seeing performances of some of the scripts she or he has read provides the most efficacious basis of comparison. Stage directions that seem impossible upon first read, or highly sub-textual dialogue, may come to life in surprising ways once the script has been explored and interpreted by a team of producing artists. Conversely, a playwright only knows objectively what works on stage and what does not if they regularly attend theatre. Sitting through a play that is expository instead of active, or one that has a passive protagonist, too many set changes, or is filled with author commentary can be a deadly experience—but also enlightening in what it reveals. Studying the point at which the audience is transfixed and when people shift in their seats helps a playwright begin to see the science behind the art.

Finally, watching audiences watch plays is usually a far more instructive exercise than interviewing them later (though it is possible for a savvy interview to supplement the former). In post-show feedback sessions, individuals may wish not to offend the writer, may be embarrassed to hazard a question or opinion, or may simply be unable to fully articulate a response. During the play, however, the audience is less guarded. As Hamlet famously expresses: "the play's the thing / Wherein I'll catch the conscience of the King."

Above all, I believe that a playwright must be a generous and brave collaborator. A writer is much more likely to create those coveted moments or that entirely dynamic play, if she or he is able to extend trust, put aside vanity and the need for control, and remember that the initial process of writing a script is only the very beginning of its journey.

Literature references

Alcott, L. M. (1868–69), *Little Women*, Boston: Roberts Brothers.
Babe (1995), Directed by Chris Noonan, Kennedy Miller Productions, DVD.
Barrie, J. M. (1995), *Peter Pan and Other Plays*, ed. Peter Hollindale, Oxford: Oxford UP.
Bend It Like Beckham (2002), Directed by Gurinder Chadha, British Sky Productions, DVD.
Breslaw, A. (2016), *Scarlett Epstein Hates It Here*, New York: Penguin.
Buffy the Vampire Slayer (1997–2003), Produced by Joss Whedon, David Greenwalt, Marti Nixon, Fran Rubel Kuzui, and Kaz Kuzui, Mutant Enemy Productions, TV series.
Catch That Kid (2004), Directed by Bart Freundlich, 20th Century Fox, DVD.
Despicable Me (2010), Directed by Pierre Coffin and Chris Renaud, Illumination Entertainment, DVD.
Goonies, The (1985), Directed by Richard Donner, Amblin Entertainment, DVD.

Hugo, V. (1995), *The Hunchback of Notre Dame*, Philadelphia: Running Press. [Originally published 1883].

Inside Out (2015), Directed by Pete Docter, Walt Disney Pictures and Pixar Animation Studios, DVD.

Jennings, C. A., ed. (2005), *Theatre for Young Audiences: 20 Great Plays for Children*, New York: St. Martin's.

Little Prince, The (2015), Directed by Mark Osborne, Paramount Animation, DVD.

Nanny McPhee (2005), Directed by Kirk Jones, StudioCanal, DVD.

Ness, P. (2015), *The Rest of Us Just Live Here*, New York: HarperTeen.

Polar Express, The (2004), Directed by Robert Zemeckis, Castle Rock Entertainment, DVD.

Sachar, L. (1998), *Holes*, New York: Farrar, Straus and Giroux.

Saar, D. (1997), *The Yellow Boat*, Louisville, KY: Anchorage Press.

Shakespeare, W. (2012), *Hamlet*, ed. Barbara A. Mowat, New York: Simon & Schuster.

Seuss, Dr. (1957), *The Cat in the Hat*, New York: Random House.

Sound of Music, The (1965), Directed by Robert Wise, 20th Century Fox, DVD.

Tarkington, B. (1916), *Seventeen: A Tale of Youth and Summer Time and the Baxter Family Especially William*, New York: Harper and Brothers.

Toy Story (1995), Directed by John Lasseter, Walt Disney Pictures and Pixar Animation Studios, DVD.

Watering the Gardener [*L/Arroseur arose*] (1895), Directed by Louis Lumière.

Willy Wonka and the Chocolate Factory (1971), Directed by Mel Stuart, Wolper Pictures, Ltd., DVD.

Zootopia (US)/ *Zootropolis* (UK), (2016), Directed by Byron Howard, Rich Moore, and Jared Bush, Walt Disney Pictures, DVD.

Tales We Live By

Suggested texts to read or view alongside this chapter

Bishop, Gavin, *Taming the Sun: Four Māori Myths; Riding the Waves: Four Māori Myths*.

Ocelot, Michel, dir., *Kirikou and the Sorceress; Tales of the Night*.

Sachar, Louis, *Holes*.

Scieszka, Jon and Smith, Lane, *The Stinky Cheese Man and Other Fairly Stupid Tales; Squids will be Squids*.

Yeahpau, Thomas M., *X-Indian Chronicles: The Book of Mausape*.

Children's literature critics John Stephens and Robyn McCallum (1998: 3) begin their book, *Retelling Stories, Framing Culture*, with the claim, "When compared with general literature, the literature produced for children contains a much larger proportion of retold stories." I'm not sure that's categorically true; it seems to me that, under their infinite surface variety, most narratives, for children *and* adults, consist of some riff on the stories humans have been telling for as long as humans have been telling stories. Consider the example of the story most commonly known by Charles Perrault's title, "Little Red Riding Hood" (1697). Aside from numerous folk versions from many lands, the core narrative forms the basis of Beatrix Potter's *The Tale of Jemima Puddleduck* (1908), is self-consciously referenced in Lois Lowry's realistic middle-grade novel, *Number the Stars* (1989), and is playfully reworked as one of Roald Dahl's *Revolting Rhymes* (1982) and in Peter Stein's *Little Red's Riding Hood* (2015) as well as countless other children's picturebooks. In YA literature, there are any number of novels, such as Elizabeth Scott's *Living Dead Girl* (2008), Nova Ren Suma's *17 & Gone* (2013), and Kim Savage's *After the Woods* (2016) that feature girls who encounter predators, go missing, and either live to tell the tale, or don't. But "Little Red Riding Hood"'s formula is ubiquitous in adult literature as well, finding its way into scores of horror, erotic, and literary novels, comic books, video game scripts, television series, advertisements, and films. The beginning of the 2008 movie for adults, *Taken*, for instance, is a subtle but unmistakable intertextual variant of Perrault's version of the tale as a caution to young women: a teenage girl, traveling to Europe on her own, is given a series of warnings by her father regarding how to keep safe on her journey. She promptly ignores these warnings when she meets a boy named Peter (a name that evokes an **intertextual** reference to the Russian children's symphony, "Peter and the Wolf") at the airport and tells him where she and her friend are staying. Peter comes back later and kidnaps the girls into sex slavery, surfacing the subtext of Perrault's version that it is the young girl's virginity that is at stake in her encounter with the wolf. Her father, in tracking her, spots her distinctive jacket—her red riding hood, as it were—as a clue that eventually leads him to finding and killing her attackers.

But are folk narratives for children?

Despite both the manifest and latent content that lends itself to such violent and sexual retellings, however, folk and fairy tales are most often considered youth literature, as if the seemingly simplistic nature of their narrative structure alone makes them suitable for young listeners and viewers. Obviously, ancient stories and folk narratives were not originally produced for children, but children would not usually have been excluded from hearing them. I say usually because there are some cultures that only permit the transmission of certain stories to young people who have undergone a rite of passage into adulthood, for instance, or to boys and men, with other stories told only in the company of girls and women. But it is clearly the case that contemporary storytellers, publishers, and filmmakers consider both the content and the structures of these ancient and enduring tales not only appropriate but also beneficial and even necessary for even the youngest readers and listeners.

Scholars disagree as to why that might be. J. R. R. Tolkien, for instance, rejects the idea that "there is a natural connexion between the minds of children and fairy stories" arguing instead that

> Actually, the association of children and fairy-stories is an accident of our domestic history. Fairy-stories have in the modern lettered world been relegated to the "nursery," as shabby or old-fashioned furniture is relegated to the playroom, primarily because the adults do not want it, and do not mind if it is misused. . . . It [a preference for fairy-stories] is a taste, too, that would not appear, I think, very early in childhood without artificial stimulus; it is certainly one that does not decrease but increases with age, if it is innate. (58)

Educational philosopher Kieran Egan (1997) disagrees. Drawing from an interdisciplinary range of research in philosophy, linguistics, and cognitive psychology, he argues that there is indeed a natural connection between the way children think and the structure of folk narratives. Research in cognitive development shows that children's first categorical distinctions are binary and without nuance; they sort the objects in their world according to relationships of similarity and opposition. This implies that, contra Piaget, very young children think abstractly rather than concretely; in fact, language development depends on the innate abilities to place individual items into abstract categories, which are initially organized according to binary oppositions based on a child's embodiment and experience—for instance, me/not me, in/out, up/down, wet/dry, full/hungry. Moreover, children are able to entertain counterfactuals as early as eighteen months of age, and they prefer fantasy to reality, as is demonstrated by the way they treat their toys, and the way they transform the ordinary events of their day into fantasy play. Ellen Winner (1988) has also noted an early aptitude for metaphor, as noted in Chapter 4, where we have also elaborated on children's attraction to rhythmic language that carries over into structured narrative. Taking all of these processes together—binary structure, abstract thinking, a predilection for fantasy, a grasp of metaphor, and a somatic grasp of the rhythms of story—you have what Egan calls mythic understanding, which is the name he gives for children's preferred method of accessing their world until around age eight. Researchers have also noted that children develop their story-making skills in stages during these years as well (Trabasso and Nickels 1992). Their stories up to age four or five are sequences of events rather than plotted narratives, and even when they begin creating goal plans for their stories, their grasp of logical cause and effect or psychological reality is not fully developed. Therefore, most children are untroubled by magical intrusions to solve problems, at least until they are seven or eight. These same processes of understanding and making stories, then, are in fact a more or less direct match to the structures of traditional folktale and myth.

Egan's (1997) conception of the progress of children's thinking tracks with the ways in which folklore is written and rewritten for different ages. In middle childhood, for instance, mythic understanding begins to give way to what he calls romantic rationality. Binary thinking has opened up into more expansive structures, and, sadly, metaphoric thinking goes into decline (Winner 1988: 103). Instead of accepting magical interventions from a transcendent realm, children begin to be interested in the extreme limits of actual reality and lived experience, which, as we will see in Chapter 9, prompts the consumption of certain types of nonfiction. But in their continuing fascination with folklore, older children become interested in characters who walk between the binaries of the human and the nonhuman, between the ordinary and the fantastic: superheroes with mild-mannered alter egos, cheerleaders who can slay vampires, supersleuths, über-rich celebrities, and athletes who seem unencumbered by gravity. This is the time when the magic in their stories has to make sense, when villains and heroes need to become psychologically real with recognizably human motivations. Adolescents then move on to become system builders, interested in the manners, politics, and intrigues of fictional worlds, all the while building on those first structures of myth and folktale until finally their thinking takes an ironic turn, and they are ready to see those structures exposed and challenged in radical ways. While Egan links this ironic understanding to a postadolescent age, I have suggested in Chapter 2 that we live in an increasingly ironic social milieu, such that expansions, parodies, and twists on folk literature have become as common as the folktales themselves. Thus, insofar as children's and YA literature apprentices its readers into the values of their culture, both the traditional tales and their ironic spins participate in this complex initiation into our pluralistic values.

Respecting diversity

Age distinctions aside, though, as we have noted in Chapter 6, to be human is to tell stories, and telling stories is what makes us human. But since the practice of retelling stories is even more broadly true than they suggest, Stephens and McCallum (1998) are quite right in focusing their attention on the cultural and ideological function of traditional stories. Ancient myth, heroic sagas, and all manner of folktales convey the values, beliefs, and hopes of a culture. Students whose main focus is anthropology, ethnic studies, or folklore seek to position traditional stories within their original contexts as much as possible, ferreting out the cultural conditions and living belief systems that inspired and continue to inspire oral tellers to invent and share the stories that lay the framework for their understanding of their social and natural environments. This is hugely important work, particularly in light of the silencing, desacralizing, and disenfranchizing of indigenous voices that take place when modern interpreters appropriate and market the stories of other (and sometimes their own) cultures. Without extensive study of the cultural systems within which the literature, customs, and social relations of a people develop, it is nearly impossible to understand the precise nature of the conflicts that traditional stories address, the problems they set out to confront, and why their proposed solutions seem wise or why the punishments are considered just and ethical. The unfortunate result of sharing the stories without due attention to such contexts, and without a frank acknowledgment that the retellers and illustrators are drawing on their own largely unconscious **ideological**, visual, and conventional contexts for story creation, what we have is what Richard Dorson (1950, 1976) called "fakelore," which, according to Eliot A. Singer (n.d.), comprises the majority of indigenous folktales retold in picturebooks for children.

But even Stith Thompson, one of the inventors of the Aarne-Thompson classification system of folklore **motifs**, admits that fidelity to original contexts is a mostly futile endeavor:

> On the whole, however, a quest for meanings outside the tale or myth itself is doomed to failure, because we simply do not know the frame of mind of the unknown person

in the unknown place and the unknown time and the unknown culture who first contrived the story. The search for the original meaning of any folk story is quite as impossible as the search for the origin of the story. (1955/1958: 178)

Contemporary theory in literary and cultural studies seems to want to have it both ways. On the one hand, we have gleefully concluded that what an author intends to say does not matter as much as how a reader responds or makes meaning from a text; or, to put it more forcefully, "the birth of the reader must be at the cost of the death of the Author" (Barthes 1977: 148). Moreover, our contemporary impulse with regard to European folk and fairy tales is to incessantly rewrite them, parodying their happy endings and updating their worldviews. For instance, in the hands of Jon Scieszka and Lane Smith (1992: n.p.), the revised conclusion of Hans Christian Andersen's "The Ugly Duckling" becomes: "Well, as it turned out, he was just a really ugly duckling. And he grew up to be just a really ugly duck." We have been taught since the modernist period (late nineteenth and early twentieth centuries) that originality and innovation are what matter in literary and visual art; we must continually find ways to "make it new" through the exploration of multiple perspectives and pluralistic dialogue.

But on the other hand, we tend to reject similar innovation when it comes to the arts of the indigenous people groups whose lands have been colonized by Western nations. The imperial actions of European nations and the consumptive global reach of the media empires of the United States have all but destroyed their stories and traditions, turning them into quaint, theme-park-style attractions, such that the scholarly impulse has been to try to recover unadulterated, authentic versions from a past before their unsought interaction with outsiders. However, as Joseph Bruchac (2011) notes and Gavin Bishop elaborates in the talkback to this chapter, even members of these cultural and ethnic groups must learn their heritage as outsiders to some degree, since most of them or us have not today been reared in a traditional community. In addition, the stories told by these insiders must conform to Western standards and expectations for children's literature in order to be considered "publishable," so some adaptation, as Bishop relates below, is inevitable. But the dangers take on the character of a Scylla and Charybdis dilemma; either co-opt and dilute the stories into modern, marketable versions that are so far removed from their origins that they utterly misrepresent the values of their origin, or freeze the stories in the past as relics of a people group that is so "other" that their pristine worldviews can only be damaged by adaptation, growth, and engagement with alternate perspectives. It is somewhat ironic that those with the most progressive attitudes toward the revision of European traditional forms for purposes, say, of contemporary Western feminism, often seem to favor preservation over revision of other cultural forms.

Betsy Hearne (1993) proposes something of a middle path through this controversial minefield. She argues that the adaptation and evaluation (and I would add the reading and teaching) of folklore require respect and balance. "Respect," says Hearne, "is not synonymous with reverence, adulation, sentimentality, nostalgia, or solemnity. In fact, humor is an important part of taking folklore seriously" (33). Instead, respect requires crediting the specific cultures and sources from which the story derives, while seeking balance between knowledge and experience, both of the culture and traditions "from which it [the story] is drawn, and the one that it is entering" (33). One of the "traditions" of children's and YA literature is, in fact, to interrogate the stories of the past and revise them to reflect the culture we want to build going forward. While many children's and YA texts have in the past continued and continue to reinforce what Stephens and McCallum (1998: 9) claim are "androcentric, ethnocentric, and class-centric" worldviews, a comparison of, say, Frances Hodgson Burnett's *A Little Princess* (1905) with Gail Carson Levine's *Ella Enchanted* (1997) suggests that something in the way we imagine middle-grade readers will relate to the story of Cinderella has significantly changed. A more controversial example is Thomas M. Yeahpau's YA text, *X-Indian Chronicles: The Book of Mausape* (2006). In a series of interconnected short stories, Yeahpau takes an unflinching look at life for contemporary Native American teens reared on a reservation. His fluid blending of native storytelling and folkloric characters with the grim contemporary realities of drugs, alcohol, domestic abuse, and media culture both challenges the practice of telling prettified stories of Native American traditions and pushes the boundaries of and within YA literature: there's a paranormal romance, but it's gritty and sordid; an allegorical trial that attacks sentimental views of Christianity with grim irony; an unexpected twist on the vision quest; and a darkly funny **intertextual** reference to Sherman Alexie, a fellow Native American author who is much more widely known. Reader expectations are continually challenged as Yeahpau deftly negotiates the balance between the culture from which he draws his stories and the culture he is writing into. In fact, Yeahpau's text enacts, in a creative way, the task Adrienne Rich sets for feminist critical practice:

> Re-vision—the act of looking back, of seeing with fresh eyes, of entering an old text from a new critical direction—is for us more than a chapter in cultural history: it is an act of survival. Until we can understand the assumptions in which we are drenched we cannot know ourselves. . . . A radical critique of literature, feminist in its impulse, would take the work first of all as a clue to how we live, how we have been living, how we have been led to imagine ourselves, how our language has trapped as well as liberated us; and how we can begin to see—and therefore live—afresh. . . . We need to know the writing of the past, and know it differently than we have ever known it; not to pass on a tradition but to break its hold over us. (1972: 18–19)

Our goal in this chapter, then, will not be to lay out a narrative of origin for these tales—there are many books and articles that do this work, some of which are referenced in the suggestions for further reading—but to look at the ways in which they have been taken up in the content and study of children's and YA literature. Part of the work of this chapter, then, will be to follow Thomas Bullfinch's lead: As he expresses it in his preface to *The Age of Fable* (1855: 5), his goal was to enable the busy, practical people of the nineteenth century to "comprehend the allusions so frequently made by public speakers, lecturers, essayists, and poets and those which occur in polite conversation," to which we add children's and YA literature. You are busy, practical people, and while some of you may decide to pursue an in-depth study of ancient texts along with their **intertextual** sources and subsequent retellings, *everyone* who reads, studies, teaches, and writes children's and YA literature should have a broad-based familiarity with the bits and bobs that have been tossed into what J. R. R. Tolkien (1966: 54) calls "the Cauldron of Story" from which all storytellers draw. Of course, we can only provide here the briefest overview of these stories with their **motifs** and structures, with the hope that these summaries will in fact inspire further research.

But in addition to a survey of the kinds and content of traditional tales, we will also consider why and how these stories, structures, and **motifs** are taken up in retellings for children and YAs, as well as how they have been studied. After all, traditional myths, epics, fables, folktales, sagas, ballads, and legends contain themes and elements that we might consider questionable for children, even under a kinship model; the gods and goddesses of ancient myth, for instance, were both randy and violent. But also, we live in a secular, scientific age, so what use could ancient myths, exaggerated legends, and magic-laced folktales possibly have for twenty-first century children? Fables, sure, because they have detachable morals, but the rest? Epics lionize their heroes through violence, some legends perpetuate debilitating fear, and folk and fairytales simply reek of sexism and entitlement, replacing an ethic of hard work resulting in modest gain with a wish-fulfillment fantasy of immense wealth granted on the basis of good looks, privileged birth, or magical intervention. Objections such as these demand to be addressed.

Definitions and descriptions

Before we go much further, though, we must clarify our terms as best we can. Brian Attebery wisely notes that "genre names are both descriptive and constitutive"—that is, they create the distinctions they purport to describe—and that these distinctions are best thought of as "fuzzy sets: categories defined not by a clear boundary but by a resemblance to a single core example or group of examples" (2014: interlude). There is simply too much integration and overlap between myths, epics, sagas, and folktales to definitively place a story in one camp or another. Moreover, categorical distinctions may change based on who is doing the categorizing; a cultural insider might see a story as something that actually happened, while an outsider, separated either by time, ethnicity, or **ideological** stance, may view it as legend or myth. That said, however, we can make some provisional analytical distinctions based on form and function.

Folktales, then, are something of a super category that contains many types of highly structured narratives that may or may not have magical elements in them. They may be comical or serious, and it is almost never possible to trace their origins back to a single author; rather, they are circulated orally among the folk. However, as Ruth B. Bottigheimer (1996) notes, folktales appear regularly in the ancient literature of many cultures, such as the Tanakh and the Christian Bible, the Indian *Panchatantra* (circa third century BCE), and the *Aesopica*, better known today as Aesop's Fables (circa fifth century BCE). And just as written versions of folktales eased the transition of preliterate people steeped in oral traditions into the developing print culture of the sixteenth, seventeenth, and eighteenth centuries, retellings and new stories inspired by their forms make up a robust segment of the picturebooks published for preliterate and newly literate children today. Although there is much blending and overlap of character types and plot structures among different kinds of folktales, folk literature tends to be subdivided according to structure or purpose, or, in the case of the Aarne-Thompson-Uther tale type index, by their **motifs**. This classification system, used worldwide by folklorists, groups tales by types, such as Animal Bride, or Unnatural Cruelty, and then further subdivides tales into more specific subtypes, assigning each type a number. Here, however, we will focus on form and purpose to highlight a few types that show up frequently in children's and YA literature. Only retellings that are original to their authors are referenced by their specific titles and included in the bibliography; the rest have many oral, print, and online versions to choose from.

- *Cumulative, repetitive, circle, or chain tales:* As described in the previous chapter, these are stories in which new characters or problems are added in until the climax is reached. While cumulative tales need not return the characters or situation back to its original state, circle stories do. Some familiar tales include "Chicken Little" (also known as "Henny Penny" or "The Sky is Falling"), "The Mitten" (Ukraine), "Chad Gadya" (Hebrew and Aramaic), "The House that Jack Built" (British), "The Little Red Hen" (probably Russian), "The Gingerbread Man" (American variant of the Fleeing Pancake story that is known throughout Europe), *Perez and Martina: A Puerto Rican Folktale* (Belpré 1932), and *If You Give a Mouse a Cookie* (Numeroff 1985).
- *Animal fables:* Drawing from the tales of the slave Aesop, animal fables amplify and use the stereotyped behavior of animals—for example, sly foxes, diligent ants, slow tortoises, and quick rabbits—to create a clever, sometimes ironic demonstration of a human frailty or moral lesson. Fables are generally quite short, and most presentations for children today include an explicit statement of the moral at the end, which sometimes becomes a stand-alone platitude, such as "slow and steady wins the race" or "familiarity breeds contempt." Not all characters in fables are animals, but most of the ones that are can speak. Examples include "The Tortoise and the Hare," "The Lion and The Wolf," "The

Dog in the Manger," "The Wolf in Sheep's Clothing"; new picturebook editions of Aesop's Fables are published each year.

- *Talking beast tales:* These are usually more elaborate than fables, and occasionally have more ambiguous morals. "Goldilocks and the Three Bears," "The Three Pigs," "The Three Billy Goats Gruff"—are you sensing a pattern here? While many talking beast tales follow the **Rule of Three** (described below) in their character constellation, others feature a singular main character, such as the twelfth-century German and French hero, Reynard the Fox (who shows up as the wily but noble Robin Hood in Walt Disney's 1973 film), Puss in Boots, the serpent who talks to Eve in Genesis, and the donkey who talks to Balaam in Numbers (these last two are books in the Torah, or the Old Testament of the Christian Bible). These talking animals share with their fable cousins the dual qualities of their animal nature and a human capacity for speech; their folk literature legacy is part of why children seem to almost instinctively distrust the character of Hiss (a snake) in Disney's *Robin Hood* (1973), and expect both humor and wisdom from Donkey in the movie version of *Shrek*. Authored books for older readers that draw from the talking beast tradition include *Black Beauty* (Sewell 1877), *Charlotte's Web* (White 1952), The Chronicles of Narnia (Lewis 1950–6), *Watership Down* (Adams 1972), and *The Amazing Maurice and His Educated Rodents* (Pratchett 2001).

- *Trickster tales:* Tricksters are figures that use their cleverness or secret knowledge to outwit stronger or more powerful opponents, making them very appealing to children for obvious reasons. Tricksters appear in sacred myth as well as folktales; Loki, for instance, though a god, is also a trickster figure from Norse mythology. Trickster characters in folktales can be animals, humans, or shape-shifting spirits, and they are characterized by their amoral and capricious behavior. They can be specific, named characters with distinct personalities, or whole species of mischief-making folk. Sometimes they are cultural heroes who perform great acts of service for humans, as Raven does when he brings light into the world in the tale from the Pacific Northwest. Other times their services are less well-intended, as is that of the duppy (a trickster figure of Jamaican origin) in Delia Sherman's *The Freedom Maze* (2011). The trickster Br'er Rabbit has antecedents in the African, Cherokee, and Algonquin traditions that interacted in the American South. High John the Conqueror is also an African American trickster and folk hero born out of the antebellum period of slavery in the United States. Coyote, Nanabozho, and Iktomi are Native American tricksters. Anansi the spider is a West African trickster; so is the precocious human infant Kirikou. Brownies or hobgoblins are tricksters from Scottish tradition who have morphed into Terry Pratchett's Wee Free Men and the House-elves in the Harry Potter series. Interestingly, there are more fairies in trickster tales than there are in what are called fairy tales; the fey folk are creatures whose malevolence must be guarded against through the use of wards, or appeased through the leaving of gifts lest they perform tricks that range in seriousness from souring the milk to carrying off a young person or replacing a human child with a changeling. Trickster figures appear in every folkloric tradition, suggesting that there is something in humans that will always find ways to resist and challenge oppression and authority, and that there is always some unseen force that loves to disturb our peace and scuttle our best-laid plans.

- *Pourquoi tales:* These are stories that purport to tell why things are the way they are; however, they don't usually go after the big whys—that is, they don't address matters of great import or religious significance. Instead, they are generally limited to animal characteristics or landscape features. Pourquoi tales are common in indigenous folklore, and are favorites of professional storytellers as well as teachers, who encourage their young students to write their own. Perhaps because they are meant to be fanciful and imaginative, and are divorced from sacred tradition, there is less controversy regarding cultural appropriation with pourquoi tales, although crediting sources should still be a priority. Some well-known literary pourquoi tales are found in Rudyard Kipling's *Just So Stories* (1902) and Verna Aardema's *Why Mosquitoes Buzz in People's Ears* (1975, also a cumulative tale).

- *Droll or noodlehead tales:* These are stories about characters who are exaggeratedly stupid, foolish, or naïve, but most often, their ridiculous solution to the problem is what saves the day. Similar to tricksters, their behavior often challenges those in authority by pointing out the absurdity of the situation in which they find themselves. Unlike tricksters, however, their send-up of rules and conventions is not intentional. Traditional tales include "The Three Sillies," "Lazy Jack," and "Mr. Vinegar." The populist Mullah from Turkey, Nasreddin Hodja, often appears as a droll figure, but he is also something of a trickster as well as a wise man. Jack of the Cornish, English, and Appalachian Jack Tales is often portrayed as a noodlehead, as is Mr. Toad in Kenneth Grahame's *The Wind in the Willows* (1908). Noodleheads often show up in picturebooks such as Harry G. Allard, Jr.'s books about The Stupids, and Dav Pilkey's Dumb Bunnies books, and the early reader character, Amelia Bedelia, giving children the opportunity to enjoy their own superiority over the silly characters and nonsense wordplay.

- *Ghost stories:* These stories turn on the presence of a ghost or haunted object that helps or hinders the main character of the story. Most ghosts haunt specific localities, but some have achieved widespread familiarity through vigorous storytelling, such as La Llorona, the Weeping Woman known throughout Latin America, who drowned her children and then killed herself. Seeing or even being spirited away by the ghosts of the Wild Hunt is a fear prevalent throughout

Northern, Western, and Central Europe and the British Isles. The Headless Horseman seems to have come by way Scottish and German mercenary soldiers to fight in the American Revolutionary War, where he found himself immortalized in print by Washington Irving's "The Legend of Sleepy Hollow" (1820). Ghosts are generally sweet and somewhat beleaguered in books for young children, becoming scarier in middle-grade fiction, and then filling a range of affective roles, from the frightening to the funny to the annoying to the sexy in YA texts.

- *Tall tales:* These tales feature characters who are larger than life, either physically or through some amazing ability. Paul Bunyan, for instance, is an American figure who is so large that, with the help of Babe, his blue ox, he created the Grand Canyon (so this is also a pourquoi tale). Pecos Bill and John Henry, also American, perform amazing feats of skill and strength. Swedish Pippi Longstocking, the strongest girl in the world, continues in the tall tale tradition.

- *Legends:* Legends begin with real people and events, but over time, their stories are exaggerated into fiction. Davy Crockett, for instance, was a real person, but he probably did not "kilt him a b'ar when he was only three" as the song goes (Bruns and Blackburn 1954). The real figures that became King Arthur and Robin Hood are the subject of much speculation, and legends have been built around other "once and future kings" like Arthur, such as the Welsh prince Owain Glyndwr (Owen Glendower in Maggie Stiefvater's Raven Cycle [2012–16]) and Cadwaladr (the source of the name of Rowling's Cadwallader, Hufflepuff's Chaser in *Harry Potter and the Half-Blood Prince* [2005]). Robin Hood and Arthur are continually reimagined in literature for middle-grade and YAs (and let's be honest, contemporary politics!). The first retelling of the legend of King Arthur specifically for young readers was probably Sidney Lanier's *The Boy's King Arthur* in 1880; a current search of King Arthur limited to juvenile literature in WorldCat, a database that itemizes the library holdings of seventy-two thousand libraries in one hundred and seventy countries, yields more than three hundred and eighty separate titles, with many more spin-offs that feature minor characters from the legend. Robin Hood's legend began in the ballad tradition (see below), but became a staple of literature for the young with Howard Pyle's illustrated *The Merry Adventures of Robin Hood* (1883), which turned the sometimes villain of the ballads into a genuinely noble and heroic figure. As with Arthur, young readers today have over three hundred titles to choose from in their quest for Robin Hood stories. The *Mabinogion*, which features an Arthur quite different from the well-known King of Camelot and the Round Table, is a collection of Welsh folkloric legends that had long circulated as oral tales before being compiled and written down in the twelfth and thirteenth centuries. These tales inspired Lloyd Alexander's Prydain Chronicles and Alan Garner's *The Owl Service* (1968). In addition to real people, though, legends often develop around purported sightings of unusual creatures, such as the Loch Ness Monster, Sasquatch (also known as Bigfoot), windigos, werewolves, vampires, chupacabras, and jackalopes, among others.

- *Parables:* Parables are most often used to illustrate a religious principle or lesson. Jesus, for instance, used parables extensively throughout his ministry. Parables are effective in teaching because they use scenarios that are familiar to the listeners to demonstrate a more generalized principle. The parable of the Good Samaritan, for instance, exposed the prejudice and hypocrisy of supposedly religious people toward someone in need by contrasting it with the generosity and kindness of a person who was considered an ethnic enemy. The story follows the **Rule of Three**, and remains relevant in contemporary culture because hypocrisy, prejudice, generosity, and kindness are human attributes that continue to give us trouble both within religious frameworks and outside of them.

- *Wisdom tales:* Wisdom tales are drawn from the ranks of all of the varieties of folklore: parables, fables, proverbs, and even trickster tales and jokes. The major qualification that makes something a wisdom tale is that it imparts some truth drawn from practical experience regarding how best to negotiate social or spiritual life. That is, wisdom tales, though many are drawn from religious traditions, offer good guidance that is not necessarily tied to that tradition. So, for instance, a Zen kōan, which is a story, dialogue, or statement that is used to test or challenge a student, might stand alongside a Sufi anecdote featuring the Nasreddin Hodja (also known as the Mullah Nasrudin), a Taoist parable, a British or Native American folktale, etc. Most published collections of wisdom tales are in fact ecumenical in this way, and offer source material for multiage storytelling sessions. Collections include *Wisdom Tales from Around the World* (Forest 2005); *Doorways to the Soul: 52 Wisdom Tales from Around the World* (Pearmain 2007); and *Elder Tales: Stories of Wisdom and Courage from Around the World* (Keding 2007).

- *Wonder or Fairy tales:* Fairy tales are longer (but still short!) narratives that take place outside of normal time and space—long ago and far away, or once upon a time in a far-off kingdom. They feature stock characters called **archetypes**, and are often concerned with enchantments or transformations of some kind: human to animal or object, rich to poor to rich again, or simply from poor to rich. Fairy tales almost always include some sort of magical intervention that either helps or hinders a character, and they often involve a test or challenge that proves a character's worthiness to receive his or her reward.

   Literary fairy tales, such as those by Charles Perrault, Hans Christian Andersen, and Oscar Wilde, build on the oral tradition of tale telling, but they change both the structure and language of their tales to suit their literate audiences. Early filmmakers, including Georges Méliès and Walt Disney, drew from fairy tales, at least in part to tie their radical experiments in form and technique to stories that would be familiar to their audiences, but also because the fantasy aspects of the tales enabled the development of nascent special effects to depict transformations and otherworldly creatures and characters; today's CGI animators continue to push that envelope.

The greatest objection to traditional fairy tales since the 1960s has been their undeniably sexist and classist biases. In most tales, males voluntarily go on journeys to seek their fortunes while females are confined to home. If girls leave home, it is in response to some threat, and their journeys involve disguising themselves and performing domestic labor of some kind until they are rescued by some outside force, be it a supernatural helper or a prince. Sometimes, they just wait or sleep until they are saved. Occasionally, a girl will show cleverness that effects her own rescue, but that is the exception rather than the rule. Older women are portrayed in competition with younger ones, and physical beauty is valued over all else. The ultimate reward in a fairy tale is a heterosexual marriage that usually involves a character marrying "up"—that is, into a great fortune and/or outside his or her social class.

Largely because of these uneven gender and class portrayals, scholars have interrogated the practices of great tale collectors of the nineteenth century— Jacob and Wilhelm Grimm (Germany), Alexander Afanasyev (Russia), Joseph Jacobs and Andrew Lang (England), and Peter Christen Asbjørnsen and Jørgen Moe (Norway)—and have found that their selection and editing processes tended to reproduce only the tales that supported the **ideological** messages they wanted to establish about national character and desired domestic arrangements. Humbler, nastier, or sexier tales, or the ones that focused on strong, independent females, didn't make the cut. Hence, recovery efforts— that is, finding and restoring old tales that tell different stories—as well as contemporary feminist revisions have been underway at least since the 1970s. However, it could be argued that such revisions of traditional tales started as early as 1697, when Madame D'Aulnoy and other women writers chose the fairy tale as a literature of protest against arranged marriages, lack of education for women, royal excesses, and war (Warner 2014: 47).

Despite these early feminist interventions, Marina Warner contends that "the fairy tale grew up in 1979" (2014: 141) with the publications that year of Jack Zipes's *Breaking the Magic Spell,* Sandra Gilbert and Susan Gubar's *The Madwoman in the Attic*, and Angela Carter's *The Bloody Chamber and Other Stories.* Even before then, though, *fractured fairy tales*, which take traditional fairy tale elements and characters and turn them on their heads with ironic twists and inverted outcomes, were officially introduced by name into children's culture through the television program *The Rocky and Bullwinkle Show* (1959–64), and have become a staple of children's literature.

Other retellings of traditional fairy tales involve a restoration or creation of psychological and moral complexity. For middle-grade and older readers, for instance, novel-length adaptations that flesh out motivations, build extensive worlds, and challenge conventional portrayals and plotlines are perennially popular. Robin McKinley, Diana Wynne Jones, Donna Jo Napoli, Emma Donoghue, Gail Carson Levine, and Patricia Wrede are just a few of the many authors who reimagine fairy tales for older readers.

- *Ballads:* Folkloric ballads are an ancient form of folk poetry of the British Isles set to music. They embedded tales of love, death, family strife, and supernatural enchantment into tunes that were easy to memorize and sing. Like folktales, they underwent changes when they appeared in cheap, printed broadsheets of the nineteenth century, prompting scholars known as song catchers to seek out folk versions still in use among people who wouldn't have had access to the printed versions. These older ballads often tell tragic, violent, and romantic tales that provide juicy plotlines for YA novels. A ballad often retold for teens, for instance, is "Tam Lin," which details the story of a girl who rescues her true love from the fairies by holding on to him as he changes into various animal shapes. Retellings for young readers include *Red Shift* (Garner 1973); *The Perilous Gard* (Pope 1974); *Fire and Hemlock* (Jones 1985); *Tam Lin* (Yolen 1990); *Winter Rose* (McKillip 1996); and *Tithe: A Modern Fairy Tale* (Black 2002).

This list of types does not exhaust the folk traditions relevant to the study of children's and YA literature, and it only scratches the surface of the critical conversations that surround this literature. Proverbs, shaggy dog stories, riddles, knock-knock jokes, playground games and taunts, jump rope rhymes, camp songs, lullabies, and nursery rhymes are all part of what Iona and Peter Opie call "the lore and language of schoolchildren" (1959). What is fascinating is the persistence of this lore through cultural change; there are countless rabbit holes to go down when studying the folklore of childhood.

Other kinds of traditional stories

The next three types of traditional story that I want to draw attention to are sometimes classified as types of folktale, because they are drawn from the folk and have defined structures. However, these story forms are less subject to the fluid dynamics of the oral tradition, for reasons we will examine as we describe them. These are *myths*, *epics*, and *sagas*.

Let's begin by thinking about *myth*. In ordinary language, the word "myth" has several usages. For instance, when we call something a myth, we might be referring to a widely believed rumor or lie that is subject to testing by the Discovery Channel's MythBusters team or the researchers at Snopes.com. Another way we might use myth is to consider it as an **ideological** messaging system that underwrites our beliefs or values—that is, a cultural myth is a way of seeing that seems natural to those people who have been reared in that culture. For instance, when we see children as deficient adults, and consider the changes they undergo as they get older as unproblematically good, we are operating under a myth of progress with regard to maturity and development. Because this way of using the term is filtered through **ideology**, we tend to reserve the word "myth" for other people's beliefs and values, taking the **ideological** myths we believe in not as myths at all, but as self-evident truths.

In terms of traditional story, however, the word "myth" refers to a sacred story that describes (or, more precisely, constructs) the belief system of a culture. Myths tell the stories of gods and goddesses, how the world was created, how it will end, how humans entered the picture, and what their relationship to their gods is and should be. Because such myths are believed to be divinely inspired, adherents to a living mythic tradition are often committed to preserving the myths in their original form, whether that form be oral, as in the case of indigenous religions of the Americas, Asia, and Australia, or written, as is the case of the religions of the book founded in the Middle East, including Islam, Judaism, and Christianity. In most religious traditions, rituals form around how and when myths can be conveyed and by whom, and appropriations and retellings of the myths by outsiders can thus be perceived as betrayal or sacrilege. When myths become divorced from widespread belief, however, such as is the case of Greek, Roman, Norse, Celtic, and some other pre- and para-Jewish, Christian, and Islamic mythologies, the stories undergo reinterpretation as allegorical rather than descriptions of actual supernatural beings, though pockets of revival and reconstruction of religions not beholden to established and authoritative sacred writings continue to surface throughout the world. And here is where definitions and distinctions get very blurry—folk religions draw from a number of sacred texts and stories, including folktales with no references to gods or goddesses at all, and can be polytheistic, monotheistic, or even atheistic.

Epics are traditional narratives, usually in poetic form with elevated style, that showcase heroes performing deeds of courage and valor, often blending history and mythology. They are built on events that have historical importance to the expression of national character, but that doesn't mean they are factual records. Instead, they often create what we might call the secular mythology of a nation or people group. Epics often begin by invoking the gods or muses to speak through them, thereby establishing the storyteller's authority to tell the story. They also often begin ***in medias res***—that is, in the middle of the action—and then proceed to move back and forth in time to create the story, which usually involves extensive descriptions of battles, trips to the underworld, and digressions of various kinds. Famous epics include *The Epic of Gilgamesh* from ancient Mesopotamia; the Homeric poems *The Illiad* and *The Odyssey*, which tell of the Trojan War and the fraught journey of Odysseus as he struggles with Poseidon on his return home; the *Mahābhārata* and the *Ramayana*, the two Indian epics that were most influential in structuring Hindu mythology, identity, and history; Ovid's *Metamorphosis*, which revised the Greek and Roman gods into more accessible, human-scaled beings; *Beowulf*, an epic claimed by both British and Nordic countries as an expression of dauntless national character; the *Kalevala* of Finland, which was instrumental in creating a Finnish national identity in defiance of Russian aggression; and the *Shahnameh*, which is considered a masterful statement of the cultural identity of Iran and Afghanistan.

Saga is a word that today usually refers to a long, drawn-out story, but it originated in medieval Iceland. The Icelandic sagas treated family histories, the lineage of kings, and the origins of the gods of Norse mythology. In the Poetic and Prose Eddas, for instance, you will find accounts of Yggdrasil, the World Tree, the two races of gods called the Aesir and the Vanir, and the frost giants. One couple of frost giants gave birth to Odin. Odin is the father of Thor, who will lead the Aesir, and the adopted father of Loki, who will lead the Vanir, in Ragnorak, the battle that will end the world. The Volsunga Saga charts the adventures, betrayals, and heroics of the Volsungs and the Guikings, two lines of descent from one of Odin's other sons, Sigi. A German version of these events is the *Nibelungenlied*, which contains stories of Siegfried and Brunhild that inspired the composer Wagner, the cartoon character Bugs Bunny, and the fantasist, Tolkien, among many, many others. New collections of these myths, epics, and sagas appear in handsomely illustrated volumes for young readers every year, and they are also mined for inventive contemporary revisions. Since they consist of action-packed tales of larger-than-life heroes, they are especially frequent in comics and graphic novel formats.

Common structures, characters, and motifs

All of these types of stories are highly structured, playing out the story structures and character arcs that we have discussed in Chapter 6. This is one of the reasons why folktales perform good service as apprentice texts for young listeners; they use and repeat story patterns and figurative language, creating expectations for what makes a satisfying story. Figures of speech are also called **tropes**, a word that has come to mean a commonly recurring convention or pattern, and many familiar **tropes**, such as the damsel in distress or slaying of the dragon, have their origins in folk literature. Similarly, folk literature introduces both the concept and the content of common **motifs**, which are recurring themes, elements or ideas in literary works. **Motifs** and **tropes** take on symbolic significance in a story through their repetition. In contemporary criticism, these terms overlap and their distinctions blur, and that's okay (unless, of course, your teacher says it isn't). Authors of both fantasy and realistic narratives build on and play with these **tropes** and **motifs**, using the well-known patterns to establish expectations and then shake things up. Let's turn, now, to a few of these recurring conventions.

The Rule of Three (and other numbers)

In your experience with folk literature, you will no doubt have noticed that the number three shows up an awful lot: a farmer has three sons; a rich merchant has three daughters; there were three bears, three billy goats, three pigs; a joke begins with three people of different religions, nationalities or hair color; our hero must perform three tasks. Divine triads are quite common, from the Christian trinity of Father, Son, and Holy Spirit to the Egyptian triad of Isis, Osiris, and Horus, the Druidic deities Beli, Taran, and Esus, and the Greek Zeus, Poseidon, and Hades. There are three Deathly Hallows in the Harry Potter series, corresponding to the three ways in which the three brothers try to evade death.

There are lots of theories for the significance of the number three. For instance, Plato cited a tripartite structure of the soul consisting of the appetitive, the high-spirited, and the logical faculties. Cognitive theorists relate the number three to embodiment, citing ways in which brains function by locating patterns and responding to rhythm as well as a spatial awareness of the stability afforded by three points of contact with a surface. Social constructivist thinkers hold that we are conditioned from childhood to recognize three as significant because of its ubiquity in our lives and stories. In terms of story structure, though, the first incident or character introduces the terms of what will be recognized as a pattern when the second reinforces it, and then the third breaks the pattern in such a way as to create a surprise or resolution. This is the way the parable of the Good Samaritan and the stories of the "Three Billy Goats Gruff," "Goldilocks and the Three Bears," and "The Three Pigs" work. When three tasks are involved, each task becomes progressively harder to build tension, such as in the story of Rumplestiltskin. This pattern of three is a boon for both tellers and listeners of oral stories because it is both compact and memorable.

Many discussions of story structure refer to a five-stage plot that consists of exposition and inciting event, rising action, climax, falling action, and resolution. Given that many readers, young and old, have little patience for exposition, authors often build their stories on a three-stage model of separation, transition, and reintegration, or the home-away-home structure that Nodelman and Reimer

(2003: 197–99) point out as ubiquitous in children's literature. Stories that follow this structure tend to focus on the section that affords the most action. For instance, Homer's *Odyssey* is perhaps the earliest version we have of a perilous, attenuated journey home, although a good portion of the story is given over to his reintegration. Walt Disney's *Sleeping Beauty* (1959) draws out the story of Aurora's childhood (which culminates in the separation phase), and then truncates the transition phase, probably because one hundred years of sleeping doesn't provide much action to animate. Fairy tales such as "Beauty and the Beast" and "Snow White" end with the construction of a new home rather than a reintegration into their former communities.

Interestingly, this three-stage structure forms the basis of Arnold Van Gennep's (1977) description of rites of passage in traditional societies. He writes, "I propose to call the rites of separation from a previous world, *preliminal rites*, those executed during the transitional state *liminal (or threshold) rites*, and the ceremonies of incorporation into the new world, *postliminal rites*" (21). These stages are clearly visible in fantasy narratives such as *Alice's Adventures in Wonderland* (Carroll 1865), *Peter and Wendy* (Barrie 1911), *The Lion, the Witch, and the Wardrobe* (Lewis 1950), *Tom's Midnight Garden* (Pearce 1958), *The Dark is Rising* series (Cooper 1965–77), and the Harry Potter series (Rowling 1998–2007), where the thresholds are passages into other worlds and times. However, they also feature in reworkings for young readers of Daniel Defoe's *Robinson Crusoe* (1719), called **Robinsonades**, as well as realistic coming-of-age narratives, such as Jean Craighead George's *My Side of the Mountain* (1959) and *Julie of the Wolves* (1972), Cynthia Voigt's *Homecoming* (1981), Gary Paulsen's *Hatchet* (1987), and Nancy Farmer's *A Girl Named Disaster* (1996). In these realistic texts, the liminal spaces of transition are most often unpopulated natural spaces that act as metaphors for their emotional distance from their families and communities. The repetition of this narrative structure thus poses the question: Do we organize our stories around our actual experience of moving from childhood to adulthood, or do we organize those experiences around our stories?

Other numbers also appear frequently in the **tropes** and **motifs** of folk literature. Binary structures are common in terms of establishing strong moral or otherwise starkly differential themes. When two sisters meet an old woman at a well, for instance, the kind sister who offers the woman water is rewarded with diamonds and pearls, while the mean sister is punished with snakes and toads—no ambiguity there. The city mouse and the country mouse find themselves equally disconcerted when they are in the other's home. These binary structures, such as good/evil, home/away, freedom/oppression, young/old, wise/foolish, and rich/poor are common ordering principles throughout myth and folklore, and, as Nodelman and Reimer (2003: 199) note, children's literature as well. But when two characters are twins, something different may be happening. Twins appear in all world mythologies. In some cases, they represent the dual nature of humans and/or the universe; that is, they may be an acknowledgment that we are both body and spirit, or they may, like the Greek Apollo and Artemis or the Xingu Kuat and Iae (Brazil), indicate day and night through association with the sun and moon. Other twin pairs are responsible for creating earth and sky, or plants and animals. Renè Girard (1981: 85) suggests that, "When myth resorts to twins, it must be trying to make a point and this point cannot be the difference between the twins, because otherwise why resort to twins? The point is obviously the absence of difference." His implication here is that we are accustomed to think of ourselves as unique, so that when a story employs twins, it is saying something about the inherent similarity in people we consider "other" that we tend to repress. In a comic story, this refusal to admit similarity might result in mistaken identity with humorous effects. But in a more serious vein, it may suggest a fundamental connection, or absence of difference, between genders, good and evil, or civilized and wild in a human being. Twins, best friends, sidekicks, and doppelgangers in children's and YA literature may point to any and all of these themes.

Seven and four are also significant numbers in world folklore and mythologies. In Western culture, there are seven notes on a musical scale, seven days in a week, seven deadly sins and virtues, seven hues on the color spectrum, and, of course, seven dwarves (just seeing if you were paying attention!). Many cultural traditions believe that magical powers attach to the seventh son of a seventh son. The number four shows up in the directions on a compass or the four winds, the four seasons, and the four elements—earth, air, fire, and water. While anthropologists, folklorists, literary theorists, cognitive scientists, and mystics all attempt explanations for the persistence of these numbers from their various perspectives, what is inarguable at base is that they reflect a tendency we have to divide and order the world of complex, manifold sensory experience into manageable chunks, to which we then ascribe meaning that we are eager to share with our children through stories. Literature for older readers often highlights the arbitrary nature and constructedness of these patterns. For instance, Sophie, in Diana Wynne Jones's *Howl's Moving Castle* (1986), is resigned to the fact that, as the eldest of three daughters in her family, she will not have any adventures or be able to seek her fortune, because that is the fate of eldest siblings in fairy tales. Jones also flips the young/old binary and the male/female tropes, as Sophie is turned into an old woman and enjoys it, and Howl, the young male wizard, spends an inordinate amount of time trying to make himself physically attractive.

The (not so) monomyth

In *The Hero with a Thousand Faces* (1949), Joseph Campbell details a structure of mythic narrative that he calls "the hero's journey" or the "monomyth" that follows a male hero as he ventures forth from the ordinary world into a world of supernatural wonders and dangers in order to secure a boon for his fellow man. So, Moses leads the Israelites out of captivity into the Promised Land; Christ enters death to defeat Satan and secure eternal life for all who believe; and Luke Skywalker becomes a Jedi and destroys the Death Star. Campbell's theory has been attacked and even discredited by scholars (see, for instance, Dundes 1984), particularly feminists and comparatists. The complaints stem from three related problems: (1) the theory is thought too general to be analytically useful, and (2) while it accounts for some broad similarities, it erases cultural particularities that are the focus of comparative mythologies in contemporary scholarship, and (3) it essentializes Western values of masculinity as the norm. To counter this last problem, Annis Pratt (1982) and Maureen Murdock (1990) have proposed changes to the monomyth so that it conforms more accurately to stories about female heroes. Despite scholarly critiques, however, the hero's journey in both its male and female guises has been widely employed by authors and screenwriters, so my own position is that it is a useful structure to have as a baseline in order to understand how stories conform to and deviate from it. Therefore, I will present it here, with the caveat that while it's a fun analytical tool to play with, it is far more interesting to discover how authors dip in and out of, fiddle with, and otherwise challenge the pattern.

The monomyth includes seven basic character types. The first are *heroes*. They most often start as ordinary people or underdogs of some sort, so that readers can identify with them. Dorothy from *The Wonderful Wizard of Oz* (Baum 1900), Will from *The Dark is Rising* (Cooper 1965), and Harry Potter are all examples of heroes who begin their stories as ordinary children, or at least as unaware of their backgrounds or powers. Over the course of the narrative, they will encounter trials that will reveal these powers or help them gain the wisdom they need to triumph. A *herald* is a character, object, or event that changes the course of the story by starting the hero off on his or her adventure. Dorothy's tornado, Harry's letter to Hogwarts, Buffy the Vampire Slayer's disturbing dreams, or the discovery of a prophecy or magical object can all be heralds. A herald can also arrive in the guise of a *mentor*. Gandalf chooses Bilbo to accompany the dwarves on their quest to regain their homeland; Hagrid acts as Harry's first mentor on his journey to Hogwarts, where he finds second mentors in Dumbledore and Hermione; and Dorothy is given guidance by the Good Witch of the North. Of course, the hero's journey cannot run smoothly, because of the presence of *threshold guardians* whose job it is to stop the hero until he or she proves his or her worth. The hyenas in Disney's *The Lion King* (1994) act as threshold guardians, as do the wolves, crows, bees, Winkie soldiers, and winged monkeys that the Wicked Witch sets against Dorothy, and the various Death Eaters and dementors that Harry and his pals must confront along the way to the final battle. *Trickster* figures can create mischief along the way, but they can also provide comic relief and act as supportive sidekicks. Dorothy has three such companions; Simba has two. The infant Kirikou is a trickster who uses his cleverness to become the adult hero of his village (*Kirikou and the Sorceress* 1998). Hence, these characters can also appear as *shape-shifters*, that is, characters who change roles in the story. In the case of the Scarecrow, for instance, he moves between trickster and mentor. Severus Snape's shape-shifting in the Harry Potter series is only apparent; while he seems to be Harry's enemy as well as a threshold guardian, he is actually an ally. The final character that is a fixture in the hero's journey is the *shadow*, which is the main enemy that must ultimately be defeated. Like the herald, the shadow need not be a person. It can, for instance, be a force, like IT or the Black Thing in Madeleine L'Engle's *A Wrinkle in Time* (1962).

Campbell divides the plot of the monomyth into a three-act structure of departure, initiation, and return. Each section is further subdivided for a total of seventeen stages. The departure stage for both males and females begins with a call to adventure. Although the female hero is more likely to begin in a space of domestic imprisonment than her male counterpart, both initially wish to refuse the call. Here again, there is a difference: females often have less choice than males to make the decision to accept the call. Snow White does not wish to go with the huntsman into the woods; Katniss does not want to be chosen for the Hunger Games. Bilbo, on the other hand, chooses to sign on as company burglar, and Harry is desperate to escape life with the Dursleys. Hence, the female hero's guides often double as captors. Both males and females receive some sort of supernatural aid, however, and cross a threshold that functions as a point of no return. The next step is called "entering the belly of the whale." By this point, male heroes have assembled a trusty band of companions and embark on a journey in reasonably high spirits; girl heroes, by contrast, descend into a green or wild world (a forest, for instance, or the Zuckerman's barn in *Charlotte's Web* (White 1952), or hell in the myth of Persephone) on their own, and the next phase of the journey begins.

During the initiation phase, the heroes undergo a series of tests and trials. While male heroes engage in battles with aspects of themselves (known as "brother battles") or battles against unknown and superior powers ("dragon battles"), girl heroes typically undergo some sort of rape trauma or challenge to their virginity. Their test involves the ubiquitous (and by now quite annoying—can we please move on already?) **trope** of the love triangle, where they must choose between a bad and a good "green world lover." Alternately, they may have a generally positive relationship with an animal—a feisty horse, wolf, or dragon that only they can tame. Both boys and girls meet with an outwardly different but psychologically similar temptation in this stage: the temptation of the regressive return to a maternal space. For boys, this comes in the form of an encounter with a goddess, who offers comfort at the cost of imprisonment, such as Edmund finds with the White Witch; for girls, a similar, imprisoning comfort within a domestic enclosure beckons—think Rapunzel, or Snow White with her seven dwarves.

But here is where the stories seem to diverge most sharply: male heroes must now assert their power over a symbolic father figure. Once the father has been bested or the hero has achieved the father's approval through some heroic action, the male hero achieves what is called apotheosis, or the elevation of his status to that of a god. Apotheosis may involve a symbolic death and rebirth into a new status, but whatever form it takes, the hero is now ready to stand for the final battle to acquire the ultimate boon. The girl hero, on the other hand, must slay the myth of romantic love by leaving her green world lover behind, as does Aerin in Robin McKinley's *The Hero and the Crown* (1984) and Buffy when she puts her relationship with Angel on more or less permanent hold ("Chosen" 2003). She may search for a father, but what she usually finds is a substitute mother figure (sorry, Peeta) or some inner strength that leads her to the ultimate boon, which for the female character is often the discovery or recovery of female tradition or community. To effect the final defeat of her "other mother," for instance, Coraline stages a tea party with her childhood dolls to lure her evil hand to its ultimate doom (Gaiman 2002: 159), a scene that stages a complex psychological shift—an apotheosis if you will—from innocent childhood to self-aware adolescence for Coraline.

After all this, both male and female heroes enter the final stage of return. At first, they are tempted to refuse to return, preferring to stay in the place where they have felt powerful, or just too worn out from the fight to face the long journey home. However, they must return now with their treasure, so they are once again given magical transport or rescue from a previously unknown entity. They cross the return threshold, where they may once again meet with some small trial, but the male hero is now "master of two worlds" and has achieved the "freedom to live" as he pleases. The successful conclusion of the female hero's journey, which is not as often achieved in realistic fiction as it is in fantasy, is the "release of creativity" and "a world transformed." Sometimes, the world is literally transformed by the expulsion or death of the Shadow, as is the case for Katniss and Snow White, but in other cases, such as Dorothy's in *The Wonderful Wizard of Oz,* the transformation of the world is more an act of creative reinterpretation.

The importance of setting

In the description of fairy tales above, we have noted that fairy tales take place outside of normal time and space. While we tend to think of time and space as two separate things, Mikhail Bakhtin (1981) encourages us to consider that in stories, these concepts are interdependent. He introduces the term **chronotope** to indicate "the intrinsic connectedness of temporal and spatial relationships that are artistically expressed in literature" (84). Maria Nikolajeva (1988, 1996) has explored the idea of the **chronotope** in children's literature more thoroughly than we have space for here, but the important point for this chapter is that the spatial elements of any given story, which include the characters, objects, and places, and the temporal elements, which include the actions and behavior of the characters within that space, do four important things:

1   They set intrinsic, logical limits on each other. For instance, if a story is set in a time and space outside of normal lived experience, then all manner of magic is possible and accepted. However, if the story is set in this world and features realistic characters, then any deviation from the natural laws of the reader's existential **chronotope** has to be accounted for in some way; a fantasy world must be built that establishes the story's logic, or some mechanism of transport or enchantment must be in place for the characters to be able to act in opposition to real-world experience.

2   Story **chronotopes** in myth and folklore tie the lived experiences of the cultural insider to the story world. So, for instance, Norse creation myths feature frost giants, while mythologies from Middle East have the world beginning in gardens. Seasonal myths depend on how their region of origin experiences seasonal change.

3   Certain minor **chronotopes** accrue symbolic significance. Castles, woods, roads, and cottages are determinative of the kinds of activities that will happen in those spaces, which in turn create emotional responses that readers ever after associate with those **chronotopes**.

4   The **chronotopes** of the story's telling affect their transfer and reception. Stories that come from cultures who understand time and space as cyclical and holistic often feel unfinished to audiences reared in clock-and-calendar-driven and densely carpentered environments. Even stories like the Jack Tales, which were originally told in settings, that encouraged continuation and pickup by the next teller may have that effect of a lack of closure on the listeners.

As a result of these four aspects, the inner landscapes and psychic space-time of children are deeply influenced by the **chronotopes** of folk literature.

Conclusion

As students of children's and YA literature, it's wise to take an ecumenical view of myth, epic, and saga, and to familiarize yourself with a range of traditions, particularly as you encounter retellings and allusions to traditions with which you are unfamiliar. As Maurice Saxby (1996: 167) argues, "Myth and legend, being truly multicultural, introduce children to a diversity of national temperaments and to different ways of confronting universal and ongoing questions about life and human nature." Contemporary multicultural **discourse** is allergic to terms like "universal" and "human nature," but there are certain structural aspects of our experience, such as our mortality and the tensions between individual desire and social life, which all human beings must confront. What comparative mythology enables is access to multiple ways by which human communities have used the arts to render their lives meaningful. As a result, then, for instance, to fully understand and analyze Gene Luen Yang's graphic novels, you would need to research the legend of the Monkey King, the color symbolism and purpose of the masks used in traditional Chinese opera, and something of the cultural history and values his various characters embody. Tracing their various sources gives you greater insight into how George MacDonald and C. S. Lewis combined Christian mythology with other folk and mythic traditions to tilt the moral imaginations of their readers toward Christian themes. Strong background knowledge can enable you to see how the masculinized values of heroic individualism from Greek, Roman, and Norse mythology, carried into children's and YA literature by way of Nathaniel Hawthorne's *A Wonder-Book for Girls and Boys* (1851), Geraldine McCaughrean's extensive oeuvre, and Rick Riordan's Heroes of Olympus series (2010–14), meet specific **ideological** challenges in Nalo Hopkinson's *The Chaos* (2012). Understanding the sources that these writers draw upon enables a fuller understanding of their work, as well as how the values, conflicts, and character types are being reimagined for young readers.

But knowing the sources is only half the fun. As Brian Attebery argues:

> Noting that Shakespeare borrowed plots from Ovid, for instance, is mildly interesting. . . . But the more important questions all have to do with what Shakespeare did with his borrowings. How did they allow him to comment on current events, challenge his contemporaries, create what amounts to a new model of the mind? (2014: Introduction)

If we believe that children's and YA texts have an influence on creating new models of the mind, we need to reflect knowledgably on what authors and illustrators are doing with the folk narratives they borrow from, how they are inviting their readers to know the past, as Rich invites, but ultimately, to know it differently.

Extending your study

Reading:

Bettelheim, Bruno. *The Uses of Enchantment: The Meaning and Importance of Fairy Tales* (New York, NY: Vintage, 1975).
    While there is much controversy surrounding Bettelheim's methods, this text remains required reading for those who want to understand the importance of fairy tales in a child's emotional life.

Tatar, Maria. *Enchanted Hunters: The Power of Stories in Childhood* (2009); *The Hard Facts of the Grimm's Fairy Tales* (2nd Ed., 2003); *Off with Their Heads: Fairy Tales and the Culture of Childhood* (1993).

Throughout her body of work, Tatar explains how the "shock effects of beauty and horror" (2009) continue to lure children into their full humanity. Her writing is both scholarly and accessible, attending to the themes behind the material facts of traditional tales.

Warner, Marina. *Once Upon a Time: A Short History of Fairy Tale* (2014); *No Go The Bogeyman: Scaring, Lulling and Making Mock* (1999); *From the Beast to the Blonde: Fairy Tales and their Tellers* (1996); *Six Myths of Our Time: Little Angels, Little Monsters, Beautiful Beasts, and More* (1995).

Warner approaches the fairy tale from a gender studies perspective, focusing on the presentations of men, women, and children in the tales. She is also quite interested in the grotesque.

Zipes, Jack. *The Irresistible Fairy Tale: The Cultural and Social History of a Genre* (2012); *Why Fairy Tales Stick: The Evolution and Relevance of a Genre* (2006); *Breaking the Magic Spell: Radical Theories of Folk and Fairy Tales* (2002); *Fairy Tales and the Art of Subversion* (1983).

Zipes proceeds from a cultural materialist theoretical perspective for his extensive work on fairy tales, focusing particularly on how the tales of European origin have continued to evolve and transmit certain types of values. He is widely recognized as the preeminent expert in the field, so if you want to study fairy tales, you have to confront, if not necessarily accept, his scholarly conclusions.

Writing:

1   Analyze a reality TV show of your choice for its relationship to traditional literature. What character types are present, and what character values do they demonstrate? What are the goals of the show, and how do these goals compare to the goals of traditional stories?

2   Joseph Campbell's monomyth is not the only means by which to analyze the component parts of a traditional story. Research Vladimir Propps' thirty-one functions of folktales and seven character functions. You could start here: http://changingminds.org/disciplines/storytelling/plots/propp/propp.htm
Write a paper comparing the two structures, basing your comparison on a children's or YA book or film that you think includes some or all of the functions and/or steps.

3   Read a book that is a self-conscious retelling of a traditional story for children or teens, such as *The Paper Bag Princess* (Munsch 1980), *Ella Enchanted* (Levine 1997), or *Kissing the Witch: Old Tales in New Skins* (Donoghue 1993). Write a paper in which you focus on the specific elements that the revision chose to pay

attention to. Discuss how these revisions change or add to traditional forms of the tale. Develop an argument as to whether you think the material changes in the revisions, such as changes in a character's appearance, gender or sexual orientation, affect the thematic elements at stake in the messaging.

4   After reading Gavin Bishop's author talkback below, write a review or an analysis of a book of traditional tales written for young readers since 2000, such as Gavin Bishop's *Taming the Sun: Four Maori Myths* (2004), Gillian Cross's *The Odyssey* (2012), or George O'Connor's *Zeus: King of the Gods* (2010). Research some versions of the tale not written for children, and focus on why you think the elements chosen in the retellings will appeal to contemporary readers.

5   Read a book where a knowledge of traditional stories is essential for the characters, such as *Watership Down* (Adams 1972), *The Amazing Maurice and His Educated Rodents* (Pratchett 2001), and *How I Became a Ghost* (Tingle 2013). Write a paper in which you explore how stories are used in these tales. For instance, do they help develop character or group identity, point the way to solutions to problems, or facilitate greater understanding of a character's motivations or a culture's values? How so?

Discussing:

1   What is your definition of a good life? What are your minimal needs for such a life, and what would count as an epic win? How have your ideas of a good life and your expectations for what it will take to achieve it been influenced by fairy tales or other traditional myths? (Think deeply about this—Will your epic win require struggle and hardship, the delay of desire as on a journey, or the help of hardy companions? What is the treasure you seek?)

2   How does popular culture perpetuate what you consider to be the positive values of fairy tales? How does popular culture perpetuate what you consider to be the negative aspects of fairy tales?

3   Think of the ways in which the stories of King Arthur have crept into contemporary ways of using language. Be on the lookout for modern Arthuriana throughout a week or so and bring examples to a "round table" discussion (see what I did there?).

Responding:

1   Prepare a traditional story for oral telling. Seek out a story from a culture that interests you, and do some research on the culture, getting an idea of their ways of thinking about time, their material culture, and their belief systems. Retell the story in whatever fashion seems respectful to that culture. For instance, if the culture values humor, progress, and parody, you can do a goofy or updated

telling, but if the story you choose is part of their wisdom traditions, you will want to treat the story with more seriousness.

2   Create a story art box from a traditional story. Look at the work of Joseph Cornell online for inspiration, and choose those objects and images that highlight the most important elements of the story. Write a paragraph that explains why you chose to isolate those moments of the story for your art box.

3   Choose five folktales or traditional stories in whatever format you like (i.e., print or film). Collect the following data from your tales: settings, gender or species of heroes, gender or species of villains, gender or species of helpers and other side characters, and colors used for each type of character's hair (or fur) and clothing. Other data points to collect might include use of magic, voice quality, age, or whatever you come up with. Once you have collected your data, create an infographic that allows you to compare the data. Consult the internet for inspiration and even infographic generators. What do you learn from your comparison? What surprised you?

Online exploration:

1   The Encyclopedia of Myths: A searchable reference work of articles about specific myths, names and motifs associated with mythology and mythic traditions from around the world.
    http://www.mythencyclopedia.com/index.html

2   SurLaLune Fairy Tales: A site maintained by Heidi Anne Heiner featuring annotated fairy tales, including their histories, similar tales across cultures, modern interpretations, over 1,500 illustrations, and more than 40 full-text books of tales from around the world. Also included are essays, a discussion board, and a blog.
    http://www.surlalunefairytales.com/

3   Aarne-Thompson-Uther Tale Type numbers: While the actual ATU guide is available through most university libraries, here is a place to start to give you an idea of the kinds of stories the ATU guide identifies.
    http://oaks.nvg.org/folktale-types.html#atu

4   Retired University of Pittsburgh professor D. L. Ashliman has created an extensive, usefully organized and subdivided classification of folk and fairy tales, with links to the tales themselves as well as essays by Ashliman and advice on searching for primary and secondary sources.
    http://www.pitt.edu/~dash/ashliman.html

5   Just for fun, here's an online folktale generator using Propp's system:
    http://www.stonedragonpress.com/vladimir_propp/propp_generator_v1.htm

Case Study: Locating the Monomyth

This case study is left to you. I have created a template for you to do a comparison of two stories of your choice, one with a female protagonist, and one with a male, to see how they conform to and/or disrupt the elements of the monomyth. The texts you choose needn't be fantasy; I think you will be surprised by what you find in a realist text.

The Monomyth for Boys	The Monomyth for Girls
Characters: Hero: Heralds: Mentors: Threshold Guardians: Tricksters: Shape-shifters: Shadows:	Characters: Hero: Heralds: Mentors: Threshold Guardians: Tricksters: Shape-shifters: Shadows:
Departure	
Call to Adventure	Call to Adventure
Refusal of the Call	Refusal of the Call
Supernatural Aid (Mentor)	Supernatural Aid (Mentor)
Crossing the Threshold	Crossing the Threshold
The Belly of the Whale	Fortunate Fall
The Road of Trials	Road of Trials
Initiation	
Meeting with the Goddess	Discovery of the Mother
Temptation Away from the True Path	Temptation to Regressive Return
Atonement with the Father	Search for Father
Apotheosis	Discovery of Female Tradition/Community
The Ultimate Boon	The Ultimate Boon
Return	
Refusal of the Return	Refusal of the Return
Magic Flight	Magic Flight
Rescue	Rescue
Return Threshold	Return Threshold
Master of Two Worlds	Release of Creativity
Freedom to Live	World Transformed

Author talkback: Gavin Bishop

In this talkback, Gavin Bishop, prolific children's writer and illustrator and Officer of the New Zealand Order of Merit, writes of the differences he finds when he retells tales of European origin versus when he works with traditional stories from his Maori heritage on his mother's side. He is tribally affiliated with Ngati Mahuta (Tainui) and Ngati Pukeko, Ngati Awa. You can learn more about his life and work at www.gavinbishop.com.

A sense of place: Retelling stories of the Maori for children

From my studio window I look down into Bowenvale. This valley leads up to a prominent rocky outcrop the local Maori call Te Tihi o Kahukura, the home of Kahukura the rainbow god. When I first heard this name it entirely changed the way I saw my surroundings. It also made sense of the number of rainbows that appear in Bowenvale when the sun comes through departing rain clouds and lights up this valley below my house.

Te Tihi o Kahukura reminds me too that every centimetre of this country, Aotearoa, New Zealand, was "clothed with words, names and stories" by the first Maori settlers over a thousand years ago. Subsequently, European explorers laid down another layer of language over the top when they arrived here about 250 years ago. Aoraki became Mount Cook, Taranaki became Mount Egmont, and Aotearoa became New Zealand. It is this layer that most people are familiar with today. Getting beneath it to the original stories of this land is something I have been trying to do as a writer and illustrator of children's books for many years.

I have retold and illustrated European folktales such as "Chicken Licken," "The Three Pigs," and "Mr Fox." My job of retelling these was not difficult because these particular stories have been thought of as children's stories for a very long time. Much of the material originally aimed at adults in fairy stories has been softened. Little Red Riding Hood is no longer raped and murdered by the wolf and the wicked queen in the story of Snow White often runs off in a rage instead of dancing to death in red-hot iron shoes. These stories have become international and no longer reflect a culture in a specific part of Europe. If we imagine them coming from a particular place it is probably Disneyland.

These stories have been isolated, connected only by being clustered together as children's fairy stories. Like most traditional tales, many of them would have been part of an intricately entwined collection from a specific country or region. And they would have related to a belief system held sacred and practiced by a group of people as the myths and legends of the Maori still do today.

Maori myths, legends and folktales are interwoven into one big on-going saga—the creation of darkness and light, of the earth and the sky, of gods and men—continuing to the present day and into the future. These stories are intimately connected to whakapapa / genealogy. And unlike the fairy stories mentioned above they are connected to a place. Hence my delight in learning of the ancient stories that flow over the valleys and hills outside my window, in the shadows of the English names we used every day.

Within this huge saga there are identifiable cycles of stories. One of the most well-known involves Maui the demi-god, the trickster and the enfant savant. Specific stories tell of his birth, the finding of his family and parents, his taming the sun and many other adventures. They are heroic stories, but several are not suitable for children. So a modern writer retelling these tales tends to leave out the episodes that deal with the sexual jealousy between Tunaroa and Maui or Maui's attempt to reverse the birth process by trying to enter Hinenui te Po's vagina to steal her heart.

The few stories that are plucked out and retold for children have to stand alone and if told well make a satisfying tale, but when one knows that they are part of a bigger and more profound picture, one is left with a sense of loss. This selective process also gives a false representation of the traditional structure of the Maui myth cycle and its connection to the main body of Maori myths and legends.

For example, many of the characters that appear in the Maui cycle go on to have adventures of their own. Hinauri leaves her husband Irawaru, who is turned into the first dog by Maui, and swims off to a new place to live. There she marries Tinirau and goes on to have many adventures of her own as do lots of other characters that first appear in the Maui stories.

Tribal variations occur in most Maori myths and legends according to the area of New Zealand where they are told. Maori folktales, though, are usually very localized and are often known only in a specific area where they can be pinned to a local geographical feature such as a mountain, headland or river. (The rock that Kura ngai tuku scratched with her fingernail when she was chasing Hatupatu can still be seen on the road between Tokoroa and Taupo.)

Most English retellings of Maori stories are by writers with knowledge of European literature and sometimes readers will come across references that suggest incidents from certain European fairy stories. When details in an English version of "Hatupatu and the Bird Woman" closely resemble "Hansel and Gretel" one suspects that the writer brought more than just the English language to his or her work.

But in my own retellings I've taken liberties too, slightly twisting events to suit my needs and to suit my audience of children. All storytellers do this and as previously mentioned, the many variations in traditional Maori myths and legends from around the country reflect this too.

However there is one thing all of the stories, woven with the Maori and English thread, have in common – a sense of place. They are all set in Aotearoa where they have been told for hundreds of years. They have grown out of this land, water and sky.

They give New Zealanders a sense of identity. They tell us who we are and show the rest of the world what it is to live here and where we come from.

So does it really matter that children only hear some of these stories? Maybe it is more important to think of these modified tales as an introduction, (to be explored more deeply later in adulthood), to the enormous wealth of myths, legends, folktales and local histories that come from the centuries of lifetimes in this part of the South Pacific.

Literature references

Aardema, V. (1975), *Why Mosquitoes Buzz in People's Ears*, New York: Dial.
Adams, R. (1972), *Watership Down*, London: Rex Collings.
Alexander, L. (1964–68), *The Chronicles of Prydain*, New York: Holt, Rinehart and Winston.
Allard, H. G. (1974), *The Stupids*, Illus. J. Marshall, New York: Houghton Mifflin.
Baum, L. F. (1900), *The Wonderful Wizard of Oz*, Chicago: George M. Hill.
Barrie, J. M. (1911), *Peter and Wendy*, London: Hodder & Stoughton.
Belpré, P. (1932), *Perez and Martina: A Puerto Rican Folktale*, Illus. C. Sanchez, New York: Warne.
Bishop, G. (1996), *Maui and the Sun*, New York: North South Books.
Bishop, G. (2004), *Taming the Sun: Four Maori Myths*, Auckland: Random House New Zealand.
Bishop, G. (2007), *Riding the Waves: Four Maori Myths*, Auckland: Random House New Zealand.
Black, H. (2002), *Tithe: A Modern Faerie Tale*, New York: Simon and Schuster.
Bullfinch, T. (1855), *The Age of Fable: or Beauties of Mythology*, Boston: Tilton, Project Gutenberg.
Burnett, F. H. (1905), *A Little Princess*, New York: Charles Scribner's Sons.
Carroll, A. (1865), *Alice's Adventures in Wonderland*, London: Macmillan.
Carter, A. (1979), *The Bloody Chamber and Other Stories*, London: Gollancz.
"Chosen" (2003), *Buffy the Vampire Slayer*, Season 7, Ep. 3. Dir. Joss Whedon.
Cooper, S. (1973), *The Dark is Rising*, New York: Random House.
Cooper, S. (1965–77), *The Dark is Rising* series, New York: Random House.
Dahl, R. (1982), *Revolting Rhymes*, Illus. Quentin Blake, London: Jonathan Cape.
Defoe, D. (1719), *Robinson Crusoe*, London: W. Taylor.
Farmer, N. (1996), *A Girl Named Disaster*, New York: Orchard.
Forest, H. (2005), *Wisdom Tales from Around the World*, Atlanta: August House.
Gaiman, N. (2002), *Coraline*, New York: HarperCollins
Garner, A. (1968), *The Owl Service*, London: Collins.
Garner, A. (1973), *Red Shift*, London: Collins.
George, J. C. (1959), *My Side of the Mountain*, New York: E. P. Dutton.
George, J. C. (1972), *Julie of the Wolves*, New York: Harper & Row.
Grahame, K. (1908), *The Wind in the Willows*, London: Methuen.
Hawthorne, N. (1851), *A Wonder-Book for Girls and Boys*, Boston: Houghton Mifflin.
Hopkinson, N. (2012), *The Chaos*, New York: Margaret K. McElderry.
Irving, W. (1820), "The Legend of Sleepy Hollow," in *The Sketch Book of Geoffrey Crayon, Gent.*, New York: Putnam, n.p.

Jones, D. W. (1985), *Fire and Hemlock*, London: Methuen.

Jones, D. W. (1986), *Howl's Moving Castle*, London: Methuen.

Keding, D. (2007), *Elder Tales: Stories of Wisdom and Courage from Around the World*, Westport, CT: Libraries Unlimited.

Kipling, R. (1902), *Just So Stories*, London: Macmillan & Co.

Kirikou and the Sorceress (1998), Written and Dir. by Michel Ocelot. French 3 Cinéma.

Lanier, S. (1880), *The Boy's King Arthur*, London: Scribner.

L'Engle, M. (1962), *A Wrinkle in Time*, New York: Farrar, Straus & Giroux.

Levine, G. C. (1997), *Ella Enchanted*, New York: HarperTrophy.

Lewis, C. S. (1950–56), *The Chronicles of Narnia*, London: HarperCollins.

Lewis, C. S. (1950), *The Lion, The Witch, and the Wardrobe*, London: HarperCollins.winter

The Lion King (1994), Dir. Roger Allers and Rob Minkoff, Walt Disney Productions.

Lowry, L. (1989), *Number the Stars*, New York: Houghton Mifflin.

McKilip, P. (1996), *Winter Rose*, New York: Ace.

Numeroff, L. (1985), *If You Give a Mouse a Cookie*, New York: HarperCollins.

Parrish, P. (1963), *Amelia Bedelia*, Illus. F. Siebel, New York: Holt , Rinehart and Winston.

Paulsen, G. (1987), *Hatchet*, New York: Bradbury.

Pearce, P. (1958), *Tom's Midnight Garden*, Oxford: Oxford University Press

Pearmain (2007), *Doorways to the Soul: 52 Wisdom Tales from Around the World*, Eugene, OR: Wipf and Stock Publishers.

Perrault, C. (1901), "Little Red Riding Hood," *The Tales of Mother Goose*, Boston: D.C. Heath & Co, pp. 80–84. [Originally published in 1697].

Pilkey, D. (1994), *The Dumb Bunnies*, New York: Scholastic.

Pope, (1974), *The Perilous Gard*, New York: Houghton Mifflin Harcourt.

Potter, B. (1908), *The Tale of Jemima Puddleduck*, London: Frederick Warne and Company.

Pratchett, T. (2001), *The Amazing Maurice and His Educated Rodents*, London: Doubleday.

Pyle, H. (1883), *The Merry Adventures of Robin Hood*, London: Scribner's.

Riordan, R. (2010–14), *Heroes of Olympus* series, Glendale, CA: Disney Hyperion.

Robin Hood (1973), Dir. Wolfgang Reitherman, Walt Disney Productions.

Rowling, J. K. (1997–2007), *Harry Potter* series, London: Bloomsbury.

Rowling, J. K. (2005), *Harry Potter and the Half-Blood Prince*, London: Bloomsbury.

Scieszka, J. and Smith, L. (1992), *The Stinky Cheese Man and Other Fairy Stupid Tales*, New York: Viking.

Sewell, A. (1877), *Black Beauty*, London: Jarrold & Sons.

Sherman, D. (2011), *The Freedom Maze*, Somerville, MA: Candlewick.

Shrek (2001), Dir. A. Adamson and V. Jensen, Dreamworks Pictures.

Sleeping Beauty (1959), Dir. C. Geronimi, L. Clark, E. Larson, and W. Reitherman, Walt Disney Productions.

Stein, P. (2015), *Little Red's Riding Hood*, Illus. Chris Gall, New York: Orchard Books.

Stiefvater, M. (2012–16), *The Raven Cycle*, New York: Scholastic.

Taken (2008), Dir. Pierre Morel. 20th Century Fox.

Voigt, C. (1981), *Homecoming*, New York: Ballantine.

Wellingtons, The (1954), "The Ballad of Davy Crockett," by George Bruns, Thomas W. Blackburn, Walt Disney Studios.

White, E. B. (1952), *Charlotte's Web*, New York: Harper.

Yeahpau, T. M. (2006), *X-Indian Chronicles: The Book of Mausape*, Somerville, MA: Candlewick.

Yolen, J. (1990), *Tam Lin: An Old Ballad*, Illus. Charles Mikolaycak, New York: Harcourt.

9

"The Web Itself is a Miracle": Nonfiction and Informational Literature

---

Suggested texts to read alongside this chapter

A Magic School Bus or Horrible Histories title.

Bell, Cece, *El Deafo*.

Sidman, Joyce, *Dark Emperor*.

Jenkins, Steve, *Actual Size*.

A selection of alphabet and counting books, such as *Anno's Counting Book* (Anno), *This Jazz Man* (Ehrhardt), *Alphabet City* (Johnson).

Sheinkin, Steve, *Bomb: The Race to Build—and Steal—the World's Most Dangerous Weapon*.

Winter, Jonah, *Lillian's Right to Vote: A Celebration of the Voting Rights Act of 1965*.

In her memoir entitled *El Deafo* (2014), Cece Bell tells the story of how she lost her hearing at age four and struggled to come to terms with the dilemmas this entailed during her early years of schooling. She describes the awkwardness she feels over wearing a bulky hearing aid and the trials of resisting her mother's desire for her to learn sign language and learning to read lips instead. She also showcases the difficulties of managing elementary school friendships and a massive first crush. Her memoir is a fairly accurate representation of her early life, though she admits to taking some liberties with characters, conversations, and the chronology of events. She insists, however, that the feelings and fantasies she had as young child are all presented truthfully, so this book is clearly classified as a work of nonfiction—a *true* story. Interestingly, however, her memoir is presented in a comics format with all of the characters depicted as cartoon rabbits.

How, then, can this text be considered a true story, or, in literary terms, a work of nonfiction? After all, the first question to ask of nonfiction, presumably, is whether and how it tells the truth of any situation. It is safe to say that Cece Bell and her family members, doctors, teachers, and classmates are all human beings, so depicting them as rabbits distances the memoir from any sort of *literal* truth. However, Bell's use of rabbits enables her to tap into an *emotional* truth of her situation in a way that a more literal depiction might miss. For Bell, the most pressing aspect of her early life has to do with her hearing, so choosing to depict people as animals who have large ears conveys this preoccupation as a visual **metaphor**. She uses other kinds of visual **metaphors** and markers throughout the book as well. Speech bubbles, for instance, enable her to visually depict her gradual hearing loss by having the font become progressively lighter until it fades away completely. The empty speech bubbles emanating from the TV, the mouths of her mother and the health care professionals, and her own mouth let us know that while people are talking, Cece can't hear what they are saying because there is a blank space where we expect oral speech to be. When she gets her hearing aid and learns to read lips, the words that appear in the speech bubbles clue readers in to the level of clarity with which her hearing can be corrected by the various devices and accommodations, while thought bubbles allow us to see what she is thinking as she attempts to process her experiences. When her friend offers her a drink, for instance, she hears "Doo yoo wan sunding do dring? We haff Jerry's mop . . ." (2014: 25). Readers can see in the picture that the can says "Cherry Pop," but they also see a thought bubble that shows a preliterate Cece thinking about a mop in a glass, indicating her confusion as she tries to process meaning from the way the words sound to her.

At school, Cece feels lonely, which she represents by putting herself in a circle that visually indicates the feeling of being in a private bubble that pops when she makes a new friend, but returns when managing friendships proves difficult. The electronic device that enables Cece to hear her teacher wherever she is in the building, however, leads her to fantasize about having superpowers, which is where the character of El Deafo—an imaginary version of herself as a superhero, complete with cape—comes from. Her fantasies are enclosed in panels with borders that differ from the borders depicting real life scenes. This visual shift indicates their status as imaginary, but Bell assures us in the author's note that these fantasies were in fact true—that is, they were an actual part of her experience as a young child.

So what's going on here? Cartoon rabbits, superheroes, borders, and bubbles: these are not the kinds of things we typically associate with nonfiction. Nonfiction relies on objectivity, language that can be taken to mean what it says, images that present photographic evidence of people and events, or graphs, charts, timelines, and/or diagrams that represent data and abstract processes, right? Right? Well, yes, but that does not tell the entire story of nonfiction for young readers. Nonfiction can also draw on the elements of poetry and fiction, such as figurative language and story structure, for its presentation. It is fitting, therefore, for the word itself to contain its opposite as a reminder of their interdependence, both as a form and as a way of understanding the world around us. In fact, when conceiving the structure of this book, I decided to include the chapters on story and folklore prior to a discussion of nonfiction because much of the new neuroscientific research points to the fact that we use narrative understanding rather than objective or reality-based understanding to make sense of the world; the story form is intellectually and emotionally prior to nonfiction or scientific understanding, and encases it even after the science takes precedence. (There is, of course, an irony in that last sentence, as I invoked the nonfictional research protocols of neuroscience to justify the fact that story is prior to understanding the science, but that's my story and I'm sticking to it.)

Until very recently, nonfiction has often been pushed to the side in discussions of children's and especially YA literature. It carries the taints of serious and useful (read: boring) instruction of the sort found in textbooks rather than **trade books**, which is what books by commercial publishers intended for a general readership are called. Presupposed to be devoid of narrative tension or poetic language, nonfiction is not generally analyzed in the same way as literature and poetry. In fact, in most discussions of nonfiction in children's and YA literature textbooks, commentators focus on two things: cheerleading for this often neglected genre, and listing the factors necessary for the evaluation of nonfiction for curricular use rather than aesthetic analysis (although one of those factors is usually writing style). In the most updated textbooks, attention is paid to concerns about race, gender, socioeconomic class, and ableist bias as well. Since these evaluative concerns are important, we shall give them some attention here as well, but we will also consider why and how they are important in the first place. First, however, let's start with some broad-based terms and definitions.

Defining nonfiction

In colleges and universities, major fields of study are usually demarcated into categories by the types of knowledge under study. The natural sciences, for instance, concern themselves with the properties and processes of the physical world, such as chemistry, biology, physics, earth sciences, and space sciences. Clearly, books that focus on knowledge in these areas are classified as nonfiction; while the information presented through such work is inevitably based in a particular theory or has a specialized focus or perspective, it still concerns itself with observable data and ethnographic research carried out under strict protocols to guarantee as much reliability as possible. The formal sciences, which include mathematics, statistics, logic, and computer science, support this data gathering and analysis in various ways, generating models and abstracting patterns that have practical and predictive value. Sometimes the models presented as facts turn out to be wrong: new information upends old assumptions; empirical data doesn't support a theoretical hypothesis; further research or more precise instruments and methodologies reveal unforeseen complications. Science is never settled, but that doesn't mean that the presentation of its current state at the time of a book's publication is fiction, even after the facts or observations have been updated. *The key distinction between fiction and nonfiction is that in nonfiction, nothing is intentionally made up.*

In addition to the natural and formal sciences, nonfiction can also include work done in the social sciences and the humanities. Social sciences look at how people function individually and in groups, so these include areas such as anthropology, cultural studies, economics, political science, psychology, sociology, and sometimes history. The humanities include the study of linguistics, literature, philosophy, the arts, and comparative religions. History is also considered by some as a humanities discipline, depending on how it is studied and presented. And while literature and the arts include fictional stories and fantasied representations, critical discussion about these things and their creators falls into the category of nonfiction. In all of these disciplines, the distinction between fiction and nonfiction holds: while nonfiction in these areas of human experience is always going to be presented from a particular perspective, the key factor in nonfiction is that nothing gets made up—everything presented as a fact or an actual event should be able to be documented, traced through to at least one and preferably more than one **primary source**. So, even though it reads like a Victorian novel, every snippet of conversation in Deborah Heiligman's *Charles and Emma: The Darwins' Leap of Faith* (2009), for instance, is documented through a **primary source**. A **primary source** is a document or artifact that was written, created, or used during the time and/or by the person under study. For instance, a diary or a letter would count as a **primary source**, as would a photograph (even though scenes in many historical photographs were in fact staged), an article of clothing or other aesthetic or practical object, or an official record of some sort. Personal interviews are also afforded privileged status as **primary sources**, even if they are conducted years after the event; however, given what we know about the vicissitudes of memory, experienced authors of nonfiction look for ways to corroborate information they receive from a memory-based personal testimony. Beyond accounts of events, there are also nonfictional elaborations in the humanities of ideas and customs and how they have developed over the course of human history. These include books that focus on philosophies of language, art, science, and metaphysics; histories of aesthetic trends or movements; historical and contemporary comparisons of fashion, food ways, and other cultural customs; descriptive how-to manuals of historical and contemporary arts and crafts, etc.

Private libraries have existed since antiquity, but when public lending libraries were first established in the early 1700s, the books were most often arranged according to the order in which they were acquired, and the library holdings were small and dedicated to the kinds of nonfiction that would, as the Reverend John Sharpe argued, "advance both learning and piety" (qtd. in Keep 1908: 52). Since novels, or indeed fiction of any kind other than perhaps parables or fables, did not fit with such a mandate, most of the books were nonfiction. Additionally, while some borrowing was permitted, library patrons didn't have the same kinds of browsing access to the books that we have in libraries today. Collections were closed, and librarians knew exactly what books they had and where to find them when patrons asked. As the public library system developed and more books were printed and acquired, this accession system of organization (i.e., books numbered by their date of acquisition) became unwieldy, and new systems based on broad subject area classifications were developed. The one most often used in Anglosphere public libraries today is the Dewey Decimal System, developed by Melvil Dewey in 1876. This system uses a three-digit number to classify books by subject, and then uses decimals to further subdivide each broad subject heading into more specific topics under that heading. Given the proliferation of print literature, the system has undergone considerable refinement since its first publication, graduating from a four-page pamphlet to four massive volumes of intricate detail. While some libraries are attempting to institute more user-friendly classification systems, such as ones used in bookstores, Dewey remains king, and therefore it's useful to familiarize yourself with its categories, particularly when you are looking for nonfiction on specific subjects, but also as a means for thinking about how we divide up the world of knowledge.

Here, then, are Dewey's broad categories:

000—General works, computer science, and information
100—Philosophy and psychology
200—Religion
300—Social sciences
400—Language
500—Pure science
600—Technology
700—Arts and recreation
800—Literature
900—History and geography

Within each category, subjects are subdivided into topics. Additionally, most public libraries have a dedicated children's section, so the call numbers there are preceded by the letter J to indicate that the book is part of the juvenile collection. You will notice that there is a category for literature, but the remainder of the categories are varieties of nonfiction that correspond to the kinds of academic subject distinctions we have noted above—natural, social, and formal sciences, and then arts and humanities, with history being considered by some a social science and by others a humanities discipline. When Dewey composed his system, folding literature into a single category likely made sense, given the relative lack of novels available or considered appropriate for inclusion in library collections. Nowadays, however, most libraries separate out prose fiction as a category unto itself, and do not give those books a Dewey Decimal number at all. Furthermore, in children's and teen sections, separate categories are often created for picturebooks, easy readers, and series books, leaving the 800s mostly for dictionaries and rhetoric guides, literary history and criticism, drama, essays, some short story collections, and poetry, in English and other languages. Other distinctions that might strike you as strange include the cataloging of folk and fairy tales in the 300s, 398.2 to be more specific, and the shelving of graphic literature and comics, including fiction and nonfiction, under the 741.5 classification.

The remainder of the categories offer a breathtaking range of nonfiction topics for children and teen readers to explore, organized in ever tightening circles of specificity. Say, for instance, you wanted to find a children's book on snakes. You could wander over to the J500s, locate animals in the J590s and reptiles in the J597.9s, and, if you didn't get distracted by iguanas in J597.954, you would find snakes classified as J597.96. Once you get there, you will find that all of the many books on snakes would be further specified by the first few letters of the author's last name and perhaps include the date of publication.

At this point, then, let's just pause and take a moment of silence to express our gratitude to librarians, search engines, and databases that make our lives easier in ways Dewey never imagined, because nonfiction for young readers poses particular problems for library cataloguers and student researchers. Take, for instance, Thomas Locker's *Water Dance* (1997). This is a picturebook that includes nonfiction information about the water cycle. In some libraries, it is shelved with the fictional picturebooks, and given a call number of PIC LOC. Other libraries place it with the science books, designating it as J551.5 LOC, and still others catalogue it as an easy reader, E LOC. Similarly, many of Joyce Sidman's elegant poetry picturebooks contain factual information about their subjects, which include animals, plants, and insects, and yet they are found only in the American poetry section, J811. And some books, like those in Joanna Cole's Magic School Bus series, are classified within the same library as either E for Easy Reader, which doesn't always distinguish between nonfiction and fiction, or according to their nonfiction subject matter in the Dewey system. These varying and hybrid formats in which nonfiction appears cause confusion not only for shelvers and browsers but also for teachers and literary critics who want to distinguish between types of nonfiction.

Let's start with a point of agreement: Nonfiction can be defined as work that aims to communicate current, factual information about the world at the time of its publication. It strives to tell the truth about its subject, whether that subject is a verifiable process or fact about the physical world, the tracing of an idea, or the account of a historical event. How it tells that truth or communicates that information, however, is wildly variable in terms of form. Moreover, in contemporary culture, we have become very skeptical about anything that presents itself as absolute truth or fact; we want to know whose "truth" is being conveyed, or to what small segment of the world this supposed truth applies. We also hate to be bored by the presentation of information. In light of these current sensibilities, adult trends in nonfiction have led to the creation of a literary category called "creative nonfiction," although there is wide dispute about both the term and its definition. Doug Hesse and Becky Bradway (2009), for instance, prefer the term "literary nonfiction" even though they agree that "creative nonfiction" is more likely the preferred term among writers. Elizabeth Partridge (2013), who writes nonfiction for young readers, disagrees, finding both terms troubling:

> I think the term creative nonfiction is misleading—we don't create anything that isn't there already, and *literary* sounds pretentious to me. So I prefer narrative nonfiction. It boils down to this: making sure we are telling a story. The author of narrative nonfiction uses all of the best techniques of fiction writing: plot, character development, voice, and theme. . . . So narrative nonfiction takes people, places, and events, builds bridges between them, gives them meaning and emotional content. Without making anything up.

Despite their disagreements about terminology, though, Hesse and Bradway agree with Partridge that the most important thing for nonfiction writers is to tell a good story, arguing that creative nonfiction is "prose with a narrative trajectory of some kind . . . in which how something is said is as compelling as *what* is said" (2009: 4). This leads, of course, to the problem that Partridge highlights about the use of the term "creative"—the reliability of the facts is called into question if the goal is to tell an entertaining story. But these practitioners also agree that the aim of nonfiction is not to convey facts or information, but to move the audience emotionally. Hesse and Bradway argue that "creative nonfiction nearly always pleads for understanding, whether it be of a social problem or something as mundane as the isolation of childhood" (8). Cece Bell's narrative certainly accomplishes that goal, making it a textbook example of creative, narrative nonfiction the way these critics and writers understand the term.

Another aspect of creative nonfiction that Hesse and Bradway (2009: 3) emphasize that is worth considering for children's and YA nonfiction is the importance of authorial voice: "Unlike types of writing that aspire to objectivity, concealing that a person produced them, works of creative nonfiction wear their making and makers on their sleeves." This sense of "writing with a teller" (4) can be critically important in nonfiction for readers in the elementary and middle grades. When presenting the natural and formal sciences in textbooks, the tendency is to distance the knowledge of these subjects from the human beings that produced it. Young learners have traditionally been presented with pictures of sharks without an indication of who took the picture and how he or she did it; they learn Avogadro's Law without ever hearing of Amedeo Avogadro; they memorize the date of the signing of the Declaration of Independence without learning about the agonized and compromised process of its writing and ratification. As a result, both the emotional content and the progression of thought—that is, the very things that are most interesting to readers who are wondering how their own emotions and thought processes might make a difference in the world—are evacuated from consideration. Contemporary creative nonfiction, such as the books in Houghton Mifflin Harcourt's Scientists in the Field series, reintroduces a human knower into the realm of information, enabling a stronger kinship with both the subject matter and the intellectual search that leads to the discovery of knowledge.

However, the problem with both Partridge's and Hesse and Bradway's definitions of creative nonfiction as interchangeable with narrative nonfiction is that not all nonfiction for young readers possesses a narrative structure. In fact, much nonfiction for children encourages a browser's approach—that is, it is not designed to be read from beginning to end like a narrative, but can be dipped into according to specific interests. Furthermore, this storytelling approach has its pros and cons in nonfiction literature for children and teens. For instance, narrative nonfiction appeals to readers who are inclined toward fiction, and who would otherwise turn up their noses at books that present a dry factual account of events without attention to emotional content, personal motivations, or well-wrought, imagistic prose. But for readers looking for quick access to facts, names, places, timelines, and formulas, narrative connections can be annoying distractions, burying the important bits in a wordy storyline concerned with psychological motivations and side plots. Because let's face it: nonfiction bears a significant educational burden. Knowing that Amedeo Avogadro started college at age thirteen and studied law before he got interested in physics won't help you use Avogadro's number to solve for x. Furthermore, people take in and process information in different ways. A person with highly developed visual and spatial intelligence is going to respond more readily to a graph of comparative data than a person who is more interested in how interpersonal relationships affect decision-making processes.

Fortunately, there is enough diversity in the presentation of information in nonfiction literature for young readers to accommodate many types of information seekers. This is why, from my perspective, "creative nonfiction" is the most useful term for our purposes, as long as we understand that the creativity lies in the *manner of the information's presentation*, not the information itself. From early-concept board books that provide pictorial representations of simple concepts and day-in-the-life type narratives of straightforward activity sequences for babies, to picturebook histories and biographies, to science and math concepts rendered in poetry, to illustrated reference books on everything from dinosaurs, art history and the human body to crafts and cooking, to themed fact books, to graphic narratives of natural disasters, to verse memoirs, to engrossing YA narratives of historical events and the lives of the famous and infamous, nonfiction literature for young readers is not always narrative, but it is always in some way *creative* in form. It blends illustration and text, humanizes the knowledge it presents, and engages various kinds of readers with various kinds of literary and pictorial styles. All without making things up.

While I would argue that all nonfiction for children and YAs is creative nonfiction, I think it's useful to make three distinctions within the broad category of creative nonfiction for young readers: **informational texts**, **expository nonfiction**, and **narrative nonfiction**, each of which includes various types of books with various purposes. I will also note that while I use the words "text" and "books" interchangeably, many of these sorts of nonfiction texts also appear in magazines, websites, and DVDs.

- **Informational texts** are defined by their purpose, which is to convey facts about the natural and social world. They address their subject matter as a class or type, rather than as individual instances, and they present the information in a timeless way. For instance, in *Actual Size* (2004: n.p.), Steve Jenkins writes, "The **Alaskan brown bear** is the largest meat-eating animal that lives on land. Height: 13 feet. Weight: 1,700 pounds." He's not talking about any individual Alaskan brown bear, and he's not placing his facts about the species in a historical context or geographic location (other than land, and the assumed connection that these bears were named for their habitats in or around Alaska). Furthermore, the facts about the height and weight are generalized statistical averages or extremes, as in, bears of this type have been known to conform to these averages. Types of informational texts include:
  - **Early-concept** and **concept books**: These are usually nonnarrative books that feature pictures with labels for very young children. The pictures are selected and grouped according to a concept or category, such as color, barnyard animals, and things found in bathrooms, or brought together to show a relationship or pattern, such as opposites or number concepts. These books might have movable parts to encourage interaction, such as the lift-the-flap, wheels or simple pull tabs found in Matthew Van Fleet's sturdy board books. In addition to helping very young children develop fine motor control, such mechanisms encourage children to see books as sites of discovery and pleasant surprises. They also facilitate the organization of the world into culturally meaningful categories, being what Peggy Heeks (1996: 438) calls "induction guides to daily life," so it is important to pay attention to the way they do this in order to ensure that the books aren't presenting and reinforcing stereotypical associations with regard to race and gender.

What is confusing and blurring in terms of generic categories here is that oftentimes concepts and other informational material are embedded in stories or introduced through characters. For instance, Joanna Cole's Magic Schoolhouse books enfold their nonfiction concepts with made-up characters and situations, and books like *This is Your Life Cycle* (Miller 2008) personify their creatures in order to embed their information in a story form. The long-running Horrible Histories series started out as a "joke book with a history theme" and ended up as "a fact book with jokes" (McKay 2009). A pure definition of nonfiction, where nothing is made up, excludes these from the nonfiction camp, but their purpose and their information let them back in. So I will simply wimp out here and say it's up to you to decide where you think they fit.

- Alphabet books and counting books: At first blush, it would seem that these books are pretty straightforward in terms of purpose: they offer an attractive way to teach kids their numbers and letters under the mandate to "make learning *fun*!" But when you pick up a few of these books, you have to challenge that straightforward assumption and ask yourself: If the purpose of this book is to teach the alphabet or numbers, how is it doing that, and how successful will its method likely be? And if you come to the conclusion that this book would not be a good vehicle for that basic purpose, then what else is going on here? It's a fascinating question to ponder, as authors and illustrators seem to find ever more intriguing ways to present the letters and numbers that comprise the building blocks of basic literacy and numeracy. So ask yourself instead: What aesthetic and philosophical ideas and values are hitching a ride onto this task? How do alphabet and counting books present the relationship of letters and numbers to the material world? How do they communicate cultural values to and about children, childhood, and language itself? As Patricia Crain (2000: 11–12) notes, "Alphabets and alphabetization are deeply implicated not only in our relationship to language but also in our relation to children and in our discourses about children and childhood. . . . To be attuned to the way in which we think and write the alphabet is to witness the small change of cultural capital at work."

- Fact books: Especially appealing to the late elementary and middle grader, these books are collections of facts, sometimes random, sometimes organized around a topic. Examples include *5,000 Awesome Facts (About Everything!)* (2012), by National Geographic Kids, *TIME for Kids BIG Book of Why: 1001 Facts Kids Want to Know* (2010), and *The Lonely Planet Kids Travel Books: Mind-Blowing Stuff on Every Country in the World* (2015). According to Kieran Egan (1997: 94), the appeal of these books corresponds to a shift in children's understanding of the world from fantasy to what he calls "romantic rationality"; that is, whereas the young child is comfortable with his or her belief in giants and fairies, the older child accommodates a belief in these unreal creatures to a passion for learning about the quirks and extreme limits of actual creatures rather than their metaphorical equivalents. What, for instance, is the fastest land mammal; who were the tallest and smallest humans to ever live; who scored the most home runs in a single season? Knowing such facts accrues psychological benefits for the school-aged child, since his or her peer relationships depend on certain kinds of playground "cred" in which specialized knowledge plays a significant role when it comes to both fitting in and standing out. But as Egan suggests, the collecting of facts goes even deeper: "By learning about something exhaustively, one gains the security that the world is in principle knowable. So one reduces the threat that one is insignificant or at the mercy of an unknowably vast reality" (87). While he admits that not everyone achieves this sense of security, it is important for teachers and parents (as well as partners and those of us who self-reflect!) to understand what may be at stake for these (us?) fact hoarders.

○ Topical science reporting: This isn't really a category that you will find in any other textbooks—I made it up to distinguish these sorts of books from other kinds of science writing that I will discuss below as more expository in nature. The kinds of books that I am talking about here deliver a set of facts about a topic without much elaboration. Comenius's *Orbis Pictus* fits this category; like a fact book, it simply presents its facts about the natural world without offering any explanation of how those facts have been gathered or verified. Unlike fact books, though, these books are not intended for the purpose of amassing trivia, but for conveying knowledge about certain aspects of the natural world that will address or awaken scientific curiosity. So, books like Jonathan London's *Hippos Are Huge!* (2015) hit the highlights of their topic—in this case, what hippos eat, where they live, what they care about, and how they defend themselves, how they fling their poop around (don't you just love children's books?), their family structures, habits, and place in the food chain. The information is generalized and timeless, and no photographs of actual hippos are included. Instead, the pictures are stylized scenes of hippo actions and interactions rendered in vivid watercolor illustrations. Nonetheless, it doesn't tell a story about hippos. In a similarly abstract form, Steve Jenkins isolates the steps in how various animals get a meal in *How to Swallow a Pig* (2015), placing his signature collage illustrations against a white background to foreground the discreet activities of the animals rather than presenting them in a realistic setting. He also uses an interactive style to engage readers: "So you want to learn how to swallow a pig. You've come to the right place." In fact, these books often use such a conversational and/or humorous style to engage readers, as in Scholastic's

You Wouldn't Want to Be series that details various dirty jobs and lowly positions humans have held throughout history and uses brightly colored cartoon-style illustrations to amp up the humor. The thinking seems to be that the facts themselves need to be dressed up in either beautiful artwork or grotesque, wacky fun in order to be interesting to young readers. Given the barrage of information that vies for our attention in contemporary culture, this is very likely true, though little empirical research has been done to assess the qualities that make for interestingness in information processing (Hidi and Baird 1986).

- **Expository nonfiction** includes books that explain and describe processes and ideas. This is the kind of writing that students are most likely to find in textbooks rather than **trade books**, but there are **trade books** that present their subject in this way—that is, as writing without a teller, or in which the teller's participation is as an outside observer whose style of address purports to be reporting more than interpreting or imposing meaning. Like informational nonfiction, these books tend to present their subjects in a generalized fashion, but unlike those books, they may relate a historical progression of the process of discovery, or concern themselves with customs or processes that are not timeless or fact based. Most textbooks don't isolate these types of books as a separate category, and I admit that this may be a fuzzy distinction, but I think it is useful to consider books that focus on theories, social customs, instructions, and procedural methods of inquiry as a separate category from books that present already established empirical, scientific facts or concepts, as well as from those books that fashion their information into plots, especially when discussing nonfiction for older readers. Well-presented expository nonfiction is particularly critical for children in the stages Erikson dubbed as "industry vs. inferiority" and "identity vs. role confusion" because these books present real-world passions and occupations and give information about how one might pursue them.
  - How-to books: This category includes what you might expect, such as cookbooks and books that teach various kinds of arts and crafts techniques. But it also includes books about how to manage personal relationships, get organized, develop self-esteem or a more positive body image—those books that we call "self-help" books. Some of the first books written especially for children were in fact of this type—the *Babee's Book,* for instance, written in the 1400s and hand-copied, was a book of conduct for noble children, and there were others like it concerned with such things as courtly manners, how to serve at table, and what improving books to read. These books still exist, although more contemporary offerings are often spritzed with humor, such as Sesyle Joslin's *What Do You Say, Dear?* (1986) or Steve Antony's *Please, Mr. Panda* (2015). Over the course of the twentieth and twenty-first century, you

will find books that instruct tween and teen readers how to pursue their entrepreneurial goals, such as Travis Nichols' *Punk Rock Etiquette: The Ultimate How-to Guide for DIY, Punk, Indie, and Underground Bands* (2008), which includes advice and instruction on how to develop your band's identity, how to record and market your music, how to silkscreen T-shirts, and how to behave while on stage and on tour, and the more general *Start it Up: The Complete Teen Business Guide to Turning your Passions into Pay* (Rankin 2011). There are also books on how to write fiction and do literary criticism targeted to specific ages, genres, and demographics, such as Gail Carson Levine's *Writing Magic: Creating Stories that Fly* (2006) for fantasy-loving middle graders; Ralph Fletcher's *Guy-Write: What Every Guy Writer Needs to Know* (2012) for tween boys frustrated with limiting school assignments; and Thomas C. Foster's *How to Read Literature Like a Professor: For Kids* (2013), which, despite its title, is suitable for high school students learning analytical reading techniques and practices. For teens, the writers of the Merry Sisters of Fate blog, Maggie Stiefvater, Tessa Gratton, and Brenna Yovanoff, have produced two books that blend original short stories with instructions on craft, providing prefaces that comment directly on how they develop ideas, create characters, and build worlds, and integrating notes from each other on critique and revision throughout the stories.

○ Art, music, and literature appreciation books: These are books that explain and interpret artistic masterworks while guiding readers through a process of learning how to understand and appreciate the arts. They provide explanations about techniques and materials or instruments, and pose questions that encourage readers to look or listen more closely to the work under examination. Sometimes books combine the two. For instance, in William Lach's *Can You Hear It?* (2006), readers are invited to look at a painting while listening to a piece of classical music on an accompanying CD and compare what they see with the images created by the various instruments and melodies within the music. Some of these books, such as the *Oxford First Book of Art* (Wolfe 1999), *The Usborne Art Treasury* (Dickins and Butler 2007), and *The Lego Architect* (Alphin 2015), double as how-to books in that they include instruction for readers to try techniques that mimic the styles of the masterworks they are exploring. In terms of literary criticism, while there are many picturebooks and scholarly books devoted to author's lives that are accessible to multiaged researchers, nonfiction books devoted to literature and explicitly written for young readers are rare. However, a few do exist. For instance, Michael Rosen has collaborated with illustrator Robert Ingpen on two books for middle graders, entitled *Shakespeare: His Work and His World* (2001) and *Dickens: His Work and His World* (2005). These works contain chapters that focus on the titular author's life, the contexts in which his works appeared, commentary on the major works, and his cultural and literary legacy and influence over the years. With timelines, illustrations, and an index, these are books that facilitate dip-in consultation as well as a comprehensive read-through. *Inside Charlie's Chocolate Factory: The Complete Story of Willy Wonka, the Golden Ticket, and Roald Dahl's Most Famous Creation* (2014), by journalist and fan Lucy Mangan, takes a slightly different approach by focusing on the many aspects of one book, from its genesis and drafting, to its multiple illustration styles and translations, to the various adaptations for stage and screen, to the literary and film criticism that has attached to it and the product lines it has spawned.

○ Reference works: These books go beyond the presentation of facts to provide context and history to their subjects. Children's online and print encyclopedias fall into this category, as do books like *Sister Wendy's Story of Painting* (Beckett 1994), which describes the major aesthetic trends and developments in the visual arts from the first cave paintings to the late twentieth century. The text is richly illustrated with reproductions of exemplary paintings which are highlighted and explained, but unlike the art appreciation books described above or the philosophy books described below, the aim of these types of books is to offer brief, comprehensive introductions to their subjects. *A Young Person's Guide to Philosophy* (1998), for instance, explains in two pages what philosophy is and what kinds of questions philosophers ask before introducing readers to the cast of characters that have shaped and informed Western thought from six hundred years BC to postmodernism.

○ Books about sex and development: Books that tackle these subjects are the most controversial expository nonfiction precisely because trying to tell the truth without making anything up always involves making value judgments about what is appropriate to show and tell children about gender, development, and reproduction at what age. The most widely known books on this topic are probably those by Robie H. Harris. She has written a series of books for young readers of different ages, starting with *It's Not the Stork: A Book about Girls, Boys, Babies, Bodies, Families, and Friends* (2006) for 4–6-year-olds, *It's So Amazing! A Book about Eggs, Sperm, Birth, Babies, and Families* (2014) for 7–10-year-olds, and *It's Perfectly Normal: Changing Bodies, Growing Up, Sex and Sexual Health* (2014) for ages ten and up. The information contained in these books is accompanied by comics-style illustrations, which, while certainly less controversial than the black-and-white photographs of children exploring their bodies and teenagers having sex included in the widely banned German text, *Show Me!* (Fleischhauer-Hardt 1975), are still often challenged for their depictions of full frontal (cartoon) nudity. Finding the sweet spot between children's curiosity and adult comfort levels is never easy.

○ Science methodology: This type of science writing stands in contrast to a simple reporting of research findings and discoveries described above. Instead, it focuses on the processes that lead to the knowledge that we have. Houghton Mifflin's Scientists in the Field series is exemplary in this respect. Exploring kid-friendly topics such as spiders, volcanoes, wolves, and cute flightless birds that smell like vanilla (kakapos), these books follow scientists from around the world, giving a picture of what doing research looks like in various conditions. The plentiful photographs make the books initially browsable, but readers drawn into the narratives will find lively writing about people doing interesting things, and thus charting a path to how one might follow in their footsteps. *The Many Faces of George Washington: Remaking a Presidential Icon*, by Carla Killough McClafferty (2011), for instance, tells two stories—a history of George Washington and the process through which forensic anthropologists used measurements from death masks, clothing, locks of hair, and other **primary sources**, worked with tailors, leather-workers, and artisans skilled in historical reproduction, and employed the kinds of computer-assisted modeling software that facilitate age progression photography in criminal investigations to create wax models of what George Washington looked like at age nineteen (quite the hottie!), age forty-five as a general, and age fifty-seven as president of the United States.

○ Philosophy: These are books that present influential abstract ideas in a topical way. While they may provide a history of the subject under discussion and present historical figures who have helped shape the discussion, their emphasis is on the subject itself rather than using a story form. Sharon Kaye and Paul Thomson's *Philosophy for Teens: Questioning Life's Big Ideas* (2006) divides its areas of inquiry into topics of love, beauty, truth, justice, and God, posing questions with regard to each topic and exploring divergent viewpoints. Like the sex books, books that tackle such potentially divisive issues are bound to attract criticism. Marc Aronson's *Race: A History Beyond Black and White* (2007), for instance, presents the many facets of how humans have learned to distinguish between races and have thus developed racist **ideologies**. While his presentation aims for objectivity, his ideas are necessarily informed by his own interpretations of the consequences of certain beliefs such as the monotheism of the Israelites; hence it, like all books that fall into this category of nonfiction, is a book for discussion, not a straightforward presentation of verifiable facts.

• **Narrative nonfiction** is nonfiction that presents its subject as a story. It is increasingly popular in children's and YA fiction for a host of reasons. The idea that nonfiction can be creative, for instance, has freed writers to exercise their aesthetic literary skills on behalf of their subject. Fueled by new research into the nature of human understanding—that, as we have noted in the previous chapters, we come to understand the world through story and that language and images are always to some degree metaphorical—nonfiction writers can unapologetically write memoirs and biographies in the form of lyric poetry or sequential art, engaging both right and left hemisphere activity in the process of reading. And while this category includes narratives in verse, the trajectory of story is what distinguishes the subgenre. Here are some of the subgenres that use narrative nonfiction to good advantage:

○ Life writing: Life writing is a broad category that includes biography, autobiography, memoirs, diaries, letters, testimonies, personal essays, and blogs. In literature for children, it also includes picturebook biographies. Occasionally, the subject chosen for a biography will have some sort of connection to children's literature or culture; there are picturebooks and chapter book biographies of writers such as Louisa May Alcott, Mark Twain, J. R. R. Tolkien, L. M. Montgomery, and E. B. White. Most often, however, biographies focus on people famous for their work in the culture at large as scientists, artists, musicians, dancers, architects, athletes, celebrities and/or activists, and their biographies for young readers focus on their childhoods. An especially popular kind of biography follows the fiction tradition of the Künstlerroman, which is the story of how an artist grew up into his or her craft. Obviously, these books are meant to encourage children to pursue their own passions with the kind of zeal that characterizes the biographical subjects. However, biographies are often written about notorious folk as well. Greg Pizzoli's *Tricky Vic: The Impossibly True Story of the Man Who Sold the Eiffel Tower* (2015) makes particularly effective use of picturebook techniques such as visual **metaphors** and nonfiction features such as sidebars, a glossary, and facsimile documents to tell the story of an infamous con artist. Writers pick and choose details to include depending on their chosen form and their ideas about what is interesting and appropriate for children. Appropriateness is, of course, a moving target, particularly when it comes to the nature of a subject's behavior and relationships; *John's Secret Dreams* (Rappaport 2001), a picturebook biography of John Lennon, for instance, doesn't dwell on his drug use or mention his abusive behavior toward women, while a biography for older readers, Elizabeth Partridge's *John Lennon: All I Want is the Truth* (2005), is forthright about both of those issues. Autobiographies are life stories told by the person who has lived them; these are not as common in children's and YA literature as biographies, although many children's and YA authors have composed their autobiographies, clearly borrowing heavily from their fiction writing and illustrating skills to tell the stories of their lives. *Self-Portrait: Trina Schart Hyman* (1981) is a picturebook autobiography that hits the highlights of Hyman's life from her childhood through her divorce and experiences as a single mother. Chris Crutcher's *King of the Mild Frontier: An Ill-advised Autobiography* (2004) reads like one of his YA novels, with raw humor and an unflinching look at the difficulties of growing up. More common than full-blown autobiographies are memoirs, which focus on a significant period in a person's life rather than trying to give a comprehensive picture. Cece Bell's *El Deafo* falls into this category, as does Jacqueline Woodson's verse memoir, *Brown Girl Dreaming* (2014). Recently, biographical blogs are being published as books for young people, including *Regine's Book: A Teen Girl's Last Words* (Stokke and Larsen 2014), which reprints the blog entries and photographs of a seventeen-year-old dying of leukemia.

○ History: Just as nonfiction about people tends to focus on famous and infamous people, or people who stand out from the norm in some way, so the stories chosen for nonfiction history texts focus on filling in context for out-of-the-ordinary events. For middle graders and teens, disasters loom large, such as Jim Murphy's *An American Plague* (2003), Deborah Kops' *The Great Molasses Flood: Boston, 1919* (2012), and Don Brown's *Drowned City: Hurricane Katrina and New Orleans* (2015). Interestingly, in many cases, topics such as these are often introduced to young readers through youth magazine articles or fictionalized versions before someone takes up the task of writing a book-length nonfiction account, as is the case with these books. In terms of readership, the brief or fictional version may pique interest, and a desire for the facts or the whole story follows. While the subject itself has to be unusual enough to hold readers' interest, the real art in narrative nonfiction is in the storytelling. Steve Sheinkin's *Bomb: The Race to Build— and Steal—the World's Most Dangerous Weapon* (2012) is organized like a novel, with a captivating narrative hook, and then an analepsis (flashback) to the genesis of the Manhattan Project, introducing the scientists and spies as characters in the unfolding drama, and doing an impressively clear job of explaining the science behind the building of the atomic bomb. The storytelling creates suspense for events that have known outcomes, enabling readers to share an evolving emotional experience while they learn about the history. And this, really, is the beating heart of narrative nonfiction— that quality of emotional engagement that is missing from expository nonfiction. The stories told in narrative nonfiction are often emotionally challenging, taking readers deep into violent periods of history such as the Holocaust and the world wars, American slavery, Reconstruction, and the Civil Rights movement, and the more recent conflicts in Korea, Vietnam, and the Middle East. While some of these histories focus on heroic actions and successes of youthful resisters, others highlight the tragedy of those who were victims of these conflicts.

Blurred lines between facts, fictions, and forms

While the subjects and the **forms** of these books in many ways determine their tone and the type of reader who will respond to them, their diversity ensures that no reader needs to approach trade nonfiction books with the fear that he or she will be bored by a dry recitation of facts. As Hesse and Bradway note, "People read creative nonfiction not because they have to but because they want to. They read it not to exhume information or ideas (although though they may well) but rather for the quality of the reading experience itself" (2009: 6). But this is where questions of ethics arise, especially for sharing nonfiction with young readers whose limited experiences and feeling-based mental processing make them vulnerable to ideological manipulation. While we remain committed to a kinship model of childhood rather than a deficit model as we have discussed in Chapter 2, it's still important to acknowledge that children are susceptible to understanding the world as adults present it to them. On the one hand, we want to tell them the truth, but most adults shy away from telling the whole truth and nothing but the truth. Moreover, we are each committed to our own **ideologies** to such a degree that they seem like truth, even if they are very different from those of our neighbors or of those from people in other parts of the world. When we see these **ideologies** play out in ways that conflict with ours, we call this an author's "agenda" that he or she is trying to "push onto the reader"; when we are in agreement, we tend to just read them as affirmation that we have been right all along.

Indeed, one of these truth or **ideological** blurs has to do with our views about the distinction between scientific facts and personal opinions or interpretations. In contemporary Western culture, we like to believe that these are sharply separable, and that the ability to distinguish between the two increases as we grow older. Fantasy is okay for young children, but as soon as readers have reached an age or level of development where they can take their nonfiction straight up rather than as a sugar-coated pill, any sort of decorated storytelling or fancifully embellished explanations of the world's historical or scientific processes are more likely to be excluded, suspected of demonstrating bias, or dismissed as anecdote rather than data. In terms of **form**, then, the line from fictional or other literary forms such as poetry to nonfictional forms such as expository prose appears to be developmental. This is, of course, a false binary. So why do we feel the need to present science and history to children in pretty packages like brightly colored picturebooks, graphic memoirs, and zany, energetic fantasies, and why might we distrust those **forms** as vehicles of truth for older readers?

Part of the answer to this question is of course the fact that we have been through the scientific revolution and the European Enlightenment and have accepted the sharp distinctions between science and superstition as an established truth about the way knowledge should be pursued. The spectacular variety of myth and folklore that has been the focus of the previous chapter gives us a pretty good idea of the webs of tales people have spun around the natural processes that confront us daily. The change of seasons and weather, the purposeful activity of animals, the fecundity of plants, the contours of the land, the mysteries of the seas—all of these natural phenomena have called forth the powers of human imagination to explain, animate, and, in many cases, give us some sense of power and control over our world. We might thus imagine a time when there was no distinction between nonfiction and fiction, when all science was steeped in myth, all history retold as legend, and all instruction embedded in superstition. Hence one reason why we might allow science for children to be presented in a story form is the alliance we imagine between children's thinking and the thinking of those from a prescientific age. But we are fairly firm in our insistence that this blur between myth and reality is not the case today; we draw a line between established facts and historical truths on the one side, and opinions, beliefs, superstitions, and theories on the other, and we want our children to do likewise.

But let's do a little thought experiment that challenges that binary: It is hideously frightening to think that our planet might be naturally evolving toward its own expiration date. Like our ancestors, we feel called to *do* something, to believe in our own effectiveness in the face of a universe that will respond to our actions in some way. Unlike them, however, we don't resort to superstitious myths of an animistic universe, or come together to chant and perform ritual sacrifices in hopes of appeasing some angry god. Or do we? Consider how our scientific account of global climate change bears striking similarities to mythic ones: We humans have neglected our responsibilities toward the planet by extracting ores, irresponsibly harvesting plants and animals, introducing destructive man-made chemicals, etc., without thinking about the consequences or taking steps to ensure the sustainability and renewal of our resources (i.e., we have sinned against the gods by taking without giving a proper portion back, or by stealing something that rightfully belongs to them). This has caused unfortunate changes in climate (the gods are now angry and are withholding their bounty and sending hurricanes, floods, volcanic eruptions, and earthquakes as punishment for our sins). Now, our political leaders (tribal elders) and environmental activists (shamans and spiritual leaders) are demanding that we reduce our reliance on fossil fuels and animal products (i.e., make sacrifices that will appease the gods, some even advocating population controls akin to the sacrifice of our virgin children) and change our lifestyles (repent) in order to save the planet (in hopes that the gods will accept our sacrifice and restore their favor).

Understand that I am not critiquing the science here, but I created this example to draw attention to the fact that the lines between nonfiction and fiction cannot be too decisively drawn in terms of both the structure of its presentation and its latent **ideological** content. The science of climate change is underwritten by an **ideology** of human power to alter a responsive universe. We respond to it emotionally as well as cognitively because it is encased in a story we are familiar with from childhood, a story that speaks to our wishes for control over unpredictable circumstances. And that has as much to do with our own methods of processing reality as it does with whether the science is accurate and effective for prediction purposes, or whether such power and control is possible or not. Similarly, nonfiction for young people makes its case by drawing on structures and **ideologies** that have been made familiar to us through fictional narratives, especially those that, like the monomyth discussed in the previous chapter, are repeatedly encoded over many stories.

Metanarratives

Understanding the connections between ancient myth and modern science neither negates nor affirms the science itself, but it does show how scientific knowledge can be understood as a version of what Francois Lyotard, in his influential book, *The Postmodern Condition: A Report on Knowledge* (1979), calls a metanarrative. According to children's literature critics John Stephens and Robyn McCallum (1998: 3), metanarratives are "implicit and usually invisible ideologies, systems and assumptions which operate globally in a society to order knowledge and experience." Such metanarratives include the one I have suggested above—that is, humans as sinners in the hands of angry gods, who can change their circumstances through sacrifice—but also some of the attitudes toward childhood explored in Chapter 1, such as the European Enlightenment narrative of rational thought being the path to universal human progress. While Lyotard (1979: xxiv) identified in postmodernity a general "incredulity toward metanarratives," one **metanarrative** that seems to stick is the belief that objective facts about natural processes if not historical events exist independently of their telling. But my climate change example calls that into question. It is therefore nonetheless work asking, as you learn to read children's and YA nonfiction critically, what guiding assumptions underlie notions of human progress and regress, and what constitutes a good life well lived—in other words, what **metanarratives** seem to be at work informing the book you hold in your hand.

Perry Nodelman, for instance, undertakes a devastating critique of the first winner of the American Library Association's Newbery Award, *The Story of Mankind*, written by Willem van Loon in 1921. While it is significant to point out that the first winner of this prestigious award is classified as a work of nonfiction, it is equally significant to point out that it presents a version of historical truth that is outdated and often outrageous in its pronouncements when viewed with contemporary eyes. It is in fact, as Nodelman emphasizes, a *story* of mankind, and like all stories, it comprises details selected for narrative and ideological coherence rather than documentary accuracy and full disclosure. In particular, Nodelman (1990: 75) points out that "the key to van Loon's conception of history is the idea of progress, based on the model of biological evolution." But even while Nodelman notes that "those historians who insist on their unbiased objectivity merely reveal a cultural bias toward a scientific approach that values 'objectivity' more than people once did" (71), his own thorough critique of van Loon's text is enabled precisely by his commitment to this scientific, presentist approach: "It is only when *The Story of Mankind* is read from the viewpoint of *logical objectivity* that these contradictions seem to be so obvious" (83, emphasis added); while most contemporary readers can't help but agree with Nodelman's reading of this text, he is careful to make it clear that it is as embedded in his perspective—a belief that logical objectivity exists—as van Loon's was in his. The writers in Betty Bacon's edited collection, *How Much Truth Do We Tell the Children?: The Politics of Children's Literature* (1988) seem less self-aware in their critiques of what they read as the uncritical embrace of capitalism in children's books; following Maxim Gorky's lead, they view capitalism and individual identity as a lie foisted on children through their literature, and see a **Marxist** worldview as an air-clearing, unarguable truth. Thus, what we see in the essays in that collection is a call to abandon one **metanarrative** for another, without the recognition that the new perspective is as much of an invested ideological position as the one it seeks to replace.

Nodelman and Reimer (2003: 129–33) condense the explicit and implicit **ideological** messaging of children's and YA nonfiction into nine general theses, smartly pointing out how some of these messages contradict each other. For instance, they argue that the world is presented to children as a "simple," "happy," "rational," "hopeful" (129, 130, 132, 133) place that is getting better all the time, which of course necessitates presenting the atrocities of the Holocaust, racism, and other kinds of oppression and exploitation as things that only happened in the past because of people who were somehow not as enlightened as the generation now reading these texts; only the good guys (or perhaps the victims) are just like us. However, if we follow these new books' "clear and obvious messages about values" (132), we can move into a glorious and conflict-free future. Books about nature, then, are invested with messages about environmentalism, and biographies are so loaded up with character values that they become "fables" (132) rather than true portraits with warts and all. But the main **ideological** contradiction lies in the fact that if the world is so simple and happy, why do we impose such a burden on children to make it better?

Are things so simple that the world's atrocities can really be placed on the shoulders of a few bad actors with attitudes that are over and done with or arise from worldviews diametrically opposed to ours? Another contradiction appears in the presentations of the world as both "homogenous" and "wonderfully diverse" (131). The messaging in much of the literature that focuses on global cultures sticks to a kind of superficial diversity that ends by emphasizing that at heart "people everywhere are really basically the same" (132).

Criteria and considerations for evaluating and reading nonfiction

By now you may be tempted to crawl under your desk and cry out with despair: But if everything is caught up in a **metanarrative**, how can there even be such a thing as nonfiction? How can we ever know anything for sure? How can we evaluate books that purport to tell the truth to children? Are we to be forever victims of Oscar Wilde's claim that truth is only ever "one's last mood" (1961: 100)? To which I reply, there, there, dear reader, it's not as dire as all that, or, not to worry—I won't dodge this difficulty.

Nodelman concludes, "Because history always advertises itself as truth, we must be particularly aware of the extent to which it always must be fiction" (1990: 85–86). I might nuance that stark distinction by saying that a history that advertises itself as truth must always be partial and embedded in a **metanarrative**. In other words, a book may tell the truth and perhaps even nothing but the truth, but no one book tells the whole truth, and the truth it does tell is limited to an author's decision-making process about which facts are relevant and appropriate, how they are connected, and how the whole package should be assembled to communicate what the author feels is important. Martin W. Sandler's *Imprisoned: The Betrayal of Japanese Americans During World War II* (2014), for instance, shines important light on the horrific treatment and tragically misguided internment of thousands of American citizens following the attack at Pearl Harbor. The story is well researched (though there is some dispute on the facts regarding the liberation of Dachau), the text is engaging, and the photographs and illustrations lead readers to understand the extent of the displacements and to empathize with the suffering of those who lost their homes and property. However, if this were the only book young people read about the Japanese internment, they would come away with the impression that while there were some ineffectual mewling protests from political figures, not a single non-Japanese friend helped care for the property of their displaced neighbors, which is just not true. Of course, the book's perspective is made plain from the title; if you want to learn about the efforts of sympathetic neighbors or church groups that did help, you need to find a different book. Indeed, it is important to remember that no book can carry the weight of telling the whole truth from all angles.

As a result, one way out of the impasse of a controlling **metanarrative** is to actively seek out diverse perspectives on any given subject. Heeks (1996: 438) notes that "the National Curriculum which came into effect in England and Wales in 1989 tended to narrow the range of subjects studied in schools, but to increase the range of resources required within each subject." This is a process-based methodology that acknowledges the need for critical thinking rather than the mere amassing of facts. It requires you to read each book with an eye toward sussing out the **metanarrative**(s) on which it is built, and also remaining self-aware of the **ideological** position(s) you bring to your reading. An example of this kind of **ideology**-based criticism applied to a fictional work is found in the case study accompanying Chapter 1; another will follow in the case study that accompanies this chapter. Such curricular shifts are in response to material circumstances; with so much information streaming into our lives, we need to become, and to train children to become, critical readers, even skeptics. In practical terms, this involves reading more books from multiple perspectives on a given subject rather than accepting one account as the authoritative truth. It also involves doing our own fact-checking—a process made both easier and harder by the ease of internet searching. However, comparing different accounts from diverse perspectives enables us to approach the learning of history and science in the way suggested by Virginia Woolf, who argued that "truth is to be had by laying together many varieties of error" (2004: 122).

You must also use your critical skills in analyzing poetic language and multimodal discourse to work out what story the language and pictures is telling the reader. What verbal and visual **metaphors** are at work in the text? How and to what ends does the author engage the reader's emotions? What are the core issues around which this text organizes its information? Focus in on the illustrations. Pictures have multiple functions in nonfiction—they are there to encourage browsing, generate interest, highlight important elements or scenes within the text, and inform readers, but they also serve **ideological** functions as well by setting a particular kind of mood, eliciting certain emotions toward the subject, or conveying implicit messages about gender, race, and socioeconomic class. A book intended to carry specific **ideological** messages about the hardships experienced by a group of people during a particular time period will complement its text with photographs and illustrations of unsmiling folk in postures of servitude, oppression or exhaustion, and carefully avoid any suggestion of care or moments of joy or celebration, even if the texts indicates that such moments are an important part of people's lives. A photograph of a baby animal nuzzling its mother is likely to engender audible responses of empathy and identification in readers, but a picture of this type suggests a personified emotional bond that may or may not be present in animals in the wild, where animals are compelled to perpetuate their species even if it means abandoning sickly or vulnerable offspring so that they can ensure their own survival. Such photographs may be conveying factual information, but they are also doing emotional work. By contrast, elements used in technical communication, such as diagrams, charts, graphs and timelines, are emotionally distancing; they abstract information rather than personifying it, giving it a different kind of weight and seriousness, and implying that the facts being presented are objective and without emotional or **ideological** bias, even if they do in fact exhibit such bias. Additionally, since gendered and racialized associations are pervasive in other media, younger readers may already come to a book with some firm assumptions about what career options and activities are available to them, so it's important to be attentive to how the small details in illustrations challenge or affirm those associations. A book like *DK Children's Cookbook* (2004), by Katharine Ibbs, only shows hands preparing food, but there is still a nice balance of various skin colors, and it is very difficult to tell whether the hands belong to males or females.

It is only once you have analyzed the various factors and the book as an ecological whole that you can make strong evaluations about nonfiction for young readers. Selection criteria for award winners include the following considerations that can be applied to any book, with the caveat that your evaluation and selection of a book depend on its intended use. If you are looking for a quick reference guide to reliable facts, for instance, clear organization and access features such as an informative table of contents, an index, and an extensive bibliography may carry more weight than writing style. If you are looking for a good read about an interesting subject, writing style is paramount. If you are looking to develop certain kinds of empathy or pose moral questions about an issue, you may actually want books that present significant challenges to contemporary ways of thinking about an issue—in other words, you might want a bias that is clear enough for young readers to see and discuss. That said, most frameworks for assessing nonfiction include the following:

- Accuracy: information is up to date and verifiable; clear distinctions are made between facts, theories, opinions, and unsettled questions; authors have appropriate credentials and/or have indicated how they did their research; a bibliography and suggestions for additional research are available for fact-checking
- Organization of material: organizational framework is clear, consistent, and makes logical sense given the subject matter; connections and interrelationship between facts and events are evident; attention is given to the placement of visual aids such as photographs, illustrations, maps, and text boxes, so that they facilitate and augment comprehension; organizational patterns (simple to complex, general to specific, assertion to evidence, etc.) allow for multiple levels of engagement, from browsing and scanning to in-depth reading.

- Visual design and access features: size and formatting of the physical book allows for appealing presentation of content; illustrations and photographs are high resolution and of good quality; captioning is informative; background images, font design, and use of color augment mood and sense of time period or content; table of contents, index, glossary, bibliography, timeline, and any additional access features are useful for locating information and aiding comprehension
- Writing or illustration style: writing and illustrations complement and reinforce each other (no irony, contradictions, or disconnect here) and are engaging, vivid and inviting; rich vocabulary is included and explained in ways appropriate to the audience; figurative language and scene setting complement rather than distract from the factual information; animals are not implicitly or explicitly personified unless the effect is clearly meant to be humorous or exaggerated; stereotypical associations in text and illustration are avoided

Taking these elements as your starting point, you can work with whatever critical theories of prose fiction or illustrated books that you prefer to analyze and assess the kinds of cultural and aesthetic work a nonfiction text seems to be doing. That is, you can deconstruct, psychoanalyze, or historicize a work of nonfiction; you can perform a critical reading of its attention to gender, race, and socioeconomic class; you can assess how its **ideological** positioning corresponds to other kinds of **ideological** positions or **metanarratives** on the same subject. In other words, you can treat it like the literature it is.

Conclusion

While reading Nodelman and Reimer's (2003) assessment of the state of **ideology** in children's nonfiction, I have to admit I got a little depressed. Most of their examples point to the horrors they presume are hidden from children, such as the reality of racial prejudice, wormy apples, irreconcilable differences, dogmatic belief systems, and homophobia, and they aver that most children's nonfiction perpetuates false ideologies of the world "by always insisting that the world is simple, happy, homogenous, easily understood, and much like the utopia adults like to imagine, and by never giving any information that would suggest anything else" (134). They are right, of course; the world is often a lousy place, and we tell our children a lot of hopeful lies and cover over a lot of troubling contradictions in the service of protection, propaganda, and wishful thinking about who children are and who we are.

But then I had some second thoughts: While what they say is undeniably true, it's not the whole truth, about either the world itself or the nonfiction literature that explores it. A lot of contemporary nonfiction, even for very young readers, does focus on the complexities of racial prejudice and discrimination, the horrors of war, and the mistakes humans have made with respect to the environment. But the natural and the human world is also beautiful and full of wonder, and its joys are sometimes simple. As Doctor Dorian tells Mrs. Avery when she asked if he understood how the words appeared in Charlotte's web: "Oh no . . . I don't understand it. But for that matter I don't understand how a spider learned to spin a web in the first place. When the words appeared, everyone said they were a miracle. But nobody pointed out that the web itself is a miracle" (White 1952: 108–09). Nonfiction for young readers includes stories about webs *and* spiders, oppressors *and* victims, similarities *and* differences, horror *and* hope, all rendered with the endless creativity of the minds who produce the literature and the minds that consume it. If, as William James (1890: 488) asserts, life for infants is "one great blooming, buzzing confusion" that requires endless sorting, discriminating, negotiating, and assessing, we would do them a great disservice to suggest any different.

Extending your study

Reading:

Bamford, R. A. and Kristo, J. V. (eds.), *Making Facts Come Alive: Choosing and Using Quality Nonfiction Literature* (Norwood, MA: Christopher Gordon, 2003).
    Sixteen essays by education practitioners examine various aspects of selection and evaluative criteria, as well as how to engage young readers. An extensive bibliography and lists of award winners are also included.
Colman, P., "Nonfiction is Literature Too," *New Advocate* 12, no. 3 (1999): 215–23.
Colman, P., "A New Way to Look at Literature: A Visual Model for analyzing Fiction and Nonfiction Texts," *Language Arts* 84, no. 3 (2007): 257–68.
Kristo, J. V., Colman, P., and Wilson, S. "Bold new perspectives: Issues in Selecting and Using Nonfiction." In S. S. Lehr (ed.), *Shattering the Looking Glass: Challenges, Risk and Controversy in Children's Literature*, 339–60 (Norwood, MA: Christopher Gordon, 2008).
The above articles advocate for critical attention to nonfiction from both aesthetic and practical standpoints.

You might also be interested in the following texts, which do not focus on literature for young readers, but provide critical insights for your own research:
Anderson, C. (ed.), *Literary Nonfiction: Theory, Criticism, Pedagogy* (Carbondale: Southern Illinois University Press, 1989).

Gutkind, L. *You Can't Make this Stuff Up: The Complete Guide to Writing Creative Nonfiction—from Memoir to Literary Journalism and Everything in Between* (Boston, MA: De Capo Press, 2012).

Writing:

1   Using the evaluative criteria presented in this chapter, write a review of a nonfiction book.

2   Analyze an informational picturebook as a visual object—that is, use the knowledge gained from the picturebook chapter regarding how pictures and composition work and how words and pictures interact to analyze how the elements of the book contribute to its purpose.

3   Analyze several children's and YA biographies on a renowned public figure such as John Lennon, Helen Keller, Winston Churchill, or Woodrow Wilson. Then, research the figure on your own, consulting multiple sources. Write an essay in which you compare and contrast the information in the children's biography with the historical record.

4   Read a critical article on nonfiction, such as Perry Nodelman's "History as Fiction: The Story in Hendrik Willem van Loon's *Story of Mankind*," or Joe Sutliff Sanders's "*Almost Astronauts* and the Pursuit of Reliability in Children's Nonfiction" (see bibliography for full citations). Write a rhetorical analysis of the article, locating specific passages that reveal the author's **ideological** position with respect to the work he or she is critiquing. Alternately, use the article as a model for writing your own analysis of a nonfiction book.

5   Read two books on the same subject that are clearly written for audiences of different ages, such as Rappaport's *John's Secret Dreams* and Partridge's *John Lennon: All I Want is the Truth*. Analyze the ways in which the material is presented in terms of format and style, and discuss how the authors chose and left out details appropriate for the age of their intended audiences.

Discussing:

1   After reading the author talkback for this chapter, discuss what types of nonfiction you like or dislike and why.

2   What literary elements might make a subject appealing to you even if you haven't had any interest in it before? What frustrates you about nonfiction texts?

3   Again, using the author talkback to seed your thoughts, discuss your personal experiences with nonfiction texts as a child. Were you drawn to a particular subject or type of book at any given time? Did your tastes change as you grew older?

4   What do you think is the most important feature of nonfiction for young
    children? For teenagers? Why?

Responding:

1   Working in groups, choose a scientific process and create a graphic novel that
    is suitable for emergent readers and that illustrates the process.
2   Choose a how-to book and follow its instructions. Were you able to complete
    the project? What features did you find helpful? What was distracting,
    confusing, or missing?
3   Locate a history textbook and choose a section that describes an event or
    introduces an important person. Rewrite the section in a manner that
    transforms expository nonfiction into narrative nonfiction. Do some outside
    research, but don't make anything up in your narrative account.

Online resources:

1   Reading Rockets: Nonfiction for Children—a large selection of resources to
    aid in finding, evaluating, and using nonfiction literature.
    http://www.readingrockets.org/books/nonfiction-for-kids
2   InkThinkTank: Ink stands for interesting nonfiction for kids, and this website
    brings together a number of well-known authors of nonfiction sharing tips,
    ideas, and insights into the creation of nonfiction among other things.
    Includes a searchable database.
    http://inkthinktank.com/
3   The following are websites maintained by prolific writers and illustrators of
    nonfiction for young readers. They each share information about their
    research and writing processes.
    http://www.seymoursimon.com/
    http://www.gailgibbons.com/
    http://deborahheiligman.com/
    http://symontgomery.com/
    http://melissasweet.net/
    http://www.stevejenkinsbooks.com/
    http://stevesheinkin.com/
    http://nicbishop.com/
4   These are the homepages for awards given for youth nonfiction in the United
    States, United Kingdom, Australia, and Canada:
    http://www.ncte.org/awards/orbispictus
    http://www.ala.org/alsc/awardsgrants/bookmedia/sibertmedal

http://www.fcbg.org.uk/non-fiction-childrens-book-awards/
https://en.wikipedia.org/wiki/Children%27s_Book_of_the_Year_Award:_
Eve_Pownall_Award_for_Information_Books
http://bookcentre.ca/programs/awards/norma-fleck-award-for-canadian-
childrens-non-fiction/

Case Study: Visual Metaphors and Ideology in Nonfiction

For this analysis, we will take a close look at Jonah Winter's *Lillian's Right to Vote: A Celebration of the Voting Rights Act of 1965* (2015), illustrated by Shane W. Evans. The first question we might ask is whether this book is nonfiction at all, even though the author's note says that his "Lillian" was inspired by Lillian Allen, the granddaughter of a slave, who was born in 1908 and, in 2008, was able to campaign and cast her vote for the first African American president, Barack Obama. However, it is unclear whether all of the things that happen to the Lillian of the book actually happened to the real Lillian, or whether she is a composite character invented to tell the story of the struggles African Americans went through as they were granted first the right, and then the protection of that right, to vote.

The action of the book centers on a strong visual metaphor: the initial endpapers show Lillian at the bottom of a very steep hill. Her posture is upright, although she uses a cane, and her head is tilted slightly upward toward her destination. The title page features Lillian with her arm raised, holding her cane aloft in a gesture that is traditionally read as triumph. This is reinforced by the subtitle of the book, which indicates that this book will be a "celebration." The first **opening**, then, shows a headshot of Lillian, looking to the right and slightly uphill, with a hand resting on her throat and a thoughtful expression on her face. The **recto** has a large sun peeping over the horizon of a hill, and the words "A very old woman stands at the bottom of a very steep hill. It's Voting Day, she's an American, and by God, she is going to vote. Lillian is her name." This delivery of information is by no means **ideologically** neutral. The repetition of the word "very" emphasizes the difficulties she faces—not only is the hill very steep, which is a challenge even for the physically fit, but the walker is very old, a fact that intensifies the

(Continued)

sense of determination that comes in the next sentence. Here, a seemingly disconnected list of attributes is given a meaningful connection through punctuation and is emphasized by the inclusion of the intensifying phrase "by God." The poetic device of emphasis through repetition continues on the next page, where the phrase "It's a long haul" is repeated three times. Here, the dominant visual character of the book is introduced: while Lillian remains brightly colored throughout the book, her history and her memories are portrayed as nearly transparent figures depicted in lighter tones to indicate that they are figures in her imagination. This visual distinction is made clearer when she meets a real person on her way up the hill; he is just as fully saturated and opaque as she is.

Lillian's story relates the collective history of the struggles African Americans have endured in American: her great-great-grandparents were slaves as was her great-grandfather until after the Civil War. He was granted the right to vote in 1870, but his wife was not. But twenty years later, "the hill gets steeper" as her grandfather is charged a poll tax and her uncle is turned away because he is unable to pass a ridiculous test. Lillian's first experience with voting is when she, as a little girl in 1920, goes with her mother to the courthouse now that women are allowed to vote, only to be chased away by a group of angry white men. She then recalls a cross set afire in her yard by white men protesting her family's attempts to vote. Later, she remembers failing the unpassable test, and admonishes a young man who passes her on the way up the hill. Her encounter with the young man is immediately followed by her memories of the funeral of Jimmie Lee Jackson, the Selma march, and the fate of Reverend Martin Luther King, Jr. Finally, she reaches the top of the hill, where the ghostly images of Dr. King and Lyndon Johnson in the process of signing the Voting Rights Act hover over her head as the sun appears in full circle. The penultimate **opening** splits Lillian into a version of her former self and her current self facing the voting booth, and the final spread is of her oversized hand with one long finger reaching out to push a lever. Given the comprehensive nature of her memories with regard to the many stories of African Americans over the course of history, it is most likely that Lillian is a composite character rather than a real individual.

The **ideology** behind this story is made clear by the visual messaging. The words indicate moments when she stumbles, or has trouble keeping her balance, but the pictures only show steady progress for Lillian—an uphill climb to a triumphant endpoint, continually emphasized by the diagonal orientation of the pictures, always moving toward the top right of the page. This method of depiction downplays the significant backward momentum of black Americans in the southern states after 1870, and says nothing of the experiences of African Americans in the northern portions of the country. While this is in keeping with the stated aim of the title to present a celebration of the Voting Rights Act, the author's note at the end takes a different tone—it is less celebratory, offering an interpretation of the Supreme Court's 2013 decision to eliminate federal oversight of states' election processes as a negative development and calling on readers to "continue this fight." This message is subtly reinforced, then, by the final endpapers, which show Lillian at the end of her day, almost back to where she started at the bottom of the hill.

Author talkback: Deborah Heiligman

Deborah Heiligman's *Charles and Emma: The Darwins' Leap of Faith* (2009) was one of five finalists for the National Book Award, received a Printz Honor Award, won the YALSA Excellence in Nonfiction award, and was a finalist for the LA Times Book Prize. She writes both fiction and nonfiction, but in this talkback, she describes how her longstanding affection for nonfiction influences the kind of books she serves up for young readers.

A Healthy Appetite for Delicious Nonfiction

By Deborah Heiligman

When I was a child, the vegetables were awful. I remember limp string beans, overcooked asparagus, spinach that tasted like a wet washcloth. My mother was not a bad cook, but she gave her vegetables little attention. They were there to augment the main course, or for their nutritional value—though I doubt they had much nutritional value by the time my mother was done with them. "Eat your vegetables!" was a threat, a punishment. The only vegetables I remember fondly are fresh corn on the cob (slathered with butter) and raw carrots. My kindergarten teacher "let" us bring in a carrot as a *treat*, the bigger the better. I couldn't wait for carrot day. As is so often the case, my kindergarten teacher knew everything.

Today, vegetables are no longer just sides, and no longer awful. In fact, each year it seems there are more cookbooks published with an emphasis on vegetables. Coming clean I must say right now that I eat mostly vegetables myself. I am a vegetarian (though once in a while, to be polite, I eat fish or seafood). I am someone who loves food, loves to cook and eat, and the reason I can be a vegetarian now is that I know how to make vegetables delicious.

I drizzle asparagus with olive oil, roast it until it's tender but firm, and then sprinkle grated Parmesan cheese on top. I roast cauliflower, parsnips, even string beans, or sauté the beans, in olive oil and garlic. Spinach gets sautéed with garlic in olive oil, too, as does kale and chard. What could be bad? The more creative we get with vegetables, the more pleasure—and nutrients—we get from them.

I think you might have guessed where I am going with this. (Not to the kitchen.) Nonfiction books are the vegetables of the children's and YA book world. They used to be bland, if serviceable. Now they are delicious!

When I was growing up, there were shelves of nonfiction books. We needed those books, and some of them were good, but most of them were—not. And some of them were, sadly, bad: bland, boring, overcooked. Some books labeled as nonfiction were not, actually, nonfiction: they had made-up dialogue, fabricated scenes, assumptions passed off as facts. But they were all we had.

And I loved nonfiction as a girl as much as I hated overcooked asparagus.
I loved fiction, too.
I loved *books*. And people. And story.

What I wanted was to learn about the world, from the outside in and the inside out. I remember clearly the first book I took out of my elementary school library in Allentown, Pennsylvania: *What Is A Butterfly?* After that I went on to *What Is a Tree?* And *What is a Frog?* I look back at those books now, and I can see that they are pretty flavorless, but they are packed with information, which is why I loved them. I learned so much! As I grew older, what I loved most was a good story, either in fiction or in biography. I was and always have been a people person.

When I became a professional writer, I wrote what I loved best as a kid. One of my very first books, *From Caterpillar to Butterfly*, harkened back to that first book I checked out of my school library. But I made it a narrative. I tell a *story* through the eyes of children: a class watches the miracle of metamorphosis. Next I turned to biographies, and other nonfiction stories that called to me (or I was asked to do—as a working writer, that's how it goes sometimes). Many of the books I wrote were about hard subjects: genetics, evolution, ocean currents. I have always been of the opinion that you can write about *anything* for children, as long as you keep the children in mind. In fact, I always keep the child *in me* in mind. When I write for younger kids, as I did in *The Boy Who Loved Math: The Improbable Life of Paul Erdős*, I wrote for myself at six or seven. What would I find interesting and fun and funny and inspiring about a Hungarian mathematician? When I wrote about the Darwins in *Charles and Emma: The Darwins' Leap of Faith*, I wrote for the teenage me.

I am adamant about one thing, always: when you write nonfiction, nothing can be made up. Let me say that again: in nonfiction, *nothing can be made up*. To include fictionalized dialogue, thoughts you don't know someone truly had, or to change the order of events to suit your storyline, would be like serving someone string beans, saying they are vegetarian, but throwing in bacon. Now I understand that you might like (or love) bacon, but it is *not* a vegetable. So you can't call that dish vegetarian.

People often refer to *Charles and Emma* as a novel, which is gratifying, because I wanted it to read like a novel, because their lives were like a great novel. But I am compelled always to say: I made nothing up. Because I love story, I strive to have scenes and dialogue, character development, plot, suspense, arcs—all the components and qualities of fiction, except nothing is made up. I used primary sources: letters, diaries, journals, Darwin's autobiography to craft it. I can back up everything with a source.

Wherever I can, I let content dictate form. Charles and Emma's life seemed like a Victorian novel to me, so I aimed for that form. In my current book, about Vincent van Gogh and his brother Theo, I am letting Vincent's life and his work dictate form: I have written in short takes and in different styles to reflect his paintings and drawings. Some of the pieces are impressionistic, some are more traditional—he painted and drew both ways. There is white space, there is drama. I hope that the book will evoke many of the same feelings that his art does. Again, nothing is made up, and I even present "competing" versions of events, where applicable. (Sort of like roasting some brussels sprouts, and sautéing others. Are you hungry yet?)

What's next for nonfiction?
What do I hope is next?

I hope more and more people will take chances with nonfiction: experimenting with form, combining different kinds of styles, textures. (Just like with a great vegetable dish!) I hope we continue to be creative—as long as we don't cross the line into messing with facts. There should be all kinds of nonfiction for children. Some kids love expository nonfiction, some love narrative nonfiction. Some kids read better if there are pictures interspersed, or even mostly pictures. Others get too distracted by photos. Some people (like me) love a narrative flow, others love sidebars and boxes and even graphic-novel-like designs. We must encourage authors to let their creativity loose with nonfiction, and encourage teachers and parents to fill shelves and shelves with all kinds of great nonfiction. I would love to see the nonfiction sections become a cornucopia of deliciousness.

Pass the roasted brussels sprouts, please.

Literature references

Alphin, T. (2015), *The Lego Architect*, San Francisco: No Starch Press.
Anno, M. (1977), *Anno's Counting Book*, New York: HarperCollins.
Antony, S. (2015), *Please, Mr. Panda*, New York: Scholastic.
Aronson, M. (2007), *Race: A History Beyond Black and White*, New York: Atheneum.
Beckett, S. W. (1994), *Sister Wendy's The Story of Painting*, London: DK Publishing.
Bell, C. (2014), *El Deafo*, New York: Abrams.
Brown, D. (2015), *Drowned City: Hurricane Katrina and New Orleans*, New York: HMH Books for Young Readers.
Crutcher, C. (2003), *King of the Mild Frontier: An Ill-advised Autobiography*, New York: HarperCollins.

Dickins, R. (2007), *The Usborne Art Treasury*, Usborne Pub Ltd.

Ehrhardt, K. (2006), *This Jazz Man*, New York: HMH Books for Young Readers.

Fleischhauer-Hardt, H. (1975), *Show Me!: A Picture Book of Sex for Children and Parents*, New York: St. Martin's.

Fletcher, R. (2012), *Guy-Write: What Every Guy Writer Needs to Know*, New York: Henry Holt.

Foster, T. C. (2013), *How to Read Literature Like a Professor: For Kids*, New York: HarperCollins.

Harris, R. H. (2006), *It's Not the Stork: A Book about Girls, Boys, Babies, Bodies, Families, and Friends*, Illus. Michael Emberley. New York: Candlewick.

Harris, R. H. (2014), *It's Perfectly Normal: Changing Bodies, Growing Up, Sex and Sexual Health*, Illus. Michael Emberley. New York: Candlewick. [Originally published 1994].

Harris, R. H. (2014), *It's So Amazing! A Book about Eggs, Sperm, Birth, Babies, and Families*, Illus. Michael Emberley. New York: Candlewick. [Originally published 1999].

Heiligman, D. (2009), *Charles and Emma: The Darwins' Leap of Faith*, New York: Henry Holt.

Hyman, T. S. (1981), *Self-Portrait, Trina Schart Hyman*, New York: HarperCollins.

Ibbs, K. (2004), *DK Children's Cookbook*, London: Dorling Kindersley.

Jenkins, S. (2004), *Actual Size*, New York: HMH Books for Young Readers.

Jenkins, S. and Page, R. (2015), *How to Swallow a Pig: Step-by-Step Advice from the Animal Kingdom*, New York: HMH Books for Young Readers.

Johnson, S. T. (1995), *Alphabet City*, New York: Puffin.

Joslin, S. (1986), *What Do You Say, Dear?*, Illus. Maurice Sendak. New York: Harper & Row.

Kaye, S. and Thomson, P. (2006), *Philosophy for Teens: Questioning Life's Big Ideas*, Waco, TX: Prufrock Press.

Kops, D. (2012), *The Great Molasses Flood: Boston, 1919*, Watertown, MA: Charlesbridge.

Lach, W. (2006), *Can You Hear It?*, New York: Harry N. Abrams.

Levine, G. C. (2006), *Writing Magic: Creating Stories that Fly*, New York: HarperCollins.

Locker, T. (1997), *Water Dance*, San Diego, CA: Harcourt Brace & Co.

London, J. (2015), *Hippos Are Huge!*, Illus. Matthew Trueman. New York: Candlewick.

Lonely Planet Kids (2015), *The Lonely Planet Kids Travel Books: Mind-Blowing Stuff on Every Country in the World*, London: Lonely Planet Kids.

Mangan, L. (2014), *Inside Charlie's Chocolate Factory: The Complete Story of Willy Wonka, the Golden Ticket, and Roald Dahl's Most Famous Creation*, New York: Puffin.

McClafferty, C. K. (2011), *The Many Faces of George Washington: Remaking a Presidential Icon*, Minneapolis, MN: Carolrhoda.

Miller, H. L. (2008), *This is Your Life Cycle*, Illus. Michael Chesworth, New York: Houghton Mifflin.

Murphy, J. (2003), *An American Plague: The True and Terrifying Story of the Yellow Fever Epidemic of 1793*, New York: Clarion.

National Geographic Kids (2012), *5000 Awesome Facts (About Everything)*, Washington, DC: National Geographic.

Nichols, T. (2008), *Punk Rock Etiquette: The Ultimate How-to Guide for DIY, Punk, Indie, and Underground Bands*, New York: Roaring Brook Press.

Partridge, E. (2005), *John Lennon: All I Want is the Truth*, New York: Viking.

Pizzoli, G. (2015), *Tricky Vic: The Impossibly True Story of the Man Who Sold the Eiffel Tower*, New York: Viking.

Rankin, K. (2011), *Start it Up: The Complete Teen Business Guide to Turning your Passions into Pay*, Illus. Eriko Takada, San Francisco: Zest.

Rappaport, D. (2004), *John's Secret Dreams: The John Lennon Story*, New York: Hyperion.

Rosen, M. (2001), *Shakespeare: His Work and His World*, Illus. Robert Ingpen, New York: Candlewick.

Rosen, M. (2005), *Dickens: His Work and His World*, Illus. Robert Ingpen, New York: Candlewick.

Sandler, M. W. (2013), *Imprisoned: The Betrayal of Japanese Americans During World War II*, New York: Walker.

Sheinkin, S. (2012), *Bomb: The Race to Build—and Steal—the World's Most Dangerous Weapon*, New York: Roaring Brook.

Sidman, J. (2010), *Dark Emperor and Other Poems of the Night*, New York: HMH Books for Young Readers.

Stokke, R. and Larsen, (2012), *Regine's Book: A Teen Girl's Last Words*, San Francisco: Zest.

TIME for Kids Magazine (2010), *TIME for Kids BIG Book of Why: 1001 Facts Kids Want to Know.*, New York: TIME for Kids Books.

van Loon, H. W. (1921), *The Story of Mankind*, New York and London: Liveright.

Weate, J. (1995), *A Young Person's Guide to Philosophy*, Illus. Peter Lawman, London: Dorling Kindersley.

Wolfe, G. (1999), *Oxford First Book of Art*, Oxford: Oxford UP.

Woodson, J. (2014), *Brown Girl Dreaming*, New York: Penguin.

9 ¾

The In-Betweens of Children's and Young Adult Literature

By now you will have noticed that many works of children's and YA literature fit into multiple categories despite the fact that I have separated out different types of literature into different chapters. For instance, you will find novels, memoirs, and nonfiction rendered in poetry, poetry presented in picturebooks and sequential art, fiction and nonfiction picturebooks that appeal to all ages, prose novels with graphic insets, novels based on ballads and folktales, narrative nonfiction, informational picturebooks with fantasy plotlines, picturebooks and novels on film, and interactive multimodal fiction—and the list of blended and hybrid **genres** will expand into the next couple chapters.

Definitions, distinctions, and **genre** taxonomies such as I discuss in the various chapters can be useful for both scholars and young readers insofar as they set expectations for the kind of book we are reading, and enable us to form some evaluations about how successful the book is within its category. But they can also be troublesome for a number of reasons. For instance, as I have noted in the chapter on nonfiction, it's difficult for librarians to decide where to shelve certain kinds of books, based on whether they are conceived primarily as artfully constructed picturebooks or conveyors of scientific information. The conundrum here is whether the main emphasis will be on **form** or **genre**, with the added problem of whether books should be separated according to conventional age levels. So, for instance, my local library places all biographies for young readers in a single section, giving a main emphasis on **genre**. This means that picturebooks for new or prereaders sit beside middle-grade chapter books. Other libraries shelve chapter book biographies next to adult biographies with a special letter added to the call number, such as J for Juvenile or YS for Youth Services, but they put picturebook biographies in a separate section.

The distinction between **form** and **genre** also becomes a problem for awards committees. The American Library Association's Caldecott Award, for instance, faced some controversy in its choices of Brian Selznick's *The Invention of Hugo Cabret* (2007) as its 2008 winner, and Mariko and Jillian Tamaki's *This One Summer* (2014) as a 2015 honor book because neither of these is a picturebook as the category is traditionally understood. In 2016, the same picturebook, *Last Stop on Market Street* (de la Peña 2015), won both a Caldecott Honor and a Newbery Award, the latter being an award traditionally given to a children's novel. In that case, while the choice was surprising in terms of **form**, the Newbery award criteria specifies only that the winner should be a text appropriate for children under the age of fourteen. The Carnegie Medal has no such age cut-off, prompting some confusion when David Almond's YA novel, *A Song for Ella Grey* (2015), won an award that has traditionally gone to literature for a younger demographic. At *The Bulletin of the Center for Children's Books*, we regularly discuss the problems of comparing YA literature to middle grade and early readers in the same category of fiction, and work hard to ensure that books for each age group are given equal consideration for excellence in their own way as we prepare our annual Blue Ribbons Awards list. A film like *Sita Sings the Blues* (2009), while it focuses on its creator's marital breakup, is exemplary of the types of concerns faced by texts that cross over from youth literature to something like "literature for all ages"; as an animated film that draws from Hindu folklore, early twentieth-century blues music, and Saturday morning cartoon violence and heroism, it hits audiences at different levels and shows the ongoing relevance and transformative capacity of traditional narratives.

Given the vast range of types of texts, therefore, I am interrupting this book to highlight three key terms that you must consider, together and separately, as you study children's and YA literature: **form**, **genre**, and **mode**. These terms are sometimes used interchangeably, and I don't pretend to have the last or most authoritative word on what they mean; in fact, my definitions may seem idiosyncratic or at least at odds with those of other critics in the various fields in which they are studied. However, I think it's worthwhile to at least tease out some distinctions and offer working definitions for purposes of analysis, since any given text you study will have its specific blend of the three. Hence, when you write about or discuss a text, you need to pay attention to how they work separately and together.

Let's start with **form**. **Form** refers to the physical way a text is presented, its means of conveyance, if you will. So, for instance, a picturebook or a sequential art narrative is a **form**. While Lewis Turco (2012) calls poetry and prose **genres**, I think it's more accurate to call them **forms** of written or oral expression, for reasons that will become clear when we discuss **genre**; prose is straightforward discourse delivered in paragraphs, while poetry is the artful use of language, sometimes as a means of personal expression, sometimes in dialogue, sometimes as a story. Different ways of writing poetry, such as sonnets, haikus, or concrete poems, are also called **forms**. Film is a **form**, as is a chapter book or an early reader or a puppet show or a play. **Form** is thus the material means of expression, and as such each type of **form** has its own affordances and limitations—that is, the properties of the **form** that define its possibilities. People who study various **forms** develop specific vocabularies to facilitate close reading and observation, some of which I have shared with you in this book. Analysis of a text should take these affordances into account, paying attention to the ways in which the **form** shapes and otherwise interacts with the content.

Genre refers to the content or subject matter of a text. There are broad **genre** distinctions, such as fiction and nonfiction, that branch into various subcategories. Any of these subcategories can be presented in any **form**, as I have highlighted. For instance, a memoir, which is a subgenre of nonfiction, can be presented in the **form** of a graphic narrative. A lament or a sermon can be expressed in poetry or prose. A fairy tale may be delivered through the **form** of a film, or as a short story. What **genres** do is establish certain baseline expectations. That said, it is wise to heed the words of Mal Peet: "I see genre as generating sets of rules or conventions that are only interesting when they are subverted or used to disguise the author's intent. My own way of doing this is to attempt a sort of whimsical alchemy, whereby seemingly incompatible genres are brought into unlikely partnerships." (in Eccleshare 2015). K. A. Holt's *Brains for Lunch* (2010) is a good example of this kind of mash-up; while you might think that the main characters being a zombie is a strong indicator of the horror **genre**, this is actually a sweet, funny romance that takes the **form** of an illustrated middle-grade novel. Moreover, the entire story is told in haiku, which upsets **genre** expectations for haiku, a **form** that usually features subject matter related to isolated images for the purpose of enlivening the sensory experience of everyday life.

Mode is what I call the attitude of approach to the subject matter. For instance, a YA novel written in prose (**form**) about the impossible love between two people (romance **genre**) can be approached as a tragedy or a comedy (**mode**). Holt's mash-up, for instance, treats both horror and romance **tropes** humorously. While J. K. Rowling crafts an immersive fantasy series earnestly concerned with real-world ethical dilemmas, Mal Peet's *The Murdstone Trilogy* approaches the fantasy **genre** and the series **form** in a fully satiric **mode**. Mike Cadden (2005: 286) argues persuasively that studying **mode** as a complement to **genre** "helps students understand why two stories might produce the same emotional response despite their being in different genres, and why it's limiting to assume that all science fiction stories are alike despite being in the same genre." Northrop Frye famously worked a taxonomy of fictional and thematic modes that you will want to study more carefully if you want to write about **mode**, but here's the quick and dirty: The emotional and thematic content of stories can be presented as tragedy, **comedy**, **romance**, or **irony**, depending on what type of character we are dealing with. As Cadden points out, these **modes** often "entwine," which is his way of saying that you will most often find more than one **mode** in a book depending on which character you focus on. For the most part, realistic children's and YA texts feature what are called "low mimetic" characters, which are characters who are neither better or worse than an average person. In the retelling of legends or some fantasy genres, however, we find heroes and villains who are a cut above or below the common run of humanity. Tragedy with low mimetic characters occurs when bad things happen to relatively good people, creating an emotion of pity. Tragedy turns ironic when the bad things that happen seem accidental, undeserved, or piled on; this is arguably the dominant **mode** of the middle-grade boy novel, such as *Diary of a Wimpy Kid* (Kinney 2007), if you trust the narrator's assessment of himself as unfairly put-upon. Tragic events are often situated somewhere in the middle or even prior to the beginning of a story for younger readers so that a romantic or comic resolution can be achieved by the end. Not so with YA fiction; while some books feature comic resolutions, many, such as Cormier's *The Chocolate War* (1974), feature characters who are scapegoated by their community, which places them in the **mode** of tragic irony. Others, such as *The Outsiders* (1967), give us characters in several different **modes**: Dally's fate, for instance, is conventionally tragic, in that, while he is at times admirable and heroic, he dies as a result of a fatal flaw in his character, while Johnny's fate is somewhere between ironic and romantic, given that he is a whipped puppy who nevertheless makes a noble and ennobling sacrifice. Ponyboy's ultimate fate, however, is comic, in that he is reintegrated into his family and his community.

It's important to note that, as a **mode**, **comedy** does not necessarily mean that a book is humorous. It means instead that the book ends with the redemption, restoration, or reintegration of the character into community. Similarly, the **romance mode** doesn't mean the same as the **romance genre**. Characters in the **romance mode** are better or more powerful than the average person; Cadden suggests Charlotte the spider as an example, and we might consider Harry Potter or Dumbledore in this way as well. A character like Charlie Bucket (Dahl 1964), on the other hand, is ironic in both the tragic and comic **modes**; at first, this fairly ordinary boy is a victim of bad luck in his abject poverty, but then his fate shifts due to the good luck of finding a Golden Ticket. While children's and middle-grade texts lean more toward comic outcomes, Cadden's model of entwining modes is more suggestive of the rich complexity afforded by novels that lead us through several different emotional trajectories on the way to resolution.

Obviously, these brief definitions of **form**, **genre**, and **mode** don't come close to exhausting the possibilities for discussion and dissection of how they work in children's and YA story worlds, but I hope they provide inspiration for research projects to pursue as you deepen your study of children's and YA literature. Interestingly, people sometimes use the term **genre** to refer to children's literature as a whole, and posit YA literature as a separate and distinct **genre**. This usage implies that there are some similarities of subject matter or content that one can expect from literature that is intended for a young audience. In fact, Perry Nodelman (2008: 76–81) has come up with a list of forty-five qualities that he finds consistent across a text set that includes books from various time periods and national origins, targeted to young children, middle graders, and YAs, and that take different forms. His exploration enables him to conclude that children's literature might be defined by something more than its audience, which is a common argument for its specificity. He says:

> [Children's literature] might, in fact, be a specific genre of fiction whose defining characteristics seem to transcend specifics of time and place, cut across other generic categories such as fantasy or realism, and even remain consistent despite variations in the ages of the intended audiences. (81)

After thinking through the various types of literature we have already discussed in this book as well as what's to come in the next two chapters, and considering the historical variations as well as the wide variety of subjects, modes, and forms that are written for young people, I still have unresolved questions about what may be considered children's and YA literature's defining characteristics, so I am not sure I can agree with his conclusion at this point, but it's a question worth considering.

Now to return to our regularly scheduled book.

Literature references

Almond, D. (2014), *A Song for Ella Grey*, London: Hodder.
Cormier, R. (1974), *The Chocolate War*, New York: Pantheon.
Dahl, R. (1964), *Charlie and the Chocolate Factory*, New York: Alfred A. Knopf.
De la Peña, M. (2015), *Last Stop on Market Street*, New York: Penguin.
Holt, K. A. (2010), *Brains for Lunch: A Zombie Novel in Haiku?!*, Illus. Gahan Wilson. New York: Roaring Brook.
Kinney, J. (2007), *Diary of a Wimpy Kid*, New York: Amulet.
Selznick, B. (2007), *The Invention of Hugo Cabret*, New York: Scholastic.
Tamaki, M. and Tamaki, J. (2014), *This One Summer*, New York: First Second.
Peet, M. (2014), *The Murdstone Trilogy*, London: David Fickling.

10

Narrative Fiction: As Real as it Gets?

Recommended texts to read or view with this chapter

Alexie, Sherman, *The Absolutely True Diary of a Part-Time Indian*.

Fish Tank, Directed by Andrea Arnold, DVD.

Edgeworth, Maria, "The Purple Jar" http://etc.usf.edu/lit2go/68/fairy-tales-and-other-traditional-stories/5098/the-purple-jar/.

Fitzhugh, Lois, *Harriet the Spy*.

Saenz, Benjamin Alire, *Aristotle and Dante Discover the Secrets of the Universe*.

Tharp, Tim, *The Spectacular Now*.

When I ask my university students to read Melvin Burgess's YA novel, *Doing It* (2003), I tell them to turn off their internal censors and any sense they have of reading "on behalf of" some imaginary teenager. Instead, I suggest that they have a glass of wine and try to enjoy themselves. As the title suggests, this is a book about having sex, and there are some sexy bits that will very likely engage readers' mirror neurons and . . . well, enough said. But it is also a book that invites the counter-pleasures of disgust, pity, and possibly even an energizing anger and outrage, depending on which characters readers identify with. In the end, though, what we discover as we talk about the book in class, once we get past any objections to teenagers having sex and/or reading about it, once we get past talking about how reading a book like this induces curiosity, pleasure, censure, and anxiety, is that this is a highly moral book. That is, the sexual activity in this book has explicit emotional motivations and consequences, and readers are called upon to both empathize with and sit in judgment over the characters' behaviors, words, and thoughts. It is a book that questions and critiques parents' and other adults' choices and their effects on teens trying to learn acceptable behaviors and coherent values, as well as adolescent concerns with body image, holding both adults and teens up to an unflattering mirror that is ultimately sobering and instructive. Is it sexist? Yep. From both sides—girl's bodies are objectified and subjected to vicious critique, which in turn makes the boys who pass these judgments via competitive gross-out humor come across as despicable jerks. Anne Fine (2003), who was British children's laureate at the time of its publication, called it "filth, which ever way you look at it," arguing that "all of the publishers who have touched this novel should be deeply ashamed of themselves." And yet it won the *Los Angeles Times* Book Prize for Young Adult Fiction in 2004. Judging from my American students' varied responses, I don't think this discrepancy reflects a difference between American and British values, but I do think it opens up an interesting discussion about realism in children's and YA fiction: How real do we want literature for young people to be? Does realistic fiction always (have to) embed moral lessons? Whose reality and whose morality are acceptable, and whose deserve critique and condemnation? Does realistic literature really represent reality, when each of those variants on the world "real"—realistic, really, and reality—has different meanings for different people in different contexts? These are the questions that concern us as we consider what is referred to as realistic youth literature.

Realism and moral danger

While the controversies surrounding fantasy have made more recent headlines (objections, for instance, to the depiction of a friendly and appealing occult realm, as in the Harry Potter series, or the bleak violence of dystopias like *Hunger Games*), the **ideological** controversies that swirl around the depiction of characters and situations that strike us as possible or imitative of the world we see around us every day are similarly manifold, especially when it comes to literature for young readers. Why should this be so? What could be wrong with showing young people the world as it is, warts and all, in an age-appropriate way? Or, to come at the concern from the opposite direction, isn't it better to present an ideal world in literature that young readers can aspire to, even if such a world contradicts their experience?

One reason people object to the depiction of a warts-and-all world is that we have an abiding belief that children will imitate the behaviors they see in books. We have good reason to believe this—who hasn't seen a child acting out a story he or she has just heard, watched or read? Moreover, we have the example of advertising—if people don't imitate or desire to imitate what they see in ads, then a whole lot of money is being wasted creating scenarios that depict real people enjoying products and services that viewers can likewise enjoy if they purchase what's on offer. So representations do in fact affect behavior. This effect is intensified if the scenario seems possible or analogous to real life. When a young reader pretends to slay a dragon, she knows that she is acting out a fantasy and her adults think it's cute and empowering. But when she reads about and then imitates a girl being sassy to her mom, we don't accept that as a similar kind of pretending. The former is an acceptable form of playing with power, the latter not so much. So we fear that if a fiction is presented as believable, young readers might not only believe it, but strive to enact it in the real world, with real-world consequences. Is such a fear justified? Here again, look to advertising. We know that a model's hair and skin have all been perfected in postproduction. We might even know, from watching it happen on YouTube, that her neck and legs have been elongated and her waist slimmed and contoured through the magic of Photoshop. And yet we hope and imagine that if we buy the products and clothes in the ad, we can somehow attain or at least approximate a standard we know to be impossible.

C. S. Lewis (1966: 28–29), in his defense of fantasy, addresses the dangers inherent in the desire to imitate realistic texts:

> I think what profess to be realistic stories for children are far more likely to deceive them. I never expected the real world to be like the fairy tales. I think that I did expect school to be like the school stories. The fantasies did not deceive me; the school stories did. All stories in which children have adventures and successes which are possible, in the sense that they do not break the laws of nature, but almost infinitely improbable, are in more danger than the fairy tales of raising false expectations.

He goes on to argue that while both fantasy and realistic fiction engender a kind of longing or desire, the fantasy story points to a world beyond this one, while the realistic story sets up expectations about the self or the circumstances and possibilities of one's life that are just as likely to go unrealized, and are more damaging and disappointing because of that. He continues:

> The real victim of wishful revers does not batten on the *Odyssey*, *The Tempest*, or *The Worm Ouroboros*; he (or she) prefers stories about millionaires, irresistible beauties, posh hotels, palm beaches and bedroom scenes—things that might really happen, that ought to happen, that would have happened if the reader had had a fair chance. The one is an *askesis*, a spiritual exercise, and the other is a disease. (30)

In his view, then, not only the imitative behaviors that might result from reading realistic fiction but also the expectations such reading engenders are likely to put readers in psychological, moral, and perhaps even physical danger.

What's implicit in Lewis's argument is a deep distrust of texts that present themselves as analogous to experience, but really aren't—that is, just because a text doesn't feature dragons or interplanetary travel, or in any other way deviate from consensus reality, it doesn't mean that it's realistic. Possible is not the same as probable or even likely. Fine (2003), for instance, scoffs at claims that Burgess's text is realistic, taking particular issue with the relationship between Ben and his teacher as a ridiculously exaggerated fantasy that would never happen. The problem here is that we know from news reports that things like this *do* happen. They are admittedly rare, which is why they qualify as "news," but they are verifiably true to someone's experience somewhere. The plotlines and issues of middle-grade and YA realistic fiction, which at least since the 1960s have explored some of the darkest and saddest sides of human experience such as debilitating grief, abuse, bullying, rape, kidnapping, murder, mental illness, and suicide in explicit detail, are all possible; they have all happened to someone—indeed, lots of someones. The same goes for the more wish-fulfilling forms and themes of realistic fiction where, for instance, middle graders solve local mysteries and teens fall in love with people they meet while traveling; it could happen, and maybe sometimes it does, but it's rare. The worry behind Lewis's assertions is that these sorts of books, because they *seem* to imitate reality, idealize and normalize such experiences as the only kinds worth having, and that one's life is somehow incomplete or inadequate if it hasn't been touched by some great tragedy or triumph.

This fear then seems to grow tentacles: Will reading these books engender the belief that the world is actually like the world created by imaginative authors? More worrisome is the fact that books follow **intertextual** trends, so will the proliferation of books with teenagers having sex with their teachers (there are quite a few), or having sex with each other (this is almost all of the ones written in this century) engender the belief that the world is *always* like this, for everyone, and any reader whose experience differs is aberrant and somehow out of step with his or her peers? And it's not just sex that is at issue. Other stereotypes abound in realistic fiction: for instance, cities are perfectly safe and interesting if you are a wealthy or middle-class white tween with a subway card; those same cities are full of danger if you are black and poor; Latino males and females are part of gang culture; parents are dysfunctional, distracted, and either abusive or neglectful; white girls are consumed with status and appearance to the extent that they will self-harm or mercilessly bully others; impossibly beautiful boys prefer geeky, socially awkward girls; you will meet your soul mate in high school; if you don't life isn't worth living, unless you are gay or transgender, in which case you will have your heart broken repeatedly and have to look forward to life being better once you get away from your hometown; the list could go on. Equally distressing are the absences in realistic literature; as we have noted in our discussion of illustration, "representation in the fictional world signifies social existence, absence means symbolic annihilation" (Gerbner 1972: 43), so a severely limited number of depictions of, say, contemporary middle-class Native American kids who don't live on reservations, or teens who take their religions seriously, creates stereotypes by exclusion.

On the one hand, these sorts of stereotypes appear and solidify because of the sheer number of books that adopt them, a repetition that leads us to call books with similar characteristics **genres**. The word **genre** is used broadly and somewhat carelessly, and it's especially tricky when talking about children's and YA fiction as we have seen in the interstitial chapter preceding this one. But what's important for us here is to note that **genres** that adopt real-world settings and characters set expectations for their readers that can, over time and many books, become formulas and stereotypes that can come to seem very realistic simply through repetition. I once had a student, for instance, who didn't like M. T. Anderson's *Thirsty* (1997) because the vampires didn't behave like *real* vampires. She had read so many vampire novels that she had developed a sense of what they were really like, and to her mind, they don't live in suburbia and have potlucks. In the same way, reading a lot of realistic novels might give us a stereotypical sense of what high-school cliques are like, or what farm kids are like, or what black urban boys are like, etc.

Add to that the fact that readers who enjoy **genre** novels set in the real world with fully human characters, such as mysteries or romances, don't read just one. They read many, unconsciously absorbing a plot formula that publishers and writers consciously follow, relying on specific details in character and setting to differentiate stories that are basically the same or have broadly similar outcomes. With an established **genre** such as mystery or romance, readers may operate with a double consciousness; that is, on the one hand, they would believe in the characters, settings, and plots as if they were real because they don't do anything that isn't possible. In fact, authors often take pains to establish the possibility of their plots. For instance, Nancy Drew knows how to pick locks because her father, an attorney, once had a criminal client who has taught her how. Therefore, when a situation calls for this supposedly normal small-town teen to pick a lock, she is up to the job. But while Nancy is supposedly normal, she is by no means ordinary, and her back story includes not only lock-picking, but all of the skills and tools she needs to solve the crimes that come her way. So, on the other hand, while readers might believe in Nancy as a realistic character, they also know that what happens to her will not happen in the course of an ordinary life. Such double consciousness is harder to maintain for readers of romance novels, however; after all, few readers expect their days to be full of crimes to solve, but they do expect to have some romantic experiences over the course of their lives. While they know that most encounters are not full of glib conversation and violent passions, they still build their expectations for such encounters at least partially through books that script them. And since books rely on drama to be interesting, readers thus have at least some desire or expectation that "the course of true love never [will] run smooth" (Shakespeare, 1.1.134). Then, like the toddlers acting out the fantasies of their stories, tweens and teens (and, alas, many adults) strive to create lives of romantic drama built on these expectations, and woe to the partner that disappoints them. Thus, insofar as these **genres** don't violate natural laws, they are still debatable in terms of their realism, and they also pose the psychological, moral, and even physical danger of trying to make real life imitate fiction.

In addition to aggregated stereotypes in realistic **genre** fiction, though, another perhaps more pernicious problem with expectations in **realism** is what we might call the **one-book fallacy**. That is, if the only book teens read about contemporary Native American boys is *The Absolutely True Diary of a Part-Time Indian* (Alexie 2007), or about black teens in Harlem is *Monster* (Myers 1999), or about Somali immigrants in London is *Where I Belong* (Cross 2011), or about tweens in Afghanistan is *The Breadwinner* (Ellis 2000), then they can operate on the mistaken belief that they can generalize that experience to most or all such teens in those situations, especially if they are outsiders looking in. These authors are either writing from their own experience or they have done their research, and most often both, but they are still only writing about individuals in a particular situation with a conflict interesting enough to warrant a novel. Insiders to such situations are going to be more attentive to detail, and more critical when an author writes something that doesn't ring true to their experiences. In addition, professional reviewers may react negatively when a book doesn't depict the experience of the individual characters in ways that offer a flattering mirror to the group. As we have noted in Chapter 1, people from marginalized or oppressed groups are often thought to have a collective identity. This can devolve into a denigrating and even dangerous stereotype when it is imposed on members of a group by outsiders. However, it may also be promoted and protected by cultural insiders as a means of establishing collective power, preserving a heritage and/or passing on strong communitarian values.

In either case, though, a collective identity creates a double bind with regard to characters who are not often represented in youth literature. Think about it: fewer books means that each book that is available carries a greater weight of representation for a particular demographic. So when, for instance, 93 percent of the over five thousand books published for young readers in the United States in a given year feature white protagonists, you can expect a lot of different portrayals of individual characters in individual situations, and no one character is thought to represent the entire group. However, if only four books are published that year featuring Native American protagonists, then readers have fewer opportunities to encounter diverse experiences of individuals within that culture. Moreover, such books are harder to access unless they have received some sort of press, positive or negative. And the one-book problem is self-perpetuating when publishers make their decisions about accepting a book from a member of a non-majority culture; as we have noted in our discussion of folktales, a book has to be recognizable by the mainstream culture— that is, it has to meet mainstream expectations regarding what is realistic in a particular situation. Our expectations are often so ingrained that we don't even recognize them as having been built by our intertextual experiences with other books depicting themes, attitudes, and ways of talking about the lifestyles and dominant concerns of people from cultures that are not our own. In the end, then, fiction that is accepted as realism might not be realistic at all.

So what is realism anyway?

It is important, ultimately, to recognize that **realism** is an –ism. That is, it is a distinctive way of writing fiction that proceeds from an **ideological** stance and has a specific history of emergence and development. So we start there: literary **realism** is a way of writing about things that did not actually happen as if they did or could have happened in the consensus reality that we inhabit. As a literary term, **realism** is usually applied to a style of writing for adults that developed in the nineteenth century. Emphasis was laid on replicating natural speech and depicting the setting and events with a journalist's eye for detail. While events in realist novels are unarguably plotted, the plots might not follow a traditional climactic pattern that builds on a single overriding conflict; instead, they often depend more on the **episodic** nature of everyday experience. Thus, this style of writing arose as a kind of protest to the idealized or overly stylized novels and **romances** that were more common prior to the mid-to-late 1800s.

Realistic fiction for children, however, could be said to have started much earlier, with the works, for instance, of Anna Laetitia Barbauld, Mary Wollstonecraft, and Maria Edgeworth, among others, in an effort to compete with the lurid **chapbooks** and **romances** that these Locke-inspired moralists found objectionable for the development of a rational intellect. While their books were more or less educational tracts or fables written in a realistic style, advocates of **realism** for adults, such as Henry James and George Eliot, sought to write honestly about characters drawn from real life, though for different purposes. Broadly speaking James wanted to explore psychological motivations, while Eliot was more concerned with exposing social ills. However, we will need to go beyond this limited usage of the term to consider special concerns and motivations for **realism** in children's and YA literature. In fact, literary **realism** has worn different guises in children's and YA literature over the years. For instance, Catherine Sinclair's *Holiday House* (1839) stands out as an early exception to the moral slant of realistic fiction for both adults and children as she wanted to portray with good-natured humor the high-spiritedness and gentle naughtiness of her aristocratic child characters, and she embedded the telling of fantastic stories within her narrative as a realistic pastime of children. But as realism took hold for adults in the late nineteenth and early twentieth centuries, children's writers such as Samuel Grisewold Goodrich (writing as Peter Parley), Mark Twain, Louisa May Alcott, and L. M. Montgomery solidified the tradition in youth literature. Here are some of the major variations:

- **Classic or bourgeois realism** is a term used to refer to books that, by virtue of presenting their characters and situations as if they were real, encourage readers to accept their **ideological** messages about middle-class values, behaviors and aspirations as common sense. Edgeworth's stories are particularly notable here. As Lucy Pearson and Kimberley Reynolds (2010) note, this type of **realism** has received robust critical attention from Catherine Belsey in *Critical Practice* (1980), and been further interrogated with respect to children's texts by Peter Hollindale (1988) and John Stephens (1992). Without too much risk of caricature, you might think of **classic realism** as the kinds of books that feature morally upright children making good decisions about their mild problems, or who learn their lesson when they don't. Then, you will have to go back and critically examine these children—they are most likely white and middle class, and some of them are insufferably boring. Others, however, are delightful old friends, like Eleanor Estes's Moffat family, Maud Hart Lovelace's Betsy and Tacy, Robert McCloskey's Homer Price, and Beverly Cleary's Henry Huggins and Ramona Quimby. Because of the lovable nature of these characters, Lois Fitzhugh's *Harriet the Spy* (1954) caused quite a stir, featuring as it does a strong-willed girl who is not all that likable.

- **Psychological realism** is characterized by close attention to the inner thoughts and motivations of a character or characters. Because children develop a more nuanced **Theory of Mind** as they grow older, **psychological realism** is more common in novels for middle graders and YAs, although writers such as Shaun Tan and Michael Rosen have introduced **psychological realism** into their picturebooks with *The Red Tree* (2000) and *Michael Rosen's Sad Book* (2005), respectively. Some of the YA novels in this style can be quite introspective, and in your more cynical moments, you might call them exercises in self-indulgent navel-gazing. However, given the imperative for tweens and YAs to understand themselves and function socially with a range of other personalities, these books are vastly popular, and can even be therapeutic. While middle-grade **psychological realism** tends to follow **bourgeois realism** in its optimistic approach to problem-solving and resiliency (and of course there are exceptions), YA **psychological realism** often has a fascination with extreme conditions, such as the mental illnesses explored in John Neufeld's classic *Lisa Bright and Dark* (1970), and Neal Shusterman's *Challenger Deep* (2015). More often, though, these books explore complex psychological conundrums that teens find somewhat relatable (and beware, your teacher probably hates that word—ask him or her why!), such as the nature of intersectional identities or life with a disability, with grace and humor; Hannah Moskowitz's *Not Otherwise Specified* (2015), Alexie's *The Absolutely True Diary of a Part-Time Indian* (2007), and Eric Lindstrom's *Not if I See You First* (2016) offer good examples. Because we are so intimately involved with the character's perspective, the **psychological realism** might not correspond with the external world, as is the case with the unreliable narration of Sutter Keely in *The Spectacular Now* (2008), giving readers a chance to exercise critical distance.

- **Social realism** critiques social structures and conditions that negatively affect groups, such as poverty, racism, and other forms of prejudice. Since these larger social problems obviously affect individuals as well, these books can also feature **psychological realism**. Jesse C. Jackson's *Call Me Charley* (1945), S. E. Hinton's *The Outsiders* (1967), Mildred D. Taylor's Logan family books, Todd Strasser's *If I Grow Up* (2009), as well as any of Deborah Ellis's fictional accounts of children in difficult circumstances take on the project of social critique through exploration of children's and teens' experiences.

- Not to be confused with social realism, a specific movement in Soviet literature called **Socialist realism** was instituted by Joseph Stalin in 1934 and championed for youth literature by Maxim Gorky. Children's literature written under this paradigm was strictly monitored. Utopian in spirit, it glorified the goals of the Communist Party to create a new society based on the elevation of the common worker.

- **New realism** is a name given to youth literature beginning in the 1960s that explores aspects of human experience that were formerly considered social taboos. New realism includes those books designated "problem novels," which tend to focus on one central difficulty, like a teen pregnancy, suicide, bullying, the death of a parent, school shootings, sexual abuse, or drug addiction. It also includes books that surface the interconnectedness of these problems. Often, it's the endings of these books that indicate the level of their commitment to **realism**. When a bully gets his or her comeuppance or a problem is resolved without residue, for instance, the book may feel emotionally satisfying, but ultimately unrealistic. More often in contemporary books, such as Meg Medina's *Yaqui Delgado Wants to Kick Your Ass* (2013), there is a recognition that solutions to most social problems are compromised and partial. New realist texts are therefore regularly taken to task for being too edgy or only focusing on the more depressing side of human experience.

Offshoots and variations include:

- **Magical realism** may more properly be understood as a type of fantasy, because it does contain fantastic or magical elements. However, these elements intrude into an otherwise realistic setting, and are treated with a realistic tone. The category is harder to distinguish in children's books that it is in adult literature, since children's books regularly feature talking animals or toys in realistic settings. Nonetheless, books like *Corduroy* (Freeman 1978) or *Charlotte's Web* (White 1952) are not generally considered magic realist texts, while those of E. Nesbit, P. L. Travers, and David Almond generally are.

- **Fake realism** refers to the types of stories Lewis objected to above. Mike Cadden (2011) sources the term to Ursula Le Guin (1989), and elaborates the category to include those books where the plot turns more on wish fulfillment than logical development of character and circumstance. He cites typical sports stories, bully takedowns, and slickly marketed adolescent girl series where the teens have bottomless bank accounts and no interfering parents as belonging to this seductive genre. I would add to his list the type of **realism** that focuses on rendering reality zany and hilarious, such as we find in books like Louise Rennison's Georgia Nicholson series, Liz Pichon's Tom Gates books, Jeff Kinney's Diary of a Wimpy Kid series, and T. S. Easton's *Boys Don't Knit* (2015). While I personally might wish that life were as funny as these writers make it, and/or I might wish that "new realism" had room for the lighter aspects of experience, it seems that the exaggerations in these books tip them over into **fake realism** territory.

Within each of these categories, you will find types of books that have become subgenres in children's and YA fiction, such as the school story, historical fiction, the vacation story, the domestic tale, the group or family novel, the survival story, the career novel, nonfantastic animal stories, and the everyday life book. Each of these subgenres carries expectations that help readers identify what they need and like from their realistic literature. There are, of course, many books that fall outside and between all these categories, and you may not agree with my placement of some of the titles. While it could be that I am just not that good at categorization (my files certainly attest to that), it might also be the case that realistic literature is as various as the life it depicts, so any categories will need to have fuzzy, permeable borders. Where, for instance, would we put the works of John Green or Jenny Downham, which are certainly about white, bourgeois subjects, but are also by turns tragic, funny, stylized, psychologically complex, and wish-fulfilling? Rather than think about these categories as file boxes, it is better to think of them as heuristic devises that call attention to the different aspects of reality that a literary work might emphasize—its particular marriage of storytelling style and purpose. Because telling children about the world as it is always has a purpose.

The ideological core, and deeper history, of realism

Each of these types of realistic literature for children and YAs has been founded on a perception of what literature does in and for society, and in particular, society's youth—that is, literature is believed by many to be something more than a temporary escape or diversion from the real business of life. It is believed to have actual effects on that business, operating as something other than a mirror, a lamp, a window, or a beguiling fantasy, and behaving more like an engine of change. As I have argued in previous chapters, stories don't just reflect our experiences; they shape them. If that's true, then if we want our experiences to change, we need to change the stories we tell about ourselves and others. You might have noticed that each of the claims made for **realism** in its various guises could also be made for different types of fantasy—that is, there are fantasies that critique social conditions and expose psychological ones, and some books that seem real are nothing other than fantasies wearing real clothes. But while fantasy can offer certain kinds of scenarios that we can envision as desirable or horrific, we don't really believe they are possible. Realistic fiction, however, by not breaking any natural laws, by offering what seems to be analogous to photographic evidence of things that could actually be happening, may have quite different effects.

Although the genre of literary **realism** is most commonly associated with nineteenth-century developments, **realism** starts with a belief that a literary work could, should, and does reflect external reality, an idea that has been around since ancient Greece. Plato refers to literature and art as **mimesis**—a form of imitation— and argues that they are an inferior imitation of the world that is already an inferior imitation of an ideal realm of what he called the Forms. These Forms can only be accessed and understood by using the rational part of our minds rather than our senses, which can deceive us. The Forms are thus the only true reality, and since mimetic art is nothing more than a representation of the world that we can perceive through our senses, literature is a copy of a copy. Now, this view of the Forms opens the door to fantasy as well as **realism**, because fantasy can point to ideals beyond human experience, and convey moral, emotional, and psychological truth through metaphors. But this idea that mimetic literature is only a pale or imperfect copy of what reality actually is or should be gives us a critical tool with which to consider realistic literature for young people: Is it really representative of the world, or is it a picture motivated by the author's **ideologically** charged view of what the world is, should be, or shouldn't be like? Thinking about these questions drills down to your core ontological beliefs—that is, what you believe about reality and your place in it. Is what we experience with our senses and imagine in our minds all there is? Or, like Plato (and many others), do you believe there is a reality outside this one that is more perfect? What role does literature then play in conveying those core beliefs to young readers?

Plato had some of the same concerns that we have discussed at the beginning of this chapter—he felt that literature appealed to the parts of our soul, namely our emotions and passions, that interfered with our reason, and this presented a moral danger. Plato argued that our emotions can be called into service by our rationality or our appetites, depending on which values we choose to adopt and which characters we choose to imitate. He believed that we are more vulnerable to the ignoble passions that literature excites, that we have a tendency to "enjoy and praise" in literature that which we would consider "unworthy and shameful" in real life (1992: 605c-e). Because he recognized that literature gives us that kind of pleasure, he worried about spillover. Poetry (and certain kinds of music? first-person shooter games? violent movies? YA books about sex and suicide?—just to bring things up to date) "nurtures and waters" those passions "that ought to wither and be ruled" and "won't be easily checked when we ourselves suffer" (606b-d), a fear shared not only by C. S. Lewis but by many thoughtful readers of youth literature today.

Aristotle agreed that literature was mimetic, but he had a different take on the value of literature's capacity to imitate reality. He argued that literature selects the bits of reality that are important to create a unified but still complex whole of action and impression. In contrast to Plato, however, he believed that the emotions we feel as the story progresses—specifically, pity and fear—are beneficial. By taking us through the whole life cycle of an emotion, a good tragedy (or, for our purposes, a good YA novel about dying young or bullying) helps us locate the sources and effects of these emotions in our lives, and thus leads us to a greater understanding of the truth of our reality. He also argued that such imitation should not be simplistically manipulated to construct a happy ending. He wasn't against happy endings per se, but they had to grow out of a carefully plotted recognition of some truth that averts a tragic or otherwise unhappy ending. For instance, Junior's and Rowdy's separate and hard-won recognitions of Junior's identity as something other than a betrayal of his Native heritage at the end of *The Absolutely True Diary of a Part-Time Indian* (Alexie 2007) allows for the two boys to reconcile rather than remain enemies. On the other hand, Jerry Renault's recognition of the kind of hero he's not comes too late in *The Chocolate War* (Cormier 1974), and Sutter Keely's recognition of his predicament in *The Spectacular Now* (Tharp 2008) doesn't come at all. In both those cases, the acknowledgment of the book's emotional and psychological truth must come from the readers, who recognize what the characters do not.

Both Plato's and Aristotle's views of **mimesis** plant the seeds for a view of **realism** more in line with what we have today—realistic literature for young readers both imitates and shapes sensual and emotional reality to create a unified impression. This impression is meant to appeal to a reader's intellect through his or her emotions, and as such it can bend what a reader believes to be true or analogous to actual experience, and influence the way the reader approaches reality outside the book. The ability of literature to marry emotion with representations of the world is the feature Plato distrusted but Aristotle applauded. Interestingly, the literature that Plato was upset about wasn't what we would call realistic at all; he was talking about epic tales delivered through poetry and performed as drama; the prose novel about everyday life had yet to be invented. But his definition of **mimesis** remains relevant in that it conveys the sense of showing reality through directly represented actions rather than narrating or telling about those actions. This definition is thus directly applicable to the kind of realistic depictions of actions that we find in contemporary picturebooks and novels for young people written in either first- or third-person omniscient voice; these purport to describe actions as they are occurring, without any overt sense that there is an external narrator or author controlling the narrative, making it seem as if the text is a direct rendering of a character's reality. By contrast, Plato referred to the narrating of events, complete with reflection and knowledge of the characters' feelings and motivations, as **diegesis**. Realistic texts for young readers combine **mimesis** and **diegesis** to create their emotional effects. When these emotional effects are managed within the whole of the text in such a way that they leave the impression of authentic truth and credibility, authors have achieved something called **verisimilitude**.

Verisimilitude is related to **realism**, but not identical to it. Rather, it is the maintenance of an illusion of truth in a work through consistency *within* the world the author has constructed rather than consistency *between* the real world and the world of the text. Thus, **verisimilitude** can exist in forms and genres other than straightforward **realism**, and we often recognize it most when the illusion of truth created is shattered. For instance, in *Boy Meets Boy* (2003), David Levithan creates a world that seems in all respects completely realistic, except that all forms of sexuality and gender identity in this world are considered completely normal. He is therefore able to craft a fairly typical romance plot for his main character without any of the complications of homophobia that might overlay such a relationship in the real world. **Verisimilitude** is never breached because the emotions and situations are consistent within that world. On the other hand, Benjamin Alire Saenz sets his coming-of-age and coming-out book, *Aristotle and Dante Discover the Secrets of the Universe*, in 1987 America. His writing is by turns lyrical and prosaic, with poetic dialogue that does not always ring true to the characters he has created—an artistic, poetic soul who embraces his orientation with grace and insight, and an angry, nonbookish loner who enjoys stereotypically masculine activities and signifiers like fighting, drinking, and driving a truck. That these two dissimilar characters strike up an immediate, increasingly intimate friendship is odd enough, but more difficult to accept is the scene where Ari's parents sit him down to inform him that he is gay. This sort of calm frankness and positivity about their son's sexuality in 1987 is hard to credit as realistic within the setting and characters Saenz has established. Setting aside the fact that his father is a Vietnam vet with PTSD that includes rage as a symptom, sullen Ari has not indicated any prior willingness to discuss his relationships, his sexuality, or much of anything else with his parents. Moreover, in 1987 AIDS was still being called a "gay plague" with only the faintest glimmer of a very expensive treatment in the offing, so that loving parents encouraging their son to pursue his affection for a boy in that environment strains credibility. Hence, this book breaks **verisimilitude** on multiple levels even as it satisfies reader emotions.

These potential schisms between **mimesis**—that is, how closely a book imitates the real world—and **verisimilitude**—whether it is consistent within the parameters it sets for itself—remind us that the use of realistic details drawn from actual life is an aesthetic choice with **ideological** underpinnings, and a culture's **ideological** wish list changes over time. As we have noted in Chapter 1, children's and YA literature has always been concerned with passing on the morals of the adults who write it. But questions arise regarding the best way to do that through literature. After all, much folk literature is threaded through with moral instruction. However, between the widespread acceptance of John Locke's philosophies regarding the dangers of fantasy and the Puritan's rejection of fairy tales, both fiction and poetry for children took on a realistic cast. Although today one might have doubts regarding the **realism** of Thomas Fleet's popular English chapbook, *The Prodigal Daughter* (1736), which features a rebellious young girl who makes a deal with the Devil to poison her parents after her father confines her to her room, books such as these, which combined sensationalism with moral instruction, had realistic settings and reflected the actual beliefs of the people writing them. While most fiction was considered out of bounds for Puritan parents, works by Mary Martha Sherwood such as *The History of the Fairchild Family* (1818, 1842, 1848), especially part I that focused on the children recognizing their need for salvation, were permitted as entertaining religious training precisely because they were considered realistic.

But more troubling for parents and critics in the early 1700s was the popularity of the melodramatic **romance** novel. In those early days of print literature, novel reading was at the center of a "scandal," as William Warner (1994: 1–2) puts it, with commentators reviving Plato's concerns that young readers, especially "young women not exposed to a classical education," would strive to emulate the overwrought heroines of the French **romances** they were gobbling up, and expect their young men to play the role of romantic hero. (I hope as you are reading this you are thinking about the present day, perhaps even of Ryan Gosling standing in the rain, as these fears are still with us, nor are they wholly unjustified.) In response to strong criticism of the **romances** and "secret histories" that were in wide circulation at the time, writers for adults seeking a more respectable reception drew from the earlier forms familiar in children's literature, including conduct books, nonfiction memoirs of pious children, and letters, essays, and sermons penned by parents for the edification of their young to create a new kind of novel that hewed closer to real life than overwrought drama. Samuel Richardson's *Pamela* (1740), for instance, claims on its original cover that it is "a Narrative which has its Foundation in TRUTH and NATURE" which has been written "in order to cultivate the Principles of Virtue and Religion in the Minds of the Youth of Both Sexes," marking it as an early work intended for teenaged readers. Thus **realism**—fiction located in truth and nature—began usurping the place of nonfiction as the site of moral instruction.

While works like Sarah Fielding's *The Governess; or, The Little Female Academy* (1749) and Catherine Sinclair's *Holiday House* (1839) embedded literary fairy tales in their narratives as stories told by indulgent adults and circulated among the child characters, this practice actually enhances the novels' claims to **realism**, since such stories are a large part of children's lives. In fact, it is a notable departure from **realism** in contemporary novels when the characters *don't* reference TV, movies, or the music they listen to as part of their daily activities. However, the move toward the ideal that moral character could best be achieved without the interference of fiction was given a booster shot by Rousseau, who argued in *Émile* that children should be educated in and by nature rather than books. Ironically, this ideology came to represented in books such as Thomas Day's *Sandford and Merton* (1783–89) and Maria Edgeworth's stories in *The Parent's Assistant* (1796), which took realistic depiction further than it had ever gone before by mimicking actual child language in conversation. As we have noted in Chapter 1, Locke's influence on Edgeworth and other writers, including Mary Wollestonecraft, Anna Laetitia Barbauld, Sarah Trimmer, and Hannah More, cannot be overemphasized; in this chapter what is important to note is that his primary influence was on fostering **realism** in children's literature.

According to Katherine Hume (1984), Locke's influence on realism in literature is even more far-ranging. She cites three major developments that emerged out of the European Enlightenment that conditioned the growth of literary **realism**. The first is Locke's insistence that "each person is the sum of his or her unique experiences" (34). By now most academic thinkers take this viewpoint as writ—we call it **social constructivism**. But what it rejects is Plato's notion, and indeed the notions of many religious thinkers, of a transcendent ideal undergirding the real of experience, some external force calling you toward your destiny. You may have had some version of this existential crisis in your own life, where you ask whether you have a calling or destiny to fulfill; it's certainly all over fantasy literature for children and YAs. But the idea that your personality and future is in some part determined by the sum of your experiences contradicts the idea of a destiny written in the stars or somewhere outside yourself. The fact that social constructivism has a history, then, enables us to see it for what it is—a present attitude or way of thinking about the self that may or may not be true. But its impact on literature is an increasing focus on individual experience. That is, quality **realism** should insist that characters be more consistent with their own histories than with any stereotyped group affiliations, although group affiliations will certainly have some level of influence. But individual characters' emotional responses must be properly motivated, and their personalities and appearances aren't manipulated to serve simplistic moral ends as they might be in fairy tales or **fake realism**. Realistic fiction thus must have a claim to **psychological realism** as well as **social realism**.

A second development, Hume (1984) argues, comes from Descartes. You may remember from Chapter 5 that Descartes's mediations on reality resulted in a new emphasis on the interaction of the individual mind with the world of sensations, and the belief that you can't trust either one on its own. Nor can you trust traditional or communal explanations for things; instead, it was imperative that each individual work out his or her understanding of the world on his or her own. According to Hume, this emphasis on self-understanding had several implications. First, it enhances Locke's emphasis on the individual, rather than the community, as the source and end of storytelling, and those stories are meant to be directed toward uncovering truth or reality as it actually is rather than as a tradition handed down. Second, an exploration of one's own mind and natural circumstances without concern for social traditions and taboos can take a writer, and a reader, to some formerly forbidden places. This breaking of taboos is clearly seen in the edgy topics taken up by **new realism**. But Hume also contends that the outcome of Descartes's emphasis on the thinking brain is that the reader is ultimately not who is important for literature. The goal for a new kind of literary art shifts from a transmission of conventional morals or values through a well-made plot arc to the amoral, unvarnished expression of an individual author's or narrator's mind. While most children's books remain primarily a vehicle of purposeful communicating through a shaped story, many YA texts foreground a granular, stream-of-consciousness account of experience, largely eschewing story shape in favor of the minute-by-minute narration of events. This prose style is what we find in works such as Tanuja Desai Hidier's *Bombay Blues* (2014) and Isabel Quintero's *Gabi, a Girl in Pieces* (2015); such books require acceptance of the character's narration as a mode of personal expression that isn't trying to create a unified impression. They also reflect a new way of conceiving reality as the sum of fragments and roles we play rather than a meaningful trajectory toward a desired end of coherent identity.

This type of narration is perhaps where the realist novel departs most forcefully from formula fiction or other strongly plotted novels. In a realist novel, we might spend as much or more time in a character's head as we do in world of events—big things don't have to happen, tension needn't build to a climax. Reflecting on and making sense of the stuff of everyday life is quite enough. This type of **realism** is finding its way into chapter books for new readers as well as YAs. Writers like Claudia Mills, Karen English, Hilary McKay, Annie Barrows, and Julie Steinberg compose gentle school and family stories, most often in series, that feature characters who encounter small problems with a rhythm of action and reflection, mirroring children's ongoing thought processes as they go about their days. While it might not seem like it, these books are actually participating in an **ideological** shift about the way in which fiction presents human experience. Rather than portraying life as a series of epic battles that we can plan for, confront, and ultimately win out over, these stories convey the message that challenges are relatively small and ongoing, and that our character and personality develop through our responses rather than prior to them.

The third development that Hume (1984: 36) suggests sets the conditions for the privileging of **realism** is what she calls "the aesthetic distancing of knowledge." That is, literature, especially youth literature, once served as a means for conveying moral and religious instruction, for passing on knowledge of a culture's traditions and expectations. As we have noted in Chapter 1, children used to be taught to read so that they could read their scriptures. You could pretty up such instructive literature with sensational plots or aesthetically pleasing poetic language, but reading still served a purpose beyond entertainment; it provided knowledge unto salvation. The emphasis on the individual and the development of scientific knowledge outside of religious traditions brought new purposes to the acquisition of knowledge. If knowledge was no longer only directed at eternal salvation or present goodness, then it needed to become useful in other ways—to make life easier or to simply be pleasurable for its own sake. Literature also began to serve functions other than religious contemplation as well. In an increasingly secular, scientific culture, literature began to function as a way of knowing human beings and the real world. Hence, the psychological novel was born, with authors putting characters in complex and difficult situations and exploring plausible rather than necessarily desirable responses. Moreover, increased interaction with cultures and traditions within and outside the West through colonization and warfare required a greater understanding of how diverse people experience the world and how conflicts arise and can be avoided. Thus, though Hume doesn't take this up, both the historical and the multicultural novel are impelled by this quest for aestheticized knowledge of human experience, and the more realistic, the better. While historical novels do allow their authors to make stuff up about the people and periods they are exploring, the need for **verisimilitude** in realistic historical fiction remains, requiring extensive research into the daily habits, customs, and ideologies of the past as they differ from our own.

Of course, in literature for children, the morally didactic impulse remains, but instead of being directed at improvement through the diligent attention to work and moral rectitude in preparation for the life to come, the purpose of children's and YA books has become more human-focused, aimed at creating racial, class, and global awareness and facilitating social critique. The realistic novel has its work cut out for it as it offers one of the most effective ways for getting inside the head of another person in order to develop understanding and empathy. In this service, literature has to combine its scientific purpose with an aesthetic one: "The realistic novel is successful as long as the knowledge it offers of human nature seems interesting to readers, and as long as the artistry compels our aesthetic admiration" (Hume 1984: 37). In other words, the characters and stories presented in realistic novels can't rest on clichés and formulas, and they have to be well written. But they also have to explore those psychological extremes and social conflicts that we have mentioned earlier, because it is these edges that readers find interesting.

As educators and readers, we often seek novels that allow us to relate to characters, believing that this is crucial to ensure interest and empathy. However, when it comes to social critique, the best way to do this may be to break identification with characters, to reveal the story as constructed so that readers have sufficient distance from which to critique the reality it depicts. In other words, if you are living vicariously through a well-drawn, realistic character, learning what his or her life is like, you are more likely to try to imagine the ways in which the character could respond to the social injustices he or she is experiencing. This puts the impetus for change on the individual rather than the system that is oppressing him or her, and this can be problematic especially if you are in some way complicit with that system. If, on the other hand, an aesthetic distancing mechanism is included—perhaps an intrusive narrator or a character using direct address, you are placed outside the story and are more likely to consider ways to respond to the knowledge you are gaining about the unjust world as well as the oppressed character. Hmmm . . . discuss.

The growth of socially conscious realism for young readers

If Hume is right that these three conditions—the greater emphasis on the history of an individual, increased attention to individual thoughts and feelings and one's ability to express them, and the aestheticization of knowledge—set the philosophical conditions for the development of some of the kinds of realistic novels we have today, they don't tell the whole story. Material conditions emerged as well. While the new emphasis on the individual and the growth of secular society promised to free people from the tyranny of strict social hierarchies and oppressive superstitions, new tyrannies of economic stratification, isolation, and social injustice took their place. Writers like Charles Dickens and George Eliot championed **realism** as a method to call readers to moral sympathy with common people, such as rural folk and the working poor in cities, who were not often represented faithfully in literature but were instead used for comic relief, demonized as criminals, or idealized as the sainted poor. In America, writers like Harriet Beecher Stowe, Louisa May Alcott, and Mark Twain wrote realistic novels for young people that, to greater or lesser extents, emphasized democratic attitudes and exposed social injustice in the 1800s. At the same time, romanticized historical fiction and adventure books of G. A. Henty and Howard Pyle that glorified war happily coexisted with the socially conscious novels. After the American Civil War, however, a trend toward **realism** with a fairy tale structure, exemplified in books like *Rebecca of Sunnybrook Farm* (Wiggin 1903), *Anne of Green Gables* (Montgomery 1908), *A Secret Garden* (Burnett 1911), and *Pollyanna* (Porter 1913), as well as the **fake realism** of the mystery series books written under the auspices of the Stratemeyer Syndicate, flourished. These writers seemed bent on constructing the reality they hoped for rather than faithfully documenting the reality they experienced. This hoped-for reality was built on optimism and materialism, and relished naughty but ambitious boys and community-minded girls in the bourgeois realist tradition.

Very few writers of realistic fiction were paying attention to the children who fell outside the white middle-class demographic. In the spirit of George Eliot's desire to wed moral sympathy with faithful representation of neglected groups, W.E.B. Dubois published a magazine for African American children called *The Brownies' Book* from 1920 to 1921, which included both nonfiction and realistic fiction; Lucy Sprague Mitchell published her groundbreaking *Here and Now Storybook* in 1921; Arna Bontemps and Langston Hughes published *Popo and Fifina* in 1932; and Eve Garnett portrayed a large working-class family in her 1937 *The Family from One End Street*. New attention to research and authenticity was given to historical fiction in the first half of the twentieth century, which saw the publication of Laura Ingalls Wilder's Little House series, Esther Forbes's *Johnny Tremain* (1943), and Elizabeth Coatsworth's many books in America, and Rosemary Sutcliff's stirring, authoritative historical novels in England. These books, however, emphasized the histories of white people and cultures. Following the Second World War, a flight into fantasy strained the cause of socially conscious realistic fiction until the emergence of the **new realism** in the 1960s, although African American author Jesse C. Jackson published several realistic novels between 1945 and 1971. But for the most part, the books written for children from the 1920s to the 1960s were steeped in bourgeois and **fake realism**. Edward Stratemeyer's daughter, Harriet S. Adams, who falsely claimed authorship for many of the Nancy Drew books, proudly said of her company's voluminous output, "'They don't have hippies in them. . . . And none of the characters have love affairs or get pregnant or take dope.'" (in Klemesrud 1968). But as Michael Cart notes, teenagers were hungry for books that reflected the new realities they faced daily, and writers like Virginia Hamilton, Nat Hentoff, S. E. Hinton, Rosa Guy, Walter Dean Myers in the United States, and John Rowe Townsend, Nina Bawden, and Jan Needle in England took up the challenge of writing frankly and memorably about race relations, sexual identity, class warfare, mental illness, teen pregnancy, and drug addiction, among other things.

Conclusion

If we were to trace the trajectory of children's and YA literature from its earliest history to the present we would find, I think, that it is something like a pendulum swing, in Michael Cart's words, "from romance to realism" (1996). Realistic fiction originally grew out of a desire to protect children from the spiritual, moral, and emotional dangers of fantasy and facilitate religious instruction. But as society became less traditional and more secular, the goals of reading fiction changed. It became an activity valued for its own sake, providing insight into the lives and thoughts of other people, and the reality that mattered most became the reality of our own emotions.

Our emotions, however, are not always satisfied by the here and now realism of our world, so the pendulum swings back toward fantasy and romance. But fantasy seems ineffective for facilitating social change, so we swing back toward **realism**. Each time, the pendulum swings wider, expanding the edges of both fantasized worlds and real human experience. In our ethical quest to expose real-world ills and give voice to psychological and social pressures and problems, we break taboos, pursue outrage, court extreme experience all in the pursuit of new stories to tell.

Extending your study

Reading:

Brown, Joanne, "Interrogating the 'Real' in Young Adult Realism," *New Advocate* 12, no. 4 (1999): 345–57.

Cadden, Mike, "The Irony of Narration in the Young Adult Novel," *Children's Literature Association Quarterly* 25 (2000): 146–54.

Hughes, Felicity, "Children's Literature: Theory and Practice," *ELH* 45, no. 3 (1978): 542–61.

Rochman, Hazel. "And Yet . . . Beyond Political Correctness." In Betsy Hearne and Roger Sutton (eds.), *Evaluating Children's Books: A Critical Look: Aesthetic, Social, and Political Aspects of Analyzing and Using Children's Books*, 133–48 (Urbana-Champaign: University of Illinois, 1993).

These articles take up a critical stance toward accepting realistic children's and young adult literature as truly reflective of experience.

Cart, Michael. *Young Adult Literature: From Romance to Realism* (2010).

A historical survey of YA literature and teen reading habits and preferences from the 1960s to the early twenty-first century.

Writing:

1   Choose a topic that has been treated in both a nonfiction text and a realistic fiction one. For instance, you might pair Jim Murphy's *An American Plague* (2003) with Laurie Halse Anderson's *Fever 1793* (2000), or *Imprisoned: The Betrayal of Japanese Americans during World War II* (Sandler 2013) with *When the Emperor Was Divine* (Otsuka 2003). Write an essay in which you compare and contrast some elements of the texts—for instance, you might compare writing style, knowledge gained, or thematic emphasis.

2   Compare and contrast a particular theme, such as the death of a parent, as it is treated in a realistic text versus a fantasy.

3   Research and analyze the authenticity of a historical fiction text such as Rosemary Sutcliff's *Blood and Sand* (1987).

4   After reading the blog post found at the following address, write your own response to the topic of gender in realistic fiction. You may choose to write from your own experience, do additional research to verify the author's claims, or write an opinion piece where you speculate as to why there is a problem. http://www.fromthemixedupfiles.com/2013/01/realistic-girls-fantastic-boys-middle-grade-fantasy-realistic-fiction-great-gender-divide/

5   Revisit a realistic novel that you recall from your own middle-grade years. Write a personal narrative where you reflect on how that novel influenced your perceptions of yourself or the people and places the novel depicted.

Discussing:

1   What are the advantages and disadvantages of contemporary realistic fiction for kids who spend a lot of their time interacting with screens?

2   How do blurred genres, such as time-travel as a way to enter a realistic historical event, affect the sense of realism in a text?

3   In the second decade of the twenty-first century, the pendulum swung back from the fantasies and romances of the first decade. What factors do you think influenced that swing?

4   Consider a persistent contemporary problem, such as racial and ethnic discrimination or lack of representation of certain people groups. Discuss what happens when this problem or people group is only presented through historical narratives.

5   Generate a list of stereotypes that are prevalent in YA fiction under such headings as: white girl problems, boys and sex, black male problems, mothers, fathers, boys and violence, and black girl dreams. Reflect on how easy or hard it was to generate your lists, any disagreements that arose, and any headings that you think need to be added. Discuss how these stereotypes affect how you see yourself and your peers.

Responding:

1   Working in groups, enact a scene from a realistic novel. Stay as close to the written text as possible in terms of following spatial cues and exactly replicating dialogue. Critique how "realistic" the passage feels.

2 Create a map from the descriptions given of the setting in a realistic novel, or, if the setting is a real city, trace a character's route through a map of that city. Discuss the problems you run into with trying to transfer realistic description to a spatial medium.

3 Research and create a visual timeline of the world depicted in Elizabeth Dulemba's *A Bird on Water Street*.

Online exploration:

1 A brief interview with Jacqueline Woodson where she discusses her process and purposes of writing tough realistic fiction and how she imagines her texts reaching kids.
https://www.teachingchannel.org/videos/realistic-fiction

2 A commercial site, but it features authors answering the question "what makes your book real?" Their answers are surprising enough to spark conversation.
http://www.fiercereads.com/realityreads/

3 A site that features over 100 award-winning realistic books for middle graders and YAs.
http://www.booknixie.com/best/childrens/realistic-fiction/books

Case Study: Creating an Annotated Bibliography

This case study showcases how one might assemble an annotated bibliography of fiction, nonfiction, and web resources organized around a particular contemporary issue for a particular age range. For my example, I chose transgender for middle grade to YA.

Fiction:

I am J, by Chris Beam: A transgender boy beginning to transition while in high school.

George, by Alex Gino: Middle-grader Melissa, known to the world as George, seeks to find a way to get her parents and classmates to see her true identity.

Almost Perfect, by Brian Katcher: A small-town boy falls in love with a girl named Sage. After they kiss, she reveals that she was born male.

Parrotfish, by Ellen Wittlinger: Grady is transgender. When he comes out in high school, he experiences rejection, but manages to find support and community with a few classmates.

(Continued)

Becoming Alec, by Darwin S. Ward: Alex grows up believing she is a lesbian, but when she is thrown out of her house she realizes that she is really a straight man.

Luna, by Julie Anne Peters: Focalized through Regan, the sister of a transgender boy named Liam, this book explores the feelings of a young woman who is not sure she is ready for her brother to transition.

Freakboy, by Kristin Elizabeth Clark: A novel-in-verse featuring three voices—Brendan, a gender-fluid boy, Vanessa, his girlfriend, and Angel, who is a transgender without having had a gender reassignment surgery.

Beautiful Music for Ugly Children, by Kristin Cronin-Mills: Gabe is slowly and cautiously starting his transition from being Elizabeth, hoping to get through graduation so he can start his new life. The book suffers from a few clichés and a rushed resolution, but it is still a tender exploration of community.

Alex as Well, by Alyssa Brugman: Alex is intersex, a fact that her parents chose to hide from her and which makes negotiating high school a challenge. Her parents are pretty awful, as her father leaves home and her mother blogs about her experiences in between trying to control her daughter.

Jumpstart the World, by Catherine Ryan Hyde: Sixteen-year-old Ellie falls in love with an older man in her building until she finds out he is a trans man. While the book is somewhat maudlin, Frank's gentle forgiveness of her reaction and her evolution of compassion are sensitively rendered.

Nonfiction:

Transgender Explained, for Those Who are Not, by Joanne Herman: Accessibly written by a transgender woman for family members and allies.

Beyond Magenta: Transgender Teens Speak Out, by Susan Kuklin; Six transgender teens describe their experiences in their own words with little intervention from the editor. What she does provide, however, are beautiful photographs that inspire empathy and an interview with a doctor who has worked with several of the interviewees.

Some Assembly Required: The Not-So-Secret Life of a Transgender Teen, by Arin Andrews: A witty memoir of a FtM transgender teenager undergoing reassignment in high school.

Websites:

http://www.transyouthequality.org/: Trans Youth Equality Foundation, a nonprofit organization that advocates for transgender, gender nonconforming, and intersex youth aged —two to eighteen.

(*Continued*)

http://www.imatyfa.org/resources/youth-resources/: TransYouth Family Allies was founded in 2006 to help children and families find supportive environments.

http://www.mermaidsuk.org.uk/ : Mermaids is a registered charity in the UK dedicated to the support for young people with gender identity issues and their families.

https://community.pflag.org/transgender : PFLAG has been a resource for over twenty years for people who are gender expansive.

Author talkback: Elizabeth O. Dulemba

In this talkback, Elizabeth O. Dulemba describes the process she went through in writing *A Bird on Water Street*, from getting her idea to doing the research to writing the novel. She has written or illustrated over two dozen books for children, including her historical fiction debut *A Bird on Water Street*, winner of twelve literary awards. She received a BFA from the University of Georgia, served as Illustrator Coordinator for the southern region of the Society of Children's Book Writers and Illustrators, and served as a Board Member for the Georgia Center for the Book. She holds an MFA in Illustration from the University of Edinburgh in Scotland. During the summers, she hops across the pond to teach Picturebook Design in the MFA in Writing and Illustrating Children's Books program at Hollins University in Roanoke, Virginia. She enjoys traveling and seeing new sights with her husband, Stan. Visit Elizabeth online at www.dulemba.com.

Creating *A Bird on Water Street*

By
Elizabeth O. Dulemba

It seems that I can't stay out of the southern Appalachian Mountains. As a kid, I visited my grandparents in the Virginia Mountains, breathing in the boxwoods. I went to camp in the mountains of Alabama, thick with mountain laurel. I taught "Creating Picture Books" at the John C. Campbell Folk School in North Carolina surrounded by mountain culture. And I currently teach in the MFA in Writing and Illustrating Children's Books at Hollins University again in Virginia, the heart of Appalachia. So it was really no surprise when my husband and I moved to a log cabin in the north Georgia Mountains. It was a life-long dream.

We ended up near Copperhill, Tennessee, known as McCaysville, Georgia on the southern side of the state line, which happens to run through the IGA grocery store parking lot. Our cabin was tucked into the Copper Basin surrounded by blue mountains. It was a lush, verdant place with a deep creek, tall trees, and a long view of a cow pasture. But it hadn't always been so. As with many dreams, reality proved to be complicated.

Landing where we did, there was no avoiding the topic of the copper mine for which the town was named. The mine's impact on the people and the landscape over the decades before we arrived was everywhere. We heard about the widespread denuding of the land caused by a hundred years of open copper ore roasting and the resulting sulfuric dioxide fumes, which poured back down as acid rain in the Basin. The smelters were enclosed in the early 1900s, but there were still leaks and the environmental damage continued long into the 20th century. I'd actually seen it. I used to pass the site on camping trips. We called it the "rape of the land." Miners sat in lawn chairs outside the mine holding up strike signs and we honked to show our support. They fought for more than their jobs, they fought for their homes and their lifestyle in the one-industry town.

It was a powerful story, but it didn't grab me completely until we moved to the area and were invited to attend a town meeting. We thought it would be a good chance to make friends, so we went. A potential scenic railway was being discussed for a train to travel north from Copperhill around a rare and interesting corkscrew track over a tall mountain. It was to be funded by one shipment of sulfuric acid per week—which would require the mine being reopened.

One might think the miners would be thrilled by the prospect, but they weren't. Men stood up like bent and gnarled trees in their flannel and denim, sharing heart-breaking stories of loss from the cancers they believed to be caused by the mines. The miners made thinly veiled threats that the tracks would be sabotaged if plans moved forward. I sat in shock, wondering what I had stumbled onto.

A Bird on Water Street chose me to write it that night, but with it came tremendous responsibility. I hadn't grown up in the Copper Basin. I didn't have any miners in my family. How could I dare to tell these people's story? And yet, it needed to be told, because similar horrors of man-made environmental devastation were still happening all across America. The townspeople and the environment needed a voice, and that voice turned out to be mine.

I stepped into the research lightly at first. Telling the story accurately and with true understanding would be no easy task. There was so much to study—the copper mines began in 1843 and ran almost continuously until 1986. It's a long swath of time. The history of the copper mining region is a proud one, but a tough one to digest. I had to submerse myself in the scientific studies and politics of the time—an uncomfortable and often depressing place to exist.

I heard a story about an entire crew of miners who all died around the same time from identical cancers, only to be told that it wasn't related to the mine. Some miners lived their entire lives in debt to the company store. And of course, the destruction of the land was simply shocking. There were no trees, no bugs, no birds for 50 square miles. I couldn't imagine growing up like that.

I decided the only way to share the story would be through the eyes of the people who lived it, which meant I needed to conduct interviews—tons of interviews with locals, former miners, and experts about what it was like to grow up in the moon-like landscape. I'd never done anything like that before, but I quickly picked up some tricks.

At first, when I told folks what I was doing, they were reticent. Who was this nosey stranger? But then I met a few key people, mainly Doris Abernathy and Grace Postelle—eighty-year-old sisters who had lived in the area from the beginning. They told me to drop their names when approaching people I needed to talk to, and it made all the difference.

I'd invite folks to lunch, or sit with them on their porch swings. I took notes on a small pad and scribbled as they spoke. I asked them about the smells of things, since our olfactory senses hold our strongest memories and can work as triggers. I asked how things sounded, tasted, and felt. What was the light like? What was their favorite food? How was the air? In a town polluted by sulfuric dioxide, that was a profound question—the polluted air often smelled like rotten eggs and the acid rain would sting if you got caught in it.

The biggest trick I learned was to keep my pen handy as our interview time headed towards its close. Something about running out of time would trigger a wave of memories to rush in at the last minute. I watched their eyes. When their gaze drifted up and away, I knew my subjects weren't with me anymore, but were instead, back in time reliving their pasts. I gathered so many stories that covered lifetimes of experiences. Surprisingly, I often encountered differing viewpoints from those who hated the environmental destruction to those who loved their Red Hills. They had no snakes, no poison ivy, no allergies, and they were proud of the stark but stunning vistas.

As for me, I was overwhelmed. I had to make the piles of information I'd gathered into a digestible and entertaining story. I chose to write the book as historical fiction so that I could compress the decade it actually took for the mine to close into a year, and tell the story through the eyes of an innocent, 13-year-old Jack Hicks, to make the story accessible to young readers and remind older readers of that time of awakening to our complicated world. I also needed to relay the environmental implications without beating anybody over the head with the subject.

The result was *A Bird on Water Street*—a coming of age story about Jack, the son of a miner growing up in a Southern Appalachian town environmentally devastated by a century of poor copper-mining practices. After a tragic accident and a massive company layoff, the miners go on strike. When nature begins to flourish as a result, Jack fights to protect it, but the cost could be the ruin of everything he loves.

The Director of the Ducktown Basin Museum, Ken Rush, was a tremendous help to me during my studies. He said my fiction had been better researched than many of the non-fiction projects that he'd been a part of. A former Copperhill Mayor attended every book launch event from Benton, Tennessee to Blue Ridge, Georgia and made it clear how proud he was of the book. At every event, locals who had lived the history came out, told even more of their stories, and thanked me for sharing their history with the world.

I couldn't have been more gratified, for truly, the book is a tribute to the community and its history, which had both bad and good aspects to it. It's won twelve literary awards including a Green Earth Book Award honor, and for me, Georgia Author of the Year. But the true reward will be the impact the story has on future generations in helping them to become better stewards of our precious earth. That will be a legacy that all the folks I interviewed can be proud of.

Literature references

Alexie, S. (2007), *The Absolutely True Diary of a Part-Time Indian*, New York: Little, Brown and Company.

Anderson, L. H. (2000), *Fever 1793*, New York: Simon & Schuster.

Anderson, M. T. (1997), *Thirsty*, Cambridge, MA: Candlewick.

Bontemps, A. and Hughes, L. (1932), *Popo and Fifina: Children of Haiti*, New York: Macmillan.

Burgess, M. (2003), *Doing It*, London: Penguin.

Burnett, F. H. (1911), *The Secret Garden*, New York: Frederick A. Stokes.

Cormier, R. (1974), *The Chocolate War*, New York: Pantheon.

Cross, G. (2010), *Where I Belong*, Oxford: Oxford UP.

Day, T. (1783–89), *The History of Sandford and Merton*, London: J. Stockdale.

Dulemba, E. O. (2014), *A Bird on Water Street*, San Francisco: Little Pickle Press.

Easton, T. S. (2015), *Boys Don't Knit*, New York: Macmillan.

Edgeworth, M. (1796), "The Purple Jar" in *The Parent's Assistant*, London: J. Johnson.

Ellis, D. (2000), *The Breadwinner*, Toronto: Groundwood Books.

Fielding, S. (1749), *The Governess; or, The Little Female Academy*, London, England: A. Millar.

Fitzhugh, L. (1964), *Harriet the Spy*, New York: Harper & Row.

Fleet, T. (1736), *The Prodigal Daughter*, Boston, MA: Heart and Crown.

Forbes, E. (1943), *Johnny Tremain*, New York: Houghton Mifflin.

Freeman, D. (1978), *Corduroy*, New York: Viking.

Garnett, E. (1937), *The Family from One End Street*, London: Frederick Muller.

Hidier, T. D. (2014), *Bombay Blues*, New York: Push.

Hinton, S. E. (1967), *The Outsiders*, New York: Viking.

Hughes, T. (1857), *Tom Brown's School Days*, London: Macmillan.

Levithan, D. (2003), *Boy Meets Boy*, New York: Random House.

Lindstrom, E. (2016), *Not if I See You First*, New York: Little, Brown and Company.

Medina, M. (2013), *Yaqui Delgado Wants to Kick Your Ass*, Somerville, MA: Candlewick.

Mitchell, L. S. (1921), *Here and Now Storybook*, New York: E. P. Dutton.

Montgomery, L. M. (1908), *Anne of Green Gables*, Boston: L. C. Page.

Moskowitz, H. (2015), *Not Otherwise Specified*, New York: Simon Pulse.

Murphy, J. (2003), *An American Plague*, New York: Clarion.

Myers, W. D. (1999), *Monster*, New York: HarperCollins.

Neufeld, J. (1970), *Lisa Bright and Dark*, New York: Penguin.

Otsuka, J. (2003), *When the Emperor was Divine*, New York: Alfred A. Knopf.

Porter, E. (1913), *Pollyanna*, Boston: L. C. Page.

Quintero, I. (2014), *Gabi, A Girl in Pieces*, El Paso, TX: Cinco Puntos Press.

Richardson, P. (1740), *Pamela: or Virtue Rewarded*, London: C. Rivington.

Rosen, M. (2005), *Michael Rosen's Sad Book*, Somerville, MA: Candlewick.

Rousseau, J-J. (1762), *Emile ou de l'éducation*, Paris, France: Duchesne.

Saenz, B. A. (2012), *Aristotle and Dante Discover the Secrets of the Universe*, New York: Simon & Schuster.

Sandler, M. W. (2013), *Imprisoned: The Betrayal of Japanese Americans During World War II*, New York: Walker.

Shakespeare, W. (1988), *A Midsummer Night's Dream*, New York: Bantam.

Sherwood, M. M. (1818, 1842, 1848), *The History of the Fairchild Family*, London: Sherwood.

Shusterman, N. (2015), *Challenger Deep*, New York: HarperTeen.

Sinclair, C. (1839), *Holiday House*, New York: Robert Cater.

Strasser, T. (2009), *If I Grow Up*, New York: Simon & Schuster.

Sutcliff, R. (1987), *Blood and Sand*, London: Hodder and Stoughton.

Tan, S. (2000), *The Red Tree*, Melbourne: Lothian Books.

Tharp, T. (2008), *The Spectacular Now*, New York: Random House.

White, E. B. (1952), *Charlotte's Web*, New York: Harper and Row.

Wiggin, K. D. (1903), *Rebecca of Sunnybrook Farm*, New York: Houghton Mifflin.

11

Are We Posthuman Yet?: Fantasy and Speculative Fiction

Suggested texts to read alongside this chapter

Harry Potter and the Philosopher's Stone, by J. K. Rowling.

The Sword in the Stone (Book 1 of *The Once and Future King*), by T. H. White.

Feed, by M. T. Anderson.

Shadowshaper, by Daniel José Older.

Defining fantasy

One would think that **fantasy** literature would be easy to define—there's a separate section for it in most bookstores, after all. But when it comes to producing a precise, coherent, inclusive definition of **fantasy** as a literary **genre**, we are faced with several sticky problems. First, we might say that all fiction is in some way fantasy, since fiction consists of stories that have never really happened, and, as we have noted with mysteries, **romances**, and other kinds of **fake realism**, many of those stories are highly improbable. Second, as with poetry, there are so many varieties of **fantasy** that it is difficult to capture all of the possibilities in a single definition. In addition, however, since avid **fantasy** readers and taxonomers are highly protective of the distinctions they draw between types of **fantasy** texts, it's even risky to revert to what people usually do with poetry—that is, to skip defining and stick to sorting. Not everyone agrees on what the subcategories should be or what types of texts should be in them, or even whether some **genres** should be included under the umbrella of fantasy at all. Science fiction, for instance, is one of those contested **genres**, as are books that propose alternate histories in this world, or are set in worlds that are not this one but don't have any magic or nonhuman characters. A third problem is that fantasy, **realism**, and even nonfiction blur in literature for younger children. There's nothing really fantastic about a young girl being a fussy eater or creatively delaying her bedtime, unless that young girl happens to be a badger who talks and walks on her hind legs. Is having anthropomorphic animal characters enough to make a book a **fantasy**, or is the animal character merely a visual metaphor emphasizing a particular quality of a human, as is the case in *El Deafo* (Bell 2014) or Art Spiegelman's *Maus* (1980–91)? Finally, a more pressing problem in a pluralistic society is that defining a work that contains supernatural elements as **fantasy** can be disrespectful of a culture's living belief system; disbelief in a responsive supernatural realm may be characteristic of secular-scientific cultures, but that is only one way of perceiving reality, and even folks reared in such a culture may accept that both physics and a living God active in human affairs are absolutely real.

Despite these difficulties, we should probably start somewhere. The major theorists of **fantasy** have all come up with complicated definitions that use phrases like "an absolute freedom from belatedness" (Bloom 1982: 206) or works that cause readers "to hesitate between a natural and a supernatural explanation" (Todorov 1973: 33), which leave me scratching my head not only as to whether I agree with their meaning, but also whether it has relevance to children's and YA fantasy. I prefer instead to start by following Edward James and Farah Mendlesohn (2012) in adopting Brian Attebery's (1992) definition, who based his on one from W. R. Irwin (1976) (and from there, really, it's just turtles all the way down . . .), of "fantasy as a group of texts that share, to a greater degree or other, a cluster of common tropes which may be objects but which may also be narrative techniques" (James and Mendlesohn 2012: 1). This reminds us that, like **realism**, **fantasy** is a literary **genre**, that is, we know it when we read it because we recognize the common **tropes**—dragons, wizards, heroes, etc.—and the narrative techniques—elevated diction, names with too many consonants, lots of capital letters, maps—as belonging to **fantasy**. But that definition is rather too inclusively vague as is, so I will add to that definition Kathryn Hume's (1984: 21) point that among these common **tropes** must be ones that depict a "departure from consensus reality." The use of the word "consensus" reminds us that reality is a contingent formation, constructed through widespread agreement in a certain place and time.

Within those broad parameters, then, we can move on to sorting. Mendlesohn (2008) offers a set of useful bins for **fantasy**: the portal quest, wherein characters enter a new world; the immersive **fantasy**, in which the action is in an alternate world from the start; the intrusion, wherein fantastic elements break into the primary world of the story; and the liminal, where the unusual things that happen may or may not be the result of magic. She concludes with a category she calls "the irregulars," gamely "subverting" her own taxonomy by admitting that there are some texts that simply don't fit any of the four other categories. Her categories offer an advantage over the more traditional distinction between "high **fantasy**," which is typically set in a secondary world and features characters of elevated stature who speak with similarly elevated and/or antiquated diction, and "low **fantasy**," where the setting is this world, the characters are more like ordinary people, and the supernatural or magic elements are met with some degree of surprise because they are not part of normal, everyday experience. Mendlesohn's distinctions are more useful since the characters in any of her categories may be exalted or ordinary, human or nonhuman. In addition, the words "high" and "low" inadvertently imply measures of quality that are unfortunate; there are good and bad books in each category. Other taxonomers sort children's and teen **fantasies** into animal **fantasies**, toy and doll **fantasies**, time-travel **fantasies**, horror and suspense, **magical realism**, fairy tale adaptations, alternate world fantasies, sword and sorcery, paranormal romances, antihero **fantasies**, religious **fantasies**, ghost stories, utopias, and dystopias, although contemporary dystopias tend to merge into science fiction. Science fiction has its own subgenres and categories, including steampunk, alien invasions, apocalyptic and postapocalyptic stories, climate disaster (also known as cli-fi), space opera, and mad scientist tales. Monster stories can lean more toward **fantasy** or science fiction depending on the origin of the monster. Falling into the cracks would be superhero comics and movies, novelizations and adaptations of traditional mythologies, and science fiction parodies. Did I leave out your favorite? Some people lump the whole genre under the inclusive term speculative fiction (and some people argue strenuously for their distinct differences—do you get it?—there is no one definition or method of carving up the **genre** of **fantasy** literature that pleases everyone, but you can have a lot of geeky fun arguing for your preferred method). Each of these subgenres has a specific appeal and often attracts an intensely loyal readership who understand its conventions so deeply that it becomes an important identity marker for them. In fact, fans sometimes inhabit their favorite fantasy worlds with as much knowledge and ownership as the authors themselves; as fantasy author Ellen Kushner quipped to me one night over dinner when discussing the research for her next novel set in a world she invented, "Oh well, if I get something wrong I'll hear about it from the fans."

A dearth of diversity in fantasy literature

One of the things that fans have be clamoring for, and with very good reason, is the need for fantasy literature with more diverse characters (see, for instance, Obeso 2014). When writers, literary critics, and publishing and library professionals drill down into the dismal numbers of diverse writers and protagonists of youth literature, an even more depressing phenomenon is revealed. The vast majority of books written by and about characters of color and indigenous people are historical, realistic texts wherein race and ethnicity constitute the central conflicts of characters who are living in a culture where their identities are not valued. While this storied grasp of history is certainly important, it presents a problem for many if not most child readers who, as I will argue in this chapter, have very good reasons for engaging in fantasies that enable them to think toward a future and beyond the conditions of their embodiment and present social environments. As Daniel José Older notes in his talkback for this chapter,

> Representation is a matter of life and death for some communities, especially when it comes to young people. The publishing industry, which is currently about 90% white, has focused inordinately on white protagonists, white communities, white stories, particularly when it comes to fantasy fiction. The white savior, the quick-to-die sidekick of color, and helpless damsel in distress are all clichés. Besides being failures on a human level, they signify lazy, shallow writing.

From the point of view of the literary critic or teacher, we have to make sure that our readings of fantasy texts don't engage in equally lazy, shallow critiques that ignore thinly veiled **tropes** that suggest superiority or inferiority based solely on race or gender affiliations or implied through absences. As we have discussed in Chapter 5, Debbie Olsen (2011) notes the absence of black children in science fiction film; if our stories are projecting a white-only future for life on earth or other worlds, or worse, if these stories portray any characters who are not white as literally alien in their embodiment, what ideological messages does that send about our cultural mythologies?

The need for diversity in fantasy literature goes beyond representations of race, ethnicity, and gender into challenging forms of neurodiversity toward a goal of establishing what Ralph James Savarese (2013: 193) calls a "neurocosmopolitan" ethics: "the feeling of being at home with all manner of neurologies." One of the implicit expectations of fantasy literature is that it primes us for futures that may look very different from the past, and that we need to be mentally prepared for. As our understanding of neurological differences such as those found in people with autism and either temporary or chronic mental conditions develops, our social environments become more aware and inclusive of individuals who think outside of normal ranges. While realistic fiction more often follows a narrative path where these differences constitute a problem that must be solved or accommodated by both the **protagonist** and other people, **fantasy** is better able to imagine possible scenarios where such thinking is necessary, valued, and even heroic. We can already see inklings of neurocosmopolitanism in Richard Adams's *Watership Down* (1972), Dia Reeves's *Bleeding Violet* (2010), Sean Beaudoin's *The Infects* (2012), and Pete Hautman's Klaatu Diskos series (2012–14).

Approaches to criticism

This deep affective and cognitive investment in literature that departs from consensus reality demands investigation: What is it about **fantasy** literature that constitutes its appeal, especially for young readers? Why are some of its **tropes** and **motifs** so resonant and lasting over time? Why do some readers absolutely hate it? How does **fantasy** literature work? What messages do these texts convey to readers at the time in their lives when they are (arguably) most open to **ideological** manipulation? What did early **fantasy** novels look like, and how has the **genre** changed over time?

Structuralism, rhetorical criticism, and narratology

As with all of the **forms** and **genres** we have discussed so far, there are multiple perspectives from which to view these questions. In Chapters 6 and 8, we have focused heavily on story grammars and structural patterns; this method is often taken up by critics to talk about **fantasy** narratives, since quest narratives with initially reluctant but ultimately heroic figures abound in **fantasy** literature. Barbara Ripp Safford (1983), for instance, draws heavily from Northrop Frye to examine five aspects of "high" **fantasy** novels: the plot pattern, the character of the hero, dialectic symbolism (i.e., symbols and images that align with either good or evil, innocence, or experience), cyclic symbolism (imagery that corresponds to cycles in the natural world, the progression of a single human life, and the broader cycles of history), and the resolution of the quest and the plot. Her graphic organizers consist of charts and subdivided circles that can be filled in with plot points to highlight how each aspect is realized in a fantasy novel. Once such an analysis is completed with a set of novels, a reader will not only gain **genre** knowledge, but also might more readily see how certain character types, settings, and situations take on metaphoric significance through repetition, and speculate how that might affect real-world expectations with regard to gender, place, and ethnicity. On the lighter side, Diana Wynne Jones reinforces while poking gentle fun at the **tropes** of literary **fantasy** in *The Tough Guide to Fantasyland* (2006).

The **structuralist** focus on patterns and similarities reveals two paradoxical things about **fantasy** texts: first, that their success as stories must in some way be dependent on their adherence to certain patterns of readers' expectation, and second, they need to do something interesting or original within that pattern to maintain readers' interest. From here, then, the rhetoricians and narratologists take over from the story grammar folk, asking how both of those things can be accomplished at once. How does a fantasy writer make his or her reader believe in the world of the book, particularly when it departs, as it must, from consensus reality? As Daniel José Older points out in the talkback to this chapter, worldbuilding that is both convincing and inventive is one of the most important narrative techniques of **fantasy**. To successfully negotiate between the familiar and the strange, Tolkien (1965: 55) argues that the world of a **fantasy** novel has to be "founded upon the hard recognition that things are so in the world as it appears under the sun [in the author's sociohistorical moment, that is]; on a recognition of fact but not a slavery to it."

Why is this hard recognition of reality necessary in a novel whose defining characteristic is that it departs from it? Because readers bring their existing **mental models** with them to a text, the challenge of the **fantasy** author is to craft a world that has enough points of contact with those **mental models** to anchor the reader even as he or she goes on to surprise, shift, and expand those **mental models** with new variations that depart from consensus reality. My students often talk about **fantasy** texts as spaces where young readers allow their imaginations to "run wild." But I have to push back on that—our imaginations don't really ever run wild; instead they run in tracks set down by two powerful forces: the senses and language. Imagination and fantasy play in the in-between and just-beyond spaces that these forces allow. Consider, for instance; humans can't imagine a wholly new color, but we can imagine any color that exists anywhere on the spectrum that light permits the human eye to perceive; that's a hard recognition of fact. From there, though, you can imagine a bunny or an elephant or a jackalope in any of those colors. Similarly, when creating unreal creatures or nonsense words, it's very difficult to come up with something that doesn't consist of recognizable body parts, or couldn't be a pronounceable word in any of the languages that you know (although Shaun Tan does just that in *The Arrival* (2006), so we might call that an exception that proves the rule). However, you can recombine phonemes, graphemes, and bits of existing things into imaginary words and images that are beyond your perceptual experience.

Fantasies, therefore, take their details from consensus reality, but they put them in front of a funhouse mirror. Catherine Butler (2012: 233) suggests five ways in which J. K. Rowling transforms aspects of existing reality to create a world that is "at once excitingly different from our own and reassuringly similar to it." Butler takes her examples directly from Rowling, but the methods she isolates can be usefully applied to most fantasy texts. They are: *Realization*, wherein objects from our imagination, such as centaurs, mermaids, vampires, enchanted glasses, and rings of power are made real; *Substitution*, where something that has a functional equivalent in our world takes on a different aspect in the fantasy space, such as Quidditch as a sport or Dumbledore's Army as an after-school activity; *Exaggeration*, which is a common feature in dystopias where it entails a real-world situation, such as climate change or expanding government authority, that grows beyond its present proportions, or, in other types of **fantasy** and science fiction, when a skill or physical attribute, such as intelligence or physical strength, is taken to a hyperbolic extreme; *Animation*, which means granting speech and/or movement to inanimate objects, such as talking mirrors or trees, and dancing dinnerware; and *Antiquation*, which often has to do with setting, diction, costume, political organization, and modes of transportation, communication, and commerce (234). Animation and antiquation seem to be two places where **fantasy** and science fiction most often part company, especially if we move sentient robots and other forms of artificial intelligence from the category of animation to the category of realization. In fact, although Butler's description of things in this category is limited to objects from myth and folklore, we might argue that realization is in fact a moving target for science fiction, as things we once thought imaginary—space tourism, for instance—are on the horizon. I will explore these ideas further as I apply them to *Feed* (Anderson 2002) in the case study for this chapter.

Perhaps the most interesting thing about worldbuilding in fantasy novels is the need for consistency and **verisimilitude** within that world. A secondary world may transform details and elements taken from consensus reality in whatever way the author chooses, but the structuring principle of cause and effect must be maintained. What I mean is that the world of the book must have its own rules, and an author cannot change them willy-nilly, although he or she can create a series of events that logically lead to a change. This is especially important in a series: if resurrection from the dead is not possible in book one, it cannot happen in book three (or seven) unless there has been some convincing development in the plot that enables it. Otherwise, you break the contract established between a writer and a reader. As Donnarae MacCann (1969: 134) points out, **fantasy** "makes a special demand upon the reader," quoting E. M. Forster (1954: 159): "other novelists say 'Here is something that might occur in your lives,' the fantasist says 'Here's something that could not occur. I must ask you to accept my book as a whole, and secondly to accept certain things in my book.'" MacCann argues that such layered acceptance is simpler for children than adults simply because their imaginations are more flexible, but that blanket assertion is not empirically true; rather, the author bears much of the responsibility for creating a world that earns acceptance from the reader through establishing and following its own rules. It helps a world, then, to have a history and a mythology so that the author has something on which to base the rules. Those histories and mythologies can be as elaborate and deep as, say, Ursula Le Guin's, Terry Pratchett's, Philip Pullman's, J. K. Rowling's, or J. R. R. Tolkien's worlds, or they can be as quickly canvassed as the history of *Zootopia* or *Zootropolis* (2016), but the more broadly and deeply familiar an author is with the world she or he creates, the more the reader will buy into it as well.

Acknowledging the dialectic between consensus reality and the estranging circumstances of a **fantasy** novel, Mendlesohn (2008) turns our attention to how readers are invited into these texts. Are we plunged into a secondary world from the start, or do we, like Lucy, Edmund, Susan, and Peter (Lewis 1950), like Harry Potter (Rowling 1997), like Meggie (Funke 2005), have to find a way in? Portals matter, but so does tone, so Mendlesohn focuses on both language use and methods of invitation and persuasion that an author uses to convince a reader that an alternate world is real, or that intrusive magic is possible. M. T. Anderson's *Thirsty* (1997: 9), for instance, begins by literally drawing vampires from the air into the mundane world:

> In the spring, there are vampires in the wind. People see them scuffling along by the side of country roads. At night, they move through the empty forests. They do not wear black, of course, but things they have taken off bodies or bought on sale. The news says that they are mostly in the western part of the state, which is lonely and rural. My father claims we have them this year because it is a mild winter, but he may be thinking of tent caterpillars.

There's a lot of explanation going on here, which can spell death to engaging world-building, but Anderson employs multiple rhetorical tricks. His first sentence is startling in its difference from what a reader might think arrives on the wind in spring. Fresh air? Allergens? Nannies? At any rate, few readers would be expecting vampires in that sentence. However, the next sentence changes the level of veracity; now it's not just the narrator who notices the vampire, but *people* see them. Then the narrator comes back and shifts the level of mystical presence by telling us that *of course*— thus ordinary after all—vampires wear clothes, stolen or discounted. Wait, what? Vampires *shop*? Before we can cast a skeptical eye on this narrator, we are alerted, once again, to the fact that people who are part of the story can see the vampires, and this time it's not just people, because people can be unreliable witnesses. This time it's the news, objective and trustworthy, and not even trying to scare their audience, but instead trying to comfort them. Finally, then, it's time to meet this narrator—he's not some omniscient outsider; he's a person with a father and perhaps a sense of humor or at least an unwillingness to believe what he's told.

So where does that leave us as readers? Remember the technique we have discussed in the film chapter about being flown into the story from the top right corner down into the story world? Recall, in addition, the discussion of the shot-reverse shot method of stitching us into the story? Both techniques are enacted here. In portal and intrusion **fantasies**, the mechanisms of suture are even more evident. By starting in an ordinary world, we learn what we need to know alongside and at the same time as the character who will be crossing the threshold or on the receiving end of a supernatural visitation. In both the film and the book of the first Harry Potter novel, there is no coy pretense that magic is ordinary; we experience the wonder of magic right alongside Harry, with whom we have traveled from the Muggle world to Hogwarts, and who is just as excited by the wondrous things that are happening to him and around him as we are. But in the immersive fantasy of *Thirsty*, well *of course* there is an uptick of cheap-clothes-wearing vampires; everybody knows that. As Mendlesohn (2008: xv and *passim*) argues, rhetoric and language, that is, the call and how it is issued, matter differently in different kinds of **fantasies**.

Psychoanalysis, cognitive poetics, and reader response

We've accepted the call to adventure and entered the portal to an unknown world, or we've been taken by surprise by a supernatural visitor, or we've learned to function in a world where we live side by side with creatures who are ontologically different from ourselves, but other questions for other types of literary and cultural critics remain: Why? What is it about fantasy that attracts some and repels others? Rhetorical analysis can lead us to a greater understanding of how we are taken in by texts, but they can't tell us why we opened the book in the first place. And of course there are many reasons, not least among them the playground capital that comes from having read the books and seen the films that everyone else is reading and seeing. But since my critical twig is bent in the direction of **psychoanalytic criticism**, my questions often turn to how a literary text or **genre** meets a psychological need. So for a contemporary **psychoanalytic** view of the appeal of fantasy for children and teens, let's begin with three premises drawn from **psychoanalysis, cognitive poetics,** and **reader response criticism**:

1   Freud and other **psychoanalytic** theorists argue that fantasy emerges through a process of displacement and condensation of repressed material; we transform our insistent bodily drives and threatening affects (emotions) into culturally acceptable forms that enable us to simultaneously exercise and exorcise those repressed thoughts and feelings.

2   Kieran Egan (n.d.) argues from the perspective of **cognitive poetics** that **fantasy** results from our attempts to mediate between the binary opposites that arise out of our earliest experiences to understand the physical world in relation to ourselves. That is, a child learns conceptual oppositions such as hot/cold, big/little, alive/dead, animate/inanimate, human/ animal, real/imaginary to categorize experiential perceptions in relation to his or her own body and other objects he or she encounters. Once these oppositions are acquired, the concepts can become nuanced in greater detail along a spectrum between them as our brains stretch, seeking novelty as part of their natural growth trajectory. Between hot and cold, we get warm or cool; between living and dead we get ghosts and vampires; between human and animal we get talking, clothed animals and hybrid creatures like mermaids, werewolves, and centaurs.

3   Neo-Freudian Jacques Lacan and other cultural, psychological, and literary theorists argue that our sense of self is performative; that is, we become who we are by adopting, innovating on, and repeating certain ways of presenting ourselves until they feel natural and inevitable. Language and other modes of expression and representation provide the culturally available forms that we use to construct our sense of self. This means that what we consider most

intimately ourselves is really our enactment of a culturally constructed fantasy. Our **reader responses** are part of a feedback loop that keys to those aspects of literary texts that represent privileged signifiers and/or associations we make from personal memories and the feelings that accompany them.

If we start from these three premises, certain things about children's and YA **fantasy** come into view. First, we could follow Egan to argue that children, in the course of finding out about themselves and their world, must use the tools available to them, the most important of which is language, to divide the world into acceptable and unacceptable behaviors and possible and impossible affordances (by which I mean abilities and limits that are imposed by the kind of material existence we and other objects have). **Fantasy** allows children to find the edges or limits by going past them, and also to experiment with the in-betweens of the opposite ends of binary spectrums. Humans can't live underwater, for instance, but they can imagine beings that can, and consider the advantages and perils of such a life through story. Children realize at some point that they are mortal, so they imagine what life would be like for themselves or others if they could live forever. What would the benefits be? And more importantly, what are the costs?

Second, if we combine Egan and Freud, we can see how mediating between the binaries of conceptual language is used as a means to displace and condense the internal and external pressures that threaten to overwhelm young readers. In other words, **fantasy** texts give children a displaced and condensed way to express pressing existential concerns for which they may not yet have words, or which would be too difficult to express in a straightforward way. One persistent **trope** in **fantasy** literature for young readers, for instance, is some version of the loss and refinding of home. As I have argued elsewhere (Coats 2007), this is no idle fear—at some point, most children will leave their present home and find a place of their own. It would be unrealistic, or perhaps too close to a painful reality, to set such a task for a child in a middle-grade realistic novel (although, I have to admit, it does happen quite frequently, especially in quasi-realistic **Robinsonades** as well as novels that focus on the deaths of parents). But by casting the entire process into a **fantasy** narrative where, despite difficulties, the protagonist achieves his or her goal, the psychic need for venture and reassurance is satisfied; the journey won't be easy, and in fact it might be quite fearsome, but you will find the strength, wit, and help you need when you need it.

Fantasy author Tamora Pierce (1993) takes up the mantle of **reader response** theorist when she makes a stirring argument for why teens read and respond to **fantasy**; her approach dovetails nicely with Egan's model of the idealistic, cause-oriented thinking he sees in the teen reader. Pierce argues that because teens "haven't spent years butting their heads up against brick walls" (50), their passion and their appetite for idealistic challenges hasn't been blunted, and thus they respond to **fantasy** as "a literature of *possibilities*" (50), and in particular the possibility to make a world in which the disenfranchised are empowered. Ordinary or even normally unsuccessful people become heroes, and magic serves as "the great equalizer between the powerful and the powerless" (51). Finally, she says, the draw of **fantasy** for some readers is to escape an unsatisfactory reality, especially one marked by the trauma of a dysfunctional family. If you examine the reasons when and why children find portals into other worlds, I think you will find one of these three, more often than not: to escape transient or existential boredom, as in *Alice in Wonderland* (Carroll 1965), *Peter Pan* (Barrie 1911), *The Lion, The Witch, and The Wardrobe* (Lewis 1950), *The Phantom Tollbooth* (Juster 1961), and *Coraline* (Gaiman 2002); to escape from an overwhelming trauma, as in *The Marbury Lens* (Smith 2010) and *The Graveyard Book* (Gaiman 2008); or to leave behind an unsatisfactory, limited life, as in *The Subtle Knife* (Pullman 1997), *Harry Potter and the Philosopher's Stone*(Rowling 1997), and *Percy Jackson and the Olympians* (Riordan 2005). And just as the characters slip through portals for these reasons, so readers fall into big fat **fantasy** books.

But perhaps a more prosaic reason for encouraging young people to read **fantasy** emerges from cognitive science. The simple fact is that fantasy is a necessary activity for human development, both individually and collectively. For individuals, imagining possibilities beyond everyday reality grows the developing brain like doing reps with weights grows muscles; putting stress on existing pathways forces them to adapt, causing new neural connections between different parts of the brain to be activated and thus stimulating brain growth. For the group, **fantasy** spurs collective problem-solving and develops the skill of prospective cognition—that is, the ability to think into the future and work together to embody as-yet-unrealized agendas.

History, philosophy, **ideology**

Even with all of these advantages, fantasy has always had, and still has, its detractors. Some people just don't like it. They may find the in-betweens of conceptual binaries off-putting, weird, and/or unnecessary to contemplate among the mundane details of daily life. Or they may be afraid of or jaded toward the call to idealism that fantasy issues; they don't see, or actively resist seeing, the deeper truths and possible futures that have been squeezed out of everyday existence. As Ursula Le Guin (1979: 44) argues:

> For fantasy is true, of course. It isn't factual, but it is true. Children know that. Adults know it too, and that is precisely why many of them are afraid of fantasy. They know that its truth challenges, even threatens, all that is false, all that is phony, unnecessary, and trivial in the life they have let themselves be forced into living. They are afraid of dragons because they are afraid of freedom.

For many, the question turns on ethics. If **realism** takes its ethical marching orders from a mandate to face life's intractable problems and social ills squarely and soberly, then what value can a trip to Neverland, a flight to the Mushroom Planet, or vicarious participation in an epic battle against inhuman forces possibly have? As I have hinted all along in this book, children's and YA literature bears a burden beyond entertainment; beyond its surface trappings, it is a method of seduction, if not outright indoctrination, into a culture's values by way of an author's individual vision. So what arguments can be made in favor of filling young reader's heads with the ridiculous ideas that animals can talk, that toys have longings, and that ordinary kids just like them may be under a geas that will ultimately lead to a great destiny?

Indeed, the rational educators and moralists eager to promote eighteenth-century European Enlightenment principles to the young, such as Barbauld, More, Edgeworth, Wollestonecraft, and Trimmer, were adamant that children be kept away from **fantasy** of all kinds, including the folktales that are the wellspring of much contemporary **fantasy**, as we have noted in Chapter 8. Objections ranged from the class-based distaste that they were considered "peasant crudities" to religious objections that they were "untrue, frivolous and of dubious morality" (Townsend 1987: 32). We hear echoes of these objections today: peasant being replaced with popular (uttered with a sneering lip), frivolous with escapist, and the moral question coming from both far left and far right fundamentalist positions. However, with the Romantics came a revaluing of imagination and a revival of interest in ancient forms, as well as a view of the child as one who "beholds the light, and whence it flows," (Wordsworth "Intimations" line 70), so that in the early 1800s, there were more or less two strands of children's literature. One was perhaps best represented by Peter Parley, the pseudonym adopted by American writer Samuel Griswold Goodrich, who produced cheerfully realistic tales and nonfiction with clearly deduced morals that inspired many imitations. The other strand was taken up by advocates of amusing, imaginary literature, such as Catherine Sinclair and Henry Cole, who produced his *Home Treasury* (1841–49) in explicit protest against Peter Parley's style of storytelling. Both sorts of stories were popular with children, but by the Victorian era, the shift in sensibility from children as irrational sinners in need of rational and moral education to heaven's own creatures in need of delightful entertainments was enough, most genre historians agree, to usher in a robust new genre for young readers, the modern **fantasy** novel (see, for instance, MacCann 1969; Carpenter 1985; Townsend 1987; Nikolajeva 2012).

I think we can dig a little deeper than that to get a more complex understanding not only of **fantasy** literature's emergence, but also of its dominant concerns in children's and YA literature. As Safford (1983) notes, modern fantasy literature takes its exigencies from older storytelling forms, such as folktales, myths, and epics, that are rooted in "the confused perception of divinity within the profane, and profane man grappling with his gods" (please excuse the universal masculine—people of every gender grapple with their place in a grander scheme of things). By either definitively separating the sacred from the profane or insisting on a privileged narrative as the only truth, Enlightenment rationalist and empiricist thinking attempted to repress imaginative theories of the interconnectedness of human and divine reality. As a result, storytelling suffered from what I flippantly call the Spanx™ effect. Spanx is a brand of elasticized undergarments that are intended to contain the "gush" of soft, seemingly unnecessary, and aesthetically embarrassing flesh to create a more ideal body shape. But that altered shape does not tell the whole truth: the gush still exists, so it has to go somewhere. The kind of imaginative pondering with respect to our place in the universe and our relationship to the divine is the excess and embarrassing mythic storytelling and superstition that reason tries to repress. However, repressing questions that can't be answered through the scientific method or logical reasoning doesn't make them go away. But do you see how a profane, perhaps even silly material metaphor can help us see a profound problem? Play it out, then: **fantasy** literature often functions as a secular, material metaphor for the kinds of spiritual and metaphysical questions that logic can't answer; it provides concrete embodiments, for instance, of the abstract notions of good and evil, and gives expression to the felt experience many people have of being answerable to something outside themselves. Indeed, perhaps the real fantasy of human existence is similar to the body contained in Spanx; that is, our perceptual universe, what we can see, smell, hear, taste, and touch, even with prosthetic devices like microscopes and telescopes, is in fact not all there is to being human. What children's and YA fantasy offers is an opportunity, then, as Victoria Nelson (2012) points out, perhaps *"even the only allowed one*, a predominantly secular-scientific culture such as ours has for imagining and encountering the sacred, albeit in unconscious ways" (xi, emphasis added).

That's where we are now, but how did we get here? In the seventeenth and eighteenth centuries, secular-scientific and Deist thinking was on the rise; Deists of the time accepted God as creator, but they believed that the creator had set natural forces in motion and no longer intervened in the affairs of earth, and that the nature of this creator could only be known through reason, not revelation. Thus the focus shifted to what could be known and achieved by humans using scientific means and measurements, rather than trying to puzzle out humanity's relation to its gods. As we have noted in the Chapter 10, Locke argued that people were nothing other than the sum of histories that could be orchestrated solely by human intervention. This separation between faith and destiny on the one hand and human knowledge and intervention on the other opened the door to rational unbelief as well as the rise of democracies based on human will rather than monarchies secured by divine right. In 1765, an anonymous French writer offered the term **humanism** to refer to this ideology that was more lateral than vertical so to speak, writing, "The general love of humanity . . . a virtue hitherto quite nameless among us, and which we will venture to call 'humanism', for the time has come to create a word for such a beautiful and necessary thing" (qtd. in Giustiniani 1985: 175). The consolidation of forces that resulted in the development of secular **humanism** marked, in some sense, the culmination of a long overthrow of the divine as the chief object of love, fear, attention, and reverence, with humanity installed in its place.

In many ways, then, modern **fantasy** for young readers is responding to the same conditions that gave rise to **realism**, as we have discussed in the Chapter 10. But it is a wholly different method of response, predicated on a different understanding of the nature of human reality and the limits of human agency. **Realism** confines itself to depicting history, the here and now, cause and effect, and/or psychological and social reality from a secular-scientific mindset, even when it attends to humanity's relation to gods; for instance, when a character in a realistic novel prays, the focus is on her interpretation of situations and signs as answers or nonanswers to her prayers. **Fantasy**, on the other hand, questions the adequacy of our present understanding within that **ideological** frame; in fantasies, the gods may speak directly through oracles, swords are pulled from stones or sorting hats, the dead return to life. In terms of the historical conditions that enabled the development of the kinds of **fantasy** that find their place in the modern novel for children and teens, we should consider that the sense of humanity's centrality and worth engendered by the development of secular **humanism** extended to an optimism that still resonates in some quarters today about the perfectibility of human systems of governance, a faith that collective rationalism will always carry the day, and a belief that science holds the answers to a sustainable future. On the other hand, however, Freud (1915/2001: 284–85) argues that humanity has suffered a series of three major blows to its "naïve self-love." The first came through the discovery that "our earth was not the center of the universe but only a tiny fragment of a cosmic system of scarcely imaginable vastness." The second blow came via Darwin (1859), who successfully promulgated the theory that humans were not the product of an exceptional creation, but more or less accidentally evolved from an animal nature that they were not completely separate or freed from. The third blow came from psychoanalysis itself, which decentered people from their own minds through its theory of the unconscious. In other words, the very sciences we believed would save us carry within them the seeds of our most profound doubt.

In addition, I would argue, market forces come into play, as speculative investments in sea voyages and other ventures changed the nature of how money was made and circulated. The idea of investing in an uncertain future payoff was nothing new; farmers have always done that. But the products of a harvest are real and tangible, so that money paid for them resulted in something you could eat or drink, or transform into cloth, so the whole business had an air of unquestioned materiality. In the early 1700s, however, unscrupulous businessmen were selling shares for imaginary and impossible ventures, such as recovering sunlight from vegetables, railroads in South America that were never intended to be built, and other projects so secret that shareholders paid their money on faith for nothing more than a piece of paper if not a simple handshake and a verbal promise. While such practices were made illegal through the Bubble Act that lasted through 1825, Anthony Trollope (1875) castigated this shift in thinking about the real value of a product as a devolution from gold to paper to words, depicting in his novel *The Way We Live Now* a realistic critique of the effects such economic tricks had on drawing room culture and the arts. For our purposes in thinking about the role this economic shift played in the development of the themes of **fantasy** in literature for young readers, we might speculate that it was a sign, like the growing fin de siècle interest in spiritualism, of a will to believe in unseen things even as it points to a suspicion that Lewis Carroll plays on repeatedly in his Alice books, that of the insecure relationship between words and the reality they purport to represent. Finally, then, I would argue that it joins Freud's other three crises of belief to provide the conditions under which modern fantasy for children and young adults emerged and found its feet in the late 1800s, and from which it continues to take its **ideological** mandates to this day.

Let's unpack that bold and broad assertion. I think our understanding of children's and YA fantasy is enhanced if we consider how it addresses four broad themes:

What are the limits of our universe (after Copernicus)?
What does it mean to be human (after Darwin)?
What is beyond or behind our rational minds (after Freud)?
What is the relationship between language and reality (after the stock market)?

While these questions are treated extensively in folk literature, the ways in which they are posed in modern **fantasy** are filtered through secular-scientific understandings (hence the afters). Taking the last question first, then, if the utterance of a specific word or name has the power to call forth a demon, for instance, or bind a sorcerer, or trigger a locator spell, then we are in some world other than this one; names in this world nowadays are no longer holy or demonic. As a result, language play, as in *The Phantom Tollbooth* (1961), and questions about language's power to affect perception, as in *Charlotte's Web* (1952), or whether a word actually has to mean anything, as in *Alice in Wonderland* (1865), become sites for exploration in fantasy. Considering the difference between the rational mind and its unconscious depths, dreams in fantasies are not usually considered supernatural oracular visions so much as they are the result of fevers or being hit on the head, and they reflect and transform material from waking life, so that farmhands can be transformed into scarecrows, tin men and cowardly lions, nutcrackers can come to life or White Rabbits can yell at you for being late. When they *are* portents or visions, they indicate that the dreamer has some sort of special, superhuman power or destiny; in other words, the dreamer falls outside normal, rational human parameters. And as for the first question, the perceived limits of our universe may have been altered by the discovery that we are not its center, but the idea that we might travel to the earth's core or leave its atmosphere, or that we might be visited by aliens, is informed by the possibilities of modern technology.

But perhaps the most significant theme of **fantasy** for children and teens has to do with what it means to be human—that is, what kind of being am I? Where do I belong? Who are my people? How am I like and unlike the other animals and objects in my world? How am I related to these other things in my world? The first few of these questions are at the heart of animal fantasies for the very young, such as P. D. Eastman's *Are You My Mother?* (1960), Marilyn Sadler's *It's Not Easy Being a Bunny* (1983), and Kevin Henkes' *Little White Rabbit* (2011). As children get older, these questions persist, and the stakes are often raised as children broaden their understanding of limits and threats: What kind of power do I have, and who has power over me? What is death, and why do we die? Think, for instance, about Fern's impassioned argument with her dad over his intention to kill Wilbur, which suggests the existential urgency when these queries come together:

> "But it's unfair," cried Fern. "The pig couldn't help being born small, could it? If *I* had been very small at birth, would you have killed *me*?" (White 1952: 3)

Children and teens are constantly being hailed in their **fantasies** to imagine themselves as something other than human. Early **fantasies** such as "The Little Mermaid" (Andersen 1837), *The Water-Babies* (Kingsley 1863), and *The Adventures of Pinocchio* (Collodi 1881) posit human form as a goal to be achieved through morally upright behavior; inadvertently, they anticipated and participated in promoting the **ideology** behind the theory of evolution. Throughout the twentieth century, animal **fantasies**, anthropomorphized machines, and shape-shifting children mostly promoted a respect for limits and species distinction on the one hand, and the superiority of a humanist way of thinking and being on the other. Madeleine L'Engle's *A Wrinkle in Time* (1963), for instance, promotes human imperfection and love as superior to the dehumanizing influence of totalitarian control enforced by the pulsing brain of IT, and yet the most lovable character in the book is Aunt Beast. And yet other **fantasy** narratives embedded the possibility for subversion of the humanist position. Roald Dahl's *The Witches* (1983) is a case in point. When the unnamed boy is turned into a sentient mouse by a witch, he is able to uncover and thwart the witches' plot to transform all of the children in England into mice and kill them. Upon learning that there is no way to change him back into a boy and that as a mouse he will likely have a shortened life span, he is not distressed, figuring that he wouldn't want to live longer than his grandmother anyway. Mowgli (Kipling 1894) does not want to return to the man village. Horton the elephant (Seuss 1954) argues for the rights of creatures no one can see. Eva (Dickinson 1988) has had her brain transplanted into a chimp named Kelly, and she eventually orchestrates her escape so that she can live out her life in the wild among chimps, mating and producing intelligent offspring, as the humans destroy their environment. Aliens were even made cuddly when *The Iron Man* (Hughes 1968) and *E.T.* (1982) showed up.

In the first decades of the twenty-first century, we have seen a tremendous increase in **fantasies** that feature in-between species such as werewolves, vampires, and chimeras. Only a few of these nonhuman creatures retain their status as horror **tropes**. In fact, we might say that in the twenty-first century, monsters have moved from under the bed to in the bed in YA literature. Even in children's literature monsters are friendly, necessary even, for helping children face down the other *humans* in their lives. Moreover, we have more and more picturebooks that use animals as metaphors for self-selected rather than species-specific identity. Skippyjon Jones (Schachner 2001), for instance, is a cat who imagines himself as a Chihuahua, and despite some pushback that declares Skippyjon to be offensive to Latinos, the character has become an industry. Rachel Vail's *Piggy Bunny* (2012) is a pig who has decided that he wants to be the Easter Bunny, and no amount of reassurance from his parents that they love him just the way he is will change his mind; he argues that just the way he *is* is a piglet who is going to be the Easter Bunny. If you are hearing echoes of transgender in these narratives, I don't think you are wrong.

So let me put forth an untested hypothesis: According to many cultural theorists, **humanism** is transitioning to **posthumanism**. By deploying the term **posthumanism**, these theorists are mounting a critique against traditional notions of **humanism** and human nature. Is human nature inherently gendered, for instance? Is racial identity inevitable? How close are we to other animals in terms of behavior, especially when it comes to ethics and desire? As the human interface with technology changes, how will that affect our understanding of our bodies? We may never be brains in vats, but might we become happy cyborgs, brains transplanted into chimps or supermodels, gamers going into virtual spaces and having adventures? My hypothesis, then, is that since before Darwin, children's and YA fantasy has been putting the question of the human to the test, priming generations of readers to wonder what constitutes our nature and our limits, and planting the **ideological** seeds that are even now blooming into a **posthumanist** ethics. Discuss.

Conclusion

You're probably wondering why, in a chapter about **fantasy**, I didn't talk about the latest blockbuster dystopia. Well that's because by the time you read this book, that block will have been busted, and there will be some new trend on the horizon. This, perhaps, is the true nature of **fantasy**—its continuing ability to speak to young readers about the things that transcend time in storied **metaphors** and metaphoric stories that remain absolutely timely. In this chapter I have introduced multiple ways of approaching **fantasy** critically, and here I will mention one more, and that is the study of a single author or a close reading of a set of texts of a particular type. As with picturebooks, children's and teen fantasy is so varied and rich that I thought it unfair to single out favorites. And of course, as with the other chapters in this book, I will remind you that this is but an introduction to a wealth of scholarship that has come before this writing and will develop in exciting ways as you and your colleagues enter and expand the conversation. Your quest from this point, should you decide to accept it, is to find your **genre**, find your author, and find your critics, and enter into the portals that lead to wonder.

Extending your study

Reading:

Attebery, Brian. *Stories about Stories: Fantasy and the Remaking of Myth* (Oxford: Oxford University Press, 2014).
   Describes the historical and ideological shifts in our relationships to myth and reality as they work themselves out in the kinds of fantasy literature produced in the Romantic, modernist, and postcolonial or postmodern literary traditions.
Levy, Michael and Mendlesohn, Farah. *Children's Fantasy Literature: An Introduction* (Cambridge: Cambridge University Press, 2016).
   Canvasses significant fantasy texts and key themes in children's fantasy from sixteenth century to the present.
MacRae, Cathi Dunn. *Presenting Young Adult Fantasy Fiction* (New York: Twayne, 1998). Working with young adult readers, MacRae presents close readings of fantasy in various subgenres. Each chapter is focused on a prominent author in that subgenre.
Mendlesohn, Farah. *Rhetorics of Fantasy* (Middletown, CT: Wesleyan University Press, 2008). Focuses on how language and rhetoric function within four types of fantasy: portal quest, intrusion, immersive, liminal, as well as various outliers.
Sandner, David. *Fantastic Literature: A Critical Reader* (Westport, CT: Praeger, 2004). Contains substantial excerpts from all of the major theorists of fantasy.

Writing:

1 Write a humorous personal essay that answers the question: Are you Team Zombie or Team Unicorn? Discuss, with examples.
2 Write a persuasive essay that provides a rationale for a text that has received criticism or threats of censorship. Instead of responding directly to the censorship, discuss what about this text makes it worth fighting for.

3 Write an essay wherein you take a position with regard to my thesis on **posthumanism** in one or two texts. Do the texts you have chosen champion **humanism** or challenge it? In what ways?

4 Choose five fantasy or science fiction texts—books or films. Do close analytical readings of the first paragraphs or scenes. How do they invite a reader into the world of their texts?

5 After reading the case study, consider how Butler's five techniques work in a fantasy novel of your choice. Write an essay in which you discuss how the author uses the various techniques to create various effects, such as humor, satire, estrangement, or comfort.

Discussing:

1 Do you have a preferred subgenre of speculative fiction? What do you like about it? What makes it stand out against other kinds of speculative fiction?

2 Why do you think that nonhuman characters have become so alluring in the twenty-first century?

3 What are some specific features of dystopias that speak to contemporary culture? Do you think that they are effective in making young viewers aware of the dangers they are warning against? Why or why not?

4 Flesh out the last paragraph of Daniel José Older's talkback for this chapter. What are some of the implications for the future of most fantasies featuring white protagonists? If you have read Older's book, what do you notice that is distinctly different about it compared to other fantasies you have read?

Responding:

1 Create a musical playlist to go with a fantasy novel of your choice. Write a rationale for each song you choose.

2 Draw or find pictures that represent the settings of a fantasy novel. Reflect on how visualizing the settings helps you understand the world.

3 Create a storybox using significant objects from a fantasy novel. How did you make your selections? What metaphorical weight do these objects carry in the story?

4 Draw or actually construct a costume for one or more of the characters in a fantasy novel. How did you know what to put into your design? How does the clothing of a character enable you to understand him or her better?

Online exploration:

1 Sketchy overview of fantasy types, but good list of secondary sources to consult for research:
   http://childliterature.net/childlit/fantasy/
2 Terrific website for book lists, helpfully divided by subgenres:
   http://bestfantasybooks.com/best-young-adult-fantasy-books.html
3 Annotated list of popular middle-grade fantasy books:
   http://fangirlnation.com/2014/08/25/the-geeky-goodness-of-middle-grade-fantasy/
4 Discussion orchestrated by Malinda Lo on the differences between middle-grade and YA fantasy and science fiction:
   http://www.sfwa.org/2013/02/an-introduction-to-middle-grade-and-young-adult-fiction-part-1-definitions/
5 Publisher Lee & Low has an imprint called Tu that is specifically dedicated to multicultural fantasy. Their website not only highlights the books they publish but also features articles dedicated to the topic. Find out more here:
   https://www.leeandlow.com/imprints/3
6 Most authors now have websites, so when you find an author you like, simply do a search!

Case Study: Fantasy Techniques in *Feed*

Catherine Butler (2012) describes five fantasy techniques used by J. K. Rowling in her Harry Potter series to bridge the gap between our world and the fantasy space of Hogwarts. In this case study we will look at how M. T. Anderson deploys three of those techniques in his satirical science fiction novel, *Feed* (2002), to hold a sobering mirror up to our present-day lack of critical thinking and our addiction to consumerism. The three techniques that I will focus on are realization, exaggeration, and substitution.

The opening chapters of *Feed* alert us to the fact that things that are currently impossible have been realized in this futuristic world. For instance, the main characters are spending spring break on the moon as tourists. Further, one of the boys, Link, has been cloned using Abraham Lincoln's DNA. As we learn more about this world, we discover that technology has advanced to the point where people are "wet-wired" to the internet with a chip implant that enables them to communicate, watch media, shop, and even alter their states of consciousness without an external device or drug. Butler argues that realization is one of the most common transformations used in fantasy fiction. Realizations can be wish-fulfilling, dangerous, or ambivalent. For instance, who wouldn't want a magic wand, but a vampire is a creature of nightmare, even if he sparkles. In the case of *Feed*, the realization of the technologies is presented as mostly negative, although readers may not be entirely convinced. We spend so much of our time online these days that it may seem attractive to be able to shop, chat, and watch our favorite shows at the speed of thought without a device. However, the skin lesions, the loss of intellect, the environmental devastation, the boredom, and finally, the ultimately fatal malfunctions that Violet experiences are perfectly logical consequences that Anderson highlights through the realization of these as-yet imaginary technologies.

Interestingly, the characters still interact face to face, and physically drive cars and go to malls. When they do, however, we find examples of exaggeration, such as when Titus buys a hot cross bun so enormous that he has to transport it in a wheelbarrow. Calista, Loga, and Quendy disappear into the bathroom to change their hair styles whenever the stars of their favorite show change theirs, and they buy disgusting fake skin lesions when these begin trending. As we can see by way of these examples, exaggeration is particularly effective for satire, as Butler notes (234). Anderson is clearly taking aim at our contemporary tendency to "super-size" fast food as well as our desire to imitate media images and follow trends, augmenting and speeding these things up through exaggeration. The images are funny, if convicting.

The chapter entitled "The Dimples of Delglacey" (109–118) starts with Titus worrying about whether he is smart enough to date Violet. Here, Anderson continues his trenchant satire through substitution. Titus says, "School™ is not so bad now, not like back when my grandparents were kids, when the schools were run by the government, which sounds completely, like, Nazi, to have the government running the schools?" (109). This is an example of what Butler refers to as substitution. Substitution is when something in the fantasy world is similar enough to its analogue in the real world to be recognizable, but with certain variations. In this case, schools have been taken over by the corporations rather than the government. This detail works as satire because of the way Titus describes it. Government-run schools are ideally meant to be disinterested, democratizing institutions, publicly funded so that they can be independent of any political or economic interference by special interests. Their purpose is to foster critical thinking so that children develop into educated citizens capable of independent judgment on the issues that affect them. Titus's reference to

(Continued)

Nazis suggests that having the government run schools turns them into totalitarian institutions with a huge potential for state-sponsored evil. In such a scenario, independent thinking and criticism of the institution could be fatal, rather than a responsibility of citizenship. And yet, Titus displays a lack of critical thinking and independent judgment, and the corporations who are running the schools have brainwashed him into complacency with regard to the environment and income inequality. His use of language, which is imprecise and full of slang and clichés, demonstrates further both the similarities and differences between our world and the future-world Anderson forecasts.

Later in the chapter, Titus hears the story of his conception. In a funny analogue to a real-world teen, he is repulsed at the thought of hearing how his parents made him; the twist of substitution is that they didn't have sex, but instead selected DNA from a movie actor they like, and then went into separate rooms to donate some of their own. The reason they are even telling the story is to salve Titus's feelings that he is unworthy of Violet; instead of acknowledging that his education hasn't provided him with adequate support, his mom calls him "a nontraditional learner" and redirects his attention to how good-looking he is, based on their selection of DNA from an actor who they thought was going to make it big but whose career fizzled. What finally works to bring him out of his funk, however, is the promise of a new car that, in the end, is really not all that different from how we distract ourselves from more uncomfortable thoughts today.

In many ways, *Feed* depicts a world that operates with radically different technologies than those available at present. However, these technologies could be seen more as extensions than differences. By combining things as they are now with things as they might be, Anderson realizes the limited potential of science fiction as framed by Fredric Jameson (2005: xiii):

> Even our wildest imaginings are all collages of experience, constructs made up of bits and pieces of the here and now. . . . On the social level, this means that our imaginations are hostages to our own mode of production (and perhaps to whatever remnants of past ones it has preserved). It suggests that at best Utopia [and therefore science fiction] can serve the negative purpose of making us more aware of our mental and ideological imprisonment . . . and that therefore the best Utopias are those that fail the most completely.

Anderson's pointed satire of the future we seem to be headed toward works primarily because he draws on values and situations that exist in the real world, but renders them slightly different through realization, exaggeration, and substitution.

Author talkback: Daniel José Older

Daniel José Older is a newcomer to YA fiction, but he's made an impressive debut. His first YA novel, *Shadowshaper* (2015), was a New York Times Notable Book of 2015, won the International Latino Book Award, and was shortlisted for the Kirkus Prize in Young Adult Literature, the Andre Norton Award, the Locus Award, and the Mythopoeic Award.

Young Adult Fantasy Fiction
Daniel José Older

Every story is the chronicle of a turning point, a crisis wherein some aspect of our dominant mythology is shattered and replaced. In YA literature, the movement is always towards adulthood. The hero sets out on a journey, and though it may not take her much further than her own backyard, the challenges presented will somehow tackle one of the fundamental beliefs we cling to as children—be it our own invincibility, the infallibility of our parents or society, or what we are capable of.

The best stories harmonize internal and external conflicts into an overarching and seemingly impossible challenge for the protagonist. In the realm of fantasy fiction, we have the benefit of being able to make literal monsters and superpowers from the wildest hopes and fears of our characters. The challenge is to do so in a cohesive way, one that pays as much attention to the details and lifeblood of the fantastical elements as it does the metaphor. This is called worldbuilding, and it's one of the most fun and difficult skills in the fantasist's toolkit.

Worldbuilding is why most fantasy writers become fantasy writers. Most of us want nothing more than to sit around all day making up amazing and ridiculous new places and populating them with new forms of magic, intrigue, and creatures. But then we have to fit all that worldbuilding into the ever-changing structure of a narrative. This usually requires discarding about 80 percent of the cool stuff we've come up with, and then somehow trying to explain the remaining 20 percent in a way that isn't boring or a blatant infodump.

Ideally, our fantastical elements function in dialogue with the deeper internal challenges our protagonist faces. This results in layers of mythology, all conversing and competing and adding an underlying wave of tension and meaning beneath the action of the story. There are the everyday myths, the social mores and personal beliefs that our protagonist must shed as she faces her destiny, and then there are the imaginary mythological aspects we bring with our worldbuilding. Finally, there is the great, neverending river of human mythology that we are always taking part in as storytellers: the way Frankenstein's monster echoes the Golem of Prague which echoes Pygmalion which echoes the original creation myths—each strikingly different and still engaged in an ongoing, centuries-long dialogue about the terrible, beautiful power of creativity.

And this is where context comes into play. Consider context the intersection of place, time, and power. Context is where worldbuilding gets really interesting, if we let it. A setting on its own, a simple place and time designation, can mean so many different things it becomes essentially meaningless. Here in New York, socioeconomic statuses can vary intensely within a single building, not to mention from block to block. When we enter into the nitty gritty realm of power dynamics—that's when we can really allow setting to become more than just a place, more than a character even: it becomes an integral part of the conflict. Most settings are in some form of crisis, whether it's actual war or a slower form of violence like mass displacement through gentrification, or political wrangling. Places are dynamic, in constant motion, and even when they're not, that stagnation itself is usually fraught with tension. Tension feeds conflict and conflict, as Robert McKee wrote, is the music of story.

Literature is an experiential art form. Our job as writers is to bring to life that contextual tension, as well as the internal and external conflicts of the story, vis-à-vis the lived experiences of each character. What does the street tell us about the changing world? What stories do the brand new highrises amidst dilapidated train stations imply? What secrets does the sudden increase in police presence whisper of? Each characters' view and analysis and, most of all, emotional response, to their world, can give us reams of information about both the realm we have created and the characters themselves.

Besides the context within the story itself, we YA writers must always be conscious of the world around us, and the literary/publishing industry in which we are taking part. This *doesn't* mean write to the trend—whatever's hip now will definitely not be hip by the time your book comes out anyway. It means we don't write in a vacuum. If we're quick to acknowledge the power of words to uplift, we have to also understand the damage our stories can do. Representation is a matter of life and death for some communities, especially when it comes to young people. The publishing industry, which is currently about 90 percent white, has focused inordinately on white protagonists, white communities, white stories, particularly when it comes to fantasy fiction. The white savior, the quick-to-die sidekick of color, and helpless damsel in distress are all clichés. Besides being failures on a human level, they signify lazy, shallow writing.

When we are honest about how diverse and complex this world is, we breathe new life into these layers of mythology and meaning we've constructed within our stories. The result is a more passionate, more truthful, and more necessary YA literature for the whole world.

Literature references

Adams, R. (1972), *Watership Down*, London: Rex Collings.

Anderson, M. T. (1997), *Thirsty*, Somerville, MA: Candlewick.

Anderson, M. T. (2002), *Feed*, Somerville, MA: Candlewick.

Barrie, J. M. (2011), *Peter and Wendy*, London: Hodder & Stoughton.

Beaudoin, S. (2012), *The Infects*, Somerville, MA: Candlewick.

Bell, C. (2014) *El Deafo*, New York: Harry N. Abrams.

Carroll, L. (1865), *Alice in Wonderland*, London: Macmillan.

Cole, H. (1841–49), *Home Treasury*, London, England: J. Cundall.

Collodi, C. (1986), *The Adventures of Pinocchio*, trans. Nicolas J. Perella, Berkeley: University of California Press. [Originally published 1881].

Dahl, R. (1983), *The Witches*, New York: Penguin.

Dickinson, P. (1988), *Eva*, New York: Doubleday.

Eastman, P. D. (1960), *Are You My Mother?* New York: Random House.

E.T.: The Extra-Terrestrial (1982), Directed by Stephen Spielberg, Amblin Entertainment, DVD.

Funke, C. (2005), *Inkheart*, New York: Scholastic.

Gaiman, N. (2002), *Coraline*, London: Bloomsbury.

Gaiman, N. (2008), *The Graveyard Book*, London: Bloomsbury.

Hautman, P. (2012–14), Klaatu Diskos trilogy. Somerville, MA: Candlewick.

Henkes, K. (2011), *Little White Rabbit*, New York: Greenwillow.

Hughes, T., (1968), *The Iron Man/The Iron Giant*, London: Faber and Faber.

Jones, D. W. (2006), *The Tough Guide to Fantasyland*, New York: Penguin.

Juster, N. (1961), *The Phantom Tollbooth*, New York: Random House.

Kipling, R. (1894), *The Jungle Book*, London: Macmillan.

Kingsley, C. (1863), *Water Babies*, London: Macmillan.

Lewis, C. S. (1950), *The Lion, The Witch, and The Wardrobe*, London: Geoffery Bles.

L'Engle, M. (1963), *A Wrinkle in Time*, New York: Farrar, Straus & Giroux

Older, D. J. (2015), *Shadowshaper*, New York: Arthur A. Levine.

Pullman, P. (1997), *The Subtle Knife*, New York: Random House.

Reeves, D. (2010), *Bleeding Violet*, New York: Simon Pulse.

Riordan, R. (2005), *The Lightning Thief*, New York: Disney Hyperion.

Rowling, J. K. (1997) *Harry Potter and the Philosopher's Stone*, London: Bloomsbury.

Sadler, M. (1983), *It's Not Easy Being a Bunny*, New York: Random House.

Schachner, J. (2001), *Skippyjon Jones*, New York: Dutton.

Seuss, Dr. (1954), *Horton Hears a Who*, New York: Random House.

Smith, A. (2010), *The Marbury Lens*, New York: Macmillan.

Spiegelman, A. (1980–91), *Maus*, New York: Pantheon.

Tan, S. (2006), *The Arrival*, London: Hodder.

Trollope, A. (1875), *The Way We Live Now*, London: Chapman and Hall.

Vail, R. (2012), *Piggy Bunny*, Illus. Jeremy Tankard, New York: Macmillan.

White, E. B. (1952), *Charlotte's Web*, New York: Harper & Brothers.

White, T. H. (1938), *The Sword in the Stone* (Book 1 of *The Once and Future King*), New York: G. P. Putnam.

Wordsworth, W. (1807), "Ode: Intimations on Immortality" in *Poems in Two Volumes 1807*, London: Longman, Hurst, Rees, and Orme, Paternoster-Row, pp. 147-158.

Zootopia/Zootropolis (2016), Directed by Byron Howard and Rich Moore, Walt Disney Pictures, DVD.

12

Entering the Professional Conversation

Where to study children's literature

Children's and YA literature has a vibrant and growing presence in universities around the world. If you want to pursue your study further, you may do so in several areas that offer opportunities for advanced degrees focused on youth literature, including English, Education, Literacy Studies, Media Studies, Theater, Interdisciplinary Children's Studies, Creative Writing and Illustrating Programs, Publishing Studies, and Library and Information Sciences. Despite its popularity and importance in the wider culture, however, you might meet with some resistance in some of the programs within these fields as many aren't yet convinced of the complexity of literature for young audiences, the rigor with which it can be studied, and the influence it has on culture at large. Even some programs within areas where you would expect children's and YA literature to thrive, such as Literacy Studies, may be resistant to considering the role quality multimodal youth literature plays in facilitating literacy acquisition and development—give young readers something that interests them and excites their imagination and you will be amazed at how their literacy skills develop. Alas, however, scholars don't always look over their disciplinary fences to see what tricks and tips they can share with each other to enliven their study and/or improve the lives of young people.

Fortunately, there are organizations, programs, and online discussion groups where you can find kindred spirits to help you expand your knowledge and interests, find support for your research, and even map a career path related to children's and YA literature. However, because the field is growing even while the global economy is contracting, I will focus on a few methods of research that begin from established entities rather than attempting to create comprehensive lists of all the graduate programs, blogs, and other websites that may not be current when you pick up this book; there's nothing more frustrating than a dead link (okay, that's hyperbole, but still . . .).

In light of the changing landscape of the field, then, suppose you want to pursue graduate research in children's and/or YA literature, either on its own or as a subfield within an area. The best way to find a program is to track down the authors of the books and articles you have found helpful or that touch on areas within youth literature that interest you. Most academics are easy to find via a simple internet search. Once you have located a person, click around the institution or department website to find out about his or her program. What you will find is that some institutions have MA or PhD programs where you can focus on children's and YA literature as a major field of study, while other programs have only one or two faculty members that teach occasional classes in the area. Within Library and Information Studies programs, for instance, you will want to look specifically at what they offer in terms of Children and Youth Services. In programs where there doesn't seem to be a specific focus on youth literature, send the professor an email introducing yourself and explaining your goals and simply ask what the opportunities and climate are like for graduate study focused on youth literature at that institution. Depending on your career aspirations, for instance, you might be happy with youth literature as a secondary focus within the broader study of the literature of a period, region, or ethnicity in an English department. In other words, you may not want to limit your search to programs that specialize in youth literature, but it would still be good to know if the climate is friendly to the field since, as I have noted above, not every institution is.

Another thing to consider when you think about graduate school is how you want to be involved in children's and YA literature, both in school and when you graduate. Programs that are housed in Education and Library Studies will likely include opportunities for **empirical research** or other work with real children and teens, while programs in literature departments probably will not. Many creative writing programs are resistant to mentoring writing aimed at young audiences, so in that case, it is generally best to find a program that specializes in the writing and/or illustrating of children's or YA literature; start your search with children's literature MFA programs, and zero in from there. Some programs offer different levels of residency requirements; a low-residency program means that you can complete most of your degree in your own community through a combination of online classes and brief on-campus stays. Some are offered as fully online degrees, while others have a more traditional model where you can be engaged in teaching or as a research assistant while you take classes and write your dissertation. Talk to people who have pursued these different options, and consult with professors who teach in different kinds of programs to get a feel for what might be a good fit for you.

Professional organizations devoted to youth literature

Most college and university professors belong to one or more professional organizations that host conferences where they can share works in progress and network with like-minded colleagues. The organizations are open to anyone; they charge an annual fee for membership, and most of them have reduced rates for students or, in the case of the Society of Children's Book Writers and Illustrators, people whose work has not yet been published. Most of these organizations also publish peer-reviewed journals with articles suitable for use in your research papers, and many also include reviews of scholarly books. Access to the journals and a reduced fee for conference registration are two of the perks of membership, but most of the journals are available through university library databases or can be obtained through a separate subscription. The ones that are open access, of course, are available in full text, free of charge with an internet connection. Here are the major associations that focus on children's and YA literature, even though most of them do not have YA in their title. All of them have websites so that you can explore what they offer beyond these brief descriptions.

Professional Organizations You Can Join:

- Australasian Children's Literature Association (ACLAR): hosts a conference every two years; emphasis is on literary and theoretical approaches
- International Research Society for Children's Literature (IRSCL): hosts a biennial congress in the summer in various locations around the world; emphasis is on literary and theoretical approaches to global literature
- Children's Literature Association (ChLA): hosts an annual conference, usually in the United States; emphasis is on literary and theoretical approaches
- International Board on Books for Young People (IBBY): a network with chapters in seventy-seven countries devoted to the promotion and dissemination of youth literature—that is, getting good books into the hands of kids, especially in developing countries; hosts a biennial congress with regional congresses held in off years; sponsors the Han Christian Andersen Awards to an author and illustrator who have made significant contributions to children's literature; emphasis is on diverse approaches, including literary and theoretical as well as concerns from the fields of education, literacy, translation, publishing, writing and illustrating, librarianship, access, bibliotherapy, social work, etc.
- Association for Research in the Cultures of Young People (ARCYP): focus is on but not limited to Canadian contexts; annual conference; interdisciplinary approaches

- Association for Library Service to Children (ALSC): a division of the American Library Association; emphasis extends beyond literature to other aspects of youth services librarianship
- Young Adult Library Services Association (YALSA): a division of the American Library Association; emphasis extends beyond literature to other aspects of youth services librarianship
- Libraries for Children and Young Adults Section of the International Federation of Library Associations and Institutions (IFLA): hosts an annual conference; emphasis is on youth services librarianship
- Children's Literature Assembly (CLA): an affiliate group of (US) National Council of Teachers of English (NCTE); hosts events at annual NCTE conference, offers research and professional development grants; emphasis is on literary analysis tied to secondary education concerns
- Assembly on Literature for Adolescents (ALAN): an affiliate group of (US) NCTE; hosts events at annual NCTE conference; emphasis is on literary analysis tied to education concerns
- Children's Literature and Reading Special Interest Group (CL/R SIG): members must also be members of International Literacy Association (ILA—formerly the International Reading Association)
- Special Interest Group Network on Adolescent Literature (SIGNAL): members must also be members of International Literacy Association (ILA—formerly the International Reading Association)
- Society of Children's Book Writers and Illustrators (SCBWI): membership opens doors to reliable advice, support, networking, mentoring, critique groups, etc.; when you or a student or a friend of a friend wants advice on how to get a manuscript published, this is where you send them

Online Discussion Groups and LISTSERVs

In addition to professional organizations that require membership fees, there are online discussion groups that you can join and participate in for free, including:

- CCBC-NET, http://www.education.wisc.edu/ccbc/ccbcnet/commands.asp: Moderated discussion list of the Cooperative Children's Book Center at the University of Wisconsin
- Child_lit, https://email.rutgers.edu/mailman/listinfo/child_lit: Active discussion list with participants from all over the world, run by Michael Joseph of Rutgers University
- *Children-literature-uk,* https://www.jiscmail.ac.uk/cgi-bin/webadmin?A0= CHILDREN-LITERATURE-UK: academic discussion list based in the UK
- *PICTUREBOOKRESEARCH,* https://www.jiscmail.ac.uk/cgi-bin/webadmin?A 0=PICTUREBOOKRESEARCH: an international, multilingual group devoted specifically to the academic study of picturebooks

Other Types of Organizations Devoted to Children's and Young Adult Literature:

Besides these professional organizations and LISTSERVs open to membership, there are nonprofit groups in many countries that promote children's and YA literature through sponsoring awards and awareness events, such as the Children's Book Council of the United States, which sponsors Children's Book Week and selects the National Ambassador for Young People's Literature, or the Children's Book Council of Australia, which sponsors annual conferences, awards, and a book week celebration. Moreover, there has been an enormous proliferation of awards chartered by and selected by professionals in the field as well as by young readers themselves. Awards are given annually to individual books according to subject matter, genre, age group, and form, as well as to authors, illustrators, and organizations who have made significant and long-lasting contributions to children's and YA literature. Rather than listing the awards here, which would be an impossible task, I refer you to a remarkable database in the Online Exploration section, which indexes, at the time of this writing, over eleven thousand books drawn from one hundred and twenty-nine awards granted in English-speaking countries. The records are helpfully searchable by nationality, genre, age group, ethnicity, format, and publication year as well as other limiting categories. One of the advantages of being active in the professional conversation through organizational membership is the opportunity to serve on the committees elected to make these awards.

Researching and writing about children's and young adult literature

Obviously, entering the professional conversation about children's and YA literature involves writing about it in some way. The beginning of this section is mostly for people who are facing an assignment and don't know where to begin, but the tips at the end and the special circumstances when researching children's and YA literature are also useful for people who wish to present at conferences or submit articles to journals. The case study for this chapter provides more specific guidance on things to remember when writing a paper to deliver orally at a conference.

In the end, start with close reading

Hopefully, by this point you have given a lot of thought to what kind of children's and young literature or media that you are curious about, and what kind of theoretical wonderer you are. You've been reading books, watching films, and researching theories, but now you need to write a scholarly research paper about a children's or

YA text. Where do you start? There are any number of good handbooks and guides that offer techniques for writing about literature, but they usually do not address the special joys and challenges of researching and writing about children's and YA texts. Let's start, then, with the good news: children's and YA texts are usually pleasurable to read or view. This is great, because to write about a text, you need to read it or view it more than once. Rereading is crucial to performing good close analysis, and since it is part of the nature of children's literature to appeal to its audience in some way, rereading a children's or YA text isn't usually an odious task. When the time comes to decide on a text you want to write about, you have some choices: you can either choose a text that you really loved, or one that puzzled or offended you on first encounter. Either way, choosing a text that provoked some sort of affective response in you is usually a good idea, since you will be living with it for a while.

To make the most of your rereading, though, you will want to have an idea of what to focus on. If you have been paying attention to the kind of response you generally have to texts, you have a good starting point, but here's an exercise to help you zero in on your particular type of wonder, or the type of wonder generated by the book itself: After completing your first reading, take some time to freewrite in response to these two prompts:

1 What was the book about?
2 What does it remind you of?

Now, do an analytical reading of your responses. If your response to the first question focused on a character, then that alerts you to a line of inquiry that might develop into an essay on the construction or development of identity or the methods of depiction and development of a character. If your response included more of an emphasis on events or how this book was similar or different from other texts you've read, you might find a structural analysis of the plot productive. Alternately, if you thought the book was about a particular theme, then you are in the territory of **ideology** or philosophy, the beliefs or values a book is trying to convey to its reader. If you feel in love with, or hated, or were puzzled by the language of the text—either why it was written in that form or why it affected you—then a rhetorical choice might be your best avenue to pursue. As you do this for a number of books, you will start to see patterns in your noticing that might lead you to a sense of what types of theory you care about and want to pursue further as a literary critic.

The second question leads you into different areas of analysis. Nodelman (2008) has argued that children's literature is recognizable as a **genre** due to a set of assumptions or patterns that repeat with small variations across time and national origin. Like mystery or romance novels, children's books tend to follow formulas; part of the pleasure we take in reading children's books is in recognizing and analyzing the formulas, while yet another pleasure is finding a book that breaks the formula, or does something really interesting within it. As we have noted in Chapter 2, children are pattern-seeking machines, so that even very small children recognize **intertextual** connections between the stories they read. But they, too, are also looking for those flashes of novelty or pattern-breaking in order to maintain their interest and grow their experiences. As you read, you draw on your entire range of experiences, including prior experiences of youth literature, to make sense of the text in front of you. **Intertextual** connections and ideas floating around in the culture at large offer rich opportunities for research and writing about children's and YA texts. For instance, if the current book you are reading reminds you of another book set in the same time period or geographical area, you could compare and contrast the portrayals of the period. If it seems to follow a familiar plot pattern, such as a heroic quest, or a method of delivery that you have seen before, such as being written in letters or other accumulated documents, you can begin to think about how it uses that particular **form** to tell its story. If it's an acknowledged adaptation or riff on a specific story, or merely uses passing references or allusions to other texts, or even just reminds you of another book, you could explore how **intertextuality** is working in that text. Thinking outside the realm of literary **intertextuality**, you might be reminded of a particular social situation or developmental process that the book is engaging with directly, such as school shootings or rape culture, or replicating through **metaphor**, as in road trip novels or fantasy quests. Each of these general areas can lead to a promising topic to write about. It's even more promising if there's a "but" in your response: "The book seemed to be about this, but . . ." or, "It reminded me of this, but. . . ." What elements of the book led to the contrast or contradiction that you noticed? There is often a paper topic to be found in analyzing the answer to that question.

Once you have an idea of what interested you about this particular book, go back and reread it with that idea in mind, taking notes on things that stand out to you as important. You will likely be amazed at how different this second reading is due to your focus; you have put on a filter that makes certain elements stand out with particular clarity. This is also where things start to get tricky, though, precisely because you are reading a text written for young people. Authors make implicit and explicit assumptions about their readers' needs and abilities. Adults writing for other adults, for instance, don't tend to see their readers as intellectually needy or inexperienced in the ways of the world. That is, they may be telling their stories in ways that elicit certain kinds of emotional or aesthetic response somewhere along the scale from discomfort to delight, but they aren't assuming that their readers are either innocent or inexperienced, or that they need to be protected from anything. Adults writing for children, on the other hand, may be assuming all of these things, while adults writing for teens may be more interested in bringing their readers up to speed on the wretched unfairness of the world. So one of the things you need to be attentive to is the implicit assumption or assumptions an author is making about the audience in the text. Indeed, this is the first of a list of forty-five qualities that Nodelman (2008: 76–81) argues are present to one degree or another in all texts identifiable as children's literature. Whether or not you agree with all of the qualities on his list or can locate them in the text you are considering, it is important to remember that what you are reading rests on a set of assumptions by authors and publishers about what children in the time period of the writing needed and liked, and what their parents and teachers would buy for them.

As we have noted in Chapter 1, since Comenius there has been a gradual growth in the belief that young people "require special forms of address" (Nodelman 2008: 76). These special forms of address are another area where writing and researching about youth literature requires special consideration. As we have noted, most children's and YA literature is multimodal and hybrid in terms of **form**, **genre**, and **mode**—from oral stories and nursery rhymes to picturebooks to graphic novels and novels in verse, all three of these aspects of a text matter. Recall that David Lewis (2001: 46) employs the metaphor of an "ecosystem" when discussing picturebooks, and I think it has utility in discussing a range of multimodal texts. In thinking of a text as an ecosystem, you are acknowledging a complex interplay of relationships between individual organisms and the environments in which they live; change one thing and it creates a ripple of changes throughout the entire ecosystem. Authors and readers are part of the ecosystem, as are all of the systems and practices that inform the **form**, **genre**, and **mode** of the text and the **ideological** and material aspects of the context. As you are doing this second close reading, you'll want to begin to ask yourself what effect **form**, **genre**, and **mode** have through the filter of your topic. For instance, if you are focusing on plot structure within an illustrated novel, what scenes are depicted visually and why? How does the style of the art contribute to the mood of the story? Does it serve to intensify the **genre** expectations of this type of plot or render them ironic? If you are tracing character development through a novel-in-verse, how does the use of poetry enhance your understanding of the way a character grows? More specifically, how does the shape or form of the poetry act as a visual **metaphor** to the character's embodiment or inner qualities and concerns? If you are working with a film, how do the details in the set design and costuming enable you to get to know a character?

Authors and illustrators choose their **forms**, **modes**, and **genres** carefully as communicative and aesthetic tools. Depending on the assignment and the focus of your research, you may need to limit your analysis to a particular aspect, but you should always acknowledge the importance of the entire package. For example, you might say something like, "In Sherman Alexie's *The Absolutely True Diary of a Part-time Indian*, Junior's character is developed through both his witty narration and his illustrations. For purposes of this analysis, I will limit my focus to the illustrations and demonstrate how they highlight Junior's key concerns and conflicts."

By the time you have completed your focused second reading, you should have enough information and notes to form a thesis statement, that is, a statement that identifies your topic and includes a stance on that topic that is discussable. Don't stress overly much about whether your topic is original (it probably isn't), or controversial (different papers have different goals). What you are aiming for is an opportunity to practice a more tightly focused and complex way of looking at a text most people take for granted as straightforward. But what you will find is that writing a paper on a children's or YA text is a challenging prospect. It *often* requires that you do a multimodal analysis, or an isolated analysis of one mode in a multimodal text. It *always* requires that you analyze a text with a complex nature of address and an awareness that you are not the target audience. In light of that, there are some definite dos and don'ts when writing about youth literature:

- Don't speak in overly broad generalities about childhood experience or what children like. If you are using a currently accepted developmental model, point out that you are working with research-based theory, cite your sources, and then admit that individual experience will of course vary.
- Don't speak on behalf of an imaginary child, or assume that children won't see multiple layers of meaning in a text.
- Do historicize your arguments if you are talking about older texts, but here again, don't overgeneralize about the qualities of that "back-in-the-day" audience (of which your professor may be a member!).
- Don't impose present tastes and sensibilities onto older visual or verbal styles.
- Don't ignore one or more aspects of the **form** in a multimodal or hybrid text. As I have demonstrated in the Alexie example above, you can finesse your focus, but acknowledge that while you know there are other things to deal with, you are zeroing in on one aspect of the text.
- Don't ignore inconvenient textual or contextual details that challenge your thesis.
- Be aware that analyzing a children's or YA text may be personally uncomfortable. Closely examining the **ideologies** and ways of seeing the world in a text from your own past may reveal things about yourself that you have never faced before; you are taking apart the texts that you used to put your sense of self together. Remember that greater self-knowledge is a wonderful gift, even if it's sometimes painful to unwrap.

Special circumstances when researching children's and young adult literature

In order to avoid some of the pitfalls mentioned above, you will certainly need to seek out relevant research and secondary sources to incorporate into your papers. Running your title through a typical internet search engine will lead to all kinds of public writing on your book, but not necessarily the kinds of research you need for a scholarly paper, which is **peer-reviewed scholarship** (more on this below). Your best friend for locating relevant, peer-reviewed research is a flesh-and-blood librarian. Children's and YA literature is studied in programs devoted to literature, education, and library and information sciences, all of which have different journals whose articles are indexed through different research databases, so it is important to have a knowledgeable guide to help you find the information you need. Even typing "literature for children" and "children's literature" into some search engines will yield different results, so your second best friends are diligence and flexibility in trying as many search terms as you can think of. Finally, though, after you've consulted the experts and done all your creative searching, you still might not find any articles directly related to the book you want to write about. What do you do?

First, try talking to your professor. Explain what avenues you have tried, and ask for help; he or she might know of an unpublished conference paper that a colleague might be willing to share. Second, while it's true that you may not find a study that specifically cites your text, there is nonetheless a wealth of material to draw from to write a decent textual analysis, thanks to the intertextual nature of children's and YA literature and its engagement with cultural forms and **ideologies**. For instance, say you want to write an essay about Sean Beaudoin's *The Infects* (2012). There are no peer-reviewed articles about this text at the time of this writing. There are, however, many books and articles on the horror genre, zombie literature, dystopias, and parody. If you combine those search terms with YA literature, you can narrow your choices. Presuming that you have already done your first reading, your response writing, and your second, focused reading, your foray into secondary materials will have a similar focused approach, and you will be able to write a well-researched paper on how Beaudoin uses the zombie hoard as a parodic horror **trope** to call attention to our uncritical acceptance of the real horrors of fast-food culture and mass-produced personalities.

Sorting what you find

Your research is likely to turn up many types of writing about children's and YA literature. Beyond the confines of a class assignment, these offer avenues that you might explore for your own professional development. However, I want to issue a few cautions and draw some distinctions between levels of professionalism in the field. Children's and YA literature is a creative endeavor, an object of academic research, a tool for education, and a commodified art form that belongs to popular culture, so you will find writing that engages with it at all of these levels, from scholarly analysis to support, advice, and opinion writing. The rising popularity of YA literature for readers of all ages, for instance, has prompted a number of articles with "click-bait" headlines by online journalists who are dismissive of a field they seem to know very little about. As a result, they perpetuate stereotypes with regard to YA literature's lack of sophistication, calling it out as nothing more than "escapism, instant gratification, and nostalgia" (Graham 2014) and making categorical statements about all YA novels based on their subjective impressions of a few. While these people are paid for their opinions, they demonstrate the kind of writing you don't want to do or even take too seriously—shallow, one-sided research based on personal opinions or surveys with no attention to literary quality or close reading that is not "vetted" by professionals in the field.

Vetting is the key point here. A vetted or refereed manuscript means that the work has been checked by experts in the field for accuracy and validity. In scholarship, this is called **peer review**, and it is crucial to ensuring that a scholarly article is up-to-date, well supported, persuasively argued, and fair to its subject matter. To facilitate fairness in the process, most peer reviews of articles are "double-blind," although a "single-blind" method is also used, especially with book proposals and manuscripts. In double-blind peer review, an editor of a journal or press sends out a submission without any identifying marks on it, and the reviewer is not made known to the author. A single-blind review means that the reviewer knows who the author is, but the author doesn't know who's reviewing his or her manuscript. This process ensures as much objectivity as possible as well as making sure that the article or book offers a perspective about a topic that is not only well supported but also fresh or different, that is, something worth putting in print because it advances the state of knowledge within the field. When I review a manuscript, I am also looking for what I call detachable theory—that is, a brilliant analysis of one text using a particular theoretical paradigm isn't very useful if it only fits that text. But if the author's way of reading makes me think of other instances where the theory will be applicable or through which it might be challenged, then I am more likely to give it the thumbs up. Because that is what peer reviewers ultimately do: they make recommendations to publishers as to whether or not the manuscript should be accepted for publication with or without specific revisions (usually with), or substantially revised and resubmitted, or rejected, perhaps with a note that it would be better suited to another journal. In each case, the reviewer is asked to give specific advice on how a piece could be made better. So if you think that your professors sit at their computers and spew forth masterpieces on their first try while you are forced to slave away, learn to take criticism and rejection with grace and humility, and revise endlessly, um, think again.

Peer-reviewed research, then, is what you are looking for as you write your papers. There are other kinds of writing and quality sources of information that I want to highlight, however. Children's and YA literature has developed a substantial presence in the blogosphere. You will find not only sharp, insightful reviews but also longer commentary from authors, illustrators, publishers, librarians, and academics among others. The key here is to be careful and do your own checking on the credentials of the writer. There are good reasons why an academic might use a blog or a social media site to "publish" his or her writing rather than submit it to the **peer review** process. One problem is that of access. Academia, like publishing, is still a majority-white, majority-upper-middle-class enterprise, so people from various ethnic and socioeconomic backgrounds who bring alternate values, perspectives, and writing styles to their work sometimes don't fit into or agree with the mainstream expectations of academic writing. In fact, both scholars and authors face a similar dilemma: As Zetta Elliott notes in her talkback to this chapter, self-publishing is for many writers an act of protest against a publishing establishment that is not keeping up with demands for texts that tell diverse stories and critical perspectives that readers need to hear. Scholars know that while **peer-reviewed** books and articles might get them tenure, fewer people who need to read or would benefit from their work on diverse texts for young readers, for instance, will find it in university libraries than if they put it out in public, online, for free. To give an example, one of the most prominent blogs that focuses on children's and YA literature is Dr. Debbie Reese's *American Indians in Children's Literature*. Started in 2006, the blog contains articles by Dr. Reese and other scholars and authors, book lists, guidelines for evaluating texts, lesson plans, and reviews. I would wager that a lot more people read Dr. Reese's blog than regularly read peer-reviewed articles published in scholarly journals that they can only access through membership in an organization or a university library. There are many other blogs that contain solid information about children's and YA literature, and they are particularly helpful in finding out about what's new and trending, or pursuing a special interest in a theme or genre. However, if you intend to use blog posts as authoritative sources to cite in your own writing, remember that these sources are not vetted by other researchers in the field, so you should check the background of who is writing and sponsoring them.

Another kind of writing that may be somewhat useful in writing research papers are reviews found in professional review journals. Here again, though, there is a difference between writing that has cleared an editorial review process and writing that has been posted on a social media site or private blog. *School Library Journal*, *Booklist*, *Kirkus*, *Publisher's Weekly*, *The Horn Book*, and *The Bulletin of the Center for Children's Books* all hire professional reviewers whose credentials come from academic degrees and long experience as librarians or teachers of children's and YA literature. These reviewers are obviously not the target audience for the books they review, but they have enough familiarity with both young people and the various **genres** of young people's literature to offer candid assessments of the quality of a work that are grounded in a context of having read more books than is considered quite normal for people who do other things like sleep and eat. Moreover, their reviews are overseen by an editor who is not beholden to any particular publisher and whose expertise in the field is widely recognized. Hence these are reviews that you can usually trust to be knowledgeable and fair, but they are not literary analyses. So the best way to use professional reviews is to help you locate books relevant to your project and keep up with what's new. Amateur reviews such as those found on bookseller sites and Goodreads.com, on the other hand, are limited to their usefulness for understanding and perhaps participating in fandom culture. Occasionally, you can use either professional or amateur reviews as a springboard from which to launch some analytical point, but if your professor requires scholarly research as part of your analysis, reviews are not what he or she is looking for.

As I have mentioned in the chapter on mass media, a good way to find additional material once you have found one or two relevant sources is to check their bibliographies. You will likely see a few texts that people refer to over and over again—these go on your must-read list. I am an inveterate collector of bibliographies. Since I am old school, I make photocopies and glue the copies into composition notebooks. Then I take highlighters of different colors and code the books and articles according to what they might be useful for—such as researching different topics for teaching, or collecting for a future project or article I might like to write. Lastly, I go through and see where these resources are—if they are not available in full text online, I jot down call numbers and make notes of books or articles I need to request through interlibrary loan.

The very last thing you can try when seeking resources on your topic is to do targeted crowdsourcing through social media. The Child_lit LISTSERV is a great resource for this, and there are also blogs, Facebook groups, and Twitter hashtags and handles that are dedicated to specific areas of interest within the field. However, I caution you to use good internet etiquette when approaching these groups—the members are not there to do your research for you. It's best to introduce yourself and briefly describe your project, including what avenues you have already explored, before you pose your query. Collect the responses you get, and be prepared, if there seems to be a lot of interest, to share your compiled and neatly formatted list with the group. Members of these groups are remarkably generous and knowledgeable, so make sure you share in kind. I have listed the most active and established LISTSERVs above, so what follows is a list of peer-reviewed journals wherein you will find articles that you can model and draw from in order to write terrific papers on children's and YA literature. Generally speaking, the more of these articles you read, the more you will understand the rhythms of academic discourse, how polished writers establish their arguments, what kinds of evidence they draw from, and how they incorporate primary and secondary sources into their writing. In fact, if you are thinking of submitting your own work to one of these journals, you should take some time to perform the kind of rhetorical analysis that I just described of several of the articles recently published, so that you know how to speak the language, as it were, of that particular journal. I should note that some journals that focus on other things, such as *American Literary History* and many journals devoted to media studies, are youth-literature-friendly so that you might find useful articles here or there, but the ones listed here take children's and/or YA literature as their main subject.

Peer-Reviewed Journals:

- *The ALAN Review,* three issues per year, included with membership to ALAN, who need not be members of NCTE, older issues available online
- *Barnboken: Journal of Children's Literature Research,* open access, online-only journal published by The Swedish Institute for Children's Books, annual since 2012, (two issues per year before then), not all articles available in English, but all non-English articles have an abstract in English
- *Bookbird,* four issues per year, included with membership to IBBY
- *Children and Libraries,* four issues per year, included with membership to ALSC, archived issues available for free online
- *Children's Literature,* one issue per year, included with membership to ChLA or via Project Muse Premium Collection
- *Children's Literature Association Quarterly (ChLAQ),* four issues per year, included with membership to ChLA or via Project Muse Premium Collection
- *Children's Literature in Education,* a quarterly published by SpringerLink, subscription or institutional access required
- *The Dragon Lode,* two issues per year, included with membership to CL/R SIG
- *International Research in Children's Literature (IRCL),* two issues per year, included with membership in IRSCL or via institutional subscription
- *Jeunesse: Young People, Texts, Cultures,* two issues per year, included with membership to ARCYP or by individual subscription or via Project Muse Premium Collection
- *Journal of Children's Literature,* two issues per year, included with membership in CLA
- *Journal of Research on Libraries and Young Adults,* open access online journal of YALSA, number of issues per year varies
- *The Lion and the Unicorn,* three issues per year, Johns Hopkins University Press, subscription or via Project Muse Premium Collection
- *The Looking Glass: New Perspectives on Children's Literature,* open access, number of issues per year varies
- *New Review of Children's Literature and Librarianship*: two issues per year, published by Taylor and Francis, subscription or institutional access required
- *Papers: Explorations into Children's Literature,* open access publication of ACLAR, two issues per year
- *Signal,* two issues per year, included with membership to SIGNAL, archived articles available online
- *Study and Scrutiny: Research on Young Adult Literature,* open access, two issues per year
- *Write4Children*: open access, two issues per year

Archives and special collections

Some research projects require you to go to the original sources of the texts and explore the conditions surrounding their writing and publishing. For this you need to seek out special collections and archives dedicated to children's authors and illustrators. These collections include materials such as original manuscripts and illustrations, letters to and from publishers, and rare historical books that are unavailable anywhere else. Librarians all over the world are busily digitizing these materials so that they are more durable and accessible, but many of the archives offer grants and fellowships so that people can travel to their sites and pursue their research with original materials. ALSC maintains a wiki called "Special Collections in Children's Literature Wikiography" that lists the major archives housing materials related to children's and YA literature.

Special considerations for writing and delivering conference papers

As you will have noticed, most of the professional organizations listed above sponsor annual or biennial conferences. The case study for this chapter shows how some of the key elements of a specific conference paper work, but there are also some general things to consider. Normally, conferences consist of seventy-five-minute sessions where three or four people read fifteen to twenty minute papers that somehow pertain to the main topic of the conference, followed by a Q & A, and sometimes by a respondent giving an overview and summary of how the papers fit together. Conferences are both exhilarating and exhausting; they offer great opportunities for networking and getting feedback on your work. Be warned, though: you will likely come home from a conference with a notebook full of must-read titles and far, far too many ideas. Conferences can also be expensive, so my best advice is that, unless you are independently funded, you should be strategic in choosing the conferences you will attend. And while it's perfectly fine to attend a conference at which you are not presenting, you should consider the conference papers you do give as seeds that can be watered into publications. In today's very tight job market, peer-reviewed publications carry more weight than a slew of conference presentations.

The first step in delivering a paper at a conference is to get your abstract accepted. An organization will issue a call for papers with a description of the conference theme and some suggestions for topics to consider. They will also contain two very important things: a word length, and a deadline. Stick to them both. I mean it. Your proposal should indicate three things: your awareness of the larger conversation surrounding your topic, your thesis or particular intervention into this larger topic, and what primary texts you will be talking about as evidence of your thesis. That first bit is the tricky part—you want to give enough detail so that you sound like you know what you are talking about, and in particular that you know you aren't the first person to think about your topic, but you don't want to sound like you are just dropping Big Theory Names. Also, you want to be concise. Conference planning committees have to read hundreds of these abstracts, so get in, say something smart and say it clearly, and get out.

Many people shear off sections of a larger paper to give as a conference paper. This is almost always a bad idea. A conference paper should be between eight and eleven pages of Times New Roman 12-point font, so around thirty-five hundred words give or take, and you should practice reading it aloud to time yourself. Almost every veteran conference-goer I know has the following pet peeves: a speaker went over time; a speaker talked too fast because his or her paper was too long; a speaker kept saying things like "in a longer version of this paper I" or "if I had more time I would . . ." These things amount to a lack of professionalism and courtesy. Everyone has the same amount of time, and everyone knows this going in, so if you go over, you are cutting into someone else's time. If you try to talk too fast, your listeners can't process your ideas. Finally, if you keep referring to what you would do if only you had more time, the impression you give is that you think your work deserves more consideration than anyone else's.

The solution, then, is to write the conference paper as a self-contained conference paper—that is, a piece that can be delivered orally in the allotted time. If you have slides or other visuals, such as handouts, plan for set-up time, and allow for a little extemporaneous talk about what is being projected on the screen or circulated. That might mean you should plan for fifteen minutes rather than twenty. Believe me, it's better to leave them wanting more than to go on too long.

Conclusion

Ha! I wonder if I have followed my own advice in that last sentence in the writing of this book! This final chapter was meant to give you guidance for continuing to pursue your study in children's and YA literature. I know that this has been a long book, but it offers just a small sampling of the wealth of avenues through which to study and enjoy the rich, complex, funny, moving, socially important, informative, immersive, life-changing stories that appear in literature for children and teens, so I hope I have left you wanting more. The final author talkback suggests one of the important ways the literature itself will move forward, keeping it vibrant and welcoming for all young people. As critics and readers, educators and parents, librarians, publishers, and book-buyers, we need to be as adaptable and smartly engaged with our publics as the literature we study, always challenging the mirrors, keeping the lamps lit, and opening ever wider the doors and windows of children's and YA literature.

Extending your study

Reading:

Nodelman, Perry, *The Hidden Adult* (Baltimore, MD: Johns Hopkins University Press, 2008).
  Focusing on six texts written for different age groups in different eras, Nodelman discerns a set of shared characteristics to develop a comprehensive theory of children's literature informed by insights drawn from various disciplines.
Wolf, Shelby A., Coats, Karen, Enciso, Patricia, and Christine A. Jenkins, *Handbook of Research on Children's and Young Adult Literature* (New York: Routledge, 2011). Over forty essays from contributors in Education, Literary Studies, Psychology, and Library Services, as well as short statements from authors and illustrators, are gathered in this collection that seeks to showcase the various methods and concerns that emerge from the study of youth literature in different disciplines.

Writing:

1 Locate a call for papers for a conference relating to children's and/or YA literature by doing an internet search. Compose an abstract for a paper according to the conference organizer's guidelines. Putting the call together with your abstract, exchange your work with your peers and offer advice to each other.

2 Write a 3,500-word conference paper based on your abstract. Exchange papers with a classmate and perform an assessment of the various techniques that will translate well out loud, and what might be problematic. If possible, deliver your paper orally to the class or at a department forum, and write an analysis of the experience, including your own feelings about the process and the feedback you have received.

3 Select one of the journals listed above, and read all of the essays in a single volume. Perform a rhetorical analysis of each of the essays by taking notes that answer the following questions: Who is the writer? What are his or her credentials? What is the subject of the essay? What is the writer's purpose? In what ways does the writer establish her or his argument (for instance, through ethos, i.e., through a personal statement about his or her ability to make the

case or argument; logos, a seemingly impersonal appeal to the logic of the argument or its relation to statistics or a particular kind of theoretical model; pathos, an appeal through emotions—outrage, perhaps, or by engendering fear that a book may be offensive, triggering, or too complex for young readers by citing anecdotal or even imaginary evidence)? What stylistic features does the writer use (analogies, metaphors, repetition, emotionally charged language, diction)? How does the writer address arguments that may be in opposition to his or her interpretation? How is the piece constructed as a whole—for instance, is the theory or analytic framework front-loaded, or interwoven with the textual examples? Finally, are you convinced by the writer's argument or interpretation? Once you are finished, compare and contrast the various elements for each essay and craft a statement about what seem to be the preferred rhetorical methods of the journal.

4   For advanced students: Write a 6,000–7,500-word paper that adopts the style of the journal on which you have performed your rhetorical analysis. After getting feedback from your professor and making any suggested revisions, send it to the journal. Learning to read feedback from peer reviewers is a skill in and of itself, so share the feedback you receive with your professor for his or her advice.

Discussing:

1   What is the hardest thing about writing a scholarly paper? What strategies have you learned in this chapter that might make that aspect easier?
2   What experiences have you had with reading the work in academic journals in your field?
3   What gaps in this book have you noticed, or what specific ideas would you like to pursue further?

Responding:

1   Join one or two of the online discussion groups for a month. What are the similarities and differences?
2   Research children's literature-based theme parks, attractions, museums, and virtual spaces, such as Disney and Universal theme parks, Astrid Lindgren's World, American Girl Museums, Pottermore.com, Seven Stories: The National Centre for Children's Books (Newcastle, UK), the Eric Carle Museum, and The Rabbit Hole in Kansas City, Missouri. What sorts of ideas do these sites generate for local multimodal projects or career options?

Online exploration:

1 Each of the professional organizations listed above has its own website. Locate and explore one or more of the groups to assess how it might be useful to your career.
2 Locate and explore the awards offered for children's and YA literature. A comprehensive list is available through Lisa Bartle's searchable Database of Award-Winning Children's Literature (http://www.dawcl.com/), or you can search via the various award-granting organizations.

Case Study: Preparing a Conference Paper

This case study consists of a conference paper that I wrote and presented at the Modern Language Association conference. It's not the most terrific conference paper ever written, but I've annotated it to highlight some special considerations for writing a paper that will be delivered orally and that could be turned into something more substantial.

The process began with an abstract. I was allowed five hundred words, and I used four hundred and ninety-one:

"Empathy and the Early Reader Chapter Book"
Proposal for a paper to be delivered at MLA
Submitted by Karen Coats

I borrow my title from Suzanne Keen's recently published *Empathy and the Novel* (2007). In that book, Keen synthesizes theory from psychology, philosophy, cognitive literary studies, and discourse analysis to explore how and indeed if reading novels leads to more empathic and altruistic responses to others. For this paper, I will extend her argument to include a developmental perspective, examining how authors of early chapter books deploy specific techniques to generate empathy in their readers. I argue that this challenge is greater for authors writing for this particular audience, because their task is to create situations and use language and images in such a way as to scaffold growth in this area for readers who are still in the process of developing a full-fledged theory of mind. Nascent child readers are in the process of developing the literary competencies necessary for them to track longer narratives, work out causal relationships, and understand how conceptual and literary metaphors reflect states of mind in fiction. Their perspectives are informed by their emerging theory of mind, but also limited by it, in that while they can imagine others having an inner life, they tend to expect that inner life to look and respond a lot like their own. Thus the task of these writers is to create characters with whom children can relate, but to also impose a critical distance so that children can conceptualize differences as well as similarities, and test out imaginative responses that might be alien to their own experience.

I start from the premise that increasing the range of empathetic and altruistic responses in child readers is the central project of these books, that they aim to educate and help clarify diffuse and sometimes inaccessible emotional responses in their readers, thus expanding their capacity for understanding the emotional world of themselves and others. In this way, they operate at what Vygotsky termed a "zone of proximal development" with regard to increasing emotional maturity. The popularity of these books, and children's engagement with them, argues for taking a fresh look at children's capacity for empathy and their emotional complexity and range. However, it also begs reciprocal investigation into how these particular books educate the emotions into acceptable cultural scripts, teaching kids how they should be feeling in specific situations, as well as what the acceptable parameters of emotional display look like.

Should this project be selected for the panel, I would like to know which texts the other panelists will be focusing on, so that I can attend to other texts. My preference will be to draw my close readings from Lenore Look's books, focusing particularly on the characters of Alvin Ho and Ruby Lu and Look's discourse strategies, but if someone else is working on those texts, I will shift my attention to other books written for this age group.

The following is the paper that I presented, based on that abstract. I have annotated it so that you can see what I was thinking as I wrote the piece for an oral delivery.

Empathy and the early reader

Literacy researchers agree that if children do not learn to read fluently by the end of their third grade year, they will have manifold difficulties throughout their school lives, and they aren't likely to become lifelong readers. Between the ages of six and nine, most children transition from "learning to read" to "reading to learn," and if this transition is not managed effectively, it becomes a lost opportunity that is exceedingly difficult to remediate. Given the importance of this particular stage of reading development, it is both surprising and not that surprising that more critical attention is not paid to the books that are produced and have uptake for the newly independent reader. Not surprising, of course, because these books are designed to reward new readers with a sense of accomplishment and playground capital largely in terms of pages read, to entertain and affirm rather than to challenge their mental abilities, and as such, they are formulaic, predictable, and easily consumable; they are not, to cite E. M. Forster's defining quality of great literature, "inexhaustible to meditation." Instead, they are generally viewed as tools for developing fluency in reading. The literacy goals of books for this age group include providing practice in newly acquired decoding skills, and helping readers sustain attention, understand more complex cause-and-effect sequences, and chart character development over longer narratives.

But as literature scholars and cultural critics, we need to ask what else is going on in these books and their readers as they approach these narratives. After all, these are the books that help develop not just competence in literacy, but *literary* competencies as well. They draw on the oral and pictorial characteristics of children's storytelling and picturebooks, but they repackage those features into written language that children have to learn to hear inside their heads. Thus, they have to engage what members of the New London Group (NLG) have termed "multiliteracies." The NLG's definition of multiliteracies

> The title should give some sense of the content.

> Begin with something that is easy for listeners to orient to, something that they should already have some familiarity with, but haven't necessarily thought about recently, to bring it to the front of their minds, so to speak.

> Here is the rationale for the paper itself—should be quick and clear.

> Expansion of rationale, still bringing things to the front of the mental stage for listeners. Remember that they have just heard another paper on a completely different subject, so they need to readjust to enter your argument.

> Here's the turn from what has been thought to what this paper will think about.

> Chief claim that needs to be defended.

> New term—give both credit and definition, maybe with a visual that repeats the definition.

includes the traditional skills of linguistic and visual literacies, but expands to include audio, gestural, tactile, and spatial literacies as well. Writers of good literature for this age group alternate between mapping explicit links between these embodied practices and their expression in words, and allowing readers to draw on their own experiences to make the necessary inferences. Lenore Look, for instance, will sometimes have her second-grade character, Alvin Ho, explain what he means with his gestures: "I tipped my head to one side. That's 'hey' in body language" (*Birthday Parties* 36), but sometimes she requires readers to make inferences in order to understand the emotion that is being conveyed through gesture: Upon discovering that his beloved Johnny Astro doll has been destroyed, Alvin's father has this set of reactions: "Then my dad opened the box. His whistling stopped. His breathing stopped. His feet stopped. Then he staggered backward. 'WHAAAAAAAAAAAT IS THIS?' he wailed. 'Johnny Astro what happened to you?' he cried. Then he really cried. He put his head in his hands, and his shoulders went up and down" (90–91).

> Use textual examples from primary texts to support your argument.

> The citation won't be spoken aloud, but it's still good to include it for future reference.

She also manages space eloquently in her settings for the Alvin Ho series, deploying exaggeration as her main technique for exploiting place in narrative. For instance, Alvin has a spatially dependent anxiety disorder; he can't talk in school or, at first, in his therapist's office. On the bus and at home, he is perfectly able to express himself, but when he gets to school, he can't say a word. He is also desperately afraid of natural disasters, which he equates with the world outside his neighborhood, a place that then acts as a safe home base for him, even though some pretty awful things happen there, such as his being left dangling from a tree in his backyard, and trussed in rope and duct tape in a box in his basement while attempting a Houdini stunt. Alvin equates certain places with certain experiences, an awareness that his brother wisely exploits in helping him study for a test. As they walk through the town, Calvin associates historical facts with specific places, and then instructs Alvin to mentally walk through the town when he's taking his test, so that he'll remember the facts by recalling the places where Calvin explained them. It works. Most significantly, though, Look uses the history and tourist attractions of the town of Concord to situate many of Alvin's fears as well as provide the contexts for his play and his understanding of difficult concepts. Alvin is a little freaked out by the fact that dead authors such as Henry David Thoreau and Louisa May Alcott still give tours of their homes, and he and his friends perform historical reenactments of battles that took place in their town, thus in effect demonstrating the value of multiliteracies for learning history by having the characters perform them and readers read about these performances that they could potentially imitate.

In erecting a bridge between the multiliteracies of sound, gesture, space, and vision with words that substitute for these embodied experiences, early chapter books set the stage for a new kind of aesthetic development—activating, as it were, an inner aesthetic, where pictures are replaced in large part by images created through words and drawn from reader's own experiences and memories. The illustrations in early chapter books do continue to help illuminate unfamiliar or difficult concepts and provide context, but they appear as spot art, and the words are what matter, requiring readers for the first time to rely heavily on their ability to transmediate from words on a page to a moving picture of the action in their heads. In the Alvin Ho series, for instance, LeUyen Pham's illustrations often zero in on concepts that might be difficult for a new reader to follow, as in figure 1:

> A handout is sometimes useful. Especially if there are pictures, or you want to do several things with a longish passage, as I do here. My handout for this presentation was a photocopy of the page from the book that included the illustration and the long quotations. I might have chosen to use a PowerPoint slide instead.

The wheels on the bus went round and round.

Scooter and Jules's thumbs went up and down in a thumb-wrestling match.

Then their fists went left-hook, right-hook in a boxing match.

Then Nhia, who is a ninja from Cambodia, slipped a head-hold on Pinky, who has the biggest head in the class on account of he's the biggest boy, and Pinky screamed into Nhia's armpit, which made Hobson whack Eli on the head, which made Sam karate-chop Scooter with a loud "Aiyah!", which made our teacher, Miss P, who was sitting at the front of the bus turn around and yell, "SIMMER DOWN, BOYS, OR YOU'LL GET A NOTE SENT

HOME!" How she knew who was doing what, all the way from the front of the bus and facing the other way, I'll never know. But she's very smart and smells like fresh laundry every day. Maybe she has eyes in the back of her head, just like my mom.

The noise on the bus simmered down.

(Look, *Girls* 4–5)

The picture depicts the described actions in a fairly straightforward way, but it also reinforces cause and effect through its linear arrangement—as one thing leads to another in time, the same activities are shown in a linear progression in space—and, more subtly, depicts the fact that the actions are going to lead to trouble, since their trajectory of movement goes against the standard direction for progress in cultures that read from left to right.

But the language is important here, too. It plays to the inner ear by initially evoking a song that readers will likely be familiar with. It goes on to depict actions that replicate the rhythms of the movement of the bus—as the wheels go round and round, thumbs go up and down, fists go left hook, right hook, creating a sense of movement in balanced tension that is then escalated by the domino effect of the interactions. The increasing tension culminates in the "aiyah" and the teacher's shouting, which then resolves itself in balance once again through the echoed repetition of the teacher's words with the rhythm and near-rhyme of the sentence that closes this episode, rendering it as a mini-poem—you can almost sing "the noise on the bus simmered down" to the same tune as "the wheels on the bus went round and round." This sort of literary language subtly evokes the communicative musicality that characterizes children's first exposures to the sounds and rhythms of their interactions with others and with their own bodies; it's appealing at an unconscious level to the comforts of early experience which consist of familiarity mixed with the mild excitation of novelty and tension that is as quickly resolved as it is evoked. Looking forward, it helps develop the kind of aesthetic appreciation for literary language that geeks like us deem important and civilizing and therefore want to inculcate in our children.

> A little surprising vernacular helps to snap people to attention after a longish passage of academic speak. Use judiciously.

Perhaps most importantly, though, early chapter books introduce children to a new kind of moral education at the time that they are just beginning to be able to understand it. Recent research in cognitive literary studies cites Theory of Mind as a necessary condition for reading well, but also implies that reading itself helps develop a robust Theory of Mind. Theory of Mind is the ability to attribute mental states—beliefs, desires, intentions, etc.—to oneself and others, and it really starts to develop in children around the age of five. Since mental states aren't visible, we have to learn to infer them through their expression, which is why it's called a *theory* of mind. Philosophers like Shaun Gallagher contest the mentalization aspect of this theory, arguing that the meaning of a gesture or expression is self-evident, immediately perceivable without the necessity of running it through a mental script. This is certainly true to an extent, as even infants pick up clues to emotional states through embodied interactions and will display a nascent form of empathy—the vicarious, spontaneous sharing of affect with another being.

> Situate what you are doing within a broader theoretical lens.

> Define new terms as they come up, rather than all up front.

> Use your font to help with 'stage directions' for oral reading.

> Didn't directly cite, so no need for in-text citation in MLA. In ALA or Harvard, you would put a date in parentheses here.

But the process isn't as straightforward as it might first seem when we consider, for instance, that smiles and shrugs, coos and cries, can mean many different things. Indeed, we often default to narcissistic explanations of what people mean when they produce a certain gesture or expression. For children, this is especially true, since their early emotional states lack the nuance that narrative understanding provides. Reading offers an opportunity to experience other minds, and to clarify what's going on in our own heads. Lisa Zunshine posits that "The enjoyment of fiction may be predicated—at least in part—upon *awareness* of our 'trying on', so to speak, mental states (of the characters) *potentially available* to us but at a given moment *differing from* our own" (132). As with most literary theory, this idea needs to be run through a developmental schema to assess its value for children's literature, and indeed we find that many early chapter books offer new readers the experience of getting inside another person's head at a time when a reader is newly aware that other minds, with ideas and feelings and beliefs that *differ from one's own,* might potentially exist.

> Use critics sparingly, but do use them.

> My insistence that we need to consider the child in children's literature criticism.

Often the way this works is for the author of early chapter books to set up two or more characters who are decidedly different from one another, such as Bink and Gollie, or Ivy and Bean. Alternately, the author might construct a character who has a single dominant characteristic that inflects all of his or her actions, such as Alvin Ho's intense fear of, well, mostly everything. This quality of isolating characteristics appeals to the child's archaic psychological pattern of what Melanie Klein called "splitting"—the dividing up of experience into congenial and uncongenial experiences or objects. As children enter later stages of childhood, they move toward what Klein called the "depressive" position, wherein they begin to see that people and objects can have both good and bad qualities, which is what often characterizes the plot trajectories or character arcs of early chapter books. For instance, Alvin Ho begins his first book believing that girls are alien creatures to be avoided at all costs, and while this attitude persists in words throughout the series, his actions belie the simplicity of his aversion—he spends enjoyable time playing with both Flea and his sister Anabelly, and even attends, briefly, a girls' birthday party instead of the boys' that he had longed to go to. Similarly, he begins the fourth book simply terrified of death and funerals, proceeds through a series of related adventures that reveal experiences with death to be scary, sad, funny, poignant, and sweet, and ends by accompanying his grandfather to the funeral he has been dreading.

> Indicate how your argument might apply to other texts.

> Define terms and attribute them to their originator or most prominent expositor.

The tendency of these books to appear in series allows the author to either reinforce the dominant characteristics with further nuances or situations, or to have the character demonstrate progress in perspective-taking and moral or intellectual development, though this is less often the case in early chapter books. Cognitively speaking, the ability to put things into more than one category is also developing at this age, so it makes sense that this ability to group objects according to more than one characteristic would bleed over into character development and understanding. Morally or ethically speaking, though, the immersion in a series can be read as the child's equivalent to Bakhtin's theory of the long Russian novel, where wisdom is gained through a complex understanding of where norms of

> This is a reference that most people will either know, or know of, so it adds rhetorical force to your paper, but only if you make it clear why it matters. Otherwise, it's just name-dropping.

behavior and belief fall short. For Bakhtin, the moral education a novel offers is superior to any abstract philosophical discussion of rules and their consequences, but also to the parsing of real-life situations for their ethical ramifications, because novels offer us insight into the motivations and states of minds of the characters before and after an action is completed. For instance, in each book in the series, Alvin makes some seriously questionable decisions—he takes his father's most prized possession to school and breaks it, he appropriates a costume that was meant to be given as a gift, he puts an enormous amount of money for camping supplies on his father's credit card. In each instance, his fears and/or desires for acceptance override his common sense, which is still on a shaky foundation as that part of his brain hasn't really developed yet. Nor has it for the intended reader, but seeing the consequences and cause-and-effect sequences can spur thought toward the development of more rational responses to emotional stress.

> Here's why Bakhtin was brought in—his ideas for adult lit are useful for understanding children's lit. The example that follows drives the point home.

The practice of reading about others can also stave off the existential boredom that tends to emerge at this stage of development. Once the inner tensions that mark early childhood have been more or less resolved, the child's psychosocial development begins to turn outward to the world of objects and other people, namely, peers. Partly because the elementary schooler can interact more independently with his or her environment and partly because he or she *has to*, intellectual energies turn toward understanding that world, which includes a richer range of other people who sometimes behave in inexplicable ways. In order to start to understand the behaviors of their teachers and peers, children need to develop their skills of mindreading, to stretch their ToM to include states of mind that are unfamiliar to them. Adults, of course, hope that this development will lead the child out of egoism to a more altruistic frame of mind; indeed, according to Michael J. Parsons, all models of development involve an increased capacity to adopt the perspective of others. Suzanne Keen begins her study of *Empathy and the Novel*, from which I draw my title for today's presentation, by introducing a healthy note of skepticism into the empathy-altruism

> This is more of the original argument of the piece—it draws on psychological work that is pretty much accepted as true, but hasn't been applied to literature in just this way. But, for listeners, it also appeals to common sense or experience with elementary school children.

> Refer to other theorists as needed to give credit and expand argument.

hypothesis—that is, the belief that "empathic emotion motivates altruistic action, resulting in less aggression, less fickle helping, less blaming of victims for their misfortunes, increased cooperation in conflict situations, and improved actions on behalf of needy individuals and members of stigmatized groups" (vii), and the claims that novel reading that leads to narrative empathy can trigger these prosocial attitudes and behaviors. Her review of the available research supports no such claims that empathetic responses to characters in fiction necessarily lead to action of any kind. However, narrative empathy can and does lead to an increased capability to understand multiple points of view, which is what children (and adults) need to explore alternatives to their own ways of looking at things. *What they do as a result* is a matter of their own consciences.

> This is where I got my idea and my title. She has written her book about adult literature, and I wanted to see how her argument applied or didn't apply to children's literature.

To cite a case in point, one might examine the evidence presented in Po Bronson and Ashley Merryman's *Nurtureshock* that found that children who are exposed to educational television shows such as PBS's *Arthur* (which is, arguably, a kind of text for early readers) are more aggressive than children with less exposure to such shows. The researchers speculate that the problem comes when children lack the cognitive capacity to track cause-and-effect sequences in narrative structure. So, for instance, in a fifteen-minute show that features bullying behavior that gets resolved and punished in the last three minutes of the show, children have been exposed to twelve minutes of models of the bullying behavior and only three minutes of consequences which they may or may not be able to connect to the negative behavior in a meaningful way, especially if the other characters have responded positively (through laughing or encouraging the bullying, for instance) to the behaviors of the offending character. In books, however, this can be mitigated in ways that Bakhtin suggests, through exploring and understanding the motivations and states of mind of the characters.

Keen's findings demonstrate that empathy is a tricky animal, as it does not necessarily depend on multiple points of identification for characters or complex or even realistic characterization. Nor do the lines of empathy necessarily follow the paths the author charted for it. For instance, empathy is more likely to be evoked in readers for negative feeling states, whether or not there are any points of identificatory details at all, or by some small detail of chance relevance to a reader's circumstances. Writers thus cannot consciously predict the success of their "lessons" in making their readers better people. What they can manipulate, however, is the use of gesture and expression in ways that will invite readers to empathize with characters so that they can better understand how feeling states appear externally, and how external actions indicate mental states. In other words, authors can expose children to the multiliteracies of emotional expression, and thus lead them to understanding, but they can't make them good.

Sources

> I am not entirely pleased with this conclusion, but it'll do.

Bakhtin, M. M. *The Dialogic Imagination: Four Essays.* (Michael Holquist and Caryl Emerson, trans.). Austin, TX: University of Texas Press, 1982.

Bronson, Po and Merryman, Ashley. *NurtureShock: New Thinking about Children.* New York: Twelve, 2009.

Gallagher, Shaun. "Simulation Trouble." *Social Neuroscience* 2.3-4. (2007): 353–65.

Keen, Suzanne. *Empathy and the Novel.* Oxford, UK: Oxford University Press, 2007.

Klein, Melanie. *Love, Guilt and Reparation: And Other Works 1921-1945.* New York: Simon and Schuster, 1975.

Look, Lenore. *Alvin Ho: Allergic to Girls, School, and Other Scary Things.* New York: Random House, 2008.

Look, Lenore. *Alvin Ho: Allergic to Birthday Parties, Science Projects, and Other Man-Made Catastrophes.* New York: Random House, 2010.

New London Group, "A Pedagogy of Multiliteracies." *Harvard Educational Review* 66.1 (Spring 1996) http://wwwstatic. kern.org/filer/blogWrite44ManilaWebsite/paul/ articles/A_Pedagogy_of_Multiliteracies_Designing_ Social_Futures.htm. Accessed June 29, 2015. Web.

Parsons, Michael J. *How We Understand Art: A Cognitive Developmental Account of Aesthetic Experience.* Cambridge, UK: Cambridge UP, 1989.

Zunshine, Lisa. "Richardson's Clarissa and a Theory of Mind." *The Work of Fiction: Cognition, Culture, and Complexity.* Ed. Alan Richardson and Ellen Spolsky. Ashgate Press, 2004. 127–46

> In a longer essay, I try to cite everything I consult, but in a short piece like this, especially one delivered orally, I refer to sources I have learned from but didn't necessarily cite in the text. It's not exactly what you are supposed to do according to MLA, but by being inclusive, it allows me to have access to all of the sources I consulted if I want to expand the paper.

Author talkback: Zetta Elliott

In this final talkback, Canadian-born Zetta Elliott discusses the current and future state of children's and YA publishing from the perspective of an author and an academic committed to expanding the availability of diverse literature for children against significant odds. You can read more about Dr. Elliott at http://www.zettaelliott.com/.

"Living Room"

I can't breathe.

I am a Black feminist writer committed to social justice. I write stories about Black children and teens, but within the children's literature community I struggle to find what poet June Jordan calls "living room." In "Moving Towards Home," Jordan empathizes with the Palestinian people as she envisions a space free from persecution:

> I need to speak about living room
> where the talk will take place in my language
> I need to speak about living room
> where my children will grow without horror
> I need to speak about living room where the men
> of my family between the ages of six and sixty-five
> are not
> marched into a roundup that leads to the grave
> I need to talk about living room
> where I can sit without grief without wailing aloud
> for my loved ones
> . . . .
> I need to talk about living room
> because I need to talk about home

I have been asked to write about the future of children's literature but right now I need to talk about home. If "home" represents sanctuary—a safe space where one can speak in one's authentic voice and not only survive, but thrive—then the children's literature community is not my home. I must make my predictions as an outsider.

By industry standards, I am a failed author. Since I started writing for young readers in 2000, only three of my thirty stories have been published traditionally. I turned to self-publishing as my only recourse, and then faced the contempt of those who see self-publishing as a mere exercise in vanity. Last year a white woman Facebook "friend" suggested that my decision to self-publish was analogous to Blacks in the civil rights era choosing to dine in their segregated neighborhood instead of integrating Jim Crow lunch counters in the South. In her mind, self-publishing is a cowardly form of surrender; to be truly noble (and, therefore, deserving of publication) I ought to patiently insist upon my right to sit alongside white authors regardless of the hostility, rejection, and disdain I encounter.

Since 2009 I have used my scholarly training to examine white supremacy in the children's literature community where African Americans remain marginalized, representing less than 2 percent of children's book authors published annually. *Publishers Weekly*'s 2014 salary survey revealed that only 1 percent of industry professionals self-identify as African American (89 percent self-identify as white). It's no coincidence that the homogeneity of the publishing workforce matches the homogeneity of published authors and their books. The marginalization of writers of color is the result of very deliberate decisions made by gatekeepers within the children's literature community. These decisions place insurmountable barriers along the path to publication for far too many talented writers of color.

Armed with these facts, I know better than to turn to the publishing industry when I seek justice for Trayvon, Renisha, Jordan, Islan, Ramarley, Aiyana, and Tamir. I know not to hope that industry gatekeepers will publish books for the children of Eric Garner as they struggle to make sense of the murder of their father at the hands of the NYPD. I know that children's literature can help to counter the racially biased thinking that insists Michael Brown was "no angel," but rather "a demon" to be feared and destroyed. I believe there's a direct link between the misrepresentation of Black youth as inherently criminal and the justification given by those who brazenly take their lives. The publishing industry can't solve this problem, but the relative lack of children's books by and about people of color nonetheless functions as a kind of "symbolic annihilation." Despite the fact that the majority of school-age children in the United States are now kids of color, the publishing industry continues to produce books that overwhelmingly feature white children only. The message is clear: the lives of kids of color don't matter.

Many members of the children's literature community clamor for greater diversity but remain silent whenever another Black teenager is shot down. They cling to the fantasy that white supremacy has shaped every US institution *except* the publishing industry. They look at the reality of racial dominance in the field of children's literature and pretend that the innocence ascribed to white children extends equally to Black children. At a moment when 75 percent of whites have no friends of color, the need for diverse children's literature—which can foster cross-cultural understanding at an early age—is greater than ever.

When Jacqueline Woodson won the 2014 National Book Award for her beautifully crafted memoir, *Brown Girl Dreaming*, she was almost immediately assaulted by the white male emcee's racist watermelon joke. Daniel Handler apologized via Twitter and donated $110,000 to the We Need Diverse Books campaign. In a blog post titled "Being a White Guy in Children's Books," *Horn Book* editor Roger Sutton wrote about how sorry he felt for Handler and his impatience "with all the talk of him stealing Her Moment" because Woodson ultimately benefited from "a *way* longer moment than any children's National Book Award winner has ever gotten before." Sutton admitted in a subsequent post that his ideas were "half-baked and clueless," but his confidence in publishing those initial, offensive remarks reminds me that the current children's literature community is, without question, *his* home.

Meanwhile, my search for "living room" continues. Am I hopeful about the future of children's literature? It depends on the day. The fledgling We Need Diverse Books movement appears to be sustaining its momentum and has successfully mobilized thousands of people. Their goals, however, seem incompatible with what Cathy J. Cohen calls "transformational politics": "a politics that does not search for opportunities to integrate into dominant institutions and normative social relationships, but instead pursues a political agenda that seeks to change values, definitions, and laws which make these institutions and relationships oppressive."

In her essay, "How to Uphold White Supremacy by Focusing on Diversity and Inclusion," Kÿra similarly condemns the liberal impulse to position "marginalized groups as naturally needing to assimilate into dominant ones, rather than to undermine said structures of domination." At the recent Day of Diversity held during ALA's Midwinter Convention in Chicago, I once again heard calls for best-selling books that will "prove" to the recalcitrant publishing industry that there is demand for diversity. Yet Kÿra rightly observes that, "When we work for justice and liberation, we can't accept progress that is conditional on being economically beneficial."

As a writer who prioritizes social justice over popularity and/or profit, I find "living room" in alternatives to the existing system. Like racism in police forces across this nation, racism in publishing is cultural and systemic; the problem cannot be solved merely by hiring a few (more) people of color. I am partnering with other artist-activists to develop a model of community-based publishing that uses print-on-demand technology to transfer power from the industry's (mostly white) gatekeepers to those excluded from the publishing process. I am hopeful that public libraries will embrace such a model and assist patrons as they learn to tell their stories, becoming *producers* and not just *consumers* of books.

Public libraries have served as a sanctuary for me since I was a child. I had a library card in this country long before I had a green card. The Brooklyn Public Library sends me into dozens of schools every year, enabling hundreds of working-class kids of color to meet an author who lives in and writes about the magic in *their* community. Most of my thirteen books for young readers aren't part of the library's collection, but perhaps that will change over time. I am hopeful that in the future the bias against self-published books will diminish as gatekeepers realize that it is unfair to punish writers of color for failing at a game that's rigged. Until then, I will continue to self-publish and I will offer my "organic" writing to the members of my community. I will seek out and/or create the safe spaces where my creativity can flourish. I will insist upon my right to breathe.

Literature sources

Alexie, S. (2007), *The Absolutely True Diary of a Part-time Indian*, New York: Little, Brown.

Beaudoin, S. (2012), *The Infects*, Somerville, MA: Candlewick.

Glossary

adaptation theory the study of how texts change when they are conveyed through a new form or medium

aesthetic of or relating to the artfulness of a text and how it appeals to the senses

aetonormativity term coined by Maria Nikolajeva to indicate that adult thinking is the norm against which other perspectives are measured

alliteration the repetition of similar sounds either at the beginning of words or in stressed syllables in close proximity

animal studies interdisciplinary study of the past and present relations between human and nonhuman animals, how these are represented in literature and the ethical implications of such representations; in youth literature, special attention is given to anthropomorphic depiction of animals

annotated edition a text that includes background information, explanatory notes, and critical commentary on the main text

archetypes the original model or pattern on which other examples are copied, but more specifically in literary theory, character types often repeated in the stories of a culture

assonance repetition of similar vowel sounds in close proximity

authoritative edition the most trustworthy and accurate version of a text, supported by documentary evidence and agreed upon by experts in the field

bibliographic criticism study of the series of steps that go into producing a published text, focusing on archival research regarding drafts, sketches, manuscripts, and editorial exchanges that have resulted in the final product

biological determinism the idea that all human behavior is innately determined by genes, brain size, or other biological attributes

broadsides large sheets of paper printed on one side that sometimes contained news, but more often ballads, poems, and woodcut illustrations

chapbooks short, poorly made pamphlets sold by peddlers in Britain, usually for a penny, starting in the sixteenth century

chronotope the interconnectedness of time and space in a work of literature

classic or bourgeois realism a term used to refer to books that, by virtue of presenting their characters and situations as if they were real, encourages readers to accept their **ideological** messages about middle-class values, behaviors, and aspirations as common sense

climactic plot features an originary stasis or exposition, an inciting event, mounting tension, a climactic moment, falling action, and resolution

cognitive poetics (also **cognitive literary theory**) a theoretical framework that seeks to understand our responses to literature through what we know about how the brain perceives and processes language and image

collective unconscious a term coined by psychoanalytic theorist Carl Jung to refer to the unconscious structures, **archetypes**, and images shared by members of a species

comedy (mode) a story that ends with the redemption, restoration, or reintegration of the character into community

concept books informational books organized by concepts, such as opposites, weather, and animal habitats.

conceptual metaphors a comparison wherein one idea or concept is understood in terms of another

concrete poetry poems that depend for their meaning and effects on their typography (visual), phonetic (sonic), or kinetic (movement) form

condensation combining numerous thoughts or meanings into a single symbol or word

consonance repetition of similar consonant sounds in close proximity

contextual concerned with the ideas, events, settings, and language that surround a particular text

cumulative plot the action in a story progresses through a series of repetitions and accumulation

deconstruction a method of literary criticism that posits that all surface meanings are unstable because they rest on the instability of language itself

developmental age a measure of a child's development (physical and psychological) charted in terms of peer norms

didactic (also **didacticism**) specifically or overtly designed to teach something

diegesis the narrating of events, complete with reflection and knowledge of the characters' feelings and motivations

diegetic in film criticism, elements of storytelling that are accounted for from within the world of the story

discourse systematic and extended expression of thought on a subject

dramatic irony when the audience knows more than the character, or knows the character to be wrong

dramatic poetry poems that stage a dialogue between one or more speakers

dynamic character a character who undergoes an arc of development that leads from a state of innocence or immaturity to a state of greater knowledge or maturity

early concept books informational books for very young children that are organized around simple concepts, such as color, body parts, shapes, everyday activities, or items

ecocriticism the study of the relationship between literature and the natural environment

ecosystem a group of interconnected elements formed and reformed through the dynamic interaction between the community and its environment

empirical research a method of gaining knowledge through direct and indirect observation

episodic plot a plot consisting of multiple incidents, each with its own mini-**climatic** structure

essentialism the belief that people belonging to certain categories (such as a particular race or gender) have intrinsic characteristics that are dependent on those categories

expository nonfiction books that explain and describe processes and ideas

eye rhyme two words similar in spelling but pronounced differently

fake realism those books where the plot turns more on wish fulfillment than logical development of character and circumstance

fanfic short for fan fiction, refers to the fiction written by fans of an original work of fiction, featuring the characters and settings from that work but producing alternate plot lines and relationships

fantasy literary **genre** characterized by characters and other **tropes** that depart from consensus reality

feminism a theoretical and activist-oriented paradigm that engages in gender analysis and critique, and advocates for all people's rights to equal dignity and fair treatment in political, social, and economic realms

fidelity criticism focuses on how a text conforms to or departs from its appearance and meanings in its original form; seen by most as a limited and limiting method of conceiving **adaptation theory**

flat characters uncomplicated, one-dimensional characters who do not change over the course of the story

focalizer the perspective through which the action is seen

form the physical way a text is presented, the material means of expression

formalism (also **formalist**) the study of the structural patterns and purposes of a text without considering outside or **contextual** material

full-bleed illustrations that do not have borders, but take up the entire page of a picturebook

gender studies interdisciplinary study that focuses on how gender identity, power, and sexuality are represented and related, in the case of youth literature, through language, image, and story structure

genre the content or subject matter of a text that establishes baseline expectations, rules, or conventions

hornbooks sheets of vellum or paper pasted onto wooden paddles and covered with a thin layer of transparent horn or mica usually containing an alphabet, the Lord's Prayer, common vowel and consonant combinations, and Roman numerals

hue the exact shade of a color

humanism an ideology that focuses on human rather than supernatural matters or forces; believes in the dignity, potential, and evolving goodness of human beings both individually and collectively, and focuses on rational solutions to human problems

ideology (also **ideological**) a set of conscious and unconscious ideas, beliefs, and values of an individual, a class, or a culture

implied author the character or qualities that the reader attributes to the author of a text based on the way the book is written

implied reader the reader the author seems to believe would have the skills and dispositions to understand and appreciate the text

in medias res a storytelling convention that means to start in the middle of the action

infant-directed speech spoken language used by adult when speaking to babies, characterized by heightened emotional inflection; slower, simpler utterances; exaggerated vowel sounds; and higher pitch

informational texts convey facts about the natural and social world

intersectionality the acknowledgment that race, ethnicity, class, embodiment, gender, and sexual orientation combine to create complex social identities that result in multiple forms of discrimination and oppression

intertextuality the practice of evoking or alluding to one text within another

irony the use of words to mean or imply the opposite of what they say

lyric poetry poems characterized by musicality and expression of personal emotion

magical realism may more properly be understood as a type of fantasy, because it does contain fantastic or magical elements; however, these elements intrude into an otherwise realistic setting, and are treated with a realistic tone.

Marxism a set of political and economic ideas developed by Karl Marx and Friedrich Engels that focuses on class struggle and the ways in which people's material circumstances affect their ideological positions

mental model an internal representation of external reality

metafictive works that call attention to the fact that they are constructed or fictional

metanarrative an expression of an implicit ideology or set of assumptions that legitimate a cultural practice or belief

metaphor direct comparison of one thing to another based on similar attributes

meter pattern of stressed and unstressed syllables in a line of poetry

metonymy a word or phrase that stands in for another word that is closely related to it

mimesis consistency between the real world and the world of the text, or how closely a book imitates the real world

mode the attitude of approach to the subject matter

modernism many definitions apply here, but the relevant usage in this book refers to the optimistic belief that human beings can create, improve, and reshape their inner and external worlds through scientific knowledge, experimentation, and productive introspection

motifs recurring themes, elements or ideas in literary works

multiliteracies attention to the verbal, auditory, visual, gestural, spatial, and tactile ways we have of creating and conveying meaning

multimodal employing different sensory inputs and outputs, including visual, aural, gestural, and tactile activities and expressions

multimodal discourse analysis (MDA) an approach to texts that focus on how meanings are made through the use of many modes of communication instead of just language

narrative poetry poems that tell stories

narrative nonfiction nonfiction that presents its subject as a story

narrative theory (also **narratology**) attends to how people make sense of and use stories as well as how stories represent and structure experience

new historicism places a literary text in its historical contexts, including the ideologies of the time as well as the material conditions under which the book was written and disseminated

new realism a name given to youth literature beginning in the 1960s that explores aspects of human experience that were formerly considered social taboos.

non-diegetic in film criticism, an element of storytelling that comes from outside the story space

one-book fallacy the idea that one book that depicts the experiences of a character is representative of all similar characters from that socioeconomic or cultural group

onomatopoeia words that imitate the natural sounds of a thing

opening an alternative to considering picturebooks by individual pages, this refers to the entire book laid flat to see both pages at the same time

pantomime a theatrical entertainment that involves music and comedy, often based on a fairy tale or other familiar story

peer-reviewed scholarship scholarly articles checked by experts in the field for accuracy and validity

performance theory a method that draws attention to and analyzes the fact that we are always enacting roles or playing parts in a larger cultural drama that in many respects scripts or determines the forms and limits of our actions; also emphasizes how our actions can be performed in resistance to social prescribed roles

peritext images and text that surround the main body of a work, such as introductions, prefaces, author and illustrator notes, and endpapers

personification when a thing, idea, or animal is given human attributes

postcolonialism examines the legacy and effect of colonial exploitation on indigenous peoples, their lands, and their arts

postfeminism can refer to either a rejection or transcendence of the **feminist** movements of the 1970s and 1980s; the rejection model sees the earlier claims of the women's movement as largely irrelevant or no longer worth supporting, while the transcendence view argues that gender binaries and roles themselves are no longer sufficiently definitional in any argument for personal or collective empowerment

posthumanism multiple definitions apply here, including (1) a critique of traditional ideas about the centrality and superiority of humans; (2) an expansion of moral concerns and subjectivities in the service of ethical treatment of animals and other nonhuman forms; (3) a way of conceiving what life will be like when cyber technologies are more fully incorporated into the human experience of embodiment

postmemory the transmission of memory from one generation to another, especially of personal, collective, and cultural trauma

postmodernism a rejection of grand narratives and theories that suggest the possibility of the certainty of knowledge and human progress; emphasizes interpretation, relativity, fragmentation, contradiction, and individual truth

poststructuralism a variation on structural approaches that critique them for being too tidy and for attempting to totalize meaning, emphasizing instead the instability of structures and the plurality of meanings across cultures and histories

primary source in nonfiction, an artifact or document that was written, created, or used during the time and/or by the person under study; in literary study, a **primary source** is a work of literature

prosumers amateurs who produce rather just consume high-quality content for distribution through social media

protagonist the main character of a story, usually but not always the "good guy"

psychoanalytic criticism though this type of criticism uses different vocabularies depending on the school of thought it is based on (such as Sigmund Freud, Carl Jung, Melanie Klein, etc.), the focus is on the elements of a text that mirror or illuminate processes and structures of the human psyche

psychological realism characterized by close attention to the inner thoughts and motivations of a character or characters

queer theory broadly speaking, this paradigm seeks to expose the **social construction** and imposed rigidity of norms of behavior by focusing on how sex, gender, and desire are fluid, unstable, and capable of many different constellations

reader response criticism focuses on the reader's experience of a text, arguing that a text has no inherent meanings, but only becomes meaningful when a reader experiences and interprets it

realism a way of writing about things that did not actually happen as if they did or could have happened in the consensus reality that we inhabit

recto in an **opening** of a picturebook, the page on the right

rhetorical criticism focuses on the ways the delivery of a message produces effects on its audiences; includes attention to words, phrases, images, gestures, **forms**, and the **contexts** of a text's delivery

Robinsonades a literary genre derived from Daniel Defoe's *Robinson Crusoe* (1719); survival stories often but not always featuring a desert island setting

romance (genre) depending on context, this can refer to a medieval tale based on legend, chivalric love and adventure, or the supernatural or a love story especially in the form of a novel

romance (mode) a prose narrative wherein the characters are better, more powerful, or more heroic than the average person

round characters characters who demonstrate multiple traits and facets and undergo development over the course of the story

Rule of Three writing or storytelling principle that features a series of three parts; used for emphasis, memorization, or the establishment of a pattern with the first two elements that is broken by the third to create a surprise or resolution

saturation the level of intensity of a color; fully saturated means that a color is at its most opaque and pure

schema a pattern of thought or behavior that organizes categories of information and the relationships among them

scripts mental representations of the basic actions needed to complete a more complex action that is common to daily experience

semiotics the study of the signs and symbols of human communication

signifiers sonic or visual images or words, whether spoken or written, that refer to mental concepts

social constructivism (also **social construction, social constructivist**) the belief that children are products of their environment

social realism critiques social structures and conditions that negatively affect groups, such as poverty, racism, and other forms of prejudice.

Socialist Realism instituted by Joseph Stalin in 1934. Utopian in spirit, it glorified the goals of the Communist Party to create a new society based on the elevation of the common worker

speech act theory originated by J. L. Austin and developed by John Searle and others; analyzes the levels of actions that utterances perform; useful in understanding the conditions necessary for speech to have effects and make changes in the way we perceive the world

structuralism a theoretical paradigm that focuses on the patterns and relationships between elements in a system that remain similar despite surface variety

synecdoche to refer to a whole thing by a word for one of its parts

synesthetic metaphors a comparison that relies on the crossing of two sensory domains

textuality (also **textual**) concerned with what is actually on the page or screen

textual criticism like **formalism**, this method of interpretation starts by analyzing the patterns and purposes of the work itself rather than bringing in outside information

theoretical paradigms sometimes called critical lenses, these are extended, systematic, and particularized ways of conceiving how a text works or what is important about a text from a specific **ideological** perspective; examples include **feminism, Marxism, ecocriticism**, etc.

theory an overarching system of ideas or a model that serves to explain a group of things

Theory of Mind (ToM) the ability to ascribe motives, beliefs, and intentions, including ones that differ from their own, to other people

tone the quality of a color that has been mixed with white, black, or gray

trade books books by commercial publishers intended for a general readership

transmediation the process of translating a work into a different medium

trauma theory attends to the experience and artistic representation of both personal and cultural traumas

tropes a commonly recurring convention or pattern

unreliable narrator a narrator whose credibility has been compromised

vectors in **MDA**, these are visible and invisible lines that show relationships between figures; this term is problematic, however, in that it refers to something completely different in computer-generated art, which is an increasingly significant method in picturebook illustrations

verisimilitude the maintenance of an illusion of truth in a work through consistency *within* the world the author has constructed rather than consistency *between* the real world and the world of the text

verse writing characterized by a specific pattern of metrical lines

verso in an **opening** of a picturebook, the page on the left

Academic References

Abrams, Meyer Howard (1953), *The Mirror and the Lamp: Romantic Theory and the Critical Tradition*, New York: Oxford University Press.

Adelson, Rachel (2005), "Hues and Views," http://www.apa.org/monitor/feb05/hues.aspx [accessed October 28, 2016].

Agosto, Denise (1999), "One and Inseparable: Interdependent Storytelling in Picture Storybooks," *Children's Literature in Education* 30: 267–80.

Allen, Cherie (2012), *Playing with Picturebooks: Postmodernism and the Postmodernesque*, Houndsmill: Palgrave Macmillan.

American Academy of Pediatrics (2016), "Media and Children," https://www.aap.org/en-us/advocacy-and-policy/aap-health-initiatives/pages/media-and-children.aspx [accessed October 28, 2016].

Ariès, Phillipe (1962), *Centuries of Childhood: A Social History of Family Life*, translated by R. Baldick, New York: Random House [Original work published in French, 1960].

Arizpe, Evelyn, Colomer, Teresa, and Martínez-Roldán, Carmen (2014), *Visual Journeys through Wordless Narratives: An International Inquiry with Immigrant Children and The Arrival*, London: Bloomsbury.

Arizpe, Evelyn and Styles, Morag (2003), *Children Reading Pictures: Interpreting Visual Texts*, London: Routledge.

Attebery, Brian (1992), *Strategies of Fantasy*, Bloomington and Indianapolis, IN: Indiana University Press.

Attebery, Brian (2014), *Stories about Stories: Fantasy and the Remaking of Myth*, Oxford: Oxford University Press.

Austin, John L. (1962), *How to Do Things with Words*, Cambridge, MA: Harvard University Press.

Bacon, Betty, ed. (1988), *How Much Truth Do We Tell the Children?: The Politics of Children's Literature*, Minneapolis, MN: MEP Publications.

Bader, Barbara (1976), *American Picture Books from Noah's Ark to the Beast Within*, New York: Macmillan.

Baillargeon, Renee and DeVos, Julie (1991), "Object Permanence in Young Infants: Further Evidence," *Child Development* 62, no. 6: 1227–46.

Bakhtin, Mikhail (1968), *Rabelais and His World*, Boston, MA: MIT Press.

Bakhtin, Mikhail (1981), *The Dialogic Imagination: Four Essays*, Austin, TX: University of Texas Press.

Ball, David (1983), *Backwards & Forwards: A Technical Manual for Reading Plays*, Carbondale: Southern Illinois Press.

Bang, Molly (1991), *Picture This: How Pictures Work*, San Francisco: Chronicle.

Barthes, Roland (1977), *Image—Music—Text*, Essays sel. and translated by Stephen Heath, New York: Hill and Wang.

Beckett, Sandra (2012), *Crossover Picturebooks: A Genre for All Ages*, New York: Routledge.

Bell, Elizabeth, Haas, Lynda, and Sells, Laura (1995), *From Mouse to Mermaid: The Politics of Film, Gender, and Culture*, Bloomington, IN: Indiana University Press.

Belsey, Catherine (1980), *Critical Practice*, London: Methuen.

Bickerton, Derek (1981), *Roots of Language*, Ann Arbor, MI: Karoma Publishers.

Bishop, Rudine Sims (1990), "Mirrors, Windows, and Sliding Glass Doors," *Perspectives* 6, no. 3: ix–xi.

Bissel Brown, Victoria (1999), *Twenty Years at Hull House with Autobiographical Notes by Jane Addams*, Boston, MA: Bedford/St. Martin's.

Bloom, Harold (1982), *Agon: Towards a Theory of Revisionism*, Oxford: Oxford University Press.

Bloom, Paul (2013), *Just Babies: The Origins of Good and Evil*, New York: Court.

Bond, Douglas (2013), *The Poetic Wonder of Isaac Watts*, Sanford, FL: Reformation Turst Publishing.

Booker, Christopher (2004), *The Seven Basic Plots: Why We Tell Stories*, London: Bloomsbury Academic.

Bottigheimer, Ruth B. (1996), "Fairy Tales and Folk-tales," in *International Companion Encyclopedia of Children's Literature*, edited by Peter Hunt, New York and London: Routledge, 152–65.

Bourdieu, Pierre (1991), *Language and Symbolic Power*, Cambridge, MA: Harvard University Press.

Boyd, Brian (2009), *On the Origin of Stories: Evolution, Cognition, and Fiction*, Cambridge, MA: Harvard University Press.

Brown, Noel and Babington, Bruce (2015), *Family Films in Global Cinema: The World Before Disney*, London: I. B. Tauris.

Bruchac, Joseph (2011), "Point of Departure," in *Handbook of Research on Children's and Young Adult Literature*, edited by S. A. Wolf, K. Coats, P. Enciso, and C. A. Jenkins, New York: Routledge, 342–44.

Bruner, Jerome (1983), *Child's Talk: Learning to Use Language*, New York: W. W. Norton & Company.

Burke, Michael (2012), *Literary Reading, Cognition and Emotion: An Exploration of the Oceanic Mind*, New York and London: Routledge.

Burroway, Janet (2003), *Writing Fiction: A Guide to Narrative Craft*, New York: Longman.

Butler, Catherine (2012), "Modern Children's Fantasy," in *The Cambridge Companion to Fantasy Literature*, edited by Edward James and Farah Mendlesohn, Cambridge: Cambridge University Press, 224–35.

Cadden, Mike (2000), "The Irony of Narration in the Young Adult Novel," *Children's Literature Association Quarterly* 25, no. 3: 146–54.

Cadden, Mike (2011), "Genre as Nexus: The Novel for Children and Young Adults," in *Handbook of Research on Children's and Young Adult Literature*, edited by S. A. Wolf, K. Coats, P. Enciso, and C. A. Jenkins, New York: Routledge, 302–13.

Cadden, Mike (2014), "'But You Are Still a Monkey'; *American Born Chinese* and Racial Self-Accceptance," *The Looking Glass* 17, no. 2: n.p. http://www.lib.latrobe.edu.au/ojs/index.php/tlg/article/view/477/427 [accessed August 18, 2014].

Campbell, Joseph (1949), *The Hero with a Thousand Faces*, New York: Pantheon.

Capshaw, Katherine (2014a), *Civil Rights Childhood: Picturing Liberation in African American Photobooks*, Minneapolis: University of Minnesota Press.

Capshaw, Katherine (2014b), "Ethnic Studies and Children's Literature: A Conversation Between Fields," Francelia Butler Lecture, Children's Literature Association Conference, June 21, 2014.

Carpenter, Humphrey (1985), *Secret Gardens: The Golden Age of Children's Literature*, London: Allen & Unwin.

Cart, Michael (1996), *From Romance to Realism*, New York: HarperCollins.

Chambers, Nancy, ed. (2009), *Poetry for Children: The Signal Award 1979-2001*, South Woodchester: The Thimble Press.

Chatman, Seymour (1978), *Story and Discourse: Narrative Structure in Fiction and Film*, Ithaca, NY: Cornell University Press.

Chukovsky, Kornei (1965), *From Two to Five*, translated by Miriam Morton, Berkeley, CA: University of California Press.

Coats, Karen (2007) "Between Horror, Humour, and Hope: Neil Gaiman and the Psychic Work of the Gothic," in *The Gothic in Children's Literature: Haunting the Borders*, edited by Anna Jackson, Karen Coats, and Roderick McGillis, New York: Routledge, 77–92. Print.

Coats, Karen (2013), "The Meaning of Children's Poetry: A Cognitive Approach," *International Research in Children's Literature* 6, no. 2: 127–42.

Collins, Fiona M. and Ridgman, Jeremy (2006), *Turning the Page: Children's Literature in Performance and the Media*, Oxford: Peter Lang.

Crago, Hugh (2014), *Entranced by Story: Brain, Tale, and Teller, from Infancy to Old Age*, New York and London: Routledge.

Crain, Patricia (2000), *The Story of A: The Alphabetization of America from* The New England Primer *to* The Scarlet Letter, Stanford: Stanford University Press.

Crews, Frederick (1963), *The Pooh Perplex: A Freshman Casebook*, New York: Dutton.

Crews, Frederick (2001), *Postmodern Pooh*, New York: Farrar, Straus & Giroux.

Crisp, Thomas and Hiller, Brittany (2011), "Telling Tales about Gender: A Critical Analysis of Caldecott Medal-Winning Picturebooks, 1938-2011," *Journal of Children's Literature* 37, no. 2: 18–29.

Cunningham, Hugh (2014), *Children and Childhood in Western Society since 1500*, 2nd ed., London and New York: Routledge [Original work published in 1995].

Cysarz, Dirk, von Bonin, Dietrich, Lackner, Helmut, Heusser, Peter, Moser, Maximilian, and Betterman, Henrik (2004), "Oscillations of Heart Rate and Respiration Synchronize During Poetry Recitation," *American Journal of Physiology: Heart and Circulatory Physiology* 287: 579–87.

Damasio, Antonio (1999), *The Feeling of What Happens: Body and Emotion in the Making of Consciousness*, Orlando, FL: Mariner.

Darwin, Charles (1859), *On the Origin of Species*, London: John Murray.

Descartes, Rene (2007) "Meditations on First Philosophy," http://www.earlymoderntexts.com/assets/pdfs/descartes1641.pdf [accessed October 28, 2016] [first published 1647].

DeCaspar, Anthony J. and Fifer, William P. (1980), "Of Human Bonding: Newborns Prefer their Mothers' Voices," *Science* 208:1174–76.

Dissanayake, Ellen (2009), "Root, Leaf, Blossom, or Bole: Concerning the Origin and Adaptive Function of Music," in *Communicative Musicality: Exploring the Basis of Human Companionship*, edited by S. Malloch and C. Trevarthen, Oxford: Oxford University Press, 17–30.

Dobrin, Sidney I. and Kidd, Kenneth B. (2004), *Wild Things: Children's Culture and Ecocriticism*, Detroit: Wayne State University Press.

Doonan, Jane (1992), *Looking at Pictures in Picture Books*, Exeter, UK: Thimble Press.

Dorson, Richard (1950), "Folklore and Fakelore," *American Mercury* 70: 335–43.

Dorson, Richard (1976), *Folklore and Fakelore: Essays Toward a Discipline of Folk Studies*, Cambridge, MA: Harvard University Press.

Dresang, Eliza (1999), *Radical Change: Books for Youth in a Digital Age*, New York: H. W. Wilson Co.

Du Gay, Paul (1997), "Introduction," in *Doing Cultural Studies: The Story of the Sony Walkman*, edited by P. du Gay, S. Hall, L. Janes, H. Mackay, and K. Negus, London: Sage, 1–5.

Dundes, Alan, ed. (1984), *Sacred Narrative: Readings in the Theory of Myth*, Oakland: University of California Press.

DuPlessis, Rachel Blau (1997), "The Blazes of Poetry: Remarks on Segmentivity and Seriality with Special References to Blaser and Oppen," *Boxkite: A Journal of Poetry & Poetics* 1: 35–50.

Dusinberre, Juliet (1987), *Alice to the Lighthouse: Children's Books and Radical Experiments in Art*, Basingstoke: Macmillan.

Eccleshare, Julia (March 5, 2015), "Mal Peet obituary," http://www.theguardian.com/books/2015/mar/05/mal-peet [accessed October 28, 2016].

Egan, Kieran (1990), *Romantic Understanding: The Development of Rationality and Imagination, Ages 8-15*, New York: Routledge.

Egan, Kieran (1997), *The Educated Mind: How Cognitive Tools Shape our Understanding*, Chicago: University of Chicago Press.

Egan, Kieran (n.d.), "Fantasy and Reality in Children's Stories," https://www.sfu.ca/~egan/FantasyReality.html [accessed October 28, 2016].

Ehrlich, Hannah (2015), "The Diversity Gap in Children's Publishing, 2015," http://blog.leeandlow.com/2015/03/05/the-diversity-gap-in-childrens-publishing-2015/ [accessed September 08, 2016].

Eliot, Lise (1999), *What's Going On in There? How the Brain and Mind Develop in the First Five Years of Life*, New York: Bantam Books.

Elliot, Amy (2015), "Power in our Words: Finding Community and Mitigating Trauma in James Dashner's *The Maze Runner*," *Children's Literature Association Quarterly* 40, no. 2: 179–99.

Erikson, Erik (1950), *Childhood and Society*, New York: Norton.

Evans, Janet (2009), *Talking Beyond the Page: Reading and Responding to Picture Books*, New York: Routledge.

Fine, Anne (March 29, 2003), "Filth, which ever way you look at it," http://www.theguardian.com/books/2003/mar/29/featuresreviews.guardianreview24 [accessed October 28, 2016].

Fish, Stanley (1973), "How Ordinary is Ordinary Language?" *New Literary History* 5, no. 1: 41–54.

Forster, Edward M. (1954), *Aspects of the Novel*, New York: Harcourt.

Foucault, Michel (1969/1977), "What is an Author?" in *Language, Counter-Memory, Practice*, edited by Donald F. Bouchard, Ithaca, NY: Cornell University Press, 124–27.

Fraustino, Lisa Rowe (2014), "The Rights and Wrongs of Anthropomorphism in Picture Books," in *Ethics and Children's Literature*, edited by Claudia Mills, Surrey: Ashgate, 145–62.

Freud, Sigmund (2001), "Introductory Lectures in Psychoanalysis," *Standard Edition*, vol. 15 [Originally published in 1915].

Friedman, Alan (1966), *The Turn of the Novel*, New York: Oxford University Press.

Friedman, Norman (1955), "Forms of the Plot," *Journal of General Education* 8: 241–53.

Furay, Conal and Salevouris, Michael J. (1988), *Methods and Skills of History: A Practical Guide*, Oxford: Wiley-Blackwell.

Gee, James Paul (2003), "What Video Games Have to Teach Us About Learning and Literacy," *ACM Computers in Entertainment* 1, no. 1: 20.

Gerbner, George (1972), "Violence and Television Drama: Trends and Symbolic Functions," in *Television and Social Behavior, Vol 1: Content and Control*, edited by G. A. Comstock and E. Reubenstein, Washington, DC: U.S. Government Printing Office, 28–187.

Gilbert, Sandra and Gubar, Susan (1979), *The Madwoman in the Attic: The Woman Writer and the Nineteenth-Century Literary Imagination*, New Haven, CT: Yale University Press.

Girard, René (1981), "Comedies of Errors: Plautus—Shakespeare—Molière," in *American Criticism in the Poststructuralist Age*, edited by Ira Konigsburg, Ann Arbor: University of Michigan Press, 66–86.

Giustiniani, Vito (1985), "Homo, Humanus, and the Meanings of Humanism," *Journal of History of Ideas* 46, no. 2: 167–95.

Goldberg, Moses (1974), *Children's Theatre: A Philosophy and a Method*, Englewood Cliffs, NJ: Prentice-Hall.

Goldsen, Rose Kohn (1977), *The Show and Tell Machine: How Television Works and Works You Over*, New York: Dial.

Gooderham, David (1995), "Children's Fantasy Literature: Toward an Anatomy," *Children's Literature in Education* 26, no. 3: 171–83.

Gopnik, Alison (2009), *The Philosophical Baby: What Children's Minds Tell Us about Truth, Love, and the Meaning of Life*, New York: Farrar, Straus and Giroux.

Gottschall, Jonathan (2012), *The Storytelling Animal: How Stories Make Us Human*, Boston: Houghton Mifflin.

Graham, Ruth (2014), "Against YA," *Slate*, http://www.slate.com/articles/arts/books/2014/06/against_ya_adults_should_be_embarrassed_to_read_children_s_books.html [accessed October 28, 2016].

Grenby, Matthew O. (2009), "The Origins of Children's Literature," in *The Cambridge Companion to Children's Literature*, edited by M. O. Grenby and Andrea Immel, Cambridge, UK: Cambridge University Press, 3–18.

Gubar, Marah (2009), *Artful Dodgers: Reconceiving the Golden Age of Literature*, Oxford: Oxford University Press.

Gubar, Marah (2013), "Risky Business: Talking about Children in Children's Literature," *Children's Literature Association Quarterly* 38, no. 4: 450–54.

Guijarro, Arsenio Jesus, Moy (2014), *A Multimodal Analysis of Picture Books for Children: A Systemic Functional Approach*, Sheffield, UK: Equinox.

Guthrie, R. Dale (2005), *The Nature of Paleolithic Art*, Chicago: University of Chicago Press.

Hall, G. Stanley (1904), *Adolescence: Its Psychology, Anthropology, Sociology, Sex, Crime, and Religion*, New York: D. Appleton.

Harris, Thomas J. (1989), *Children's Live-Action Musical Films: A Critical Survey and Filmography*, Jefferson, NC: McFarland.

Hearne, Betsy (August 1993), "Respect the Source: Reducing Cultural Chaos in Picture Books, Part Two," *School Library Journal* 39, no. 8, 33–37.

Heeks, Peggy (1996), "Information Books," in *International Companion Encyclopedia of Children's Literature*, edited by P. Hunt, London: Routledge, 433–42.

Henderson, Laretta (2005), "The Black Arts Movement and African American Young Adult Literature: An Evaluation of Narrative Style," *Children's Literature in Education* 36, no. 4: 299–323.

Hesse, Doug and Bradway, Becky (2009), Creating Nonfiction: A Guide and Anthology, Boston: Bedford/St. Martin's.

Hewins, Caroline M. (1888), "The History of Children's Books," *The Atlantic*, http://www.theatlantic.com/magazine/archive/1888/01/the-history-of-childrens-books/306098/ [accessed August 18, 2014].

Hidi, Suzanne and Baird, William (1986), "Interestingness—A Neglected Variable in Discourse Processing," *Cognitive Science* 10, no. 2: 179–94.

Hogan, Patrick Colm (2003), *The Mind and Its Stories: Narrative Universals and Human Emotions*, Cambridge: Cambridge University Press.

Hollindale, Peter (1988), *Ideology and the Children's Book*, Stroud: Thimble Press.

Hollindale, Peter (1996), "Drama," in *International Companion Encyclopedia of Children's Literature*, edited by Peter Hunt, New York: Routledge, 206–19.

Howarth, Michael (2014), *Under the Bed, Creeping: Psychoanalyzing the Gothic in Children's Literature*, Jefferson, NC: McFarland.

Horning, Kathleen T. (2013), "I See White People," http://ccblogc.blogspot.com/2013/07/i-see-white-people.html [accessed October 28, 2016].

Hume, Kathryn (1984), *Fantasy and Mimesis: Response to Reality in Western Literature*, New York: Routledge.

Irwin, William R. (1976), *The Game of the Impossible: A Rhetoric of Fantasy*, Urbana, IL: University of Illinois Press.

Jackson, Kathy Merlock (1986), *Images of the Child in American Film: A Sociocultural Analysis*, Metuchen, NJ: Scarecrow Press.

James, Edward and Mendlesohn, Farah, eds. (2012), *The Cambridge Companion to Fantasy Literature*, Cambridge: Cambridge University Press.

James, William (1890), *Principles of Psychology*, New York: Henry Holt.

Karp, Harvey (2003), *The Happiest Baby on the Block*, New York: Bantam.

Katz, Phyllis A. (2003), "Racists or Tolerant Multiculturalists," *American Psychologist* 58, no. 11: 897–909.

Keen, Suzanne (2007), *Empathy and the Novel*, Cambridge, MA: Oxford University Press.

Keep, Austin Baker (1908), History of the New York society library, with an introductory chapter on libraries in colonial New York, 1698–1776, Printed for the Trustees by the De Vinne Press.

Kelly, David J., Quinn, Paul C., Slater, Alan M., Lee, Kang, Liezhong, Ge, and Pascalis, Olivier (2007), "The Other-Race Effect Develops During Infancy: Evidence of Perception Narrowing," *Psychological Science* 18, no. 12: 1084–89.

Kiefer, Barbara (2011), "What is a Picturebook? Across the Borders of History," *New Review of Children's Literature and Librarianship* 17: 86–102.

Knight, Karenanne (2014), *The Picture Book Maker: The Art of the Children's Picture Book Writer and Illustrator*, London: Institute of Education Press.

Kohlberg, Lawrence (1984), *The Psychology of Moral Development: The Nature and Validity of Moral Stages*, New York: Harper & Row.

Kolata, Gina B. (1984), "Studying Learning in the Womb," *Science* 225: 302–03.

Kress, Gunther and van Leeuwen, Theo (2006), *Reading Images: The Grammar of Visual Design*, New York: Routledge.

Kristeva, Julia (1980), *Desire in Language*, New York: Columbia University Press.

Kümmerling-Meibauer, Bettina, ed. (2011), *Emergent Literacy: Children's Books from 0 to 3*, Amsterdam, John Benjamins.

Kümmerling-Meibauer, Bettina, and Meibauer, Jörg (2011), "On the Strangeness of Pop Art Picturebooks: Pictures, Texts, Paratexts," *New Review of Children's Librarianship* 17, no. 2: 103–21. Reprinted in E. Arizpe, M. Farrell, and J. McAdam (2013), Picturebooks: Beyond the Borders of Art, Narrative and Culture, New York: Routledge, 23–41.

Lacan, Jacques (1988), The Seminar of Jacques Lacan Book I: Freud's Papers on Technique, 1953-1954, translated by J. Forrester, New York: Norton.

Lacan, Jacques (2006), "The Mirror Stage as Formative of the *I* Function as Revealed in Psychoanalytic Experience," in *Ecrits*, translated by B. Fink, New York: W. W. Norton & Co [Original work published in French in 1966].

Lakoff, George and Johnson, Mark (1980), *Metaphors We Live By*, Chicago: University of Chicago Press.

Larrick, Nancy (September 11, 1965), "The All-White World of Children's Books," *The Saturday Review*, 63–65.

Le Guin, Ursula K. (1989), "Why are Americans Afraid of Dragons?" in *The Language of the Night: Essays on Fantasy and Science Fiction*, Edited and with introduction by Susan Wood, New York: Harper Perennial, 34–40.

Leitch, Tom (2003), "Twelve Fallacies in Contemporary Adaptation Theory," *Criticism* 45, no. 2: 149–71.

Lerer, Seth (2008), *Children's Literature: A Reader's History from Aesop to Harry Potter*, Chicago, IL: University of Chicago Press.

Lesnik-Oberstein, Karin (1994), *Children's Literature: Criticism and the Fictional Child*, Oxford: Oxford University Press.

Levitin, Daniel J. (2008), *The World in Six Songs: How the Musical Brain Created Human Nature*, New York: Dutton.

Levy, Jonathan (1992), *The Gymnasium of the Imagination: A Collection of Children's Plays in English 1780-1860*, Westport, CT: Greenwood Press.

Lewis, C. S. (1966), "On Three Ways of Writing for Children," in *Of Other Worlds: Essays and Stories*, edited by Walter Hooper, San Diego: Harcourt Brace Jovanovich, 22–34.

Lewis, David (2001), *Reading Contemporary Picturebooks: Picturing Text*, London and New York: Routledge.

Livingston, Myra Cohn (1984), *The Child as Poet: Myth or Reality?* Boston, MA: Horn Book.

Lyotard, Francois (1984), *The Postmodern Condition: A Report on Knowledge*, Minneapolis: University of Minnesota Press [Originally published in 1979].

MacCann, Donnarae (1969), "Wells of Fancy," in *Only Connect*, edited by Sheila Egoff, G. T. Stubbs and L. F. Ashley, Toronto: Oxford University Press, 133–49.

Mackay, Constance D'Arcy (1918), *Patriotic Drama in Your Town: A Manual of Suggestions*, New York: Holt.

Mackey, Margaret (2007), *Literacies Across Media: Playing the Text*, New York: Routledge.

Mackey, Margaret (2011), *Narrative Pleasures in Young Adult Novels, Films and Video Games*, London: Palgrave Macmillan.

Mackey, Margaret (2011a), "Spinning Off: Toys, Television, Tie-ins, and Technology," in *Handbook of Research on Children's and Young Adult Literature*, edited by Shelby A. Wolf, Karen Coats, Patricia Enciso, and Christine A. Jenkins, New York: Routledge, 495–507.

Malloch, Steven and Trevarthen, Colwyn (2009), *Communicative Musicality: Exploring the Basis of Human Companionship*, Oxford, UK: Oxford University Press.

Marcus, Leonard (2012), *Show Me a Story!: Why Picture Books Matter: Conversations with 21 of the World's Most Celbrated Illustrators*, Somerville, MA: Candlewick.

Martin, Carol Lynn and Ruble, Diane (2004), "Children's Search for Gender Cues: Cognitive Perspectives on Gender Development," *Current Directions on Psychological Science* 13, no. 2, 67–70.

Martin, Michelle H. (2004), *Brown Gold: Milestones of African-American Children's Picture Books, 1845-2002*, New York and London: Routledge.

Mazokopaki, Katerina and Kugiumutzakis, Giannis (2009), "Infant Rhythms: Expressions of Musical Companionship," in *Communicative Musicality: Exploring the Basis of Human Companionship*, edited by Colwyn Trevarthen and Steven Malloch, Oxford UK:, Oxford University Press.185–208.

McCabe, Janice. Fairchild, Emily. Grauerholz, Liz. Pescosolido, Benice A., and Tope, Daniel (2011), "Gender in Twentieth Century Children's Books: Patterns of Disparity in Titles and Central Characters," *Gender and Society* 25, no. 2: 197–226.

McCloud, Scott (1994), *Understanding Comics: The Invisible Art*, New York: HarperPerennial.

McGavran, Jr., James Holt (1991), *Romanticism and Children's Literature in Nineteenth-Century England*, Athens, GA: University of Georgia Pres.

McKay, Sinclair (2009), "Horrible Histories." *The Telegraph*. http://www.telegraph.co.uk/culture/books/6120942/Horrible-Histories.html [accessed October 28, 2016].

Mendlesohn, Farah (2008), *Rhetorics of Fantasy*, Middletown, CT: Wesleyan University Press.

Miall, David S. (2006), *Literary Reading: Empirical and Theoretical Studies*, Bern, Switzerland: Peter Lang.

Miall, David S. and Dissanayake, Ellen (2003), "The Poetics of Babytalk," *Human Nature*, 14, no. 4: 337–64.

Moebius, William (1986), "Introduction to Picturebook Codes," *Word and Image* 2: 141–58.

Murdock, Maureen (1990), *The Heroine's Journey*, Boston, MA: Shambahala.

Neighbors, R. C., and Rankin, Sandy (2011), *The Galaxy is Rated G: Essays of Children's Sciene Fiction Film and Television*, Jefferson, NC: McFarland.

Nel, Phil (2003), *Dr. Seuss: American Icon*, New York: Continuum.

Nel, Phil (2012), *Crockett Johnson and Ruth Krauss: How an Unlikely Couple Found Love, Dodged the FBI, and Transformed Children's Literature*, Jackson, MS: University Press of Mississippi.

Nelson, Victoria (2012), *Gothicka*, Cambridge, MA: Harvard University Press.

New London Group (NLG), (1996), "A Pedagogy of Multiliteracies: Designing Social Futures," *Harvard Educational Review* 66, no. 1: 66–92.

Ngai, Sianne (2012), *Our Aesthetic Categories: Zany, Cute, Interesting*, Cambridge, MA: Harvard University Press.

Nikolajeva, Maria (1988), *The Magic Code: The Use of Magical Patterns in Fantasy for Children*, Göteborg: Almquist & Wiksell International.

Nikolajeva, Maria (1996), *Children's Literature Comes of Age: Toward a New Aesthetic*, New York: Garland.

Nikolajeva, Maria (2002), *The Rhetoric of Character in Children's Literature*, Lanham, MD: Scarecrow Press.

Nikolajeva, Maria (2010), *Power, Voice and Subjectivity in Literature for Young Readers*, New York and London: Routledge.

Nikolajeva, Maria (2012), "The Development of Children's Fantasy," in *The Cambridge Companion to Fantasy Literature*, edited by Edward James and Farah Mendlesohn, Cambridge: Cambridge University Press, 50–61.

Nikolajeva, Maria and Scott, Carole (2001), *How Picturebooks Work*, New York: Garland.

Nodelman, Perry (1988), *Words About Pictures*, Athens, GA: University of Georgia Press.

Nodelman, Perry (June 1990), "History as Fiction: The Story in Hendrik Willem van Loon's Story of Mankind," *The Lion and the Unicorn* 14, no. 1: 70–86.

Nodelman, Perry (1992), *The Pleasures of Children's Literature*, New York: Longman.

Nodelman, Perry (2008), *The Hidden Adult: Defining Children's Literature*, Baltimore: Johns Hopkins University Press.

Nodelman, Perry and Reimer, Mavis (2003), *The Pleasures of Children's Literature*, 3rd ed., London: Pearson.

Oatley, Keith (2011), *Such Stuff as Dreams: The Psychology of Fiction*, West Sussex: Wiley-Blackwell.

Oatley, Keith (2012), *The Passionate Muse: Exploring Emotion in Stories*, Oxford: Oxford University Press.

Obesa, Dionne (2014), "Science Fiction and Fantasy 2014: How Multicultural is Your Multiverse?" http://www.publishersweekly.com/pw/by-topic/new-titles/adult-announcements/article/64261-science-fiction-fantasy-2014-how-multicultural-is-your-multiverse.html [accessed October 28, 2016].

Ochs, Elinor (1988), *Culture and Language Development: Language Acquisition and Language Socialization in a Samoan Village*, Cambridge, UK: Cambridge University Press.

Olson, Debbie C. (2011), "Last in Space: The 'Black' Hole in Children's Science Fiction Film," in *The Galaxy is Rated G: Essays of Children's Sicene fiction Film and Television*, edited by R. C. Neighbors and Sandy Rankin, Jefferson, NC: McFarland, 64–82.

Op de Beeck, Natalie (2010), *Suspended Animation: Children's Picture Books and the Fairy Tale of Modernity*, Minneapolis, MN: University of Minnesota Press.

Opie, Iona and Opie, Peter (1959), *The Lore and Language of School Children*, Oxford: Oxford University Press.

Painter, Claire, Martin, J. R., and Unsworth, Len (2013), *Reading Visual Narratives: Image Analysis of Children's Picture Books*, Sheffield, UK: Equinox.

Paley, Vivian Gussin (1979), *White Teacher*, Cambridge, MA: Harvard University Press.

Paley, Vivian Gussin and Matlock, Resa (2002), Storytelling and Story acting with Vivian Gussin Paley. Part I. Ball State University: Covenant Productions, DVD.

Pantaleo, Sylvia and Sipe, Lawrence R. (2008), *Postmodern Picturebooks: Play, Parody, and Self-Referentiality*, New York: Routledge.

Papazian, Gretchen and Sommers, Joseph Michael (2013), *Game On, Hollywood! Essays on the Intersection of Video Games and Cinema*, Jefferson, NC: McFarland.

Parry, Becky (2013), *Children, Film and Literacy*, Basingstoke: Palgrave Macmillan.

Parsons, Michael J. (1987), *How We Understand Art: A Cognitive Developmental Account of Aesthetic Experience*, Cambridge, UK: Cambridge University Press.

Partridge, Elizabeth (April 23, 2013), "Narrative Nonfiction: Kicking Ass at Last." *The Horn Book*. http://www.hbook.com/2013/04/choosing-books/horn-book-magazine/narrative-nonfiction-kicking-ass-at-last/#_ [accessed October 28, 2016].

Pearson, Lucy and Reynolds, Kimberley (2010), "Realism," in *The Routledge Companion to Children's Literature*, edited by D. Rudd, London: Routledge, 63–74.

Piaget, Jean (1963), *The Origins of Intelligence in Children*, New York: W. W. Norton & Co.

Pierce, Tamora (October 1993), "Fantasy: Why Kids Read It, Why Kids Need It," *School Library Journal*, v39 n10, 50–51.

Plato (1992), *Republic*, 2nd ed., translated by G. M. A. Grube. Revised by C. D. C. Reeve. Indianapolis, IN: Hackett.

Postman, Neil (1983), *The Disappearance of Childhood*, London: W. H. Allen.

Prashad, Vijay (2001), *Everybody Was Kung Fu Fighting: Afro-Asian Connections and the Myth of Cultural Purity*, Boston: Beacon P.

Pratt, Annis (1982), *Archetypal Patterns in Women's Fiction*, Bloomington, IN: Indiana University Press.

Pratt, Mary Louise (1977), *Toward a Speech Act Theory of Literary Discourse*, Bloomington: Indiana University Press.

Prince, Gerald (1987), *A Dictionary of Narratology*, Omaha, NE: University of Nebraska Press.

Ratelle, Amy (2014), *Animality and Children's Literature and Film*, Hampshire: Palgrave.

Reynolds, Kimberley (2007), *Radical Children's Literature: Future Visions and Transformations in Juvenile Fiction*, Basingstoke: Macmillan.

Rich, Adrienne (1972), "When We Dead Awaken: Writing as Re-Vision," *College English* 34, no. 1: 18–30.

Robinson, Marilyn (1998), *The Death of Adam: Essays on Modern Thought*, New York: Houghton Mifflin.

Rollin, Lucy (1993), *The Antic Art: Enhancing Children's Literary Experiences Through Film and Video*, Fort Atkinson: Highsmith.

Rose, Gillian (2012), *Visual Methodologies: An Introduction to the Interpretation of Visual Materials*, London: Sage.

Rose, Jacqueline (1984), *The Case of Peter Pan, or The Impossibility of Children's Fiction*, Basingstoke: Macmillan.

Rosen, Michael (1996), "Radio, Television, Film, Audio and Video," in *International Companion Encyclopedia of Children's Literature*, edited by Peter Hunt, New York: Routledge, 530–38.

Rudd, David (2013), *Reading the Child in Children's Literature*, Basingstoke: Palgrave Macmillan.

Safford, Barbara Ripp (1983), *High Fantasy: An Archetypal Analysis of Children's Literature*, Ann Arbor, MI: University Microfilms International.

Salisbury, Martin (2004), *Illustrating Children's Books: Creating Pictures for Publication*, London: Quarto.

Salmon, Edward (1888), *Juvenile Literature As It Is*, London: Henry J. Drake.

Sanders, Joe Sutliff (2015), "*Almost Astronauts* and the Pursuit of Reliability in Children's Nonfiction," *Children's Literature in Education* 46 http://link.springer.com.libproxy.lib.ilstu.edu/article/10.1007/s10583-014-9241-z#. [accessed October 28, 2016].

Saussure, Ferdinand de (1959), *Course in General Linguistics*, translated by W. Baskin, New York: The Philosophical Library.

Savarese, Ralph James (2013), "From Neurodiversity to Neurocosmopolitanism: Beyond Mere Acceptance and Inclusion," in *Ethics and Neurodiversity*, edited by C. D. Herrera and Alexandra Perry, Newcastle upon Tyne: Cambridge Scholars Press.

Saxby, Maurice (1996), "Myth and Legend," in *International Companion Encyclopedia of Children's Literature*, edited by Peter Hunt, New York and London: Routledge, 166–76.

Schank, Roger C. (1990), *Tell Me A Story: Narrative and Intelligence*, Evanston, IL: Northwestern University Press.

Schwarz, Joseph (1982), *Ways of the Illustrator: Visual Communication in Children's Literature*, American Library Association.

Serafini, Frank (2014), *Reading the Visual: An Introduction to Teaching Multimodal Literacy*, New York: Teachers College Press.

Shklovsky, Viktor (1990), *Theory of Prose*, translated by Benjamin Sher, Normal, IL: Dalkey Archive Press.

Shulevitz, Uri (1985), *Writing with Pictures: How to Write and Illustrate Children's Books*, New York: Watson-Guptill.

Simms, Eva M. (2008), *The Child in the World: Embodiment, Time, and Language in Early Childhood*, Detroit, MI: Wayne State University Press.

Simpson, Birgitte Vittrup (2007), *Exploring the Influences of Education Television and Parent-Child Discussions on Improving Children's Racial Attitudes*. Doctoral Dissertation, Austin, TX: University of Texas at Austin Repository.

Singer, Eliot A. (n.d.), "Fakelore, Multiculturalism, and the Ethics of Children's Literature," https://www.msu.edu/user/singere/fakelore.html, Retrieved 15 October 2015.

Sipe, Lawrence (1998), "How Picture Books Work: A Semiotically Framed Theory of Text-Picture Relationships," *Children's Literature in Education* 29: 97–108.

Sipe, Lawrence R. (2008), *Storytime: Young Children's Literary Understanding in the Classroom*, New York: Teachers College Press.

Smith, Michelle J. (2011), *Empire in British Girls' Literature and Culture: Imperial Girls, 1880-1915*, Basingstoke: Palgrave Macmillan.

Stearns, Peter N. (2006), *Childhood in World History*, London and New York: Routledge.

Stephens, John (1992), *Language and Ideology in Children's Fiction*, London: Longman.

Stephens, John (2013), *Subjectivity in Asian Children's Literature and Film: Global Theories and Implications*, New York and London: Routledge.

Stephens, John and McCallum, Robyn (1998), *Retelling Stories, Framing Culture: Traditional Story and Metanarratives in Children's Literature*, New York and London: Routledge.

Stevenson, Deborah (1997), "Sentiment and Significance: The Impossibility of Recovery in the Children's Literature Canon or, The Drowning of *The Water-Babies*," *The Lion and the Unicorn* 21, no. 1: 112–30.

Stockwell, Peter (2002), *Cognitive Poetics: An Introduction*, New York: Routledge.

Sutton, R. (2015), "Are we doing it white?" *The Horn Book*, http://www.hbook.com/2015/02/blogs/read-roger/are-we-doing-it-white/#_ [accessed October 14, 2016].

Tarr, Anita and Flynn, Richard (2002), "'The Trouble isn't Making Poems, the Trouble's Finding Somebody that will Listen to them': Negotiating a Place for Children's Literature Studies," *Children's Literature Association Quarterly* 27, no. 1: 2–3.

Thacker, Deborah C. and Webb, Jean (2002), *Introducing Children's Literature: From Romanticism to Postmodernism*, London and New York: Routledge.

Thompson, Stith (1955/1958), *Myth: A Symposium*, edited by Thomas A. Sebeok, Bloomington and London: Indiana University Press, 169–80.

Tobin, Joseph (2000), *Good Guys Don't Wear Hats: Children's Talk about the Media*, New York: Teachers College Press.

Todorov, Tzvetan (1973), *The Fantastic: A Structural Approach to Literary Genre*, translated by Richard Howard, Cleveland: Press of Case Western Reserve University.

Todorov, Tzvetan (1977), *The Poetics of Prose*, translated by Richard Howard, Ithaca: Cornell University Press.

Tolkien, John Ronald R. (1966), "On Fairy Stories," *The Tolkien Reader*, New York: Random House, 33–99 [Originally published in 1947].

Townsend, John Rowe (1987), *Written for Children*, 3rd ed., Great Britain: Kestrel Books.

Trabasso, Tom and Nickels, Margret (1992), "The Development of Goal Plans of Action in the Narration of a Picture Story," *Discourse Processes* 15, no. 3: 249–75.

Trautner, Hanns M., Ruble, Diane N., Cyphers, Lisa, Kirsten, Barbara, Behrendt, Regina, and Hartmann, Petra (2005), "Rigidity and Flexibility of Gender Stereotypes in Childhood: Developmental of Differential?," *Infant and Child Development* 14: 365–81.

Trites, Roberta Seelinger (2007), *Twain, Alcott, and the Birth of the Adolescent Reform Novel*, Iowa City, IA: Iowa University Press.

Trites, Roberta Seelinger (2014), *Literary Conceptualizations of Growth*, Amsterdam: John Benjamins.

Tumbokon, Chacha (2014) "The Positive and Negative Effects of Video Games," *Raise Smart Kid*. http://www.raisesmartkid.com/3-to-6-years-old/4-articles/34-the-good-and-bad-effects-of-video-games [accessed October 28, 2016].

Turco, Lewis Putnam (2012), *The Book of Forms*, rev. and expanded ed., Hanover, NH: Dartmouth College Press.

Turner, Mark (1996), *The Literary Mind*, New York: Oxford University Press.

Van Gennep, Arnold (1977), *The Rites of Passage*, translated by Mokia B. Vizedom and Gabrielle L. Caffee, East Sussex, UK: Psychology Press. [Originally published in French in 1960].

Vermeule, Blakey (2009), *Why Do We Care about Literary Characters?*, Baltimore: Johns Hopkins University Press.

"Video Game Addiction: 81% of American Youth Play; 8.5% are Addicted" (2007), *Metrics 2.0: Business and Market Intelligence*. http://www.metrics2.com/blog/2007/04/04/video_game_addiction_81_of_american_youth_play_85.html [accessed October 28, 2016].

Ward, Winifred (1950), *Theatre for Children*, Anchorage: Children's Theatre Press.

Warner, Marina (2014), *Once Upon a Time: A Short History of Fairy Tale*, Oxford: Oxford University Press.

Warner, William (1994), "Licensing Pleasure: Literary History and the Novel in Early Modern Britain," in *The Columbia History of the British Novel*, edited by J. Richetti, New York: Columbia University Press.

Weitzman, Lenore, Eifler, Deborah, Hokada, Elizabeth, and Ross, Catherine (1972), "Sex-role Socialization in Picture Books for Preschool Children," *American Journal of Sociology* 77: 1125–50.

Weir, Ruth H. (1962), *Language in the Crib*, The Hague: Mouton.

Wertham, Frederic (1954), *Seduction of the Innocent*, New York: Rinehart & Company.

Westman, Karin E. (2007), "Children's Literature and Modernism: The Space Between," *Children's Literature Association Quarterly* 32, no. 4: 283–86.

Wilde, Oscar (1961), "The Critic as Artist: With Some Remarks upon the Importance of Doing Nothing," in Wilde, *Selected Writings*, edited by Richard Ellman, Oxford: Oxford University Press, 39–119.

Wimsatt, William K. and Beardsley, Monroe C. (1954), *The Verbal Icon:Studies in the Meaning of Poetry*, Lexington, KY: University of Kentucky Press.

Windling, Terri (2015), "'Into the Woods' Series 48: The Child Ballads (Part II)," *Myth & Moor*, http://www.terriwindling.com/blog/2015/07/into-the-woods-series-40-the-child-ballads-part-ii.html [accessed October 28, 2016].

Winn, Marie (2002), *The Plug-In Drug: Television, Computers, and Family Life*, New York: Penguin.

Winner, Ellen (1982), *Invented Worlds: The Psychology of the Arts*, Cambridge, MA: Harvard University Press.

Winner, Ellen (1988), *The Point of Words: Children's Understanding of Metaphor and Irony*, Cambridge, MA: Harvard University Press.

Winnicott, Donald W. (1965), *The Family and Individual Development*, New York: Routledge.

Wojcik-Andrews, Ian (2000), *Children's Films: History, Ideology, Pedagogy, Theory*, New York: Routledge.

Wolf, Shelby A. (2003), *Interpreting Literature with Children*, New York: Routledge.

Wolf, Shelby A., Coats, Karen, Enciso, Patricia, and Jenkins, Christine A. (2011), *Handbook of Research on Children's and Young Adult Literature*, New York: Routledge.

Woolf, Virginia (2004), *A Room of One's Own*, London: Penguin [Originally published in 1929].

Zipes, Jack (1979), *Breaking the Magic Spell: Radical Theories of Folk and Fairy Tales*, Lexington: University of Kentucky Press.

Zunshine, Lisa (2006), *Why We Read Fiction: Theory of Mind and the Novel*, Columbus, OH: The Ohio State University Press.

Index